The Andrew Street Mob

To David and Katie
All the Best
Brian

The Andrew Street Mob

☀

Kids in the Fifties Growing Up Inside Johannesburg Experiencing Multiple Black Tribes, European Cultures, American Influences through Music and Movies

Brian Marais

MARAIS MEDIA INTERNATIONAL

Printed in the United States of America

First Printing, 2010

ISBN 10: 0982673205

ISBN 13: 9780982673201

Marais Media International

www.MaraisMediaInter.com

Author's Note

The book has taken an enormous amount of time to write. It evolved through the normal cycles of many scenarios, but always with the major theme of a group of kids growing up and experiencing all the wonderful and tough circumstances that confront us as we learn many basics of life. It was written because as I travelled, I found people were not aware of the complexity of life, the complicated history, and the magnificent beauty of the land and the seas that surround South Africa.

This book is not about apartheid. There are many books written on the subject of apartheid, but that is not necessarily the only life that existed. There is a profound history attached to the simple aspects of life in the 40's and 50's. Most of our parents never had a car. There was no television available. There was an explosion and diversification of music and movies from America, and a profound changing of new technology in the world—read on!

Acknowledgements

Every book, major report or study requires an enormous amount of work and research. Plus there are many contributors to the final product. My list is no different to any other accomplishment. I truly thank you all, from the attendants in the Johannesburg Library who were surprised at the large amount of copies I made, to the many, many friends who read and typed the ugly written pages of text. I wish to thank my niece Shirley van Straaten, also a close friend for so many years, who drove me to finish the book and made a major contribution in editing, reviewing and through discussion. To my friends in the Andrew Street Mob, Bobby's Group and friends in life—Thank you so much!

Contents

The Andrew Street Mob

＊

CHAPTER 1

Andrew Street I

THERE WERE ABOUT SEVENTY of us kids growing up on Andrew Street in the block between Main and Lindhorst Streets, but there were arguments as to the actual number. So we counted, more than once. There were twenty or so kids in arms and carriages, about twelve between five and eleven, fifteen around twelve to fourteen, and the rest fifteen to twenty and some of those were married with a kid. But we were not sure of that breakdown. Every time the total number was always different! So we decided to agree, and after much debate, agreed that the number was seventy!

Andrew Street was located in the suburb of Kenilworth about fifteen miles south from the center of Johannesburg. It was tree-lined on both sides with eight-foot wide sandy sidewalks and the tarmac street was a four-car width with clearance—but not much of it! The southern suburbs of Johannesburg, a large area of land, maybe twenty square miles, consisted of slightly rolling hills and valleys. There always seemed to be a gradient of some sort; very seldom could you find level ground. All the big buildings, like schools, were built on banks, built-up ground, or graded hills, as were the tennis courts, soccer, cricket, and rugby fields.

World War II was raging and there seemed to be little food and no money. To bolster nutrition, all kids were forced to drink milk and eat caramel candies supplied by the school. We hated the candy, it gave you the same feeling as when you had to take Epsom salts or eat cabbage! Photos were taken of kids, and nurses stuck sticks on our tongues, looked down our throats, examined our chests and measured pulse rates. The kids at school talked about the war, and to keep up with everyone I listened to the radio every night at 6 PM to get the latest news. I didn't understand the war. I knew it was bad because people were being killed. But it was good when bad people died. War was very confusing. So I wanted to know everything about it. At home I would always try and get my head close to the radio loudspeaker by lying on the floor.

During the years of WWII, radio was our communication with the rest of the world. It blared news of the war with Germany and Japan every day. The war in Europe was more interesting to us kids because our fathers and relatives were in the fight. We didn't care about Japan. Letters to mothers and sons and daughters were very exciting events. We would sit around and listen to someone read a letter. The newspaper articles were never really read by kids, but we followed the arrows on the maps in the paper. They showed the Allied Forces driving the Germans back to their country. My mom was now, and throughout the war period, very busy: working during the day, and volunteering in the evening with the Women's Auxiliary. This organization did everything they could to help the soldiers: preparing food packages, arranging the knitting of sweaters, pullovers, scarves and socks for the troops. In addition, they helped soldiers, sailors and airmen who were on home leave. They also entertained a large number of British Servicemen who were being sent to South Africa for rest and recuperation. Many of them had been in the war for years and the British Isles was short of food and not necessarily a good place to rest: South Africa was not rationed severely with food and had no ongoing local conflicts.

World War II was continuing as the United Kingdom and the Commonwealth countries were fully committed to battle. The Japanese attacked Pearl Harbor, and America entered the conflict. The grown-ups in South Africa were glad about America's entry because the British and their allies were having a tough time. We learned of these events by listening to adults and to the radio. The war was also affecting lifestyle in South Africa and taking its toll on the family.

My dad joined the Army even though he was not that young. My uncle Dennis joined the South African Air Force and went to England to fly with the Royal Air Force squadrons. Families in Andrew Street had sons 'going off to war'. Many families made clothes, knitted sweaters and scarves and supported Women's Auxiliary groups. All the women in our family knitted. They did it while sitting chatting, while listening to the radio, and even on buses. My sister could knit a sweater in two days. The house was full of balls of wool. They were fun to kick around barefoot in the house.

Now the Movietone Newsreels at the movies started to become important. We understood more, as it had started to affect families and the kids in the Southern Suburbs of Johannesburg. We hated the Germans and the Japanese. We didn't know why the Italians joined the Germans; we knew some Italians who lived on Main Street, opposite Andrew Street, and they didn't seem like fighters. It was just a big game adults were playing and we had started to see the right and wrong of it. But, as much as we talked, we didn't understand the horror.

◆

Our area of Johannesburg was a mixture of people, especially during the day. Many non-whites were working in different jobs involving labor and services. We had milk delivered by black men, fruit and vegetable carts were driven by Indians, refuse from houses was picked up by black men, and ice cream carts could be driven by Indian or black men. White journeymen and black helpers did construction and building work, plumbing and electrical repair work. Our street was very busy and doors were essentially open during the day and locked at night. We were aware of stealing and burglaries. We had been burgled ourselves one time. Our parents taught us to be careful even though we walked to school and caught buses by ourselves. We knew from stories in the paper that there were many crimes being committed. We were aware of some cruel happenings.

Although our lives were centered on Andrew Street, all the kids in Andrew Street were reminded every day that we were growing up in a complex society and in a country where the people were predominantly black. The blacks out-numbered the whites by a factor of almost 4. There were more than eight black languages and as many tribes in Johannesburg. None of us understood anything spoken in a native tongue. The different tribes didn't necessarily get on with each other. Fighting between them was frequent and resulted in wounded and dead: Sundays had the highest toll and usually involved excessive drinking. In Johannesburg, the black and white people were split into very definite areas for living purposes. We were living amid a kind of segregation with changing rules. Included in our city were first, second and third generation English, Scottish, Irish, Welsh, Dutch, Greeks, and other Europeans, Indians, Chinese, Jews, and Middle Easterners, such as Lebanese. The Andrew Street kids included quite a few of these ethnic groups. The mob derived from Afrikaners, Huguenots, English, Yugoslavian, Irish, French, German, Dutch, Jewish, and Belgian peoples, many of them who could be up to eighth generation South Africans. Added to the complications for kids growing up was all the religious backgrounds and beliefs in what a person should be and do in life, which was inherent in the cultures of the parents. Most of the parents were qualified tradesmen: plumbers, machinists, electricians, carpenters, butchers, diamond cutters, and miners. There were also bookkeepers, accountants, shopkeepers and owners of small businesses: middle-class (whatever that meant). Our parents were looking to the future knowing the black population would always be greater than the white population. The edict of our parents was that we learn and become qualified at something, so that we end up being better than laborers. We understood what they meant, we agreed many times, because they told us many times! Kids grew up like us all over the world and with different languages and traditions and all skin colors. We saw that in shorts at the movies, read about it, and teachers told us how other people grew up. We knew our situation through our daily life encounters, which touched all these things in many ways. We often talked about the mixes of race and personality and behavior, but the talk was kept short and only touched on quickly; we did not want all these things to interfere with our fun. We happened to be white, and spoke mostly English, peppered with Afrikaans and South African colloquiums.

Our parents, our teachers, adults everywhere discussed the segregated life and all aspects of the roles that different people played and what these people should be doing: All of this was done endlessly. The newspapers were filled with stories and changing rules and this was followed by unending discussions by adults . . . As kids we listened, but in many ways it was all very confusing and we wished to ignore the 'negatives', so we played the games of the day and just witnessed daily life.

◆

My mom, my sister Yvonne, my brother Bazil and I lived with my gran and her husband Uncle Mick at number 65. Gran was twice the size of her husband. Her hair was black and gray. She had soft eyes with a touch of green. Gran was a big woman all over, much larger than my thin mom. They both had long hair, and Gran always wore her hair on top of her head, while my mom rolled her hair into a bun. Gran wore mostly black dresses. My mother loved colors and never wore black. My mom was very pretty and always neat; her nails were always polished, she wore lipstick and powder on her face, and she very seldom went out without gloves. Yvonne was tall, slim, long brown hair, beautiful olive skin and a slim, pretty face with dark eyes and a sweet smile. Bazil was taller than Yvonne, handsome, masculine face, brown hair, strong arms and legs. Even though he was mostly serious, he also had a pleasant smile. Gran's marriage to Mickey Flynn was her second. They had two sons: Dennis and Rob, both living elsewhere. Gran's first marriage produced my mother, my aunt Amy and my uncle Bill.

Uncle Mick was of Irish descent, a small man with sharp features, short gray hair, flat and parted on one side. Even though he was small he was very tough, a real Cousin Jack (a term for Welsh miners, who had a worldwide reputation as tough, hard workers). Uncle Mick had worked in the gold mines of Johannesburg all of his adult life. He was gone early in the morning and came home a little after I got home from school.

Another member of the household was Lena, a black servant girl. (African people or natives, terms used primarily for indigenous people, were called girl and boy even though they might be fifty years of age! They were also known as blacks despite the numerous tribes and variance in color.) She was employed by Gran to clean and cook for the family.

I went to Kenilworth Junior School: a primary school for kids. Helen and Bobby from next door would join me on the way to school almost every morning. Helen was dark haired, with beautiful, deep brown eyes and an athletic build. She was the same age as me. Bobby had light brown hair, was slighter than his sister and a year younger. Helen was always in full spirits. Bobby was quieter. The three of us would walk along Andrew Street, away from Main Street, to the end of the block; every house was different. The houses were basically brick construction with a corrugated galvanized zinc roof, a verandah, small doors and windows. They were all different as though designed by fifty different architects with different tastes in colors and street front designs, and reflected the taste and economics of the early part of the century. They were also graced with narrow pathways and flower gardens or large ceramic pots with flowers. Every house we passed had a different fence around it; however, they were all low in front, less than four feet, and as high as six feet on the side and at the back. We got to know the names of all the people that lived in these small houses. They were proud of their houses. Many had come from living on the mine sites. Almost every house on Andrew Street was a large upgrade of the dreary mining houses that were built in rows of ten houses or more, all the same design and located in row upon row on the mine properties.

At the end of Andrew Street we would turn right on Lindhorst, go down three blocks and then turn left into school. Kenilworth Junior School was almost a whole block in size, a "U" shaped barrack style brick building, and one story high. It had a large playground surrounded by tall Eucalyptus trees. We walked this way every day by ourselves. Sometimes we met others from Andrew Street going to school. But it was guaranteed that walking back from school we'd see the Adams kids: Brian and Graham, mild, quiet blond kids with English parents; Zoni and Juni, Yugoslavian boys with dark complexions, smiling eyes and Eastern European flat heads; Donald (Doc), a big, strong, tight-curled redheaded Irish kid just full of freckles; and Mel who was a very quiet, light brown haired boy, thin and brittle as a dried leaf. Also, we might see one or more kids, from the Jooste, Matthews or van der Merwe families.

Although we may have walked to school with girls, we never ever mixed once we were there . . . that was not done. Boys and girls were even seated separately in class.

We walked unescorted to and from school, as we knew the way and it was safe. Doc, Bobby, Helen, Zoni, Mel, Juni or whoever was in the same group going to our inevitable classes walked and talked. This was always nice if you weren't late. There were always groups of people outside the school waiting for the bell. There was a loud sound and we all shuffled in. The classrooms had blackboards, a platform, a chair and desk for the teacher. Students had wrought iron and solid wood desks with a no-lift top for writing: they were never, ever comfortable. The floor was wood and the walls were brick. Sometimes there were posters on the walls. After school, we went to the koppies (low hills) or played in the street, those were essentially the choices for recreation.

And so the Andrew Street Mob was born!

The Andrew Street kids and other kids from the neighborhood mostly loved the walk home from school, which we intentionally prolonged to include very critical things: find tennis balls, steal fruit, look in houses and gardens, and sit on the corner and talk. People who lived near school became tired of our antics and trimmed branches of fruit trees so kids would have to come onto the property to get fruit. This could also be discouraged by either a dog or trespassing warnings. We came up with an ingenious design to defeat this plan. We got an old grass broomstick, removed the grass, and nailed an empty can to one end so that the can was perpendicular to the stick. It resembled a beggar's cup with a long stick on it instead of an arm. We then filed the lip of the can until it was like a razor blade. This worked very well for collecting fruit. Three kids would hold the stick and put it over the fence, position the can under the fruit and simply saw the stalk by moving the stick backwards and forwards. The stalk broke and the fruit, usually a peach or plum, fell into the can. The stick was retrieved and the process repeated. It worked like a charm! But of course, whenever we did things like this, something bad would happen. We found out the hard way. When we took a lot of peaches and plums, we would have to put them under our shirt and above the belt, to carry them away. The peaches, especially, caused an itch on the stomach that lasted for days!

One day, two black girls got into a huge fight on the corner of Andrew Street and Lindhorst. They yelled, arms flailing. They didn't punch, but hit with the flat of the hand, and grabbed each other's clothes, tearing them off. The crowd, including Brian and Graham, the Adams kids, the Joostes, Zoni, Juni and Doc and me, soon grew to about thirty kids. We ended up shouting for one girl or the other. They eventually tore each other's blouses off, didn't stop fighting and didn't care. We loved it! We boys got our first look at bare-breasted women fighting. We cheered loudly until some white adults came out and broke up the fight and told us kids to go home.

"That was fun."

"Wow!"

"That was really good."

"Adults are stupid sometimes," said one kid.

We all agreed.

◆

My brother went away to boarding school and my sister to a convent. This was hard to understand. I asked many times but nobody told me why! Mom and Gran said it was just for a short while. Bazil went to a boys' school on the other side of Johannesburg in a suburb called Malvern, and Yvonne went to a Catholic girls' school in Rosettenville, a next-door suburb to Kenilworth. My mom and I went to see them on Sundays. These schools were horrible places in my mind, reminding me of the dark dungeons and cold castles that I saw in comic books. The nuns and priests were serious and stern. They never smiled, except when my mom and I were leaving. Then there was a vague, thin, superior smile, which I never understood.

◆

No matter what I was doing, I had to meet my mother at the bus stop with an umbrella, each evening that a 'Highveld' storm took place. These storms were unpredictable, but generally came in the early evening when everybody got home from work. You could tell it was coming because the sky turned dark blue-black and everything became mysteriously somber. The tumultuous downpour of water usually lasted for fifteen minutes but anyone caught without an umbrella had no need to take a bath that night. The skies opened up typically between 4PM and 6PM. So I would go to the corner and meet the no. 32 bus from Johannesburg on the left side of Main Street going south. The bus would stop just before Andrew Street and then continue on further south on Main Street. The buses and cars, of course, traveled on the left side of the road in South Africa like they do in England.

I reviewed them from the bus stop: we faced Diering Street on the right and Andrew Street on the left. Over the road, looking from right to left was Liebe's Grocery Store and next to that and in sequence was a butcher shop, Mrs. Flynn's Cleaners, Coronation Fish and Chip shop and the shoemaker. Then came the lane that separated the two rows of houses and Tony's Vegetable shop from the lane to Andrew Street. I had been to these shops a hundred times for my gran, my uncle Mick and for my mom. The owners all knew me as Charl and I knew them as 'Mr.' or 'Mrs.'

There were not many cars in the neighborhood at this time. Most people walked to the stores on Main Street every day for food and household items, or they went to Rosettenville Corner for more expensive things like shoes and clothes. If needed, they planned a big trip to downtown Johannesburg on a Saturday, by bus, where the shops were open only a half-day. It was a major delight to go to 'Town'. The shops around the corner on Main Street looked as though they were built in the twenties or even earlier. Single storey brick buildings, with sloping, corrugated, galvanized roofs, gutters and downspouts, round cement posts that support the overhang every fifteen feet. There was nothing special about these shops; there were two windows for display, and a single doorway to enter or leave. People knew the shopkeepers' names. The shopkeepers also knew the neighborhood people by name. Everyone addressed each other as Mr. and Mrs. This was the formality of the day and seldom did you hear a first name unless the people were very close friends. During the day it was alive; it was very busy on Saturdays, and after 6 PM it was dead. So the kids from the nearby streets and Andrew Street would then walk up south on Main Street to the Good Luck Cafe on the corner of Verona and Main where the shop stayed open later. The favorite candy was a black jawbreaker: a one-inch hard sugar sphere that changed colors as you licked away each layer. Milk shakes, ice cream sodas and fountain drinks were also a favorite along with all the different kind of candies that the world produced.

The bus came and my mom arrived, she gave me a kiss. There was no rainstorm, so we walked up Andrew Street. I told her about my review of our area.

"I know all the names of the families on the street."

"Name them! Let's see if you're right!"

"Okay!" I took up the challenge. "On the north side is Tony's Vegetable store, an empty house, the Murray's, Mel's home, the two older sisters, the Schumachers, Mary Jooste, the Loxtons and then us. Then there is the old, crabby Scottish couple, the Robinsons, next to us."

"Don't say things like that!" instructed my mom.

"Well they are!" I continued: "David and Denise's place, Tom and then Doc Gilberts, the Jooste's big, big family, and the Ziemans up the road." I pointed.

"That's right so far," agreed my mom.

"Going back to the corner of Andrew Street and Main Street on the left side is the spooky, old abandoned house, then crazy Mimi, Zoni and Juni's home; a set of flats, don't know who lives there, and then the Hanekoms. Mr. Gore lives in the small house and next is Mr. Cloete, the cowboy, who plays the amplified electric guitar. And then Mom, is the Blooms with all the money, and the biggest house with a high cement wall . . . so we can't see in! The Adams across the street from us, Brian and Graham and family, the Mathews, then in the semis are the Van Der Merwes and Edgertons and another old house on the corner. Is that right?" I asked.

"Yes, Son! You're right. But you be careful what you say about the neighbors."

"Okay," I sort of agreed.

My mom and I reached the house. "Thank you for the tour of Andrew Street!" said my mom sarcastically.

"I'm going to play!"

"Be home in time for dinner!" she added.

◆

On Sundays the kids would sometimes go with their families about 15 miles out of town in a southerly direction to 'Van Wyk's Rust', a pleasure resort, which had a natural spring-fed swimming pool. The pool was constructed totally of concrete, about 100 feet in diameter and surrounded by acres of willow trees and green grass. The natural spring, at an elevation of 6000 feet, continually fed the pool. The water was cold. Throughout summer, it was an ideal place for picnics, and always heavily booked for Xmas Day picnics.

In summer after school, kids numbering between six and twenty played cricket in Andrew Street, with a tennis ball, a dustbin (garbage can) as the wickets and a rock as the ball delivery point, and a cricket bat. Using a cricket ball, which is very solid and much heavier than even a baseball, had got us in trouble because it dented cars and broke windows very easily. We tried 'corkies'- a solid cork ball—but that did just as much damage. Getting money for cricket balls and corkies was also a problem. Every time a car came up the road, we moved the dustbin and rock off the street, and gave the drivers dirty looks hoping they wouldn't come back. We also gave them a sarcastic wave goodbye and then continued with our game.

The rules of street cricket were simple. If you hit the ball in the street area where other players could find it, you could score runs by running between the dustbin and the rock. If you hit the ball over the fence you got six runs and you had to go get the ball yourself. The most feared hit was down the drain, which usually became a lost ball. We would jeer the batsman and walk away in disgust. Or we might applaud him—if he went home and got another ball. Other normal cricket rules applied, you were out if the ball hit the bin, if the ball got to the rock or bin before the you did, or if you hit the ball and it was caught without it bouncing. Also, you were out if you did a stupid thing like hitting the bin during your stroke of playing the ball. You scored as many runs as you could run after you hit the ball. The dustbin and the rock were easily moved, and when the neighbors got mad and yelled at us kids, we'd just move the game down the road. The competition was always furious, despite the teams being different every day. They were picked each day as we arrived on the scene. Some very good batsmen and bowlers started their skill development on this street.

Cricket was the gentlest game we played. The kids in Andrew Street and I were going through a batch system of learning different sports and activities. We had gone through the various stages of growing up and playing games. We made box carts and tried them out. We assembled junk bikes with parts from anybody and anywhere. We did street bike racing. We ended up playing, at any given time, soccer in the street, hide and seek, kick the can, and running a game called 'Hasie' (hare)—the latter included the introduction of girls playing in the street with the boys. Helen played with us no matter what game we played. She could throw, she could hit and she could run with any of us. She was my pal and I was proud she was my next-door neighbor. I went to see the Loxtons almost every day. I loved Mr. and Mrs. Loxton; they were always nice to me. Helen, Bobby and I talked together hundreds of times. We never argued once.

The making of box carts started with stealing pram (baby carriage) wheels and axles out of garages, and finding pieces of wood: the basics. We designed these carts in all sorts of strange ways so they resembled death-defying machines. We used fruit boxes to sit in, the box mounted on a on a 6-inch piece of wood. A 4-inch piece of wood, holding the back axle and wheels, was attached. Through the front end of the 6-inch piece of wood, you had to drill a hole for a half-inch bolt that had to have a double-nut. This went through a second 4-inch piece of wood with axles and wheels. A piece of rope was tied on each end, real tight, to the inside part of the axle, inside the wheels. The rope had to be long enough to reach inside the box. Finally a piece of wood was drilled and bolted to the box, and its 'swing' aligned with the back wheel, so as to serve as a brake. That was the perfect box cart. We never achieved that once, because our box carts cost nothing, and there were many substitutions for the real parts. Once the box cart was made, we were impatient to try it. We had to find a steep hill, without traffic, so that we could go roaring down the hill, hoping the brakes worked, and without damaging the carts, scraping our legs or killing ourselves. When you crashed it was important to yell (but not cry). If you could jump up quickly after falling off, examine the bruises, and walk away with a 'did not care' attitude, you had made it! The first practices with box carts by the Andrew Street Mob were held on Lindhorst Street, but that challenge was not good enough. Southern Suburbs kids knew 'Daisy Dip' had to be taken on! Daisy Street was in Rosettenville, the next-door suburb, and the dip was off Prairie Street. Parents did not allow us kids to go there. It was about a mile of walking from Andrew Street but it was worth it. It took six kids to do it: at least one at each end of the road to watch for cars, one to hold the cart and two in the dip in case of a crash. Doc, Zoni, Juni, Bobby, Brian and Graham and a few of the Jooste and van der Merwe kids stole away to Daisy Dip. We got set up in positions and Doc went off first. He was going really fast and to me it was frightening. Doc went screaming up the other side. He had made it. A Jooste kid went swirling all over the place till the speed straightened his cart out. Bobby went off and veered into the side of the street before he got going. His cart was a mess.

I went off next. I was scared. The cart started to move very fast, too fast, I was thinking. I hung onto the steering rope as tight as I could. Now I knew why triple knots were used. I was so scared. I had two hands on the rope and wouldn't dare use one to pull the brake. I wished it would end but the cart went faster, everything was bouncing all over the place. I hung on fiercely. It was so fast that everything was a blur. Then the cart went through the dip and started to slow down. I realized my heart was pounding and sending blood so fast to my temples that it hurt. I was so glad the 'Dip' was over.

Despite the very scary experience and the occasional brake failure, the Andrew Street Mob survived everything. I thought it was the most daring thing we had ever done. We agreed that the hill was really steep, and when the cart hit top speed, the twitches in the cart due to the steering side movements and bumps in the road were the scariest of all. But after you went through the dip and up the other side you felt like a hero. We didn't stop talking on the way home. Nobody suggested we do it again. We didn't tell our parents!

◆

When I got home from school, I would run through the house shouting "Hullo! Gran!" After I got a big hug and kiss, I would change and go out into the back yard. Then I would go back inside for my sandwich. I always wanted to take the sandwich into the street and go and play, but Gran would not allow that. She said that food must be eaten at the table.

There were a lot of rules about going into the street: don't play near the corner, watch for cars, and don't leave the block. So I would sit at the kitchen table and talk to Lena as Gran lay down on her bed for her afternoon nap. Lena was in her twenties, with black skin, black stubby hair like most Africans, dark brown eyes and sharper features than usual. She was slight but strong. Lena was always smiling and pleasant. She always wore an apron and a small cloth wrapped around her head, tied in a knot on her forehead. Lena was a willing worker and lived in the room in the back yard. I liked her. I asked Lena a million questions while eating lunch sandwiches she made, about where she used to play, and where her family was, and where her father and mother lived. Lena described her African village in Zululand and how they grew up, and explained that her parents still lived in the village. She and her husband had come to Johannesburg to earn money. He worked and lived on the mines and they were not allowed to have their wives living there. I didn't think that was fair, and felt sad for her. I told Lena that it was not very nice to have families scattered all over, and have your parents live in different houses, like I did. She agreed without her usual smile. I said no more.

After school one Monday afternoon I got mad and shouted at Lena, because she had done the washing late and my shorts were wet. I wanted to go and play in the street. Gran gave me hard lecture on respect for older people. It lasted a long time. I felt ashamed. Then she made me apologize to Lena. Finally she made me go sit in my room to think about it for at least an hour. I did. I was truly sorry afterwards about shouting, but Lena never, ever said anything about it again. We were even better friends after that episode.

◆

I loved talking to Gran.

"Why does Uncle Mick get up so early to go to work?" I asked.

"He has to be at the mine at 6.30 AM, just like Mr. Gilbert and a few others, so that they can catch the first cage down the mine."

"Then what?"

"Then they go and drill holes in the rock, put the dynamite in, set the fuses and then catch the hoist back to the surface and blast the dynamite," explained Gran.

"Do they have lunch?"

"Yes! While they're working."

"Do they do this every day?"

"Yes! You talk to Uncle Mick. He'll tell you what he does."

"I will," I replied. I wondered why everything was the same, each day. Everyone around us seemed to do the same thing every day. Even on weekends: the people went shopping on Saturday and to church on Sunday. I thought it was boring to do the same thing every week.

◆

The Andrew Street Mob was made up of kids from many families. The initial group, all under the age of 10, who always went around together in Andrew Street, consisted of: Donald (Doc), whose father was a miner; Brian and Graham, whose dad worked in an office; the Joostes (7 kids), the Adams kid; Helen and Bobby, whose father was a diamond cutter; Mel and his parents (we never knew what they did!) Yvonne and Bazil never participated; they were too old. Also, there was Zoni and Juni, of Yugoslavian descent, that lived with their grandmother, Mimi. Their mother and father, butcher shop owners, lived elsewhere in the city; we never knew why.

Mimi, who was also a second mother, preacher, administrator of punishment and kindness to everyone in the street, was, if not liked by everyone, feared by all. As we grew up in the street we learned that Mimi could never be taken for granted. Everyone had felt the famous wooden spoon on their rear end; girls were exempted. I had experienced a brick passing my ear within an inch one day when I opened their front gate and yelled "Zoni!" Mimi came out, threw the brick and yelled, "You knock on the door!" One word all the Andrew Street kids understood was 'out'. That meant off her property, fast and furiously, and no questions.

Mimi's house was always dark, and when friends called on Zoni or Juni we knocked on the door with apprehension, stood back three feet, and hoped Mimi didn't answer. But she usually did, forever dressed in an apron, long dress, and Afro haircut. She always met the visitor with questions like, "What do you want?"

"Zoni," Was the inevitable reply.

"He's not here and he can't come out," would be the reply, leaving us in utter confusion, because we knew Zoni was inside. We would class this as a middle-of-the-road question and answer.

Then there was the definite instructive greeting: "I don't want you coming around here, especially with your dirty shoes. I just cleaned and polished the verandah and the path so get '*out*'." That famous word just meant 'fly'. There was another sort of greeting that would melt you inside: "Come on in, Zoni is nearly ready. Would you like some toast and tea?" and it was simply the best. Flabbergasted and with unsure smiles, us kids of Andrew Street would enter, making sure we knew all the obstacles in our pathway to the front door in case Mimi uttered those letters that form the word O-U-T. There were often ten or more kids for tea and toast on these happy occasions.

◆

Yvonne and Bazil came home from school, and shortly afterwards, Bazil joined the South African Army to go to North Africa. It was really nice to have them both at home and enjoy a big family. But it was bad to see Bazil go.

◆

Playing soccer in the street was our favorite activity. We had done it forever in between all our new-idea games. We loved it. It was never boring. It started with a kid's size leather ball. After a few days we had scuffed the ball up badly. We used two bricks at each end for the goals and played in the middle of the block so that we could see cars approaching. Anyone could play. Then the ingredients had to change. The leather ball wore out too soon and Brian and Graham (the owners) got hell from their parents. The bricks were replaced with tin cans, as they were easier to move when a car came up the street. Players didn't get hurt as bad.

My mom gave me a lecture: "Charl, I'm sick to death of you tearing up your clothes and shoes in the street. You're not playing in the street anymore . . . that's it."

"Mom, I won't wear my shoes out, if you buy me some tackies (canvas sneakers). I'll use those." I pleaded like a mournful child. I didn't like that type of pleading, but my friends said it worked.

"There is no money . . . I keep *telling* you!" my mother shouted, and then left me not knowing what to do. Soccer was too important to me. I would have to work something out.

We discussed it in the street, and it seemed like the parents had had a meeting. Brian, Bobby, Doc, Zoni and some of the Joostes had all heard the same thing. We were now so used to instruction, having learned it every day, we just followed orders and avoided conflicts. We did what we were told and our reward was money, which we used to go to the movies—and we loved that so much! So, for soccer the solution was perfect: barefoot tennis ball soccer. It really is amazing how good we got at playing with a tennis ball. We learnt to put our toes under the ball and scoop it up, so we could hit it hard. We learned to curl our toes in when kicking hard and turn them up when passing the ball. We could really kick hard, especially on the volley; we broke windows. Some guys could bounce a ball 15 or 20 times on their feet and knees and off their heads. There were no exceptions; we all played barefooted. It was easier to hide broken skin from parents' eyes than broken shoes. It also circumvented the yelling and screaming about 'money growing on trees.' As if that was so important! Using our prized soccer shoes was definitely out of the question; we would never do that in a thousand years. It became apparent that every single item we used for fun was used, broken or very cheap. No item was ever wasted. Our games were the most wonderful things in our lives. Hour after hour, ten kids or twenty kids, no matter, all ages, all types of games; we participated, even two on two! The better you got, the longer you held the ball. You also got great satisfaction when someone angrily pushed you off the ball, in frustration at your ball skills!

Some kids were allowed to play all the time in the street, others watched from windows. Some stood around until they got in the game or got called home. A kid was supposed to be qualified to play based on age or size, or if they brought the ball! But the rules changed every day, so sometimes you were in and sometimes you were not. There were many games played and lots of tricks learned. We never had many toys, as kids did in affluent societies. This was a blue-collar neighborhood, so beat-up used cricket bats, old soccer balls, and shoes, were treasured items. Tennis balls were picked up from people who played badly enough to hit balls over the fence from the Alleta Park tennis courts in Kenilworth, four blocks from Andrew Street. We waited patiently outside the court until someone hit the ball over the tall fences. Adults could very seldom catch kids with a half a block's start. Sundays were really good days for miss-hit balls. If only the bad tennis players knew how appreciative we were of their wild tennis shots. Tennis balls were even dug out of drains. The worst thing for us, and we all hated it, was the 'time for supper' call from home. It inevitably took place every day. After that call, eating, studying and bedtime were on the schedule. Andrew Street was very noisy and busy after school hours but very quiet after dark, and deathly still by 9 PM.

The Andrew Street Mob was all about kids coming together to have fun, play, feel the joy of belonging together, and talking about interesting stuff. We never talked about schoolwork! This mob was a fun-loving group. This was not a fighting gang. We had very little, but we were not desperate or underprivileged to a point of requiring physical violence. There was no stealing or raiding or intimidation. However, we were no angels either. We loved to challenge the traditional ways of people and institutions. We did make noise in the quiet street, and drank the occasional bottle of milk left on the porch by the milkman. We did take a piece of galvanized iron siding off Mr. Robinson's garage, when he and his wife went to Scotland. They were my next-door neighbors, whose only conversation consisted of the words 'good morning' and 'good night'. We did it just to see what he was hiding. There was nothing. So he never knew we had looked inside his locked garage. We just did it because nobody else locked garages.

◆

Just like any neighborhood, the seventy or so kids knew each other and we knew some of the parents, especially those who were nice and who were mean. After going away from the street for any reason, when you came back it was like having been on a hunt in the wild unknowns and returning to the security of an African camp . . . the security of roof and walls, food, the love, support and knowledge of the people and the wonderful feeling of knowing the land around you. Everybody got a greeting, because the street was always full of friends, and there was always some activity going on. It was a magic street. You could tell because no matter what time you walked past other streets they were quiet. "Nothing!" one of the kids had commented.

◆

One of the Mathews' kids was very sick for quite a while; all the families in the street knew because it was said that he would not recover. It was very hard to understand this, because everyone got sick, but came back in the street playing within three weeks at the most. An ambulance came one afternoon and we knew that it was serious. There were twenty of us playing; we stopped and walked to that end of the street.

The street was very quiet. We all stood very still for quite a while. Two men got out and went into the Mathews house. We waited. There were parents from a lot of families standing around in the street and some stood on their verandahs.

Everyone watched the men wheel the boy out of the house on a gurney and put him in the ambulance; he was totally covered with a white sheet. It was a very quiet scene. We could hear the wheels rotate on the gurney and the whispers of the attendants as they loaded the gurney into the ambulance. The attendants closed the door, got into the ambulance and drove away. All of us kids went and sat on the sidewalk.

"The white corpuscles ate up the red corpuscles," one kid said. It left me hollow inside and tears came to my eyes . . . I didn't know why.

*

CHAPTER 2

Andrew Street II

THREE O'CLOCK IN THE morning: a loud knock was heard on our door. I heard Gran and Mom get up. I rolled out of bed and stood at the door to my room. I was nine. There were many neighborhood stories about these early knocks. The news was never good. We stood in fear of the worst news. The war had been going on for a couple of years.

"You answer it, Maude," said Gran.

"All right."

My mom opened the door and we saw a man in uniform.

"Mrs. Flynn?" he asked.

"I'm her daughter. She is here."

The man handed her a telegram. "Sorry to wake you up, but we are instructed to deliver these telegrams as soon as the news is received."

"What's it say?" asked my mom.

"We don't know," he replied.

"Thank you."

"All right." The man left.

My mom went through to the kitchen and switched on the light. Gran followed her. I stood in the background. My mom opened the telegram.

"My God!" she exclaimed.

"What's it say?" asked Gran.

"Dennis has been shot down over Hungary . . . presumed missing."

Mom and Gran hugged each other.

Gran, tears streaming down her face, stared across the kitchen. "He's gone! My son! He's gone, I know!"

"Not necessarily," my mom tried to comfort Gran.

A lump formed in my throat. A hollow feeling was inside my body. A tear came to my eye. I hardly knew my Uncle Dennis. He was so good-looking, like a movie star in his South African Air Force uniform, with badges on his lapel and on his cap. Uncle Dennis was quiet and unassuming, and never said anything about my dad when all the other uncles and grownups were saying mean things about him. He always talked to me when he came to visit. I liked him.

"Better wake up Mick," said Gran. My mom went to wake him up. Gran made some tea and we all sat around the kitchen table talking until the sun came up. Uncle Mick did not go to work that day. It was the first time in my life that he missed work. Even if Uncle Mick was sick, or it was freezing cold outside, or pouring rain, or if he had got 'drunk as hell' the night before, he would go to work. My mom didn't go to work either. Instead, she made breakfast. She suggested I go to school, but Gran said no.

It was a very solemn day. Gran would cry and then go to her room. My mom read, as did Uncle Mick. I went into the yard and thought of Wolf, my beloved dog that went away some months earlier, but that only brought about despair about things we had no control over, and the pain went deeper. I just wanted to do something, but I knew it wasn't right to go play in the street. So I just sat in the yard.

Our backyard was a very peaceful place. There were fruit trees, roosters, fowls, chickens and pigeons. The fig tree bore three crops of figs a year, the plum and apricot trees two crops each and a frail peach tree, only one crop. The peach tree, however, yielded the biggest peaches, bigger than the hole you make when you use two hands and put your two middle fingers and your two thumbs together. Each member of the family claimed a certain peach and followed its growth until they ate it.

Dinner that night was very, very quiet. I heard only the sounds of knives and forks touching the plates. Finally, we had coffee . . . no talk, just the end of the meal. We all went to bed early that evening, a black shroud clouding our thoughts.

◆

I was now ten years of age, walking down Main Road to school at 7:30 AM each day. I was going to Rosettenville Central School, located near Rosettenville Corner, the Broadway Hotel, and a variety of shops and cinemas. It was all part of a famous intersection in the Southern Suburbs. The days at Kenilworth School had ended. To get to the new school, the kids of Andrew Street could either catch a bus on Main Street or walk about a mile. This school included kids from all over Johannesburg's Southern Suburbs. It was a pre-high school with kids up to 12 years old. The new school opened up my eyes to surrounding territory, it showed an expanded horizon, which in turn increased my knowledge of where I lived. A new school with all new kids was exciting because there were different things to do and new kids to play games with.

The most exciting thing was that they had real soccer and cricket teams, which played against other schools. We had played these sports in the street but this was the real thing. Now we would have real soccer shoes and a school shirt and socks. After enduring the first few days of general harassment and initiation administered by the older kids, like 'ducking' (forcing your head under the water tap), it didn't take long for me to divide the groups in the playground into 'fun', 'quiet' and 'trouble-like'. I joined the group playing soccer with a tennis ball. I played goalkeeper and was good at it; this was a fun group. While playing on the rough grass in the playground, I met Desmond, who loved soccer and lived above Andrew Street. So we walked to school together and after school we met and walked slowly up Main Street. Desmond had hard and sharp features and black hair with white, white skin. He was not heavily built but was strong; I found out when we wrestled in fun. Helen, Bobby, Zoni, Juni, Brian and Graham, Mel and Doc were still my major playmates on Andrew Street; and they went to Rosettenville High School. After school we played in Andrew Street.

My world was now between home, Rosettenville Central School, Pioneer Park (where we played soccer and cricket), the Adelphi Cinema (where we went on Wednesday and Saturday afternoons), and Andrew Street. The park was a mile north of school, and the cinema three hundred yards from Rosettenville Corner. I went back to Pioneer Park on Saturdays to play soccer.

◆

Street bike racing started with three or four kids who had small bikes: hand-me-downs, or assembled from junk in garages. We built them to look like racing motorbikes: definitely no mudguards. The racetrack was from the tarmac street through a driveway and onto the sand sidewalk. It continued past two houses and back through a second drive-way to the street. We timed everybody to the second. We did every-thing we could to improve times. There is a tremendous art in going from a tarmac street to a sand sidewalk. You have to know how to speed up, corner the bike, and get around the bend. It was totally necessary to lean inwards, drag one foot, not slide too much, straighten up and then sprint as fast as you could. The crashes on the turns with four bike riders going from the street to the sidewalk were numerous. There was no dispute as to who won the races but there were many arguments as to whose turn it was to ride. There were only four bikes and fifteen to twenty kids that rode. The bikes were constructed by groups of kids and belonged to everybody. I didn't have a bike.

After the racing from sidewalk to street was mastered, we decided it would be more fun to try it blindfolded. Well, that became quite an accomplishment, and took a long time to achieve. A person could laugh like hell at someone else riding the bike, but when you had to do it yourself you knew you had no control. When you started to move, you had no idea as to where you were going. You became very nervous about crashing into something. This game finally came to an end after Doc, blindfolded on a bike, rode from the street onto the sidewalk, and ended up hitting a wire fence. He was propelled over the fence and into a row of beautiful flowers. We ran into the yard and got him out. He wasn't injured, but the flowers were flattened. We had to play further down the street for a very long time following that incident, mostly be-cause the garden was in the house next to Doc's home. We didn't mind moving our games down the street—as long as we could play!

The new challenges in our street were very necessary because this mob pushed the limits of every game—and then it became boring. So, our appetite to try something new was always there. I wanted to become good at all these games and worked very hard at it. I would not give up on anything we tried without getting to be good at it.

Although, I was playing all these sports, both at school and in the street, I was having a tough time with bronchitis. It all came about mostly at night. I felt the wheezing during the day, but the attacks were the worst, when I went to bed. My family was concerned.

◆

A beautiful scruffy dog wandered into Andrew Street one afternoon. He had a square face, brown eyes and light brown hair, and his tail was wagging like crazy and all the kids fell in love with him. He hung around for days mainly because the kids sneaked food out of their houses and fed him; nobody claimed him. So I pleaded with my mom and Gran and got him accepted into the family. He looked like a pal and he acted like a pal, so I called him Pal. He joined the family and Pal slept in Wolf's old kennel.

Wolf was my dog when we lived with my dad at the top of Main Street (Number 9). Wolf and I were inseparable. We never left each other from the moment I came into the yard from the house. Wolf would meet me with a wagging tail and never really leave my side. And he always wanted to play. I could wrestle with Wolf, grab his neck and run with him or lie on his stomach when we both got tired. My most favorite time ever was when I got a cowboy suit with two pockets in the vest, and chaps with fringes on the side, a gun, a holster and a cowboy hat. I put on the suit with frantic happiness, grabbed Wolf and went with my mom to the koppies near the house. My mother watched as I played 'Cowboys and Indians.' Wolf ran by my side throughout the game. Wolf hated when I tried to sit on his back and ride him like a horse. When I jumped on he'd just slide out from under me, and we'd run some more. The three of us only went a few times to the koppies, even though I asked many, many times. My dad never came to see the game. I liked the koppies and the backyard. I didn't like our house. Everything inside the house was quiet and serious. Everything outside was fun.

Wolf came with us to Gran's house when my parents split up and we moved. Wolf was my best friend. He was the first one I wanted to see when I got home from school. I would run through the house shouting "Hullo Gran!" And after I got a big hug and kiss, I would scramble into the back yard. Wolf and I would hug, then run in and out and under the trees, me laughing and shouting. I'd try to catch Wolf until I got tired.

Half our property was the backyard. Wolf and I spent so many hours there together. It was our world. Many hours were spent on the back doorstep. We just sat there. I would pat, stroke and hug him. I talked to him about becoming a famous soccer player, or a famous cowboy actor, or a runner that could beat everybody. I told Wolf I would be very good at something one day, because it is such a good feeling to do things better than anyone else! I also told Wolf about my teachers and my uncles, and that if he wanted to bite them, it was all right with me.

I also told him that I was sorry he had to stay in the backyard. Parents did not want dog fights in the street.

Each day at five o'clock Wolf would jump onto the six-foot-high brick wall between the Loxtons' duplex and our house, and walk to the pillar that was in front of the houses and facing the sidewalk. Most people who came up the street, from busses that stopped on the corner of Main and Andrew Street, would cross over to the other sidewalk, so as to avoid Wolf. One day, for no given reason, Wolf jumped off the pillar onto Helen and scratched the side of her face. This was a truly unusual event, because Helen and I were always talking or playing together. We had done this many times without problems with Wolf. Her parents were furious and called the police. There were many discussions between all the grown-ups and an agreement was made that Wolf would have to go to a farm. I was hollow inside. I cried and screamed that it was all lies and they were going to shoot Wolf. Everyone told me that was not true. Wolf would go to a farm. I very quickly sorted out the good and bad grown-ups. I tried to find a way to get Wolf somewhere safe where I could go and see him. My first plan was to find a friend at school to take Wolf. I'd untie him before going to school, deliver him to the friend, then go to school and say nothing. I decided to talk to some friends, swear secrecy, and do it. I often untied Wolf before going to bed . . . if I could do that without being seen.

All my efforts failed. Nobody would take Wolf. I felt horrible and now didn't care about school or anything. I just moped around for the longest time. I couldn't come up with an answer. Then something weird happened! The night before someone was scheduled to take Wolf away . . . he disappeared. I couldn't find him anywhere. The family searched the neighborhood, but Wolf had vanished. This was mysterious. I believed Wolf knew somehow and had run away, and that made me feel good inside. He was smarter than the grownups and it was good that he wasn't going to be forced onto some farm, no matter how nice everyone said it would be. But where was he? Or had the grown-ups taken him away? This was all very confusing and I started to feel as though I was the last one to know.

It was a long time before I could go out the back door of the house either after school or on the weekends. It just seemed so empty. The yard was dead. The chickens and birds did not do what Wolf had done to make it alive. No matter what good feelings could be generated elsewhere, it was impossible to take them into the backyard and not remember Wolf and end up being sad. I had cried many, many times.

One night there was a whining at the back door. Gran opened the door and a German Shepherd dog, very thin and drawn, was standing there wagging his tail. He didn't answer to 'Wolf'. I was ecstatic! A dog that looked like Wolf! Gran and I dried the dog with a towel, fed him, and put him in Wolf's kennel. I could not sleep and twice sneaked out of the house and into back yard to see him. Each time he wagged his tail and put his ears back. I hugged him so hard one time he yelped. Finally I went to bed and fell asleep. In the morning the dog was gone. The kids going to school and everyone at dinner discussed the dog . . . was it Wolf or not? I said nothing. I was just so happy inside . . . it was Wolf! I knew it absolutely, by the scar on his left leg above the joint, by his teeth and by his eyes. I know he didn't look as healthy as he used to be, but I was sure it was Wolf. I was incredibly happy he was alive. The loss of Wolf was very, very sad. I missed him terribly, especially in the afternoon after school and on Sundays after church. The backyard I loved to play in was empty. The trees and grass had no emotions . . . nothing was fun in this place anymore! It took me a long time before I could even think of having another dog. However, Pal seemed to be the one.

◆

As the arrows on the maps were getting closer to Berlin, the kids knew that the news of the war ending was getting better every day. Italy had surrendered and joined forces with the Allies. The Germans had surrendered at Stalingrad and the RAF had bombed Berlin. Hitler was all over the newspapers. Millions of people were free and celebrating. The atomic bomb had been dropped on Hiroshima and Nagasaki. I really didn't understand the story . . . just one bomb could wipe out a city! I had seen big explosions on Movietone news where houses and factories got blown up, but never a whole city with just one bomb. No one I knew could explain it.

We saw people celebrating all over the world on Movietone news at the cinemas. People were dancing and hugging and kissing each other in the streets in many cities of the world. We had never seen people 'kissing' in the street like that! Our parents were ecstatic that the wars had ended. After listening to all the grown-ups and teachers in our lives and their opinions on politics, black and white, heritages, English,

Afrikaans, Uitlanders (foreigners), Europeans and so on, the kids were now hoping that the final end of the wars would lift the spirits of people everywhere and bring happiness to everyone. We believed life would be easier.

Despite our continuous inquiries to the South African Air Force, the news of Uncle Dennis never got any better. Then my mom got notification that Bazil was coming home from Italy. She was very happy but did not show it in front of Gran. I went to my brother's homecoming, along with Gran, my sister Yvonne and Mom. We went by bus and made our way to the Wanderers Stadium in Johannesburg City. It was like going to an international rugby match. We sat in the stadium seats for a long time. The stadium was almost half full. The train pulled in from Cape Town followed by the soldiers who marched onto the playing fields. The generals and officers made their speeches.

A general pleaded, "Please remain in your seat. We will discharge the soldiers and they will walk to the edges of the sports field, whereupon you can observe your loved ones and go and meet them. Please honor this request."

After that the soldiers were dismissed, and despite requests for normal behavior, there was a horrendous scramble of people coming out of the stands looking for their loved ones. People ran out on the field, so did my mom and Yvonne, and I trailed them. Gran said she'd wait. People just ran randomly looking at the soldiers that didn't have anyone around them and just kept moving. Amazingly enough it worked, and everybody found the one they had waited for, for so many years. They were hugging and kissing, slapping each other on the back, staring into each face in bewilderment. There were tears of joy. My mom found Bazil with the most monstrous set of bags strapped all over his body . . . But he looked in good shape. He was embarrassed by the affection of Mom who draped herself all over him. There was a total outburst of joy! The whole stadium was full of natural affection and happiness. The feeling was unique in that our normal life was so conservative regarding display of feelings, and here everybody just let go! I truly thought that it was terrific! Everyone moving around wild with excitement and shouting! People never did that at all.

We all went home on the bus, talking and talking, and just ignoring everyone on the bus because the feelings of the stadium had not subsided. We were going to have a home cooked meal: roast beef and Yorkshire pudding, and rice pudding, the family favorite.

Bazil told us many stories and we had lots of questions. The story I liked best was the one where the Americans and the South Africans had relieved this Italian village and everyone was celebrating. The Americans were spending lots of money and had a lot of candies and therefore were meeting all the girls. A South African soldier took his shirt off, wore only his bush jacket on top, and sold his shirt; he too then had money and joined the crowd. Bazil said that within an hour nearly all his group had sold or traded their shirts and the party in the town just got better. There was a lot of happiness during this wonderful day. I liked people to be happy. I liked the story.

I noticed Gran was the quietest of us all. She was smiling but thinking deeply. I could tell because I had seen her when she wasn't happy. I knew that look, she never had it very often, but today it was very sad: Dennis was gone . . . forever.

CHAPTER 3

Vryburg

AT THE AGE OF twelve, I suffered continuously from bronchitis. It had increased in severity over the last two years. Each night I would try to sleep lying down with my head on the pillow. Sometimes sleep would come. Most nights I would feel the choking of airflow and a deep wheezing inside my lungs. I had experienced this so many times; I would play a game of counting the wheeze bumps. To relieve the wheezing I would have to sleep sitting up in bed with four pillows. When that didn't work, or I had an attack that caused really short breathing, I had to put my head over a boiling pot of some chemical, whose vapor would let me breathe more easily. Gran spent many late hours, over two years of nights, talking to me, until I would finally fall asleep. By the time I was twelve, doctors were suggesting that I go and stay for a complete year in the province of the Orange Free State. It had a dry, arid climate, was primarily farm country and the biggest producer of maize in South Africa. Although I hadn't seen my dad for a while, he had suggested that I go to Beaufort West, in the Cape, where he had grown up. My mother had said no, she couldn't afford it. Gran strongly disagreed with everyone and suggested that I go to Vryburg in Bechuanaland for school vacation, where her sister Tillie had a farm. Gran thought this could help determine if the climate would improve my condition. The decision was made. As the summer holidays were the longest and lasted from December to January, that's when I would go to Vryburg. Yvonne and her friend Delphine, and Elaine, my cousin, would also go.

Through kids at school I had developed a perception that all people in the countryside were farmers and all farmers were Afrikaners (speaking Afrikaans, which originates from Dutch). The kids also put people in categories of city boys and farmer boys, adding how dumb farmers were and that they knew nothing about city life. I had learned in school how tough and strict the pioneers were, and the kids in the playground confirmed that all farmers were pioneers. They also told me I would be treated like an outsider, especially as I didn't speak Afrikaans very well. In addition, they were determined to convince me that the Black people were out of the veld and forests and were wild and ferocious and would hunt me down. These comparisons were a contradiction and not like anything I had heard at home. I had some fears that the kids were right, despite my gran telling me that their statements were not true. My mom confirmed Gran's statements and added that we came from a long line of farmers. Still, I didn't know what to believe, so I was not anxious to go to Vryburg. I was glad that Yvonne and Elaine were going, because my sister gave me confidence, and I liked Elaine because she was about the same age and we always had fun together when our family went to visit her and Aunt Amy, her mother.

The train was to leave Johannesburg on a Sunday, and I was told I should get into bed as soon as the train pulled out and that I would wake up in a station called Warrenton. This was close to Fourteen Streams and is where they changed engines before going on to Vryburg. Vryburg railway station was where my farm cousin Southey would meet us. Warrenton was on the main line from Kimberley to Mafeking, just north of Kimberley, and you had to travel southwest from Johannesburg through Krugersdorp. The only interesting part of this trip, that I could see, was traveling on a train, and the fact that a steam locomotive pulled the train. It had great big pistons driving the cranks and enormous steel wheels. The engineers had to use coal shovels for firing the boiler. There were lots of levers and gauges all over the place. The coalbunker was at the back of the engine, followed by a water tank car. It seemed as though someone had just shined every part of the steam engine with the brass only slightly outshining the black steel parts.

I got to talk to the train driver before going to the carriage. The train driver, dressed in overalls, big horse buckle belt, a peaked cap and glasses and boots, looking like an American train driver, informed me it was a 15F engine, one of the biggest, and very popular. It was equipped with a low stack and two side fender plates. The wheels were bigger than I was!

Despite my telling my friends about the trip, and that it was no problem to travel, and that I was old enough to handle this, I was still scared when the train pulled out of Johannesburg. This was my first trip anywhere far from the Southern Suburbs of Johannesburg. It was like going into a dark tunnel with thousands of little lights flickering in the background. I felt alone. I had heard about my aunt Tillie and aunt Eileen and the farm Langenhorn from my mom and her friend Mrs. Creswell who was friendly with Aunt Tillie's daughter Mima. The family continued to be a mystery to me; there were so many people. I would have cried if I weren't with the girls. Yvonne was 18 years of age, Delphine the same and Elaine was 12.

This was going to be an exciting trip. Vryburg was in Griqualand West, Bechuanaland, close to Bophuthatswana. Kimberley was to the South and the Kalahari Desert to the North. Kimberley was famous for diamonds and the Kalahari Desert famous for animals, animal parks, and the starkness of desert country. Most of all it was famous for its inhabitants, the Bushmen. Short, thin, colored people called San who wore nothing but small cloths around the middle of their body. They were the only ones to survive in the arid desert. Pictures in our schoolbooks showed them as aborigines with loincloths. We had learnt about them at school. They fascinated me because they were so small!

Each compartment on the train had one door, two windows and six bunks, three on each wall. The middle and top bunk folded up for day travel. The top bunk was near the roof, which meant the passenger couldn't see out the window when lying down. The seat bunk, when lying down, was too low to see out the window, so the middle bunk was just right; Elaine and I fought over the middle and I lost. Elaine took the middle and put the safety board in the holes provided to prevent a passenger from falling out. I wouldn't sleep on the bottom bunk because you could end up with a foot on your body when somebody climbed out, so I slept on the top bunk. The compartment also had washing basins.

Snug in bed and lying quietly, I listened to the clicking of the train wheels going over the rail joints. It was a soothing sound. I was a lot calmer and I started to feel that this might be an exciting adventure, going to see farms in desert countryside with live animals, and meeting more people of my very large and complex family. The girls were asleep. I knew that because they had stopped talking. I too fell asleep on the train as it journeyed through the suburbs of Johannesburg, through the town of Krugersdorp, then left the Witwatersrand (Ridge of White Waters) to head for Potchefstroom. The Witwatersrand is a 60-mile-long plateau, 6,000 feet above sea level. Gold was discovered there in the 1880's and was the reason for most things that occurred since that time. Johannesburg was the center of the plateau. It had grown from mining camps into a large city of over a million people.

I woke up with birds singing: it was 6 am. The train had stopped. The bunk was not as comfortable as my bed. I lay there for a while, thinking how quiet it was and how distinct the noises were in comparison to home, where the house was always so active. I put on my shorts and shirt, climbed down from the bunk, and went down to the toilet on the train. It was a weird contraption, with just enough room, and a big sign 'Do Not Use when Train is in a Station.' Too bad! I left the toilet and walked down the corridor to see what was happening. A conductor was coming the other way.

"Good Morning Sir," I said.

"Good Morning Son," said the conductor with a smile and a perky movement as though it was a good day to be alive. He was dressed in black. He had a watch and chain around his stomach over his waistcoat and wore a cap, a long black jacket and a railway tie.

"Where are we, please?" I asked.

"Fourteen Streams, we're waiting to be attached to the engine and train that is going to Mafeking," replied the conductor. "Where are you going?"

"To Vryburg Sir, to see my aunt," I replied. The man paused and so I continued, "Can I get breakfast on the train?"

"No, the dining car is on the Mafeking train and we haven't been joined to that train yet, but you can go down to the station platform. There is a coffee shop that is open, but don't miss the train. We leave at half past seven," said the conductor.

"Thank you Sir," I said.

"Fine."

Yvonne, Delphine, Elaine and I got off the train and had to walk across a railway line, because there was no station platform. This was a rail junction consisting of sand, ties and rails. We walked towards the coffee shop that had a ground level wooden platform. The entrance had a fly screen door hanging off its hinges. The building was an old brick building in need of everything, but inside there were neat little wooden tables and chairs, oilcloth over the tables, and it looked clean.

All that didn't matter a few minutes later, because the smell of bacon, eggs, coffee and toast was exquisite. Outside the air seemed so fresh; birds were singing; the tall eucalyptus trees were very still. Everything was so crisp: the air was exhilarating, and all the sounds of the country could be heard individually. This was so different, by comparison to the noises of Johannesburg and its cars and buses.

We ate breakfast and scrambled back onto the train. The porter had returned the bunks to their storage positions. The engines had been hooked up. A loud blast of the steam whistle, then another, and a few seconds later the train inched forward almost painfully, groaning and squeaking as though a massive iron beast had been woken from its sleep. We left the eucalyptus trees behind around Fourteen Streams Junction. The railway line curved back into a straight line along a sand road, grass tufts, small trees and flat land were visible. Spring had gone and the trees were green, but there was more sand color than green and the background of the countryside was light brown. Soon we were crossing a series of streams and islands as we went from bridge to land to bridge in sequence. Elaine counted them . . . fourteen!

The train was dusty because all the windows were open. I sat with my back to the engine and didn't get as much soot and dust on me as when I faced the way the train was moving. Each railway carriage had neat little verandahs on each end open to the air. I decided to go out and stand in the complete open. I leant over the railing and the air, soot and dust flowed into my face, so I waited until the train was going across wind, when the smoke blew away from the train. The rails were 22-yards long; 80 rails meant a mile. I counted the clicks and timed them over a minute, so I could tell the train speed. It was 25 miles per hour. The South African trains run on narrow gauge 3'-6", speed is limited, and they very seldom exceeded 40 miles per hour.

Elaine joined me, and we hung on the railing as we talked to each other about the trip. Yvonne and Delphine kept to themselves and were also talking. Elaine was one of two daughters of my aunt Amy and uncle Harry, Amy being a sister of my mother. Elaine was older than me and was a plain looking girl with glasses; she had a wonderful, warm smile and was just very nice. Elaine's sister Alicia was the same age as me, a pretty blonde, and wilder than Elaine. Aunt Amy was very religious and had recently tried Catholicism; she had previously been a member of the Presbyterian Church and was presently a Baptist. I didn't care to visit my aunt Amy on Sundays because there was a hundred percent guarantee of ending up in church before the visit ended.

"Where is Vryburg?" I asked Elaine.

"It's on the line from Kimberly to Mafeking".

"What do they do there?" I asked.

"In Vryburg?" asked Elaine.

"Yes!" I replied.

"They farm cattle, and make milk and cream and butter and stuff. Everything gets shipped out of Vryburg," replied Elaine.

"Mafeking is where the British fought the Boers, and the British General or whatever he was, Baden Powell, was held under siege. He started the Boy Scouts," I said.

"Is that true?" asked Elaine.

"Yes!" I replied.

"I know all about it," said Elaine, smiling, "that's also where the famous Jameson Raid on the Boers in the Transvaal started from!" I returned her smile, thinking, *I have to learn more.* We were silent for a long while, just looking at the scenery and swaying with the coach.

"Even when you go on picnics to the countryside, you never see anything like this," said Elaine. "There's so much land and no cars and no people. The land is flat and dry with those small rocks, brown grass, and small trees looking as though they are about to die. It's so flat you can see the horizon from end to end. How do people live here?"

"I don't know," I ventured. "There's nothing to do I guess. Wonder what Aunt Tillie is like? Mom said she's as nice as Gran . . . so that would be alright."

"We're also going to visit Auntie Eileen. Southey's her son, and our cousin, you know; he's going to meet us in Vryburg," said Elaine. "He's about sixteen years old, I think."

"Wow, look at that dust cloud on the horizon." The winds had swept up sand particles from the plowed lands and formed swirling clouds that must have been 200 feet in diameter and twice as high.

"I want to ride a horse," I said. "Someone had a horse in the fields near Andrew Street and I rode it without a saddle. I'd like a black horse with a long black mane—and a saddle made of fine leather with silver tips on all the edges. Then I'd like to have a white cowboy hat and black jacket the same color as the horse, and black pants with all the tassels and things. Wow!"

"You've been listening to Grandpa Mick," said Elaine. "He gets all his stories from American Westerns. There's no such thing as a fancy cowboy!"

"Sure is!" I suggested forcibly. "I'll show you a picture."

"Okay," relinquished Elaine, "but South African horse riders don't dress like Americans, they dress like kommandoes *commandos* of the Boer War—all in khaki—and the hats are different, they're not so fancy!"

"Oh, I've seen those pictures in the history books, maybe we'll see a couple of real South African cowboys in Vryburg!" I suggested. I didn't want to argue with Elaine. I liked the American-style clothes and especially the Stetson and I also thought the hat of the Boer kommandoes wasn't bad either. It made you look rough and tough!

"Well Charl, we're not even going to stay in Vryburg. We're going to the Langenhorn farm and it's a long way from Vryburg," said Elaine.

"How are we going to get there?" I asked.

"Don't know!" Elaine replied as though she didn't care.

"Let's go and get a lemonade drink," I suggested, thinking that my cousin was going to be a drag. Girls were a drag. It would be so much nicer if I was to meet Southey and we could do things together. It would be great if only I was going to Vryburg. I felt like the youngest again. Everyone was in charge of me.

"Okay!" Elaine said with a nice smile.

Vryburg is a rail stop in Bechuanaland. It is a small town with shops, houses, a hotel, and a church steeple. The predominant church of small towns in South Africa is the Dutch Reformed Church. The Afrikaners are the main congregation and they are very, very earnest in their religion, their politics and their government. This is reflected in most of the small towns of South Africa. This power was put and held in place because of what the Afrikaners had experienced in the long, never-ending battle for South Africa, first against Dutch colonists and then English colonists. The South African small town contains the very nature of the pioneer farmer: order and religion in a free space. I was brought up to learn the teachings of the Anglican Church. People said these two religious backgrounds were different. To me it was confusing; the church was a house of God, no matter the name or the place.

Some of the roads were tarmac in Vryburg, but just off the main road, the streets became dirt roads.

The train entered Vryburg station very slowly. My first sight was of a large group of black people on the platform. The women were dressed in bright colors, usually with a scarf wrapped round their head like a turban, but with a knot tied at the back. Some had light colored blankets wrapped horizontally around the top part of their bodies, with a baby asleep in the back, legs astride their mother's back. Some women wore sandals; some had on shoes, but many were barefoot. Most women had a bag on their head or at their side, and a child with wide eyes and nubbed hair hanging on tight to their mother's skirt. The black men were dressed plainly, in khaki pants and plain shirts, and sometimes a jacket. The clothes looked clean but worn. These people were either going to Rhodesia or Johannesburg via Mafeking, or waiting for husbands, relatives and friends from either of these places or from the Kimberley mines and Free State farms.

Just before the train came to a halt, the color of people changed to white. I saw only a few whites on the platform as the train stopped, they too were bound for Rhodesia or Johannesburg or waiting to meet someone. There was a strong contrast in dress to the blacks. The whites wore fewer colors, neat business suits or Safari style suits (short pants, high socks and a bush jacket) or farmer style, short sleeves, khaki shorts, socks and shoes, and often a hat like the Kommandoes. Clothes were newer and pressed with sharp creases. The socks went right up over the calf to the underside of the knee. When the train came to a stop, the color of people on the train matched the color of the people standing at the station. That had been the same at Johannesburg station. People traveled separately according to color.

Yvonne, Delphine, Elaine, and I struggled off the train with our suitcases and stood on the platform.

"Hello there!" said cousin Southey, dressed in khaki shorts and shirt and wearing a big smile. He was strong and slender, with brown eyes and brown hair. He was also older than any one of my close friends in Andrew Street. I worried that he may not be too interested in me, and that that may not turn out to be good.

"I'm your guide! Let me have your bags," Southey suggested.

We all introduced ourselves, shook hands and slowly merged into the crowd funnel leaving the station. We walked two blocks to a group of dark red-and-cream striped buses of the South African Railways and Harbors. The windows were high off the road, and luggage was stowed below in enclosed hatches and on racks above. The racks and luggage were covered with canvas because of the dirt roads. There was also a trailer of similar design, which carried supplies for the farmers: bone meal for cattle, fuel, and lubricating oil. They would return with grain for the silos. Black people traveled in separate buses: two classes of travel, reflecting the norm.

"We're leaving right away," said Southey. "Otherwise we'll have to stay over for a day before the next bus leaves."

We clambered aboard. Elaine, Southey and I shared a three-person seat; I got the window seat. Yvonne and Delphine sat behind us. The bus pulled out with lots of noise, people yelling and waving. Vryburg disappeared very quickly as we hit the sand road going north to Aunt Tillie's farm. The dust and stones flew as the bus and trailer hit 50 mph, despite the 40-mph maximum sign on the bus. The ride would last more than two hours because of stops along the way. The stops included getting off the bus, talking and having a cup of tea or coffee with people at the stop. It was all so friendly and as though we had known everybody for years. I mostly stared out the window as Southey and Elaine talked. I looked at the dry land, the thorn trees, the brown grass, the almost non-existent small hills, the fence, post by post, and the everlasting overhead wire running from pole to pole. The road was wide and 18 inches below normal land height to make it as level as possible. The sky was blue with an occasional bird. I never saw an animal. I wondered if I would have to live in this country all my life. It all looked so barren and uninviting. I didn't know what to think, and sure wished my friend Desmond was here.

The bus kept a constant pace, spraying stones up to thirty feet onto the side of the road. Natives of the area walking from farm to farm would anticipate the bus, head into the grassy bush, and stand and wave as the dust express zoomed by! This continued until the main farming district came into view and then the bus would have to stop, a black man from the trailer bus would open a gate, and close it after the bus went through the simply constructed wood and wire doorways of the veld. In the farming district the main road was lined with a fence on each side, twenty-foot from the edge of the gravel. This kept the cattle and sheep off the main road. This was the same as farms outside of Johannesburg, but the distances here between farms were miles and miles more, and there was not much change in the landscape.

It was late in the afternoon when the bus left the main road and drove up to Langenhorn, which Southey described as 'Aunt Tillie's place.' The bus stopped; passengers got off to stretch. The bus driver helped with the baggage, everyone shook hands and thanked the driver. Before anyone knew it, Aunt Tillie was standing right next to Elaine. She grabbed her and hugged her, then went on to Yvonne and then shook hands with Delphine. My turn came next. She hugged me a little longer. Aunt Tillie was as big as my Gran. Both were round and robust. Gran was a pale white and Aunt Tillie sunburned, with more gray hair. They had the same beautiful smile.

Aunt Tillie's farmhouse was a typical example, with its stone walls, corrugated zinc roof, large verandah, polished cement entrance, immaculately clean floors, and cool dark interior. I was shown my room with its rough hand-made furniture, quilts and a single pillow. There was a bathroom, but no hot and cold running water. There were no electric lights, switches or plugs. The girls were going to sleep in a little guesthouse just a short distance from the main farmhouse. I was glad because they wouldn't be around all the time.

The bus took off. After the clothes were put away, a black woman named Elena made tea from hot water off the top of a coal stove. Aunt Tillie asked us about her sisters and life in Johannesburg, and what Yvonne, Elaine and I were doing in school. Aunt Tillie, Aunt Eileen, Aunt Violet and Gran had grown up in Tweeling in the Orange Free State, a village of around 1000 people, close to Frankfort, founded by a German named van Gordon. Their family was originally from England. The family left Tweeling and headed north and they bypassed Kimberley and the diamond diggings with all the uncertainties of beer halls, drunks, fly-by-nights, gangsters, moneymakers, and claim jumpers. For some reason, there was a split, with Gran going on to Johannesburg and Aunt Tillie, Aunt Eileen and Aunt Violet finally trekking north of Kimberley to the outskirts of Vryburg. There Aunt Tillie and her husband, Mr. Stapelberg, who was German, bought a farm, called it 'Langenhorn,' and started in the farming business. Elaine and I tried to find out what happened to her husband, but we didn't want to be rude and ask directly. All we found out was that its owner, Aunt Tillie, now operated 'Langenhorn'.

Following tea we got the tour. There was a big barn and inside it a four-wheel cart and two two-wheel carts, and enough room for hay and tool storage. There were a number of kraals (corrals) for cows and calves, a barn and large pasture for horses, a creamery, and a small guesthouse. Through a clump of trees were some native rondavels (round shaped mud-wall and grass-roof huts) set out in a random pattern. Close to the house there was a corrugated zinc water storage tank, 50 feet in diameter and 4 feet high with the traditional windmill and connecting pipes. All the water for this district came from underground. *This is a real farm*, I thought, *just like you see in the Western movies.* There were fences and gates everywhere.

Dinner was cooked by Aunt Tillie and served by Elena and her son Jacob. The servers had been trained in all the graces and etiquette of English and Afrikaans traditions and were very good at their jobs. We bowed our heads as Aunt Tillie thanked the Lord for the benefits of food and family. The room was lit with candles, all the best china was used and the food was marvelous. There were meat and potatoes, beans with corn, fresh bread, and cold water. Afterwards we sat around and had tea. I liked it because there was no cabbage. We always had cabbage at home, maybe because of Uncle Mick's Irish tradition.

Southey carried the conversation most of the night.

"Tomorrow at 6 am we're going to milk the cows, and I have something special for you, Charl. Sometime later we're going to collect the horses and go to the trading post for Auntie. Then after a few days, we will be going to the Christmas picnic," said Southey.

"What is the special thing?" I asked, savoring the excitement of a surprise.

"Wait till morning."

"I'm going to show you how to make cream," said Aunt Tillie.

"At the Christmas picnic there's going to be a small fair and sports competition. There will be races, a cricket game . . . " added Southey.

"A cricket game?" I inquired anxiously. I loved sport and at least I would know what to do in cricket.

"Yes," said Southey. "Do you play?"

"Yes!" I said excitedly.

"Do you bat or bowl?" asked Southey.

"Both," I replied. Now, this was going to be fun. I wondered if the ground would be like Pioneer Park, flat and sand. Would they put a mat down?

"Good," he said. "Don't tell anyone."

"After the three weeks here at Aunt Tillie's, we're going to stay at my mom's farm for a while," said Southey.

"Can I learn to ride a horse?" I asked.

"Yes," said Southey, "without a saddle!"

"No!" said Aunt Tillie.

"Of course he can, he's big and strong," said Southey.

"No," said Aunt Tillie. "I promised his mother I would take care of him."

The long day from Fourteen Streams to Aunt Tillie's farm started to take it's toll on the travelers and so Southey took the girls to the guesthouse and Aunt Tillie wished me a good night's sleep.

I sat for a short while and reflected on my day of adventure. It was good, and all the scariness had gone away. I took a candle and went to bed. It was weird. As I walked, shadowy figures that were in front suddenly went past and followed me. This was not like electric lights where you could see everything. The candle went wherever I went. I got into bed, and lay there for a while and then realized I needed to go to the bathroom badly. So I got up, knocked on Southey's door and asked where the toilet was.

"It's out the back door down the pathway. It's the very small house," said Southey, who then turned over in bed, faced the wall, and added, "Watch out for the snakes!"

"What snakes?" I asked. This terrified me. I wondered if he was playing with me.

"The ones that like the warmth of the building after the sun goes down!" said Southey.

I walked down the path with the candle, shielding it from the evening breeze. I had visions of snakes lying in the corners ready to strike. I had never been this scared of anything, but the pain in my belly was too much to hold everything in. I opened the spring-loaded door slowly, put the candle in and looked around. The smell was a terrible combination of disinfectant and everything else. This outhouse had a wooden seat and a hole. I searched the corners, looked down the hole, dropped my pants, squatted, and got out in record-breaking time. It was quite a feat with a candle in one hand! I crawled into bed and went to sleep relieved, but not totally enthralled. My last thoughts were questions about why snakes wouldn't come into the house!

◆

Southey woke me up at 6:30 AM. I could have slept for another two hours after the bus trip.

"Come on, we got to get going."

I jumped out of bed. *Wow! I'm on the farm*, I thought. I put on a short-sleeved shirt, short pants and tackies (running/canvas shoes) without socks: my favorite clothes.

We sat down for breakfast. Someone told me there was nothing like breakfast in the country. There were eggs, fresh bacon, freshly made baking powder biscuits (scones), porridge and coffee. The girls were present, talking and talking about everything on the farm, from the color of the sheets to the spider webs on the wall. I thought they were crazy or maybe just boring, but Aunt Tillie really loved to have them around so I thought it must be okay.

As soon as Southey was finished, we went outside. The house was surrounded with grass, trees, flowers and cement patios but if you looked further there was just sand and grass everywhere with just a sprinkling of small trees. Southey and I went through the verandah to the kraals (corrals).

"This is the surprise, Charl. We're gonna have some fun," said Southey. "See the calves in the kraal over there? Well, we're going to drive them to the big kraal where the mother cows are waiting for their babies. The calves go through the chute like salt through an hourglass. You've seen that."

"Yes," I answered, very attentive.

"The mothers will come to the chute to meet their calves, then the milkers will take the cow and calf and, while they're happy being together, they'll milk the mother."

"Why not just milk the mother?" I asked.

"They give more milk this way," said Southey. "Let's go over to the chute."

We walked over to the chute. There were five black men who would be doing the milking. One would drive the calves to the chute, one would open and close the chute gate, and the others would grab a pail and take the mother and the calf to a quieter spot to do the milking. The men who were milking would slap the calf as he tried to get his mouth on the mother's nipples for milk. The milkers had their own stools to sit on. Some of them could spray the milk three to four feet from the teat if necessary. The slapping of the calf and the milking proceeded till the cow was giving little milk. The calf could take the rest. The calf and the cow would then be left alone. There was a lot of experience in getting the cow and calf to a corner, milking, and keeping the calf away.

"Charl," said Southey. "This is the surprise, in fact, it's a game. We're going to ride a calf."

"How you do that?"

"You stand astride the chute on those two poles. As the calf comes through, you jump on his back . . . arms around his neck . . . and I'll time you to see how long you stay on!" said Southey.

"No way. You go first . . . let me see," I requested sincerely. I was not yet convinced the farmers wouldn't have fun with me.

"Okay."

Southey climbed up on the chute poles. One of the black men released a calf and he came running through the chute. Southey dropped on the calf's back, arms and legs astride of the calf's body. He stayed on for about 5 seconds. The calf went one way and Southey went the other. He fell to the ground, and then jumped up.

"See," said Southey.

"I see," I replied. I was scared, but I had to do it. So I climbed up on the chute. The calf came down. I dropped on his back. My chest hit his spine, my hands slid off his back as I slipped towards the tail end of the calf, unable to hold on. Then the calf half bucked me off. I fell to the ground. Not in sand, because these kraals were full of cow dung—mostly cow dung, maybe a foot of it and some grass. I bounced up. "Hell," I exclaimed.

"You were a little late, Charl," said Southey.

"You must fall before his head is under you. Not too early, not too late."

Southey did it again, and this time he stayed on for about 6 seconds.

My anxiety changed to feelings of a challenge. I got up on the posts. The black man at the chute encouraged me by clapping his hands and saying, "Look carefully baas."

The calf came down the chute. I dropped my arms around his neck; my left foot was on one side of his stomach and my right foot on the other side. By God! I was on the calf. In a split second the calf began wrenching. I had no control. Again my hands slipped and I felt my body go sideways. The calf had thrown me. I landed in the cow dung. I rolled a couple of times then jumped up with some of it in my mouth, shouting, "Hey, I did it!"

Southey agreed, "Great! 2–3 seconds."

The black men clapped and cheered.

We did this for about an hour with breaks while the men were milking the cows. Southey and I brushed off and went and sat under the tree to have a well-earned rest. I felt good inside, even though I never matched Southey's best time. I did get close to 5 seconds one time, though.

"God, that was fun!" I exclaimed softly, "Except the time the calf stopped half-way down the chute and then jumped over me as I fell to the ground."

We both laughed about that for quite a while.

"Good," said Southey, "You'll have something to tell your friends back in Johannesburg."

I thought about that for a while. I knew my friends wouldn't believe me, but my story was mounting up.

After lunch, Aunt Tillie took me to the creamery and showed me how they separated milk. A large machine had a center core shaft with about twenty funnels assembled in a certain order. A cover was placed on top and the milk pail emptied into a small tank above the separator. A valve was opened to let the milk flow to the separator, and then a large handle was rotated, by hand, spinning a horizontal shaft and a vertical shaft with mounted funnels. Centrifugal force caused the cream to come out one end into a cream can; the thinned milk, called whey, went through a second outlet into a large bucket.

"Don't turn the handle too fast or too slow," said Aunt Tillie. Showing me the vertical arm motion.

"Like this?" I asked.

"Yes."

I turned the handle for ages. My arm got tired, so I changed hands. I got a workout all right. It was boring.

The cans full of cream were taken to the storage room on the outside of the farmhouse in the shade. The walls consisted of one layer of wire mesh, a layer of charcoal, then a second layer of wire mesh with intermediate timber supports. Water dripped from a tank above the storage cooler into the walls. As the wind passed the room, it cooled the walls, and everything inside was kept cold. Every two or three days the bus would pick up the can of cream and drop off the empty returns.

The whey was moved to another storage house, where corn was added. I was told by Southey to load up a bucket and feed the pigs. I did just that, and took the heavy bucket to the pigpen. I got five feet inside and, as I was just about to pour the contents into the trough, a big pig hit me on my side! I didn't see him and was jolted by the power. Half the feed went into the trough and half onto the ground, and the pigs scrambled. I got knocked over a second time and fell into the pig-mud. I didn't like it at all. I scrambled out with pig feed all over my face and clothes and mad!

Southey was at the fence laughing with another bucket of feed for me to handle!

"Not funny," I said sternly, thinking I was being toyed with again. "Those pigs are nuts! Look at that one walking down the middle of the trough, while the others are eating! I could've got killed!"

"No," said Southey. "I'd have jumped in and saved you. By the way, we empty the bucket here!" added Southey, laughing. He was outside the fence at a wooden bar and laid the bucket on the bar, tilted it, and emptied the slush into the trough. This job was done. I was hoping that all the jobs were done.

We finished the day by taking a walk just outside the kraals, in the same countryside we saw from the bus. The landscape did not change, no matter which way you looked. We ended up picking some wild berries located in nearby bushes, removing the stalks and leaves, washing the berries in water and then sitting in the kitchen having wild berries and fresh warm cream. I had never tasted anything so good!

Aunt Tillie saw me in the kitchen and instantly suggested that I take a hot bath. She told me to talk to Otiend about heating some water. I went down to the rondavels and approached Otiend with the problem. Otiend was a South African Khoikhoi who was in charge of many operations on the farm.

"This is easy," said Otiend, very accommodating, and very positive. Otiend was in his 50's, I guessed, but wasn't sure. He was skinny, strong, and hard work showed in his hands. He was dressed in a minimum of clothes with a sort-of half a waistcoat, no shirt and cut-off pants (below the knees). There was a belt, but it was wrapped with the upper part of the pants and it couldn't be seen. He had no shoes. His face was filled with a scheme; he had a glint in his eye. "Come we go to get the water, and then make it hot."

Otiend and I walked down a short path with two pails to the reservoir and windmill. We made this trip a couple of times. The water was conveyed in buckets from the reservoir, and poured into two big black iron pots three feet in diameter, but resembling half a sphere with three legs each. Otiend placed some grass and dry cow dung underneath the pots. He lit the grass and smiled.

"Be ready in no time," he said with confidence in the African way, which accentuated the vowels to the beat of music.

I was concerned it would take a long time and asked, "How long?"

"One hour maybe!" said Otiend, who sat back to relax with a pipe. I wasn't sure if the pipe had some of the cow dung inside it or not. The smell was a little stronger than nature's clean air and wasn't bad considering what was burning.

"An hour!"

"Sit down," said Otiend. "Baas Charls, where are you from?"

"Johannesburg," I replied.

"Ah! Ha! The big city of gold! Many people have gone there and never come back. It is a place of good or evil?"

"Probably both," I answered defensively. "But I only know stories."

"I wanted to go but the spirits have told me No! I believe them because the word of the mouth says first you get rich, and then they can't find you."

"You mean black men get rich and then get lost?" I inquired not knowing what he meant. Then I remembered talking to Southey and he told me that Otiend was known for telling wild stories, some approaching the mystic and some that easily created shivering senses in the body.

"I am not a black man," replied Otiend.

"I know," I said. "You are a Khoikhoi, right?"

"That is right. I am talking of all peoples," said Otiend.

"I know," I said. "A lot of people who have come from tribal lands go into the city. They live in townships and work in Johannesburg, like at my school. Lots of people from other countries, but they are not lost. They have found something new!"

"Other countries. Like England?" asked Otiend.

"Yes, and Germany and Greece and Italy!"

"There are many countries?" asked Otiend.

"Yes!" I answered." Many, many countries."

"The missus always talks of England and the King and the Queen."

"That's only one country!" I said.

"Do they all speak English?" asked Otiend.

"No, they speak their native tongue, Italian or German."

"Ah! Ha!" exclaimed Otiend, sitting back on his haunches against a tree, contemplating and slowly muttering. "Uh! . . . And they are free?"

My thoughts were drifting into a confused state in trying to understand where this man was trying to go. Surely he knew these things, then, maybe not.

"Yes! I believe they are freer than where they came from!" I sat looking at the pot and the water wasn't boiling yet. Then I pushed my question. "Otiend, I don't know what you mean by . . . being lost?"

"You are saying people come to the big city Johannesburg, and are still there. But you are speaking of the body," said Otiend. "It is the soul that is lost and it never comes back. If it leaves you, Baas Charl, it leaves forever. When they come home to see their old friends, they are empty. They talk of things like fancy clothes and shiny shoes. They do not talk of their soul. It is gone, or they hide it," said Otiend, as he got up to move the cow dung, now red in color. He added more dung as we sat in silence.

I was thinking deeply. We sat for a while. I never thought anybody lost their soul in Johannesburg or anywhere else. Otiend was smiling whenever I looked up. I now did not know if I was being tested, or if Otiend wanted to know about the city. The way Otiend said what he said would make you believe that he knew everything. It was true that religion touched the soul, but it only differentiated between good and bad. How did you lose a soul?

"The rains will come soon," said Otiend in a soft voice as he looked into the sky.

Otiend didn't move very much and I was up and down all the time, looking at an uninteresting fire. He looked like a strong man to me, stronger than my uncles, and he had already talked to me and not down at me. Good!

"Rain? I heard it doesn't rain here—very much." I challenged.

"It will come in two to three weeks," said Otiend.

"I will be at Aunt Eileen's farm at that time," I said, glad to change the subject from Johannesburg.

"Missus Eileen . . . I have been there to help Baas Southey . . . that is her son."

"Yes, that's right," I replied.

"The 'Lazy Y' is Missus Eileen's place, Baas Charl. There is a woman who lives in the bush on the 'Lazy Y'."

"She lives on the farm but not in the house?" I asked.

"She has a house like a hut, small, very small, Baas, and it's in the trees and bush. She lives alone."

"A woman lives alone on Aunt Eileen's farm?" I asked.

"That is right Baas! She is small, old, and she has a beard to her neck," said Otiend, stroking his arms from his chin to below his neck.

"No Otiend! Women do not have beards!" I stated.

"This one has a long beard, Baas Charl," said Otiend. "She has a different spirit."

I had absorbed enough spirit stories, so I got up, put more cow dung on the fire, and put my finger in the water. It was getting warm.

"The cow dung must be very dry, otherwise it would smell," said Otiend. "Come on Baas Charl, we will prepare your bath."

We went into the bathroom of the house. It was weird to have a bathroom without pipes and valves and taps (faucets). There was a drain.

We fetched towels and buckets of cold water, and then put the plugs in the bath and in the washbasin. We fetched and carried the hot water to the bath and mixed in the cold water. The bath was ready. It was getting late, so candles were lit. I was ready to jump in the bath.

"Thank you Otiend for all your help."

"Tomorrow," said Otiend with a smile. He backed out the door then turned and left.

I sat in the bath thinking about Otiend's stories . . . truth or fiction. Was this just a game being played on the city boy?

I loved sitting in the dimly lit room, soaking in hot water. It was a dream compared to the pig trough. Thoughts came so easily as the warm water provided the comfort of a blanket. I knew I already had many things to discuss with Desmond and the Andrew Street Mob. I'd almost forgotten about them! I was starting to believe in many things I hadn't seen or touched before. Later I got out of the bath, dried myself, got dressed, had dinner and went to the bedroom and started to get into bed. My foot stopped halfway down, the sheets jamming my toes . . . 'apple pie sheets' (short sheeted). Who did that? I remade the bed, got in between the sheets and fell asleep, thinking of people's souls and a woman with a long beard. Not possible!

◆

The next evening Southey and I compared notes. Both beds had been apple-pied. I didn't believe Southey, but would wait and see. Yvonne,

Delphine, and Elaine had most likely done the dirty deed, so Southey and I decided to return the favor of the apple pie beds. Southey's idea was to fill their beds with thorns.

"After dinner, while they're having dessert and talking to Aunt Tillie, we'll sneak out and get the thorns and put them in their beds," said Southey.

"At night," I asked.

"Yes," said Southey.

"Where are the thorns?" I asked.

"They're in the grass. We pick up the ones that fall off the bushes when they dry out. It's easy, we'll go through the grass field barefoot, walk softly, and pick them up when you feel them," said Southey.

"You're crazy. Are your feet that hard?" I asked.

"Don't worry," said Southey, "it won't hurt . . . that much!"

That evening, shortly after the main dinner meal, Southey and I left the house and went to the field. We took our shoes off, tied the laces, and hung the shoes around our neck. Southey just walked, picking up the thorns off the ground easily as soon as he found them.

I started slowly. "Ouch," I managed to get a single thorn and put it in a paper bag. "Ooh," I said as I got two more thorns. I hated this but I learned to walk very softly, touch the thorns, and pick them up. As I got better I could just feel the thorn and then collect it with my hand. This was stupid, but it was fun.

Definitely, no one back home would believe this. My feet were now very sore and I was so glad when Southey was finished. We took the two bags of thorns, sneaked into the guesthouse, and put the thorns between the sheets, in all four corners, with a couple in the center of each bed.

"Good," said Southey. We left, went back into the house and entered with an easiness as though we'd just been talking, sat down and had some tea with everyone.

"Where have you been?" asked Aunt Tillie.

"Charl and I went to my room to look for something to read," said Southey.

"Why are you limping Charl?" Asked Aunt Tillie.

"I . . . Uh! . . . Stubbed my toe on the bed," I said.

"Is it alright?"

"It's fine," I said.

Southey wanted to go to the windows of the guesthouse and wait for the girls to go to bed, but if Aunt Tillie went for a walk and saw us peeping, it would not be easy to explain.

After the girls left to go to bed, Southey and I laughed at the various animations we came up, with imitating the girls getting into bed. Showing how they, with a candle, slipped into bed, talking of course all the way into the sheets . . . surprise!

"Ouch!" said Southey.

I countered with "Ooh! Those bad boys did it!" We doubled up laughing!

The next morning, after everyone was seated at breakfast and eating, and without a word having been said about apple pie or thorns, Aunt Tillie asked in a stern voice, "Who put the thorns in the girls beds?"

No answer.

"I want to know," she continued. "Charl?"

"Can I go get some more porridge?" I asked. I didn't want to give the game away.

"Answer me!" stated Aunt Tillie. There was no answer from me.

"Southey, are you up to your nonsense again?" asked Aunt Tillie.

"Well the girls apple-pied our beds so we had some fun," said Southey.

"Thorns can hurt you . . . some are poisonous," said Aunt Tillie.

"Not these," said Southey. "They're from the back field and all dried out."

"No more of this . . . understand!" said Aunt Tillie. She was mad at us!

"Alright," agreed Southey and I in chorus.

Poisonous, I thought, *oh my God*!

I put on two pairs of socks but it still hurt to walk. This farm stuff was getting to be a little too much, but I liked Southey, he had a sense of humor.

◆

The normal weekend was always treated as a time of rest. Most of the black people that worked with the cows and sheep were off part-time on Saturday and the full day Sunday. The white people would rest, attend church, listen to the radio and visit each other. However, this Saturday everyone was going to the 'Country Store'.

The Black men inspanned (hitched) horses to the large wagon and everyone piled into the back. I was excited. I had some pocket money and wanted to buy some sweets (candies). These were almost unheard of at Aunt Tillie's house.

The wagon and horses got onto the main road after going through a number of farms. There was a general agreement among the farmers to allow crossing each other's property instead of using the main road. This allowed cars and buses a free road to travel at higher speeds. The most responsible task in this part of the country was to close the gates properly. Every fence had a gate and every gate was opened and closed without exception. Nobody wanted the reputation of leaving a gate open.

The wagon turned up the road to the 'Country Store' in a town called Piet Plessis. There was a long verandah, wooden sidewalk, double-doors and windows the full length of the verandah. These windows were not necessarily for display, but rather for light, although they were completely covered with dust, which sat at least one-inch thick on the windowsill.

The girls, Aunt Tillie, Southey and I got off the wagon and walked into the store. It was about 60 feet wide and maybe 100 feet deep. There were a few black people inside and many black people were standing around outside with bundles at their side. It was an informal meeting place to talk, see friends and laugh. I saw two black women talking with bundles on their heads. Despite moving their heads and arms and bodies, the bundles remained upright on their heads with amazing balance, whether walking, stopping, or turning while telling a story. It was magic the way the bundles remained in balance as the bodies moved in all directions. There were also lots of small black children, 'picannins' as they are called, running around playing games. This was obviously a place of friendship for black people and the 'exchange of stories'.

"Good day, Tillie," said Mr. Burke, the owner of the store. He was known to be kind to both black and white people. He obviously had a monopoly, being the only store for 100 miles, and so he charged a little more for goods than the Vryburg shops did. The store had everything: canned food, farm tools, general medicines such as Bayer's aspirin, Eno's fruit salts, Zambuck ointment, and toiletries such as Vitalis and Brylcreem hair tonic, Pepsodent and Colgate toothpaste, and Lux and Sunlight soap. There were clothes, leather bags and belts, a whole section on hardware, flower and food seeds, a few large implements and outside were timber, fencing and diesel oils. There was nothing exciting to me. There were no games or any sports stuff. I went to the sweets counter and took some jellybeans; there wasn't even any chocolate. I asked if he had chocolate.

"Too hot to keep it around," was the explanation. "It turns white before you know it," said Mr. Burke.

I paid and went outside the store to look around. There was a house and garage with a truck. I couldn't wait to leave. This would not be the place for me to live, I thought, it is so simple and there's nothing to do.

I felt strange being the only white person outside the store watching the kids play and the women talk. There were 30 women and children outside and only one man sitting on the verandah. A good-looking old black man, with a gray haired beard and a pipe; he wasn't talking to anyone. He smiled at me. I waved back. I experienced a desperate feeling from the possibility that I might have to live in this place, and that I might not have a choice in the decision. The black people were friendly, soft, kind, and minded their own business. They were people of the Twsana tribe. I also admitted this was a role reversal, me being the only white among all these black people. I wasn't afraid; they never gave me that feeling, despite the stories from newspapers and people in general. There was a friendly feeling, and this was a happy place! Now I understood how Lena, our black servant, must feel, she being the only black amongst whites. The atmosphere wasn't unfriendly either; it was more like an invitation to be friendly. I kept looking around to continue my assessment. Yes! Closing the gap seemed always to be up to the white person. It was too confusing a thought, so I continued to look around. The old man kept smiling. He looked so comfortable.

It seemed ages before everyone got back on the wagon. Then we all clambered aboard and drove off. I felt bad that I didn't wave goodbye to the old black man sitting on the verandah.

On the way back to Aunt Tillie's, the girls talked incessantly about the store. Southey and I said nothing. When we got to Langenhorn we put the wagon in the barn, put the bridles and leather harness on the wall, closed the door and walked the horses to the pasture. We ate dinner together and commented on the store and its owner. I was out of the conversation because I was thinking more about the negative things the kids at school had said about blacks and farmers. Where were these things? They were not evident to me. I could not see any of that stuff.

It wasn't true! I believed now they really didn't know anything about farmers. I got up early from the table and went to bed.

"Goodnight Charl," came the short harmony of words from those at the table.

"Sleep well," I replied.

This was a Saturday on the farm.

On Sundays, many farmers went to church. Aunt Tillie very seldom went. Instead, she cooked, and the girls served breakfast. Fresh eggs and bacon, and what I loved most were the freshly baked biscuits and then coffee. We had it out on the verandah. The sky was perfectly blue, the air was still cool, no sounds came from the kraals and nothing had been scheduled for today. In this arid countryside it didn't get any better. It was very quiet with all of the thirty black workers gone for the day. After breakfast, everyone just sat around on the verandah.

It was hot, about 90°F, and the wind silent. This Sunday was so quiet. Again I could hear the birds. There was nothing on the horizon. No dust kicked up by cattle. They were under trees out in the pasture, if that's what it could be called. It was as if they knew it was the day of rest. No activities anywhere as the animals, people and their land were right in the middle of a hot and dry summer.

I walked down one of the roadways leading away from the farm. I went down to the main road where the buses flew, walked along it, and then walked back up Aunt Tillie's second roadway to the farm. I saw insects. That was all, not even the birds were out, and the silence was uncanny. I sat under a tree, looked at the dried-up pan and all the cracks, and decided to see if there was any wet clay. I got a broken branch and dug out a triangular piece of the pan, and found the clay was wet on the bottom. In no time at all I broke off a willow branch and made a half-inch diameter stick 3 feet long. I was going to play kleilat (clay stick or whip). I put some clay on the end of the stick, swung the stick above my head and down to my foot that was now held off the ground. The stick hit my foot and the clay flew across the pan. The first shot was a good one. I did this shooting of the clay for over an hour. Kids did this in the koppies in Johannesburg, with two teams, trying to hit the opponents. When it hit, your body stung for a long time. I walked over to the windmill and water tank. These were standard on all farms because of the subterranean water. A swim would be marvelous. The windmill was about 30 feet high. I got permission from Aunt Tillie, went to my room, changed, took a towel and climbed up the little stairs to jump into the pool. There was a green algae floating, the wind had blown it to one side of the tank. I dived in and my whole body was refreshed. Tingles of coolness enveloped my entire skin. I must have swum across the fifty-foot tank ten times when I heard a splash. It was Southey.

We stood for a long time in the middle of the tank. Water came up to my chest.

"Southey, why don't you come and stay with us in Johannesburg for a while? I have lots of friends and you must know our family is very large. Aunt Tillie's daughter Mima is there."

"I could not leave my mother. I am the only one around for both Aunt Tillie and my mother. They need some man to kick around!"

"Aunt Tillie adores you . . . you can see that!"

"Maybe once a month!" he replied, smiling. "The men are missing from Aunt Tillie and my mom's farms. I'm the only one. My mother needs me for many things. I will not go to college like everyone wants me to. The women in our family are supervisors of many black farm workers. They order all the supplies, food, buy and sell horses, cattle and pigs, and of course sell their main product, milk. Then they pay everyone. Man! They bake their own bread and cook their own specialties. They attend meetings among the farm owners and raise their kids. So I want to help!"

"Wow!" was all I could say, because to me that was a man's work. There was always a feeling of strength with Southey. I was sure he would eventually run one or even two farms.

The next three weeks went by fairly quickly. The routine settled into milking cows, separating the milk and cream, feeding the livestock, and having a hot bath. One night, when everyone was talking about the games we might play at the next Saturday picnic, Aunt Tillie brought out some 78-rpm records and the gramophone. She wound up the spring causing the turntable to rotate, placed a record on the turntable and put the needle in the groove of the record. The music was traditional Afrikaans with either a vastrap (foxtrot) or waltz beat. The black workers loved to hear the music and as Elena and Jacob had told them it was a music night, ten of them assembled on the verandah and sat and listened.

Suddenly there was a loud scream, and nearly all the black people scattered. Otiend rushed in, "Please missus Tillie, the snake, he's back!" Southey ran to the tool room, grabbed a shovel and went out onto the verandah. Otiend followed with a kerosene lamp. They searched around the verandah and house and after ten minutes gave up. They didn't find the snake.

Aunt Tillie joked, "They only come around for the music." But the girls and I didn't believe that statement, so we discussed the snake and where it might go. Nobody from Johannesburg slept well that night.

◆

Each year at Christmas time, the farming community planned a pre-Christmas event with a Boeresports (farmer sports) Tournament, including a cricket game, followed by a braaivleis (barbecue) and a party afterwards. This was primarily for children and young people and included a social gathering for all the farmers and their families in the district. Aunt Tillie told us we'd spend the whole day at the event, which would be held at Piet Plessis commonage. Now I was truly excited, sports and a cricket game. I could not wait!

Saturday finally came. Aunt Tillie had the large wagon inspanned (hitched): it was to be drawn by six horses. Southey was showing me how to fetch the horses out of the lower pasture. The horses always moved to the farthest corner of the pasture as soon as a man appeared. One of the dogs, named Jakkals (jackal, similar to a wild dog), helped to herd the horses. Although the horses didn't really acknowledge Jakkals, he was determined to show them that he knew how to guide them. The horses just seemed to know it was time to pull the wagon again. The large wagon needed six black men, Southey and I to even just nudge it out of the barn. Everyone was collecting harnesses, rings, and ropes. Southey explained to me how to place the bridle on the horse.

"Walk up gently, touch him on the nose, stroke his neck . . . don't make any fast moves. They know what's coming, so talking and petting is part of the game. Stand on the left side of the horse . . . as if you were sitting on it . . . bridle in left hand . . . stroke with the right, then slowly bring the leather straps over the nose, use both hands to pull it up, and place the bit in the mouth. That's sometimes the hard part, they will rear their head back and you have to start all over."

Southey did it to a couple of horses as I watched. Then Southey gave me a bridle and told me to inspan Robin, the older horse. I very carefully stroked the horse, and pulled the bridle over the nose and put the bit in his mouth. I moved my left arm around the other side of the neck, pushing up the bridle over the ears and my right arm on the near side. Suddenly I felt a painful bite on my upper part of the arm. I dropped the bridle screaming, "Damn you!"

Southey came running over. My arm had been punctured. I continued to scream in agony. Otiend came up to me and stood in front of my face.

"That horse has a bad spirit for new people," said Otiend as he put his hand on my shoulder. "I will put the bridle on for you."

I was almost in tears, from the fright and the pain, but held them back, too proud to cry. "I did it like you said."

"I know," said Southey. "I was watching . . . that horse is always so tame, I don't understand."

They took me into the house. Aunt Tillie rolled up my sleeve, got some antiseptic, rubbed it on, and wrapped a gauze bandage around the arm. Then she called for some tea and sat me down.

"Did you do it gently?" asked Aunt Tillie.

"Oh yes," I said.

"Maybe you caught his tongue with the bit."

"It could be. Oh! God it hurts!"

"You'll be alright," said Aunt Tillie. "Lie down on the settee and drink some tea. I'll be back soon."

"I'm fine," I said. "I'll just walk around a bit."

The six-horse wagon was ready in thirty minutes. Boxes of food and heavy clothes were loaded onto the wagon: the heavy clothes for late night winds. Blankets were placed along the sides. The wagon had two sets of seats to carry three abreast up front, and then the back had a flatbed center 15 feet long with the two sides slightly tilted upwards over the wheels. Anything loaded in the middle would not roll off the sides.

Aunt Tillie called for everyone to get up on the wagon. I got up, put my jacket on and climbed in the back of the wagon. The pain had subsided, but some numbness still surrounded the bite marks. Otiend got up and sat in the back. Aunt Tillie sat up front. Southey took the reins and Elaine, Yvonne and Delphine sat on the second seat. The black servant girl, Elena, sat in the back with Otiend and I sat next to them. The wagon moved off. An extra riding horse was taken, and followed the wagon on a lead rein.

The roads from farm to farm were made up of two wheel tracks, and the only major road that was almost two lanes wide was the road to Tosca and Terra Firma, the one the bus had traveled on. So as you went from farm to farm you courteously waved to everyone working or standing on their verandahs. The trip took about an hour and a half with many stops at the farm gates. Otiend would jump off, open the gate, the wagon would go through and Otiend would close the gate and run to catch up. It was always a game to try and leave behind anyone who had to close the gate. Otiend was pretty fast, though, and he never left the gate unlocked. Everyone was reminded again and again that closing gates is sacred in farming country. Herding cows, horses, and pigs from other farms is a tiresome task and doesn't please any farmer.

Finally we arrived at the Piet Plessis commonage. There were a large number of wagons, over a hundred people, kids, countless dogs, and many activities going on. A few flags moved slightly in the breeze, and dust from the roads was scattered into clouds by incoming wagons. I sat up in the wagon, wondering where the cricket field was located. I couldn't see it. As the wagon stopped, I saw a man behind a big table, and a sign "Entry for all Events." All signs were in Afrikaans, the predominant language of the area. He was taking names for all the events. Southey grabbed me and said, "Come on, let's put our names down."

I put my name down for the 100-yard dash and for the cricket team. I addressed the man in English. "I would like to play cricket, Sir."

"You can bat or bowl?" asked the bearded man, in broken English with the heavy accent of a man whose mother tongue is Afrikaans.

"Both," I said.

"Are you a fast bowler then?"

"No, spin bowler," I replied.

"You must be a good bat?"

"Middle of the order," I answered. I was excited about a game of cricket in another place with different people and grownups.

"Well, we will put your name down and let you know at 1:00 PM," said the man, and then he continued with a smile on his face. "So my friend, there are other events you can enter. There is a tug–of–war, egg spoon race—but that's for the ladies. There is a sack race using mielie (maize) bags, Jukskei (horse shoe toss) and vinger trek (finger pull), are you interested?"

"What is the last one?"

"Oh! Two fellows just hook their middle fingers of the right hand. Then they stand like sword fighters and try and pull each other into the ground."

"I never heard of that. I know all the others. Can I come back later? Oh! By the way, where's the cricket field, Sir?"

"We'll put the mat down after the races . . . over there." He pointed to a sandy cow pasture with brown grass, four inches high.

"Oh," I said. "Thank you Sir!" Thinking about my teacher's description: "A cricket field has to be like a smooth, level blanket. The wicket has to be like a billiard table." All I could see was an open cow pasture. There was nothing that resembled a cricket field. God, even a tractor might have troubles negotiating parts of it!

At 10 o'clock, the running events started. The track looked like an old road: flat, with 3 to 6 inches of sand, commonly known as "very heavy." No South African records for the 100 yards today. The first event went off and I ran my hundred yards. I pushed hard and came in second in my heat and went to the finals, making the last six. I sat down in the shade knowing that just being fit didn't mean you could win. These farm kids were tough and did not give up. Sitting in the shade was wonderful, but it ended very quickly as we were called to line up again for the final. I got a good start but it was like running in deep, loose beach sand. I lost by many yards. The farm kids ran barefoot and just skipped across the sand with probably only two toes touching each time the foot came down. My tackies were a disadvantage in the sand. I went and sat down in the shade of a tree; it was very sunny, very dry and very hot. A thought crossed my mind, *Isn't that what Shaka, the famous Zulu chief, made his soldiers do, run through the hills barefoot without leather sandals, unlike the other tribes?* Everything was new here. I was frustrated because I had to learn that everything was different, and done in a special way, and I didn't know all the special ways. *Maybe I'll do better in the cricket game.*

I went down to another field where the horse races were being held. Southey had entered in the milk carton race, which was held over 200 yards. In the middle of each contestant's track was a milk carton. Like the knights of old, the horseman was required to spear the carton with a sharpened broomstick and then carry the carton over the line on the stick. Simple!

There were four heats. In Southey's heat there were five riders. They took off at a fast sprint for sixty yards, and then slowed slightly as they approached the cartons. The riders leaned over the right side of their horses, drove their sharpened stick through the carton, lifted it up as soon as possible to prevent the carton falling off, and rode as fast as they could to the finish line. Two riders carried their carton over the line, including Southey; he qualified. The other three riders either missed or dropped the carton.

"Okay Southey!" I shouted.

The final run-off would be before lunch. I ran over to Southey. "Where's the cricket ground?" I asked.

"It's usually over there."

"Wow, are you sure?" I exclaimed.

"No, I'm not sure, but they will pick a place somewhere and wherever it is, it'll be fun," said Southey, just smiling all over. I didn't like that smile; I had seen it before, when we went to ride the calves.

Otiend came over. "Missus Tillie wants to see you, baas Southey."

"Okay, thanks," said Southey.

I followed him over. There were a lot of people around Aunt Tillie. They opened a pathway for us.

"Charl," said Aunt Tillie, "this is George Harvey, Eddie his brother, and Willie. They are all very good friends of mine."

"Hello Charl, Welcome to Vryburg. Are you enjoying yourself?" said Eddie.

"Thank you. Yes, Southey is showing me many things."

"We came over to invite you for tea at our farm, Stonehedge, sometime." said Eddie. "Maybe you and Willie and Southey would like to go hunting!"

"Wow! . . . Yes sir!" I said wondering what hunting meant . . . lions? I didn't think there were any lions in this part of the country.

The Harveys had the biggest farm in the area. Along with beef, they produced over ten gallons of cream a day.

Aunt Tillie said, "We should have lunch soon. Elena and Otiend will set up blankets under the tree and we'll put the food out there."

"I have to ride in the milk carton final," said Southey.

"I want to watch," I exclaimed. "Can I go, please?"

"Yes," said Aunt Tillie.

Southey joined the other finalists. I watched from the sidelines among all the farmers and their wives. The black people, mostly from Botswana, the very few Bushmen, and the Khoikhois, all stood together in one area. The milk cartons had been positioned. Eight riders and horses were ready. This was believed to be the most exciting event of the day. The gun went off and the riders and horses raced at full speed leaving behind a beige dust cloud. Southey had said that being first at this stage of the race was important, but not as critical as being on a good pathway to your milk carton, the positioning of the body and the broomstick lance. The ground was not smooth and one horse stumbled slightly, the rider's broomstick hit the ground and shot out of his hand, twisting into the dust: he was out of the race. He slowed and let the others pass. I saw that it wasn't Southey. The crowd became silent as the riders approached the cartons; the riders' 'steady-as-it-goes', the lances down, then spearing the small wax box sitting on the ground. Now the advantage of being first was apparent: no dust, clear vision, and an open pathway. The seven riders went through all right but we could not tell who had successfully lanced his carton until 20 to 30 yards down the track, when the broomstick lances were held horizontally. Some riders let their sticks slip down in their hand until a grip could be made about half way down the stick; this was to create a better balance for riding a fast horse.

The carton was on Southey's stick and I screamed. "Go! Southey, Go!"

Three riders crossed the line together. Southey was second. I was so proud. I ran to Southey but couldn't get close because of all the officials. I waited. Where were Elaine, Yvonne, Delphine and Aunt Tillie? A hand touched my shoulder. It was Aunt Tillie, "God, he's a good rider."

"I know," I said. "He's great."

Finally Aunt Tillie and I reached Southey, congratulating him and shaking hands. I wanted to hug him but restrained myself. I didn't know whether it was the right thing to do.

Southey answered my twenty questions with, "The horse ran beautifully, just so responsive to the reins." Now I knew why we took the spare horse with us.

We walked back to the wagon, sat in the shade and ate lunch, relishing good, homemade sandwiches and homemade lemonade. There was also the traditional braaivleis with boerewors (farmer sausage) and meat of all kinds. We ate until we were full. We were enjoying the beautiful hot summer day in December, in the thorn bush and sand-grass country of the district of Vryburg. To me it was a million miles from Johannesburg. I was truly getting to enjoy this vacation, even though I missed Gran and Uncle Mick and my friends.

Southey went away but came back shortly. "We're both playing in the cricket game!" he exclaimed.

I jumped up and said, "Alright, thanks!"

After lunch the cricket game started. I was amazed. They had actually set a mat down over the tall grass, pulled it tight and driven spikes into the ground to pull it taut. The field sloped by 5 percent. The fence was the boundary and it therefore formed a rectangular field and not an oval. The sides had been picked. One team from Stella district and a local team from the farm district called Tlakgaming. Stella won the toss and elected to bat. I was in the Tlakgaming team and so we went in to field. The two Stella batters got ready to bat while their other nine team members disappeared into the beer tent to await their turn to bat. Lots of people pulled up chairs to watch, drink beer, finish their lunch and relax. This was going to be an afternoon of relaxed enjoyment for most of the crowd.

Aunt Tillie said, "Now it is time to talk, sit in the shade, drink some beer, meet with old friends, and, through the corner of your eye, watch the players. This is done so you're not embarrassed when someone asks you about the game!"

I noticed the girls were talking and wondered, again, what else do girls do?

The Tlakgaming team started to bowl. In the first over the batsman could not hit the ball because it bounced all over the place. Being young, I played way out in the field on the downside. All the older team members were close to the wicket and close to the crowd, who sat only on the upside of the sloping pasture. The game proceeded. It was more of a hit and miss game. If the batsman hit the ball, he would score because it was impossible to field the red erratic spherical leather missile bouncing randomly from right to left and up and down! If the batsman missed the ball he had a good chance of being out. I was trying to work it out in my head. The ball sometimes just hit the mat, stayed low and slid through on the surface towards the wicket. Other times it would bounce high or go left or right. It was obvious this was not a 'true wicket', it was not a sticky wicket, and it was not Lords where the ground looked like a billiard table. Well, all the players were not in white pants, white long sleeved shirts and white cricket boots either. Most of the players wore short khaki pants and tackies or boots, although some had attempted to dress in cricket's white, formal style. Some had white shirts, some had white pants, a few had the combination, but no one wore long pants.

The game went on. A couple of careful batsmen went out with low scores, and a couple of aggressive batsmen got a few good hits and scored, but also were subject to bad luck, and were sent back to the tent for beer. It was no secret that you had to have a hell of a lot of luck to survive. Southey was a good fielder. He and I covered the downside and kept the runs down. Near the middle of the Stella innings, with six batsmen out, a ball was hit hard towards me. It bounced about ten yards ahead of me and then suddenly veered to my left. I was scared I might miss it but kept my eyes focused on the ball. The batsmen were yelling, "Two runs," the Stella supporters were clapping for the good hit (the bat had hit the ball solidly). I could hear them. It was a safe hit as the ball had already hit the ground. The batsmen completed one run, and, noting the ball's changing direction, the furthest batsman from the ball confirmed the challenge and yelled, "Two." I dived like a goal-keeper to my left, eye on the ball, got my fingers over the far side curve of the ball and held on. My body hit the ground . . . I rolled over . . . and came up like a cat, knowing which way I had to throw. I planted my right foot while changing the ball from the left hand to the right. I paused for a split second and fired the ball to the wicket keeper, exactly as my teacher had taught me. I had done this many times on the sand pitch of Pioneer Park in Johannesburg. The ball was off-line to the wicket but the wicket keeper moved away from the wicket to the line of the ball. The batsman, running towards the wicket keeper, saw that the ball had been stopped, panicked and increased his running speed, then slowed down, as he saw the wicket keeper move away from the wickets, feeling safe that the run would be made. The crowd was hushed by the sudden stop of the ball in the outfield. And I had been shocked that it was in my hand. The throw was routine, we had practiced that till we could do it in our sleep. Suddenly the ball took a turn away from the wicket keeper's position and headed into the wicket taking the bails off. They must have flown six feet in the air. I jumped upwards as far as I could and shouted, "Yeah!" Not the gentlemanly thing to do! The batsman was out. He paused for a second in utter amazement. Then in good tradition, walked towards the crowd and the imaginary pavil-ion. The players on our Tlakgaming team yelled, "Howzat!" "Good throw Charl!" "Ja Boetie! (Yes Brother)". The wicket keeper put the bails back. Southey ran over to shake my hand and then slapped me on the shoulder.

"Oh, your arm," he said, worrying about the horse bite.

"No, it's the other one," I laughed.

After the Stella team was all out for 76 runs, and the players had retired for the traditional tea and biscuits, the wicket keeper walked up to me. "What a throw, Charl, but man the ball curved so much in the air."

"I know," I said. "I can't throw it straight. My teacher has been trying to get me to throw straight, but it's pretty hard for me. I can't do it. So I aimed for five yards to the right of the wicket."

I felt so good all over because I had at last done something well here in the Vryburg area. Everyone here was so nice. There were no forceful instructions, like at school. The adults were all so helpful and friendly: they were kind. This was the true South African farm hospitality: a tradition from the Dutch Voortrekkers (pioneers). Aunt Tillie hugged me for the catch. I was embarrassed. I excused myself and went to look at the scorebook to see where I was batting. I was 9th in order, which meant 7 batsmen would have to go out before I batted, so I went for a walk around the 'country fair'.

"I saw you Baas Charl," said Otiend, not approaching me, but standing under a tree. I went over to the tree, thinking that the natives never really mixed with the white farmers; they were always slightly removed from the scene.

"Thank you Otiend," I said. "I was lucky."

"No Baas, you have the natural way . . . many, many people would not have stopped that ball. It was a strong hit."

"Do you know the game of cricket?" I asked.

"I come every year. Every year I learn something of the white man's game," said Otiend.

"What do you think?" I asked.

"It is good. It teaches man many things," replied Otiend.

"Tell me please," I asked.

"It is a waiting game . . . patience . . . for the mistake. The man that bats, he waits for the bowler to throw bad. The fielder waits for the batter to make a bad hit. The batter hopes for the fielder to miss, but to do that, you must have patience . . . be very quiet. Then the action is like the lion striking the buck. It is fast and it must be good."

"Interesting," I said, then teasingly, I asked, "What spirit do you see?"

"The spirit of the English, quiet and patient, but watch out if you break the rule," replied Otiend laughing and slapping his knee with his hand. I loved it.

"Wow!" I thought. Nobody I knew had ever told me about the patience and the strike. Nobody had described cricket as a game of patient predators. But I could see it now, clear as can be, and I had played cricket for a whole year.

"Where are you from?" I asked.

"The Cape Province is where my grandfather worked on the farms. In the bad years he moved to the Orange Free State and then here to these farms. This is where I am," said Otiend.

"Forever?" I inquired.

"That is not for me to say. The Gods will decide," replied Otiend.

The cricket game had started. Otiend and I sat silent for quite awhile, resting under the tree.

"Baas Charl, when you bat today, move one foot closer to the bowler when he starts to run. Then, when the ball is good, step back and stop the ball. When the ball is bad, move one more foot forward and hit it hard, man!" Otiend demonstrated this, but not very eloquently or with a great amount of style. I laughed. Otiend smiled with a wide-open mouth and finished his instructions with "Howzat!"

"Very good," I agreed. "I must go to the game, it is not polite to not watch the game. Even if you bat last!"

"Is that true?" Asked Otiend.

"Yes! There are many, many rules" I replied, and walked back to the game.

What did Otiend mean? I asked myself. *Sounds like a good idea. Just avoid the bounce if you can. It's so much easier to hit the ball before it bounces. Or you just scramble back and stop it when it bounces. Huh! Easier said than done.* How did Otiend know all this? The natives of the area never played cricket. The Indians in Johannesburg played it, but never the black people. I thought maybe only the West Indies and New Zealand had black players.

As I got back to the crowd, I heard "Howzat! Another batter out!" I looked at the scoreboard: 3 men out, 20 runs; I turned and saw that the fourth man out was walking towards the crowd. The scoreboard only showed the score in increments of ten runs, except when a wicket was taken. Then the actual score was shown. Towards the end of an inning they sometimes showed the score as it progressed.

"Four wickets, 28 runs," said the scorer. Someone changed the numbers. The sixth man going to bat was Southey. I stood in the crowd to watch. This partnership started slowly. It took half an hour to put on ten runs. The score was now 38 runs, more than half the score required. Piet van Rensburg hit a hard shot and it hit the fence; four more runs. Southey had only seven runs at this point. Then Piet was bowled; he had 22 runs. He was our best batter. It was now 42 for five wickets. We had to get 77 runs! The crowd clapped in appreciation of a good innings by the batsman. In went the seventh batsman, and I went to look for pads and gloves and a bat, hard to find for a young boy. I put on two different sized pads and found some sweaty gloves. I was dressed, if not ready. Southey kept trying. The seventh player came in and immediately hit everything that came towards him. He went out with nine runs to his credit with the score six wickets for 54. The eighth batsman went in. Southey scored two more runs and was caught in the deep outfield. Southey had nine runs and he had worked hard to get them. I went out toward Southey. We stopped. Southey advised, "Stay in there, Charl, James is a good bat. He could save the day!"

"Okay," I said. I was so damned nervous I was shaking. The crowd was ominous and I didn't want to disappoint the team.

A big lump came to my throat as I took center from the umpire, lining my bat just off-center towards me and then looking at the crazy cricket ground. Remembering what my teacher had told me: to know more about the pitch in front of you, you need to walk out to four or five feet from the crease and feel the mat with your feet. I did this and to my surprise, the mat caved in at least an inch in all kinds of places . . . meaning the ball would stay low if it hit those areas. Then I remembered what Otiend had told me. I stood a foot beyond the crease. This made me vulnerable to be put out if the ball went past me and I didn't get behind the crease before the wicket keeper collected the ball and knocked the bails off the wickets.

"You can stump him!" said one of the players, laughing.

"*Not much etiquette*," I thought.

The umpire's hand dropped, the bowler ran up and delivered. The ball was over-pitched, meaning it would not hit the mat. I stepped back and hit it hard. The ball bounced twice and hit the fence. Four runs on the first hit!

The crowd clapped. I was amazed that I did that!

I went back to the crease, remembering what Uncle Mick had told me: after a big hit, stop the next ball and settle down. I did just that . . . stepped back in the crease and stopped the ball: end of the over. The bowler came on from the other side.

James played carefully and we scored two runs in the over. The score was creeping up; we now had 62 runs. Fifteen more runs were needed to win. The crowd quieted. I faced the same bowler for an over without score. I kept moving up the wicket and back into the crease as Otiend had told me. James scored no runs either the next over. This was becoming a standoff. Then I cracked another hard shot, straight ahead; I had kept my left elbow high and driven through the ball, and we ran two. Again I sat back for two balls and then really stepped down the wicket and hit a towering drive to the offside and towards the downside of the field. Two fielders were trying to get to the ball to catch it. While James and I were running furiously, the ball hit the ground and scooted to one side. James and I took another run . . . three more runs. Half the crowd was cheering and half the crowd was silent. James took one more run off the over and faced the next bowler without score. We had to get ten more runs . . . 77 runs to win.

I started off with a ball going by, just missing the wicket. My confidence sank. Then a second ball went past. The bowler was bowling short so the ball would definitely hit the mat way before the batsman, easier to see than a well-pitched ball, but it was shooting low from a soft spot in the mat. I faced six balls without hitting the ball . . . very disconcerting. The bowlers changed. James scored once more. I was relieved. I felt better facing this other bowler. I took an extra step out of the crease and hit the ball past the bowler; two runs. The crowd clapped, but I felt really nervous and was still worried about getting to 77. The next ball bounced normally, my eye lost it, the ball went between my bat and pad, I stepped back and put my bat up to meet the ball and hit my wicket with my bat! I put myself out! How stupid! I was so mad at myself. Of all the ways to go out! James came over, "Well done Charl."

I walked towards the crowd. They clapped and I felt good and bad; I had wanted to pass the score of 76. Pietrus, coming in to bat, shook my hand. "Good," he said, with a smile.

Southey slapped me on the back. Aunt Tillie cheered. Yvonne said, "Good Charl!" Delphine agreed. I took off the pads. I was still so mad at myself. Elaine came up and added, "See! I knew you were good."

James did what Southey said he would. He took the Tlakgaming team past the score of 76. He scored 11 runs, same as me.

After all the clapping and talking, James came over to me.

"We did well," he said.

"Yes," I said. "I would like to have finished with you."

"But then Pietrus would not have batted," said James.

"That's right," I said, and thought, *How true.* "And we won!" I added with excitement.

"Yes," said James. "See you tonight."

"Bye! Thanks!" I said.

In the evening everyone attended the big braaivleis and the men drank beer, told stories, and laughed. My thoughts were on how much fun we were having! I felt good about my throw, but missing that ball that bounced so normally made me mad at myself. It was true what Otiend had said about mistakes and pouncing on the weakness. I felt awkward that I didn't understand a lot of the jokes told by the farmers. They laughed so much, the jokes must have been good. Even though they mostly spoke in Afrikaans, they would switch to English if you didn't understand. However, the jokes I did understand were a lot funnier than when told in English. In Afrikaans you could really express a personality or action, whereas in English, it always sounded so formal. In fact most of the jokes lost the feeling completely. I knew I had to learn more Afrikaans.

This event was a great get-together for many, many people of the two districts. There were almost a hundred people gathered. Farming, progress, problems, politics; thousands of words filled the sunset glow. In the evening the crowd drifted into the church hall where a six-piece boeremusiek band was playing the accordion, bass, guitar, drums, ukulele, and concertina. The players were all local farmers who had learned the traditional music of the Afrikaans, the main pioneers of South Africa. They played all the famous Afrikaans folk songs: Sarie Marais, Bobbejaan Klim die Berg (baboon climbs the hill*)*, Ou Tante Jacoba (old Aunt Jacoba*)*, Brandewyn Laat my Staan (brandy leave me alone*)* and on and on. There are hundreds of South African folk songs.

There was to be a surprise for the kids at 8:30 PM. The band leader stopped the band and spoke over the microphone, "Please, your attention, the moment you have been waiting for . . . the gifts and the surprise!"

All the kids ran to the front. Parents stayed behind. A big box was wheeled into the center of the hall. All the kids got a small gift first. Then, with everyone quiet, someone opened the box. It was full of bananas! I thought this was crazy.

"Yvonne," I said, "why such a gift?"

"This is not a tropical area Charl. It's unusual to have bananas here . . . or any tropical fruit," said Aunt Tillie.

"Oh!" I said. *Still, crazy*, I thought.

People danced into the night, kids fell asleep on the floor, and men fell over each other drinking and laughing. I had drunk a lot of home-made ginger beer, it was so good and nothing like the drink you bought in stores. I had also eaten lots of meat from the braaivleis. I had done my share. Aunt Tillie had seen enough. "Let's go," she said.

We jumped into the wagon. All the girls got into the back of the wagon. Everyone was covered with blankets. Aunt Tillie and Southey sat up front. The wagon moved slowly down the road. The bumps were taken in slow motion. The nights was beautifully clear, as always, and quiet, except for the sounds of horses, movements of the harnesses, the creaking of the wagon and the rolling wheels. We sang a few songs. Southey threw the reins over the front step board. The horses knew exactly where to go. Otiend jumped off and on the wagon, opening and closing gates. I lay so comfortably in the back of the wagon. Again I wondered about all the negative things that kids at school had told me about blacks, about farmers, and how they would treat me. Where was it? I didn't see it. It just wasn't true! I had had such a wonderful day with all these people. I now believed my Mom and Gran were right! I remembered helping to put away the cart and seeing the horses walk away into the fields, but not getting into bed. We all slept well that night.

◆

Christmas day was spent quietly. There was no big celebration, other than a wonderful Christmas dinner. We talked about everything and in a random manner; there were no limits on either the time or the subject. Southey was looking forward to going home the next day. I was going with him to Aunt Eileen's. The girls were to stay on with Aunt Tillie, with perhaps a visit later in the week to Aunt Eileen's.

The next morning Southey and I left in a Skotskar (two-wheel cart). I said good-bye and looked over my shoulder for Otiend. I was hoping to talk to him before leaving. As we went through the gate, Otiend appeared and waved. I responded. We headed away from the main road and further into the bush country. There were only two tracks, no cut road, and the tracks were not well worn. The trees and their branches of thorns sometimes hung over the road. As the cart traveled your eyes became your safety warning sensors, low branches and you ducked out of the way, arms above your head and over your eyes. Southey and I talked for a while and then fell into silence.

The cart shook and bumped. Absolutely every sound of the cart, the horses, and the leather harness could be heard. I was awed by the silence. You could hear insects and birds, but not much else. There was a scary feeling that nothing happened here, but I knew there were animals, snakes, and birds out there. Still, I wasn't experienced enough to tell where they were. I was glad I was with someone that knew all the sounds of the country, just as I knew the sounds of the city.

There was so much land. But what could you do with it? How could you start a farm? Aunt Tillie and Aunt Eileen worked really hard, owned lots of property, but weren't very well off. They didn't have a car or truck. Certainly they owned lots of things, but maybe a lot of the farm was inherited. Aunt Tillie worked hard, 6:00 AM to 10:00 PM, every day of the week, a little less on Sundays. These people were true pioneers who chose to stay and live an independent life from all of us that lived in cities, where things were easy to get. My eyes roamed the countryside looking for life, but there was just nothing. I saw nothing but silent trees, grass and bushes all in shades of browns, sandy colors, and not much green. Although it was summer, it looked like a dry winter-brown landscape. Otiend had said it would rain, I remembered. Sure didn't look like it; the sky had been that beautiful clear blue without a speck of anything in it ever since I arrived.

"Southey, will it rain soon?" I decided to test Otiend's forecasts.

"No," said Southey, "This is not the time, but sometimes the weather changes quickly."

"I haven't seen any animals," I said.

"There was an antelope in the trees over there next to the small hill, but he's gone."

"Really?" I said. "What are we going to do at your Mom's place?"

"Well, I have to catch up with my work," replied Southey, "I have to mend the fence, put some poles in the ground and string wire."

"Could I help?" I asked.

"Well I'm not suppose to work you too hard because of your arm!" Said Southey laughingly.

"Who said that?" I asked.

"Aunt Tillie," replied Southey.

"My arm is fine and I can help… please," I pleaded.

"Sure," said Southey.

"Great!" I felt happy about learning new things.

We rode for a while, and then Southey surprised me by asking, "Why were you so upset at being put out in the cricket game?"

"Oh, I don't know," I spurted out. Then, I paused and sat silent.

"Come on Charl, speak up. Nobody out here can hear you, only me," encouraged Southey. I decided to be honest about what I felt inside. After all, I wanted Southey as a friend.

"Yes, maybe I was. I don't like playing cricket very much. It's so frustrating sometimes, you make the slightest mistake and you're out. I mean for the whole game. Then you field, drink tea, and discuss everything in boring detail."

"That's only the batting," said Southey.

"Well I don't bowl that much. At school the teacher always uses fast bowlers. I'm a spin bowler. I have no control with the fast ball."

"Everyone was talking about your stop and throw to the wicket. They say you could be good," said Southey.

"Yeah really? Well that was lucky, especially the stop."

"You should keep playing, who knows?" suggested Southey with a grin on his face.

"The game is too slow, I get bored. Maybe the batting is exciting, but everyone is so 'La-de-da,' you know? Like, above you. I don't like those kinds of people. They're so different to people in other sports. Like rugby or like soccer . . . now I love that!" My voice uplifted with excited tones. "There's lots of action! You hit the players, take the ball and control it, run, and kick. You get hit and you just get up and fight back. It's fast and it's fun, and there's lots of interaction with other players, shoving and pushing. The contact makes it alive and the speed of the game makes it exciting!"

"It's true, you'll have to learn to bowl well to enjoy more in cricket," said Southey.

"Otiend says everyone is waiting for a mistake," I said without thinking.

"Otiend said that?" asked Southey.

"Yes, and I think he's right."

"He's a very smart Khoikhoi, and he says very many things," said Southey, "but still, not everyone understands all his stories. He has a funny, indirect way of saying things. He describes lots of earth things with emotions, like 'the tree loves birds and not snakes'."

I wanted to ask about the bearded lady but decided I didn't want to be caught believing something like that without someone else telling me.

"Maybe that's true in lots of games. We're always waiting for a mistake, then take advantage of the person," said Southey.

"Yeah, like in soccer, I always look at the ball and the foot, just waiting for the ball to get away from the player, then attack like a lion!" I explained, adding some of Otiend's suggestions.

"Soccer is not always the rushing of the ball," said Southey.

"No, I don't mean that. I mean you have to wait for the chance," I replied.

"Sports are so exciting when you do something well. But it's hard. There is so much to learn and so many things to do well. You know, like in the milk carton race, you have to learn to ride, hold a stick, lean over without falling, aim right, spit out the dust, pierce the carton, and ride like hell. All just to come in second place . . . and then you get a cotton shirt for a prize. I actually could've killed my horse . . . Aunt Tillie's horse," exclaimed Southey. "If the spear went onto the ground by mistake. One of the farmer's horses got injured badly in one of these events when the stick went between the horses legs."

"You mean the horse stumbled or something?"

"Yes," said Southey. "The rider came down as well. There was a lot of panic at that race."

"Wow! But it must be great to ride like that," I said.

"You can learn," said Southey.

The ride continued in the hot, hot sun, which was now getting up in the sky and depositing its millions of rays onto the ground. Southey's thoughts were probably on seeing his mother and getting things done. My thoughts were on why anyone would think of introducing cricket to Africa. Only the English could do a stupid thing like that. Imagine explaining the complex game to anyone for the first time . . . just stupid . . . and then they play it here in this bush country? Were these people laughing at the English or were they just crazy, like the kids at school?

The cart came to a stop. I jumped off, opened the gate, and then closed it behind the cart. We were very close to the "Lazy Y" ranch farmhouse. And within minutes we went through a final clump of thorn trees, saw the usual windmill and water tank, house, storage barns, and a tennis court.

"You have a tennis court!" I screamed.

"Almost everyone has a tennis court," said Southey, "except Aunt Tillie. It's a popular sport around here!"

In two more minutes we were outside the house, having opened and closed one more gate.

Aunt Eileen came running out, "My God Charl, you're so big! Last time I was in Johannesburg you were that size!" indicating a two-foot long baby. She hugged and kissed me, then Southey, but with an unmistakable mother's compassion.

"Come inside. Charl, that's your room."

Two black servants put the luggage away. Tea was being prepared and sandwiches were on a plate on the table in the middle of the kitchen. The house was smaller than Aunt Tillie's, with one large breakfast-dinner room with a fireplace, three bedrooms off one side, a kitchen, and the 'Vryburg Bathroom' as I called it, outside the house. One door led out the back of the house to the milking kraals. Another led out of the front of the house, which had eight steps leading to the ground. The main floor of the house was at least six feet off the ground. Twenty feet away from the house was the tennis court and three big, beautiful trees about forty feet high. The hard sand courts were made from clay and anthill sand. The anthill sand was used because the hills were formed with small homogenous pebble-size particles limited by what an ant could move or carry. These were ideal as the last layer of soil on the court, making a great sliding surface.

I asked why the house was up on stilts and four feet above the tennis court.

"Because of the Lazy Y River," said Aunt Eileen.

"River?" I questioned, "I haven't seen water anywhere."

"Well, when it rains the river runs right in front of the house," said Aunt Eileen. "My father found out a long time ago when he first built the house. It seems it got flooded, so he raised it."

"Will I see it?" I asked again thinking of Otiend's tales of rain.

"No," said Aunt Eileen. "It won't rain."

I got up from the table and went to my room, unpacked, and then went walking around. Southey and Aunt Eileen had got into a deep conversation about things that needed to be done. I heard them say they would play tennis on the weekend with some guests. I would have loved to have Otiend with me, so I could ask about the farm and the bearded lady, and question him about the forecast of rain. It was not because Southey wasn't nice or not always friendly. But there were the usual older and younger teenager feelings, I had experienced so many, many times. At least now I knew how to handle these situations. Always acting, I thought; with teachers, with parents, with relatives. As a kid you always played different roles for different situations, so you had multiple personalities, and most of them were 'weird'. With Otiend I felt comfortable; even though he was so much older, he never demanded respect, but he sure got it from me. 'Respect your elders,' I had been told so many times. There is a great flaw in that somewhere. Why not respect what a person is, or does? There was warmth in the natives of Africa as well as the European (expression denoting white people) behavior. However it was not necessarily taught to everyone in Johannesburg. There was always rough stuff at school, especially between older kids and younger kids. Warmth was taught in my family. And Otiend had it. Otiend was honest, even if others said to watch out for his stories. I decided that my thoughts during this walk were just too confusing. I went inside and washed my face in cold water.

At dinner we sat around and talked. I told them about life in Johannesburg. It was really easy to describe, and that was a good feeling. The two black servants served us unceremoniously, with Aunt Eileen conducting all their movements. I learned that the next day Southey and I were to fetch the horses from the large pasture. Aunt Eileen was going shopping. Then the following day work would start on the fence before the visitors got here on Sunday.

We sat inside with the doors open and the screens in place. When it got dark the kerosene lamp was turned on. Bugs from the surroundings tried desperately to get through the screen doors, almost blocking the cool night air from entering the kitchen and circulating in the rooms. We finished the final cup of tea for the day. The candles were lit, and everyone drifted off to bed. Aunt Eileen took the kerosene lamp to her bedroom.

I woke with sunlight on my face and birds singing. They were perched in the tall trees, and my room was closest to the trees. It was 7 AM, and I could hear cattle moving and other activities in the yard. I jumped up, washed my face in the basin on the washstand, got dressed, brushed my teeth, and went into the kitchen. Southey was already eating breakfast.

"Eat breakfast and we'll go and get the horses. Mom has to leave early to be back tonight."

Southey and I were soon on our way to the far corner of the large pasture. We could see the horses and when the horses saw us, they started to walk away. Southey and I were carrying bridles.

"After we corner them we'll put the bridles on," instructed Southey.

"Okay," I said, thinking that we would have to walk back.

After 20 minutes the horses were in the corner. Southey had such a wonderful way: he talked, cajoled, and whistled until my horse almost came to him. He hugged the horse, and the horse's head went up and down, his tail swishing, and on went the bridle. The second horse was not that easy. I stood by the first horse tied to a tree, and then carried the bridle over to Southey, who had coerced the horse next to the first one.

"Put the bridle on Charl."

"Me?"

"Yes, who else is around here?"

"You," I said.

"No! You do it."

My mind went back to my previous experience and the instructions. I moved very slowly, gently touching the horse on the flat part of the nose, bringing up the bridle with my right hand, the bridle going over the mouth. The horse backed away, then a second time, and a third.

"Keep doing it," said Southey. "You must show you're the master."

I felt as though I was too short and that the horse was playing with me by putting his head down and then pulling it up. I finally grabbed the horse's mane and, almost in frustration, whipped the bridle on, then gently moved the bit into the mouth, and tied the straps under the head. I was amazed. I had done it without hesitation.

"Good," said Southey.

"Now we have to walk back, right?" I said hopefully.

"No, we're riding," said Southey.

"Without a saddle? Really?" I asked.

"Yes, without a saddle. Here's my hand. Left foot in it, up you go," instructed Southey. I was on the back of the horse in a second and immediately grabbed the mane. Southey threw me the reins.

"Hook your toes on the underside of the belly when we ride, but most of all, stay in rhythm with the horse going up and down. Get that rhythm right and you won't fall. Stay upright on straight runs, lean forward uphill, and backward downhill."

So many things, I thought, but this was exciting. Scared again, with butterflies in my stomach and my heart pounding, but I liked it. This was absolutely new.

First we had the horses walk. I was sliding all over. Southey stopped the horses and got off, then took off my tackies.

"Put these in your shirt."

I stuffed them in the front of my shirt. We took off again. I could feel the horse's skin sliding over its rib cage, which was better.

"When we trot, get that rhythm," said Southey, as he slapped my horse and nudged my horse with his feet.

Oh God! This was awkward. I was really bouncing, one hand on the mane, the other holding the reins. I was out of rhythm, then in rhythm, and then the horse stumbled on the grass tufts. I grabbed the mane with both hands, and survived. The horse immediately walked. I grabbed the rein. Southey was waiting for me about 20 yards away.

"Shit," I said with high emphasis, but not much volume. After the horse got into a trot again, slowed and got into a trot again, my rhythm finally came and only went away occasionally. I started to see where he was going. I noticed gullies and grass and natural pathways. Finally Southey came alongside, slapped the horse, and he broke into a gallop. This was a lot easier, even though the gallop was slow. As we rode into the farm, Aunt Eileen said, "Charl, that's incredible!"

"Told you he was a natural," said Southey.

I jumped off the horse with relief. I was hurting everywhere, despite the short ride. There was pain in my toes, my knees were burning and my crotch and butt ached, but I produced a smile. I really felt now that I had accomplished something. The horse was so big and yet he went where I wanted to him to go. That was a powerful feeling!

"That was great," I said. It was true, but I was glad it was over for now!

The two horses were inspanned to a Skotskar. Aunt Eileen got up on one side, the black manservant got up on the other side, and off they went to the trading post, and perhaps a visit to one or two farms. Despite the apparent calmness of this land, it was always wise to have two people travel together, because if the cart broke down, or problems occurred, the second person could go for help. After all, some roads were only traveled on once a month.

I walked around the house and ended up going through the kitchen to the back of the house. As I descended the steps, I saw two

Bushmen standing about thirty yards away. They made no movement. The black people on the farm had decided to stop work and look. A couple of black kids came to look and stood back some 15 yards. The Bushmen were silent. I didn't know what to say or do, so I went to look for Southey. We almost collided going around the side of the house.

"Two Bushman are standing in the backyard," I said.

"Yes, I know," said Southey. "Masilo will speak to them. They have been here before."

"What do they want?" I asked.

"Not much," said Southey. "Just some water, maybe a bit of food."

Southey and Masilo spoke to them. It took a long time because of the language difference. Masilo had worked in the Kalahari with the South African Governmental Office, so his Khoisan language abilities were related to his five years in the Kalahari. Southey finished and came over to me and we decided to go into the cool of the house and have some tea.

"I know about the Bushman from school," I said.

"Oh Yes! Tell!" challenged Southey.

"We learnt at school that Bushmen were the original South Africans, along with the Khoikhois. Then the blacks came down from the north. And whites landed in the Cape and came up from the south. Then all the cattle wars took place. Because the Bushman were not a powerful tribe they were driven or disappeared into the Kalahari," I replied.

"Very good! Yes, they are nomadic and could survive there. The Khoikhois joined or melted in with everyone else," said Southey.

"They also said there are many paintings by the Bushmen all over South Africa, from the Drakensberg mountains to the Kalahari. Like the mystery painting of the "White Lady," which is hundreds of miles . . . maybe a thousand . . . from where they live now. It's a cave painting of a white lady looking like a Pharaoh's daughter. I mean at the bottom of Africa . . . still nobody knows why!" I added. I had just had this history lesson, along with the Zulu Nation exploits in the history of South Africa. So! It felt good that I knew something about these tribes.

"I've heard of the Painted Lady," said Southey. "We also hear stories from people who go into the Kalahari. In fact there are Bushman paintings in the Vryburg district."

"Close to here?"

"Not too far."

Southey and I stood for a while and looked at the two Bushmen. Then I broke the silence because actually seeing them fascinated me.

"How do they really live in the desert-like country? Have you heard?" I asked.

"The Bushmen stick to their traditional way of life. They live by many good principles, are very close in family, and every person is very important. They have learned to live off very little desert food and water. The Bushmen get moisture from plants, store the water in Ostrich eggs, and bury them underground. They're very good with that poison arrow and small bow that you see over their shoulders. About this size." Southey had his hands about two feet apart. "The farmers talk about their phenomenal stamina for chasing an animal who's been struck by their poison arrow. Even the farmers that work near the Kalahari say they can run up to 15 miles before dropping."

"Across the desert in the hot sun?" I questioned. "I mean, you can hardly walk 150 yards in the hot sun!"

"Yes!" said Southey. "Barefoot!" He paused. "The Eland is a big prize. So the Bushman, after sinking his arrows into the buck, will run for miles and miles until the antelope drops from the poison in its body. Then they carry it back to the camp for a three-day celebration of eating and dancing. This is a religious hunt and a survival event. They share everything with everybody. I guess you can say they learnt to live there because they had to. But you know, they seem to want to live that way."

"They look so frail—small and wrinkled, like old people." I observed.

"True . . . but their children are very beautiful," said Southey. "You know, the truth is, we are their neighbors. And they are a mystery even to us." Pausing again for a while, Southey looked at me as though he was going to sum up the stories. And that is what he did. He concluded by saying, "Somebody wrote, after coming back from one of the expeditions into South West Africa and the Kalahari, that he had asked an old Bushman how old he was . . . and the old Bushman replied: 'I am as young as the most beautiful song in my heart, and as old as all the unfulfilled longings of my life.'"

"Wow!" was all I could say. I didn't understand the last part but I liked the first sentence.

Southey added, "I've always remembered that!"

I looked at the two Bushmen. Strange-looking because of their tan skin. It was wrinkled more than the average native and it made them look old. They wore loincloths only. A bow was strung over their shoulders next to arrows in a pouch with a strap. A second skin bag over their shoulders was empty. The Bushmen were barefoot, covered in dust, and looked very weary. But they stood proudly and erect. They looked very intense in their discussion. Suddenly, Southey said something and moved his arms, and Masilo took them to the water. Southey went into the house and returned with some food. The Bushmen half bowed. Their faces changed and they seemed very happy. They took the food and water to a group of trees about 100 yards from the house. They squatted under the tree and were talking and smiling and their heads were bouncing up and down as they spoke, obviously happy.

"What's happening?" I asked.

"They asked to stay near the house for the night and to get some water. I agreed and gave them some food."

"What are they doing?" I asked.

"Looking for a member of the family who has run away. They usually don't get down this far from the Kalahari. They don't like the fences and stay away from strangers," Southey replied. I looked at him and when he saw a question on my face, he added, "They're not the two Bushmen who were here before, but they said that other people from their family had been here before. Maybe we'll become a Bushman's roadhouse!" Southey smiled.

"No, seriously, it's an honor that they like us. My mom has always been kind to the natives of the area. We're sure that it doesn't take a long time for the other native people to know that."

I sat for almost an hour watching them. Fascinated by their simple movements while sitting, the moving of their heads, one talking, and one listening. I was spellbound. These two people were very content. They squatted with their knees up near their head, their rear end almost touching the ground, and moving their body slightly, but never rising. They were in a state of happiness!

Again, I wished Otiend were there. I could have asked him a lot of questions about the Bushman. I was sure he would know. My thoughts and questions were driving me crazy, so I decided to go for a swim. I went to find Southey. He was in the house.

"Want to go for a swim?"

"No! I have too much to do."

"Can I help?" I asked.

"No, you go ahead. Cool off. I'll see you at lunch."

I changed and went over to the tank and dived in. The coolness enveloped my body. As my head came out of the water there was a feeling of being in a pure state of pleasure. It came about as the much lower temperature of the water-cooled my hot skin. I loved to swim, so I moved around in the water for about half an hour, then sat on the side of the tank. I could hear the small noises of people working and farm animals moving from one place to another, seeking coolness from the hot African sun. Mid-summer had no mercy on those who stood in its open pathways. I looked at the Bushmen. *Fascinating people,* I thought. I'd never seen anybody like them. Maybe in a school book, but I probably skipped past the page so fast, I didn't notice. Anyway the drawings were sometimes in brown or in black and white. Seeing people live and in color was so completely different. *Maybe when I grow up, I will travel and see all the different kinds of people. Learn how they live.* It was hot, so I disappeared back into the water.

Aunt Eileen got home at dusk. At least six people helped her carry, unpack, and put away boxes.

"Not that box, Masilo. That's for Mrs. Bezuidenhout," said Aunt Eileen.

"Who's Mrs. Bezuidenhout?" I asked.

"That's a lady who lives close by," was the reply.

It was *her*, so I decided not to pursue the matter.

"The tennis matches will take place on Sunday," said Aunt Eileen.

"That will give us an extra day to work on the fence," said Southey. "We'll start tomorrow."

At 6:00 AM the next morning, Southey yelled at me to get out of bed. I jumped up and had a wash, then ran outside to help inspan the horses. They had been tied up close to the house overnight. Masilo and Tau loaded posts onto a trailer cart that was connected to the Skotskar. Masilo and Tau were two black African men who worked the farm for Aunt Eileen. They were strong looking, with big muscles, and about six feet tall. They looked like brothers. Aunt Eileen had employed them both for five years. After we had prepared everything, Southey and I went and had breakfast. Masilo and Tau went to eat near their kraal. They had mielie pap (similar to grits). Southey and I had eggs and bacon, toast and coffee, in the house. At 7:30 AM we moved out.

Southey and I jumped up on the Skotskar; Masilo and Tau sat on the trailer. After going through the gate, we went along the road towards Aunt Tillie's, then broke off to the left for about a mile. Sure enough, there was the broken fence. Termite ants had destroyed the posts in the ground, and the wind had done the rest. About 16–20 posts had to be replaced. I felt useful doing this. It was more exciting than going camping.

We unloaded the posts and started digging new holes. When the hole was two feet deep, the post went in. It was aligned with big rocks hammered into the hole on each side of the post with a 16-pound hammer. Then small rocks were set around the post and the big rocks, closing the hole as much as possible. I fetched the rocks from wherever I could find them. The rocks were hammered in with a long iron bar. Sand was poured in to fill the rest of the hole, and the sand was tamped. The post was tested for movement and the barbed wire was hooked up to the posts. The team never said very much, we just worked, especially after doing four posts.

"There was a cold wind late last night Baas Southey," replied Masilo. "It is very different." It started to get even cooler, and the wind was blowing stronger. It was not the bright, hot day of yesterday. Eight poles were in place and wire hooked to all of them. I wanted to go to the bathroom. Feeling shy, I signaled leaving my position and went into the middle of a group of thorn bushes.

"Watch for snakes . . . I'm not lying," said Southey.

I looked around on the ground.

"In the bushes, they like to lie in the branches," warned Southey.

Masilo and Tau showed no signs of laughter. This was serious. I looked everywhere, twice. Then the bushes started to move. I panicked, finished quickly and pulled up my pants. There was water on my head. I looked up; the branches were being whipped by the wind. There was more water. I ran out of the bushes and a shower of sprinkles hit my head, arms, and legs.

"It's rain!" I yelled with joy. "Otiend was right!"

"Damn it!" said Southey. "Look at those clouds. Where did they come from? They're dark."

Masilo grabbed the horses and held them. They were getting nervous.

"Let's wait a minute, it may pass," said Southey.

We four stood close to the cart on the downwind side. The wind and rain were warm, but hit hard against the body, getting heavier and heavier. We stood, bent over, close to each other and with our heads buried in our arms.

"Let's load the cart with the tools and head home," said Southey.

Tau and Masilo loaded the tools and jumped on the trailer. Southey and I mounted the cart. Southey slapped the reins on the horses' rear ends. They moved off into a trot, but straight into the wind. This caused the horses to stop and start awkwardly. The rain came down harder. Southey jumped off the cart, fed a small riempie (thin leather string) through the bridles, and led the horses down the road. Tau, Masilo and I huddled very close together, behind the seats of the cart and the side of the trailer. The rain didn't quit. Finally we reached the farm. It had taken an hour and a half. The horses were led into a small barn, Tau and Masilo went to their huts and Southey and I went into the house.

Hot coffee was boiling in an enamel pot; I pulled it off the stove, and poured it into my cup. I was shivering. The coffee went down my throat and I could feel it warming the body all the way down.

"Put on something dry, Charl," suggested Aunt Eileen.

"I will," I said. I went to my room and changed, came back to the table in the kitchen, sat and sipped on the coffee. It had never tasted better. Now you could hear the rain on the galvanized iron roof . . . the same as in Johannesburg. It was always a sound that varied according to the wind flow and the downpour. It was very consoling to know you were protected from the rain.

"You will see the 'Lazy Y' river today," said Aunt Eileen. "It'll come out of the trees north of the farm. If you grab a wash tub you can go up to the gate area, jump in the tub and float in the river, and come right in front of the house."

The rain stopped about two hours later and that's just what Southey and I did. We went to the washroom, dumped the dirty clothes on the floor and carried the tubs to the gate area. The galvanized washtubs were about 3 feet by 2 feet, oval and flat-bottomed, with a two-inch bottom rim. The water was running like crazy in the ditch. It was going to be tricky getting into the tub, into the river, and staying afloat. We threw the tubs in water, ran alongside the tubs, and then jumped in. The tubs swayed, but with good co-ordination of body, arms and feet, the tub finally became stabilized. This didn't prevent the tubs from rotating, so hanging on desperately and trying to look ahead was a difficult feat. We frequently bottomed out or hit the sides of the ditch, and many times nearly tipped over. This was great fun; you were never really in control. In what seemed just a few minutes, I floated right in front of the house between the tennis courts and the front door. *Amazing*, I thought. You couldn't tell that the water would flow this way when it was dry. As Southey and I passed the house, we yelled loudly. The water carried us further, so for the next 400 yards we went through the tree and native hut areas. Then we jumped out of the tubs and dragged them to the bank. We were soaking wet but the water was warm and so was the air; amazing transitions in just a few hours. Southey and I repeated our adventure three more times, limited only by the burden of carrying the tub approximately 800 yards upstream.

"What a storm," said Aunt Eileen at supper.

"We could hardly walk with the horses," said Southey. "It's gone now though, so we'll finish the fence tomorrow."

I dared to add with a soft voice, a little hesitation, "Otiend said it would rain."

"What? When?" asked Aunt Eileen.

"When I was at Aunt Tillie's," I replied. "He told me it was going to rain soon."

"He's got a spirit in him. Maybe he's a witch doctor!" laughed Southey.

"No!" I said, being protective. I had read about witch doctors and how they coerced people.

"How do you know he's not?"

"He's . . . not . . . mean," I stuttered.

"That's true," responded Southey, "but we don't know if witch doctors are mean . . . they're so clever. Otiend's a good storyteller."

I went to bed a little mystified by what had happened. I didn't know how Otiend could tell it was going to rain, but I was really happy that his prophecy came true, and so did Aunt Eileen's story of the 'Lazy Y' River. I was looking forward to the tennis on Sunday and the braavleis.

The posts went into the ground fairly quickly the next day, and by one o'clock the fence was finished.

"Let's head home for lunch," said Southey, "I think Mrs. Bezuidenhout is coming. How's your Afrikaans, Charl?"

"Not good," I said. "We don't speak it at home. I only have it at school."

"She doesn't speak English," said Southey.

"Why not?"

"Her husband was a Dutchman from Holland, and she is from an Afrikaans family that spoke a lot of Dutch."

"My mom was taught Dutch, not Afrikaans, at school," I said. "But I guess nobody speaks "High Dutch," as my Mom calls it. Everyone speaks English or Afrikaans in the city. Her husband…is he dead?"

"Nobody is sure, but he hasn't been around for as long as anyone can remember. Some say he died and she buried him. But natives of the area, and a few farmers who have been to her place, have never seen a grave. It is traditional for the Afrikaans to have a funeral and a Predikant (minister) and to have a casket. But none of that has been done. Everyone knows the people who do these things. It really has been a long time since he disappeared or died! Maybe he is in the house— nobody has ever been in there, not even my mother," said Southey.

I just couldn't ask. Could Otiend be right again about the bearded lady?

The four of us reached the farm. Aunt Eileen came out the back of the house to greet Southey.

"The fence, is it finished already?"

"Ja, Ma!" said Southey.

"Come inside, you too Charl. Mrs. Bezuidenhout is here."

My heart sank as I walked into the room. There was Mrs. Bezuidenhout, five feet tall, Dutch Pioneer hat, big sprawling dress, and boots. There was very little lace or frills. She was dressed in Voortrekker (Pioneer) style. Her clothing could be right out of the Great Trek. Her hands were wrinkled and her face old and she had a beard at least five inches long. She looked like a little man but for the dress and the hat. I didn't know what to do and especially where to look.

"Mrs. Bezuidenhout, this is our nephew, Charl," Aunt Eileen said, doing the introduction.

"Goeie dag, Charl."

"Good day . . . Uh! Goeie dag, Mevrou Bezuidenhout," I stuttered, still having a hard time trying to look in her eyes. We shook hands and I backed off. *Oh wow!* flowed through my head. What a mystery! She is just like the pictures in the history books.

We sat down for tea. The conversation was in Dutch and Afrikaans; I picked up the meaning slowly, but was unable to answer anything fast. I continued to feel embarrassed to look at her. The little old lady was very polite as she drank her tea, except she poured her tea into the saucer and drank from the saucer.

"Baie warm (very hot)" she explained. President Kruger was supposed to have done this in presence of the Queen of England, when negotiating the problems of the Uitlanders (foreigners) within the Transvaal Republic. When asked politely by the Queen why he drank tea that way, he replied that there were two reasons: firstly, it cooled the tea, but secondly, and more importantly, it kept the nose out of the cup of other people's business!

Farmers had all kinds of strange habits, such as dunking rusks in their coffee. I loved to do that, but had a hard time getting away with it in front of my mom and Gran, who would both yell at me.

The bearded lady never took her hat off all the time she was there. She looked at me a number of times, which made me feel hollow inside. Yet she wasn't threatening, and actually was very gentle in her actions, although it was awkward for me the whole time. The tea continued and the politeness never subsided. It was formal, a ritual. Aunt Eileen, usually carefree, maintained the formal tea proceedings in respect for the lady's way of life.

The tea was finished when the lady said "Ek moet huistoe gaan (I must go home)." We all stood up; she took her bag containing her groceries. Southey said he would walk her to the far gate in the pasture. I went too, but sort of trailed behind. Mrs. Bezuidenhout walked slowly. We reached the gate and Southey refused to leave her there, so we walked into the bush. It got thicker and trees were taller. In a clearing was a small house and there were chickens and a couple of dogs that ran with wagging tails toward their mistress, barking at Southey and me. The grass was long around the house, unkempt. Southey said he would to come by and clear the land a little. She thanked him and invited us into the house.

"Nee dankie, (no thank you)" said Southey. We all said "Totsiens, (good-bye)" and she waved, no smile, no emotion.

Southey and I walked for a while. I might have been scared to, but would have gladly gone inside the house just to see it.

"She lives alone?" I asked, "Isn't she afraid?"

"No. Well, she doesn't show it. It's not clear, but some say she's been here almost all her life," continued Southey.

"The beard...the clothes?" I questioned.

"She is very religious, Dutch Reformed Church. She has no family, or nobody knows if she has!" replied Southey and quickly added, "The beard is probably from a family with lots of hair. My mother is her only friend. We treat her like family."

"Oh, that's why you call her Ouma! (Grandma)" I suggested.

"Yes Charl. But also out of respect."

"I'm sorry," I said, "but it's so strange."

"I know."

I went to bed that night with a multitude of thoughts. I lay there with my legs stretched out and my arms behind my head, thinking. This trip was becoming so different from anything anyone had ever told me, and I was dying to talk to someone who had had something like this adventure. Desmond hadn't, neither had any of my Andrew Street friends. I so badly wanted to talk to Otiend. It was unheard of to talk to a native on the phone. I had never heard of an African having a phone. In fact, not everyone even *had* a phone line to their farm, only those near the main road, like Aunt Tillie.

"Tennis, that'll be great." I changed my train of thought. I closed my eyes, and sleep took over very quickly.

On Sunday everyone was up early in anticipation of the guests' arrival. I got up and washed, had breakfast, and walked out to the courts. We were all ready for match play. The surface had been swept, more sand placed on top, and swept again. The lines had been whitewashed. The height of the net had not been set, but that would be done before the matches started.

The first to arrive was Aunt Tillie and the girls. Otiend was not with them, and my heart sank. I greeted everyone pretending to have missed them.

"Having a good time?" asked Aunt Tillie.

"Yes, thank you," I replied.

They all went into the house and Aunt Eileen conducted the tour inside and then outside. I felt lost. I wanted to talk to Otiend, and I already knew I wasn't as interested as the others were in playing tennis. More people turned up and there must have been thirty people with about 16 tennis players. Teams were picked and doubles and singles matches were scheduled. By mid-day, when the sun and heat were at their peak, everyone had gone through the ritual of playing tennis, going for a swim, and relaxing under the three big trees drinking the famous barley lemon cool drink. Tennis stopped and everyone sat around talking, eating sandwiches and fruit, and drinking lemonade. No further games were scheduled until between 2:00 and 3:00 PM, whenever someone decided it was time. A small breeze came across the land surface and everyone sighed. The story of the 'Lazy Y' river and the thunderstorm held everyone's attention.

"Was Charl out there?" asked Aunt Tillie.

"Yes, he's alright. He handled it well," said Southey.

"Didn't have to wash that night, right Charl?" teased Elaine.

"Well, only under my arms!" I replied.

"So that is what you do in the bathroom," said Yvonne with a smile.

"No, I just go in and wet my face. Nobody knows the difference!" I added.

I did not understanding girls; I thought they were so complicated. All they did was talk. Even when they got older, they never stopped yapping! Whereas boys did sports, like swimming and it was so simple and enjoyable. Diving into water and away from that hot, hot sun, even if just for seconds, and then sitting on the side of the tank with the slight breeze till the body got warm again, and then back into the water to cool off. Just outstanding! You didn't have to talk very much either!

I went over to the clump of trees. A game had started and everyone had fallen into a relaxed position watching the game. Good shots or pretty plays were appreciated and applauded or whistled at. The overall background of Sunday and 'Africa Silence' at noontime was again being disturbed by the entry of a silly human game, I thought. Fluttering of wings and screeching birds were now interrupting the tennis sound.

"The birds are really noisy," I said, looking up into the tree.

"Yes, they are making a lot of noise," said Aunt Eileen. "Southey, come here!"

"Okay. What do you want, Mom?" asked Southey.

"The birds are being disturbed and flying out of the trees!"

"It might be a snake," said Southey.

That got everyone's attention. They all stood up and moved back to potential safety. The birds were screeching, flying away from their nests, and coming back to the branches. I moved away from the trees. I couldn't stand snakes, and was petrified by them. They were scary even at the zoo behind glass.

"It's a snake alright!"

"Oh God!" said one of the girls.

"What's the matter?" I asked, sarcastically as though it was nothing at all.

Southey ran into the house and came out with a machete-style knife.

"Use a gun," said Aunt Eileen.

"No, it's a boom slang (tree snake*)*."

Southey went up the trunk, without shoes, and out on one of the branches. The snake was big, at least two inches in diameter and eight-foot long. Southey's action had caused the snake to move further out on the branch, closer to the nests. The birds were flying around in a frenzy. Everyone had moved away from under the tree in case the snake fell to the ground. The snake went to another branch, moving very fast. Southey carefully moved to the same branch, and in one quick move, took two steps, grabbed a branch nearby with his left hand, and brought the knife down on the snake. It fell to the ground with leaves and pieces of tree tumbling down. After the snake hit the ground, it quivered for quite awhile, nerves and muscles dissipating energy. It was in two pieces.

Everyone applauded and Southey came out of the tree. Aunt Eileen just looked at him.

"Don't you do that again," she said.

The tennis games resumed, but only a few people sat under the tree. It seemed that suddenly a crowd of people had something else to do. Southey took the snake's remains to the back of the house, put them into a tin barrel and closed the top.

I lost every game I played. Tennis was not my sport. Even though I had good reflexes and certainly played a number of ace shots, I was terribly inconsistent and muffed the easy shots too many times. I just did not play well and became disinterested.

In the evening as it cooled off, the braaivleis was started and the seats were now moved to the front of the house. Some people decided to played tennis and others chose swimming. It was a beautiful African evening, equaled only by those other arid semi-desert regions of the world where the solitude of the earth meets the ending activities of the day. Rest is contemplated and the animals, birds, and humans of the world turn to the time to relax, having survived another day. Only the nocturnal start their day.

As twilight was reached, the horses and carts that had brought the visitors were disappearing through the gates of the 'Lazy Y' farm into the darkening trees, bushes, land and fading sky. Everyone had thanked Aunt Eileen for her hospitality, commended Southey, and wished for another gathering soon.

I was headed for bed.

"Come on," said Southey.

"Where to?" I asked.

"We have to burn the snake. Otherwise its mate will come looking for it and we'll have another snake in the house."

We fetched the snake that had been left at the back of the house and placed it on the ground clear of the house. We fetched a burn barrel. It was not that heavy but I was tired and moved it slowly. We put paper, sticks and then bigger wood pieces in the barrel. Southey lit the paper and when it was burning well, I lifted the parts of the snake with a stick and put them in the barrel. It was not long before the smell was bad. We then went to bed and let the snake burn. I thought the whole process was bizarre and only participated because Southey insisted it had to be done.

◆

A week later I was packed to go. The Skotskar was ready. Everyone stood outside the house. I said good-bye to the two black servants and then Tau and Masilo. A big hug and kiss followed this from my Aunt Eileen. Southey and I were headed to Eddie Harvey's farm called "Stonehenge" for a day and a night, before my return to Aunt Tillie's.

"See you in Johannesburg," she said.

"Thanks for everything," I said. "Especially the rain shower."

"Thank you for mending the fence. Bye!"

"Bye," I said.

I turned once more to look at the house and Tau and Masilo. This is their life, I thought! They live like this all the time, and it seems so hard, but they're so good at it. Everyone was happy in whatever they did, so what else mattered? I was thinking of these things because I knew I might have to come and live here. I wondered again, if I did come and live in Vryburg, whether it would be at Aunt Eileen's or Aunt Tillie's.

Southey slapped the reins and the horses took off. Masilo ran and opened the first gate and waved good-bye. I got the second gate and then we headed down the two-track road toward Aunt Tillie's, back the way we had come about a week ago. The time had gone fast, and it seemed as though the adventure could still go on and that there were still many things to discover.

Southey started the conversation. "The Harveys have the most modern farm in the district. Man, is it big. Uncle Eddie has more cattle than Aunt Tillie and my mother plus four or five other farmers all together. They probably have a hundred black people working on the farms. Uncle Ed has a brother, George, as well as five sons: Willie, Jackie, Kenny, and the twins Teddy and Athol."

"What are we going to do there?" I asked while wondering how I would be able to remember all these names.

"Spend a day and a night. Willie wants us to go rabbit hunting."

"That should be fun," I said. I was glad to hear it was rabbits.

"Yes, and it'll be at night," replied Southey.

"At night, how do you do that?" I asked.

"Wait and see," said Southey with a wry smile on his face, the same look as he had when we went to milk cows, feed pigs and collect thorns! "The girls will be there as well," added Southey. His smirk became even more intense.

"On the hunt? No!" I pleaded.

"No," said Southey, "Just for the two-day visit."

"Good," I said.

The ride continued through the trees and thorn bushes. I had become familiar with a second level of sounds, now that I knew the first. My eyes, also sharper, panned the landscape for life in Africa's sunny silence. The mornings were beautifully fresh. It was part of the enjoyment of living here. Again, I thought, All *this countryside undisturbed by man's cars, buses, boats, and planes—this is what the pioneers wanted to live in - away from the rules-away from the confusion and complicated mixtures of cities —maybe I could come and live here?* A movement in the bush caught my eye.

"A buck," I said.

"Antelope . . . lots of them," said Southey.

I saw about five of them. The antelopes watched the cart, their ears pricked and outstretched as high as the skin would allow. Like a radar dish, their heads were squared at all times with the moving cart. Southey brought the horses' trot to a walk and then pulled to a stop.

The antelope didn't like this, and became restless. They were not more than 30 yards away.

"It would be easy to shoot them from here," said Southey.

"What for?" I asked.

"What for is right!" agreed Southey. "Some people hunt just for hunting's sake. It's so easy to kill them with a high-powered rifle and a scope."

"I wish the hunters would try a bow and arrow and give the buck a chance," I said. "They should be made to walk through the bush without guns! Maybe with only a stick in their hands," I added. I always got mad at the concept of shooting animals.

"That's unfair," said Southey.

"To whom?" I asked.

"To the hunter" he said with his familiar smirk. "How could he tell his friends he's been in the bush for a week and come out with only grass stains and dirty boots!"

"That's right!"

We laughed, and it was a good feeling.

"Yeah, they'd have to go straight home and hide and not go to the bar, or the Carlton Hotel in Johannesburg," I said.

"Carlton Hotel?" asked Southey.

"That's where most of the professional Safari hunters hang out," I replied. "They take the so-called hunters to the bush. Americans, some British, some Europeans - whoever has the money!"

"Interesting," said Southey. He flicked the reins, the horses moved and instantaneously the antelope took off, not knowing the danger, but anticipating the move toward them. The horse and cart continued along the backcountry road.

Live and let live, I thought. *Who said that? Mom? Gran? Uncle Mick?*

After some reflection, Southey suddenly became serious. "I hope these tourists can shoot. It is terrible to wound an animal. For instance, if you shoot a baboon in the chest and you do not kill him . . . he will dig the bullet out with his hands and scream all the time."

"Oh my God!" I was shocked. "How terrible." I didn't even want to talk about it.

"A professional hunter would take care of that, they would not let the animal suffer. So it is a good thing they go with the tourists," said Southey.

"God! What a horrible scene that would be!" I added.

"Yes!" confirmed Southey, with a somber look.

Through more gates, finally we arrived at the main road. Instead of going right to Aunt Tillie's, we turned left, and about six miles down the road from our turn we entered Stonehenge. Our cart and its dust had been seen by two picannins (small black boys), who raced against each other to see who'd get to the gate first. They both opened it. Southey threw some coins and the boys scrambled for them in the sand.

"Thank you Baas," they yelled in harmony.

The cart approached the Harvey's house and their son Willie came out to meet us. I thought they were nice handsome-looking people, with an air of wealth. I had seen the difference in Johannesburg when I had met some my Mom's friends. Wealthy people had elegance and a sureness that seemed so natural. We shook hands and greeted each other, and upon suggestions made by the hosts, we went into the house. Black servants carried the suitcases to the rooms and then brought tea. Yard boys, black men, took the horses and cart, outspanned the horses, and took them to the barn for water and feed.

The house was big and constructed of stone/mud walls and thatched roofing that made the house cool inside. A breeze blew through the house, as all the doors were open. Fly screen doors were the only obstacles to the wind. The couches were big and deep cushioned. There were paintings on the walls and some beautiful furniture including pieces of famous Stinkwood furniture, in a rich deep brown/black color. I had seen this beautiful wood before. I kept looking around, thinking that this house was so beautiful. I couldn't stop looking. It beat any movie scene of African farms.

"Lemonade?" asked Mrs. Harvey.

I stood up from the couch, "Yes please."

"Don't get up," pleaded Mrs. Harvey. "Are you enjoying your vacation?"

"Yes, very much, thank you," I answered.

"The girls will be here soon."

"That will be nice," I said. I was not pleased to hear that they were coming!

A lot of conversation went on between Southey and Willie. Then Aunt Tillie and the girls arrived and everyone went through the greeting ceremony again.

Following lunch, Willie, Southey, and I went to a back area of the farm. We took a couple of cans and practiced shooting. This was more for my sake, or so they told Mrs. Harvey, but we all enjoyed it. I had shot a .22 rifle before and was pretty good at it. Willie showed me how to handle the rifle safely.

"Are we going on the rabbit shoot tonight?" I asked.

"Yes, about 9 o'clock. But they are Springhase (Springhares)," said Willie.

"After dinner?" I asked.

"Yes, when it's dark."

"Why?"

"You'll see. Be a little patient," said Southey, with that smile again.

I felt like I was a guinea pig again. Back to the teacher/older person syndrome, a tease, keeps you in the dark. Oh well!

Everyone turned up at the house about 3:00 PM. Eddie Harvey suggested going for prickly pears. "They are an interesting fruit. We use them to feed cattle and they make the milk better. The skin can be candied. You can put them in the cooler and have them with breakfast. If the black kids eat too many they get stomach trouble and come and ask for castor oil!"

All the girls, Southey, Willie, and I, got up and walked down a side road to the prickly pear patch. It was enormous; the leaves were big enough to walk on. Willie gave the instructions. "Look for dark red-mauve colored prickly pears, don't fall, walk slowly, support yourself at all times, especially when cutting the pear. Don't touch the hairs on the pear."

Slowly, everyone moved within the prickly pear patch. We each cut a pear, marked it with our initials and dropped it in a canvas bag. I thought it was like being on some planet that grew enormous plants, which could swallow you up. They were 15 feet high, surrounded by rocks and thorny trees. The thoughts were scary!

"The Thorn Planet!" I said softly.

"What did you say Charl?" asked Elaine.

"The Thorn Planet," I repeated. "We're on the Thorn Planet in Prickly Pear City!" Nobody laughed.

The next event was to get out of the giant cactus field safely, wash the pears, take the skin off and eat them. We walked back to the house, enjoying the hot sunny weather and cooling breeze.

One of the picannins came running down the road, "Baas Willie, the turkey is dead!"

"Where?"

"At the water, Baas."

"Southey, go and see what's happening. I'll go to the house and get the shotgun."

"It's a snake!" I said hesitantly, because I was guessing.

"Yes, it's probably a snake," said Willie.

Willie caught up with us and we cut through the bush following the picannin toward the usual windmill, tanks and troughs. Sure enough, the turkeys were scattered.

"Don't go any further, there's the dead turkey. But where is the snake?" None of the girls moved an inch.

"There, in the tree!" I shouted.

"Look at that!" said Southey; "He wants another turkey. He's not satisfied with one."

"Charl spotted him in the tree," said Southey.

"Then he should shoot him," said Willie.

"Me?" I asked, surprised that they would consider me.

"Yes, why not?" asked Willie.

"I only shot a few rounds with the other gun," I pleaded, but truly hoping they would let me do it.

"You can do it."

Willie took me to the side, told me how to get close enough for the gun's range and what direction to shoot so I wouldn't kill the rest of the turkeys. This was now really exciting! I was a little scared because I hated snakes. But I was trembling all over with excitement.

"If you're too far away you'll just injure the snake," said Willie, as he loaded the gun, put on the safety catch, and gave it to me. They all stood back, some sat down to watch.

I took the gun and walked slowly through grass. I now became serious and didn't act like a movie star. This was really, truly happening. It was like in soccer when you got the ball and you had a chance to score, the goal would be something good for your team. You eliminated the crowd and the background noise. People's shouting went unheard. The gun was pointed down and rested under my armpit and on my left forearm. I watched my pathway and the snake alternately. As I got to fifteen yards, my heartbeat quickened. I stopped and relaxed; I knew I had to get closer. My heart was pounding but I wanted to remain calm. I changed the gun's position and now held the barrel in the left hand and the butt in my right hand. My finger was on the trigger.

Willie turned to Southey, both of them close behind; "He's doing it like a professional."

"He learns quick," said Southey.

I took one step at a time, and very slowly. The tree was small, four inches around with not many branches. The snake was still in the branches, moving very slowly. I raised the shotgun and released the safety catch; I saw the snake move on the other side of one of the branches. I held the gun and looked through the sights. It was like looking through a camera. My heartbeat was loud; I knew I was shaking, but not visibly. The snake curled back around the near side of the branch. I had the snake's body, two feet from the head, in the sight. I pulled the trigger. I heard the noise as my mind and eyes lost sight of everything for a split second. Then I heard everyone yell.

"Great Shot! Good Shot, Charl. You got him!"

The snake fell to the ground in two shattered pieces. The tree branches came down after the snake. I stood frozen, after being kicked back by the gun's recoil. Willie ran up and took the gun away.

"See man! Easy huh?"

"Yes," I agreed, still in a trance of excitement and relief. It was like scoring a goal.

The story was continued in detail at dinner. I felt proud of what I had done, especially when somebody else told the story. Eddie Harvey congratulated me and related a number of his escapades. So did Willie. Southey was not a big talker and just listened. The girls wanted another subject, so as soon as coffee was served, they broke away from the table. The men sat around. I felt important inside. Usually I departed from a dinner table as soon as possible, but this was intriguing.

"How are you going to hunt the springhase?" Mr. Harvey asked. I was all ears. What did he mean?

"Can't tell you," said Willie, with a secretive smile. Mr. Harvey returned his smile.

After the festivities of dinner, Willie and Southey took me to the back of the house. They grabbed light sports jackets and went into the backyard, through some of the buildings to an old garage. Willie unlocked the door and opened it wide. There was a 1936 Ford 2-door, complete with a rumble seat at the back. Southey carried the guns. Southey and I got in. Willie took the driver's seat and started the car. It just purred. A beautiful beat coming out the back. I was in dreamland. Sixteen to twenty five year-olds prized these cars. "Own one of these," some guy had said, "and you're guaranteed a date." I thought it would be nice just to drive it . . . anywhere.

When I related this quote, Willie replied, smiling and almost laughing, "They still have to be good-looking! To ride in a car like this." Nobody seemed to disagree.

We drove to an area of the farm center that was not plowed and the ground was very natural. There were trees and bush and it did not look as though it was used at all. Southey jumped out, opened and closed a gate, and then we took off deep into this open field. It was rough riding. After about 15 minutes Willie stopped the car and got out. Southey followed. By the lights of the car they loaded the rifles, which were .22 caliber and carried a magazine holding twelve bullets. Willie took out a wrench and loosened the headlight assembly bolt on the left fender. The headlight was loose enough to turn.

"Get onto the fender Charl. You have to operate the light," said Willie, "Southey will do the shooting. Now listen carefully. When we drive off, you scan the horizon, and then bring the light back to about 20-30 yards from the car. Look for eyes; the springhaas are mesmerized by light. If you get two eyes in the light, hold it there. Southey can then take a shot, okay?"

"Okay," I replied.

The car moved off slowly, bouncing, rolling. My legs tightened on the fender to prevent sliding off. I turned the light sideways and tilted until I got a 30-yard distance, then moved it sideways.

"Not so fast!" said Southey.

"Okay," I said.

It was ten minutes before we saw any flickering in the light.

"Fireflies," said Southey.

Then the car turned slightly and I got overexcited.

"Eyes . . . look Southey! Lots of them!"

"Steady Willie," said Southey, as he raised the gun. "Crack, crack," the sounds of two bullets down the barrel and through the air. The eyes disappeared.

"Nothing," said Southey. Still, we drove over to look, dismounted and walked around. 'Nothing' was right.

We continued to drive around. Now my legs were more relaxed. I had learned to balance on the fender. Only when the car hit a large grass tuft or sank into a hole did I tighten my legs. Southey nearly fell off a couple of times. We had been at this for about an hour. Willie stopped the car and everyone stretched. I was given the gun. Willie was going to operate the light and Southey was going to drive the car.

"Number one, Charl," said Willie, "safety catch on. When you see the springhaas eyes, put the left arm under the barrel, butt of the gun on your shoulder, squeeze your legs on the light."

"Right," I said. I took the gun, got up on the car fender and practiced holding the gun, which was unwieldy.

Southey drove off and the gun waved all over the place until I put it across my lap with the barrel at an angle pointing toward the car's oncoming pathway, away from Willie on the other fender.

"Eyes!" said Willie. I raised the gun, it was moving all over. Then I steadied it on the eyes. Off went the safety latch. Two shots fired.

I wasn't sure where they went. We stopped again. Nothing.

"I knew you had missed, but we always stop to make sure no springhaas is just wounded!" said Willie. "Put the safety catch on."

"Oh yes, okay," I said.

I got a little better with the gun, but after thirty minutes we stopped and stretched. It was painful sitting on the fender no matter what you did.

"You drive," said Willie.

"I can't," I said. "I have never driven a car."

"Come on Charl," said Southey, "You never rode a horse either."

Despite my "No's," I soon found myself in the driver's seat: I wasn't scared at all; this was too exciting.

"Anyone can steer," said Willie. "It's clutch and accelerator that's the trick." I practiced the clutch and accelerator without the engine running.

"Okay, if you panic, just turn off the key."

Willie and Southey exchanged whispers. They agreed to first let me try to drive around, before they got on the fenders. After all, they did not want to be that stupid!

I stalled twice. The third time it worked. Once I had got it in low gear I felt fine. I drove in a circle while Willie and Southey watched.

"Let's do it," said Willie.

Now I became nervous as Willie took the gun and Southey positioned himself over the loose headlight.

"Let's go," yelled Willie.

The clutch came out too fast. The car lurched. I got a cold shiver of sweat down my spine as I saw Southey and Willie do back bends and lurches forward with their heads almost disappearing at their feet.

"Sorry! I'm Sorry!"

"Not too much trouble," said Willie, "Slowly now."

I was so careful as I held the accelerator steady and withdrew the clutch pedal. The car moved as smooth as a go-cart starting down a hill without a push.

"Super!" yelled Willie.

The car bounced as I negotiated through the field traveling at 10 mph. I was sweating. I was excited. I couldn't believe the feelings of power going through my body. This was so great!

Two shots and then another two shots: Willie never had to wait for someone to yell, "Eyes."

I stopped the car. We all got out and looked around. Nothing! Then we got back into our respective positions. I noticed Southey and Willie had both hands on the headlights as I drove off. But I did it smoothly and smiled along with my thoughts of, *don't trust me, hey!*

For three quarters of an hour we drove around, shooting followed by stopping and searching. It all produced nothing.

"It's the springhaas' night tonight," said Willie. "Let's go home hey!" Willie tightened the bolt on the left fender after setting the light straight. The bullets were removed from the gun. We all jumped in the Ford and rolled back to the farm, opening the gate, putting the car away, and going to bed. Two seconds in the bed was enough for me to fall sound asleep.

I woke the next morning knowing the trip to Vryburg was ending fast. I was very interested now in getting to talk to Otiend; the upcoming events of the day, my nice hosts, the Harveys, my cousins, and even breakfast were not important. My excitement was my frustration. I couldn't wait to get back to Aunt Tillie's. I knew the vacation was over, but I would just die disappointed if I could not meet and talk to Otiend.

Southey and I talked for a good fifteen minutes. I thanked him profusely.

"Thank you! You don't know how much I liked doing things with you! I've learnt so much and my friends at home are not going to believe what we did!"

"It was wonderful, man, to have you, and I enjoyed it very much as well. You must come back soon!"

"I will, and you must come to Johannesburg . . . it's not that bad!" I laughed.

"Okay—we will meet again then!"

"Thanks so much to your Mom, hey!"

Southey took off in the cart to 'Lazy Y'.

In turn, I thanked Willie and all the Harveys for everything they had done. Willie was the force. I liked him. He had a power and you would be glad to follow him. He was fair and I was always looking for that in anyone. Willie was as old as some of my uncles and so much nicer. Why did I even think of them? We shook hands and hugged.

Everything dragged: time, conversation, getting the horses, saying the final good-byes and all the words of thanks. I went with Aunt Tillie and we left. Horses were always willing to go home so there was no problem with their speed.

As we approached Auntie Tillie's farm, the now familiar group of Aunt Tillie's farm workers was fast gathering outside the house. By the time the cart got through the gates they were standing waiting to greet, take the bags, and talk to everyone.

I jumped off the cart, helped Aunt Tillie down and then walked very quickly to Otiend.

"Hello Otiend, I must talk to you, please!"

Otiend stood in his dirty farm clothes. He was barefoot with his legs together, arms close to his body, and elbows in his stomach, and his two forearms extended horizontally towards me. Otiend's hands were vertical and he clapped very slowly. I bowed my head slightly and really didn't know why.

"Yes Baas Charl."

"As soon as I get out of the house," I replied.

I ran off to the house to do a few things. I unpacked only one bag, because I knew we'd all be leaving soon, maybe tomorrow.

"Lunch at one o'clock," yelled Aunt Tillie, as I ran out the door.

I ran down the yard, passing the cows in the kraal. I looked for Otiend but couldn't find him, and after an hour was desperate. I ran back inside the farmhouse and confronted Aunt Tillie.

"Where's Otiend? He said we could meet and I can't find him."

"He's gone on horseback to the store to fetch some groceries we forgot to get."

"Damn," I muttered, after I had walked away.

"What's your problem?" asked Yvonne.

"Nothing," I replied.

"What are you cooking up?"

"I just want to talk to Otiend."

"He'll be back Charl. Relax! My cute brother!"

"Yvonne . . . stop!"

I was lost. So I walked around the farm until I resolved within myself that Otiend would be back and everything would turn out all right. When Otiend did arrive, he still had a lot of work to do so I followed Otiend around as he worked, but that was not what he wanted me to do.

Otiend recognized my frustration and said, "Baas, come to the huts at the end of the day."

"Okay! Yes! Okay," I agreed.

I waited. I was frustrated. My mind was full of questions! Time was running away fast! I didn't want to go swimming, so I just walked and drifted away from the farm to a dried-up lagoon and sat in the shade of a tree. Ants were crawling in and out of an anthill away from the lagoon and on high ground. They're not stupid, I thought. When it rains the anthill will not be flooded. The buzz of insects and noise of birds came and went and I thought of the silence of this dried-up land, with its red-brown-beige soil, clumps of grass that looked as though moisture would double their size, not many flowers, and very little green. So what was so intriguing? There were thorn bushes with white-tipped thorns and tall grass and short grass, but nothing had richness for the eye, none of it had any more than sand color, unless water was close by, and that disappeared quickly. Yet this was cattle country! And people just loved it all. The challenge! The lifestyle! The freedom maybe ... I never thought about that!

My thoughts drifted back to Johannesburg and school. Then I remembered the 'Vee Gang'. They had sort-of beaten me up once or twice, nothing bad, but they had roughed me up a little. It happened to all new students. I had stood up to the little punk they had sent to irritate and goad me. The plan, of course, was to get me to a point where I would hit the creep, so that the big boys could come to the little one's rescue. I remembered the little punk's pimply face as he challenged me.

"Why don't you do it, ugly?"

But I resisted and just pushed him away. The big boys answered this by pushing me around with a few light punches. My strength and ability to get away quickly saved me: soccer training paid off.

I had a few feelings that caused me to think that I didn't want to go back to school or Johannesburg. There were many things I would love to change, like their understanding of farmers, which was so damned wrong! I liked living with my Gran and Uncle Mick, and I loved Pal. I liked Desmond, and my friends: Helen and Bobby, Doc, Zoni and Juni were especially nice. I didn't like a lot of life-things . . . the way everyone treated black people . . . the harshness of people like the Vee Gang . . . the fact that everyone got more spending money than me . . . my uncles who thought they knew everything . . . the fact that you had to go to church every Sunday . . . the continuous instructions on what to do. What was missing? I would ask Otiend.

I finally wandered back to the farmhouse and drifted into my room. It was nice and cool and I slumped down on the bed and fell asleep.

When I awoke the sun had hit the horizon, but it was still light outside. I jumped off the bed and ran out the back to avoid dinner. I ran fast towards the huts and as I came through the trees to the six or seven rondavels, I slowed down. There was Otiend at the second hut. A fire was burning with a pot over it, Otiend's dinner. My heart pounded from the excitement. My run from the house was not enough to produce the strength of this pulsating beat in my chest.

"Hello Otiend."

"Hello Baas Charl. Sit here." Otiend offered me a seat on a log. He then squatted on his legs to one side of me. At our back was a slight breeze that sent the smoke of the fire away from us. Otiend was smoking a corncob pipe filled with his kind of tobacco. I did not recognize the smell and thought I'd never get used to it either, but I was in someone else's home so I would not say anything.

"Can I ask you some questions, please?"

"Yes," said Otiend.

"This is my first time away from Johannesburg and my first time in the farm country. I have read a lot of history about South Africa and I'm not sure I understand it. It's mostly about all the cattle wars, the Europeans coming here, the Great Trek up to the Transvaal. Then also, all the wars with the black people."

"I am not black," said Otiend.

"Yes I know. I meant natives," I said, nervously. I did not want to offend Otiend.

"We are many people," said Otiend, "we come from everywhere in Africa." Otiend's hands circled wide. The Bushman came from up there," he pointed to the north, "a very long time ago. The Khoikhoi from down there," he pointed to the south. Then he paused, and poked the fire. "The black people also come from there," he pointed to the north, but it was not the same north that he had indicated before. "After the Bushman and the Khoikhoi . . . they came."

"I read that," I said, "my teacher told me too."

"Has he been to Bechuanaland?" asked Otiend.

"No, he is from England and lives in Johannesburg."

"England is the place for the English," said Otiend.

I didn't know if this was a statement or a question, but I knew that Africans often spoke that way, saying something that can mean two things. Gran had told me that I should speak little, and listen a lot, and think a lot, because many things are hidden in what Africans tell you. They always honor you in assuming that you have the sense to know what is being said. So they leave it up to you to interpret the meaning. She also said that simple language means a lot, but I didn't understand all that.

"Yes," I replied.

"He knows us?" asked Otiend.

"No, I don't think so. He lives in Johannesburg and hasn't traveled a lot. Only from England," I replied.

"How can he teach you about us?" asked Otiend.

"I don't know; he has been to many schools. He is older," I replied but realized this was a stupid answer.

Otiend just smoked his pipe.

"He knows cricket," I defended.

"That is a game for a green field, not for Africa. Africa is brown and when it is green, it is jungle," said Otiend. "But Baas Charl, you did not come to talk about the English."

"No, definitely not!" I said. "I really don't like them because they think we are a colony of theirs and their Queen rules over us . . . that they are better than us!"

"No one can be better than you," replied Otiend as a puff of smoke drifted up and away.

Now, nobody had ever said that to me. I stopped thinking about that statement and replied. "I have seen so many things here in Vryburg. I do not know what they mean. I don't know why people live here or why they come here."

"Why do you live in Johannesburg?" asked Otiend.

"I was born there."

"I was born on the farms," said Otiend. "I don't know the big city of Johannesburg."

"The city has lots of things like buildings, schools, theater, hot and cold water," I suggested.

"Is that important?" queried Otiend. Then he looked down and stared into the fire. "It has a lot of people, I don't know them or what they do. I know people here, the animals, the land."

We two sat in silence for sometime. The thoughts in my mind were in turmoil and still I had no answers. I wanted to say something to Otiend to show my feelings but none of my thoughts made sense. Suddenly, it just came out, very naturally.

"Can I be your friend, Otiend?" I asked.

Otiend's face very quickly changed from the 'wise man' look to that of a person receiving a gift.

"I would be honored Baas Charl," he paused. "You are the first white man who wants me to be a friend. It is my honor," said Otiend. "It is my honor."

"No," I said. "It would be my honor. You have been so kind to me and I would like to learn from you. How you know about the rain? How you know about the cricket game? I see no books in your house, no papers." I paused, scraped a stick in the ground without any pattern, then, looking up, "And why do you like me?"

"You are a good young man," said Otiend. "You should be liked." He paused, "You should learn."

I was just so warm inside. How I wished Otiend lived in Johannesburg.

"Otiend, where is your wife?" I asked.

"She is near Kimberley."

"You have children?"

"Yes, six," said Otiend. And before his last sound on the "X" went away, I asked.

"Why do you live away from your family?"

"Baas Charl, you have many questions."

"Why is it that . . ." I didn't know how to ask, so I scraped the stick some more. There was no pattern on the ground at first but I could see a circle forming. I looked up determined to ask what I wanted to know. "It seems, Uh! I mean --- I don't understand why people live here on the farm. You live away from your family, and what do you do for fun . . . or, Uh, I don't know!" I stammered, really feeling like I had messed up the conversation. And I just wanted to talk. I just wanted to talk to someone who showed no force towards me. Otiend adjusted his sitting position and drew from his pipe. I was nervous.

"You are a strong young man," said Otiend, "but you are troubled. You have a lot of things on your mind and sadness is in your eyes. You are not asking what you want to ask."

I had kept a lot inside. Especially about my mom and dad and what had happened. Everything seemed to break up at that time and I didn't understand that either. After looking into the fire for some time I looked up at Otiend. His face was soft, not stern, and he took his pipe out of his mouth and cleaned it. He said nothing. I knew it was up to me.

"I'm scared. I have asthma and doctors say I must live in a place like Vryburg because it is dry."

"Asthma!" exclaimed Otiend.

"Yes, it is a disease that stops you from taking all the air into your lungs."

"It is the smoke in Johannesburg," said Otiend.

"Yes! Maybe! I don't know," I replied. "But I have my family and lots of friends in Johannesburg and I don't want to leave." I tried to explain my problem.

"There is someone you love there?" asked Otiend.

"Yes, my granny. I would rather die than leave her." The statement surprised me in that it came up without thought.

"Where are your father and your mother?" asked Otiend.

"My mother lives with us, but my father lives away," I replied.

"You love your mother?" asked Otiend, looking straight into my face, as though it was a most important question.

"No! . . . Yes! I don't know sometimes. No! Yes! I do! . . . I do!" I knew deep down I did love her, but she was always so busy.

"What of your father?"

"No, he doesn't care. I don't know him. He has never been around for anything." It was clear that I didn't know.

"You have food?" asked Otiend.

"Yes," I said.

"You have a place to sleep?" asked Otiend, as though he was going through a definite set of questions.

"Yes. Definitely!" I confirmed.

"Well, that is good. Then it is not important that your father is there. Your grandmother is there. Your mother is there," said Otiend. Then he asked, "You want to stay there?"

"Yes," I said.

"You don't want to stay here?" asked Otiend, drawing deeply on his pipe.

"There is nobody I know. Everything is so far away . . . the store . . . Vryburg . . . there are no boys my age." Now I was answering some of my own questions!

"You can make friends very easily."

I didn't answer. I didn't think so. It was so far away to other people. We sat for another while. After gathering up some courage. I asked, "But why do you live away from your children?"

"It is very hard to live away but there is no work, the land is not good where they live."

"Why can't you bring your wife and children here?" I suggested.

"It is not allowed," replied Otiend.

"It is not allowed!" I exclaimed exasperated. "Why? You mean Aunt Tillie?"

"No, Baas Charl, the man with the paper for work. He is in Vryburg."

"I see," I said. "Is he in the government?"

"Yes, I believe that."

"It is the same in Johannesburg," I said. "Our house girl cannot bring her husband to her place. But I know she does because I hear them sometimes on Saturdays. He takes a chance because he must have a pass for the area and if he is caught he goes to jail. I don't believe this is right. Why must they be separate? Why all these rules, Otiend? Why do we have all these rules to live? Do your people have rules?"

"I don't know that one about the white man's rules," replied Otiend.

We sat for a while watching the smoke. I felt better, more relaxed. I was totally enthralled at all the things we were talking about. Otiend never took his eyes off me now.

"You like to work here?" I asked.

"It is a good place."

"Why?"

"Missus Tillie is very good to us. We can eat well and she treats us good. The missus gives us clothes and sometimes presents. Also, Baas Charl, I can go home every three months to see my wife and children."

"Only every three months?"

"Work people on the farms . . . they go home once in a year," replied Otiend.

"When you go home, do you play with your children?" I inquired softly.

Otiend slowly and very gently started his answer. The expression on his face changed from a serious one to a softer look.

"It is a wonderful time. Yes Baas! We play games all day. Then we walk and then we talk about the trees, the land, and the stories of the animals. We talk many hours about my father and mother. We tell of our friends and we dance. We talk about the God of the sky and of the land. The children fall asleep by the fire as the story goes on..."

There was a silence as the fire crackled. It lasted for quite a long time. I felt the story inside my body. I liked this man and the way he talked with so much feeling.

"Is it sad to leave?" I asked.

"No . . . because there will be another time, and I can carry the song of love in my heart for many months . . . it does not go away."

The atmosphere changed as I stood up, walked around and came back to the fire. I thought about the movies, cameras, pictures, jazz music, ice cream parlors, soccer, and schools; all these things were missing. Did I miss them? Yes! Man, the greatest things that happened here was everybody visiting and talking. Even here they talked about black and white and English and Dutch and Afrikaans and Uitlanders (Foreigners). The 'Boere' (Farmers) they would call them. What did that mean? It was a very complex word I had learned and it meant so many things from a nation to a peasant. It was very deep within the soul. I was damn sure I didn't know!

How could I live here? Why wouldn't Otiend tell me about this place? Did I have to come and live here to find out? Was that what Otiend was saying . . . but not saying?

"You are happy?" I asked.

"Yes Baas Charl. Every day the heavens smile at us . . . and every night the heavens close their eyes slowly. I do not want Johannesburg.

It is a big cave where people go. They never come back with happiness. You are from there and you are not happy."

"Is Aunt Tillie happy?" I asked.

"She always smiles," he answered, with an upbeat voice. I believe he was relieved to change the subject.

"You are not scared here?" I pressed.

"No! Baas, but I would be scared in Johannesburg. I know everything here . . . the sounds, the trees, the animals, the roads of this place, and the God of this heaven. I can live here because I grow here, like a tree, each year a little bigger. One day I will not grow, but I will not die."

"Everybody dies," I said. Nobody had ever told me that, but I had already realized death would come.

"In the city, Baas Charl, everyone dies in the city. Here your soul lives forever."

I thought about that for a while. "You mean the black man's soul dies in the city?"

"The African man and the white man," said Otiend.

I realized my mistake of using 'black man' all the time. "The white man's soul lives forever . . . here in this place?" I stated, with a little question in it,

"I am not sure," said Otiend. He opened his hands. "Perhaps if he becomes a child of Africa."

"Like Aunt Tillie!" I suggested.

"That is truly possible," said Otiend.

"Will I die?" I asked.

"You have a chance to live forever because your heart is open," said Otiend.

"Oh boy!" I thought, but then I didn't know what it meant.

"When you are in trouble, how do you get out? I mean, if you have many problems, how do you fix them?" I asked.

Otiend looked at me for a long time. I felt now I had asked too many questions, so I poked the fire. I sat back and waited for a long time in Otiend's silence. Then I said, "I'm sorry Otiend, I know, too many questions."

"The problems . . . you must fix . . . Baas Charls. You must think of the most important one and fix that one first. . . . You must be the man."

"There are so many rules!" I exclaimed as I went into thought. "All the rules: at school, at home, on the bus. Black man must do this . . . White man must do that. We must not do this or that. Don't play in the street. Always, the adults tell you, but they never give you freedom. I enjoy freedom very much." I caught myself saying too much.

"It will be like that for a long time . . . it is up to you . . . to choose the rules you like," stated Otiend like an African king.

I was satisfied with this wonderful talk. I did not want to stay late because people on the farm got up very, very early. I would have liked to embrace this man, but I knew it was not courteous to do this, until you had known someone for a long time. I stood up.

"Otiend . . . I thank you with all my heart and I am glad we are friends."

Otiend stood up and put his hands together. "I am glad we have met. You will do good . . . Baas Charls. Thank you for your friendship."

We said goodnight and I walked into the dark trees a very, very happy person.

◆

The trip back to Johannesburg started with all the expressions of gratitude and the good-byes.

Aunt Tillie had tears in her eyes. The girls were all hugging her. I think Aunt Tillie liked having them around. We were saying goodbye to the people on the farm and, as tradition dictates, we all stood outside the house. Otiend was in the background. I hugged Aunt Tillie and thanked her.

The bus came.

I walked over to Otiend and said, "Thank you so very much again."

"Go Well, Baas Charl!"

"Goodbye!"

"Goodbye," said Otiend with a small smile. He backed off.

The bus moved off. I waved at everyone, and lastly at Otiend. He waved back. Dust turned everyone to face the other direction and walk off. I crawled up in my seat.

After an hour my thoughts drifted over this marvelous trip. I really liked Aunt Tillie, Aunt Eileen and Uncle Willie. I would truly miss being around Southey, who was like an older brother who cared. I had learned so much from him. Mostly I now believed that farmers were not stupid, not strict and mean, and I hardly got treated like an outsider. In fact I thought they were very strong people, very brave in working the land that was unforgiving . . . I learnt things had to be done in a certain way. Everyone had been extra nice to me. All the strangers at the picnic made me feel at home and as though I was one of them. They spoke English because I didn't speak Afrikaans. I would have many, many things to tell the kids in the playground and I was going to enjoy every moment when I told them, just to see the changing expressions on their faces: That made me feel good. But all through the bus ride to Vryburg and the train trip to Johannesburg, I thought about Otiend, and I felt sad. He was a wondrous person to me. I had gone over the conversations, the predictions of rain, and how Otiend was so calm. Most of all, it was all the time that he spent with me, and the long interesting talks, matched only by Gran and Uncle Mick. Otiend had been like a nice father to me, and I wished I had someone like that in my life every day. It was now going to be very hard for me to understand the dislike that many people had for African people. To me this had been an amazing trip!

My mother met us at the train station. She gave Yvonne and I long hugs and kisses. Delphine's mother picked her up, Aunt Amy picked up Elaine and they all went home. We went back to Andrew Street, talking about everything. Gran gave me a forever hug and was so excited to see me. I was so glad to be with her. Uncle Mick gave me a hug with a big smile, and had a few questions as well. We had such a nice dinner, all together, everyone so happy about all the happenings. Especially about what Yvonne and I had learned, and all the news of our family in Vryburg. Funny, I thought, I just found out, from Yvonne's story at the dinner table, what Aunt Tillie and the girls had done all the time. I answered every one of Gran's questions until she got tired and went to bed. It was not long after that that the whole family went to bed. I lay in my bed thinking how quickly we had gone from one life to another. I was now back home and everything had changed in just 24 hours. Everyone in Vryburg would be getting up tomorrow and doing what they did. I would be going back to school in a couple of days. I truly felt so different now, compared to the time when I was leaving to go to Vryburg. I had such a nice time with everybody . . . the people at the picnic . . . the Harveys . . . the natives of that world. Aunt Eileen and Aunt Tillie were perfect and Southey had taught me so much and had made my vacation exciting, in so many ways, it wasn't possible to say. Uncle Willie letting me shoot guns and drive a car. I guess I was being tested as a young man, but so what, they seemed to enjoy it, and I was so very glad to have all these grown-ups challenging me. Finally Otiend, with his ways and his wisdom, had made me think differently about almost everything.

My birthday was coming up soon and I already felt so much older!

✳

CHAPTER 4

Andrew Street III

I T WAS SATURDAY MORNING and there was nothing to do, so I walked down Andrew Street to the corner of Main Street and sat down on the sidewalk looking at Zoni's house. This is where the kids of the street usually gathered. I was becoming a strong-bodied kid with brown hair, hazel eyes, and dark tan skin and just loved activities with my friends. It was almost a year since I'd come back from Vryburg. Even after all this time, I was still amazed that there was very little reaction to what I had experienced. Nobody was particularly interested in farm life or the people. Even Desmond didn't comment very much.

The trip had definitely affected me. My understanding increased phenomenally about the different life everyone lived in the Vryburg area. I had thought about this so many times. I wondered what Otiend was doing, and what it would be like if he and Southey lived here. I knew it would be very complicated with Otiend because whites never mixed with black and native South Africans on a social basis. We never had dinner together. We never actually mixed at night. We were together during the day at school or at work, and then went our separate ways at night. They didn't go to our cinemas, didn't ride our buses and were only seen in cars as chauffeurs. Thoughts of why it was like this got too complex, and I had many other issues to solve without working on black vs. white. I had school; I had to avoid the 'roughies' that hung around school and Broadway Corner, uncles I didn't like, a missing father and no money for anything. I hated begging for money. I would never ask my dad because I wouldn't get it. I mean, to have twelve pennies in my pocket would have been just marvelous. So I thought about

Southey. He would make a great brother. My own brother took very little interest in me on a day-to-day basis, whereas Southey had helped me with many facets of farm life, and with riding, sports and having fun; Southey was challenging and never forced you to do new things, although I never refused either. Then I realized that Zoni and Juni and I had something in common. Primarily our grandmothers were raising us. Except that Mimi, their grandmother, was on a different planet than Gran.

Bobby came down the street and told me my mom wanted to see me. I reluctantly went home to see what she wanted.

"Your dad called and wants to meet you in the city," my mom informed me. I was completely surprised. I didn't know what he wanted.

"Dad really called! Do I have to go?" It had been a long time since I'd seen him. It would take me away from the street and I never gave in easy.

"Yes!"

The arrangement was that he would meet the bus in the city, and put me back on the bus later. I got dressed in shorts, socks and shoes and a neatly pressed short-sleeved shirt; I had no long pants. They were too expensive, my mom had explained. I wanted a pair because everyone else at my age had long pants. I went to the bus stop, got on the double-decker bus, went upstairs, down the aisle, and got the front seat. I liked this seat because the windows were right in front of you and it felt like you were driving.

I sat on the bus thinking how co-incidental it was to have thought of my dad, and then find that he had called. When I was little I had lived with my dad and mom on Main Street, most southern end of the suburbs and close to the kopies. My mom and dad had argued almost every night. Eventually, my mom, Bazil, Yvonne and I left with my dog Wolf, after my dad went to work one night. It was scary going out at night and walking down to Gran's house on Andrew Street. I was worried about leaving my house and my room. I didn't know anything about going to Gran's. I thought it must be a big move because we never took this many suitcases anywhere. I wondered about my Dad. Was he at work? Why wasn't he coming? Why were we going to Gran's house so early in the morning? It was 5AM, still dark. There was nobody on the streets. I had never seen it like this. I had never been out in the real dark. It was like a large tunnel with lights, ghosts shaped like houses looking at you, each with a different face. None of them looked happy.

I was scared and glad everyone was with me, especially my dog Wolf; I didn't want to think about him because it made me so sad inside. But I do remember Gran meeting us at her door and picking me up into her arms, flooding me with warm feelings.

To get from Kenilworth to Johannesburg City, I caught the bus at the corner of Andrew Street and Main Street going north. I looked out the window intensely as we went down Main Street. I hadn't done this trip for some time. The first landmark was Rosettenville Corner, an intersection for streetcars, filled with shops and movie palaces, and the famous Broadway Hotel. As we approached the corner, I could see lots of streets with small houses, churches and Rosettenville Central School. It was very busy, because it was Saturday and people were shopping. After getting out of the Rosettenville Corner traffic the bus sped up because it was now a straight run for quite a distance. Past 'The Corner' the bus passed one of the highest concentrations of entertainment and recreational areas in Africa. Immediately on the left was the Turffontein Race Course, and on the right were the houses and shops of the suburb La Rochelle. Further in and behind these houses were Regents Park and the City Deep Gold Mine. Beyond and away from this area the bus veered left and drove past the Rand Stadium, a large soccer stadium that could accommodate about 20,000 people. It was the dream of kids to play here. It was the top venue for soccer in South Africa. I wondered if I would ever play there. I ran a dream through my mind, as I had done many times before, of entering the field from the stadium tunnel and being cheered by the crowd. I could see myself beating players and hearing the noise of the crowd grow louder. I crossed in front of the goal with the ball at my feet and suddenly turned on the defenseman chasing me. I looked down and shot the ball hard. When I looked up it was sailing past the goalkeeper's hands and into the net. The crowd goes wild. I came back to reality: the dream was a long way to go, for one thing, I was still a young teenager.

Behind the stadium was Pioneer Park, with swimming baths and a man-made lake called Wemmer Pan, surrounded soccer, rugby, and cricket fields as well as tennis courts. They trained sea cadets at Wemmer Pan. I thought this was funny; it was 500 miles and six thousand feet up from the nearest sea! Past the Rand Stadium on your left was the suburb of Glenesk, the Olympia ice rink and the Wembley Stadium, where they had motorcycle and dirt track racing and more rugby fields. The ice rink was one of only two in Africa. I had been there twice and in that time I had learned to skate without hanging onto to the boards at the side. It was nice in summer because it was so cool inside. The bus then headed directly towards Johannesburg City over a bridge that crossed railway lines and on to Eloff Street Extension. At the bridge I saw the headgears of Robinson Deep Mine and Chris Mine. My uncle Mick had worked at both of these mines; the same mines where parents of many a Southern Suburbs kid had spent a lifetime working. On both sides of the street and set way back were large man-made hills called 'tailing dumps.' These hills stood out on the skyline; they were hundreds of feet high and thousands of feet in length and width. They consisted of a light yellow waste rock from the Robinson Deep, City Deep, Chris and earlier gold mines that had operated since the 1800's. These dumps were the source of yellow dust that continually floated with the wind and fell to the ground everywhere. The mining companies had tried to grow almost everything on the dumps but were not very successful. They were now part of photographs of Johannesburg. Beyond the bridge we went through an industrial area with its one- to six- or eight-storey buildings and factories, and into Johannesburg City, where there were automobile stores one after the other, and many, many shops. Finally, the bus stopped near the theaters in downtown Johannesburg outside of Escom House, the electric utility headquarters. The offices, retail shops and apartment buildings were now up to about twenty stories high.

My dad was on the platform waiting, and he was smiling. He was a short man, under six-foot, well built, and very good-looking, with black hair combed straight back. He was immaculately dressed in a gray jacket, gray pants, white shirt and red tie. He wore a hat and looked just like the Mafia in the movies! I laughed quietly. Adults always dressed up when going into the city of Johannesburg.

"Hullo Dad!" I had seen him a few times since moving to Andrew Street. I felt he was my dad; the difference to other kids' dads was that he wasn't around all the time. I envied the other kids having a father at home. Of course I didn't want the fighting or rigid discipline that my friends talked about. It always seemed when you asked an adult a question, they answered by saying that you didn't need to know. I had now got used to not having a father in the house and so I didn't know how to treat him when we got together.

"Hullo Son!" He gave me a hug and a kiss, which embarrassed me. I didn't like seeing other fathers kiss their sons either. "I wanted to have lunch with you and take you to see something that *happened during the war.*"

"What's that?"

"Well, wait and see."

We had lunch together at the East African Pavilion, it was a very famous for serving curry, and I loved it. The servers were all from Kenya and very tall. My dad was very pleasant. He asked me what I was doing, and then told me of his work at the Johannesburg Rand Daily Mail and Star Newspapers. He was always proud of working there and took pride in his work. We left the restaurant and he explained that what I was going to see was not very nice, but important to experience. It would make me grow as a young man. Also, it was necessary in a way, because he and many South Africans had helped fight Italy and Germany, and many of our men had not come home. He wanted me to understand why.

I was sneakily maneuvered into the theater. I learned later that the news broadcasters had recommended not taking children to see these pictures. It was a series of short films on the final days of the war in Germany, and the worst part was about the results of all the atrocities of the concentration camps. It was a frightening experience for me. I could feel the total control of the uniformed man over the weak and frail men and women. Where were the children? I had never seen anything like it. I was disgusted that people treated people that way. I thought it was a terrible, terrible thing to do! The film was in black and white and showed the miserable camps, showers and barbed wire fences. However, the buildings did not matter to me. It was the people standing and looking into the camera. They were so thin; their skin was tightly stretched across their bones like a cellophane wrap. It seemed as though there were no muscles left in their bodies. There were no exceptions . . . Worst of all; their eyes seemed too big for their head. I could not get the expression in their eyes out of my mind, all the way from the cinema, down the street and into the ice cream parlor. My dad and I went into the parlor to finish our day before I caught the bus. We talked quietly and about little things. He said he was sorry it was not a happy movie, but he wanted me to know what had gone on during the war. He also added that it was his hope I would never see or go through any of that in my life. He hoped the world would not see it again . . . ever. My dad put me on the bus, gave me some pocket money and said that he would guarantee a fun movie next time. I thanked him for the time we had spent together.

On the bus home I wondered why my dad had suddenly wanted me to see the movie. I thought about how little we knew by just living in Andrew Street. The trip also confirmed my dad wasn't a monster. That is what some of my uncles had said, and my uncles were definitely wrong. I was glad they were wrong!

I remembered that some time ago the news of World War II had inspired my friends and the grownups in our lives to talk about places in foreign lands. Kids at school knew about the United States, and the surprise attack on Pearl Harbor. We learned about the bombing of London and the struggles of England, the domination and aggression of Germany, the puzzling entry of Italy, the sad situations in many countries of Europe and North Africa, and the big turnaround of Russia after it had been under siege for years. These were pictures in our eyes and words in our ears. We didn't know what it all meant. The term that described it best was 'far away'. We had seen the war movies and ended up with a fascination for tanks, ships and planes. Zoni and I knew all the names, such as Spitfire, Hurricane, Lancaster Bomber, Mustang P51, Navy Corsair, and B17, B24 and B29 Bombers. When they were available, about five of us kids built these planes out of kits. We cut and glued the balsa wood, laid the tissue paper over and wet it, and after it dried, we assembled the planes. We gave it up when Zoni got a plane kit that included a 15-foot wingspan; it would have taken a lifetime just to cut out the pieces.

Two weeks later, Zoni, Juni, Doc, Mel and I were talking in the street. They confirmed having seen the films of the concentration camp atrocities and had experienced the same frightening feelings.

Zoni said. "It was a black and white horror movie of unbelievably thin human beings, actually standing up and moving around."

We all agreed. We were so glad to live in South Africa.

"I don't know why this is done to people," Doc added. So we also talked about this a lot. Then we got into how England and Europe was so crowded and so dreary, when compared to America. We liked the 'American Scene' because it looked bright and upbeat, with newly shaped cars and wide streets like South Africa.

"America looks good in pictures but it looks just the same as pictures of places in South Africa; like Cape Town, the Garden Route, the Drakensberg, the Kruger National Park, Durban and the South

Coast. We don't know anything about these places . . . we haven't seen them . . . we only know the Southern Suburbs and downtown Johannesburg. We haven't been anywhere else! I think we should go!" Mel concluded.

"Agreed! We'll do it when we're older!"

Our group of the Andrew Street Mob then agreed that if we couldn't do it, it didn't matter.

◆

I was now playing organized soccer with the St. John Ambulance Brigade, an organization that attended major sports events and provided paramedic help in case of injuries. They were at all the professional soccer games in England too. The organization was an alternative to the Boy Scouts. As a member you could earn merit badges in subjects such as swimming, soccer, camping, fire fighting, etc. with the main merit badge being first aid. Among the twenty-five of us in the soccer team were Brian, from Andrew Street, Henry and Otto. We met a kid named Chris, a very friendly boy, big and with a pleasant, rounded face and positive approach to all we did. He liked our class leader, Mr. Davis, and was always around him.

In the first-aid classes we learned the order of importance when reaching an injured person. First was to stop the bleeding. Second was not to move the patient if the body was contorted. Third was to cover the patient with blankets for shock. There were many more of these actions, but the most important thing to remember was that you were not the doctor. To be on the first aid team you had to learn the pressure points in the body, the different types of fracturing, and every conceivable method of bandaging. We seemed to be practicing these interminably.

To me the only reason to belong was to play soccer. The team played on Saturday mornings at Pioneer Park, and then you could change and go to the Adelphi or Grand Cinema in the afternoon. Included with St. John's activities was the annual athletic competition between different branches of St. John Ambulance. Swimming, running and jumping were the main events. In our branch's trial runs to choose a team, I won many running and jumping events. The leader, Mr. Davis, ended up picking Chris as the goalkeeper in our team, despite the fact I played goalie in the school team; also he picked Chris for a number of the events I had won in athletics. It took some time to work that out in my head. My thoughts were that it wasn't fair! I resolved it by not caring, as long as I was on the soccer team. Nothing like this had happened in our 'street sports'. If you were good it was acknowledged 'silently'. It all ended up with me not having any more respect for Mr. Davis. I just concentrated on getting better at soccer.

Then there was camping where all the kids learned about fires, snakebites, and camp food. Little Falls, east of Johannesburg, was the favorite camp spot. I loved the swimming there, it was just marvelous; the rest of the camping activities were not that interesting to me, despite everyone else really loving everything about it.

◆

The Andrew Street Crowd grew dramatically in size. We started to mature at 14 and 16 years of age. We were going to parties, first with cousins and families, then with friends to birthday parties. Boys and girls from surrounding streets joined the fun. New kids from other places moved into the street and everyone became part of the family.

Three blocks down from Andrew Street was a group of girls: Beryl, Grace, and Ann. They had already joined the crowd and became known as the 'The Kennedy Street Girls'. Beryl had dark hair, parted in the middle, was very pretty, shorter than most and always smiling and laughing. Grace was thin and tall, with traditional quietness, a beautiful face and pleasant smile. Ann was heavier than Beryl and Grace but pretty and always very pleasant and quiet (my mother said she would grow up to be an elegant lady).

Billy and Johnny joined the group, and Billy brought in Tommy. Billy was short and stocky with blond hair combed straight back; he looked like an older English gentleman, and acted like one, but with a naughty approach to everything. Johnny was tall with red/brown hair, good looking, and forever smiling and positive. Tommy was medium height with sharp, good-looking features, and had the devil in his eyes and devilment in his soul.

Norman also came into the Mob through one of the parties. Norman was tall with blond hair, was good-looking in a manly way, smiled a lot and loved to do anything anyone suggested.

Thelma and her mother moved into the flats next to Zoni's and Juni's house. The gang decided to get to know them so one Friday, Juni applied his technical expertise, set up a large search light, and beamed it on the windows of Thelma's apartment, which was on the second floor. There was no response. At the same time, a bus stopped on Main Street and two people got out and walked passed our crowd standing around the light. They inquired why the light was being shown on their window. Embarrassed introductions followed, and Thelma, a shorter girl with brunette hair, a pretty face, a very friendly smile and a great personality, joined the crowd and also joined the parties.

Gloria and her mom moved into the house opposite to Mimi, as did Julius from Belgium, a relative of Gloria's and our first foreign import. Gloria was thin and a very pretty blonde, she walked with a spring in her feet and was a happy person. Her mom, a single mother, was an older copy. Julius was short, pleasant looking, thin, and smiled all the time. He wore funny glasses that looked upside down, but was always a kick to be around. The second import was Guy, a Frenchman from Mauritius. Guy was a tall man, a little steeped in his walk, with light hair and Latin looks, and very expressive in his mannerisms. We thought there might have been some Italian blood there, but never said so!

Suddenly we were starting high school, we were into racing bicycles and getting a whole new focus: girls!

The bicycles facilitated riding past the koppies on Rifle Range Road, although parents forbade it because it was a main traffic artery going south out of Johannesburg's Southern Suburbs. We could now cycle to soccer and to explore other parts of the southern suburbs we had not walked, such as Kenilworth, Rosettenville, Turffontein, Hill Extension, La Rochelle, and Wemmer Pan.

The Andrew Street Mob took underwent a big change. Many of the earlier group of *play street kids* were going in different directions, forming new groups and opening up their range of activities. High school took a toll on our free time in the street. The mix of kids was revolving and changing. It didn't change our feelings for each other, but growing up was spreading us in directions never experienced before.

Things were changing fast. Although girls had entered our lives some time ago, parties had caused everyone to dress like they were going to church or their aunt's birthday party. This became a quandary. With every new activity came a hitch: with bikes . . . not enough money for parts, with girls . . . you had to dress up and needed more money, with all these friends . . . not enough time!

At the parties, all the girls would sit in one corner, and all the boys would sit in another. Some grownup would then bring us together to learn to dance a waltz, a foxtrot or a tango. After several parties, we all got better at those dances. We progressed to the samba, conga, the Mexican hat dance, and the swing. It was fun to dance. We hardly spoke; we just laughed. At first, we were embarrassed at tripping or missing a step; when we messed up, everyone else laughed. These close encounters with girls gave rise to a whole new set of feelings! Liking a buddy was easy: you could be as sarcastic as you like and feelings were understood, but with girls that was impossible. Showing any warm feelings towards girls was different. So the liking of a girl was only transmitted through a smile or a laugh. It was also unheard of for boys to just walk over to the girls we liked and say "Hullo!" I would just sit talking in a group and hope and wait for the slim chance to dance, maybe made possible by an adult introduction. It was very, very wise not to show your affection—I found *that* out after being nice to a girl; the guys ragged me constantly afterwards.

The parties with grownups were always so formal. The girls wore pretty dresses and (usually white) socks and shoes, and the boys put on neatly pressed pants and shirts. We nearly all wore the same clothes to every party. We would enter, sit, dance, and mix just a little, and then we'd have cold drinks or tea and biscuits (cookies) or cake, and then it would all be over. It never seemed worth it to get so dressed up. After a while, the parties became like school, like a class, and deep down inside, the discontent grew. None of the adults seemed to realize that it came about from the fact that 'rock and roll' was the new thing. Formal dances like the waltz and the fox trot were on the way out for our generation. In our predominantly English-speaking neighborhood, Afrikaans and traditional South African music was not that popular. We knew how to dance to it because we'd been taught. It was not regarded as much fun to go to an Afrikaans friend's party, mainly be-cause of the music. American music and music by South African black musicians interpreting American music, was the 'In Thing'. Swing, jazz, jitterbug, rock and roll, and slow dancing were perfect. This was the era of dancing and the Andrew Street kids were growing up *—on this stage of life*; other dances belonged to grownups.

We may have loved Glen Miller, Tommy Dorsey, and Artie Shaw, Nat King Cole's "Nature Boy" and "I Love You," Doris Day's "It's Magic," The Ames Brothers "You, You Are the One," and Perry Como's "Till The End Of Time," "Prisoner Of Love," "Blue Moon," and "Wonder Who's Kissing Her Now." But, modern versions of boogie-woogie, such as Arthur Smith's "Guitar Boogie" and the tremendous multi-recording antics of Les Paul and Mary Ford with "Brazil" and "Lover", now excited the crowd. Wherever possible, modern music was sought out. Jukeboxes in restaurants, records bought in stores and the few radio programs that played it. Two dance themes evolved in the Andrew Street Mob: hard swing music, and boogie-woogie, which were fast dances similar to the Jitterbug, and of course romantic music, which lured us into slow dances.

Although the Andrew Street Mob planned to have parties without parents many times, we found it was hard to do. Throwing a party without a place and without parents knowing seemed impossible. Rock and roll was suffering from parents' outrage. We heard comments such as 'no melody' or 'too loud' or 'the beat is monotonous and driving me crazy'. The radio announcers for the South African Broadcasting Corporation said that rock and roll would be dead within a year. We just laughed!

The first opportunity for a 'real' party came about after a year of parties chaperoned by adults. An old, single-storey Victorian house located on the corner of Andrew and Main Street had been vacant for many months. It had thigh-high grass and a narrow pathway leading to the doorstep. There was no electricity or plumbing, and it was dirty inside. The house was set back off the street and we were sure no one would hear the noise. Also, not many people would want to come through the tall grass and bushes up to the old house. Workmen had begun to dismantle the house but it was being done so slowly, progress couldn't be seen. The house was next door to Zoni and Juni.

Ten of us worked like crazy all Saturday afternoon cleaning. We set up candles on the windowsills in three of the seven rooms because there was no electricity. The others were closed off. A portable record player was begged and borrowed, and two old tables with tablecloths were brought in to hold the food and drink. The pathway was only slightly trimmed. It was a labor of excitement. We closed the door at about 5 PM and headed home to wash, eat, and get spruced up. There were some intriguing thoughts about being alone with girls . . . no parents! It would be our first party without chaperons, and some of my friends and I agreed that being free from older people and mixing the whole crowd in one place was exciting; sort-of a test to see how far everyone might go.

At 8:30 PM, everyone who was invited was already there. Helen, Gloria, Beryl, Grace and Ann, a couple of girls in Andrew Street who never hung out with us, and a few I didn't know. The boys were there before any of the girls. Doc, Zoni, Juni, Mel, Billy, Johnny, Tommy, Norman, Julius, Guy, Brian, Graham, Bobby and a couple of new faces. The girls dressed in short skirts, blouses, sweaters, flat shoes and socks (very close to Bobby-Sox styles). The boys wore sweaters and long pants; some wore jackets. Fancy sweaters with crew necks were in. Zoni had a red sweater with an enormous yellow 'Z' on it. There were soft drinks, cakes, sandwiches, salads, and cheeses on the table. Someone had swiped a bottle of whisky out of his parents' liquor locker. He knew he was doomed on Sunday, but he didn't care, and the risk made him very popular. He had the most fun, dividing it up in one of the dark rooms. Actually, he had been challenged by the boys to see which of the girls was brave enough to go in there.

Two girls went in together and all the boys thought it was a 'go'. The unpredictable feminine gender fooled the young men. The girls didn't stay in the dark room for long.

The party had 20 or 30 kids dancing at a time. Those invited had brought some of their friends. They were all welcomed. This new type of party was great. The dance floor was always full. I liked Beryl, and danced with her as frequently as I could without being tagged for hanging in there. I also danced with Gloria, who was the best dancer, and we 'clicked' on the floor as dancers. It was exciting. The party crowd was truly having a wonderful experience. This was just what all of us would have loved to do every weekend. We were dancing, laughing and talking. Everyone was loose and informal, walking everywhere and talking to everyone, totally unheard of! The kids were unmolested by thoughts of what should and should not be done. Swing, popular, and rock and roll music from the cheap record machine filled the room. I thought it was great just to walk across the floor and ask someone to dance. The girls always said 'yes'. No adults, and no program of events, caused a free atmosphere. I felt a new freedom, same as the soccer in the street and just as exciting. I felt like a man guiding his own progress in choosing a girl to dance. I noticed my buddies matching up with girls; some of the choices were surprising. Most surprising of all was the lack of shyness.

The party progressed into a wonderful atmosphere of excitement. We were all enjoying the hell out ourselves; it was wilder, noisier and loads more fun than anyone had thought. No one sat in corners all night! New rock and roll steps were being taught to those who didn't know. We were getting good at it even in such a short time. The freedom of not being watched was hard to believe. We became even more enthusiastic, yelling and stomping on the floor. The bottle in the dark room seemed to never run out. The owner obviously enjoyed his role. Some boys were acting drunk. No one believed them. At 11:00 PM everyone was on the dance floor, having danced into a sweat to the upbeat Frankie Laine's "Sunny Side of the Street", and now we were into the slow romantic song "Blue Moon" sung by Perry Como. It was quiet and couples were slow dancing close.

"What the hell are you doing?" The adult shout rang through the air, reverberating throughout the Victorian mansion . . . it took forever to die out!

The dancers turned to the voice-noise; it was so loud, and it belonged to an adult. A ripple of fear ran through all the kids, the instant fear you get when caught in an awkward situation. It's like a quick stomach surge, and then your mind's reactive sensing of what you should do creates waves of nauseous feelings in your body. The fear didn't subside. There in the entrance stood Mimi, whose Afro hair-do seemed to stand up even higher than normal. She had a kitchen apron on, horrible beige-colored stockings and shoes that looked like slippers. She was sloppy!

She continued to yell! "You rotten kids! I'll tell your mothers and fathers, and I'm going to." The boys knew she could get violent.

"Where's Zoni and Juni?"

"They're not here," I answered. I was mad at her! Why did she have to come here and spoil our fun? I didn't care what she was going to do!

"You too. Charl."

"We're just having fun." I snapped. I was not sure if I was being brave or stupid.

"This is not fun, this is bad," Mimi yelled, waving her spoon at me. I didn't back off. I was so mad! I stood there in front of her. The girls slipped behind the boys.

Mimi started to walk around. Silence fell over the three rooms. Those in the dark room, lucky for them, had slipped out the window. The song "Blue Moon" ominously came to an end, as the record player clicked, and clicked, and clicked. The perspective of the scene crumbling into an abyss came to mind. Then Mimi yelled again.

"I smell whisky. You are all going to get it. You girls! Shame! What will you grow up to be? You want me to tell your parents?"

"Mimi . . . " I said loudly, "please!"

"Shut up! I don't want to hear from you. Shut up! I don't want to hear from you boys; you are so rotten," she paused, "you always making up all these things! Always getting in trouble. I'm always seeing you! Looking after you! I want to know where's Zoni and Juni?"

"We don't know," said Doc.

"Liars! I know they were here. Hell! They are going to get it."

Unexpectedly, she lunged slightly forward yelling. "Get out! . . . Get out of here! Don't come back!"

We hardly moved, having nowhere to go. Mimi stood in the doorway anyway, and who would leave the girls? I looked back across the room and sought out the faces of Doc, Johnny, Billy, and Beryl, my dance partner. I judged we all had the same look of amazement and disappointment, eyes dropping to the floor.

"Oh! . . . Well! . . . Then!" she said in a lower voice, as though total calm had come over her. She surveyed the room again. She seemed to raise her body higher and with a fairly quick movement, but with an awkward stride, started to walk around the room. She raised her wooden spoon, some kids moved. Bang! She hit a candle off the sill, stood on it, put it out. Then she went to the next one, until all the candles were put out. We grabbed what we could, left through the front door and down along the narrow pathway. All of us were confused, but really mad that our first real party had been stopped. Mumbling voices furiously touched on Mimi. We were surprised she would stop us from having fun. The beautiful party was killed! I stood in the street for a short while with all my friends. Finally, we split into different groups and walked the girl's home. Mimi had won . . . but she had also lost! She had fully represented the adults. I walked home with Beryl, Ann and Grace; they had never gone for tea at Mimi's. They didn't know what we had experienced. We hardly said a word after we had agreed what a wonderful party it had been. Beryl and I talked for some time. We had talked at her front gate many times, because kids just never went inside to talk. Girls were allowed to go out of the house to the gate . . . and that was it! I liked Beryl very much, but besides our friendship, there was something else that made it stop there.

I walked back to Andrew Street, thinking about what Grandpa Mick had said one day, after I told him how I disliked some of my uncles. "After you grow up . . . in your heart and soul is a place for old people, who were around when you were a child. Some of them will have been mean and some of them nice." I never knew what he meant. I know I didn't have any grownups that fell into the in-between category. But Mimi definitely existed in both; she had been part of my thoughts for as long as I knew her. There were so many curious situations that we got into when she was around. Sometimes it seemed as though she was sent to keep the Andrew Street kids in line by totally confusing our minds. She seemed to be part of all of us; nothing seemed to escape her. She made us mad . . . and especially tonight! She made us happy, she also made us sad, but she was always there. Maybe that's why we liked her or loved her . . . although, I wasn't sure of that either!

◆

Down at Rosettenville Corner were two cinemas, The Grand Theatre that was older, with slightly cheaper tickets, and the Adelphi Theatre, which was more modern and more expensive. Front row seats were best at the Grand, because they were a long way from the screen, and good because you could get up anytime and go out of the theater, get a pass and come back. The Grand was close to Rosettenville Corner and the most popular with the younger kids. The movies were always preceded by advertisements, the current trailers such as Gene Autry or Roy Rogers, Zorro followed by Gaumont or Movietone News. This took about 45 minutes and was followed by an interval, when you could leave the theater to buy cool drinks and sweets. When the little shop next to the Grand Theatre was full, everyone went over to the Crystal Cafe on the other side of the street. The Greek owners served the best Banana splits and Parfaits ever. They also had the best variety of sweets and candies from all over the world. Unfortunately for them, the counter was very long and while one kid was selecting sweets from one side, his friend would put a few sweets in his pocket at the other end! Further down the road, and very close to Rosettenville Corner, was another milk bar and they were famous for a drink called 'Panther Piss'. The color was predominantly yellow! The drink was simply a touch of all flavors from his counter. The owner would just zip down the bar adding flavors at will. The kids loved it.

The Adelphi Theatre did not have all these choices, as there was only one cafe and it was attached to the theatre. The Adelphi was about three blocks from the 'Corner' going east. When the kids went to the

Adelphi, some of them would make a run, at the interval of the show, to Rosettenville Corner to the cafes there, just to get their favorite sweets and Panther Piss.

The Andrew Street kids had been going to the movies for some time, and we were familiar with the Tarzan, Zorro, and Batman trailer series and the Gaumont and Movietone News. There was also a large choice of movies, which mostly fell into two categories: English and American. The English movies we had agreed were stuffy, righteous and sad and seemed to be shot in one room and one house, whereas the American movies were bright and happy with beautiful clothes, lots of music, jazz, big bands and love stories. There were always large places, deserts, trees and hills with a ranch house and no other place for miles. The gang knew all the actors and actresses. Favorite stars were Rita Hayworth, Doris Day, Jennifer Jones, Ingrid Bergman, Olivia de Havilland, Loretta Young, Ava Gardner, Judy Garland, Bette Grable, Gary Cooper, John Wayne, Spencer Tracy, Van Johnson, Ray Milland, Humphrey Bogart, James Cagney, Dirk Bogarde, Richard Burton, Terry Thomas and James Mason. The most hated by our crowd was Bette Davis. We had names for her: 'Moaner', 'Bitch Woman', 'Hateful Wife'.

The opulent scenes, dresses, houses, cars, lifestyles and personalities of the movies impressed us no end. It was so much better than what we had and saw in real life. We discussed it all to death. Many of us agreed it was dreamlike. It was a fairy tale existence far away from where we were.

When we went to high school, there were many movies to see. There was "It Happened in Brooklyn" with Kathryn Grayson, Jimmy Durante, Frank Sinatra and Peter Lawford; "New Moon" with Nelson Eddy and Jeanette MacDonald; "Carnival" with Stewart Granger and Jean Kent. These shows opened at the Metro, the Bijou, the Plaza and Curzon Theatres in Johannesburg City. Movies were always played first in Johannesburg City, before coming to the suburbs. It was considered a great day if you went to any of the movie theaters in the city. I was excited by any movie that had dancing and jazz music. These included "Ziegfield Follies", "Thrill of Romance" with Van Johnson, Esther Williams, and Tommy Dorsey and his band, "Anchors Aweigh" with Frank Sinatra, Kathryn Grayson and Gene Kelly, "Till the Clouds Roll Bye" Jerome Kern's biography, and "Fiesta" with Ricardo Montalban and Cyd Charrise. My favorite was "Words and Music," which had

Gene Kelly and Vera Ellen doing "Slaughter on Tenth Avenue." The dance that they did stayed in my mind forever and I kept seeing it done again and again. The influences of these movies and the lifestyle shown were discussed endlessly . . . they had a profound effect on many in the Andrew Street Mob.

One night we checked both theaters and the good show at the Adelphi was sold out. We reluctantly went to see a Bette Davis movie.

Doc suggested we take all the front seats. We all gave Zoni our money and Juni, Johnny, Billy, Trevor, Tommy, Norman, Guy and Julius went to get some Cracker-Jacks and candies for the show. We got in late and the usher took us to the front row of the Grand's glorious seats. We booed Betty every time she came on the screen. The cinema attendant threatened to throw us out at least five times. So we varied the 'boo's' for times when Betty was truly being a bitch. Finally, we were all bored with her. So on her tenth tirade, we all got up and marched out the theater, in step, swinging our arms high like German soldiers. We joined in a verbal pact to never go to her movies again. We also decided that she was the last one anybody would consider as a girlfriend, a wife or a friend.

◆

Sunday nights had become the cream of the week, the last gasp of enjoyment before the long week of school, homework and housework. The list of ideas for games and exciting activities never shortened, despite our getting older. We could fill a book-and-a-half of things to do. We were driven by the creative minds of youth to achieve the single goal of having fun.

The corner of Main and Andrew Street was the place where most of it took place and where everyone met. It was right in front of Mimi's house. Kids were coming from Hill Extension, Kennedy Street, Rosettenville and Turffontein suburbs, all within a radius of 10 miles. We walked or road bikes. Very few caught the bus because it cost two pennies to ride and was too costly. Double-decker buses had conductors and there was little chance of sneaking a ride. But we did beat that when the bus was full, or the conductor was upstairs collecting fares. We could ride two or three stops. This situation was best when the bus went uphill and you could jump off if he came back down the stairs. In any other case you'd better have your money ready. So we all walked everywhere. Even though it was just pennies, they were hard to come by, as pocket money was not a regular thing. The fruit off our backyard trees could be sold to Tony's at twelve for a penny and bought back at six for a penny. We'd have to sell him about a hundred pieces of fruit to go to a movie. If you needed money from your parents, there had to be a very good reason, and fun was the last reason to be considered. Money was the hardest thing to get. It was a major concern to most of us, all the time, without doubt. But maybe the beauty of the situation was that we were all in the same boat, and that made it easier. The situation made us become very creative.

Moccasins had just hit the stores in Johannesburg. It was really upbeat to own a pair, and the six or seven who had got a pair, teased the rest of us. Some of the mob got them, but only after pleading for weeks around the house. This tended to put the parents on the ropes, or into a state of monstrous frustration. One Sunday, underneath our favorite light near the corner of Main Street outside Mimi's house, the crowd had started a competition to see how far a moccasin could fly from a foot, delivering a soccer kick. The maximum reached was 30 feet. Then accuracy was tested: to reach the middle of the street, between two rocks. Finally, the ultimate test was to stand under the street light 25 feet above the ground and see if you could hit the light. It had no cover so the light bulb was exposed. After many tries Doc hit the light and we scrambled! Glass fell to the street as the flash and darkness hit our eyes. We found Doc's shoe and then found the night had ended, as the light was a requisite of our Sunday evening fun. Neighbors complained about the light being out and the City Maintenance Department replaced the bulb.

One Sunday night a game of 'Hasie' (hare) was being played right outside Mimi's house. We had played it for years. Hasie is played in a street marked with a large diagram, 20 feet by 50 feet. It is a simple game between two teams of seven players. One team tries to get through the maze of defensive players on the diagram in one direction, and then turns around and tries to get back through the maze, without being touched. Lines are drawn with chalk, first a rectangle, then two cross lines midway on the short side and midway on the long side. A diagonal line is added from one corner to the other. These are then called 'the lines.' Once touched you are dead (out). The defenders are restricted to staying on the lines. Two defenders are placed on each cross line, this totals six players, and they cannot leave their lines. They can move from side to side but must have at least one foot on the line in order to touch any offensive player. The seventh player is 'Hasie' and is allowed to roam all lines to ward off the penetration. He must continually move through all the lines, called 'feeding'. The Hasie must also have at least one foot on the line to eliminate an offender. The offensive team must get at least one player through the three cross lines to the back of the Hasie diagram and then make it through this gauntlet again to the starting point. This frees the team. 'Freeing' means all players start afresh: 'alive to run again.' Otherwise, the teams change places and the roles are reversed.

Sunday night was our favorite night for the mob to go and play this game on the corner. There is a lot of shouting and laughter and noise generated from this fun game. Also arguments arose from the issues of truly being touched, or foot on the line, or the Hasie not feeding his lines. Of course when a player freed his team, a big roar ascended into the night air, disturbing adults!

There had been complaints to parents. Parents had told kids. Kids had told kids. The communication circle was complete.

One gorgeous summer night, when the air was warm and clear, the crowd was playing Hasie. More than thirty players stood around, so some had to watch. We usually played with mixed teams. Tommy, Zoni, Billy, Helen, Beryl, Trevor and myself were on one team, against Doc, Johnny, Guy, Julius, Thelma, Gloria and Norman. We were on defense first, with Tommy and Zoni on the back line, Billy and Trevor on the middle line and Beryl and I on the front line. Helen was the Hasie. It was common to try to get into the square without the diagonal. When the Hasie fed its lines, both sides of the middle line were attacked, making sure not to run into the Hasie coming up the diagonal in the back squares.

Julius got through very quickly but I touched Johnny trying to scrape through a corner. It is hard defending the front line and trying to stop someone because it's so open. Seven players can tease and fake runs, and when you cover them, someone else can sneak through the place you left. Beryl touched Thelma and she was gone. Doc got through the first line at the same time Julius got through to the back squares. Tommy and Zoni didn't want to let him through to the back of the rectangle because they would then have to watch players going in both directions. Helen nailed both Norman and Gloria, running the diagonals. She was a brilliant Hasie. Doc, Guy and Julius were working the back squares. Tommy and Zoni let Doc and Guy through so that we could now concentrate on everyone coming from the back of the rectangle, going in one direction only. They had a hard time getting through, and those standing on the sidelines were complaining about it taking too long. Zoni and Tommy suddenly opened up the middle purposely and Doc and Guy ran through right into Helen's quick run from the front lines . . . all planned. We had obviously been on the same team before. Julius was the only one left and he conceded. It is almost impossible to get through by yourself.

Their team went on the lines and our team took the offensive. Helen and I worked the two corners and then sailed through into the back square before they knew it. Helen shot through on my fake run to one corner, pulling Johnny over. Then she got me through by faking coming back. We decided to wait for our teammates. Tommy, also fast, was next to join Helen and me. Then Zoni got through on some of our miscues. Beryl was stuck in the middle so we started our back run. Helen ran through two lines, taking a chance going into a diagonal square. Tommy joined her and before I could make another square, the roar of the crowd told me Helen had got home. Our team could start another game.

The games went on for a long time and the shouting and scream-ing was constant. Suddenly, everyone got tired and sat down on the curbstone, talking.

The 'noise' subject came up. Comments and opinions went from one end of the spectrum to the other. Then Billy suggested, "Let's play a game where the first one who makes a noise or talks gets punched by everyone else." We agreed it was a stupid game but acquiesced. We let out a preliminary yell before the start.

Thirty of us sat there in total silence. Some got up and walked; oth-ers lay back on the grass. No noise! It was the weirdest thing. It became very hard to control. Hand signals were used. A car drove by and we waved. After only twenty minutes, a cop car came around the corner and pulled up in front of us. The cops got out the car with the typical attitudes of prime investigators of a situation that required correction.

"What the hell is wrong with you kids? We keep getting reports of all the noise you make here."

Everyone sat stunned. Nobody answered.

"Listen I'm talking to you," said the cop, with an Afrikaans accent. Nearly all the cops were Afrikaners.

The driver got out and came around to join the first cop.

"Perky little bastards, hey Piet."

"Ja (yes) man! Are we being smart?"

Silence. The only noise came from the shifting of bodies. A minute seemed like an hour.

"And nobody answers us. So what must we do to make them talk?"

Nobody answered because our games were sincere; every game we played was by the rules. You were judged by your sportsmanship. This was not only an Andrew Street thing, South Africans were known for their love of sport. You played it right, you got respect; you cheated, and your name would be remembered. No way was anyone going to answer. We knew the consequences. Everyone would punch you, but that was nothing compared to being remembered as the guy who caved in. The fear mounted as everyone realized that anyone the cop talked to directly was doomed.

"You," the cop addressed Zoni. "You tell me what's going on here otherwise I'll take you down to the station."

Silence remained. Everyone looked down. A mixture of feelings filled the group. Gladness that it was not them, and sympathy for Zoni. I wondered what he would do. There were many stories about going to jail and being treated like crap. Nobody we knew had been treated well. And we knew it was a lot worse for blacks.

"Ja! You Mister I'm talking to you!" The cop pointed at Zoni.

"Nothing, Sir."

"Nothing! Hey! You come with me." He came towards Zoni to grab him. The whole group stood up.

"Take us all! We were playing Hasie and stopped for a rest," said one person. "We're now playing a game of silence," said another in the crowd.

The cops were taken back when everyone stood up and spoke. They backed off from Zoni. Then they saw we were no threat.

"It was just a fun game of punching the first person, which spoke or made a noise," said another.

The cops showed no sense of humor. They continued in their self-important, menacing role.

"We will not put up with this kind of behavior. You will be quiet and you will not play in the street. Understand!"

"Yes Sir!" came the mumbled reply.

And so the Andrew Street Mob was warned, emphatically. Then the cops left, and as they went around the corner, we piled onto Zoni.

"Scared the hell out of us! Man!"

The crowd broke up for another week of school.

"I can't stand them," I said to Helen, as we walked up the street. "I hate their whole attitude. It's so . . . I don't know what."

"Don't worry," said Helen. "It's all over now."

I didn't think it was over. Why were they picking on us and talking to us like we were dirt? I had had too many experiences of being told what to do . . . exactly . . . and in no certain terms. But I said nothing further.

◆

One Sunday night, Gerald, a tall lanky boy who had recently joined the Andrew Street Mob, had brought some pop bottles, corks, and dry ice. The crowd was putting water in the bottle, adding dry ice and then putting the cork in the bottle, to see how high the cork would go. This had been tried before. There were bets, and every time the cork was placed in the bottle, the crowd backed off. One time, after many minutes had passed, nothing happened. What wasn't working? Finally, Gerald walked over and cautiously bent down. Everyone yelled, "No . . . Get away", but Gerald persisted. He had his arm over the bottle. The bottle exploded. Fragments of glass went into his armpit and some in his face. Gerald took off running, but he could hardly see because of the blood all over his face. The crowd chased him and caught him and took him to Dr Pienaar who lived down the road. Juni stayed with him to help pick out the glass. Despite the quick action of his friends, Trevor, Juni and Dr. Pienaar, Gerald ended up wearing the scars of this crazy idea. He truly never recovered from this accident and became a background figure, a shadow that never joined conversations or led any of the Andrew Street Mob activities.

Another Sunday evening brought the crowd to the corner of Andrew and Main Street. A long discussion was held on 'what to do'. We were tired of Hasie, and tired of sitting around. The crowd was also out of favor with Mimi. Doc agreed to have everyone up to his house for tea, and maybe play some cards. His parents were gone. We loved that situation! Doc's house was three quarters of the way up the block. The crowd of twelve started to walk, and then there was a challenge to see who would be the first one at Doc's house. We all took off running, which very quickly turned into a sprint. Billy was slightly ahead as I gained on him. When I got to the point of taking over the lead from Billy, he put out his arm and gave me a small nudge to put me off balance. I couldn't keep a straight line and my faltering steps drove me into the side of a pre-war car. My right arm got jammed between the door handle and the door. The door handles on these cars were 'L' shaped and the long end was parallel to the door. Everyone stopped running and gathered around as I pulled my arm back, and everyone who had been laughing at the incident said, "Sorry, okay?" It was a funny incident and pretty normal behavior among our group. The crowd poured into Doc's house. We enjoyed the adult-free house and were moving around, talking, and having tea and cookies.

One group was talking about the sound barrier having been broken by a jet plane, and America saying that space flight would be possible within 30 years, and nuclear-powered ships within six years.

"We're going to build an oil-from-coal plant near Vereeniging," said Billy.

"King George and Queen Elizabeth and the two Princesses are coming," said Grace.

"And their cute daughters, Elizabeth and Margaret," added Beryl.

The girls went into the discussion about the royal family trip and clothes. "Christian Dior has dropped the hemline to 14 inches above the ground," said Ann.

"Yeah, well I like it just below the knee," said Beryl.

The boys discussed the MCC tour (Marylebone Cricket Club), England's representative touring cricket club. Dennis Compton, a top class cricket and soccer player, had scored 300 runs. Len Hutton and Cyril Washbrook had an opening stand of 359 at Ellis Park in Johannesburg.

"I worked at Ellis Park at the All Blacks (New Zealand) vs. the Springboks (South Africa) game," I added

"What did you do?

"I sold Coca Cola . . . to make much money," I answered. "Well there were a large bunch of lads doing it. We had to get there early and we got one coke free (or six pennies) for every twenty four we sold."

"That's good money, Charl!"

"We'd run into the coke warehouse, hand our money in and drop the empty tray, and someone would give us a new one. A couple of us wanted to see the game, or at least the second half, so we worked hard, hoping to finish at half time. As the game began, the crowd was still coming in . . . I mean that stadium has had over 90,000 spectators . . .

it was hectic running in and out of the coke warehouse, and the fellow taking the money was very slow. I waited and waited one time, and then decided to bypass him, go and get a full tray and give him the money on the way out. I got a full tray of cokes and he was still so busy, so I walked out."

"With the money for all twenty four cokes?"

"Yes," I said. "I did it twice."

"Charl! That's bad!"

"Yes!"

"It was slow selling cokes during the game. I gave up at half time and watched the game. So did many guys."

"Do you get paid then?" asked Doc.

"Well, I had to go to the main office in downtown Johannesburg on Tuesday after school. So I went in to get paid, and the lady said that the boss wanted to see me!"

"Oh! Shit!" remarked quite a few friends in unison.

"Were you scared?" asked Billy.

"Tell us!" suggested Beryl.

"I don't know about you Charl!" added Grace

"Yes! I thought I was done for . . . and thought of just leaving. I had my money. But instead, I walked into his office. To my surprise he had a smile on his face."

"What?"

"Yeah," I answered, "he was smiling."

"So?"

"'Charl,' he said to me, 'you sold the most trays of Coca Colas. Did you know there was a prize?' 'No . . . definitely not!' I replied. I hadn't known. I didn't know what to do. My blood seemed frozen going through the door. Now it was racing as I approached his desk. 'And,' he continued, 'you get the one pound (240 pennies) prize!' I wanted to jump six feet in the air!"

"Charl, you got away with all that?"

"Yes, I was originally going to confess, but..."

"We don't believe you Charl, and thousands never will . . . You'd give it all back!"

The conversation went on for a long time on many subjects. Then someone said, "My family was really upset by Jan Smuts losing to Dr. Malan." There was an unexpected lull, as everyone had probably heard the subject discussed at the dinner tables, on the bus, in the school: we knew the negative possibilities. Apartheid would now be fully implemented, and many positions held by English-speaking South Africans would be given to Afrikaners, or so someone had said. Politicians do that! General Smuts of the United Party had carried the country through the war and was very famous overseas. He had been part of the committee that started the League of Nations. Dr. Malan of the Nationalist party stood for many dreams of the Voortrekkers. This was a very difficult subject for the Andrew Street Mob. Many of our families were integrated relationships between English and Afrikaans speaking South Africans. The kids were aware of the sensitivity of these issues, and in the Andrew Street Mob we chose to let it be, as opposed to the grownups that continually discussed politics and religion.

I disliked the overbearing politicians and religious leaders. I tuned myself out of the conversation because it would just make me speak my mind. These were my friends and they could believe in what they want. Besides, it was a very complex problem to me. I preferred the cleanliness of mathematics and design.

As I sat there I felt a trickle down my arm. I put my left arm up my right arm shirtsleeve and my fingers came out with blood on them. I had a jersey and a shirt on and the further I pushed my arm up my sleeve the more blood came out. The girls jumped up and got a dish-towel and everyone went quiet.

"You alright Charl?"

"Yes," I answered.

"Is it hurting?"

"No, I'm okay."

I got up and went to the bathroom and rolled up the sweater sleeve. The shirt was covered in blood. I rolled the sweater down. Billy, Johnny, Doc and some of the girls went with me to the emergency ward of the hospital. The nurse got me on the table. I could see she was a serious lecturing nurse.

"What were you boys doing? There's a big hole in his arm. We'll have to sew it up!"

"A hole?" I asked.

"Yes, a hole."

The handle had actually gone through my arm. I had just pulled back my arm thinking it was only jammed. But I felt okay; I was the center of attention. I somewhat liked it, and played the part.

"One of the girls pushed me while I was running," I said to the nurse.

"Now, Charl," said Beryl.

"That's true. Girls are after my right arm." I showed the nurse my right hand where there was a black spot. "A girl jammed a pencil in there when I was seven! She was mad at me at school."

"Yes, I bet you did something to her," said the nurse sarcastically.

"No! I just pulled on her hair from the back a couple of times, that's all."

"I know your kind of brat," said the nurse, slightly smiling.

I was all bandaged up, and my friends wanted to walk me home. I didn't want to go because that meant the end of Sunday. It was late and I would have to explain everything at home. So, I planned to just stick my head into the living room and say I was going to bed. I was delivered home and yet another Sunday night came to an end.

◆

Two major events took place at 65 Andrew Street within a year. My brother, Bazil got married to an Afrikaans girl. I wondered if he would learn to speak the language. It was never spoken at home. I liked her very much. She was pretty and very warm to me. I responded. After they settled, I went to see them one night. I had to catch three buses and a tram to the suburb of Melville in Johannesburg. It cost me a lot of money and my brother didn't seem to care. So, despite having a good time, I decided never to go again.

Bazil had met James during the Second World War II and together they went through the North African Desert Campaign and then into Italy. Bazil brought James to the house when he returned. James met Yvonne and they courted. They also got married, and Yvonne moved to Kensington to live with James and his family. James came from an Afrikaans family too! My question was the same. Would my sister learn to speak good Afrikaans? I went to visit them as well, but by bicycle. I met James's family, his brothers John and Peter, his sister Joan and his father and mother. I got to love James's father, Mr. van Straaten. He showed kindness and warmth every time I came to visit. We had long talks. I didn't know whether to call him 'Oom' (Uncle), a sign of respect in the Afrikaans culture, or 'Mr. van Straaten'. Everyone called him 'Van.' So I called him Mr. Van. I was also interested in the wood machines that James had in his back yard. Carpentry was interesting and I wanted to learn more about it. I loved my sister Yvonne, and was very sad to see her move. She had protected me from the roughness of the streets and always gave me sisterly advice. She had contributed to my upbringing, along with Gran, Uncle Mick and Mom.

◆

The trip to Vryburg had not resolved my problem of bronchitis neither had the events of the year, since I had gone to Vryburg. I did not want to go to the Karoo or any other place away from Johannesburg. I had Gran's backing. My mom, after much deliberation, had decided to take me to the best specialist in Johannesburg. So, after school one day, we went to Dr. Malherbe. He examined my chest, took x-rays, and asked me a series of questions. Then he said he would give my mom an answer in a week's time. It all seemed so simple. After a week my mom and I returned, entered the doctor's office and sat down.

"What is the most strenuous sport you like to play?" asked Dr. Malherbe.

I jumped at soccer, after quickly rejecting cricket. "Soccer, Sir! I like soccer very much."

"Not strenuous enough," replied the doctor.

It seemed like an age before the second suggestion evolved.

"Cycling. Yeah! If I had a bike I would ride a lot."

The doctor paused for a moment and then agreed. "I want you to get a bike and ride it as much as you can. You must do it very consistently, not just for a week but also for a whole year. In fact, if you ride it every day for a year that would be the best."

"I will," I agreed and was so relieved. I was expecting the worst: having to go and live in Vryburg or Beaufort West. Vryburg would be all right because Southey, Otiend, my aunts and the Harveys would be there, but I didn't know anybody in Beaufort West. To leave Andrew Street and my friends would have been heartbreaking. So the decision to stay was super, and there was the bike: I'd never had a bike, and I was already thirteen.

"Charl's physical body is in good shape. The lungs need to be able to do more and be in better condition. Let's try the exercise and see the results in six months," Dr. Malherbe ended his assessment.

On the way home my mom complained about the expense connected to the simple solution. Then she said, "I'm so glad you do not have to go away, son!" I was ecstatic!

A new bike was out of the question. However, a plan went into action and I got a bike. It was an old, heavy bike. Within a few weeks I had met other people riding and had suddenly noticed racing bikes: they were so beautiful. My mom rejected my requests for a racing bike. She said she had already spent too much money on the specialist, and that the doctor had not done much and hadn't promised success either. Even though my mother was very strict in many ways she was generous in allowing me to do things I liked.

The ownership of a bike allowed me to go places in the Southern Suburbs. I rode everywhere. I now had my own bike to do dirt track racing or perform in the street. The kids of the street could sit on the handlebars, facing backwards, and ride. We pedaled easily, holding the handlebars and peering over our shoulders to see where we were going. Doc was good at riding on his back wheel only, front wheel and handlebars up in the air, until one day the front wheel fell out. He was stuck in a quandary for a while because now he really had to balance. There was no way out. Finally, he came down on the forks and went over the handlebars despite his slow speed. He survived. We all laughed after his frightening stunt.

A new block of flats was being built on Main Street opposite Andrew Street. The construction of the brick walls required wooden scaffolding, with loose 8 inch wide by 12 feet long planks going from beam to beam. It was a two-storey building. It was intriguing to watch the bricklayers work. The cement was made in a cement mixer from sand piles and cement bags. The bricks were in a neatly arranged pile. To keep one white bricklayer, laying brick on a flat wall took ten black men helpers. The helpers mixed the cement, put it in a bucket, raised it to the scaffolding floor with a rope and pulley and filled a cement trough for the bricklayer. The bricks were taken from the pile by one man, tossed to another, who threw the bricks up fifteen feet to the scaffolding floor, where another man caught them. He gave it to another man who placed it near the bricklayer. The black men used inner tubes from cars, cut to fit the hand, with a slit for the wrist to go through. They wore cut-up old car tire treads, shaped to fit the foot, preferably with some tread left, and attached inner tube strips to make it function like a sandal. A good bricklayer would lay three thousand bricks a day. Walls of houses in Johannesburg were generally made up of a rough brick on the inside, a 2-inch air gap and a face brick on the outside. The inside was finished with smooth plaster.

Although it was fun watching the workers, it was more fun playing in the unfinished building at night. Then there was a dare 'who could ride their bike off the first floor scaffolding into the pile of sand'. Nobody responded so I volunteered, but not with *my* bike. The Andrew Street Mob had an all-purpose yellow bike, assembled from all kinds of parts, which had been collected from every junkyard source we knew. We were all bike mechanics and were very proud of our creation. It was named 'Tour de Andrew Street' (with reference to the Tour de France, which we followed intensely). I took the bike up the inside stairs and got it to the planks on the scaffolding. The planks had to be rearranged to look like a diving board. Bricks were placed on one end to compensate for the weight of a bike and rider going off the other end. Everything was moved away for a clear pathway onto the sand pile. I got on the bike and, to the sound of cheers; I waved and went off the end of the boards, chewing on a carrot. The bike naturally went straight down and just crashed into the sand. I went over the handlebar fell down into the sand and came up with a mouth full of sand and carrots! There was sand in my ears, up my shirt and down my pants. I was known from that day forward, suggested by Johnny, as 'Count Coco the Crusading Curry-ball.'

◆

And so we continued our Sunday nights. The tall grass in front of the old house had been discussed. This Sunday evening the traffic had died down after the flow of cars returning from the Vaal River and other picnic spots to the houses of the Southern Suburbs. Someone linked the grass, Main Street, cars traveling and general interest in creating something to do. The grass grew to 2–3 feet, and was easily pulled from the ground, bearing a large clump of soil holding the grass roots together. We pulled out twenty clumps of grass, and waited for a no-people, no-car situation. Doc, Zoni, Trevor, Tommy, Billy, and Julius placed the clumps across Main Street with just enough room for a car to pass on one side. We did this about four times in quick succession and finished with two rows of grass clumps. It looked like a two-foot high grass wall across the main road with enough of a gap for a single vehicle to go through on one side of the road. We hid in the foliage of the old house and watched. We laughed and had much fun seeing cars and buses coming to a screeching halt, and maneuvering over the grass and through the gap, waiting for safe passage. Some drivers swore. Some passengers got off the buses and walked. We disappeared before the cops came.

CHAPTER 5

✳

School Teachers
of the High School Calibre

M Y ATTENDANCE AT ROSETTENVILLE Central School included playing soccer in winter and cricket in summer. The games were played on Wednesdays after school, at Wemmer Pan Park. After the soccer games, a bunch of us who didn't have to go home, would run as fast as we could to go to the matinee show at the Adelphi Cinema. It was only about ten short blocks through La Rochelle, a short distance to run after the game. Most kids had to go straight home. I felt I was lucky, as I got to go to the theater every Wednesday afternoon. During summer this was not possible because cricket took up the whole afternoon. If a student made the highest score at cricket, or scored goals in soccer, their name was called out at the morning assembly in front of the whole school, and the honored student would have to stand up and be seen by all. My name was mentioned a few times in both sports. In the first year I was the goalkeeper in soccer. However, after the first season I changed position because our team was so good, it won every game, and I spent a whole season with nothing to do. Many of my teammates begged me to play in goal, but I just wanted to play out in the field. It proved to be a good move. The games were a lot more exciting, and harder to play, than in the street. You needed shin guards because players attacked ferociously. I learnt a lot more about beating players to the ball and passing: I loved it all.

During this time the polio scare was everywhere, and one of my classmates, Henry, got polio, and had to wear steel braces on his legs and walk with crutches. Everyone was reminded of Henry's incapacity and readily helped him up and down the stairs. I could never talk to Henry about scoring goals or the success of the team's activities. I didn't understand life's dealings in fortune and adversity. Why did God allow this to happen? I didn't like the fact that Henry was on the wrong side of the cards being dealt. This seemed so weird. Why did only a few people get this disease . . . where the hell did it come from?

My years at Rosettenville Central were coming to an end. The students in my class were in the range of 12 plus years of age. Parents had to decide which high school to send their kids to. There were a number of options for those who lived in the Southern Suburbs. Forest High School was the first choice, and it was located at the end of Andrew Street, two blocks from the Andrew Street Mob's block. If the student had good marks they were eligible. The cost was higher than for other schools. If they had low marks, or if there was not enough money, they had to go to Sir John Adamson Junior High School. This school programmed a student to catch up to usual standards within two years. Some students didn't want to go to this school because it had a reputation for being tough. I was good at Arithmetic, History, English and Geography. My not–so–good subjects were Nature Studies and Afrikaans; I had really good marks for Arts and Crafts, especially in charcoal sketching and the building of uniquely designed objects. I didn't know where I wanted to go. The kids in the Andrew Street Mob were going through many changes, similar to me. There were many conversations about 'what are you going to do?' It was discussed incessantly. Parents were talking . . . relatives were adding their comments, and naturally, kids were not included. The decisions were made and we went where we were told! Most of the boys in the crowd, Doc, Zoni, Juni and Billy, went to Sir John Adamson. Beryl, Grace and Ann, the Kennedy Street girls, went to a girls' Catholic School, and Helen, Bobby, Tommy and Mel went to Forest High School. The rest of the street crowd was split between going to Sir John Adamson and Forest High School. Johnny went to a special weekday live-in school in the city of Johannesburg.

Despite Forest High School being at the end of Andrew Street, and through a process unknown to me, the adults in my life sent me to Witwatersrand Technical High School in Johannesburg City. Billy eventually ended up in this school too, a year ahead of me. It was a school for blue-collar workers' sons who had a flair for electrical, mechanical or carpentry types of disciplines. My dad continued his quest to have me in the printing trade.

The school subjects included two languages: English and Afrikaans, mathematics, mechanical design and drafting, workshop, geography and history, plus workshop and sports activities. I had to catch a bus from the Southern Suburbs into Johannesburg, walk a distance of three miles through Johannesburg, past the railway station, up into Hillbrow, and past the Wanderers Club to the north side of the city. This was about a twenty-mile trip across the city. School started at 8:30 and finished at 3 PM. The mandatory school dress code was navy blue jacket, blue shirt with a tie, gray pants, gray socks and black shoes. I heard my mother say it was worth the expense.

I didn't know what was happening. This breakup of kids that had gone to the same school was unsettling. I wouldn't know anybody. I also decided it could be exciting. Only Johnny and I would be going into Johannesburg city. Desmond and I discussed the event to great lengths. He was going to Forest High School. I felt as though I'd been tossed out of the main stream of things that were happening. My parents did not explain why. My friends' parents didn't explain to their kids. So, as decreed, we all just did it! Leaving Rosettenville Central School was not eventful . . . it seemed like it was not important. What was exciting, to me, was going to school in the downtown city of Johannesburg!

Johannesburg was a bustling city of finance, commerce and manufacturing. Thousands of people commuted to its center every day. Almost everyone was connected in some way to the spinal cord of retrieving gold, coal, diamonds, and other minerals. Gold, after its very early discovery, could no longer be mined off the surface, and so the mines were deep underground with some as deep as 10,000 feet. Only the telltale mine headgear gave you a clue that there was a hole going down to those depths.

The parents of all the kids going to high school had the basic decision of guiding them towards a future in mining or not. Most jobs were connected in some way to the mining game. The decision was never easy! None of the decisions made by parents were ever explained. It seemed universal amongst us and often caused a separation in our understanding of what was going on. We didn't fight it; we just accepted the fate.

During the early part of high school I got into a mixture of new events and situations. Again my horizon lifted. Kids now came from the towns and cities across the whole sixty mile long Witwatersrand, to attend Johannesburg Technical High School. Students even came from other provinces such as the Orange Free State.

I was enrolled in the mechanical department, it being the closest category to printing. The curriculum included normal high school subjects, but there were workshop activities in the afternoon. This workshop work at first was boring. Every student had to take a black piece of steel 8″ x 3/4″ x 1″ and file each surface flat and perfectly at 90° to all sides. As a side was finished, it would be checked by the teacher and stamped, and so it went on. It took almost three months to get anywhere near finished. The workshop was big, with more than a hundred students with files, a vise and part of a workshop table. The instructors mostly sat in the office.

After about six months, four students, including myself, decided to skip out early from school. We exited through the workshop windows, thus avoiding the school corridors where students could be seen. We left at 1:30 PM, and it worked! We varied leaving early, and didn't all go together at the same time. When our work was up to date and stamped, we would leave. Finally, we got caught, pulled into the office, and questioned. The information they had on our activities was overwhelming and surprised us. Somebody had squealed! We were given a choice: go to the principal and get reported to our parents, or take six strokes of the V-belt. We all chose the second. The students in our class could see through the office windows as the four of us took our punishment. Bending down, we got six strokes, and twelve marks. The marks were mostly on the top of the leg, as the V-belt hit the buttocks and whipped around the edge of the body. It truly hurt; my eyes watered but no sound came from me. The four of us took the punishment with no complaints. We did not want our parents to know, because we'd be punished again. It took six weeks for the marks to go away. Nobody at home ever saw that part of my body.

The students of our class passed the first year and went on to working with machinery such as shapers, drills and lathes: we were thirteen years of age. We took the perfect, rectangular pieces of steel and machined them into parts for a solid tap wrench. This was followed by a complicated adjustable tap wrench, with one side rigid and the other with a screw and sliding blocks. The screw was cut on a lathe, where the gears had to be changed to suit the calculations on the type of screw thread. The tool had to be shaped on the grinding wheel to meet the Whitworth screw thread standards. The rest of the tap wrench was made on the shaper machines, which produced a flat surface finish. We found out how much easier it was to get a flat surface by machining, rather than by filing. Any mistake on the wrench required that you start all over from the beginning. I joined the many that made a mistake. I didn't like it that other people knew I had made a mistake: it was embarrassing and would always be remembered. I didn't do it again. We were now into manufacturing.

The English class teacher, Mr. Strang, was about 5'2" tall, very expressive in his teaching, and had feminine reactions to anything objectionable. He had the dirtiest tie because he blew his nose on the back of it. Most kids loved him though, because his class was always alive. He taught us the elements of English grammar and sentence structure, and drove us crazy with spelling exercises. He was a stickler for reading, borrowed books had to be returned on time, and he was very strong on work ethic. If a student didn't comply, there was punishment: one hit with the cane for minor offenses, two for more serious, and three if you made him really mad. Lots of students were subjected to caning; some wore two pairs of pants. They screamed or jumped when hit and yelled, 'No Sir!' or something similar. I took my punishment one day for leaving a book at home twice; three hits for each time. As Mr. Strang was short, he had to stand on the 12-inch high platform, and the student would bend over standing on the floor of the classroom. It was amazing; Mr. Strang was a small man, but he swung the cane 'from the top of the roof.' I took the first hit and it didn't hurt, I then expected the second hit to do the dirty deed and hurt . . . nothing! The class was signaling to me to scream, and then I finally got it. I screamed and grabbed my pants at the back with both hands. Mr. Strang stopped. The students told me the reason to yell and show that you were hurt was simple. Mr. Strang would feel satisfied and you wouldn't get sent to the Principal.

"Now go and sit down!" instructed Mr. Strang. I went back to my seat amazed. Now I knew why nobody worried about the caning and why the boys often snickered at students who didn't know what to expect.

I continued playing cricket but I wasn't super-interested. Cycling was in my blood, and soccer. I was riding well and I was in the second team, under sixteen, in the Marist Brothers soccer club. Desmond and I had joined the club. We were happy to be doing something together again. So, the normal routine for me was school studies during the week, practice for the soccer team Marist Brothers, and playing a match on Saturdays. I no longer played for the St Johns Ambulance Brigade. Marist Brothers was a real team, and part of the major soccer league system in Johannesburg, whose youth leagues had many teams. We were enrolled in the under sixteen group, regardless of age. I was so excited and practiced hard. The Saturday game, to me, was the highlight of the week.

Our Mob went to movies on Saturday afternoons. On Sundays in summer, the ideal was to go to Van Wyks Rust swimming hole and picnic. If not, we went to the Municipal Swimming Baths at Wemmer Pan. It cost about a penny to go swimming. Whenever it was possible to attend a party, my friends and I went. Sunday nights on the Andrew Street corner was the Mob's last gasp of fun for the weekend. It was truly a magic time. We all did our homework before Sunday night. The core group of the crowd was always there. Our parents gave up trying to keep us in the house, because we would just irritate them. We really got into the games, the talk, the laughter and friendship. I felt sorry for the kids on the block who weren't allowed to join the festivities.

One Wednesday morning at 7:15, I was riding my bike to school down Eloff Street, in the downtown area of Johannesburg. I was racing to go through on a yellow light and passing Witwatersrand Technical College, just before turning right in front of Johannesburg's Park Railway Station building. I stood up and sprinted to catch the light but realized I wouldn't make it. I squeezed the brake. In the corner of my eye I saw my front brake assembly shoot out and swing back into the front wheel . . . behind the fork. There was a ripping of steel and breaking of spokes. I went flying over the handlebars and hit the ground head and shoulders first. I rolled twenty feet. Cars came to a screeching halt. People gathered around. Traffic had stopped. I was dazed. Someone asked me if I was all right.

"Yes," I replied. A couple of men escorted me into the college building. Someone brought my bike inside; it was a mess. I was in deep trouble. This is exactly what I didn't want to happen. I heard lots of questions and answered them but I don't remember the people who helped. I was bandaged up and then took my bike, rolling it on the back wheel, and headed for the bus station some ten blocks away.

The bus conductor, feeling sorry for me, shoved the bike under the stairs. Sitting on the bus, I went over and over again my mother's strict instructions not to take my bike to school! I had worked out a way to cycle to school without my mother knowing. I timed her getting up in the morning, stealthily hid the bike on the side of the house, walked out the front door normally, sneaked around the side of the house, picked up the bike and rode off. I knew whether I was early or late, according to whether or not I saw Beryl at the bus stop on the corner of Kennedy and Main streets. The ride was usually fast, through the southern suburbs, into the city, down Eloff Street to the Johannesburg railway station, right and then left past Hillbrow and to school. I had done this so many times, and come home safely, until today. Gran met me at the bus. Someone at the college had called her. She was worried, caring and stern with me all at the same time. I didn't know what was going to happen.

My mother came home. She was furious.

"You will have to pay for the repairs!" she yelled. She was breathing hard. "You will have to pay for the repairs. I don't care about your bike riding anymore! I don't know what to do with you, Charl, you cause me so many problems!"

"I'm sorry Mom! I'll do better."

◆

The Witwatersrand Technical High School was an all-boys school. It's sister school, the all-girls Commercial High school, was located a mile away. The girls' school taught business subjects, shorthand, typing, adding machine operations, as well as high school subjects. The two schools only got together in school plays, meetings on subjects like languages, and during the Annual Johannesburg High Schools Track Competition day. Both schools always had a respectable position in the events of that day and they were usually well behaved.

This year, however, was an exception. It seemed that too many students didn't meet the second roll call in the afternoon, having disappeared into the girls' school locations. Usually the teachers took roll call only in the morning, and then students could take advantage and watch the games, leave or move wherever they wanted. This year the teachers were not to be fooled, prompted by the returning empty busses after last year's competition. The school always arranged these busses, and if you had an alternate means of transportation, you had to declare it. Most students said they would take the bus and would return by bus. Jannie van Niekerk had said he was not going by bus; he was going from his farm by horse. The students all laughed!

The following Monday, some members of my class were questioned as to their absence the afternoon of the track meet. A variety of excuses were offered: in the grand stand, in the toilet, etc. Mrs. Rube asked Jannie why he had not even made the first roll call.

"The horse was lame, Ma'am," was his reply.

The class tried to keep quiet, so as not to get her mad at Jannie, but eventually the whole class burst out laughing. Jannie just stood there without expression.

"Can I sit down, Ma'am?" Jannie asked the teacher.

"Yes," replied the teacher, without smiling.

It didn't matter in the end, as the whole student body was kept after school for an hour in the Main Hall. We had to stand motionless. The hall was full. We had been admonished. Jannie was near the wall so he slid behind the heavy, long curtains that hung from the ceiling and fell asleep standing. As there was no talking, students close to the curtain could hear his snoring. It sounded like a lone ship in the fog moving through a silent ocean. The teachers never found him sleeping!

Following the hour of standing, a bunch of my friends and I agreed, it was worth it. We decided that growing up was a series of new things, challenges, defying the rules and getting punished!

An English immigrant's son, Bert, joined my class. He had recently arrived from England. His attitude towards all of the students in the class was amazing. He continually gave the impression that he had been sent to educate the colonies, and that Johannesburg compared to London was nothing but a farm town. His attitude and remarks were tolerated for a long, long time. The end came when he got the class in trouble for talking too much and we had to stay late after school. Some of the guys warned him of the next consequence. I told him afterwards in no certain terms not to do it again.

"Who are you?" asked Bert, in an uppity accent.

"Just a member of this class."

"Oh, but you're the big shot, hey?"

I walked away, thinking I had heard that accent in English movies. He was pretending to be upper class, but the Cockney words and accent came out when Bert was pushed for words.

Two months later, one afternoon I was in a hurry to leave school, get my bike and go. I went into the boys' toilet. There was a long row of urinals and I went to the furthest one, it looked the cleanest. There was only one entrance and it was thirty feet from the last urinal. I was almost finished when Bert came in and stood at the first urinal.

"Oh, I say, it's the big shot!" said Bert dragging his forced accent on each syllable.

I said nothing. I finished up and picked up my school bag in my right hand and walked towards the doorway.

Bert continued his remarks, "So you're the one all these stupid 'Blokes' . . . as you would call them . . . look up to! Hey! You're their man, so to speak!" Then he stepped in my pathway at the door.

"Move," I said.

"Make me, Mr. Big Shot!" gazing into my eyes with an upper crust look on his face.

I didn't quite remember everything I did, but the English boy was suddenly flat on his back about ten feet in front of me and his pants were around his ankles! I did realize my bag was now lying on the floor, and my right hand knuckles hurt a little. I picked up the bag, walked around the English boy and left him there!

◆

Time flew as we attended school. We had so much to do. I had interesting subjects at school and worked hard at my homework. Cricket, soccer and cycling took care of sports activities; weekends were just completely fun. I had now spent three years at this school and it was coming to an end.

"You have to get a job, Son," said my mom.

"I don't agree," argued Gran.

"You know the situation . . . Mom!" answered my mother.

"He'll have to finish matriculation at night school," said Gran.

"That's all right," answered my mom

This discussion faded at the dinner table. I knew the story from day one. The struggling blue-collar workers trying to let their sons and daughters go as far as they could, against the costs of school, clothes, food and lost income. All my friends talked about this . . . where were we going next year . . . what were we going to do! Some of the mob was already working. We didn't see college on the horizon. I truly wanted to go to some college and do better!

The school year ended in December. I had spent three years at this school. The school exam results were issued and I received two distinctions; one in mathematics and the other in design. It was the last day of school. All students were congratulated. The students who were leaving decided that there were two teachers disliked by everyone, who should be 'honored'. The word spread fast in the playground, started mainly by the guys who played tennis-ball soccer, and when we began to stack up park benches, eight high, around the two cars belonging to the two teachers, a lot of students joined in, laughing and loving every minute of it. A sign was also posted: "Hope you get home before New Years." We left the school grounds.

There was sadness as students who were not returning walked down the hill from school to downtown Johannesburg. The big crowd slowly broke up into smaller groups. Many of my student friends came from the Johannesburg suburbs, but others came from towns close by, such as Krugersdorp and Germiston. We had been part of the school routines for three years, made friends from new places, and carved a small memory in each other's lives.

A bunch of my closer friends and I walked down to Hillbrow with our books. Hillbrow offered a European style of life in Johannesburg: out door cafés, nice restaurants and nightclubs.

"Just dreams!" said one guy, as we stopped at a tearoom for a cool drink and went and sat at one of the tables. There were eight of us. He continued, "We are looking for a long, beautiful road ahead." His lead set us talking for a good hour about different things. The stories were long and interesting and we were all enjoying it very much.

My turn came, and I started with, "Teachers are sometimes a pain. They always like to embarrass students. Let me tell you, in class at Kenilworth Junior School, at the age of seven, Peter Smith, who sat in the back left-hand corner of the classroom, wanted to go to the bathroom. The door was in the front right-hand side of the room, the farthest distance from Peter's desk. He asked the teacher if he could leave, three times.

"'Peter, you stay in your seat!' she ordered. 'We go to the bathroom during break.' I always wonder why teachers say 'We'. Well, five minutes later, Peter ran from his desk and out the door past the teacher, leaving behind him brown drops on the classroom floor. The class laughed but eventually felt pretty bad for Peter, and about what happened. We just ended up disliking the teacher. So then, the delightful lady teacher had us go out the classroom to the playground so the maintenance people could clean up. Peter went home early that day. All he had to do was face his world the next day knowing what had happened on the previous day."

"Not very nice," suggested one of the crowd.

I was on a roll, and urged the crowd to stay longer, before walking down the hill from the café to the busses that went to the Southern Suburbs and trains that went to Germiston and Krugersdorp. We had still a way to go. They gladly agreed, someone told a story, and then I continued.

"You remember our high school Afrikaans teacher, Mr. Retief, he's a big man with a beer belly, large arms and body. He is definitely equipped with continuous, but varied, stern looks. He was our first class on Mondays. 'BLOU MAANDAG' (Blue Monday) he'd write on the board. Well, he was astonished that my Afrikaans knowledge was so bad considering I had an Afrikaans name. It's actually French Huguenot in origin, but adopted as an Afrikaner name." Some of the crowd nodded.

"He always made me stand up and speak Afrikaans, and recite my stories—more often than anyone else. He used complicated Afrikaans phrases when talking to me. He probably didn't know that even my mother tongue, English, gave me trouble. It was hard to understand . . . you know . . . what good grammar meant? I still don't understand all the rules. Its crazy how they come up with all the different ways to make a sentence. It's different in both languages as well." I paused but not for long. I was not going to lose my audience. "I love mathematics, science, design, and drawing. Also, he didn't know that I hated the rough sounds of English and Afrikaans. My Italian and Lebanese friends seem to have beautifully smooth languages. French movies are the greatest. I also think English is stupid." I stood up, moved my arms and legs in various passionate stances. The group laughed. "You can't say . . . 'love' . . . in Afrikaans or English. One sounds like you're describing the removal of a wheel from a car, and the other like you're telling an army to go to war!"

The crowd giggled, ending their general acknowledgement of the stories with 'yes!' or 'you're right!' The eight of us told our stories, some about the Girls Commercial High School play, held at our all-boys school for some reason. They said that the acting was so bad, everyone laughed during the girls' presentation. We felt bad, but then so did the

actresses, and they laughed on the stage! The stories about the cancel-
lations of all the sports at school break time. "Yeah—this guy broke his
leg while a group of cricketers were trying to throw the ball through
his legs. You know, where six guys stand with legs apart on one side
and six stand opposite on the other side, then they try to throw the ball
through the legs for points. You're supposed to catch the ball before it
goes through your legs. I guess he didn't. So, off to hospital." A sip of
cool drink and another story was told. "The soccer players broke two
windows playing between the electrical shop and the hall. So much for
soccer at the break."

Finally, one of the listeners asked, "What else don't you like about
teachers, Charl?"

"Oh! Am I the only one?"

"No! But you seem to notice a lot!"

"It's not a like or no-like, they just seem so weird," I replied, and
then continued. "Hey! Another moment here at high school was with
my mathematics teacher. She is a large, fat lady who always sat with her
legs apart behind her desk, and it stands on the usual 12-inch platform
in front of the blackboard. You could see up her dress—even from the
back of the class! Man! We named her 'Ma Rube'." I took a sip of tea.
"She was either over-sweet or grumpy. She would smile when members
of her class tried to get close; she loves the 'adoration kids'. The ones
we have other names for, who always want to please the teacher. Us
'rebels' dropped pencils in front of her desk, when walking by, because
we loved to have arguments as to what color pants she wore! Sometimes
they were blue, and sometimes pink, but mostly white. One guy in the
class got us all in trouble because after going through the motions in
front of her desk, of dropping the pencil—I mean, didn't she know?
Well, he came back and sat down and said. 'They're white, mostly white
and then there is . . . yellow – yellow – yellow . . . Man!' Our group
back there exploded with laughter and then there was a second phase
of laughter, as the word got around. Despite everything she warned us
she would do, she never found out why we had all laughed so much."

The eight were ecstatic!

"Some more Charl!" suggested someone.

"Oh! Okay!" I continued. "Then one day Ma Rube was doing this
long mathematics equation on the board. She loved to go scrambling
through each line of the calculations, maybe to confuse the class; stopping every third line to explain the transposing, the simplifying, and

the deduction. One morning after she had about nine lines on the board. I raised my hand after she had explained the last three lines, and I said that there was a mistake on the seventh line. Man! I love mathematics; I can see it, as it happens, all the way . . . intriguing stuff. She disagreed, told me to sit down and continued onwards. I wondered if I had made a mistake! Then she got to the bottom of the board and the answer. Jack and some of my class friends looked up the problem in our Math's textbook. Jack stood up and told her that the answer was wrong! You know, at the end of each chapter, where the answers to the test questions are located?" "Yes! We know that," was the consensus of replies from the table.

"I don't know why I love telling stories about her. Anyway she told me to come up and show the class. I did, and worked the problem through. The answer matched the book. She just told me to sit down.

"I never could understand why mathematics was easy for me, as opposed to languages. Ma Rube never liked me again, nor did she ever. But score one for the Rebels!" I added.

The stories continued, as the group was content to sit in the beautiful summer sunshine, under clear blue skies, in Johannesburg's cosmopolitan center. I actually think we just did not want to break up. We didn't want to go home and have this all end.

"You know, if you get a distinction in the final exam, you know over 90 percent, it's sort of the unwritten rule to go and see your teacher. Two of us got distinctions that year and we went to see her. Ma Rube spoke to Joseph, a sweetheart in her definition, throughout our visit, with all kinds of pleasantries about his loyalty, good performance, good attendance, and brilliance. I just stood there. She finally turned to me and said, 'You did well.' Then while turning her head back to Joseph she continued, 'Sometimes teachers are flabbergasted because occasionally there are students they would never expect to do well,' she paused, 'but they do under very extraordinary circumstances . . . get high scores.' So much for Ma Rube, man!" I said.

"Bitch," said one of the kids.

"But you know, we're lucky that two other teachers have to moderate final exam papers. This means she couldn't mark me down. The next year we had a new math teacher, Mr. Goodman, who was happy to have students who excel in mathematics, but still treats everyone equally. He was a nice teacher. When handing out problems he would say, 'Those who wish to do problems 1 through 10 in the chapter of the day, go ahead, those that can do problems 11 through 20, try them.' We all know, I mean those of us that read that homework, that class problems get harder as the numbers go higher. What a neat way to teach a class with students at different levels. I worked so hard in his class because he had no favorites. Sound good?"

"Yes it sounds good."

"I also liked Mr. Goodman. It was amazing who did well in his class, versus Ma Rube. Joseph did well again because he was good. The Rebels liked this class as well."

It was now almost four hours after school but we still went through another bunch of stories and a round of cold drinks and sandwiches. We just wanted this to last for a long, long time. Maybe we should have done this before. We told our stories and they were flowing from everyone, and it was so interesting to know what each other thought. I finished my stories with a comment on a discussion held with my mother.

"I discussed all these things with my mother. Like teachers not being so old fashioned, like being happy and not miserable, like being confident people who know their work and just let everything flow . . . Because I didn't think Ma Rube knew her work, and Mr. Goodman sure knew *his* work . . . boy! No mistakes! I don't think teachers realize we kids know that! My mother said that I had just introduced another definition of 'love what you do', important words of life. I don't quite understand what she means."

A number of the kids said, "We know what she means." Finally someone summed it up, "Maybe that's why Mr. Goodman's car was left pretty well free of obstruction."

With that we all got up and walked to our destinations of bus stops and train stations. Something new was coming up for each of us; we had individually talked about it at the tearoom.

"It's very exciting!" said one of my friends and then asked, "What are you going to do Charl?"

"Oh! Be a dancer in the movies!"

"Yeah, like who?"

"Gene Kelly," I retorted, laughing. "No! That's a dream. There is a chance of a job in a workshop that one of my uncles knows about."

"Yeah! We all have to find something."

The group walked towards Johannesburg center in silence. I was so sad. I knew now we should have done this before. I thought about our small revenge of stacking up the benches around the cars of teachers who were not loved or respected. I smiled. It was small but significant. This walk though seemed very sad, because we were saying farewell to many friends. We had reached a departure point. We shook hands and said our good-byes as though we would never see each other again.

◆

I was glad school was over. I was now fifteen. I accepted that my mom, a single parent, could no longer support me. She had brought up three kids living in Gran's house, and it had been hard. There was just not enough money, and she needed help. I was glad that I could do something to help her. My brother and sister were married and gone. I didn't understand why even though my dad and my mom worked, there was never any money to spare. So I was going to do what had to be done and get some of my own money.

As I had spent three years at a technical high school, I would get a year off a five-year apprenticeship in mechanical work. My dad again wanted me to me to go into the printing trade because he'd spent a lifetime on the printing press; he was very proud of being in charge of those monstrous machines that produced the daily papers. It looked very boring to me to be standing and watching a big rolling press print newspaper everyday.

My dear aunt Amy got her husband, Harry, one of the nicer uncles, to recommend me for a job in a foundry and machine shop. Uncle Harry had some connection there, like knowing the owners. I was told by my mom to submit my school record, fill out the apprenticeship papers and give them to the Rowe and Monfries Company.

My uncle Harry set up the interview, and I was accepted.

On December 15, almost the middle of summer, I started work in a cold, dirty factory in Jeppe, an industrial portion of Johannesburg City. My first job was working on a drilling machine, assigned to 'Red', a senior apprentice. There were about fifty dirty white people and one hundred and fifty dirty black people in the foundry. In my first week, I was both excited at the idea of earning money and very hollow inside at the extremely gray surroundings of work and no friends. I felt so out of place, and I didn't like it even the smallest bit you can think of! Most of all I didn't like the many, many, old and dreary-looking people who were dressed in dirty gray, black and dark blue overalls, discolored boots and heavy leather gloves. The factory was a dirty place. It was nothing like the spotless shops at school. The only good difference between school and work was the ride to work; it was shorter than the ride to school. I hated it all!

﹡

CHAPTER 6

The Cycle Game

M Y DREAM OF OWNING a racing cycle while attending high school drove me to find out new and used prices, best brands of bikes, plus it opened my eyes to all the different accessories available. I approached Mr. Huth who was the owner of the local cycle shop and had the reputation of being helpful. Mr. Huth wore glasses, had gray hair, was slightly bent over but was about six foot tall and very strong-looking. He had a serious but welcoming smile, was easy to talk to and beloved by many cyclists. Mr. Huth was a sponsor and heavily involved with the Rand Roads Cycling Club. He gave me a job with Deale and Huth's Cycle Shop after school. I worked in the back of the bicycle shop and, besides learning all about racing bikes, models, parts, and prices, I learned many new things, like how to assemble custom wheels with various combinations of hubs and rims, how to straighten and balance wheels, and how to set up a bike for a rider. After my first pay-day I joined the cycling club. Mr. Huth and I negotiated a method for me to buy a racing bike. I would have to have 30% paid off before I could take the selected bike. To me the challenge was on!

There were two black men who were the cycle mechanics in the shop: William and Joseph. I was to assist them in bike repair, but according to society's rules, they would not be my bosses. All instructions came from Mr. Huth. So I repaired punctured tires, cleaned bikes, and stacked things, as well as building wheels. I noted all the bikes coming in and going out, looking for a second-hand racing cycle. Joseph taught me, through many laborious stages, how to assemble the custom racing wheels. There were many ways to damage the light alloy rims and scratch the hubs, so a lot of care had to be exercised. Everything in racing was light; even the spokes were thinner between where they went into the hub and where they went into the rim. The art of putting 36 spokes through a hub and then putting the end through the holes into the rim, in the right sequence, was not easy. Joseph showed me how to do that. I learned the better ratios of gears for racing: 48 teeth on the chain wheel and 16 teeth on the wheel sprocket were good for road racing; 52 on front and 16 on back was not good for sprinting, and therefore not good for track. Racing saddles for short distances were thin, like a broomstick handle, and long distance saddles were wider, 4 inches or so, with cutaways as the leather came to the point. I wanted a racing bike with drop handles and 27-inch wheels with racing tires. The very famous 'Conloy's' light aluminum wheels with tubular tires (tire and tube in one) would have to come later. I enjoyed working in the shop, learning, meeting different racers that came in and most of all, just talking about cycle racing.

Although it seemed to take ages, I finally saved enough money for the one-third deposit. I bought a Sun Wasp road bike—a thing of beauty. It was second hand, had forks that sloped a little too much at the wheel, but I was very happy. The forks could be changed. I bought new toe clips and cleaned and shined the bike from top to bottom. I took it home and everyone agreed it was nice. I had traded my old bike. Now I could show my friends that things were getting better. I had worked every day after school. I could now start training for actual racing: this evolved into Sundays becoming my cycle race day.

◆

Most of the bicycle races were outside Alberton, a small town south of Johannesburg. It was a nine mile ride to the starting line from Andrew Street. The races began from a side road off the main road to Heidelberg. The usual race from the start line consisted of going downhill a half mile, up a half-mile, then down about five miles, after which the road was primarily flat to Vereeniging, a city south of Johannesburg. 25-Mile race riders went over this course, turned around at 12.5 miles and headed back. The wind always seemed to blow towards riders on the return leg; the rider's time was consequently always slower on the return.

Time trial races were ridden independently, without pacing behind someone. All riders left the starting line based on a random draw, so no one knew who had won until everyone was in and all handicap times were calculated. Paced handicap races meant you could travel in bunches and riders started at predetermined handicap times. Scratch riders had zero minutes. The first one over the finish line won this type of race. There were about 100 riders on average who assembled to race on Sunday mornings. Safety was a concern so the races started about 8AM, thus avoiding Sunday car drivers who hopefully would not be on the road until after the races were finished. Good riders would finish 25 miles in close to an hour whereas the 100 km race (62.5 miles) was usually over, for a good rider, in approximately three hours.

I had a tough time in my first races even though they were only 5 and 10 miles, especially with breathing, and how and when to use strength. I loved paced handicap races; it was like racing as a team. On the other hand, I dreaded the time trial races; riding by yourself was too lonely. We quickly learned that the one going out in front of the pack all the time, and being the hero, wasn't always the one who won the race. I eventually developed a good pace that was comfortable, and found out that I was a good sprinter, especially coming out of the pack, and I also had a lot of speed when coming to the finish line. My main disadvantage was that I couldn't afford a ten-speed gear-change, and I didn't like the free-wheel cog (this allows the rider to stop peddling when going downhill). I preferred the fixed cog, which provided more control of the bike in the pack, especially with other riders jostling, changing positions and riding without care for anyone else. So I peddled all the way in a race. My legs built up and my breathing capability got better. The doctor agreed the right decision had been made. Also, there were no attacks of bronchitis. Gran was ecstatic about the progress.

A number of the Andrew Street Mob started to ride . . . Zoni and Juni, Doc, Trevor and Julius. Trevor was a well-built, moderate sized, exuberant boy from Natal, and was always full of fun, especially if there was a challenge involved. Newcomers to the gang who began to ride were Pat and Billy. Pat was a tall, dark headed boy with broad shoulders, very strong, who laughed a lot even though he was a little too serious sometimes. Billy, short and stocky, had a touch of English arrogance, was sometimes demanding but always ready for fun. My interest in racing aroused the interest in others. Zoni and Juni got bikes. Doc got a bike. Julius, a thin, wiry boy with glasses and a nice smile joined the Andrew Street crowd and the cycle group. Julius had come from Belgium and had already raced in his country. Johnny did not want to race. So the Andrew Street Mob was in. We rode to the races together and afterwards rode home together, and talked incessantly.

Even though I had ridden in many races and not come close to winning, I had gained good experience. My next scheduled race was the 44-mile Alberton-Heidelberg-Alberton, a time trial race. I trained extra hard for over a month. On the day of the race, Zoni, Juni, Doc and I left early in the morning for Alberton. The road was clear, and from the Southern Suburbs the slope was downhill. We got our numbers and started according to the draw. This race was in a different direction to our normal races and I did not know the wind patterns, though it was still 22 miles going out and 22 back. I had a nice handicap time of 10 minutes, reasonable as I was fourteen years old, a little younger than my friends from Andrew Street. The race was open to all ages.

I took off from the line in a standing start and slowly pumped my legs to bring the bike into a fast but steady pace. After a mile I settled into a rhythm; there was a crosswind blowing slightly in my face. I worked the bike harder on the down-slopes and sat back on a steady pace for the up-slopes. I reached Heidelberg (the turn) in good time; only a couple of riders had passed me, but I had not lost sight of them. There were no groups as this was a time-trial race. If you sat behind a rider and you were seen and reported, you could be disqualified.

I was riding steadily and caught up to a black man riding a racing bike in a very easygoing manner, just enjoying himself. He suddenly moved faster only a few seconds after I passed him. He caught up.

"Come on Klein Baas (small boss) jump in behind man, I can give you some pace."

"No thanks," I said, "You can't . . . I can't in this race."

"But why not? I am fast!"

"It's the rules of the race!"

"Rules . . . you cannot ride together?"

"No," I said. "Each man must ride by himself."

I stood up, to get off the saddle and to put more power into the bike, and to relax my body, which had been bent over for a long time. I passed the black man. He passed me. I sat back. He slowed down. I stood up again and rode hard. He jumped in behind me.

"Please!" I yelled, "They will kick me out of the race, if you ride with me. Please . . . my friend . . . let me ride alone."

"Are you sure, Baas?"

"Yes! Thank you! See you on the road my friend."

"See you Klein Baas . . . Ai!" The black rider dropped off. I heard him say something in his own language.

I drove the bike hard. I wasn't tired so I slowly pushed a little harder; when I felt the strain I let up. My thoughts continued on the conversation with the black rider. There were many of them on the road. They loved the high gear ratios, slow peddling even against the wind and up the hills. They were strong riders. I wondered if they had a club, because they were not allowed to be members of the white man's bike racing clubs. I had met quite a few while training; we rode together for miles, talking. I saw some of them often, but only knew them by face and by the bike they rode, and the way they rode the bike. This black and white separation didn't make sense . . . why did it cover absolutely everything people did? Why didn't politics stay out of sports? I wished I could say something about it. Then I wondered how they paid for their bikes because they earned a lot less money than whites. It had taken me a long time to pay off my bike, plus I had help in the way I bought it! I stopped thinking because I had to concentrate on the race.

I pushed hard on the pedals, feeling good, breathing well, and I knew Alberton was near. Up to now, only a few senior riders had passed me. I wanted to try and keep it that way. I looked back. It was something I had heard you should never do, as it supposedly made you nervous and you lost your pace. In fact, then I remembered, it was one of the black riders who had told me, "Don't look back Baas and don't let anybody pass!" Then he had laughed. I saw a few riders, so I put my head down and pushed hard and fast. I was concentrating deeply now. All the wandering thoughts of a bike ride were forgotten. I was co-ordinating my body reactions and movement of the bike at a much faster pace; everything started to sing, it was actually humming. Suddenly the turn-off appeared; how did it come up so quickly? I had thought I still had a long way to go. My energy was still very high and I wasn't tired in any way. I pushed even harder, feeling I could expend all my energy. I drove like crazy up to about 200 yards to the finish, and then I finally stood up. I loved the feeling of finishing a race. It was a challenge coming to an end. So I threw in every ounce of strength until I felt the painful strain in my legs and forearms as the muscles cycled through the push and pull sequence. I crossed the finish line, then every filament in the body relaxed. Hands off the handlebars and sitting upright on the seat as the legs slowly diminished their speed: it was the style . . . so I did it. After slowing down and riding back to the finish line, I put my bike against the fence, grabbed some liquids and rested against the fence with my eyes closed. It was 10:30 AM and I felt very good about finishing the longest race I had ever ridden. A rider stopped by and said he had had trouble at one point and asked, "How did it go with you?" I told him I'd had no trouble, but related the story about the black cyclist.

He stood there for a second and then said. "The stupid black bastard! Doesn't he know?"

I was amazed! In fact, even disgusted! Especially after I had told him how nice the guy had been. He left. *Some people have a terrible problem relating to blacks*, I thought.

Riders were still coming in; there was a good field of riders today. I didn't care how many; I had done what I came to do. I was so relaxed now, there was no hurt and I felt an inner satisfaction of having achieved something I never believed I could have, some time ago.

Zoni came up to me. "Have you seen the rider board?" he asked.

"No," I replied.

"You're in the lead . . . so far."

"Bullshit."

"Yes, my friend, you are in the lead, you had a pretty good time."

"Yes, I felt it was my best ride for some time. The handicap was good too, but never mind, someone will come in higher. I've never won a race."

We sat around and talked about the wind, the different bicycles, the hurting and the riders who were went out fast and faded coming back.

Doc came up. "Charl, you're first, and there's only a few riders to come in."

"You're crazy."

"No."

I couldn't believe it. I might be second or third or fourth. First didn't seem possible. So we all went to the board. Sure enough, my time, less my handicap, put me in first place. The last riders were coming in and we anxiously watched the official put the final times up on the board. I couldn't believe it! I had won. The three of us jumped around, hugged each other and laughed. This was a terrific thing to have happened. I didn't want to be too loud, but damn, I was happy.

The cycling activities were complete and prizes were being given out. As usual the cyclists stood in a very informal circle on the side of the road. It was the same formation no matter how important the race, even at the Dunlop Cup, the biggest race of the year. I had won the Alberton-Heidelberg-Alberton race with a ten-minute handicap. I got a big trophy to keep for a year, and little cup to keep forever. I felt so proud inside. The results would be in 'The Star', a major Johannesburg newspaper, the next day. Other prizes were given for second and third place and also to one of the riders for the fastest time of the day. I was little embarrassed to receive the cup. I felt that I hadn't worked very hard for the prize. But this feeling went away as I slowly justified my hard work and hard riding.

Gran was ecstatic, so was my mom.

Gran then asked me in a serious tone of voice. "Did you get out of breath?"

"No! I felt good all the way! Everything was working well. I felt strong throughout the race."

"So the bronchitis is gone?"

"I don't feel it anymore. So I guess it's gone away."

"That's lovely!"

My grandpa Mick told me that I could be in the Olympics in a couple of years. The thought sank into my head. I buried myself in cycling with my friends.

◆

The gloomy atmosphere at work in the factory of Rowe and Monfries never got any better, and was compounded by all the tricks of apprentice initiation. I saw the old men play with other apprentices. They sent one apprentice up the road to get a 'struggling bar'. The young boy of fifteen knew no better as he obeyed them and ended up bringing a heavy six foot structural bar, mounted on a wheel barrow, down a very busy street (he couldn't come down on the pedestrian walk). He was embarrassed by cars honking all the way but he was resolute in completing the job.

"Struggle enough," said one journeyman, laughing like a jackal, "take it back."

I never fell for any of these games. My mathematic sense didn't allow for illogical things and if that wasn't enough, I had the experiences of having to grow up in the street. All the tricks they tried were refused. I made them mad! They set up an older apprentice to try and get me to stand behind a grinder and catch the sparks in a paper bag to keep them lit.

"Drop dead!" I replied.

An older apprentice, Tim, threw his tea at me and I retaliated by emptying my mug of hot tea in his crotch. The fists started to fly and the journeymen quickly separated us.

"In the foundry after work . . . both of you!"

Red, a Senior Apprentice, talked to me after I had cooled down. "You've done the wrong thing," he said. I had befriended Red, even in the short time I had been there, because we had a common interest in soccer. We discussed it whenever we could. He also suggested in a roundabout way that if I hadn't signed my apprentice papers, I should find another job, because he hadn't learned a damn thing for three years, except drilling pipe flanges.

"But that's what *I'm* doing!" I replied.

"Yes! You're my first replacement in three years!"

"You are right Red, I should have just ignored Tim. But I'm not happy with this place!" I showed my frustration.

"No!" said Red, "It's okay. The journeymen love this sort of thing. There will be a big crowd in the foundry."

I didn't want to fight. The foundry was full. The black and white workers formed a ring with their bodies. They loved a fight. I was mad at myself . . . mad at the whole thing. I knew that Tim and I, as apprentices, had been tricked into the fight. Everyone yelled as Tim and I entered and the fight begun. Tim came across very aggressively, and punched with everything. I just protected my head and took all the body blows because they didn't hurt. I continued to move around and back off and never threw a punch. I just stopped as many punches as I could. Tim hurt me many times and then a hard punch got through to my head and I staggered, but kept my balance. In those few seconds I felt an urge to retaliate. I threw a hard left jab with all my body weight behind it and it landed on Tim's gloves . . . he staggered and backed off. The crowd sensed the fight had finally begun and they began to scream . . . but I backed off as well and remained upright and resistant.

"Fight back! . . . Chicken! . . . Baby! . . . Loser!"

"Ah! Forget them!" yelled a bunch of workers, and they left the foundry. I never threw another punch. The men finally called off the fight. I went home hurting badly with sore arms and a sore head but I was resolute inside about what I had done.

During the following days none of the journeymen spoke to me or acknowledged me. They walked by me as though I wasn't there. *Good!* I thought. I don't care anyway. Red never said anything about the fight; he talked about everything else. Tim was surprisingly friendly and we got to talk many, many times. Red and I went for a drink at Christmas, and I got in the bar only because I was with Red. Eighteen was the legal drinking age. The bar man turned his head and pretended not to see us. This bar was in the back streets of Johannesburg, in the industrial area of Jeppe Street and it made its most money on Friday nights.

After talking for an hour, Red turned to me. "Okay!" he said, as he stood at the bar holding his beer. Looking me straight in the eyes and with his quirky smile, he asked, "I'm curious why you didn't throw a couple of punches? You didn't seem to be in trouble, he was open many times . . . you're fast, you could've stuck it to him! Now the men at work are calling you a 'Sissy'! A wet rag! A wet spaghetti! But most of all they don't think you've got any guts."

I knew this was going to be talked about sometime, and now was as good a time as any.

"I don't care what they think. I don't give a shit! I was mad at myself. I realized too late that the journeymen had goaded me into the fight. They must have got Tim to start it all. I wouldn't give them the satisfaction. Tim did hurt me, but not badly . . . Red, I see this shit all over the place, at school, at the movies, at Rosettenville Corner! Why do I have to have it at work?"

"Hey! Man!" interrupted Red. "They do it to all newcomers. The men in the shop are okay! They're trying to have some fun . . . maybe test you."

"I hate fighting, Red, between friends, or in the family It just shows how frustration gets to you . . . or that you can't work it out. And that you don't want to look stupid or be shown up!" I retorted. We sipped our beers, silent for a while.

I smiled at Red. "I don't like it here anyway," I said, not knowing why I was admitting my thoughts. But Red had befriended me, and I trusted him.

Red didn't reply right away. He sat with his beer at the bar looking at me as though I had said something important.

"Very interesting! Nobody in the shop talked about goading you two into a fight. But that could be the motive. Hey! They all know you're in good shape and play soccer for 'Marists'. One guy said that he might go and see you play. Most of them thought you didn't know how to fight, and most of all, they didn't like it that you didn't at least throw a punch at Tim . . . when you had him open!"

"I don't know how to really street fight. Also, I like Tim. . . . I just didn't want to give them satisfaction."

"Okay that's interesting," agreed Red, but with a little reservation.

"I'm taking your advice," I said, to break yet another silence. "I've asked my brother-in-law, James, to ask his brother Peter, who works at a machine shop, to get me a job. And they have agreed to find out if it's possible."

"You're joking! You're going to work somewhere else? Aren't you under contract?" asked Red as he put his beer down.

"No Red. And I'm not joking. I'm serious as hell! I don't like it here and I haven't signed the papers. Please! Please! Don't tell anyone."

"I won't."

◆

Trevor, now a steady member of the Andrew Street Mob and a good rider with good times, wanted to attempt the Johannesburg to Durban ride. It would be close to 380 miles. This was a race against time only, and the participants would have to complete the ride in one sequence, start to finish. This meant if you slept, sat on the side of the road, read a book, these activities were counted against the ride time. All stops were included. In other words, when did you start, and when did you finish. It was done on the honor system, as official monitors were impossible to arrange for what was to be a 30-40 hour ride. The unofficial record was about 29 hours. The agreed procedure was to sign in at the police stations at all the major towns and cities. The police station could verify the time, but no one could monitor how you got from town to town.

The route to Durban from Johannesburg going in south-eastern direction included Heidelberg, Standerton, Volksrust, Newcastle, Ladysmith, Colenso, Estcourt, Mooiriver, Howick, Pietermaritzberg and then Durban. All of these towns were rich in the history of the Great Trek, Anglo Boer war and various British-Boer-Zulu power struggles, including the discovery of minerals and gold in Johannesburg and the Transvaal.

"Better check the police station clocks!" said Pat, laughing, "you know small town cops! They don't change anything till New Year's!"

"Trevor, this is exciting. That's quite a ride," I said with envy that he would actually try to do it.

"No! I'll be all right," replied Trevor.

"I might try it," said Zoni.

"This Andrew Street Mob tries everything," added Juni: this quiet boy was always thinking.

Trevor went off at 5:30 AM in the misty morning, starting from Johannesburg City Hall and riding through Troyeville and down into the flatlands of the Transvaal. The road was narrow, so cars and trucks were a constant threat. Black people walking on the side of the road, towards the traffic, were also a hazard. To miss them meant you went wide often, into the middle of the road. Going through Troyeville had been slow because of the traffic lights and people going to work. Trevor worked the pace well, stopped every two to three hours, rested, lay down and ate very little. The evening became very pleasant and even though he ached in many parts of his body, he kept riding and welcomed any down-hills. Johannesburg is 6000 feet above Durban, so at least every now and again, the legs could stop moving and let gravity take over. There were long straight roads going up and down slightly around Heidelberg, Standerton and Volksrust. He stopped for lunch and then continued his push against the varying winds. Just before Ladysmith, it started to rain and the wind was horrendous. Trevor was freezing cold, as the combination of winds and rain went through everything he wore. He stopped in the town, signed in at the police station and went to a hotel; it was midnight. He had been on and off the bike for eighteen and a half hours.

"Please be sure to wake me at 2:00 AM," he asked the clerk more than once.

"Sure Sir!"

Trevor fell on top of the bed, took off his wet clothes, and rolled under the eiderdown. He was asleep in seconds.

When Trevor woke up, he could hardly move, his muscles were so sore. It seemed he had been asleep for seconds. Then he panicked. Nobody had called him and he could see light through the curtains. He looked at his watch. It was 4:30 AM. He washed his face with hot water. His riding clothes were drier and warmer but were tighter. He hurried everything.

"Stupid bastard," he yelled at the clerk, as he went past the desk with his bike on his shoulder. Trevor jumped on his bike and peddled into a rhythm, then stopped at a restaurant and grabbed some coffee and toast. *At least it's steep downhill now,* he thought, *the famous, steep, winding road into Pietermaritzburg and down into Durban.* The ride would be a breeze now if only he could stay awake and ride all the way. After riding through the blur of trees, Trevor peddled into the streets of Durban and caught the wonderful smell of the sea. He checked in at the Durban Police Station at just after 12:30 PM. The ride had taken 31 hours.

"Why didn't you take an alarm clock?" asked Pat.

"Why didn't I do a lot of damn things?" answered Trevor.

"Absolutely great!" I said, "Could've beat the record? . . . Hey!"

"Yeah! Maybe."

Trevor was the Andrew Street Mob's hero.

◆

One Sunday, there were no races, so the Andrew Street Mob decided to ride from the Southern Suburbs to Germiston Lake, have a picnic, and get back by 5:00 PM. Five girls would go: the three Kennedy Street girls, Beryl, Ann and Grace, and two from Andrew Street, Thelma and Gloria. So with all the boys, Johnny, Norman, Trevor, Billy, Zoni, Pat, Doc and myself, there was a crowd of thirteen. The distance for the cycle racers could not even be considered a ride. This would be complete relaxation.

It was slow, almost too slow to ride with your hands off the handlebars, because the bike would swerve all over the road. In fact, for the racers, it was more fun helping the girls on the up-hill. One hand was placed under the saddle of the girl's bike and the other hand on the middle of the pusher's handlebar. Then they just pumped away with the bikes side by side. At Germiston Lake we had lunch and swam. Because some of the girls had to be home early, the group left at 3:00 PM and headed home. It was hot, around 90 degrees F. There was also very little breeze and everyone was puffing, hardly talking and just pushing one pedal down after the other. We wished we'd gone in Norman's truck instead.

"There's a river that comes off the hill and some pools, where we could swim, cool off and rest," said Pat.

"How far?" asked Beryl.

"About a mile."

"Let's go and do it."

Sure enough, there was a stream coming down the side of the hill to the drains on the side of the very new four-lane freeway (highway) between Johannesburg and Germiston.

We dropped our bikes within 20 yards of a pool, which was located 100 yards off the road. We went into the water without hesitation. It was only a few minutes later when someone remarked about a strange smell.

"Yes, I smell it."

"It's a stale sort of smell."

"Don't drink any of the water."

"No."

We got out, slowly. The heat frustration had gone away.

Pat and Trevor walked up the river. The smell got stronger. Zoni and I ran up to them.

"Yes, it's stronger," said Zoni.

We kept walking up on the side of the stream.

"Oh God! Look there!"

"It's a donkey!"

"It probably fell into the river and broke its leg or something, and drowned." Part of the carcass was above the water.

"It's a wonder the vultures didn't get to it."

"There're no more vultures in Johannesburg."

"Lots on the streets."

We walked back to the rest of the crowd.

"Yes the smell is there too. There's a dead donkey in the river," said Zoni.

The girls screamed and the volume turned to a heightened tone of panic.

"I'm going home," said Beryl.

We followed and went to get the bikes. The pace picked up tremendously on the way home. It took no time at all to get home. The girls said good-bye as they went into their houses. All the guys went to Pat's house to have a shower and a Dettol (antiseptic) scrub. I went into my house.

"Gran, do you have some Dettol (antiseptic wash)?"

"Why?"

"I want to have a bath now. I was in a river swimming with a dead donkey!"

"What did you do that for?" asked Gran.

"I thought it would be fun! Oh! So did Zoni, Thelma, Beryl, Grace and everyone," I joked.

"You kids! Honestly! I'll run you a bath, and give me your clothes. I don't want Lena to wash them with ours."

I really didn't understand the panic of the girls. I was sure there were all kinds of things in rivers and besides, I never swallowed the water.

"Yeah! Girls are different," I said aloud.

"What's that?" asked Gran.

"Nothing, I'm just mumbling."

◆

The following Friday the crowd met in the Broadway Hotel. The conversation confirmed that everyone had gone home and had a bath.

"Dettol Bubble Bath Day," said Trevor.

"Where's the party this weekend?" asked Zoni.

"I heard there is one at Joan and Denise's," I answered.

"Who are they?"

"Trevor's friend Elaine, who just joined us, introduced them to the crowd and they've decided to throw a party."

"Good."

"Are we going to the Grand Theater or the Adelphi?" asked Norman.

"I don't care what's showing at the Adelphi . . . let's just go there. I hate the Grand, it's full of bugs," said Norman

We finished our beers and went to the Adelphi. It was an easy, inexpensive way to enjoy a Friday night. Fridays with friends was a major part of our lives. The getting together with friends, talking, doing something and putting the week's work and study to the back of the mind was just so enjoyable. Friday was on the schedule without any planning. It was also very important to me to just be part of it. Friday was the start of the weekend, which gave a freedom from so many demands in life. I played soccer on Saturday afternoons, but whenever I could, I rode over to Kensington early on Saturday mornings to see my sister Yvonne and her husband James. Mr. Van, James' father, always made sure he talked to me. He would occasionally give me some pocket money. It was very helpful, because money seemed to be nonexistent; the only entertainment that was really affordable was the parties, Friday nights and social gatherings. Going to the theaters was on the borderline, going to the movies in Johannesburg city or going to special dances made it painfully hard to muster up the money. Something would have to be taken from the work week. Lunch-money, ride the bike instead of the bus, or walk. Whatever big pleasure was taken, it had to come from minimal basic earnings and any other scheme you could think up. Detailed costs were calculated in advance for the week. Would I ask my parents? Almost never!

On the Saturday we had gathered together with the full intention to go to Joan and Denise's party.

"How are we getting to the party tonight?" asked Billy.

"Nobody knows, and all the girls want to go. We need a truck," I suggested.

"Norman has a truck!" said Billy.

"It's not available. His dad's gone and didn't give him permission."

Norman, against all good sense, agreed to take the truck from his father's yard. It wasn't cleaned, but that didn't matter. It was used to haul gravel, timber, or whatever. We dug in and roughly cleaned it and threw in a couple of blankets. The boys met in Andrew Street. Norman picked us up and drove to Kennedy Street, picked up the rest of the crowd and sixteen people in the truck headed out to Joan and Denise's.

Joan was model-quality and had brown hair, sparkling eyes and a most pleasant smile. Denise was blonde, very nice looking in a more conservative way, and quieter in her actions. Both these girls were physically active and wonderful company. They lived further south of the Southern Suburbs, past Uncle Charlie's Roadhouse and Meredale Swimming Pool. Their house was located in the hills alongside the main Johannesburg-Vereeniging road, just before the road entered the flatlands.

It was a great barbecue, starting as the sun went down. There was dancing and beer. A 'braai' is truly a South African favorite pastime, done anywhere possible. The racing cyclists were very relaxed and not worried what time they got home. There were no cycling races that weekend. Joan had started to go out with Bobbie. He was a big, good-looking young man with a better body than any weight-lifter. The boys wanted to meet him because he was one of the best riders in South Africa. He too became a member of the Andrew Street Mob. So did Ron, an equal size to Bobbie, and a track cyclist predominantly, very strong and very good-looking, from Italian stock. Ron had moved in with Zoni, Juni and Mimi. The Andrew Street Mob kept getting bigger.

We danced all night . . . talked to everyone . . . drank all the beer and decided that this party was better than a Friday night out. Any dissention to that statement was drowned out. I enjoyed the music and dancing more than other activities. Our crowd of boys and girls were all dancers, and we kept it going so that the floor space was never empty. The exchange of talk was non-stop. We were in our best element and every minute counted. This crowd and its activities made our complex lives easier. We didn't want it to end, but it did! Two o'clock in the morning the truck pulled out of the front gate of Joan's place. Everyone had blankets over them. It was very cool and there was a certain amount of cuddling going on, so the blankets were perfect.

"No lights," announced Norman.

"No lights?"

The so-called mechanics got out and after half an hour, no better result.

"Let's just drive," said Norman.

Everyone jumped in and off we went. As the truck continued along the main Johannesburg-Vereeniging road, other car drivers kept flicking their lights. There were a lot of comments in reply starting with "We know they're out" and ending with some pretty bad language. This surprised the girls because we never usually spoke like that.

"What an education," commented somebody from underneath a blanket.

"What are you doing under there? I want to see," said another, as a bunch of us ripped the blankets away.

"Nothing! Just nothing! Just like we thought!"

The truck turned the corner off the main Johannesburg-Vereeniging road and headed along Rifle Range road towards the Southern Suburbs.

"We may make it," said Grace. There were very few houses until a couple of miles from the water tower.

"If we get past the tower into the back streets of Main street, we should be okay," said Ann.

"Why are you worried about that?" asked one of the boys, as he pulled the girl next to him under the blankets. She didn't resist.

A motorcycle cop sitting around the corner from the tower flagged the truck down. Norman pulled to a stop.

"Oh! Shit!" was heard many times, in very low tones.

Everyone was so silent you could hear the cop's shoes squeak as he walked towards the truck. The slow methodical movements of police always put us in an anxiety cloud. We never had good experiences with cops. They were often very abrasive with us kids. They were much rougher with black people as they bounced them into the 'Black Maria', the local name for a police pick-up van.

"What is your name?" he asked.

Norman told him.

"This is your truck?"

"It's my dad's."

"Do you have a license?"

"Yes, but I don't have it with me."

"Did your dad give you permission to use the truck?"

"Yes, Sir!"

"Where have you been?"

"We all went to a barbecue," replied Norman. The atmosphere was tense.

"What will happen now?" asked one of the girls. This thought must have crossed everyone's mind. Norman was doing a good job. He was very polite. I was sure Norman was in deep, deep trouble, with both the cops and his dad.

"Drinking?"

"Yes, Sir, a few beers," said Norman.

"And your lights are out," said the policeman.

"We tried to fix them. We were stuck in Mondeor and so we drove slowly to get home, Sir!"

"You also know you can't transport people in the back of a truck!"

"No, I didn't, Sir," replied Norman; everyone knowing it was a lie.

There was along silence as the cop walked around the truck, looking at us in the back of the truck. We were in big trouble. There wasn't a damn law we hadn't broken. We had the book covered, including under-age drinking and beer in the truck.

"Oh! God! Help us," whispered a panicked voice. A little hope lay in the fact that highway cops were more reasonable than the police station cops, who treated us kids like criminals; but this was bad, and we all knew it. Our parents would go berserk if we went to jail. I really feared going to jail . . . I'd heard too many bad stories!

"Well, I'll tell you what I've decided to do."

Everyone was so quiet you could hear people going to bed a mile away. "I'm going to assume I never saw you. You stay on the back roads of the Southern Suburbs and drive very carefully. Pull over to the side of the road when you see a car coming towards you. Good evening." The officer was stern, and as he walked away, about a dozen voices whispered loudly, "Thank you . . . Sir!" One girl said, "What a beautiful cop!"

◆

Peter, James's brother, arranged an interview for me with Mr. Funkey, the owner of Main Reef Engineering. Three or four people including the shop foreman talked to me. I got the job, and I was so relieved. The shop was bright and airy and designed to make mining machinery. The contract had to be signed and it required my mother's and father's signatures. Gran was upset because my aunt Amy had told her I was not allowed to change companies during an apprenticeship unless I changed the discipline, e.g. from mechanical to electrical, etc.

"You're not going to be able to learn a trade, and I want you to have something by the time you're twenty one. Otherwise you'll just become a 'Bum on the Street'!" Gran was almost crying. I hadn't seen her that way ever, and I felt very, very bad! But I also was very mad at my aunt for making her cry.

"Aunt Amy is wrong, Gran! The contract wasn't signed with Rowe and Monfries. I was still under two months' trial," I replied, trying to explain. Then I got a little strong. "Aunt Amy was probably mad at me because Uncle Harry got me the job there! But I hate that place!"

"Is that true now . . . you'll go to school, serve an apprenticeship and become a journeyman?"

"Yes Gran! I would never, ever tell you a lie."

"Alright then Son!"

The contract was signed. I said goodbye to Red and Tim, and was surprised to see that they didn't want me to go. I didn't miss a day of work in changing. I started cutting on a shaper machine . . . much bigger and more complicated than the one at school. I was enrolled at the Witwatersrand Technical College, downtown Johannesburg City, where I'd had my first bicycle crash! My daily routine became: up at 5:30AM . . . catch the bus at 6.00AM and travel for 45 minutes to Industria (Main Reef Engineering was located 20 miles outside Johannesburg), start work at 7AM . . . finish at 4:45PM . . . catch a bus to downtown Johannesburg to college . . . attend class from 6PM to 8 or 9PM and then catch the bus home. During the first year, this would be done on Mondays, Tuesdays and Wednesdays, so I could finish my High School Certificate and continue onto college subjects. Gran was happy! I was going to school and family emotions settled down immensely. I was on the good side of the family. Uncle Mick agreed it was a good time in the house!

◆

I was now over 16 and had to play in the under-18 league in soccer. My progress in cycling grew fast. I was riding 20 miles at every opportunity in my busy schedule. This excluded Thursdays, which was a soccer night, and Saturdays when there was a soccer game. Holding a position in the soccer team was getting tougher. Marist Brothers was a popular team; players came from everywhere. My chest was now as clear as it could be; I was very healthy and very confident in what I was doing.

A big 20-mile paced handicap race was coming up soon, followed by the Olympic trials. I had entered both these events. The 20-mile ride was within a few weeks, the Olympic trials early in the next year.

The 20-mile race was in a circle: Alberton towards Vereeniging same as always, but a turn left at about 10 miles took you back to Alberton via another road. I went off by myself between the seven riders ahead of me and the twenty behind me. I was driving my bike equipped with a 48-tooth chain wheel and 16-tooth cog. I had trained with a 15-tooth cog, meaning the ratio was higher and legs went slower. The lower gear ratio felt really good to my legs and up to now the ride had been fast and easy. At ten miles a Troyeville rider caught me and the two of us rode together. More riders were passed, but one remained, a Pretoria Wheelers rider. It was a paced handicap ride. The first one over the line wins the race. A group of riders usually outpaces single riders, so according to an unwritten rule, the pace is set, first by one rider in front, then another, and another. Those that never give pace are not very well liked. This changeover happened every 200 yards or so. The Troyeville rider and I caught the Pretoria rider.

"Let's work this together and stay away from the scratch men." I suggested. "What's your name?" I asked the Troyeville rider.

"Peter."

The Pretoria rider said nothing.

At 15 miles into the race, the wind tore into our faces and bodies and the Pretoria rider refused to go in front. Peter and I worked the front as we had before. The road was relatively flat. Near a small climb, it turned, and in that short portion of the race circle we could see riders behind us. At 2 miles to the finish, we passed the remaining riders that were in front of us and left them behind. I now realized that we might be the first group to go over the finish line. I was also getting tired, I slacked slightly from the front and Peter, also tired, slipped back as well, indicating time for the Pretoria rider to press the wind. He stood up and instead sprinted for a breakaway.

"Oh shit," I shouted, "Bastard."

"Let's go after him," yelled Peter, looking over the side of his bike, his face grimacing with disgust.

"I can't . . . no energy for the wind," I yelled, disappointed that my energy was flat. There is a hollow in the body when you feel that way and you wish the hollow would fill up. *Must train more,* ran through my splitting mind.

"Come on, I'll give pace, you sit in behind," said Peter.

"Okay," I said and pushed in behind, put my head down and kept my front wheel six inches from Peter's back wheel. I just looked at his wheel, nothing else, and pumped away, making sure the gap between our wheels did not vary. I rested for a quarter mile and then pushed down hard on the pedals to take me between Peter's bike and the side of the road. My new-found racing buddy was relieved, and jumped in behind me. We were now a team. We were working well, and gaining on the Pretoria Wheelers rider, and that inspired us even more. I didn't look up or sideways and I didn't close my eyes!

We knew that after coming off the main road it would only be about 800 yards to the finish, and that we had to catch him before that intersection. There was no thought of tiredness now.

"Let's just catch the bastard! " I yelled. Peter took pace, then I took pace, and we swapped every 50 yards now. We could see the turn-off, people on the side of the road were holding traffic back for the bike racers. The Pretoria rider turned onto the side road. We were 20 yards behind him. The side road curved slightly left for 300 yards and then there were 500 yards of straight to the finish line. We caught him at the turn.

"Come on!" I yelled, "a short jump." I stood up and short-sprinted. Peter jumped in. We caught him and the three of us leveled out across the road: three riders coming to the finish line. We all slacked off a little on the pace at 300 yards, as we couldn't be caught by any others. First one over wins the race! It was everyone for themselves now! Strategy and quick energy were key elements. I was in the middle, my eyes were flicking from one rider to the other, but more to the Pretoria rider, to make sure I was not caught by surprise. All three sitting, pushing easy but hard enough, and watching, with 200 yards to go. The Pretoria Wheelers rider jumped.

I yelled loudly, "Let's go, Peter!" He tried, but I saw his front wheel disappear from view. My front wheel was level with the Pretoria rider's back wheel cog at 120 yards, a perfect place, I was gaining and I knew I had the strength in my legs; it was just a matter of timing now. At 50 yards I stood up and applied the last dregs of conscious energy and my front wheel moved level to the Pretoria rider's crank line. This was it! I suddenly let go everything. The bike was being whipped from side to side furiously with every leg stroke, my head way over the handlebars, my eyes almost closed with the strain, my shoulders in line with my arms and over the handlebars. I was gaining. Every remaining piece of energy was in these last few seconds of thrust . . . the finish line came up so fast that as I hit it, I wasn't sure how close the two wheels were. The crowd on the two sides of the road was screaming, followed by the familiar "Ah! Wow!" Followed by the sound dying down from its peak. I hadn't even seen the crowd until after I crossed the finish line.

I felt the hollows coming back as the total relaxation of my body came about. I slipped back on the seat, arms in the air, legs going like crazy because I rode fixed wheel: no coasting. The bike slowed and at 100 yards past the finish line, one of the volunteer helpers grabbed my bike at the saddle, threw an arm around me and stopped the motion. I loosened the clips on the pedals and slipped off the back of the bike, hanging onto the shoulder of the helper.

"Wow! Thank you! Thank you!"

"What a finish," said the helper.

One of the riders I knew who hadn't ridden that day came running down. "You won Charl! You won . . . by an inch!"

"No!" I beat him! Yes! Man! Yes!!

"Yes you did!" We wrapped our arms around each other!

As we walked back to the finish line to get refreshment, I saw the outline of my new compatriot. Peter had really helped me in the race. I walked over to him, to this new face, shook his hand, put my arm around him, and said, "Thank you. I learnt about something nice to-day."

"It's alright, man . . . where did you get the energy . . . *Jussus* . . . you got some finish. Hey!"

"We caught the bastard. Man!" I said. "Come and have a drink."

We got drinks and sat on the grass watching the other riders come in. The Pretoria Wheeler rider came up, shook my hand and congratu-lated me then left quickly saying, "I broke too soon."

As he left, my new friend Peter called, "Thanks for all the pace-set-ting help!" I nodded and added, "It was us—together. It was great . . . hope we do it again."

"We will. I'm sure!"

There was no answer. Peter and I just sat there for a long time, rest-ing and talking. Inside I knew the love of sport and competition would be in my life forever, as long as there were people like Peter around. I loved sports passionately and could never understand why some people didn't participate!

◆

"Charl" the soccer coach called out, "I want to see you after practice."

"Yes, Sir," I replied. Thoughts streamed through my head one after the other—*Saturday's game was tough, the other team was good, the wing beat me a couple of times, but it was only on the outside. I reconciled that's where you force the winger to go. Besides they didn't score through me. Why do I have these guilty feelings?* The practice completed, I felt good after the closing sprints, which traditionally wrapped up the exercise and practice. I walked over to the coach.

"Charl. Yes! Let's go sit on the bench for a few minutes." We sat down. Nobody else was around and I knew this was going to be serious.

"Charl, I hear you're a pretty good cyclist and ride a lot."

"Yes, Sir! I ride quite a bit."

"Well, we practice Tuesday and Thursday, and I gave you Tuesday off. If you don't turn up to practice it affects the team, but even more so, there is a chance that you may lose your place on the starting team. If you ride a bike on Tuesday that's not fair to the team."

"Well Sir! The Tuesday is for night school. I go to college after work and the class I have to take is only given on Tuesdays. It is not for cycling," I explained. "But, I do ride as much as I can now because of Olympic trials next year . . . but that's on other days."

The coach's stern looks changed to a warmer expression. "I'm glad you use Tuesdays for school. I feel better that I gave you Tuesday off for a good reason. I guess what I should really say to you is that the two sports don't mix. You're developing different muscles and they have different effects on your performance. Running and riding are two different things and when you add soccer movements to the dimension of running it makes the difference even wider. In soccer the first three steps are very, very important. How fast you do them is most important plus, can you change direction once or twice while you're doing three steps? That is what really counts. Reaction times are also very fast in soccer, compared to running and cycling. Physically it mostly affects the muscles in your legs and tendons around your ankles."

"What does all this mean to me?" I asked.

"It means, I guess, technically your training for cycling doesn't help you for soccer, in fact, it may hurt your soccer. I mean just as an example, in your ankle, the muscles and tendons are working in a straight line on a bike. Not so in soccer, they're being twisted and turned in addition to straight-forward running."

"So what should I do?" I asked. I was now a little perplexed, especially about being on the starting team or not. I needed to know the punch line to this conversation.

"You really should give up one of the sports."

"But Sir, they're both very important!" thinking that I had friends in both sports.

"I think you could do very well in soccer," replied the coach. "Right now there are signs of stiffness, perhaps the loss of reaction and quick coordination, but these things can be worked on." He paused, smiling. "So you should make the decision. I'm glad that Tuesday is just for college. I thought you were riding. Keep it up, and our arrangement still stands. See you Saturday."

"Thanks, Coach," I said. I proceeded home, didn't remember anything about how I got there, ate, and climbed into bed. Usually I would walk home with Desmond who was playing in the same team, but he hadn't been at practice. My mind was totally focused on what would happen if I gave up soccer or cycling, or if I kept doing both. Who could I discuss this with? Not my dad; he knew nothing about any of this, neither did my mom. Nobody in the family knew what I was doing except James, my sister's husband, who was a fan of Germiston Callies (Caledonians), another soccer team on the 'Rand' (Witwatersrand).

I sought the advice of Mr. Huth, the bicycle shop owner, the man who had introduced me to and guided me through racing. I questioned him on the soccer vs. cycling aspects. I admitted not knowing what to do, and that I loved both sports, and that I had friends in both sports and wanted to continue both. Mr. Huth never really committed an answer. Finally, I expressed my thoughts about the Olympic trials. I told him that I really wasn't sure I was good enough. I knew I was very young and that there were no handicaps given.

"Mr. Huth do *you* think I should enter the Olympic Trials? I don't know if I have a chance at any of it, especially becoming a 'Springbok' (South African national team)."

"The main point is that the experience will do you good, Charl," said Mr. Huth. "The trials are a measure of how good you are in South Africa. We are not as good as the Europeans and even the best Springboks will have lots of competition and trouble keeping up in the Olympics. Competing is the only way we'll grow. Our riders will bring that experience back with them. You're very young, about seventeen, right? This is open competition you know. I would try it now, get some experience. Solve your soccer problem later."

"Thank you, that's a good idea. Thank you for your time, Mr. Huth," I felt relieved and thankful again towards Mr. Huth. I decided to leave; I didn't want to take up any more of Mr. Huth's time. He was a very busy man running both his shop and the Rand Roads Cycling Club. I was happy, I had made my mind up immediately because I did not like resolving decisions over a long time: there was no question I would enter the Olympic Trials, and I would not worry about the results. Riding home from the shop I suddenly realized I had solved my problem. The Olympic trials would tell me if I was any good. The soccer problem could be solved later. In my mind a nagging thought sat on a perch like a bird. My family knew nothing about my college, my sports; they knew only some of my friends. My dad knew nothing of anything I did . . . he had never in his life done what I had done already and I was only 16. I guessed I had to thank my coaches in soccer and cycling, and my teachers in college.

◆

The training was rigorous. Every night I could, after work or school and even as late as 9 PM, I rode about 20 to 30 miles from Kenilworth along Rifle Range road, past Uncle Charlie's and then past Van Wyks

Rust, and back. The road was lit up to Uncle Charlie's Roadhouse and then the farms started and there was not much lighting. It was dangerous because cars and trucks used the road. Many drivers probably could not see me till they were very close.

That was part of the game, I had told my friends. I didn't want to ask them whether it was good idea or not to enter the trials. I was scared they might tell me I was crazy competing against all the really good riders of the day, like Bobbie, Ron, Dennis and riders of that class, but I knew that and didn't want to worry about it.

There were no handicap minutes in the Olympics; everyone went off scratch. The track trials were to be held at the Malvern Cycle Track. I went there to practice. The banks on each end of the track were always scary; I had to get to know them. Especially in the 220-yard sprint race. The track was 440 yards long. Two cyclists started at the finish line by maneuvering for position. The ideal was to position themselves behind the other rider, at the highest position on the bank on one end of the track, because that gave a distinct advantage. There was no real limit, in time, to jockey for position. Your time only counted over the last 220 yards. You were first over the finish line, even if it was by an inch. So from that high point on the track, you could sweep down on your opponent and get a great jump with aided acceleration due to gravity, get in front of him, and hopefully out-distance him to the finish line. There were many other tactics.

I practiced on the track on Saturday mornings. I balanced the bike at the top of the track and then sprinted till my lungs had no more air. Then I trained for fitness and rode around and around the track until it was boring. I was definitely going to enter. There were a lot of riders practicing. It was scary, but new and exciting to try. To balance at the top on the sloped edge felt like you were on top of a wall on your bike. The transformation from balancing to downward sprint from the bank meant the rider and bike had to be in absolute unison, otherwise the rider fell.

The trials, to be held over two weekends, started. My first impression was that there were hundreds of competitors. My second was the excitement of upcoming competition. I looked up the schedule and found I was in an early qualifying race. The two-man, one-lap, 220 sprint.

My competitor and I balanced our bikes at the start line and the gun went off. I took off in a slow ride to the top of the bank and stopped. The other rider followed and balanced up behind me. This was not good for me. I moved forward ten yards; so did the other rider. As we did the bank was less steep, and less gravity help was available; not a good position. I faked a four pedal movement and started to sprint, but quickly slowed. The other rider broke into a sprint, cut to the inside, and I re-charged my sprint. I was right on his wheel, taking draft. We passed the 220-yard line, I was riding higher on the second bank and then as we hit the last hundred yards, I stood up and with a burst of energy went past the rider with 15 yards to go. I was in the second round. Wow! This was exciting and so quick! It was a flash of time by comparison to road racing.

Reality came back quickly as my opponent in the second heat was about 25 years old. He looked very strong. We started off into a strong ride right from the start line, I jumped in behind him, and he didn't even go up the bank. He increased the pace all the way to the 220-yard line and then stood up. I stood up as well but held back the sprint. I tried to get alongside my opponent but he just increased his speed and moved in front of me. The sprint was even and I never lost ground. But the opponent just plain kept me behind him. I was out!

I walked into the inside of the track oval, sat on the grass and looked at the scoreboards. I knew many riders by their faces; names were a blur. I felt alone in my quest . . . but that was all right . . . I had planned it that way. I got up and rode home. I had a five-mile race the next day.

On Sunday the weather was beautiful and again the cycle stadium was packed. My next Olympic trial, the five miles, 20-lap race heat, had twelve riders. I sat in the pack of twelve riders for ten laps. Each lap or half-lap, the lead rider would go up on the bank, allowing another rider to give pace. The overall time had to qualify as well as being amongst the winning riders. I gave my half lap of pace and went back in the pack. I felt good. I was half-way back in the pack at 15 laps, when about five riders went up on the bank. I found out instantly that I was giving pace again. I pushed it a bit, as I was mad at the riders who wouldn't take a turn, and I pushed harder and suddenly found myself 100 yards ahead of the pack. I knew this wasn't a good idea, but kept riding, I felt good. At 17 laps the group behind me worked harder. A rider, almost lapped, was ahead of me by 50 yards, but I just couldn't catch him. After 18 laps the group caught me. I fell into the pack. The pace had increased tremendously. I felt tired and it was hard to keep

up. I wanted to have that confident feeling for the sprint and it wasn't
there. So, I tried to rest and just concentrate on the wheel of the man in
front of me. I was sixth man back. The first two riders would go onto
further qualification. The increasing pace was taking its toll but I had
rested and felt better. Approaching the last bend before the straight and
the finish line, the riders stood up and sprinted and jostled from side to
side. This disturbed me and so I broke to the outside but my confident
feeling was not there, even though I was gaining on the leaders. My
sprint was dull and as much as I pumped the bike, I knew I wouldn't
catch the leader. I finished fourth.

The last trial that I entered was a one-lap, six-rider competition,
where the riders took off on the gunshot and sequences of sprint-
ride-sprint took place over a one-lap ride. The time for the whole lap
counted in this race. It was just like a horse race. I got into third place
quickly; my strategy was to try and stay in the middle. We rounded the
first turn, the group was tight. I was scared of the closeness. Handlebars
were inches apart. Julius had told me that in Europe, riders would try
to touch others to throw them off. Coming down the back stretch,
we were still tight. I was still in third position. On the second bend, I
got my wheel on the outside of the man in front. I stood up with all
the others. I had my good sprint feeling, but a rider on my right had
boxed me in. A second rider was on the outside of me as well. I couldn't
drop and go to the outside; there was not enough time. The inside was
closed; the continuous white line was on the left. I tried to push sideways but was too scared of crashing. The group went across the finish
line. I had all kinds of reserve energy left. I got off my bike, mad at
myself and damn disappointed. I just knew I could've beaten them. I
was mad at myself. I got my bag and rider's jacket, got back on my bike
and rode the 20 miles home, with my head over the handlebars, I was
so down. I had known I really had little chance of qualifying; I was too
young, and my bike was not the right bike, it was a road-racing bike
with curved forks. Track bikes had almost straight forks. But I felt that
didn't matter, I had made so many mistakes. The next trials were four
years away . . . that was an eternity!

"Didn't make it Gran," I said, as I entered the house. I took off my
toe-clip shoes, threw my stuff on the bed and went into the kitchen.

"I'll make you a sandwich and some tea . . . sit down," suggested
Gran.

She looked at me and smiled. I loved that smile. It was soothing . . . it could calm a country of angry men.

"It doesn't matter Son! I bet a lot of other kids didn't make it either. You tried and that is just as important. By the way, Johnny called and he says there's a party tonight."

"That's great," I said. "But Gran, all that training. I was so fit and strong. I know my bike was heavier than most others. Maybe a lighter bike would have helped, but that was not the reason . . . I was not good enough! I work things out technically, but it doesn't always make you win. They just beat me at the game!"

Uncle Mick came into the kitchen and sat down. "How did you do Son?"

"I didn't make it . . . I'm just telling Gran!"

"Too bad! Continue, Son! I'd like to hear the story," Uncle Mick suggested as he sat down and had some tea.

We did this all the time and I loved sitting at the kitchen table and talking to them. I could always talk to them!

". . .I was saying it wasn't the bike or my fitness. I made so many silly mistakes on the track!" I had to get this out. I didn't want to explode on my friends. My mom and dad, well that was out of the question. Gran and Uncle Mick were a good choice. We talked for some time about the bad judgments made, not analyzing the other rider choices and definitely not knowing the tactics. I had no tactics. I just rode!

"Did you learn anything, Son?" asked Gran as she poured three cups of tea and put a sandwich in front of me. "It's peanut butter." It was always peanut butter!

"Thanks!" I took a bite. "Yes! I learnt other people want to win as well and in these races it's more aggressive. They fight for position on the track, they push and pull, and maybe they don't care! I need to be smarter about the game and not just be fit."

"Good! You've learnt something. You're better off now than three weeks ago!" suggested Gran.

"Put this in your 'toolbox of life'," suggested Uncle Mick.

"You're both right you know! Thanks!" I replied sincerely.

So we sat in the kitchen like always. Never in the lounge or the dining room. Our life and heavy discussions were always at the kitchen table. We sat there, the three of us. I had another sandwich and more tea. Uncle Mick had tea and a sandwich. We all liked it very much. We discussed school, sports and work . . . laughing mostly. I loved them both very deeply.

◆

The legal age to hold a driver's license was 16. Cars became a new thing in the Andrew Street Mob. Johnny had an Austin A-40, his brother an Oldsmobile two-door coupé and Zoni had bought a Wolseley. Mac had joined the 'Mob' and had a half-ton truck. Mac was tall, strong and relatively quiet, but loved the fun side of life. He was rugged looking and fitted the truck to a 'T'. Norman had bought a MG-TD and was the envy of everyone. Juni had bought an MG-TC with sixteen-inch spoke wheels and Pat had an Opel. I had very deep feelings about my friends owning their own cars. I was very glad for them, but it made me feel unfortunate in many ways.

The cars had a major influence on the decline of interest in cycling . . . but so did girls. The late Saturday night out became early Sunday mornings to bed. The 6:30 AM rise was very early, especially to get on a cold bicycle saddle and ride 9 miles to start a race. A small drift away from the sport was apparent. The times that someone with a car would bring riders home after the race were beautiful, because the long ride of nine miles up the Alberton City Hill was a killer. Some cyclists even walked the steeper sections despite the fact that riders would like to say, "cyclists never walk their bike".

My deep thoughts of cycling versus soccer continued to make me look for an answer. The disappointment of failing in the Olympic trials, even with the excuses of being too young, with not enough experience, and having an old bike, began to outweigh all the suggestions of 'keep trying'.

There must be a love inside you to keep going, I thought. *I love soccer very much and don't want to give it up.* Then I pondered on the question of my bronchitis, would it come back, if I gave up cycling? I had been free of the deep suffocating breathing, and that was even more important. The dilemma continued.

The next big race was the Dunlop Cup. The actual cup was the largest trophy in South African cycling; it stood about 3 feet high. The event was very popular. It was a 100-kilometer (62.5 miles), paced handicap race. Almost every rider that could enter would apply. Riders came from all over the Witwatersrand and sometimes as far as the Orange Free State, Cape Province and Natal. The race was from

Alberton to Vereeniging and back, the same course as the usual races. The course started with a dip for the first mile, up a little hill and then downhill for five miles. The next 25 miles or so were on the flat. At the halfway mark, the cyclists would make a 180-degree turn, and head back on the same flat 25 miles to the five miles uphill and the mile and a half ride to the finish line. Sponsored by the Dunlop Tire Company, it was always well organized. It contained small elements of the Tour de France, with spectators on the side of the road, big banners across the finish line, blowing in the gentle breeze, and water handouts at points along the road. There were trucks, an ambulance and people selling bicycles and parts. It was truly the cycling event of the year.

I was seventeen and had earned a handicap of nine minutes. There were riders with 20-minute handicaps; I remembered those days. There were big packs of cyclists at the five-minute, three-minute and scratch marks. There were over 100 riders.

I prepared my old bike with the care and love of a mother for her newborn child. The night before the race I removed all the grease from the crank and replaced it with heavy oil. I checked the chain for bad links or stretching, no good on long rides. You wanted your legs to have even loading with every revolution; not varied cycles of push fast and push slow. I also removed grease from the hubs. I was lucky enough to borrow a set of 'Conloy' wheels with tubular tires; they were much lighter than my 27" steel wheels and rubber tires. I bought a 16-tooth freewheel cog especially for this race. I planned to train again on the 48-chain wheel and 15 tooth fixed cog for the race, and only on the day of the race drop to the 48-chain wheel and 16-tooth cog ratio. I had learnt this from the black riders who loved the higher gears and even rode 48 by 13, which was very slow peddling, very hard against the wind and wicked to your body on up-hills. I checked toe-clips and all the bolts and nuts. I had clean clothes and polished shoes. Nothing was overlooked; I even added a spare tubular tire, placed under the saddle, and a pump. I mounted two bottles with rubber straws on the handlebars. During all my years of racing, I had never had bottles to drink from during the races. But this was a special event to me and I had decided not to take a chance on anything.

◆

I got up at 6 AM Sunday morning and made some hot chocolate. I filled the bottles with it. Some guys put raw eggs and milk in their bottles . . . the thought of that was enough to make me sick. I put on my tight cotton shirt, black racing pants, small socks and shoes with toe-clips. I rode very slowly to Alberton. How many times had I done this, I wondered. It was always invigorating. I felt good, but a little sad, and I didn't know why. I had chosen to leave a little earlier than all my friends usually did. When I arrived at the starting line there was already an enormous crowd. I registered and got my number and went and sat on the grass. It was a beautiful day for the race. The weather was perfect; the air was clear and thin because of the 6000 foot altitude of the Witwatersrand.

I saw a lot of friends, including Bobbie, Ron and Dennis. The greetings were short as everyone was going about their business. The start of the race was announced. The scratch riders would take close to three hours, so with stragglers and picking up riders and bringing them in, the race would take 4-5 hours and would be all done by 1:00 PM.

The first riders went off and I lined up to start. I was ready to ride. I took my position on the line; there were about eight riders in my group, a nice size. The signal to go was given by the drop of a flag and the voice of an official. We started off. The first two miles were brisk, and as we hit the downhill, some coasted. Three riders and I pushed down the 5-mile hill, sometimes reaching 30+ miles an hour. I finally found the usefulness of the freewheel cog. It was good to keep the muscles working. It was also very good to warm them for the long level ride. We hit the flats and had already started to catch riders. Were we going too fast? Always a question! Were we going too slowly? I felt good as I pumped away. I had a habit of standing up every mile for a little while and then sitting back down. Somebody had told me it was a good idea. Everyone helped each other indirectly, in discussions, thoughts expressed, experience, and through arguments of course! I thought cyclists were nice people, close to each other as in all sport activities, tough in competitive spirit, but nearly all of them friendly, when the race was over. There are always the over-serious idiots who never seem to be the best. *You have to sort out who you are!* stuck in my mind. I wondered why I was thinking all this stuff in the race.

The nine-minute group was almost shredded. Five riders had dropped back and one had gone ahead. Two guys going off at eight minutes had joined the two remaining. It was only twenty miles into the race and the group was ever-changing. Some riders with lesser handicaps had also passed us.

Going out, at one of the road intersections where people gave out water, I saw some of the Andrew Street Mob girls. They waved; I waved back, but did not slow down for water. The pace had remained vigorous since the start of the race. It was still too early to consider the question of going out too fast or too slow. I did not feel any strain. As we approached the halfway turn, there were already riders on the side of the road, either finished for the day or making repairs. There were some 35 riders who had already made the turn. It seemed that during the race, the only important thing to consider was the number of riders ahead or behind. The group hit the turn and, sure enough, there was the proverbial wind in the face. The reality of competition finally hit home. This was a big race and someone would win out of all these groups. The time going out had been fast. It would be so nice just to double the time and end it like that. Now the riders had to face the wind and keep their heads down, give pace, go to the back, take draft, rest in the group and give pace again. I pushed away and felt fine, still no major strains; the bike was running great. I didn't need to rest my legs, so even on slight downhills, I just backed off the pressure to give my body a slightly different feeling.

Quite a few riders were dropping back and also taking water from the side of the road. I saw the Andrew Street Mob again. The girls were yelling, "Go man go!" One shouted that Zoni was up ahead. I kept pushing my legs, pulling on my arms, alternatively standing up. My group was gaining on the riders up front, and the 6-minute and 3-minute men had not caught our group. The wind had got stronger and no single rider or small group was trying to break away. The group I was in got bigger and bigger. We were riding two and three abreast and had passed the 50-mile mark. Zoni was in the group somewhere. Every now and again I remembered that the first one over the finish line would win that beautiful cup and keep it for a year; right in the middle of the dining room!

This unique feeling of being in a bunch of cyclists, not knowing who would win, but all working against time together, reminded me of a flock of birds flying, changing places, maneuvering, seemingly without purpose, then floating in the wind and flying against it, but always aware of position. Erratic riders, side-to-side wobblers, fast and slow instead of steady flow riders were avoided. They caused bumps and reactions. Being too close to the edge of the road or sitting in the middle seemed to me to be the worst. The riders all made their individual choices. I preferred the outside, away from the edge of the road, away from the middle. I would even take some wind before choosing to ride in the middle.

There must have been forty riders as we hit the 55-mile mark; there were 7.5 miles to go and the five miles of hills would start soon. A certain amount of jockeying took place. I noticed there were no riders on the hill. *Could this be the lead pack?* I decided it was and that to finish in the top ten would be magnificent. Wow!

The group hit the toe of the hill. After one mile, the group was down to thirty riders. The too fast . . . too slow going out question was being answered. I remembered the 100-yard uphill sprint races at the Easter Show Grounds. Two riders were battling all the way. One fell behind. The other rider, in the lead most of the way, collapsed at 95 yards and the trailing rider won. So it was all in this hill, each succeeding 100 yards of the hill taking its toll of riders. I continued to feel strong without any tiring! I had an amazing feeling of strength and power as I inched past riders on the hill. More and more power seemed to be available, but I still had a cautious feeling that the hill could consume the energy available in my body at any time. I was pretty much standing, head down, looking at my front wheel and the relative bikes on the side and in front. There was deep concentration on position and speed. I thought again about those 100-yard up-hill sprint races where you never knew whether to go out fast or slow. Where many riders collapsed ten yards from the finish, and where some went over the line so slowly you could walk faster . . . that was truly a mind over energy race. So was this one. I kept pumping, feeling good. I could see the crest and I was with five riders who had outlasted all the riders at the bottom of the hill. Where were the Scratch men? I looked back at the long line of riders. Bad idea or not, I always wanted to know where I was. Riders were strung out over the five miles of this monster hill out of hell. There was no telling who was close behind. I felt I was in a very good position despite not knowing who was where. The crest was getting closer and it would be an easy ride from there, but very competitive. There was a flat, a downhill and slight uphill to the finish, two miles from this crest. *This race is almost over. We are down to seconds!* I thought. I knew, and so did all the other racers, that once a rider hit the crest, he was gone, and there would be very little chance of catching him. A feeling of being up in the front bunch was already an accomplishment.

The crest loomed closer, the riders were moving a little faster. I moved up closer to the front. We hit the crest . . . a 'wobble rider' took off in a jump and swayed too wide. The rider behind him swerved to avoid him, causing the rider in front of me to get hit and go down. My bike went over something and down I went. I jumped up quickly, straightened my handlebars in seconds and asked the downed rider, "Are you okay?"

"Yes! Man! . . . Ride! . . . I'm okay."

I jumped back on my bike, stood up, and perhaps for the first time in my life sprinted . . . sat . . . sprinted . . . sat . . . sprinted for the longest time. I was going to try and catch the leaders. I was truly mad as hell at that absolutely stupid bastard who caused the fall. The first four riders were gone and many others had passed me, maybe fifteen riders. I drove my body as hard as I possibly could. I didn't care now, how this ended, even if I collapsed before the end and had to eventually walk over the line. I rode like hell. I was just short of sprinting. I passed rider after rider. I had no idea where all the energy came from as I stood up, driving continuously, and only sat very occasionally for a few seconds. I passed riders with no compassion! I saw the finishing line and although it was still quite a distance I pumped furiously and sprinted. I kept passing riders even as I crossed the finish line. Then I heard the shouting and clapping and I realized I had out-sprinted a strong group of five riders to finish thirteenth. I continued to ride a half-mile or so and then turned back to the finish line.

"Damn that stupid rider . . . I had a chance to be in the first pack over the line . . . what's going on . . . where's my luck gone?" I said out loud. I rode on the side of the road to avoid riders finishing. *So ironic!* I thought. *I pushed so hard and I still have all this energy left. I knew my body couldn't go faster but my energy level never dropped. I could have been in that first pack. I would've stayed with them without a problem . . . Oh! Wow! What a feeling!*

"Dammit! Could've been there in front . . . I wasn't scared of any of those guys," I said to a friend.

"Where did you finish?"

"Thirteenth."

"That's great man, that's riding. What was your handicap?"

"Nine minutes."

"Good time, my friend. But you should go down to first aid, get some stuff for your arm and leg."

"Hey! Oh yeah! Thanks! See you!"

I hadn't realized I had scratches and burns all over my body. My arm was scraped all over the outside. My leg had been churned up on the road as well; there was a scrape on the calf and one on the thigh. My hands were saved because I wore gloves.

"I never even felt the pain or realized it was this bad," I told the nurse.

"How did you do?"

"Thirteenth, off nine minutes."

"Hey, that's pretty good. How old are you?"

"Seventeen."

"Wow! You will really do well in racing," she suggested. She finished the dressings. "Now don't forget to rest for a week, including training, before you race again."

"That's alright," I replied with a smile. "This is my last race . . . I've given it up."

"Given up what?" she asked.

"Cycle racing."

"Why? You're so young."

"I've been riding for four years," I replied. I felt as though my statement had formally made my decision.

"Oh! And so now you must give it up! You're too old! Or you're too good!"

"No! No! It's a very long story. Maybe if you're free one Saturday, I could tell you all about it?"

"Oh, that would be nice, but I have a boyfriend."

"Just my luck!" I smiled again. "He's lucky!"

"You stay racing, my friend that is such a good place to finish for an 'old man!' . . . Especially at your age!!" She smiled and slapped me on my good shoulder.

"Listen, thanks very much. You're very nice!" I said. I wanted to stay. But there were other riders waiting, "I really appreciate it . . . good luck."

"You too, Charl. Think about racing again, though . . . bye!"

"Bye!"

I went back into the crowd, got a drink, met up with my friends. The Andrew Street Mob had all got together against the fence and we were just all talking. How much I loved this, nobody would ever know! To sit and talk and laugh with my friends! It blanked out all our troubles. We discussed the abnormality of having the Andrew Street girls at a race. Why! They never got out of bed till noon on Sundays! We sat on the grass against the fence, this great bunch of teenagers walking through life with a supreme spirit of loving to be together. We were on a heavy, sad note right now as we counted the small number of cycle riders from the Andrew Street Mob. It was rapidly shrinking. Perhaps the cars were causing us to lose interest. I knew that my schooling, which was getting harder and harder, would take up all my time. A car would be years away. I could continue, but only if my friends did too. I felt relieved, happy and contented that I had made the decision, and it had come about naturally. I had probably ridden in about seventy races since I was fourteen. This was my last ride and it was a good ride and I was so very happy with it.

New things were going to come . . . that was for sure!

(Bobbie went to Helsinki and won a silver medal (cycling) in the Men's team pursuit (4000m) –South Africa did well in cycling at the 1952 Helsinki Olympics)

＊

CHAPTER 7

Augustness

(An interpretation of been marked by majestic dignity)

'ROSETTENVILLE CORNER' WAS AN intersection of main arterial roads and a major area for shopping in the Southern Suburbs. All busses to our area passed through the intersection, and on one corner a tramline terminated. The tram would take you along the racetrack to Turffontein. Flanking 'The Corner' were many small shops, theaters, restaurants, and the Broadway Hotel. During the day it was always a bustling center of shopping activity, but at night a transformation evolved and it became an area for adult entertainment, and a meeting place for local young people. The bars were crowded, the famous Broadway Hotel was always busy, and the restaurants and both theaters, the Grand and the Adelphi, invariably had customers.

The young crowd was noisy and generated a vibrant atmosphere. Occasionally, hostility broke out and ended in a street fight. This was not a place for conservative people! The fights were generally confined to a certain area and passers-by were never molested. The fights were along the lines of the settlement of a personal dispute, easily decided by an all-out physical lunge, arms, head, fists, head and the boot . . . a challenge settled by 'using one's self' to coin a local phrase. The participants ignored the audience's opinions, unless onlookers cared to get into the argument in a physical way. The Broadway Hotel had a bar on street level; the location may or may not have been responsible for the start of many of the disagreements. However, it was obvious that the scuffles tended to occur nearby. The local inhabitants knew this, and only men entered the bar's noisy atmosphere. Taking your lady in there was not done. Just one floor up in the hotel was a lounge where the ladies could be entertained without problems. So, avoiding certain small areas, passage was peaceful and most things were available at 'The Corner.'

If you grew up in the neighborhood you did not need a textbook to explain these things; everyone knew. If you wished to entertain a nice lady or friend in a special way, you would preferably go into Johannesburg City Center, which had theaters, stage plays, dance plac-es, night clubs, restaurants, and very modern hotels. If cosmopolitan surroundings were to your taste, you could find the varied background atmospheres of Europe, the Middle East, and America in Hillbrow, a close-by suburb of downtown Johannesburg.

Year after year, Friday was typically 'boys night'; Saturday was re-served for ladies or for parties, and Sundays for swimming. There was no reason to change this cycle. Young people were subject to minute economics, so Friday could be tailored to suit your pocket, Saturday was a 'big spend' night, and this left Sunday as the physical exercise and fun sports day that fell into the small money category. Friday was often spent in the vicinity of Rosettenville Corner, Saturday wherever plans took you and Sunday on the grass near water. Parties were preferred over everything else at any time.

The Southern Suburbs was also undergoing a modern reformation. Once a typical blue-collar community with a steady work ethic and 'knowing one's place in life', it was changing into a mixture of things. There were many influences in the changing of this society. One of them was 'kids tired of toeing the line to absolutely everything'. Some parents blamed it on the American movie influence and the American music. It was true many of my friends preferred the American way to that of the English and also to that of the South African Pioneers. The everyday life was good. But the images from gangster movies, the jazz music, and the seemingly unlimited amounts of money that Americans had to spend, was unsettling. The comparison of wages and jobs was very humbling. The same qualification in America gave you so much more in life. The simple fact that not everyone who was working could afford a car in the Southern Suburbs, meant that our standard of living was lower. Nightclub scenes in the movies were a wonderful image to us. Big bands, beautiful singers, cigarette girls, extravagant dresses, and men in elegant suits were everybody's dream. We loved the movies! We imitated different actors in our dress as much as possible, in our South African way. Kids dreamed the experience. We couldn't explain this to our parents.

Zoni had gone through the 'Zoot Suit' phase, a little later than in America, but he played the part. He dressed in the wide shoulders shouldered, and multi-colored outfits. The rest of the crowd chose a more straightforward look. Top of the line and tremendously popular was the 'In Look.' It was based on charcoal gray and pink. The suit was charcoal gray, the shirt pink, with black shoes and pink socks, completed by a white tie. Nobody was sure if it came from America. Some of the styles and talk were derivatives of the American way. The dances were based on teenage styles. Local bands in the Southern Suburbs started up and died. Johannesburg City had the hold grip on that sphere of activities but it was very expensive. So, parties with records, and dances in local halls with bands interpreting American music, had to satisfy the Saturday night needs of the Andrew Street Mob.

There were many different crowds in the Southern Suburbs and they held parties within their own groups, much like the Andrew Street Mob. Most kids got to know each other through activities such as cycling, soccer, cricket, rugby, tennis, weight lifting, motorcycles, swimming, and ice-skating. These being the major sports activities in the Southern Suburbs. The integration of kids of their own age throughout the Southern Suburbs was inevitable. There were also a few excursions to other suburbs of Johannesburg and other cities.

Rosettenville Corner was the favorite place to meet. Adventure abounded at this busy intersection. There was the meeting of friends plus the chance of seeing acquaintances, people you didn't see very often. A dynamic, small-hometown atmosphere existed at this intersection. "What happened on the Corner last night?" was a typical question.

◆

I had met different people through my activities. There was the soccer team, friends at work, acquaintances at college, and my cycling friends. My closest friends were in the Andrew Street Mob but I also had friends from other social groups. I considered myself very lucky. Having previously met Bobby, Tom, Abie and Mickey (I called them 'Bobby's Group') at a party, we had decided the next good place to go was a Saturday dance being held at the Glenesk Hall, which was close to Rosettenville Corner. We met for a drink at 'The Corner' first, had a beer and talked about the latest, latest. After an hour, we decided to leave, jumped in Bobby's car (really his mother's car) and off we went.

Arriving at Glenesk Hall, we parked the car and approached the double doors, which were closed. Suddenly the doors opened with a loud crashing sound. Two boys were backing out fast as two gunshots went off. Bobby, Tom, Mickey, Abie and I scattered to the side of the hall and dived into the bushes. The two boys turned and ran. Three other boys, followed by another ten, came running out to pursue the two.

"Get out of here . . . you bloody bastards!" A car drove off.

The four of us slowly emerged from the bushes. People had decided to leave the dance and were filtering out of the hall.

"Whew, that was close," said Mickey.

"Yeah, they might have thought we were with the two guys," said Abie.

"Time for a drink," said Bobby.

"In here?" asked Abie.

"No way!" said Bobby. "Let's go."

We ended up back at the Broadway Hotel.

'The Vee Gang' was prominent where I grew up. What they did and where they went was never in the papers. Kids of the Southern Suburbs knew the stories. There were similar gangs in other suburbs. One Saturday when I went over to see my sister and her family in Kensington on the East Rand, I mentioned the event at the Glenesk Hall to my brother-in-law, James. He then related a similar story about a Jeppe Gang, very prominent where he had grown up in Johannesburg. He told me how that gang terrorized their dances many times. One night the dancers planned an ambush. When the gang turned up, they let them into the dance hall, then locked the doors, beat them up with baseball bats, and then threw them out: their dances were never gate-crashed again. To me, all this stuff did not seem to be a normal way of life; it was too risky. You'd eventually get beaten up, no matter how many fights you won. I guess I couldn't see the fun in it either. It was hard enough trying to make a few pennies and learn something without ending up in jail. I couldn't understand why guys would take the risk of ending up in those lousy conditions of filth and dirt. We had heard how badly you were treated in these places. I didn't like the power that the authorities had over you in jail. I know I wouldn't be able to take it. I had told this to all my friends and confirmed that I didn't want to do this kind of stuff and end up in jail. They all agreed!

Many of my friends were working now. Some, such as Johnny, Trevor, and myself, were attending downtown colleges part time. None of my friends went to the prestigious University of the Witwatersrand, in Johannesburg. Doc was working in the mines and Johnny was working with his brother in their father's business of construction equipment rental. Billy, Tommy and I were machinist apprentices, Zoni was a refrigeration mechanic apprentice, Juni an electrical apprentice, Trevor a salesman, and Pat and Guy were electrical apprentices. All the girls were working in offices in Johannesburg. Bobby was a mechanic, Mickey and Tom in construction and Abie working at odd jobs while boxing professionally. We chose what we liked because it didn't matter what type of job you did, the pay was pretty much the same at our age. The wages were pitiful, copied from the British and European systems, whereby the gap between owner/boss and worker was enormous. It seemed someone had worked out what seventeen-year-olds should earn, no matter what they did. Very few young people could afford to live alone. I didn't know anybody who did. We all lived with our parents, and those who didn't, boarded with families. The only way someone had the use of a car was if there was help from their family, or if they were allowed to use their parents' car. Very few parents of our crowd had cars. The situation was improving though, with some cars coming into the crowd. We hated buses. The real need for a car arose when going on a date. It was almost impossible to get a date without a car. Girls that would catch a bus to a dance were few and far between. Living in an apartment alone was, for this crowd, an economic impossibility. The usual was to live at home with your family, own a car or ride with your friends if you could. All the politics of the country, black vs. white, English vs. Afrikaans and all the apartheid rules that were the concern of the adults in our life, were not as significant to us as trying to etch out a living and a lifestyle different to that of our parents. It was simple! Our fathers, mothers and grandparents had worked very hard, every day of their lives, and did not even have a car to drive. The raising of large families, the Depression, and World War II bound their lives. Some of us, including myself, were looking more towards the American Style of life in preference to that of the European or traditional South African way. We were in some ways forsaking our parents' traditional South African way of life. We were intent on improving our living conditions and opportunities. It was not clear at all how we might do it, but we were determined, and it was exciting trying to get wherever we were going! It was a favorite subject in the Andrew Street Mob and the dreams were sometimes profound.

The Andrew Street Mob was growing up fast, learning something everyday. We were all in long pants and pretty dresses. We were all extremely fit looking as none of us were overweight. Being well tanned added to the picture. We were also extremely active in all directions and therefore our minds were alive. All the girls were blossoming into young ladies. None of them were in the large category and so they looked great in shorts and blouses and outstanding in evening dress. It was not hard to create a dream sequence

◆

The Adelphi Theatre was a major place of entertainment to the people of the Southern Suburbs, as well as the racetrack, and the ice rink. The Grand Theatre continued to be considered a fleabag. Only the combination of a very good movie at the Grand and a truly bad movie at the Adelphi would get the young crowd to go to the Grand Theatre. At one time the Adelphi had been the great favorite on Wednesday and Saturday afternoons, because all the kids from school would go to the matinee. The interest in girls developed slowly over the years, and boys started sitting next to girls. The advance of the boy's arm to the back of the girl's seat and then onto her shoulder was only accomplished after many, many months of trying, training, and discussion. It had always been the hot topic of the week. To miss a matinee had almost meant death to the week's fun.

Now that everyone was working, the matinees were a forgotten item. Friday night was the fun time of the week for being with the boys. So Johnny, Trevor, Doc, Zoni, Pat, Juni, Billy, Norman, Tommy and I, and many other combinations, would head out Friday night to The Corner, have a beer, meet other friends or acquaintances and go to a movie. Sometimes we would have a beer afterwards or head home. If we had a borrowed or begged car, and many times it was a half-ton truck, and had met some girls, we would end up at the drive-in at the Olympia Ice Rink. This was where the greatest pepper-steak sandwiches and milkshakes were served. You could add fries if you were really hungry. The half-ton truck was equipped with blankets, behind the back of the seat, which could be spread in the back of the truck. This would protect the girls' clothes from the ever-present construction dust.

One night when nothing was good, no truck, no good movie, the crowd went to the Adelphi and walked out with the same feeling that they had walked in— dullness. Tommy remarked that the gates to the houses on Prairie Street were all the same, and put up the same way. So everyone took a look. Sure enough, five to six houses in a row had the same basic iron gates, the same simple hinges consisting of a pin and hole. Although the gate was heavy, it just needed to be lifted in order to be removed. The gates all looked the same size. So Tommy and I picked up one side of a gate, and Zoni and Doc the other. We removed the gate and moved it to another house. Then we lifted that gate up and put it on the hinges of the gate we had removed. The gates were different colors and different designs.

Very quietly and efficiently we swapped six gates. At least one person was a lookout for people in the street, cars going by, and lights in the windows.

"That's quite a feat," said Tommy.

"Yes," said Billy. "Damn good job, chaps!"

"What do you think they're going to say when they come out of their houses?"

"'They've stolen our gate!'"

"'No, there it is on that house!'"

"'Bastards!'"

"'Who did this?'"

"'Those damn kids that go to the Adelphi!'"

The suggestions multiplied. Now everyone felt like we had done something to add to the beauty of the land, and we laughed. This event had definitely brightened up the dull evening.

One beautiful Friday night in summer, after the week's work and study, the Andrew Street boys cleaned up, got dressed in nice clothes, and gathered outside Zoni's house. As Andrew Street was about a mile from Rosettenville Corner, the decision whether or not to ride by car was usually made on the basis of whether that particular Friday had the potential for a party, or the chance to encounter ladies. Believing that neither of these things would happen, we decided to walk. It was about 6:30 PM. There were ten of us, all young men, talking and laughing. There were usually about 14 of us in the crowd, but tonight was a 'thin' night. Perhaps the others would join us later. As we walked, a discussion ensued about the party on Saturday.

"Who's throwing the party?"

"Ann and Grace."

"What about Beryl?"

"Yeah, I guess her as well."

"Who's coming?"

"The same old crowd."

"Yeah."

"Well, except some new guy."

"A new guy. You know him. Yeah! He's bringing some girls from Krugersdorp."

"Good, we need some fresh meat."

"Meat?"

"Yeah, meat."

"What's wrong with our girls?"

"We like 'em too much."

"Oh you mean they won't go."

"Well, yes and no."

"What do you mean?"

"Well, those who do, won't tell, those who don't, don't give a hell. Ha!"

"Funny."

"He's right, maybe?"

"We need some ladies that move."

"Yes, man! We need some to move!"

"Why don't we go to Braamfontein next Friday?"

"Yes! Such a good idea from such a young fellow."

"No man, the girls might go, because they would think we were great. But the boys over there don't like strangers."

"They don't let strangers mix with their girls, is what you mean?"

"That's right."

"Didn't Charl have a girlfriend over there?"

"No."

"Oh yes, he did!"

"Her name was . . . I can't remember."

"She was part of the Braamie Gang."

"Is that what they call them?"

"No, that's what I call them."

"Well rather you than me."

"Let's get some Braamfontein girls to come to the party tomorrow."

"Yeah, man, that's an idea."

"What if the boys follow?"

"They won't know."

"Huh! You believe in fairy tales? Better believe it, you tell one, and they'll all know."

"No, what we'll do is get the girls to come over to Johannesburg City and meet us there . . . like at the Carlton Hotel. Then we'll pick 'em up and bring 'em here."

"The Carlton Hotel, you're kidding."

"They'll look like a bunch of pro's next to all those people dressed up."

"Might be fun."

"Wait! What'll Ann and the girls think?"

"Be interesting."

"No. It's not worth the chance."

"Do you really think the girls think that we are just so neat and clean?"

"Neat . . . and . . . clean? What the hell is that?"

"Well you know what I mean."

"No. Not neat and clean."

"Let's say . . . I mean we're not aggressive."

"Okay! But that doesn't mean you're neat and clean!"

"Maybe if they do think what we want them to think, this will change their minds and they'll help us out when we need it most. Ha!"

"Why do you always laugh when you say something stupid?"

"I think it's funny!"

"It's not. It's stupid!"

"Yes, I also think it's stupid to put Braamfontein in the Southern Suburbs."

"Aren't there nice girls in Braamfontein?"

"Yes, but we haven't found them. Ha ha ha!"

"Oh! Shut! Up!"

"Don't get upset now."

The ideas were doomed to failure before they started. Our group so wanted to spark up the parties. They were a lot of fun, but they were always the same: nice parties, nice people. We continued walking, now with haphazard discussion, then when we reached Rosettenville Corner, without vote or discussion, we filed one by one into the Broadway Hotel street bar.

"Hullo! How goes it? Castle lager . . . Lion beer . . . Three Lions . . . Old Brown sherry."

"Wait a minute, who said that?"

No one replied. It was the cheapest drink you could buy. The rumors were that farmers ran their tractors on it. "It's good for any diesel engine with over 100,000 miles," one man had told us. "So good that the engine has twice the power as it gets older. Can't use it on a new one; too much power in the sherry, the engine will seize. Have to have some wear and tear, some gap between the piston and cylinder to allow the engine to do what sherry does to a man."

"What's that?"

"Burp!"

"Oh God! We've got to move into another social circle," said somebody. The looks on the faces and body movements of those close-by confirmed the statement.

The Andrew Street Mob met other friends and, as the beers went down, we talked about many things, including soccer, fun times, what was happening to everyone, and of course, our favorite subject: ladies. Who was cute, who was going with whom, who'd like to go with whom, what one had to do, to go with whom, and why the hell she was going with whom, when she was so cute: never an uninteresting topic.

At 7:35 we dumped the rest of the beer down our gullets and shuffled out to the Adelphi Theatre, which was three short blocks from Rosettenville Corner. We had picked up some friends from the corner, and the now fourteen-man discussions were filled with less serious subjects than that of ladies. Perhaps due to the beer, the nonsensical discussions on meaningless topics had started in the bar, and helped produce a lot more laughter because of the challenge of coming up with crazy, inane ideas.

"Who bit off the tortoise's head?" someone asked.

"I don't know," said another. "Who did?"

"What a dumb question."

"No, it's not dumb."

"The answer is the elephant."

"The elephant! That's impossible. He can't get his mouth down that low."

"He doesn't have to. In Rhodesia, tortoises live in trees."

"Bullshit!"

"I've never seen a tortoise in a tree."

"You must be a city boy."

"That may be, but I'm not stupid. Their feet are too short to wrap around a tree trunk, so how can they climb trees?"

"Nah! They don't climb trees, you see."

"How do tortoises get up in the trees then?"

"Well, eagles love tortoise eggs and pick 'em up and hide 'em in the trees . . . cause, if they fly them up to the mountain and put them there . . . other eagles will get the eggs."

"So, now . . . you're telling us . . . that the eggs stay in the trees?"

"Oh, for years, and the tortoises grow, don't fall off the trees, and can't climb down because of their short legs, and so the elephants come along and eat them."

"Jeez! I don't know if I can stand it."

"Okay, so the elephants come to eat them, but they have to wait for them to stick their heads out of their shells."

"Yeah, I know that."

"Well, how does the elephant bite the tortoise's head? What does he do with his trunk while he's biting the tortoise?"

"Oh! Elephants can eat two things at once. He's ripping off leaves from higher branches . . . the tortoises think something is going on . . . they stick . . ."

"THEIR HEADS OUT . . ." said a few of the group in harmony.

"Yes! So the elephant ends up rattling the leaves and . . . chewing on the tortoise's head. Don't you city-dwellers know anything?"

"No! It's a fact. Tortoise heads are a delicacy to elephants."

"Okay! Now we know! They do it in Rhodesia. That's enough!"

We went to the end of the line for theater tickets, which was about thirty feet from the ticket booth. Everyone was still laughing about older elephants without teeth or with false teeth that couldn't eat tortoise heads. We slowly settled into line, obviously with loud conversation, an occasional yip and yell, and some whispering and laughing—just generally having a good time. Then, fairly abruptly, there was silence in the line. We noticed the rest of the people looking across the street.

The night was clear and warm and the start of a new film had attracted many people to the Adelphi Theatre. The ticket booth, located at the front of the theater, was some 20 feet back off the street. For some strange reason, it was also located on the tip of a corner and connected to the theater only by a roof. So everybody walked between the booth and the theater when going around the corner. The theater building took up the rest of the block. The doors opened at 8 o'clock and the people waiting to buy tickets were now lined up at 150 feet back from the ticket booth to the side of the theater in a long line; there were perhaps 300 people. The theater had about 800 seats.

It was ten minutes to eight and a beautiful, black, antique convertible, top down, was slowly cruising up the street. The driver put out his arm and waved his white-gloved hand. The convertible made a U-turn and then came back down the road alongside the ticket line towards the ticket booth. The car was from Benoni, a small town 20 miles east of Johannesburg. You could tell by the license plate. In the back of the car was a man, sitting firmly erect, distinguished-looking with a neatly cut mustache. He was in the center of the back seat with a man on each side of him. In the front seat of the car, another three men sat abreast, somewhat crowded for space. From what we could see, all six were dressed in black pants, black shirts, black sweaters, and black gangster-like hats. As they came by close to the curb, we could see they were all in their early twenties.

The car stopped in front of the theater, with the back door in line with the ticket booth. Immediately, the two passengers in the front of the car stood up, their heads way above the windshield, got out, and went to the trunk. They opened the lid, removed a large, long object wrapped in paper, and shuffled onto the sidewalk with it. Then they made a gesture to the car and waited. The two men on either side of the distinguished gentleman in the back stood up, got out of the car, and went to stand on either side of the rear door nearest the ticket booth. As they reached what seemed to be a predetermined spot, they stiffened to an upright position and faced each other.

The two with the large object raised it and moved towards the rear car door. The paper was quickly removed and a large roll appeared. This was placed at the rear curbside door. The two men began to open up the roll in the direction of the ticket booth. Everyone in the ticket line alongside the theater had become very quiet, entirely absorbed in what was happening. In fact, the lady in the ticket booth had stopped preparing the cash for the register and had assumed a frozen position with her mouth wide open. We were astonished at our own silence; nearly all the giggles and chatter had subsided. As the roll opened, it showed redness, a bright redness.

It was a red carpet!

While the carpet was slowly unrolled, nothing moved, including the mysterious figure in the back seat of the car. His stoic appearance caused the audience that now surrounded these smoothly operating

men to flip their eyes continuously from the carpet to the solitary fig-
ure and back: still no movement. These men were impeccably dressed.
The beautiful shiny black automobile, open topped, looked like a 1929
Chrysler Tourer with whitewalls . . . all the essence of the American
Prohibition Days.

The carpet, now completely unfurled, had reached the box office.
People in the line moved back. The two men rolling the carpet suddenly stood erect. Click, click, of the heels of their shoes, two quick
moves and they faced each other from either side of the carpet; the
ticket window was between them. The movements of the men had
caused the patrons and spectators to shuffle even further backwards,
to see what was happening. In sequence, the two men at the rear door
of the car stiffened and clicked their heels. There was still no utterance
or movement from the distinguished man. The ranks of the crowd,
silenced by suspicion, had grown. They all shuffled forward again, no
one losing his position in the line. The four men on the carpet clicked
their heels again. The driver, ensuring all four carpet persons were in
position, moved from his seat, stepped onto the sidewalk, went around
the front of the car, moving the crowd, and proceeded to the rear door.
With gloved hands and great elegance, he opened the small door.

Silence.

The crowd waited. It was almost 8 o'clock.

The man in the back seat moved forward, very slowly, very smoothly, and with great precision, like the slow uncoiling of a large snake. He
raised himself and stood erect in the back of the car, facing forward.
Totally ignoring the crowd, he turned and moved towards the door.

It seemed as though it took a million horsepower to move his body.
Slowly, he stepped down from the car onto the red carpet. As his toe
touched the red, five pairs of heels clicked. He paused, and then walked
down the carpet, still oblivious to the crowd. His stride on the carpet
was much like that of an elegant connoisseur of the arts, who, at his
third attendance at a function of royalty, showed all the necessary experience to comport himself correctly. Not one sound came from the
crowd. We shuffled for a better view as he strode down the carpet to
the ticket booth. Expectation raised the atmosphere to a great height
of intensity. He reached the ticket booth, and again, five pairs of heels
clicked. He stared straight at the cashier, who had absolutely no idea
of what was happening. She prepared herself to speak. Her mouth was
closed, but her throat was jumping and her hands were shaking a little.

She tried to clear her throat. The crowd, still not sure of the plot, was tense. They pushed forward to witness the act, find out what was happening, and understand this live play at Rosettenville Corner. Was it a play put on by the theater as a gimmick? Maybe!

The mysterious person with gloved hands gave the cashier a stack of money. "I'll take all the remaining seats for tonight's showing."

"Yes, Sir! No Sir! You can't! I mean all these people..."

"All the seats! Madam! Now!"

"I don't know how much that is."

"Less than five hundred. You can have the rest! It's all there."

She counted the money. The news came down the line. "They've bought all the tickets."

"They can't!"

"Yeah! They're not first in line!"

"What the hell is going on?"

As the argument continued, the tickets were taken. The stoic figure transformed into a smooth, fast walker. He and his five men moved very rapidly back to the car and within seconds were driving away. The red carpet was left on the curb; the crowd was frozen with amazement.

"Where's the manager?"

Some of the crowd ran after the car, but the surprise exit had been too fast. The manager came out. He tried to get an explanation, but everybody was yelling. He said he could do nothing. People were getting mad, and started pushing and yelling. Some were really furious.

"This is outrageous."

"Not coming here again."

The ticket lady was a deep tomato red. The manager was flustered, cheeks turning the same color as the ticket lady, and unable to do anything with the people, who were full of questions and threatening to do his body some damage.

"Who are they?"

"Why don't we call the police?"

"For what?"

Someone in our mob suggested going to the Grand Theatre.

"That dump?"

"No thanks."

"Let's go back to the bar."

"Let's go into the city."

"No car."

"Yes! No car! Typical! We need a car! We don't have one!" coming out of many mouths.

"To the bar then."

"No, think of something else."

Fourteen of us stood on the corner. We questioned who the guys from Benoni were.

"Damn funny!"

"Yes, no doubt!"

"Let's go get the cars and go to the Olympia Roadhouse. Maybe some ladies there."

"No ladies, just men and ladies. Ladies don't get to go to the Roadhouse without men. The ones we know don't have cars."

"Does anyone know a girl with a car?"

"Yeah! But she's ugly!"

"So?"

Although we had become lethargic about the happenings, a number of people were peeved. They showed it by waving arms and talking very loud. The theater manager couldn't get back into his office. People just stood around him. He had turned down all sorts of suggestions, bar the ones that implied he do nothing.

"They had no right."

"It's unfair."

"Hooligans . . . gangsters! Where the hell did they get the money?"

"That's the problem with the Southern Suburbs and Rosettenville Corner. This place should be cleaned up. Get rid of these people," said one old lady.

So we educated her. "They were from Benoni."

"Really? . . . Oh!"

Some of us thought the whole thing was pretty sneaky. Trevor wondered why they had left the engine running all the time.

It was now 8:10 PM.

"Look over at the traffic light," yelled one of the belligerent men at the top of his voice. "There they are! . . . At the traffic light!"

Our group turned around and was astonished at what we saw. Thoughts streamed through our heads.

"Why come back? . . . Dumb! . . . Why is everything dumb tonight? What are these crazy people doing in this car?"

The people who had come to the theater were now standing all over the sidewalk in front of the theater, and some in the street. Those who had crossed the street froze after hearing the shout. They, too, looked down the street.

The nearest traffic light was a block away, but it was clearly visible from the theater. The big touring convertible was coming towards the theater, straight for the ticket office, it seemed. People, unsure of the situation, backed off. It was not clear now whether violence would prevail or not. There were some angry people in the crowd, who probably didn't care about what they did. There were some that didn't want to get hurt. These men in the car could maybe do something worse than buy all the tickets. The brave and belligerent men stood close to the curb. The meek people stood closer to the wall of the theater.

"Wow!" said someone, "this is fun."

Our Andrew Street Mob had been to the Corner too many times, not to know that you stay clear of crazy things. You don't go up front. Wait and see! A second and third group was strengthening the men on the curb. They were ready and mad.

"Dumb!" said one of our fourteen. "Dumb as can be! Everything is dumb tonight."

"Okay, we've heard that!"

The car came into plain view. The driver and the four assistants were seated, but the man who had walked down the carpet was standing up. The car was moving slowly, at approximately the speed of a running man. It continued in its direct path to the ticket office.

"Get them," yelled someone in the crowd.

"Wait," said another.

"No! Get them. We'll beat the hell out of 'em," said the first man, only louder.

"Wait and see what they're up to!"

"Don't be dumb!"

"Shut up!"

The crowd from over the road had stepped off the curb. The crowd at the theater stepped into the road. The path for the car was getting smaller. But still, the black car kept coming toward the theater.

The tall, erect, distinguished figure was still looking straight ahead like a dignitary in a parade. The car was getting closer. The crowd shuffled. What was going to happen? It seemed like a dream . . . a nonsensical mirage. The man in the back seat, still standing, raised his hand and leaned backwards, almost into a crouch position. Suddenly his body was twisting, his arm coming around like a discus thrower, and out of his hand came all this paper! Up into the night sky it floated and down it came, like confetti at a wedding, falling all over the street and sidewalks.

"It's the tickets!" shouted a bystander.

The men on the curb dived to pick some up . . . to make sure.

"It is . . . the tickets!"

"God dammit! It's the tickets!"

The black touring convertible changed direction and slowly disappeared into the night. Everybody from everywhere scrambled, fought, fell over, bumped, slipped and grabbed at the tickets. They hardly noticed the sign on the back of the car: 'MERRY XMAS FROM THE TOWN OF BENONI!'

Yup! It was late December.

The residents of Southern Suburbs have yet to find out who the black-clad purveyors of benevolence were.

*

CHAPTER 8

Potchefstroom

TURNING EIGHTEEN WAS A great feeling. Being seventeen had been difficult. It seemed more like a transition from sixteen-to-eighteen than a definite year of life. Legal drinking came with this new age. By some teenage convention, drinking was considered acceptable when you started work, which was usually at sixteen. Full-time school was not enough qualification to drink.

Eighteen was also a scary age because all teenagers knew about the Army system. The South African Government had a ballot system for recruiting armed services personnel (rookies) and training the youth to take part in the protection of the country. These political descriptions were used as propaganda to detract from the horrible thoughts conjured up by a teenager of going to a soldier training camp. They had a reputation of being run by hard-nosed adults, resembling police, with rules coming out of their ears, nose and throat. I knew if I was selected this was not going to be a Boy Scout camp. The worst was the total interruption of my schooling and work. I was well into college subjects by now and engineering design was so very interesting. It consumed my mind and I knew I had a flair for thinking up new approaches and concepts for projects. Industrial Systems was my favorite subject. I just hated the thought that the Army would cause me to stop or delay my progress significantly.

There was no conscription system in place. Names of those turning eighteen years of age were placed in a ballot system and the unfortunates were supposedly drawn on a random basis out of a hat. Those names that remained in the hat were free of service training forever, unless a war broke out. Those whose names were pulled were required to spend four years in whatever service they were assigned to. The program included three months of basic training, and then two- to three-week camps every year for three years. In addition, and the most undesirable service requirement, was a once-a-month Saturday devoted to further training and lectures. It was very much like the American Reserve System. Exemptions from this duty for your country could be had through attending university full time, a hardship condition such as being the only man on a farm, and of course, the usual timeless attribute of 'who you knew'. Discussion of the Army service had come up many times at parties or wherever us eighteen-year-olds met. The whole process was deeply feared, because, it would interrupt everything a person did normally. Pat had gone through this for two years already and wasn't yet finished. Most of the Andrew Street Mob were lucky and didn't have to go.

Five friends of mine had decided that we had to go together to find out. Bobby, his brother Tom, Abie, Mickey, Dai and I caught the bus outside the Broadway Hotel and headed for the Armory in Johannesburg's downtown area. Bobby was good-looking with brown hair about the same height as me, just under six-feet. He was well built and had a wry sense of humor. Tom was quiet and unassuming, tall, blue-eyed and blond and extremely good-looking. Tom looked quiet and serious but was not. Abie was average size, strong-looking, extremely fit, sometimes serious but full of fun. Mickey was smaller than most of us, a Lebanese descendant, dark complexion and black hair, strong, good-looking face with a great smile. He was slightly stooped. He was always laughing and you missed him as soon as he left your presence. (Bobby's Group.) I had been out with them many times, to parties and clubs. Dai, not part of the group, was a quiet, studious type, always sincere in his pathway through life, and the least adventurous. He lived in Kennedy Street, and hung out only occasionally with us. He and I studied at the same college. He said he also had to find out, so I invited him to join us unfortunates. The names were published in a particular room, during particular times on a particular board, and each individual had to check the drawing of his name. Phone calls were not accepted.

The bus stopped and we jumped off, talking and arguing about directions until we arrived at the Army barracks. There was a line and it was obviously the right one. It was very long. Dai went first, followed by Bobby, Mickey, Abie, Tom and me. I typically preferred that position. The line was noisy with talking and laughter and generally relaxed until about twenty feet from the list. Then it became very silent as each young man moved forward at the rate of about one a minute.

The board was finally in view. It was large with glass-covered lists of names and a light directed towards the board. Dai reached the board, everyone was silent. He went down the alphabetical list to his surname. He looked again.

"I can't find my name," he exclaimed.

"Let's see!" said Bobby. He looked "Nope, you're not there."

"Great," said Dai. He could not help his happiness. It was short-lived as he realized our feelings of predicament. I did not want to find my name. It would be a disaster in my life. I would truly resent it. It would be a heavy, heavy load and no added money.

Bobby found his name and just said, "It's there!" He walked to the side where it was dark and said nothing else. Mickey didn't see his name and in his typical manner didn't say anything. He joined Bobby. Abie found his name. He looked twice. He was mad. He walked backward and forward. "Shit, this is screwing up my boxing!" Tom confirmed his name and quietly joined Bobby. My heart went crazy as I purposely started a lot higher on the list than I needed to. There it was, unmistakably forged in black and white. It was as though somebody knew everything about you, your full name and number, G91358, and your identification for four years. I could not speak. A million thoughts of how damn hard it was to work, go to college and have so little money to spend; now this would be a tremendous interference. Would it add two years to college or what? It was like someone had just thrown a heavily loaded sack on my back and it was going to take four years to get it off. It was like a jail sentence. I walked away. I could not speak. The six of us walked silently out of the grounds of the barracks. I felt as though we had just been given a sentence. We were all assigned to the 22nd South African Irish Regiment. We had no idea what the hell that meant!

"A beer?" suggested Tom.

"Shit, yes," was echoed three or four times.

"The nearest, sleaziest bar . . . let's go," said Abie.

The first round of beers hit the table. Two minutes later, the waitress was ordered, in military tones, to deliver the next round.

"To the future defense of our country!" toasted Tom sarcastically.

"Well, somebody has to improve the damn standards of our fighting and we're from the famous fighting Southern Suburbs and that is why we are chosen . . . Man!"

I stood up and raised my glass. "Catch the stupid train to Potchefstroom on January 2nd, 8:00 AM, leave all your girlfriends at home, come to the holiday capital of the world, get up at 6AM for three months, eat well, dress neatly, and parade and drill and listen to a stupid bunch of Government Idiots tell you how to fight!"

"Take it easy Charl! They're not all stupid," argued Dai.

"Come on Dai! Most of them are left over from the Second World War and couldn't find a job, so they rejoined for twenty years," I said angrily. "I'm trying to get through college at night. It screws up everything. Three months, how can I study? Pass the exams? My soccer, what happens? I'm trying to be in the top team or the reserves. Shit! . . . It's nothing but a complete balls-up!!"

"We've also got problems," said Tom. "We're programming our horses to go through the training for racing. Who'll supervise the grooming, walking and running of them every day? What is going to be lost, who's going to train them . . . we don't know now!"

Bobby's and Tom's parents had racehorses and all those off-the-track preparations were much a part of their lives.

"My father will kill me. He told me to scratch my name off the list," joined in Abie. Abie and his brother Evie were boxers entering the pro scene. Their father had taught them boxing since before they were six years of age. "Everything in life is hard man, and it all happens to me. I knew I'd be listed . . . sure as shit! . . . I'd be in there. I hate the Government. Who are we going to fight anyway?"

"Maybe the blacks," said a man at the bar.

"Nah!" we all replied. "We'll all be too old by then."

The old man (by our standards, that was anyone older than twenty-nine) interrupted our conversation for the second time. "Excuse me! I hear your obnoxious tones of being young and disgruntled by interference in you lives. But you young men have it good. I got called up to go to North Africa in the Second World War, and we got sent off within weeks without training. Then you know what happened?" He drank some beer. "We ended up helping the British in North Africa. Yeah! Under Montgomery, whom the British thought was a good General. We didn't! You don't have it bad. We went from place to place in North Africa." He squinted and looked slowly at each one of us. "Nothing but sand dune after sand dune. We were chasing the bloody sky and nobody ever knew who was telling us what to do and where to go. And! . . . We never found out till we read books on World War II . . . ten years later!"

"You became part of the British Army, Sir?" questioned Tom.

"That's right, the Eighth Army."

We were quiet for a while, for the first time since looking at the board. We considered the old man's words.

"Well, we'll get all the modern training! Now, I hear, we'll be trained for nuclear war," said Bobby with a smirk. We all laughed. The old man shook his head and raised his beer.

"Oh sure," I said, "learn to run fast as the blast wave travels, faster than speed of sound."

We all calmed down and bought the old man a beer. "I guess we owe you!"

The six of us listened to the older man. He had an interesting story as an eighteen-year-old in the North African desert, which was rough, dirty and got sand in everything. Then he went to Italy where they had fun between skirmishes as they freed village after village.

"People just were so happy to see us, they were so full of joy, and all the way from the tip of Italy's boot to the beautiful Italian Alps, that was the good part! . . . I miss them!" He added with moist eyes.

We left the bar. Dai had entered the conversation all night. Everyone silently thanked him for that. He sure was lucky. Mickey, on the other hand, didn't feel good about being left out of the draft; we were his best friends. He even said he would volunteer, to which everyone violently suggested he was crazy. There was no guarantee that any of us would be together through this mess.

◆

The train pulled out of Johannesburg station at 8 AM. We were dressed in shorts and short-sleeved shirts. Our destination was Potchefstroom and it would be a hot, dry town in the middle of summer. I had read the city was founded by the Pioneer (Voortrekker) leader Andries Potgieter in 1838, and later became the capital of a large area later split between the Transvaal and Free State. The first Afrikaans church north of the Vaal River was built in 1851. There was supposedly the remains of a fort, which was used in the First War of Independence. This didn't matter to us Johannesburg boys, we knew it was a religious town, probably dead at night, lots of farmers, mostly Afrikaans and worst of all, no girls to take out on a date. Johannesburg was predominantly English speaking, even though most people spoke both languages. As you traveled out of Johannesburg, the balance of language changed. Generally, farming communities spoke Afrikaans. There were English farmers as well but not many in Potchefstroom. The people of this town would be far removed from the emerging social life of the 'Fifties'. Big city life was not their style and vastly different to the country life of Potchefstroom and its surroundings.

"We have to get home on weekends," said Abie.

"No car," replied Bobby.

"We'll hitchhike."

"Then you'll have to speak Afrikaans in the car with some religious family. Answer their questions on what church you belong to. Are your parents members of the church? And do you go to church every Sunday? I hate all that stuff," said Tom.

"How about the train?"

"Too much money. Also, man! It takes three or four hours, man! It's a milk run!"

"Maybe we can get some of the 'Suburbs Boys' to come and get us. It's only about 80 miles to Jo'burg."

I sat looking out the window at this arid mass of land. I liked train traveling. I liked all traveling; it always had an excitement to it. But now I had a horrible feeling this nightmare would be thick with problems. How could I enjoy it? I had one up on my friends: I had experienced Vryburg and had loved it. I believed I could survive, so I made the decision: I would just get it done. I would get to understand what had to be done and move stealthily in the shadows of this miserable lifestyle! There was no other choice!

The train cars were open-carriage and there were some 300 eighteen-year-olds on this train; camaraderie formed immediately. The talking was intense, and the noise level high. The questions on what had to be done, where everyone would go and how it would be were all asked. The answers were probably two percent correct. The mood was not a happy one, but it was upbeat. This was the start of an adventure no one really would have subscribed to. Disgruntled young people tended to be physically active. Arguments took place on varied subjects. The train was very, very hot inside. We all wondered why the hell it went at only 25 miles per hour. All windows were open. After two hours the train stopped and the open windows were jammed with heads of curious young men. There was nothing, absolutely nothing. All you could see were farmlands, arid land and very few trees surrounding the rail line. The train was stationary for a long time, about fifteen minutes. Some of the young men got off. Later almost everyone got off the train except the very timid souls. The first separation of man and boy had occurred. Bobby, Tommy, Abie and I dismounted and stretched out on the beige grass, twenty feet from the train. Some guy took a leak with various comments on the values of urine distribution on flat land.

Without warning a large dried lump of cow shit came flying through the air from somewhere close to the next carriage. Without any time lapse, three cow turds were returned. This continued for a while until the ground could yield no more turds. Besides the cow shit was on the other side of the fence. The distance to the train was getting close to the point of us not reaching the train if it pulled away. The shower of cow shit diminished. The train whistle blew. Every one scampered onto the train. We returned to our seats and settled down, wiping all the dust and cow dung from our clothes. The train moved on. About ten minutes later, the carriage door suddenly opened and two guys very sneakily threw two large turds into our carriage.

"Bastards!" yelled Bobby and Tom.

Four guys chased the two throwers, who scampered into another carriage and blocked the door. There was no way to get them.

"Remember their faces, man," yelled one of the guys.

"Won't forget," said another.

The cow shit toss changed the subject of Army to lots of other things.

Two hours later the train pulled into Potchefstroom. Trucks were waiting and the three hundred of us were taken into the camp and set off close to the parade ground. This location would be where our Army activities began each day. It would become a very familiar place. We just sat on the grass in various groups.

A voice came over a speaker. A sergeant stood on a small podium.

"Welcome to Potchefstroom. Stand up! You will now go to the barrack 'B' over there where you will be issued uniforms and be given your barrack number. You are free for the rest of the day and will re-port on this parade ground at 8:00 AM tomorrow morning, dressed in uniform. There will be an inspection and your boots must be clean and shining. The canteen is open between 1:00 and 2:00 PM and 5:00 and 7:00 PM. Go!"

"He's Afrikaans all right." Bobby suggested.

"They all are," replied Tom.

We filed through barrack 'B' and got Army clothes, boots, socks, caps, and a barrack number. Rifles were to be issued later.

"Are . . . we together?" I asked. Hoping and slurring the words, "I'm in Barrack H-8?"

"Yes," said Bobby.

"Yes," said Tom.

"Yes," said Abie.

"Thank God!"

We looked at the map and found the barrack. There were six beds, four against the windows, and two against the wall. We chose the window beds, threw our stuff down and sat on our beds.

"What now? Hope we don't get a couple of shitheads in our cabin," said Tom.

We all agreed. Then there was a noise.

Someone was coming up the stairs . . . staggering. A small guy, five foot two inches or something, thin, drawn face, heavy suntan and battling with his stuff. When he hit the top of the stairs he threw his Army bag on the floor.

"My name is Piet: Piet van der Merwe."

We shook his hand.

"I'm from Vereeniging."

"We're from the Southern Suburbs . . . Johannesburg," said Tom.

"How's it going man?" asked Abie.

"Can I take that bed?" Piet asked

"Yes!"

We all introduced ourselves. Not much else was said and a suggestion of hot tea got the five of us to head for the canteen to eat lunch.

Army routine began with rising at 5:30 AM, down to the showers located down a hill away from the barracks. Most guys went down in their shorts with a towel and toilet bag. It was January and the middle of summer, but it still could get cool. The water was never hot, never warm; all soldiers complained.

Following the shower we went back to our barracks, got dressed into khaki shirt, short pants, socks and brown boots. The boots were still hard and hurt when you walked. Everyone of authority said that once they were worn in, they'd be just fine, but it would take a long time. Someone suggested peeing in the boots, letting them soak overnight, and then washing them as a one-day process! Nobody ever claimed success from this method. The boot tips were ironed over a period of a week; a very hot iron and a 'spit and polish'. This eventually gave them that shiny, mirror-like finish.

"We finally have learnt something," I claimed.

With our dress almost complete, beds were made and blankets were stretched tight, ready for the famous coin drop. It should bounce if dropped from shoulder height. Barracks could be randomly inspected during the day while the soldiers were out.

The daily routine for the first month was: assembly at 7:30 AM, lectures to noon, lunch for an hour, and parade ground drills in the afternoon, at the hottest time of the day. The day ended at 4 PM. All this was followed by washing and ironing for the next day. Breakfast was from 6 to 7:30, lunch 12 to 1 PM, and dinner from 5 to 7 PM. Marching in the hot afternoon was very tiring, and we dragged our bodies around, but we got it done. To most of us it was just so damn boring. Nothing was interesting about the continuous repetition of moves by various sized groups of soldiers trying to succeed in perfect co-ordination, as defined by the Army.

"OH! YES!" We would hear shouted, followed by a softer tone, "We will get it right." Two expressions from the sergeant who never said very much, except, "Left turn—right turn—stay in line. Okay let's do it again, Hey!" The English words with the flat Afrikaans accent.

The first meal, the first early morning parade, the lecture and the afternoon drill experience showed us the uninteresting, mechanical, formal structure that the Army is not only known for, but hated for by a hundred percent of young soldiers. This routine was to continue for three weeks. Saturdays were spent washing and ironing, going to a movie on the base. Sunday we just mulled around. This routine went on for two weeks, and in the third week passes to go off base were granted. Accompanying the pass was the instructions of wearing a uniform. Civilian dress was not allowed. Caps off in restaurants, otherwise they had to be worn all the time.

At the end of the second week of training we badly needed to get off the base and we didn't care where. We had played enough cards. We had talked about everything and we needed some different air. Saturday night, Bobby, Abie, Tom, Piet and I left the camp and went by bus to downtown Potchefstroom. We had a restaurant in mind but when we got there it was full of soldiers. We moved onto other places, same story. Finally, we found a café that was broken down, but it served hamburgers, lasagne, spaghetti, and French fries. There weren't many soldiers in the place. We sat down at a wooden table with an oilcloth and water-stained knives and forks. I couldn't have cared less if we had to eat with our hands. This change was great. Abie exploded with his frustrations.

"This Army shit. I hate all this . . . no girls . . . everyone dressed up like police. There are rules every day, and rules every night. We've got to get to Johannesburg. Honestly man! I'm going to go crazy! This is the worst!"

We agreed! We were waiting for Abie to go through the roof, but as we were reluctant to get into the depressing subject, it died.

I got up and went to the jukebox. "Cherry Blossom and White . . . or something," said Abie.

"Cherry Pink and Apple Blossom White by Perez Prado," I corrected. I was surprised that Abie knew that song.

"Yes! . . . Great music!" said Abie.

"This place is not that bad," said Piet. "It's bigger than Vereeniging."

"Yeah, but Joh'burg's got it all," said Tom. "And, Abie you're right, we gotta get Piet to Joh'burg."

"I'd love to go to Joh'burg," said Piet. "I've never been there."

"I promise! We'll show you a good time," was my offer.

"Yeah," agreed Abie.

Bobby changed the subject. "The reason we see no girls is because they all belong to the Dutch Reformed Church and most of them speak Afrikaans. With that, my friends, there is not much chance of dancing and having some fun afterwards. Can you imagine the girl who picks up a soldier? Wow!"

"Bobby, you're generalizing like you always do. Let's go find a place to dance, or else turn off the juke box," said Tom, "it's frustrating!"

We couldn't turn it off. Anyway, no one would allow it. We sat and relaxed. There was nothing to do here, but that was okay. Finally we paid, got up and walked out of the restaurant and down the street. The places were packed with soldiers and crowded. Almost the second we were about to abandon the course and go back to camp, we saw a sleazy-looking bar with a neon sign. A big tough guy outside came into view.

"Let's go in," said Abie.

"We're behind you," Bobby agreed.

Bingo! We hit the jackpot: six women and only thirty guys. Some locals, but mostly rookies trying to re-create the fun they usually had in their home towns. The language was mixed Afrikaans and English. Not the best words in any of these languages, but very well understood. This was heaven, so we had a drink, then another, and another. We finally left as everyone decided that none of the six girls deserved 'our talent'. Therefore we would leave the girls to the lower and lousy-looking types of men, who had absolutely no idea of classy women!

It was seven miles to the camp from Potchefstroom town center. Buses had stopped a long time ago. So we walked and talked.

I liked this; we walked all over the roadway. Walking in a straight line was suddenly forbidden; that was work! We laughed as we walked and talked. The subject was the girls in the bar. How we would take them home with us and tell our parents that we were going to have a monstrous wedding with five guys and five girls from 'Potch!' Arguments arose as to which girl would marry which guy. Where we would get married was easy: the Broadway Hotel of course! Then we had to describe it to Piet. We would also have the honeymoon suite in the Carlton Hotel, the best hotel in downtown Johannesburg. Surprise the hell out of the clerk by demanding five beds side by side! We would call it "The Number One Potch Marriage."

Then we got serious! We just looked at each other with concern.

"We've got to get to Joh'burg next weekend. We can sneak out on Friday. Let's just pay someone to pick us up and bring us back," suggested Tom for the fortieth time.

"Does anyone know anyone?" asked Bobby.

"No," was the unanimous answer.

"What a waste of my body," moaned Abie. "Man! I could really go it."

"Are we going to church parade tomorrow?"

"No!"

"The group was definitely a little drunk . . . maybe more than a little, except for Piet. He looked as though he could hold his liquor. Nobody knew if Piet was religious or not. The group didn't know if he was attached to the Dutch Reformed Church. We had talked about him many times, and especially after he had gone to one of the church parades. We never found out either way, even with the most tempting statements, such as, "wonder why whenever someone drives into a small town the first thing they see is a steeple of a Dutch Reformed Church". So the group never asked and Piet never offered. Also, we were very, very interested in finding out if he was an Afrikaner who was deeply tied to traditions, or if he was just a good boetie (brother). This was important, as we might have a hard time if he was too conservative. The people of the Southern Suburbs of Johannesburg were moderate, and they mostly voted for General Smuts, the United Party that was in opposition to the (mostly Afrikaans) Nationalist party. There were lots of Afrikaans people in the Southern Suburbs, some of them conservative, but mostly they were more open-minded. In fact there were many mixed Afrikaans- and English-speaking people married, and within our families. Eventually, after discussing this topic numerous times, we finally said it out aloud to each other that we didn't care what the hell Piet was, and it didn't matter, because we really liked Piet. He had our respect; we were amazed at his fortitude. He was very small and thin, and didn't look 18 years old, but he was tough. We decided to give him a test we made up at the last moment, and because we had nothing to do!

Piet went out one night during the third week of camp. Bobby, Tom, Abie and I hooked ropes onto his bed and raised it to the ceiling with all his gear on top. Then we went to bed, put out the lights and waited for him to come back. While we lay on our beds pretending to sleep, the door finally opened. Piet came in, put the light on and, after the initial shock, very quickly noted his bed was in the air.

"Bastards!" he yelled.

Bobby asked, "What?"

Abie, with a smile on his face, asked, "What?"

Piet ran to the corner and grabbed his rifle. The rest of us sat up in our beds, calm as we knew there were no bullets. But we also knew that a rifle could be used like a cricket bat. So we grabbed our pillows for protection.

"You bastards!" yelled Piet. "Picking on me . . . Hey!" with a good strong Afrikaans accent on the last word.

With those words Piet fixed his bayonet in the rifle and ran towards Bobby, the bayonet horizontal to the ground, at stomach height.

"Don't be crazy!" yelled Bobby. He held the pillow at the same height as the bayonet.

Piet put the bayonet into the pillow with just a little effort.

"Okay Piet, we'll bring the bed down," we all yelled.

"Say you're sorry!" demanded Piet.

"No!" . . . "Well okay." . . . "We're sorry!" The four of us stammered inharmoniously as we restored Piet's bed to its right place along with everything else. This episode had settled a lot of things and increased our liking of Piet.

The long walk from downtown Potchefstroom finally came to an end; nobody had had anything to say during the last mile. As we walked up the steps and into the bungalow, and during the dropping of clothes on the floor and the climbing into bed, the conversation all centered on "never going to do that again."

"Think of Dai," I said.

"Why think of Dai?" asked Abie, who had for the past week mentioned this girl and that girl and how he missed them.

"Think of Dai having danced Saturday night away and hugging and kissing some girl in the back of a car." I suggested.

"Shut up Charl!" said Abie.

"Yeah! Shut up," said Bobby.

"Good night my friends," I added with a grin on my face.

Off went the lights.

◆

Our bungalow group was assigned to the artillery unit. The main objective was to train a crew to bring a twenty-five pound gun into action as fast as possible from a convoy position. This was usually done close to a hillside where tree cover could be found.

"This crew will definitely know how to bring the gun into action!" shouted the sergeant. The gun was usually towed by a covered truck, which carried men and a shell carrier. The training to ready the gun consisted of: driving along the parade ground, when, at a given signal, the tow vehicle would stop. The crew would scramble to unhook the gun, lower a platform on which the gun could rotate, pull the gun onto the platform, place a signaling device on the gun, rotate the gun into position, set the barrel at an elevation and load the breech with a shell. While this was being done, the tow vehicle was taken away and the shell carrier positioned behind the gun. The barrel was tilted to its final angle as the sight was aligned with some given object, such as a mirror in a tree or an antenna on a stationary truck, and the crew took their positions ready to fire. The whole operation had to be completed in two minutes. The crews practiced this on the parade ground starting from a standing position. Bobby was sight man, Tom in charge of shells, Abie and Piet the helpers and I was the acting bombardier in charge of the crew. Everyone had a number of tasks. A truck driver, Jacobus, was assigned to the crew from the Army's driver unit. The crew became very efficient and after many, many hours was one of the top gun crews. We actually had the parade drill down to one minute, thirty seconds. There would be a competition in the next two weeks. The end of this training would coincide with the big weekend in Johannesburg as the Army was granting a weekend pass. All the plans were in place. A friend of Bobby's would pick us up at 4:00 PM on the Friday.

The two weeks dragged, the nights were long and the days went by quickly. The vigorous training kept everyone running with thoughts only to complete all the operations fast and correctly, because then the instructor would leave us alone! The crew went through what seemed like hundreds of gun drills.

Friday at 4:00, the Army released its soldiers. At 5:05 PM everyone was in Bobby's friend's car as planned, talking about girls, parties and places to go. We agreed to go to a fair on Sunday morning in the northern suburbs of Johannesburg and then go to a party afterwards in the afternoon. We then had to catch one of the special busses to Potchefstroom at 8 o'clock on Sunday evening. Piet was coming too, and he was to stay with me on Friday, head for Vereeniging on Saturday and meet us at the bus on Sunday. Everyone drank beer in the car. It was amazing how we found the money and got the beer; the conversation was upbeat all the way. The Army was totally forgotten.

I took Piet home and introduced him to Gran, who was full of smiles to see me. Uncle Mick shook the hell out of my hand, and Mom gave me an unusually long hug. I wondered why they were so glad to see me; I had only been gone about five weeks. They made Piet feel at home and I was very pleased, because he was a friend to me and a complete stranger to them. Within the hour, Piet and I met with my other friends of the Andrew Street Mob and we went to the movies. It was total joy! I was in my home territory. The movies were up to date, the crowd was alive, and I saw a lot of acquaintances. We had beers at the Broadway Hotel afterwards 'til the bar closed! This was such a great thing to do, I thought, as the unusual, but very pleasant feelings of being home in my surroundings just made me feel good. The Army was such a waste of time and I hadn't read a technical book for months! I didn't like that at all!!

"Thanks," said Piet, as he left on Saturday morning.

"Fine," I replied, "Cheers boetie," I added as Piet headed for Vereeniging.

I spent Saturday with some of my Andrew Street friends: Billy, Johnny, Pat, and Trevor. The questions on the Army were few and I was glad. I was more interested in what I had missed. No major events had occurred and I got the feeling that my being away was not a major event either. Sunday morning I met Bobby, Tom and Abie and we went to the fair in the northern suburbs of Johannesburg. Walking around, we bought some beer and then headed for the party. *This has to be good,* I thought, the weekend had been relatively quiet, and somewhat of a letdown. There had been no party and it had gone too fast.

We reached our destination. I walked up the stairway in a block of flats in Rosebank. At the third floor we knocked on the door. Tom's friend Joseph and a girl, Alice, greeted us. In we went. There was one other girl in the kitchen. There was no music. I placed the beer on the counter and then put some in the refrigerator. *The fridge is empty,* I thought, *no food!* This was not good!

I decided to just drink beer until it was time to catch the bus. But the disappointment of 'no party' was strong. I wanted relief from my hatred of the Army, being placed under the bossy permanent force instructors, the useless training for war, when I already disliked the concept. I had never hated anything more. To me, Potchefstroom camp was miserable. I leaned against the kitchen counter and wondered how I could get out of this Army mess. Alice came into the kitchen, and interrupted my thoughts.

"Bring your beer and come inside. Everybody is in there, or maybe you'd like to see the view from the balcony," invited Alice.

"Yes, sure," I agreed. *Well, this is pleasant,* I thought.

We walked through the living room, and onto to the balcony. I noticed one other girl, Jackie, surrounded by all the boys. Alice and I talked on the balcony for some time. Alice explained she was working, living in the northern suburbs and generally having fun. I told her my story, in short, and refraining from explaining the frustration of the Army or my unhappiness with life in general at the moment. Alice was nice. This was sufficient reason not to kill her pleasantness, despite my disappointment in the small quiet party. She went back inside as a bunch of the crowd had decided to make some sandwiches in the kitchen.

I stayed on the balcony for some time then walked inside to the living room. Almost everyone was in the kitchen. As I brushed the curtain aside, I saw a beautiful redheaded girl sitting in a chair facing the balcony. I hadn't seen her when I first walked through the room and that puzzled me. She was really nice looking!

"Hi!" I said.

"Hello," said the girl.

"I didn't notice you before," trying hard to keep the conversation moving. A cold sweat came over my body. My thoughts raced and my heart could hardly keep up with it's own pace . . . my system was running amok! *Wow,* I thought. *She's gorgeous . . . it's unbelievable.*

"May I sit down?"

"Yes," said the girl.

"My name is Charl."

"Rosemary."

"You live close by?"

"Yes, here in Rosebank."

"I normally live in the Southern Suburbs."

"You're a friend of Tom and Bobby's?"

"Yes," I said, "Yes, and I actually like them!"

The conversation was awkward so I talked about the Army and a little about college. I started on sports, but that drew a blank.

Rosemary and I talked for some time, it still felt awkward, and then the crowd came back into the room. Jackie greeted me as she came in and sat next to Rosemary. Alice brought the sandwiches into the living room as Tom and Bobby also came in to sit near us. The group talked and laughed and had a good time. I did not want this to end!

Bobby came up close to Rosemary's chair, sat on a footrest, and started to talk to her. As he continued, I felt a pang of anguish. I knew Bobby well, and he was on the make. Discouraged, I backed out of the general conversation, fearing I might just make a fool of myself. Bobby was making progress. I thought, *Too bad.* Rosemary sure had a wonderful smile. I excused myself, went into the bathroom, stood in front of the mirror for a while, washed my face, and combed my hair. *Wow!* I supposed that though Rosemary was really too good to be true, I should, under all circumstances, get her phone number or I must make a date or something. I decided not to push hard and just to play it slowly.

I left the bathroom and went back into the living room. Bobby was still there, so I made a quick entry, in order to be noticed, smiled, and went into the kitchen. This was a new thing, I pondered. Bobby and I had never gone after the same girl, no matter what odds were stacked against us. This 'rule of friends' had been followed for a long time and it was very common in the Andrew Street Mob. Why did it bother me so much? It triggered a little anger, so I decided to get a beer from the kitchen.

"Hi," said Alice.

"Is there a beer?" I asked.

"Nope! Run out!"

"Can we go and get some?"

"Sure."

So Alice and I went down to the local store and bought a bag full of Lion and Castle Lager beer. Then we walked back slowly. *Alice is attractive and very nice*, I thought, *but Rosemary is just a knockout.* Oh! To hell with it, it's Sunday with new faces and new places. My thoughts were jumbled. *Besides, Alice may be Joseph's girl! Ah! Just let it ride.* I was glad we took a long time to get back to the party. I teased Alice and got her to laugh and that made me feel good. Alice was good fun. It was so nice to even touch a woman on the shoulder, as I pushed her aside gently and made for the stairs. She chased me up the stairs to the apartment. But I was extremely fit; I beat her, but made sure it wasn't by much, and then I realized she also had beer in her hand.

"You'd have got me without the beer!"

"No! Not with you having those nice legs!"

I was surprised: nice legs! How would she know? I had on long pants. Alice staggered by, touching me on the brow of my head with a certain amount of affection.

"What do they teach you in the Army, to walk slow?" Alice quipped, smiling, with her eyes lit up. She then laughed out loud . . . I laughed too. Then we burst into the kitchen with Alice yelling, "Beer, right here man!"

"Only for the 'Ugly People'!" I added.

Rosemary was in the kitchen. I was surprised and didn't know what to do or what to say. *How incredible*, I thought!

"Hi!"

"Did you go for beer?" Rosemary asked.

"Yes," I replied.

"Yes," said Alice.

"Why didn't you ask me?" questioned Rosemary. "I'd have gone with you to the store."

My heartbeat skipped again and again as I sought an answer. What was going on here? Bobby was after her. Was she now cutting into Alice's fun . . . Nah! Rosemary was just being nice . . . dammit! I was totally confused and definitely felt inexperienced in handling this situation! Although I could spend a lot of hours at this party!

I broke open three beers. I had to do something. I felt so damn awkward between Alice and Rosemary. I had never been in a position to choose. If I even had that choice, did I have it now? . . . Nah! The girls were just being nice. The conversation in the kitchen relaxed as Jackie and Tom came in.

Abie grabbed a few beers. "Good man, Charl," said Abie.

Abie talked to Alice, and so Rosemary and I talked and then moved out to the balcony. My body seemed to drive my mind. I wanted to put my arm around her but my mind refused to perpetrate the action. She was beautiful and more attractive than anyone I had ever seen. Reddish-brown short hair, cut to flow back in the modern style like a Ducktail but feminine; beautiful facial features; rosy cheeks, an incredible cheeky smile and her eyes—gorgeous and very penetrating. I knew by Rosemary's manner that she knew she was pretty. And I had seen lot of pictures of pretty girls, because that's what we liked to do when we weren't studying! But the pictures weren't any better than what I was looking at and, besides, even if they were, the pictures weren't real and alive. I was 'gone' and I knew it.

Time dissipated so quickly and seven o'clock came too soon. The party group had decided to see us off. We left the apartment in two cars and headed towards Johannesburg, to get to Pritchard Street, and connect with the bus to Potchefstroom at 8 PM. I hung close to Rosemary to make sure I could sit next to her in the car: I did.

"I would like to write to you, I have lots and lots of time," I suggested.

"Sure!" Rosemary replied. We exchanged phone numbers. My heart was now in gear and I had a little more confidence.

The road into Johannesburg was not even a background to me, mesmerized by this girl. The car came to a stop behind one of the buses. It was 7:45 PM. The bus was already full of men bound for Potchefstroom Army camp. Everyone got out of the two cars, grabbing bags, saying good-byes, thank-yous and "Cheers!" I stood close to Rosemary: I had decided I was going to be forward, so I put my hands on her shoulders and kissed her. She responded warmly, I backed off, "Bye! Call you soon."

Our group piled onto the bus. All the front seats were taken. We ended up on the back seat. "Where's Piet?"

"Probably on another bus."

The four of us slumped . . . there was nothing to say . . . the damn Army had our souls again. The bus pulled off. Potchefstroom camp came soon and then Monday morning within a heartbeat or so.

◆

The daily routine continued. Thursday night in the bungalow Bobby said that he had written to Rosemary. My heart dropped a thousand feet and into a chasm. I got up and went for a walk. How much I hated this situation, nobody would ever know. Army bullshit coupled with a great buddy interested in a girl that I had very deep feelings for, even though we had just met, was just too much. She was someone I could just enjoy every day. Also, this coming weekend there would be no pass. The next weekend to Johannesburg was ten days away at least with a damn dull weekend in-between. So I decided that on Friday, I would phone Rosemary, tell her that I was coming up and ask if she would meet me? I'd skip camp. The Army never checked anyway and I didn't care.

I tried to call Rosemary the whole weekend but no answer. This was the worst weekend I had experienced since training had begun. I would just have loved to go kick a soccer ball a hundred times or ride a bike for hours and hours. I wanted to do something really physical, but this place, and what I knew about it, turned up zero opportunity.

Monday came again, Tuesday passed and on Wednesday night Bobby walked into the bungalow with a letter. "It's from Rosemary," he declared. I lay on the bed with eyes of steel. There was a surge in my body, but I uttered no sound. I was resolute not to show any feelings. My mind, always extremely active to resolve things, ran the gamut, and I decided to show nothing, regardless of the news. If they were going to go out . . . so be it!

Bobby continued, "Charl, you look like you're pissed at someone."

"No! I'm not!" *Hell! Did it show?* I questioned myself.

"Well, I wrote to Rosemary, the girl from the party, I asked her to go out and she said no! Can you believe that! She said that she was writing to Charl and would like see *this* guy!" said Bobby, pointing at me. I changed from a freezing refrigerator to a hot furnace temperature within milliseconds.

"You're kidding . . . you're full of full of bullshit Bobby! Let me see!"

"No," said Bobby. "It's private!" He had a smirky smile that was the best.

"Bullshit . . . Bobby!"

"No, my friend! It looks like the pretty one is all yours."

"That sounds okay then . . ." I said with some of the disbelief going away. My face had obviously been an open book! I didn't like that situation, but what the hell, I was so glad.

For the next three weeks, we spent the weekdays looking forward to the weekends. Bobby, Tom, Abie, Piet and I would slip out of camp even when no passes were given. We were very creative in arranging various modes of transport, including hitch–hiking. It was exciting taking the different risks of not being in camp. The Army had very seldom checked before. If they did check, did we care? I disappeared with Rosemary into Johannesburg's young people's night scene. Sometimes Tom and Bobby would join us, along with Alice and Jackie. I was on an unbelievable high and only scared of one thing: running out of money on a date with Rosemary. We kept to the local dance clubs, local hangouts or hung around at home, not that expensive, but the fear of running short was always there. Dancing sent my heartbeat very high. Touching Rosemary was not measurable. I didn't believe there was such a heartbeat rate despite my sport activities. I believed my blood just flowed fast continually when I was with her . . . there was no beat. I was 'in love'. My first real love and my socks were knocked off. I was barefoot in the sand, nowhere to hide, all emotions came out, there were no protective devices for my feelings, this was it, I loved it, and I knew it showed. My family even thought I was a nut! I spent six hours at home between Friday and Sunday. My friends in the Andrew Street Mob were being grossly ignored.

One weekend was devoted to Johnny's twenty-first birthday. The Saturday had been planned to include a maximum number of members of the Andrew Street Mob for the celebration. Johnny was very popular with all of us. A very large bunch of guys went to the East African Pavilion, in Johannesburg's downtown, for curry and rice (the best anywhere), and Castle Lager beer. This restaurant had the tall Watusi Kenyans serving the most delectable curried meat and rice with condiments including dried fish, coconut, mango chutney, spring onions, and so on, and so on. My dad had taken me there. The event took three hours and we rolled out at four to go and get ready for the party. There must have been a hundred people at the party; well it just seemed that way! Johnny had promised to get me home because I had no transport. We had heard there would be a check on Sunday and I had to be back in camp by then. The boys at 'Potch Camp' had already taken a lot of chances by slipping out of camp. One thing we realized is that if one person was caught, it could truly ruin it for everyone. The party was so good and no one would leave. I couldn't care; I was with friends. Finally the group got smaller, I pleaded my case to Johnny but that didn't work, however, Pat volunteered to take me to my 'Potch' home if Johnny came with him to keep him company on the return leg. At some inglorious hour we left Johannesburg and Pat drove me to Potchefstroom. He reached the gate of the Army barracks as the sun came up. I was truly, truly thankful.

◆

A certain animosity had built up in the camp between the Afrikaans- and the English-speaking South Africans. It was difficult to name any specific element: the Army-induced competition, the cricket games, the mess hall, the speaking in Afrikaans and the separation of the two groups all contributed.

One night there was almost a tragedy when two bungalows were having a friendly pillow fight. Someone put a half brick in a pillow and hit a soldier on the head. He collapsed immediately. The players all hovered around. The ambulance was called and he was taken to the hospital. The next day at the morning parade the commander banned any pillow fights or anything like that. All passes were canceled. A special assembly at 4:30 PM extended our day. All soldiers had to attend. We were told to stand quiet with absolutely no movement. The officers walked up and down while the whole camp stood motionless. It was an age before we were dismissed.

That weekend about twenty buckets of water were thrown into the bungalow of the Afrikaans soldier who had wielded the brick-laden pillow. This compliment was returned to three other bungalows and the mess continued. Two Afrikaans soldiers were beaten up in the nearby park area on the Sunday. This was retaliated by the roughing-up of three English-speaking soldiers. The parks were not a place to go except on Sundays.

Our bungalow group never got into this mess and neither did most of the other barracks. However we took a lot of defensive action. Doors were locked, and when there was no lock, the bungalows were always occupied by four or five young men.

The old Potchefstroom stories circulated and included stories of the raids on the local girls' school and similar problems they had during the Second World War. The interesting stories of the Ossewa Brandwag (Wagon Sentinel), a group of paramilitary people, who hated the British for their crimes against and persecutions of their grandparents and their parents during the Boer war. This group was purported to have even been supportive of the Germans against the British during the beginning of the Second World War. No wonder soldiers, of any kind, were unpopular in Potchefstroom. Bobby had heard from rumors that it was local gangs, rather than Afrikaans soldiers, that had actually beaten up the three English-speaking soldiers. All of these stories were confusing, and indirectly started further frustrations in camp. We didn't know where the root of trouble was located. Everyone we knew in camp got along great. A question floating around the dinner tables was whether it was older grown-ups in Potchefstroom or what?

I discussed the confrontation with a friend whom I talked to almost every day in the mess hall.

"Johannes, we're all South Africans," I said, "we're all here together. This is our land. We are three hundred years old and we are still forming. It doesn't belong to the Dutch or the English anymore. Why must we worry about the past so much?"

Johannes, who was from the Northern Transvaal, answered, "The roots are deep, Charl. It is only about sixty years since the South Africans fought that dirty war with the British. There were many women and children who died in the English concentration camps. My father would be very mad at me, even now, if I married an English girl, even if she was South African!"

"Is it true?" I asked.

"Yes Charl . . . it's true." Johannes paused for a moment "Do you dislike the English, Charl?"

"My family is half English . . . how can I? Well! . . . But I don't like the ones that come to our country and treat us like colonists, who think we are nothing, and treat us though we are stupid." I agreed to that easily.

"Oh! I don't like those English either. They treat the black man as though they were slaves to them . . . as though it was their right. I have a lot more feeling for the blacks. I have to work very close to them on the farm every day. In fact sometimes it's truly sad . . . the way some of the South Africans treat them. I think they are too hard on them as well," said Johannes with an unusual softness. Then he continued with more straightforwardness, "I live on my father's farm and we have to treat them hard, otherwise they don't work. You cannot allow them to drink either . . . Man! Then you are in trouble. That's the worst, they can't get going for days afterwards. There are some that just come and go, others stay forever, but you never know. Also my friend . . . a farm is a business. It allows us to live, but you have to work the land and it is hard work. Our biggest problem is to know which black man will stay with us . . . after we have taught him everything."

"Yeah! You're right on that. I work in a machine shop and you can smell their homemade beer from the night before. The smell lasts for days. In fact we have showers at work to make sure some of them take a shower after the night out; but that is another subject. I don't know what to make of all this stuff. We are a mixed family of English and Afrikaans people. Actually my grandfather from my father's side spoke French, Afrikaans and English. My grandmother from my mother's side speaks English and Zulu. I was never brought up to fight traditions. I now realize that, and I'm happy that stuff in our family is gone. Although you never know how deep some feelings are! We are also descendants from the Huguenots from my father's side. The Huguenots came from France. They were persecuted by the Roman Catholic Church in France and moved into Belgium and Holland. Then they came to South Africa with their dreams. My grandfather, who spoke French, lost his farm for supporting the South African Kommandos against the British. The family was dispersed. My father doesn't even know what happened to some of his brothers and sisters."

"Where was the farm?" asked Johannes.

"Oudtshoorn."

"Ostrich farm?"

"Yes," I said. "It took three days and three nights to cover it on horseback. So I was told."

"Why was it confiscated?"

"After the raids on the British camps the Kommandos would ride like hell. A horse will only last about forty miles at a fast pace."

"Now I know that's true about horses," interjected Johannes.

"So they would need to change horses. My grandfather helped them. The British became the laughing stock of Europe, because the great British Army couldn't stop these raids by the South African Kommandos for over two years. These Kommandos, they were just a bunch of farmers man! But they knew how to ride, fight and shoot."

"Regtig (Really) Charl?" asked Johannes

"Really!"

"Your Grandfather was a Boer?"

"Ja, my friend. So if the British, to continue the story, found horses full of sweat on a farm, they would burn the farm to the ground, shoot the men and put the women and children in concentration camps. As I said, my grandfather helped, and the British caught him. My father escaped to Beaufort West. My grandfather survived as well. I don't know how. The rest of the family dispersed."

"Where did they go?"

"Besides my father and one aunt . . . I don't know."

"It's a crazy world Charl, my grandfather also fought the British." He paused, smiled and looked me straight in the eyes. "So what do we know?"

"That's right! Johannes! What the hell do we know! We're still wet behind the ears!"

We laughed.

"Listen, I must go, see you later."

"See you later."

"Totsiens (bye)."

We parted.

◆

Things started to change in camp life, making it better for me. I had impressed the officers with a big innings in a practice cricket game. I was normally a steady batsman because I hated to go out early in the game. But I believe I hit the ball harder than ever before, and I was as aggressive as I could be. My frustrations with the Army subsided when I hit the hell out of the ball. It felt good! I was chosen to play in a game between two divisions. My Wednesday afternoons were now good. They were called 'sports days'. I played cricket every Wednesday afternoon. I was also getting used to better things as the breaks kept coming. College had started. I had applied to the Army to continue studies and I was given permission to attend college in Johannesburg. This meant I was given off all day Friday. Problem was that I was a few weeks late and had to catch up. So my weekends were always in Johannesburg. I had to have papers signed but that was fine. Light in a tunnel, I thought, a combination of love and hate. College was absolutely no problem when compared with Army life. I was totally enthusiastic because my weekends would be with Rosemary. Money was continually tight despite my being paid by Main Reef Engineering.

Two major maneuvers were included in basic training. One was a fully organized night patrol and the second was a major seven-day maneuver with guns and live ammunition. It would involve the whole 22nd South African Irish Regiment. Preparations were being made.

The first maneuver took place nine weeks into training. All soldiers were loaded onto trucks and transported to a river bank 20 miles outside of Potchefstroom. This area was part of the old farmlands purchased by the South African Government for training soldiers. The tents were pitched and the central camp set up for on-site operations. The exception was that meals would be delivered from base camp until the actual maneuvers took place.

The first unusual incident involved Solomon, a simple, rotund, large, slow-walking, nice person and son of a Johannesburg Jewish businessman. He became a buddy with Japie van der Zyl, a farmer's son: a tough little Afrikaans guy, quiet and pleasant. They hung around with each other all the time. No one understood the relationship. These two had been given the job of digging a lavatory pit. So they walked down to the river bank to a designated spot some 200 yards away from the main camp. As they proceeded along the pathway, Solomon was walking in front and kicked a *Rinkhals* (Spitting Cobra) snake that was coiled up, sleeping in the pathway. This is a snake that can kill chickens when it's three weeks old and grows to be 6 to 8 feet long, three inches round. The snake reared up . . . Solomon froze! Japie, in reaction, hit the snake with his shovel, which he brought down from his shoulder. He then pushed the blade into the snake's body near the head and drove it down with his foot, killing the snake. Solomon was usually very slow but he did move to the side of the action. In a slow drawl he asked Japie why he killed the snake. Japie hit his own head with his hands in disbelief.

"Man, you'd be dead soon, if I didn't do that."

"Oh! Really?"

"Yes man! Jussus! I don't believe you!"

Apparently, after Japie covered the snake with sand, they just continued walking, not saying much about anything. They went down and dug the latrine.

The second night, the first major event, a night reconnoiter maneuver was to take place after dark. Bobby was made leader of our unit. We were matched with another two groups, each with a leader. The three groups would go out on the same route at different times. The leader was to carry the compass and an assistant was to carry the instructions. The instructions had about four legs of the walk, for example the unit was to advance 500 yards at so many degrees, turn right, travel 1000 yards at so many degrees, and supposedly these various legs eventually would return everyone to base; if completed correctly. Bobby had the compass; I had the flashlight, and Tom the directions.

The summer night was definitely black as we left camp. This was in the country, no city lights, just brilliant starlight, shadows of dark and darker, and the camp lights. A small amount of light from the moon showed the background of trees. The group before us had left five minutes before; the reconnaissance had begun.

Ten minutes into the walk everyone was talking. Abie was trying to count the steps. Tom had told Bobby the yards. Piet and I were talking and just following. Bobby was out in front.

"I will keep the compass for the first leg, and then everyone will take turns. I'm being very democratic," suggested Bobby

"We are very lucky to be together in a group led by you, Bobby!" said Piet.

I added to his suggestion. "I agree with Piet. It could've been so different, so we think you should keep the compass duty!"

"No, really, if you don't take turns I'll throw the damn thing into the bush at the end of the first leg!" replied Bobby.

"I like you crazy people!" said Piet.

"Oh! So! The people of Vereeniging are not crazy?" I asked, challenging Piet.

"Not as crazy as you guys!"

"Huh!"

The group ended up all talking, walking through brush and grass as Bobby led. After an hour, the brush became thicker, then suddenly, without warning, we were all scrambling down a steep bank and ended up in twelve inches of water.

"Hell! Shit! What are you doing with us?"

"What?" asked Bobby.

"We're all in the river," said Tom. "I know . . . we're lost."

"But you knew that was water. You were leading. You went down the damn bank into the river. Why didn't you tell us? Why?" asked Abie.

"What for? I was already in the river. I thought you'd like it! And that you wouldn't mind joining me!"

The group ran towards Bobby to dump him in the river, but he had anticipated that and slipped out of reach and onto the bank. Not everyone laughed. We were all soaking wet up to our knees.

"We're definitely lost," said Bobby. "We don't have a map! All we have is a geometric shape with four sides! How far did we walk Abie?"

"Eight hundred yards," replied Abie very confidently.

"But the first leg is only 300 yards!" yelled Tom.

"You just told me to count," yelled back Abie. "Besides 800 looks like 300 in the dark!"

"Lets just walk back 500 yards," suggested Bobby.

"No! Let's look at the second leg, calculate the distance and angle, and take a cut!" I argued.

"Oh Shit! Here we go!"

Everyone commented on the next direction. "You go left. No! You go right." Eventually, it was decided to go in the second direction. Everyone continued to walk, through trees, through bushes, over roads, along pathways and further discussions brought no real solution.

"We sure screwed this up," said Tom.

"Let's just go back," said Abie. "Towards those little lights that occasionally flicker."

"Go Back! You guys from the city! That's what we're trying to do, man," exclaimed Piet.

The walk continued and the group spread out slightly. Then a flare appeared in the sky. The South African Army was not stupid enough to assume that the new recruits would do it perfectly. A number of flares were shot up. Everyone was now confident we were walking towards the camp after we turned 180 degrees in direction. Bobby and I finally ended up walking and talking and walking and not talking. Abie and Piet had headed back separately and Tom decided to do it on his own. In one quiet moment while walking, the two of us could hear the rustling of our heavy battle dress, worn even though it was summer. These British-style jackets had two pockets in front, two lapels across the shoulder, and a tight belt. Bobby and I were warm. The pants had dried, the boots however were still waterlogged and squishy. We talked about girls in Johannesburg, where the fun was, how we hated the Army, especially the atmosphere and the silly rules we were being taught.

"Just stupid," said Bobby.

"And more," I added.

We had no idea where we were. We were walking closely together, our eyes looking into the dark. It was so quiet we found ourselves whispering. In an instant, almost faster than the eye can see, Bobby suddenly disappeared from sight. He was going down quickly and screaming. I saw his shadow disappearing. In reaction, my left arm shot out, in the same split second, and by some unknown intuition my fingers touched his jacket and went through the top lapel. I held onto the lapel. The downward force of Bobby's weight hurt my three fingers holding the lapel. My right arm came around to help and grabbed some front part of Bobby's jacket. Bobby's arms were outstretched and grabbed my left leg.

"I've got you!" I yelled. "Slowly!"

"There's nothing under my feet," screamed Bobby.

I stood very still, thinking there was a hole or something. My feet were on firm ground. I was not going to move.

We continued to hold onto each other. Bobby had fallen into a well. Just an open hole covered with a corrugated iron sheet that had rusted and seen better days. It had broken in two, like the snapping of a dry twig. I kept my feet firm and leaned away from Bobby. I pulled on him as Bobby scrambled out of the hole. I found the flashlight that I had flung in the act of saving Bobby.

"Shit, look at that."

We sat down just to compose ourselves. Was this the only well? We understood now. Somebody had forgotten to check all the wells in this land when it was bought.

"Jesus! This stupid damn government," said Bobby.

"What do you expect man," I added, "They have no idea what the hell they're doing. Anyway . . . what the hell do they care about people . . . only their damn positions?"

"What?" asked Bobby.

"Oh forget it," I said. "This is my feelings about the Army . . . about politics . . . it keeps coming out . . . I don't know! Oh! What the hell! Man."

We walked back very carefully. We even suggested walking back with arms around each other's shoulders. All the carefree feeling was gone. This was serious. Both of us were talking for the hundredth time on how to get out of this mess called the Army. Bobby suggested his mother's contacts.

"Maybe just go overseas. Tell them you are going to study or something. I hear you can get out that way," I suggested.

"No, I wouldn't leave South Africa," said Bobby.

"I maybe could if this shit continues," I said firmly.

We arrived back at the camp and checked in. We diligently reported the well to the officers. We found to our surprise that Tom, Abie, and Piet were already back. In fact, the five of us were all well ahead of other groups. We went back to the tent. We told our story to Tom and Piet.

"We must investigate the matter in the morning," Bobby said in a thick accent imitating the officers.

"Solomon and Japie are also back," said Tom, "Lets go. I have a great idea for one of the groups."

We went down the pathway and dug up the snake. We dragged it back into the camp, and propped it up in the tent next to ours.

"Let's go outside and wait to see what happens," said Tom.

We went outside and sat on the ground quietly, waiting. The Army tents were bell shaped, 15 feet in diameter, with about a foot of straight side at the bottom before they tapered to a point at the top. The entrance flaps were on one side only, so we'd propped the snake up inside the tent, looking at the entrance. Whoever entered the tent would have to bend down to enter, so we arranged the snake's head just below eye level, at the back of the tent. It was perfect because no one really stood up in the tent; everyone usually crawled across the floor once they were inside.

Two recruits approached the tent talking. The first one went in, followed closely by the other. Suddenly, a phenomenal scream came through the tent walls and two men, pushing and shoving each other, burst out of the tent hitting the side of the tent, banging the door flaps aside and yelling. "A snake! A snake!"

God! We laughed and laughed and then quietly worked our way back into the shadows of our tent. We listened for over an hour to the discussions and movements of some thirty people, some with fixed bayonets. Finally, they heard someone say, "Shit! It's only Solomon's snake . . . it's dead."

After three days we returned to the routine of the main camp, ironing, washing, lectures, and drills. Another weekend with no pass, I wasn't sure if Rosemary would wait around for me on this erratic basis. Again, everyone was bored. But, after ten weeks, the whole camp had matured to the lifestyle. Young soldiers were exerting a certain amount of confidence. One morning the soldiers refused green eggs served for breakfast. The officers explained that the omelets were made of dried powdered eggs, which had turned green and were not harmful: green was still rejected. An officer was assigned to report on the satisfaction of the food. The answers would always be positive, so as not to be singled out and ridiculed, so when complaints were made, nothing was ever done. Therefore, unplanned action by the soldiers was instant, and everyone joined in, and this method became more effective.

The second major event occurred at dinner when the steaks were off-color, and the taste, which matched the smell, was peculiar. The comments became louder from table to table. Then one soldier got up, walked down the aisle and dumped his steak on the end of the table and left. A large group of soldiers, almost without hesitation, did the same thing. Eventually, all the tables had rancid steak piled at the end, almost two feet high. Everyone left. Although incidents of misbehavior were addressed in the morning parade, nothing was ever done to either correct the situation or punish the soldiers. So we considered the action a tie.

One night, news of beer in camp spread like lightning. Soldiers went down to Bungalow 25, purchased beer at an exorbitant price and went back to their bungalows to enjoy drinking in the company of their buddies. So as not to leave any trace of evidence for the officers to use against us, we had determined a place for the empty bottles under the building.

The beer loosened up everybody and topics were great that night in the bungalow. We had discussed many things, but, for some strange reason, we finally ended up on the subject of gays. Who had met them, knew them, what they did. Who really knew? A personal friend of mine was gay. I had met others. I loved to imitate them, and had acquired the mannerisms, and could talk the talk. I went on-stage in the bungalow. I told them that I had belonged to a 'concert party' for two years, formed from my friends in the Andrew Street Mob. "A man one day introduced himself as a producer of concert party shows, and convinced our Andrew Street Mob, when we were all around fourteen, to form a little theater company and rehearse. We did this and put stage shows on at the Grand Theatre in the Southern Suburbs. The producer had my neighbors doing whatever they were good at. Helen was a tap dancer and singer; her brother Bobby was the pianist, Doc, Zoni and Juni were actors and Mel was a dancer. I was one of two comedians."

I got into this story seriously. The guys kept an interest, so I added that the concert party group actually ended up touring the Witwatersrand to the cities of Springs, Boksburg, and Randfontein, and had eaten in a special section of the black miners mess hall (this was definitely not done). We got to do this because one of Zoni's relatives managed the kitchen. We had big steaks and potatoes and although the black workers looked us at strangely, we had a good time. On another occasion our bunch of entertainers ended up in Selby Hall, one of the small side halls of the City Hall in Johannesburg; this was a benefit show. There were five-minute skits, comedy scenes, dancing, and piano playing and singing. I had been one of the comedians that had to use a high voice. I got to practice that part many times!

So after the long historical introduction, I applied my smacking lips, swinging hip walk, and twanging high-pitched comedy routine in the bungalow. Beer had totally loosened me and the crew was ahead of me. The boys were in stitches and some almost got stomach cramps from laughing. It was suggested that I do it in the lecture the next day.

"Sure," I said, "Oh! . . . For sure!" Obviously helped by all the beer I'd drunk.

The next day we ended up in the radio communications class. The word of my exploits had gone beyond my friends. Piet Coetzee, a man of about 28, a corporal in the permanent force, was to give the lecture. His voice, slow, with a thick accent, monotone and direct, went on and on. Everyone was getting sleepy eyed considering the celebration and the night before. A silent wave of fidgeting and irritation began circumventing the class. Suddenly, I couldn't take it anymore. I stood up and in the high voice said, "Please Sir, I don't understand the part about the electrical part absorbing electrons . . . very, very confusing!"

"What?" said the officer.

"Sir," I said, moving my hips, "you know something about the loss of electrons. Could you please explain?"

"Ja! Man—sure!" said Piet Coetzee. "The waves just die when they hit the insulator."

"They just die, like that?"

"Yes! Man! They are absorbed by the insulating material."

"Sort've a short life like a flower?"

"Yes," answered the instructor looking at me with total amazement. I did not cringe. This was too much damn fun. The class was beside itself with my high voice. Those who didn't know what was going on were dumbstruck, I was told later.

"I could just die too," I suggested. "Sort've get totally absorbed." I said very softly, moving my arms to suit the words. Two soldiers giggled while trying to hold back laughter. Piet Coetzee and I continued the conversation. The murmuring increased even though the lecturer yelled.

"Listen to what I say and you will learn something!" Then he turned to me and commanded. "Sit down soldier!"

"Yeth Thir," I said. The class almost erupted.

"Is that clear now? Dammit man!" yelled Piet Coetzee.

"Yes Sir," said a few soldiers.

"Is it clear, Dammit?"

"Yes Sir," everyone answered loudly.

The lecture went on. It was more tolerable. The soldiers filed out of class. A small victory, I thought, the only kind that can be achieved by recruits against the hundreds of rules on behavior and actions implemented by the Army.

"Thanks," said Tom as the class left the room. "He doesn't even know, does he?"

"Nope," I replied.

At lunch soldiers close to our group discussed the event and laughed.

"What happens if he connects you, Charl the gay, with Charl the cricket player?"

One soldier answered. "Oh, he'll just tell his officer friends. Man those guys should play rugby, that'll get rid of the high voice. Ja, just one lekker (nice) hard tackle . . . and he'll know who he is."

◆

Rosemary and I continued phone calls and correspondence. I had a picture, thoughts and desires. It acted as a background, a retreat, when the Army training life became too much. But this also led to a yearning to see and touch. I wouldn't discuss her with anyone. Despite the requests for intimate information and occasional crude expressions and questions, my responses contained no information. I believed that it was too personal . . . and nobody's damn business. In my case it worked. My buddies became more sincere as I became more serious about this relationship. My feelings were deep and profound and I mostly couldn't believe my reactions to all of it.

One Wednesday of the week after dinner, we sat around, in the bungalow. I told the group, "I'm going to Joh'burg this weekend. I told Rosemary I'm coming up, she wants to see me and I'm going!"

"There's no pass, man! Some guys have now been caught out of camp," said Piet.

"Screw it," I answered. "I hear Rudy's getting his brother's car."

The story was, his brother was coming to Potchefstroom for the weekend, and Rudy could use the car and bring it back Sunday night.

"Let's all go," said Abie.

"Yeah, let's get hold of Rudy!"

The plan evolved. We'd all leave Friday 4:30 PM and come back Sunday.

Rudy's sudden popularity was amazing. Rudy liked the attention.

Everything was good. I called Rosemary.

"Lovely," she said.

We took off on Friday, and sped up to Johannesburg. It was amazing, the transition in attitude after we left the camp. We discussed this.

"You guys are a complete delight to travel with . . . once you're out of uniform! Such nice uplifting people!" I commented.

"We are Charl!"

We were all going different ways this weekend. So the arrangement was for all to meet on Sunday night at 10 PM on the Johannesburg City Hall steps.

"Okay."

"Okay."

"No," said Rudy. "Make it midnight. You're not there, I'm leaving."

"It's okay," was the reply.

Rudy's words rang in the air like Christmas bells. Midnight was great, no catching the usual bus at 8 PM. Also we didn't know if there were any busses, as there were no passes.

I ran into the house, showered, changed and got a ride from Johnny to Rosemary's. We picked her up and went dancing. I was ecstatic and full of it. Unfortunately, Rosemary brought Jackie, her friend. She was a wisp of a blonde, who could drink any man under the table. I knew it. I had been one of them. So the main idea was to plug Jackie full of liquor, regardless of cost, because Jackie and Rosemary were like Siamese twins. I had once told Bobby that I was sure the cord was still attached between them, and it didn't stretch far enough! During the dance, I got a little mad at the situation. I wondered why the hell Rosemary had to talk to Jackie all the time? Rosemary had to be home at 2 PM. I had hardly seen her for quite some time. Finally, I gave up and ignored their talking; I knew Rosemary and I were going out again on Saturday.

Rosemary did not like formal dances. We were all dressed up. Rosemary looked so beautiful. It went through my mind, what could be better in life than going out with a pretty girl to a party. The dance was at the Wanderer's Club, the very exclusive sports club with cricket grounds, soccer grounds and tennis courts. The dances were spectacular and a fortune in cost to people less than twenty years of age. I believed it was worth it. While at camp I could save. This was the first time Rosemary would meet all of my friends: Johnny and Madge, Johnny's friend Herbie and his girlfriend, Trevor and Maureen, Billy and Joy, and Pat and his new girl friend. Madge had come into Johnny's life and Joy into Billy's. Madge lived in the city of Johannesburg and Joy lived almost around the corner from Billy in the Southern Suburbs. There were about 17 at the table with Jackie as a single. The band was more into foxtrot and some swing but no rock. Jackie got to drink a lot of brandies, Rosemary not as many. I tried to keep up but at 11 PM had to go outside and take a walk as my head was swimming. A few of my friends tried to dance with Rosemary and Jackie but they refused. Rosemary said she was with me. Usually the Andrew Street Mob just danced with each other at ease, so it became awkward. Rosemary and I danced a few times but she didn't want to leave Jackie. So I talked to my buddies and went and stood at the bar for a while. Rosemary came and got me.

"What's the problem?" asked Rosemary.

"Nothing."

"Come on now!"

"Well you can see Jackie anytime."

"She's not coming tomorrow night. I brought her because I don't know any body!"

"I apologize but she buries you!"

"Charl, that's not so nice."

"Yep! I know. But I look forward to seeing *you*. Jackie is taking up precious time!"

"We'll be alright . . . Okay!"

"Yes! It's okay!"

The dance ended at 1 AM. Johnny and Madge dropped Jackie off, and then took Rosemary and me to Rosebank. I was so glad to talk to Rosemary alone and showed it. We sat on the steps of the verandah. We talked and everything went soft and pleasant, and we laughed. This is what I had wanted to do all night. I had been dreaming about it for weeks at camp.

"It's so nice that we are alone. I wanted to tell you that it made me very warm inside when I heard you wanted to go out with me!" I said in a low and soft voice.

"Couldn't you tell . . . the day we met?"

"No! I was confused . . . maybe because I was excited to meet you!" I said truthfully.

"Well! It was exciting for me too!" Rosemary said.

We hugged and kissed and I just had such incredible feelings, I could have stayed there forever.

Finally, Rosemary went in the house at 3 am and I started my 18-mile walk home. It was fun watching all the different people around this time in the morning, especially as I headed through Hillbrow. I always took the Eloff Street-to-La Rochelle road past the Olympia Ice Rink and the Rand Stadium, it was well lit: Rosettenville Road was shorter, but too dark. After passing the Broadway Hotel I was already looking forward to Saturday Night. I knew the formal dance had been a failure.

On Saturday, I chatted to Gran and Uncle Mick and my mom. I had lunch with Trevor and Johnny. In the evening I got dressed and went and picked up Rosemary. We headed into Johannesburg to 'Rock and Roll!' We went into the club, informally dressed and started to dance immediately. This club, just opened, was at the bottom of Hillbrow. The rock and roll dance places in Johannesburg moved from building to building as the noise and clientele drove the building owners to evict the club operators. It was a continuous cycle. This particular night was going to be exciting, a bunch of people were saying, because 'Louis' was getting out of jail. Louis was a well-known member of a Johannesburg white gang. He was good looking, dark and swarthy and had looks like Aladdin and a great smile. Louis was a good man to his friends. He had stolen a car some time ago, and gone to jail. Louis was always known to be with the 'special ladies'. At midnight, Louis came in with an entourage of men friends and some girls. The crowd yelled and clapped. He walked around, shook hands. I got a piece of the hand. Louis knew me by sight because we had somehow talked many times. He liked to know what you did and whom you liked. He once said I worked too hard! I agreed! Louis didn't know my name. And that's the way this Johannesburg crowd operated. If they saw you enough, they knew you. Louis ended up drinking with a beautiful blonde. The dance continued. At 1:30 AM he got up and walked out the door. The girl followed.

"Wait here," he said.

"No, don't do it," said the blonde.

"No trouble darling!" Louis left. He returned in fifteen minutes with a yellow convertible Buick, top down. The blonde got in, but she was mad at him. Louis waved to the crowd watching this, and drove off.

At 2:30 AM Rosemary and I stood outside waiting to go home, we were 'getting a ride' as the saying goes. The story being told kept us from going. Louis had been stopped by the cops and taken to jail . . . his girl driven home. It would be a mandatory two years for stealing a car: one day of freedom! Rosemary and I headed to her home with some friends. Again we sat on Rosemary's porch. We talked for a long while.

"When are you going to get out of this Army thing?" asked Rosemary.

"Soon Thank God!" I answered. "We go on a big maneuver into the bush for a week. Then it's all over. Before we come home we do a passing out parade.

"You mean with bands and everything?" asked Rosemary.

"Yes," I replied. "Then we're qualified soldiers. Ready to fight the enemy!"

"Can't you get out sooner?"

"No, if I did, I'd end up with Louis!"

"Jail?"

"Yes."

"I miss you Charl," she said with a sad look.

"I can't tell you how many hours I think of you Rosemary . . . maybe too many hey!" I whispered almost in a sheepish manner.

"I love to think that you're thinking about me. I think about you all the time . . . at work . . . on the bus . . . wonder what it means?"

"Oh nothing!" I beamed. "We're just friends and we wear nice clothes and we're compatible. We may fit!"

"Charl, you are not so funny sometimes! But it seems so complicated with all this Army and school and soccer. I love you and the way you dance . . . you're the best."

"Don't worry about the school, and definitely not the Army, and I'm not the best at dancing! I know it!" I was glad to hear her words though; the warmth inside me was phenomenal.

"Stop kidding around!"

"I know how to come second and third. I have a dancing partner, Gloria, we entered all kinds of competitions in Braamfontein even— jive -rock—boogie—stuff."

"So that's why you're so good."

"No, I just love it . . . and I love you too!"

The two of us just sat together. Hugging, kissing, this ignited the internal mystic feeling that generates warmth that is too difficult to explain.

Finally we hugged and kissed good-bye and then parted at 4 AM. Twice in one weekend, I walked home from Rosebank to Kenilworth all the way through Johannesburg. This time the streets were very quiet. There was an eeriness about all the areas I passed through, but I was not scared. I could outrun most people and sustain the run for some time. However, I did walk in the middle of the road sometimes. It was almost daylight in my hometown. The walk was a breeze due to my pleasant thoughts. I had just left her and already missed her . . . amazing!

I slept well into Sunday. Johnny and I went and picked up Madge and Rosemary. We went out with Trevor and Maureen, Billy and Joy and Pat. We spent the day at Zoo Lake, one of Johannesburg's famous parks. We went on the rowboats and walked around looking at all the families having fun, and then sauntered into the famous tearoom and had some food. Finally, we pulled away at 7 PM. We dropped off Rosemary first. This time I kissed her good-bye and headed home with Johnny, Madge, Billy and Joy.

"She's very pretty," said Johnny.

"Yes, I'm lucky," I concurred.

"Are you going steady? Hey!" asked Billy.

"No, I'm not sure," I answered.

"Chicken," said Joy.

My beautiful friends dropped me off at home.

"See you soon. Thanks, Johnny, for everything."

"Sure mate!"

I ran into the house. "Hi, Gran."

"Hullo! Son! I saved you some dinner."

"Yes, please!"

I sat down with Gran.

"Have to meet at the Cenotaph in Johannesburg."

"What time?"

"Midnight."

"What time do you get to camp?"

"About 3 am. Get up about 6 am!"

"How do you do it, Son?"

"This is the fun part Gran! This is the fun part! The Army is just the worst place. I want to get out. I yearn for it with all my heart and strength."

"Everyone has to go to the Army."

"No Gran! Dai got out and he's just going to school. Mickey also didn't have to go and he's working. Everybody is getting better at what they do while we waste our time learning to march!"

"You'll be home soon?"

"Yes Gran! Then I can drive you crazy every day."

"Never, I love you too much."

I got up and kissed her on the cheek.

"Thanks, it's nice to know that . . . and I love you very, very much too!"

I packed all my stuff in my bag and then sat and listened to the radio with Gran. There was a play on the radio and it didn't make any sense because I had come in the middle of the story, so I just sat and looked at my Gran. She was knitting. *Wow! Has she been good to me,* I thought, *probably more than anybody.* I got tears in my eyes from the feelings inside.

I got up and kissed Gran, hugged her, grabbed my bag and went out the door of 65, and walked down Andrew Street to the bus stop. I got the last bus into Johannesburg and arrived at 11:00 PM and walked to the Cenotaph. No one was there. I sat on the steps. It was really quiet. Time stopped ticking. I thought of all the good and bad things in my life. I wanted something to *stop,* such as the Army. I wanted something to *go,* such as Rosemary and I. Then I also wanted to make more money. I had definitely decided to go as far as I could in school; I had promised Gran that I would. I didn't want to play cricket anymore, but I wanted to get much better at soccer because I loved it.

Bobby, Tom and Abie turned up. "Have a good time?"

"Yes!"

"Good. Did you get Rosemary?"

"Wouldn't you like to know?"

At 1 AM we were finished talking about what each of us had done on the weekend. The panic had set in.

"Where the hell is Rudy?"

"Can't call him. Don't know where he lives."

The unknowns of getting to Potchefstroom at this early hour increased. There was no transportation. I had absolutely no money left after my expensive weekend. Who could I call? There was nobody! Hitchhiking was the only chance!

"Cenotaph? Midnight?"

"Yes!"

"Yes!"

"Yes!"

We sat back one more time. Each set of lights coming toward the Cenotaph had us looking and anxious. It was dragging into the early morning. If Rudy didn't come we would be doomed. Anxiety built up! Suddenly, out of nowhere came this big car, a wonderful sight, in the form of a big black Buick straight eight. Rudy pulled up.

"Shit Man! I'm sorry! Couldn't get away from my girl. Finally she said to me 'Go!' So anyway we can go, but I need money for petrol."

"Okay!"

"Okay!"

We jumped in and Rudy drove off, and then stopped for petrol. I sat in the front. Everyone in the back went to sleep even though it was awkward and crowded. Rudy and I talked for a while. I finally felt sleep creep into my body.

"Want me to drive?" I asked.

"No, I'm alright."

I went to sleep.

A loud noise! The car lurched into the air and then descended into a ditch! Everyone was thrown around in the car! It came to a stop pointing downwards and slightly to the side! . . . Rudy had fallen asleep. It was still early morning and not yet light outside. There was a fence along the road and nothing anywhere: just a road and a fence; there are parts of South Africa that are so flat they put a billiard table to shame, this was one of them.

"Holy Shit!"

Everyone got out. Nobody was hurt. Steam from the radiator. Bobby opened the hood. The radiator was smashed.

"It's nearly 4 o'clock."

"Oh Shit! Rudy, your brother's going to kill you."

"I know!"

"Listen, Bobby is a mechanic. We'll all chip in and pay for the radiator."

"Yeah!" Everyone agreed, not knowing where the money would come from.

"No, it's my fault. I messed up the whole weekend," Rudy continued. "You guys walk. It's not far now, maybe ten miles. I'll stay with the car."

"No, we're all in this shit together."

We sat for a long while. There weren't many travelers this time of day. All suggestions of running the car or getting it out or the ditch were deemed futile. It was becoming lighter as the sun breached the horizon.

"There's a truck coming."

We all turned and waved it down. It stopped. The driver was an Afrikaans farmer named Villiers. He had gray hair with brown sun-tanned skin from all his days in the African sun. His hands were strong and his arms made of sinewy-looking muscle that could probably toss a sack of corn ten feet. He had a pleasant face, a bit of a smile at our predicament and a wonderful attitude to help. The gang slowly got him to speak English because our Afrikaans was so bad.

"Come on . . . jus leave the car . . . all of us will go into Potch. . . I will get a tow truck and drop you fellows by the camp."

The Afrikaans farmer is legendary in his willingness to help others. "We will see you through" is their expression. The stories are true and the action taken is always with disregard as to 'who you are'; they will always help. To us, standing alongside the broken black Buick, all the bad things that had been said about these farmers dissolved as quickly as sugar in boiling water.

Everyone agreed by saying. "Dankie Meneer (Thank you Sir)." But Rudy would not go, despite all the pleading.

"I have to stay with my brother's car!"

So a plan was made to cover for Rudy at the Army base through roll call and in class until 10 o'clock.

Mr. Villiers drove off with us, and we were happy sitting inside and outside the truck cab. As a general courtesy, we stumbled through a conversation between the farmer and us Johannesburg boys in terrible English and even worse Afrikaans. We were very happy and laughed many times with the farmer, especially on the subject of 'You City Boys'. We reached camp with time to shower. We thanked the farmer profusely. The farmer told us not to worry . . . it was no trouble, and promised to send a tow truck; he did. Rudy got back to camp at about 10 AM. The Army never knew what had happened as we successfully covered for Rudy. Everyone was now concerned about getting money for the radiator; this was no small item to us.

Army training was now well into March. Daily routine and weekly routines were easier to do. It was extremely boring and although humor had its part when the training was first begun, there were no more jokes about the dumbness of the officers, stupidity, authoritarian motives, and regimentation of the Army. There was talk of how we could get revenge, but that was in low tones. The soldiers in training had forgotten about cross-town animosity, and the Afrikaans—English element had come and gone and got buried. The only thing everyone wanted to do was to get over this episode of life. Two things were yet to be done: one week of field maneuvers and the passing-out parade. We knew nothing about the maneuvers but knew the passing-out parade would not be interesting. However, when they were completed the soldiers knew the train to go home would leave Potchefstroom.

◆

I received instructions for the gun crew. It was announced that the final full maneuvers were to begin. They would last one week, going through the weekend, and end the next Wednesday. Thursday would be the parade. Friday would be travel day home, the end of March and the end of three months of training.

I told our crew about the schedule. Bobby suggested a "bombed out" party on Saturday, the day following the Friday we got home. We agreed. I phoned Rosemary—date confirmed. Bobby got Mickey to arrange for a car and to phone for reservations. He told him to get some girls for Tom and Abie. Piet had his own girl. Bobby said he would get a girl.

"How about Jackie? Tom!" I suggested sarcastically.

"No thanks," said Tom. "Drinks too much, I don't have the money!"

"Has to happen," I pleaded. "Rosemary goes, Jackie goes!"

"You take care of two, then," said Tom.

"Rosemary is cute, but she sure wants her way," said Abie. "I just want a girl who gets drunk and goes for it!"

"So what's the difference?" said Piet.

"Nothing Piet! It's too complicated to explain."

"Mickey will go too!" said Tom. "He knows."

"Who cares, after this three months of bullshit, why worry about girls, we'll all just get drunk," said Bobby.

"It's a deal, we are all going," I confirmed. "It's the deal of the year!"

"Let's go find a beer," I suggested, after acknowledging some of the truth said in jest. Thinking that Rosemary was so cute, beautiful and exciting, but always with Jackie. *So everything has a problem, if it's good. Well, what's so bad about that?* Loving someone was complicated.

Midday Thursday the crews started to prepare for the maneuvers. Everything had to be checked out in the mobile unit, the gun and the ammunition carrier. Each soldier had to carry his gun, load up with eating utensils, clean socks, groundsheet, blanket and whatever he could squeeze in his pack. Suggestions were that it not be too heavy. This was going to be a week in the same clothes.

All the gun units were lined up on the parade ground. Twenty-five pound shells were loaded in the ammunition carrier. Thursday required guard duty, as live ammunition was always secured.

Ten o'clock the next morning the crews were told that the maneuvers were about to begin. Small permanent force units, corporals and officers, would be countering the maneuvers. They would steal gun sights, rifles, or disrupt the operations in whatever way they could. The gun units had to be secured at all times. Live ammunition meant safe operations and careful handling. Those units that performed well would be commended.

"Oh yes!" said Bobby, "And we'll all be given rock and roll records for our collection!" A commendation was an insignificant offer to us, and we wondered if the officers knew we couldn't care less. Jokes were still not readily received though, and Bobby's comment faded into silence.

The 22nd South African Irish Field Regiment 25 pounder gun crews left the parade ground in sequence. We formed a long column of trucks all very neatly arranged by number. A permanent officer was in charge of each six-gun group. The officers rode in a jeep and there was a gap of fifty yards between gun groups. The column proceeded through part of Potchefstroom and into the veld (fields). One stop in the afternoon allowed for hot tea to be served with dog biscuits. The hard, nutritious biscuit was the only guaranteed food for the maneuvers. It didn't go soft in cold water, so if there was a combination of no hot tea and bad teeth, you could actually starve on this trip, if you didn't have a hammer.

Late that day, as dusk was covering the farmlands, the column reached a heavily wooded area. We had no idea where we were. Each six-gun group was required to hide and camouflage their vehicles in the trees. The other requirement was to remain close together in a group. The 20-foot-long carrier and 15 foot gun belonging to my crew got driven up into the trees. The six guns were pretty close together. The officer gave us instructions on how we would be moving out, in the dark of the night, to take a firing position ten miles further into the hills. With that, he took off, telling us to protect the guns, and that we should remain in the trucks and not wander off into the woods.

As there was still some light and we knew the officers would be gone for some time, our crew chatted to the other crews. Pretty soon there was a large crowd of guys. We posted lookouts for the officers.

We mingled in the dark and then lit a fire. An officer came down the hill screaming that everyone was totally stupid. Didn't we know that the fire would tell the enemy where we were? Then the officer returned up the hill.

"They're serious about this war game," said a member of one of the crews. "The permanent officers are all drinking. One of the guys went through the forest to see where they were. They're all in the operations vehicle drinking and laughing . . . having a hell of a good time. Just like we'd be doing on a Friday night in Johannesburg."

I wondered what Rosemary was doing. *She is certainly not sitting at home; I wouldn't. Ah well, this will be over soon.*

It was at least three hours later when the officers all came down the hill. Earlier instructions had been to tie white handkerchiefs on the gun muzzles; no lights were to be used. The column would travel by moonlight following the waving handkerchiefs. The whole column should fall back into line just exactly as we left Potchefstroom. This was to be the permanent sequence. Our officer came into the area yelling, "We are going to move now, get ready. We have to fall in line behind Gun Group Five."

"Where's my jeep?" he yelled. Then repeated the same question to the nearest gun crew.

"Don't know sir! We were in our carrier all the time."

He looked around. It was dark.

"Jesus man! Where the hell is my jeep? We'll miss our place in the column. They are already gone!"

"Don't know sir! " said the second gun crew.

He ran around yelling and asking, stumbling occasionally, he had obviously had a few drinks too many.

Every gun crew in the area knew a bunch of soldiers had released the brake on the jeep and carefully guided it down the hill, quite a distance, until it could be rolled up against a tree, so it could be assumed that the officer had left it out of gear without the brake on. We thought that was pretty smart! The officer ran over to the unit that was to follow his group. He explained his problem. Then he and the second officer ran back looking for the jeep.

"Follow the tracks, Sir," suggested a soldier.

"Can't see the tracks in the dark you stupid idiot! Where's your damn brain? Where's your damn torch (flashlight)?" asked the officer.

"Can't use it, Sir! We're on maneuvers!" proclaimed another soldier.

"Get me the bloody torch!!"

The voices carried in the night. The gun crews relayed the conversation. Anybody that heard laughed and snickered, or smiled. I felt so good inside. This was part payment for us being treated like boy scouts instead of men.

The officer found his jeep. "Bastards!" he muttered.

He started it up and drove it to a position ahead of the six-gun crews who were waiting patiently for him. He drove down the hill onto the main rode and took off fast after the main column. The gun crews could hardly keep up. The officer wanted to close the ten-minute gap in the column. The first gun crew took off. Our crew followed but lost sight of the handkerchief because of dust swirling off the road. Jacobus, our driver, said he couldn't see anything through the dusty window. I opened the hatch in the roof, climbed up through the hole and sat on top of the carrier roof. I could see just a little better than the driver, as the outline of the red-brown sand roads contrasted with the color of grass and bush and trees. A small amount of moonlight also helped but nothing was truly clear or in focus.

"This is fun at last! Finally they got the gun crew operating after the million training sessions on the parade ground!" I shouted over the noise of the trucks. The enemy could have heard us coming from sixty miles away!

"Right-right-right . . . little moves," I yelled.

"Okay," said Jacobus.

"Left-right-left," I yelled.

We were doing well but hit a couple of bumps and the crew screamed at me.

"Hey! I'm your leader!"

"Only for a week!" came out of the truck.

We continued for some time, traveling at 20-30 mph.

"Not bad . . . in the dark . . . hey!"

"Yup," shouted Jacobus. "Hope the hell we make it."

Bobby, Abie, Piet and Tom expected the truck to turn over at any time, so they held onto anything secure or stable. My anxiety was nullified by the super confidence of completing this Potchefstroom trip. There was no thought of mishap in the last week of this dumb adventure. This was the end!

Suddenly, I realized something had changed, but I couldn't see properly. A surge of anxiety and then . . . in a split second . . . a vision . . . and an immediate reaction. I yelled as loudly as I could, "Brakes! Hard! Dammit! Hard!"

Jacobus responded instantly. He had excellent reflexes. The slightest touch of a feather would have made him react. He applied the brakes, and the truck, ammunition carrier, and gun, skidded in the sand of the road, swerving from side to side. Jacobus steadied the iron monster as best he could. I was hanging onto the rim of the opening and the guys were yelling as the whole mass of people and machinery came to a halt. We were ten feet from a 25-pounder gun barrel. There was the handkerchief, all covered in sand, now brown in color, hanging from the tip of its barrel.

"Shit! The barrel could have gone through the windshield!" exclaimed Jacobus with his hand on his head. He was sweating. We were all coming down from some high feelings we'd never known before.

"So much for the theory of the handkerchief," yelled the normally quiet Jacobus. Some soldier later commented that it was South Africa's most valuable super-defense secret!

"Shit we've made so much noise catching up to the group, the enemy could have heard us if they were in Johannesburg!" suggested Abie.

"Fantastic driving, Jacobus," said Bobby.

"Yeah! Man!" we agreed.

The column continued for a long while at a snail's pace. Finally, we turned off into the hills, which spread out into a formation like teeth on a hair comb. The gun barrels were facing north to shoot over the hill. All the groups were located on the same side of the hill. The guns were brought into readiness by aligning the gun sights with a small light positioned in a tree. Night watch was ordered. Five out of six slept while one was on watch.

The morning brought hot coffee. The day brought hot weather, routine drills and a complete set-up to be able to fire the guns. The nights brought guard duty. This continued through Sunday. There was little food. Dog biscuits had been issued and that was it. They supposedly had all the vitamins required for survival. This batch was harder than rocks, and did not even dissolve in coffee. The veld was cold at night and the rubberized ground sheet was not thick enough to avoid bumps in the terrain. Ingenious methods of cutting and laying grass, and shifting sand, helped. The wind blew across the plains and up the hill. The mock-attack was scheduled for Monday and everyone was told that the infantry would possibly raid the guns. All unknown personnel must be challenged.

At 10 AM Monday the guns started firing at a designated target. Information came back on hits and misses. Our crew handled the live ammunition gently; this was our first time. We passed it between three people from the ammo carrier into the gun and then closed the breech. Bobby, after setting the sight, would say, "Okay." I would then give the order to fire. After an hour, the shells moved faster from hand to hand and into the breech. On the order of "Salvo (fire at will)," six rounds went off as fast as the breech could be opened and closed and Bobby could set the gun with the hand wheels. This was fun even though the shell burst on the target and exploded ten miles away on some open piece of land with an imaginary target.

"Fun at last," said Abie.

That night at about 11:30, Piet was on guard duty. He heard a jeep moving around in the trees nearby. The gun was located in the trees, but there was clear ground to one side. The jeep appeared through the shadows into the clearing. Piet grabbed his rifle and stood on the edge of the clearing, watching the activity in the moonlight. The jeep stopped. Piet moved out and challenged the jeep. He couldn't see inside because the top was up. "Who goes there?"

No answer!

"Who goes there?" Piet moved towards the jeep, slightly crouched, rifle in hand, hands in the correct position to shoot.

No reply!

Suddenly Piet moved beside a tree for protection, and fixed his bayonet on the end of the rifle. This farmer was at home in the bush. He didn't care about Army bullshit either. Give him an order and he'd do it . . . no philosophy required. He ran toward the jeep. The driver started the engine and the jeep began to move off. Piet ran the bayonet into the passenger side of the jeep. The jeep turned away. Piet stabbed at the top of the jeep and the bayonet went through the canvas. The driver panicked, turned the wheel and pushed down the accelerator. The jeep responded and went right into an anthill that was three feet high. The front wheels went over the top and the oil pan jammed on top of the anthill. Three wheels were in the air and the jeep was rocking.

"What the hell are you doing, soldier?"

"Who are you?" asked Piet.

"Colonel van Staaden."

"Sorry Sir! You did not answer me." Piet was firm.

"What's your name soldier?"

"Private van der Merwe, Sir."

"Get your crew and get this jeep off the anthill!"

"Yes, Sir."

Piet yelled. We were already awake from the noise and watching in amazement at this little man. He was so quiet during all our antics in camp, never leading, always just there. The crew got the jeep back to four wheels on the ground. The jeep disappeared. Piet still had a fixed bayonet on his rifle.

"You can put that away now Piet!"

"Okay!" he replied.

We were worried for Piet; we didn't know what the hell these officers would do. They were like gods in a castle in the sky; they could come down anytime and strike at you. Then they'd disappear again.

On Tuesday morning, our crew sat on a hill and got to see the action of other gun crews firing. We could also see the range where the shells landed. The explosions were all over the place. It was very apparent that the artillery needed more practice.

"Thank God they got the shells over the hill, otherwise we'd have dirt and splintered trees all over us!" commented Bobby.

Tuesday evening the crew went into action and did some night firing. This was a little more exciting as the flashes of the guns hit the dark sky. But the pleasure was short-lived. The wind still blew and the nights were cold and the veld was full of grass and sand, and whatever lived in it. We were hungry too! Wednesday the maneuvers continued with scouting, moving through the bush doing leopard crawls in low grass and whatever the officer could think off. This went on into the afternoon.

Wednesday evening brought an unexpected surprise. We were told it was the end of the maneuvers. Campfires were lit. Meat had been delivered and a braaivleis (barbecue) started. This was truly welcome after days on rations of dog biscuits. Beer was brought in. Nobody ever found out how all the beautiful cases of Castle and Lion Lager got into the camp. The different gun crews mixed and sat around the campfire talking. There were twenty-four soldiers at the campfire where Tom, Bobby, Abie, Piet, Jacobus and I sat. The stories did the rounds again about the scout treatment and the running around the parade ground with our rifles over our head. It was agreed the rifle got really heavy after one lap and seemed to double its weight when the officer told you to run around one more time. The green eggs at breakfast, the tainted meat and the continual reference to 'real war.'

"Who the hell wants to fight a war," I said, "it's so insane, nobody wins. I lost an uncle over Hungary; he was a tail gunner in the South African Air Force. Shit, what a place to be. As a tail gunner you couldn't get into the main body of the plane except when it landed. They knocked on our door at 3 AM in the morning. My grandmother said, 'Oh God, it's Dennis . . . he's been killed.' The man at the door said, 'Your son is missing.' Everyone knew what that meant. Well at least the government offered to pay her way over to Hungary to see the grave." I paused. "What the hell do we care about Hungary or any of those people in Eastern Europe, they just come here and continually tell you South Africa is so backward. Let them stay where they are! Shit, I need a beer!"

"Charl, forget that stuff," said Abie. "Here's a beer."

"Good work, Charl," said Tom. "We were the third best today. Third again!" We had come third in an earlier competition.

"Ah! Nuts! It's not me. It's all of us. Look how good we are when we have fun!" I said, laughing. "We also have the best driver in the camp!"

"Yes! Yes! Jacobus!" yelled everyone in our crew.

"These officers are something else, I know what you're saying Charl," said Abie. "Remember the time we were on the rifle range and we were all in the bunker marking the shots?"

"Yeah ... Oh you mean when the red flag went up?"

"Yeah, and the officers told us, clearly and concisely, 'the red flag means, no loading of rifles, all rifles down on the mats and everyone at least ten feet away from the rifles'."

"Sure, I remember," said Piet, "we were in the bunker, they said 'lunch'. So up goes the flag, we came out of the bunker and sat on the hill having sandwiches."

"Yeah, then the two shots were fired at the targets and into the hill where we were sitting."

"Scare the hell out of you," commented someone.

"Shit! We were down into the bunkers in two seconds!"

"Man! The stupid instructor, Smith or something, the one who was probably a cook's assistant in the Second World War," said Tom "Wasn't he to blame?"

"Yeah! He made that guy, the one who missed the target every time, lie down, take the gun, put it to his shoulder, and then told him to squeeze the trigger, slowly. Yes! There were bullets in the magazine. Then the idiot soldier, probably trying to be smart, cocked the rifle and fired a second shot, before Smith could recover from the shock of hearing the first one!"

"What the hell is a Smith doing in Potchefstroom anyway?"

"He's a British Army reject!"

"Well, the guy said the officer told him, after aiming, to shoot two bullets quickly."

"Wow! We sure scrambled off that hill."

Then someone asked the question on all of our tongues. "How do we pay these officers back?"

"We have to think of a way, we only have a couple of days," said Bobby. "Yeah, we're gone early Saturday morning. This Friday is the last Friday in Potchefstroom and probably the last time I will ever come here."

"Don't be too sure," said Piet.

"What do you mean?" asked Abie.

"Ah! You might like it! So don't forget it," murmured Piet with a big smile. We didn't know what he meant, but it was good to see the smile.

The Army stories disappeared quickly with the mention of the end of the week.

"Is everything set up for the dance party?"

"Yes," said Bobby. "Mickey has got it organized."

This started stories about girls. Army stuff died in a microsecond. We welcomed the subject and continued it well into the night. We were all enjoying the beer and braaivleis. The officers had come by and then left to go to their own party.

Stories abounded about sleeping with black women. Of course, nobody present had done it: it was always someone who was not there! This lead to sleeping with women from the mixed races, and nobody had personally done that either.

"Man, the Cape Colored girls are beautiful, some of them!"

"Yeah, but they get old quickly."

"So, you don't have to be around them for life."

"You go to jail for that!"

"No, you don't! Lots of guys have done it."

"Would you marry one?"

"No! Never! Get serious! Why would you get married to anyone? Just visit ladies . . . less trouble!"

"Even if you really want to go out with colored women, where can you go?"

"Where can you go? Take them to movies or dances and see what happens."

"Nah! I'd make it some quiet place."

"Never touch them," said one farmer.

"You guys from farms man! You don't understand, you must come to the city. We integrate like crazy!"

"No thanks man! What you do in the city is too confusing. I like the simple life."

"He's full of bullshit. I live in the city, it's nothing like he says."

"Where you from? The northern suburbs of Johannesburg? Hey!"

The banter went backwards and forwards until a tall soldier suddenly stood up. He looked as though he was 25.

"Excuse me. I've tried the colored and black women, but the best is white!"

That statement stopped everyone talking.

"Oh! Yes big man. Tell us why . . . Yes! Details my friend. Tell us in detail!"

"Ah! – Man! – Yes!" echoed the guys. We were now lying on the grass, taking in all this bullshit. We listened to this tall, good-looking soldier with daring looks and sparkling eyes.

"I'll tell you why." He got into a comfortable stance, looked around to every soldier. He stood with his legs slightly apart. He pointed his hands upwards and outwards as though to request a go-ahead.

"Go on Man!" suggested quite a few soldiers.

"I met this girl at a dance," continued the tall soldier. "She was young, white as a beautiful white rose. She was, like, 18, and we danced all night."

He had a pleasant low-toned voice. He had a slow style and used his hands to express the meaning of his words. He caught everyone's attention.

"So about 12 o'clock we go to her house and we're on the couch for an hour. Man! We're touching everything and the clothes are being opened and we're going like hell at it."

"You did it?" asked one soldier.

"In an hour, my friend!" He paused, looked at the soldier, turned and looked at the circle of slightly drunken soldiers, and continued, "You do it soon or you leave the place . . . that is the formula. It never improves after an hour, if you didn't get it . . . .."

He turned once more to study the crowd. This was his style. "Well, we're all dressed about 1:30 AM, sitting quietly, and the mother comes down the stairs. Man, I was embarrassed, my hair, my clothes were all messed up.

"'Time for bed, my dear' says the mother.

"'This is Clark, Mom!' says my young lady.

"'Hullo!' I said.

"'Hullo!' her mother says, with a blank look on her face. 'I'll show him out.'

"*Oh! Shit!* I'm thinking. *Big lesson coming up.* The daughter winks at me and goes upstairs.

"'Sit down, Clark.' the mother says . . . like an instruction. Man, I'm nervous, Jussus I don't like it man!

"'Would you like a beer?' she asks me.

"'No! . . . Yes! . . . Please!' I answered.

"So we sit, she has a drink and I have a beer. It is about a half an hour of this and man is she friendly! Her nightgown is open at the knees and she touches me on the arm."

"What?" said one drunken soldier. "What did you say? . . . What did you do?"

"Well," Clark continued, "I was nervous because I thought my date might be looking down from upstairs. Then her mother says she thinks I'm a handsome man and her hand goes to my shoulder, pulls my head towards her and she whispers in my ear. She turns down the lights, sips her second drink and I finish most of my beer. She takes the bottle and puts it on the floor and the next thing, man, . . . we're on the floor with the beer."

"What! Did you? . . . Aah! Come on!"

"Yes! Man! Her robe slips off. I rip my pants off and we're naked and going at it."

"Shit, what about the husband? . . . Are you nuts?"

"No men in the house, Man! My date told me her dad was gone, no brothers."

"You did it?"

"Well, she gets up off the floor and says, 'I'm going to bed. Sleep on the couch if you want Clark.' She smiled. 'We'll get you breakfast in the morning.'"

"You stayed? Are you crazy? No way! Man! Nobody would . . ."

"I stayed for a while. No busses and I've got nothing to do." He had the group of us mesmerized as he continued . . . "At about 3:30 AM there's a noise on the stairs."

Clark stalled, drank his beer and looked around. The crowd was quiet and listening. You could sense an aura of disbelief, but . . .

"The mother? Your date?" asked a few guys.

Clark smiled. "No, the grandmother."

"Oh! Yeah! . . . So granny is going to the bathroom?" interjected another soldier.

"No! She comes to the couch and sits down."

"Spare us all!" yelled someone.

"Bullshit!" yelled another. Most guys were laughing!

"Okay!" said Clark, and walked over to the place where he had been sitting. "Yeah! We did it as well." The tall soldier sat down, smiling and stated emphatically, "Man! white women are the best!"

Very few believed it, some laughed at it, and some were just bored, but that broke up the campfire group and we went to find our sleeping place on the ground near the 25 pounder gun.

Thursday, we returned to camp. All equipment was washed, cleaned and put away. Barracks were rendered spotless. Everyone took showers and prepared for Friday.

◆

The passing-out parade was an eight-mile march from camp to Potchefstroom and back. Best uniform, polished boots and brass buckles. The canvas leggings, straps, and boot covers had been washed with Branco and our .303 rifles were all shined and polished. There were people on the roadway. Some parents had come to pick up their soldier sons on Saturday. Our crew was going back by car Saturday morning, we had arranged a pick-up. The official dismissal was 8 AM, Saturday. The march was boring; the town was dry and hot. Summer was ending but it was hot that day. After ten miles we had passed the barricade where all of the senior officers were sitting. We became an unending column of soldiers marching back to camp. The rifles were very heavy and irritated the collarbone. Every time someone repositioned theirs, they were warned of extra duty. Some soldiers slipped a handkerchief underneath, others turned the barrel every ten minutes, and some balanced it just off the shoulder. Piet, the smallest guy, just marched the whole way, never grumbled, never complained, never moved the position of the rifle. No one could grasp this mature man in a young man's body.

Friday night the conversation continued about the great payback. We were packing our kit bags full of personal belongings. We stuffed everything in the bag, except the uniform required for the final Saturday morning dismissal parade.

Finally, Saturday came and the soldiers listened to all the accolades. Then came the one order everyone wanted, "Company dismiss!" Everybody leapt, yelled, threw hats in the air, hugged buddies, and shook hands and took off for home.

I got a taxi from Johannesburg after being dropped off. Piet was met in Johannesburg. I arrived at 65 Andrew Street at noon. I stepped out of the taxi in my uniform, kit bag in hand and backpack slung over my shoulder. I started to move towards the front gate and was met by Pal, my beautiful dog. He jumped up and was all over me, and finally flattened me to the ground and licked my face. I took on the challenge and left the bags on the ground and grabbed Pal, who immediately got out of my grip and ran 10 yards away and 10 yards back and we did this for five minutes. It was as if Pal knew I was home for a longer time now. Before, all the visits had been short, as I had dashed off to see my friends. Pal had responded very nonchalantly to this!

"Hi Gran!"

"Hi Son! You look like you've been camping."

"Yes."

"No, I mean your face has white stuff, windburn or something."

"It'll come off."

We hugged for a long time. Pal was still barking and running around us. Uncle Mick had met me at the door. My mom was at work.

That night Bobby, Tom, Abie, Mickey and I picked up all the girls and drove to Northcliff, in the northern suburbs of Johannesburg. On top of a hill was the Worldsview Nightclub, where you could take a bottle of liquor and give it to the club waiters. They would pour drinks for you and add a mix, for a high price, and everybody benefited. This got around some legal liquor issues. Johannesburg youth were used to walking the edge of legality often, and for a change it worked out to be cheap. The Worldsview always had great live music, jazz and rock. As it was located on top of a hill, the club and parking lot became very romantic when viewing the lights of Johannesburg downtown. It was also possible to see the lights of Pretoria on a clear night. Abie had once, when told of this, exclaimed, "So what, it's a just a dorp (small town)."

Before we went into the club, Bobby warned us, "This is my mother's car and if I get drunk, nobody is allowed to drive it."

"That's because, folks," I added, "one night I was driving his mom's car, Bobby was drunk in the passenger seat and we were in Johannesburg near Eloff Street. We stopped at a traffic light. This car pulls up. Guess who was in it? . . . Bobby's mother . . . I died. Well, Bobby, you tell the story."

"No car for three months. And I want the car for next week. If I get drunk, I don't drive." Bobby informed us firmly.

Everyone looked so very different, considering the last three months. We were sitting down at the table—suits—sharp ties—nice dresses—high heels—make up: a bunch of 18-year-old kids having fun.

"How come you all have this white crust over your face?" asked Jackie.

"We all got it from the Potchefstroom wind, while on maneuvers," answered Tom. "Hope it goes away."

"Have another drink, Jackie!" suggested Bobby. The guys all laughed.

"Love to! What are you laughing at?" asked Jackie.

"Nothing!" the chorus replied.

I was in heaven. Rosemary looked stunning. Everyone was talking, drinking a lot and dancing. Rosemary and I went out onto the balcony and hugged and kissed, and talked, then returned to the dancing room. The band had stopped playing. When we got to the table, Jackie, leaning into the wind a little, demanded, "I want to know what the revenge on the permanent officers was."

"Secret," said Tom, who was getting interested in this lady who drank men under the table.

"Oh, come on, you know, we won't tell anybody of significance."

"We don't know anybody of significance," said Abie.

"Tell her Piet." He had come up from Vereeniging to join the crew and had a very pretty girl by his side.

"No."

"Come on Piet," said Jackie. "You and Bettie are so quiet."

"Just in love," said Abie, who had been matched with a girl, Rebecca, from the Southern Suburbs Turffontein area. We liked her because she knew how to handle Abie, who was well on his way to being drunk.

"Don't take notice of Abie," said Rebecca.

"We are in love," said Bettie. Piet blushed.

"Great," I said. "That's the way to be." I raised my glass. "Some guy this Piet. Bettie we approve of your choice and we definitely approve of his."

"Thank you" Bettie replied. Piet just smiled.

"Charl, after trying to lead us in Potch! For once you've got something right!" added Tom with a smiling face.

"Don't be mean, I'm brain injured. I've just spent three months with the 'intelligentsia' of South Africa's Army who have convinced me to go jump off a very high bridge if South Africa ever goes to war."

"Why?" asked Bobby, who was also getting drunk.

"Because it would be too confusing to fight under their command, and you would have a better chance of survival!"

"Hey! South Africa did well in the Second World . . ."

"Hey! I'm kidding!"

"No! You're not!"

"Listen!" interjected Abie. "Forget the Army." He paused while all of us quieted down. "Let's dance."

"Yes!"

"Yes!" Margo and Mickey agreed.

"No, wait a minute," said Jackie. "How did you guys get revenge?"

"Tell her Piet," said Abie. "Come on man, be a pal."

Piet took his beer, had a sip and started the story. We were all ears. We had never seen Piet on center stage. This was too marvelous. We were more than attentive. We were all as quiet as a Teddy Bear on a child's pillow.

"On Friday night, while everyone was packing and getting ready for going home, we walked around the officers' quarters. We were just looking, and it was before 9 o'clock." Piet had our full attention. He took a drink.

He asked softly, "Should I tell?"

"Yes!" the guys replied.

"The officers always get biscuits and tea at 9 PM. We wanted to put something in the tea. It was very hard to understand how much could be put in the pot without changing the taste. So we experimented by adding more tea leaves and that helped hide the taste."

"What did you put in the tea?" asked Rosemary.

"Epsom Salts," said Bobby.

"Oh my God," said Jackie, "that stuff can make you go to the bathroom every hour, for days, if you have too much."

"So Piet, who put the Epsom salts in the teapots, was it the cooks?"

"No!" said Piet.

"How? Who did it?" asked Jackie.

"That's the secret," I said, "and nobody is going to tell!"

"All we want to say is that there were a lot of officers missing from the parade this morning," said Piet.

"I mean . . . a lot. I think the guys got them good and they're probably in bed right now!" added Abie.

We all laughed.

"Come on, you guys!" pleaded Jackie.

"Let's dance," I suggested. "The band is great."

We got up, satisfied with the last of the Army stories, and very happy with the payback. We disappeared onto the dance floor and fell into the mood of fun and the rhythms of rock music.

I enjoyed the dance so much I did not want time to pass. We had come from a small hell to heaven today, and I wanted the evening to just smolder rather than burn away.

One o'clock arrived. Mickey and his Margo were happy. He stood up and raised his glass and said. "I'm glad you're back . . . I missed you all!"

"No! We missed you, Mickey," replied Bobby. We drank and we knew what he meant.

Then what seemed like two seconds later it was two o'clock. The couples reassembled. We said good-bye to Piet and Bettie, and wished them all the best. "See you soon . . . Cheers!"

"Where's Abie?"

"He went to the car at midnight. He was drunk."

"Where's Bobby?"

"Went with him."

"Who's going to drive?"

"Tom, maybe."

"Have you got the key?" I asked.

"No, Bobby has it."

Our half-drunk group found Bobby at the wheel, asleep. After a long scramble and shaking we still couldn't wake him. We looked everywhere, even in his pockets, but could not find the key. Coffee was suggested, but the club was closed. Everyone climbed in the car, talked, sort've fell asleep. Five couples curled up. Despite the fact the girls were anxious to get home, the boys not so anxious to go. Why end something good? We hadn't been in the back of a car with a girl for some time.

"Wait for an hour, we'll get Bobby to wake up and go. He won't let anyone drive now anyway."

Everyone fell asleep.

The cold air of early morning finally penetrated the car structure and woke up one of the girls. She moved and everybody slowly entered the land of living, including Bobby.

"Let's go Bobby! Shit, the girls are in trouble! Where's the key!"

Bobby got out of the car, took off his shoe and produced the key.

"This goddamned Army stuff has made you sneaky . . . let's go!"

The car descended from Northcliff and into the suburbs. Abie was still out. The car pulled up at Rebecca's.

"Will someone walk me up the driveway. I'm scared!"

Nobody answered. Mickey said he'd walk her up the driveway.

Margo said. "Go for it!"

Rebecca and Mickey walked slowly up the driveway.

"My father's going to hit me," said Rebecca, looking very worried.

"You're not serious?" asked Mickey.

"Yes!" she replied.

"Tell him the truth!"

"He won't believe anything." Rebecca's face had lost the joy of the party.

"Do you have a key?" asked Mickey.

"No!"

"Oops! . . . Mistake maybe?"

They reached the door and it was locked. Rebecca rang the bell. Within thirty seconds the door opened.

"What the hell, it's five o'clock!"

"I'm sorry, Sir!" said Mickey.

"He didn't . . ." Rebecca stopped herself. She couldn't say she hadn't gone with Mickey.

"It's not his fault, Dad."

"Don't you show your face here again," he yelled at Mickey. Then he turned to his daughter. "You get inside Rebecca!"

As she went in the door, her father took a quick step towards Mickey. Mickey took off. Bobby started the car. Tom opened the door, in jumped Mickey, and we drove off!

"Shit!"

"See! We make such good getaway . . . you don't need good Army training . . . Ja!" I joked, but that didn't help!

Someone started with "Look what we've been through in the last three months . . . the train . . . the radiator . . . the farmer." Then someone else interrupted. "The camp shit. . . Jackie and the girls from Northern Suburbs!" We laughed! She was asleep. Again someone added, ". . . the snake . . . Charl and the instructor! . . . White girls".

This was followed by a spurt of words from others, " . . . Bobby's hole, he didn't fall in . . . stupid officers and maneuvers . . . Piet challenging the colonel . . . Getting shot at . . . The green eggs . . . The tea . . .Yeah!"

The suggestions died out as the car rolled downtown and into Johannesburg with everyone singing,

"Got along wit outcha . . . before I metcha!
Gonna get along wit outcha you now!
Ah! Ha! . . . Ah! Ha!"

◆

The gun crew dissipated fast into individual lifestyles. I got off some Saturday obligations of the Army because I pleaded about my important soccer venues and my college workload. I had been very lucky to get Fridays off . . . there *was* something good in the officers. 'Bobby's Group', as I called them, met occasionally in the Southern Suburbs and connected at parties.

Rosemary and I went out for another six months doing something almost every weekend. My problem was transport. We were in love, I knew. But then we broke up because of my studies, and the fact that she and Jackie always went out when I had to study or had to go to soccer. I believed during this time that she met a guy named Peter. He was a good looking guy who could devote a lot of time to girls, never having to be in the Army, play soccer, and study, or maybe it was just the unreasonable reason of being more available. I went through the rotten emotions of a first love break-up. Somehow blues music became very appropriate. The words of 'St Louis Blues' echoed through my head for a long time. Billy Eckstine's version made me disappear from life on earth. I buried my soul into soccer, work for survival, books for school and my friends in the Andrew Street Mob. I never knew why I had made that decision. I could have given up on all my life's complexity and stayed together with Rosemary. But I had analyzed that a million times in a million places. I just knew I didn't want to just give in to a pleasure that meant I could not do something with myself. Being a dancer remained low on my list and was disappearing as a dream. Besides, I loved engineering design, it seemed endless, and all that it entailed. But even more, I was in heaven playing soccer; I was pretty good and would not give it up. I definitely couldn't give up the studying, which would make me a better person!

"Maybe Abie was right," I said out aloud, one day during my recovery. "Yes he is right!"

He had said, "Maybe we should just have a drink and have fun."

*

CHAPTER 9

The South Coast:
Durban and Scottburgh

Durban

EVER SINCE WE COULD remember, Durban and Scottburgh had been two magic words to the Andrew Street Mob. These two resorts had long been suggested as the place to go for fun. Located in a sub-tropical region with magnificent beaches. Surrounded by hills covered in banana trees, sugar cane fields, green grass and green tropical plants; all with rivers coming down from the mountains, in what seemed like every twenty miles of coast. In the 'Fifties' it was a young person's getaway to the beaches for fun, dancing and adventure. The biggest attraction was girls in skimpy bathing suits, sometimes away from their parents for the first time! One large step removed from parents, teachers, and bosses: and freedom expanded exponentially. The first couple of trips were learning experiences. Most trips had previously been done with family. Trevor was raised there, but he didn't relate much detail to us, or we hadn't been listening when he did!

We essentially wanted to discover it ourselves.

Information from school, adults who talked about their vacations and friends taught us many aspects of this intriguing coast. We knew Durban and Scottburgh were located in the province of Natal and on the South Coast of South Africa. Durban is a large city and port. Scottburgh is one of the oldest towns along the South Coast. Natal is the home of the Zulu Nation. Shaka, a Zulu Chief born in 1787, was responsible for the rise of the Zulu Nation and the conquest of the Natal territory. Natal is also home to an Indian population first brought into

South Africa in 1860; the most famous of them, Mohandas Ghandi, came late in the nineteenth century, with his philosophy of passive resistance. Although discovered by the Portuguese and being subject to Dutch, English, Indian and Zulu residents plus the wars of Zulu-Natal tribes, Zulu-Boer, Anglo-Zulu and the Boer War, the atmosphere was very South African and had a large thread of traditional European ways.

None of us were sailors but sea stories intrigued us. We lived in a country that was about 70% surrounded by sea. There were a hundred stories of South African whaling, shipwrecks on our west and east coasts and a thousand stories on the complex oceans surrounding our land. The west coast is essentially barren like desert, the east coast very fertile. The mighty Agulhas Current flows down the East Coast of South Africa. Natal is situated between the East and South coasts of South Africa. The Agulhas Current is up to 160 kilometers wide and moves swiftly at 5 knots. It compresses a north-flowing current close to the shore causing the famous 'Sardine Run' in June as the sardines complete their migration. The strong force of the current also creates one of the world's most turbulent seas when combined with heavy southwesterly gales. The results are 'killer waves' reaching a height of 20 meters. For small vessels to 90,000-ton ships, the sea is dangerous. The warm waters attract sharks and there are many species on the coast. The Tiger, Zambezi and White sharks are among the most dangerous. The Tiger and Zambezi enter the river estuaries, with the Zambezi even swimming upstream. The historical stories I learnt were intriguing and exciting to read, but to go and swim and surf where these large species of fish swim scared the hell out of me.

◆

Our standard Friday night of going to the theater to see a movie and having drinks at the Broadway Hotel in the southern suburbs had become just a little too regular. One Friday, close to 11:00 PM, Zoni, Trevor, Johnny, Doc and I were sitting in the Broadway Hotel.

"No plans his weekend," said Doc.

"Yeah, nothing at all," said Johnny.

"Anyone else?"

"No," everyone replied.

"Whose game to go to Durban?" I asked.

"When?"

"Tonight."

"Tonight, are you crazy, it's an eight hour drive."

"What else would we do? . . . I mean who cares . . . lets do something different."

"We could leave at 12 midnight and be in Durban by 8:00 AM for breakfast. We can get a hotel room on Saturday for one, and all sneak in later."

"We could walk around and see the sites of Durban, surf all day Saturday and surf on Sunday and then leave at 2:00 PM"

"We'd be back at 10:00 PM Sunday night and refreshed!"

"It's summer, man! Have to get to the big water!"

The enthusiasm grew as the beers disappeared and suggestions flowed from one to the other. You could sense the positiveness for going, very easily overcoming the nothing-to-do atmosphere.

"We could go to Van Wyks Rust on Sunday if you want water," said Doc.

"I like the water that goes up and down in curls, smells of salt, and throws you onto a beach!" I replied. "Like when we went to Cape Town, Doc!"

"Did we swim in the sea?"

"Yes! Camps Bay . . . cold as hell!"

"I'm game," said Trevor. "How about your car Zoni. Will it make it?"

"Yes, we can go in it. But you guys buy the petrol," Zoni stipulated.

"We always do!" said the group in chorus not even missing a beat.

"Okay! Corner of Andrew Street and Main, Zoni's house --- 12 midnight. I'll bring beer and sandwiches," said Johnny.

"Sandwiches?" asked Trevor.

"Hey! Johnny always has to bring something. Relax! Man!" suggested Doc with a smile.

"Chocolate cake, then," suggested Trevor.

The five of us walked home up Main Street. Trevor cut off to go to Leonard Street. Johnny picked up his Austin A-40 at Zoni's place and went home to 'Emoyeni', his house, which was two miles north of Andrew Street. Johnny's home, built on the edge of the koppies, overhung a steep, rocky hill that sloped down into a small valley. A beautiful modern house, in comparison to all the other houses lived in by kids who hung around in the Andrew Street Mob. It had a single-lane bowling green. Johnny's parents had their own business. His dad had gone to America to gain experience before the Second World War and had landed on the day of the start of the Great Depression. After returning to South Africa, following the war, he had set up a construction supply business. Johnny and his brother were well off. Johnny was very different to his brother Allen in kindness and warm personality. Although Johnny had never been short of the material things of life, he had never showed any difference to his buddies: we liked that very much!

Trevor, who had become a steady member of the Andrew Street Mob, had grown up in the Natal Province. He spoke Zulu to some degree and it was enough to make all the Zulus laugh and love him for his knowledge of their language. Trevor was a fun raiser; he incited activity and laughter. He mixed well with girls and had no difficulty entrancing a lot of them to enjoy life, to dance, and have fun. We always thought it was due to his 'stories' but some girls had said it was due to his good looks, clean manner and wonderful smile. We agreed reluctantly but didn't care if he was better looking than us!

Our small Andrew Street group met at midnight with swim gear, pants to go dancing, towels, beer, sun cream, and whatever the refrigerator at home had on its shelves that wouldn't be missed. There were small amounts of money in our pockets. We were young people, and only starting our working life, and would still walk home up Main Street to save a three-penny bus fare. Apprentices of the business, manufacturing, and mining worlds, we had left behind the shorts and running shoes that were worn 24 hours a day, and were now working and responsible for ourselves. Our Mob contributed to the welfare of our families; we paid rent, bought our own clothes and tried to get ahead in any way we could. There was a pride in doing that for our hardworking parents. We never questioned it! As clothes were important to meet girls, to create an image, and to feel better than just working in factories, they were a top priority. Long pants of worsted wool, a nice pair of leather shoes, moccasins (definitely without a parent's approval), ties, open neck shirts with long sleeves, neatly ironed, and a good looking jacket, often called 'A Float'. We still needed help in many ways but there was a pride in trying to do it independently of our parents. Birthday and Christmas presents were predominantly clothes in pretty boxes.

Jumping into Zoni's car, we found it crowded, but what the heck—it was very exciting just to leave everything behind. The car sped off.

"First stop, Ladysmith," said Doc.

"What the hell is in Ladysmith?" asked Trevor.

"Nothing."

"Why stop?"

"Don't stop, then," said Doc.

"This is going to be a stupid trip, I know," said Johnny.

The conversation drifted into a wild party that Johnny, Trevor, Viv and I had gone to about three weeks previously. Viv had started to hang out with us because we were fun! Transportation was always a problem so I had gone with Bobby, Tom and Mickey. I hung out with them many times separately, as they were rarely a part of the Andrew Street Mob activities. Trevor related the story.

"It was in Malvern! I don't know who gave the party! Betsie van—der – Something! She lives in one of the resident houses on the mine. You know the ones built with the fly-screens on the back porch, on a small piece of ground, and surrounded by fences. Actually, dirty fly-screens! Broken fences! . . . We also had a double date that night. Shelley had asked John, Charl and I to come over after the party. Her parents were away, and she had two friends staying over for the night," said Trevor.

"Malvern to Krugersdorp, that's thirty miles. It's the other side of town," said Zoni.

"Yes! As though we had so much to do on Sunday!" I added.

"So what was wild?" asked Doc.

"Two girls at the party were taking turns."

"With everybody?" asked Zoni.

"Well, only those who found out," said Trevor.

"You went with them?" asked Zoni.

"No," I interjected. "Trevor doesn't do that kind of thing!"

"What are you two talking about?" asked Doc. "Either you screwed them or you didn't!"

"No! . . . I want to know these two girls . . . what's their names, did they want to make it?" asked Zoni.

"Yes!" I answered.

"They just went with a bunch of guys."

"Six or seven each," I said.

"Bullshit!"

"No Zoni . . . true man. Seriously . . . two girls and we don't know all the guys who went with them."

"You went with them?" asked Doc.

"I went with one," I said.

"In the house?"

"No! I borrowed Bobby's car. We drove about five blocks away to the park."

"And?"

"Well we got into the back seat and the clothes came off, man! She just rolled up her dress and it was crazy, it was over so quickly. We didn't say much . . . sat and talked for a while . . . then she said, 'I want to go back to the party.'"

"Were these girls smoking dagga (marijuana)?"

"No, but they were drinking . . . lots!"

"What about you guys?" said Doc, looking at Trevor and Johnny.

"Yes, we went to the party, but we didn't go with those girls," replied Johnny with a somewhat innocent look.

"No, we didn't go," confirmed Trevor. "Absolutely."

"Hey, the Andrew Street girls were there as well," said Johnny. "Beryl, Thelma, Gloria, Ann and Grace, anyway".

"Did they see you, did they know what you were doing?" asked Zoni.

"Who knows?"

"Girls always find out these things!" said Doc.

"Then you went to Krugersdorp?" Zoni kept pressing for information. The group was purposely letting him work for information.

"Yes," said Trevor. "Johnny drove all the way to Krugersdorp, midnight date. Charl had this idea of scaring the girls by knocking on the front door, rattling the windows and then running around to knock on the back door. So we did that! I went to the front door and knocked, rattled the windows and then disappeared. Charl went to the back door and knocked."

"The back door came open so fast," I said. "The back verandah light went on at the same time. And a double-barrel shotgun was in my stomach . . . shit!"

"Hell! Man!" interjected Zoni.

"'Shelly! . . . Shelley! It's me Charl,' I yelled, as I put my hand on the barrel and moved it out of the line with my body."

"'Don't you ever do that again,' she yelled back."

Everyone laughed!

"Scared the shit out of me," I confirmed.

"Now, he was white-white for some time," said Trevor.

"I asked her if the gun was loaded, and she said, 'Absolutely'," I added.

"Yes! . . . Oh! My God!" Exclaimed Doc.

"So you had another party? Did you get any?"

"Why do you guys always want to know that? . . . Well, it was sure quiet compared to the other party in Malvern. We drank beer in the kitchen, sat at the table eating cheese and crackers. Shelley had made them. We talked forever. After about three beers Trevor split to the living room." I answered. "Johnny was talking to another girl and left for some other part of the house. Shelley and I stayed in the kitchen. She was kind've a tease. Maybe it was because she was so pretty with her blonde hair, perky face, sensuous smile and wandering eyes. She had a figure like a gazelle . . . tight! We shared another beer, passing it back and forward, while starting to touch and kiss. Then standing right in front of me, she did back-bends on the kitchen floor! Weird! Saying this was the latest gymnastic backbend. The position though suggested a dozen other things."

"What things?"

"Well! . . .Well! . . . You guys know! Do you want me to make a drawing?" I answered. "After a while . . . you know, after beer and backbends . . . I didn't know what to make of it. If I was aggressive she backed off! So nothing happened!"

"Yes! Sure Charl we believe you!!"

"A short while after the backbend demonstration, she just suddenly said, 'You boys better get going, the sun is coming up and I don't want the neighbors to see you leaving.' I agreed. So! Johnny, Trevor and I left. I wondered why we even went there!"

"So did you two guys get anything?" asked Zoni, looking at Trevor and Johnny.

"No! Sir! A fun wasted effort," replied Johnny.

"Don't know if I believe you," said Zoni. "Who wants to drive?" he added.

"I'll drive," said Doc.

We stopped. We didn't always stop, to change drivers, but was a strange two-lane road, which turned all over the map.

So Zoni got out to go to the left front seat. Doc took the wheel and, after stretching, Trevor, Johnny and I returned to the back of the two-door car. We squirmed our way, into uncomfortable positions, with arms and legs intertwined. We found out why Doc wanted to drive.

The hours of the morning moved on and we drifted into sleep, except Doc, of course. He stopped at Ladysmith and filled up the car and nobody moved. About an hour later Doc heard something rattling in the back of the car. We were doing about 80 miles per hour. He tugged at Zoni and slowed the car down fairly fast, which woke everybody.

"Zoni, something's making a noise in the back," said Doc loudly.

Zoni, in a sleepy haze, reached in the glove compartment, took out a torch, opened the car door and got out. The car was still doing 20 miles per hour!

"Zoni!" yelled Doc, as he swerved the car away from Zoni's pathway. Trevor, Johnny and I were thrown into a lump on one side of the car and were now completely awake. We heard the sound of Zoni's body hitting the ground and the door slamming shut. Looking around out of the back window, all we could see on the unlit two-lane highway was a light bouncing all over the place. Doc stopped the car .We jumped out fast, like soldiers going into action, ran back to where we saw the light. In the mist we saw Zoni getting up.

"You okay, man?" yelled Johnny.

Trevor helped him up.

"Yes," said Zoni, shaken up, full of sand, and with a scraped arm. "I'm okay. What the hell happened?"

"You got out of the car while it was moving," said Doc. "You're lucky the side of the road is sand."

We couldn't find the rattle, didn't care, so we got back into the car. Johnny was the new driver and we kept going to Durban and we all went back to sleep.

I woke up and the car was moving. It was early morning and everything was very quiet. The dawn pre-light was everywhere.

We were traveling down through the Valley of a Thousand Hills. It was blue-gray beautiful. The large rolling hills had mist touching the top of every mountain. These were big hills and valleys, trees closely packed, all touching each other almost as if to say 'it is cold . . . stay close'. I had not seen this type of beauty and it sank into my mind. I immediately questioned living in the flatlands of the Transvaal. The road wound round the hills as it descended at a steep angle. If the car went over the side of the road it would be a long time and a long way before we'd have come to a stop. After a long while of my staring out the window, we reached Pietermaritzburg. This was beautiful. I knew about this place. Pietermaritzburg, a historical town steeped in the history of the Boer vs. British fighting. It is located south of the battle-fields of Rorke's Drift and Blood River where the Boers and British fought the mighty Zulu Impis. This was Northern Natal, Zulu country, home of Shaka, Dingaan and Cetshwayo. It was a countryside that witnessed the Mfecane (crushing/scattering) warfare that left hundreds of thousands of blacks dead through Shaka's period of extermination and monstrous cruelty to the other black clans. Pietermaritzburg had become an English-speaking town despite having an Afrikaner origin. I was glad it was peaceful now.

My mother had said that there are very few things more beautiful than a sunrise. I thought that it was incredible descending through the Valley of a Thousand Hills, through Pietermaritzburg and into Durban. The last leg with a continuing tree forest, trees close together, averaging 40-feet high, with a winding two-lane road and precipitous drops on one side. However it was different now because there was the start of sub-tropical landscape with palm trees and different vegetation.

Johnny finally drove into the outskirts of Durban. Durban was a coastal city with beaches and modern city buildings and hotels, with a magnificent history of development from Pioneer days. Vasco da Gama landed here in 1497 on Christmas Day. Just less than 400 years later in 1823 the British decided to stay and still later in the 1860's more British settled here. Indian laborers came to work the sugar cane fields and were later joined by Voortrekkers from the Cape. Durban also changed hands, according to whether British or Boer were dominant. Durban, although one of the busiest ports in Africa, to most people from Johannesburg, it was just a place for long-awaited holidays. The main attraction was the constant weather temperature, the beaches, the hotels, the nightclubs plus the surrounding recreational areas: a great combination for fun. The city and surrounding areas had almost a perfect all-year-round warm climate. The rich sub-tropical fruits, fresh fish from the sea, spices from the Far East, Indian cooking, combined with all other cultures in restaurants made Durban very popular: a true sub-tropical paradise of activities. Looking east, the sea covered the rest of the picture till it disappeared on the horizon.

What is life like over the sea? I questioned. *It's not enough to see pictures and movies, I know that!* My thoughts continued for some time on that question as I stared at this very clean and brightly painted city. *Intriguing,* I thought. *What a trip, already!* The car swept through the empty streets, a few stragglers were hanging around the corners as other people were on the way to work. South Africa had a five-and-a-half-day workweek for offices and shops. The tradesmen had a five-day week. The people in the streets were going to work until 1 o'clock.

Johnny stopped the car at a sand parking lot on the beach. We literally fell out of the car, took our shoes off and walked on the cool, moist grains of sand. The air was brisk with a promise of a hot day to come. The dawn sunlight was now above the hills, behind us, as we walked towards the sea.

"Monstrous . . . unbelievable!" said Trevor, as he jumped out of the car and ran twenty yards and purposely fell in the sand.

"Let's get some breakfast," said Zoni.

"Yes!" "Yes!" "Yes! Okay, yes!" Came the chorused reply.

Johnny locked the car, and we found a place to eat. We crunched into the bacon and eggs and toast and savored the hot Kenya coffee . . . our favorite. We talked about possible events in Durban and decided if we divided the number of events by the hours it would be impossible. After breakfast we came back to the car, changed and went body surfing. It was so amazingly easy just to go out and swim. Lifeguards were on the beach already. There were signs on the beach indicating various currents and the safety conditions. Early swimmers and beach walkers were already there. We did not venture very far as we only knew about swimming in pools and rivers: especially me. We surfed until all the muscles ached, then dragged our bodies out, lay on the beach and fell asleep. People came out of their houses and down to the beach with kids, buckets, lunch, towels and other beach paraphernalia. After a couple of hours we woke up to the sound of activities and found we were surrounded by hundreds of people. It was ten o'clock and 85°F.

Zoni had heard of a dance near the beach that night with a rock-and-roll dance competition: perfect! We spent the rest of the day on the beach surfing, swimming, and walking around looking at the girls on the beach. Then we walked down the esplanade past the hotels and witnessed the world famous Zulu Rickshaw Boys enticing tourists to ride. It was something to see the incredible number of beads that made up their costumes and rickshaws; probably in the millions. None of us had enough money to spend on lodgings. So the decision at breakfast was to hang onto money for the dance: there would be no hotel room. While looking and walking along Durban's boardwalk and esplanade, we finally witnessed the tourists going back to their hotels. It was becoming quieter now as the sun was going down and we were absorbed in the most beautiful, multicolored sea sunset. It was dream-like. Standing on a deck and leaning on the railings, it was very difficult to understand that the water actually extended thousands of miles before touching Australia's shore.

That evening we took fresh-water showers on the beach, dried off and got changed in the car. By 9 o'clock we were sitting down at a table drinking Castle and Lion Lager. Trevor won the 'Name the Five Rock and Roll Songs and Singers Competition' with a certain amount of help from Johnny and me. We knew all the answers backwards but left Trevor to fill out the card. We danced with the spare girls, usually standing in two's. We made sure these girls were not attached to a local crowd or belonging to someone, having learned those rules when venturing out to dances held in Krugersdorp, Germiston and especially certain suburbs of Johannesburg, such as Jeppe and Malvern. We followed the unwritten, but wise rule, 'don't break into the local crowd, regardless of who smiles at you'.

We had a great time dancing. Zoni hit almost every dance, I was not far behind that number and neither was Trevor. We drank too much and became friendly with some very nice girls, which just made our 43-hour day. Finally we dragged ourselves slowly back over the beach to the car. It was 3 AM. Two slept inside and three outside on towels!

Sunday morning sunrise was not as pretty as Saturday's glorious exit of the sun.

"Maybe true beauty is more of an excitation than a real thing," I suggested to Trevor.

"Too early, Charl."

End of discussion.

Our crew surfed once again. This time we became more adventurous, wanting the excitement of catching bigger and stronger waves, which translated their energy into the feeling of having more power in the water around our bodies. We were propelled faster and further. What a feeling. We did this again and again until we were exhausted. None of us would have quit except for the presence of fatigue. Then Zoni saw two of the girls from the night before. We were glad that our choices of the evening had been in good taste! We were also maybe a little worried about what would happen if all the girls we asked to come to the beach last night, actually came. However, life seldom embarrassed us that way. The girls joined us, lay on the beach and did some near-shore surfing with us. We ended up going for a short walk and, unfortunately for our pocket money, went to lunch. Later we returned to the beach and lay around talking.

"I could do this all my life," I said as I lay next to this pretty girl.

"It's 4 o'clock guys," said Doc.

"Shit, are you serious," said Zoni. "I've got to get up at 5 AM!"

"We've got to go, girls," said Trevor.

"Where are you going?" they asked.

"Home!"

"Why?"

"We've got to go to Johannesburg," said Trevor.

"Johannesburg?" one girl exclaimed. "You guys didn't tell us that! Charl said you were from Pietermaritzburg!"

"No, I didn't say Pietermaritzburg . . . were we drunk? . . . No, maybe it was some one else!" I replied with an embarrassed smile.

"No we weren't drunk."

"Charl, tell the truth!" suggested one of the girls.

"No, I don't remember saying that! Ah well!" I bowed. "I'm sorry! It didn't work Hey!" I suggested.

"No!" came back the three girls in reply.

We all laughed. We reconciled because there was something exciting in this group venture. We promised a return, invited them to Johannesburg, took phone numbers, and said our goodbyes. I actually got a kiss. This surprised me, mainly because it put a smile on the face of my friends. We slowly piled into the car after all kinds of discussion on arrangements for driving, paying for petrol, what time we would get home, and why did we do this?

"We've got to come back and go to Margate at Christmas for a couple of weeks."

"Maybe Scottburgh."

"Well, somewhere down here."

It was agreed.

The drive home was mixed with feelings of whether it was a great idea or was it worth it because we were now going to pay for it. The two-lane highway took over eight hours once you cleared the city limits of Durban. The break was at Ladysmith and still nobody ever knew why. It was perhaps just a good time to stretch before you actually screamed aloud with frustration. We had eventually cleared Durban at six o'clock and by the time we got to bed in the Southern Suburbs it was

3:30 AM. I had to get up at 5:30 AM to get to work at 7:00 AM. The whole crew would be up by 6:30 AM to be at work by at least 8 AM. No regrets, we all agreed substantially. This was the start of some new adventures. We had cleared the runway for take-off. It was time for new things to happen.

◆

Scottburgh

Talk of the second trip to the South Coast was in almost every conversation. The only consensus was that it would not be Durban because the 'Southern Suburbs Boys' said that Scottburgh and Margate were the super places to go. Very explicitly, all the talk came down to girls and descriptions of girls. The surfing was also good because Scottburgh, south of Durban, was a unique town, built close to a large sugar refinery and like most small towns on the South Coast it had a river that came down from the hills and split the beach.

"There's a great long beach but everyone settles on the sandy south end. From there you can walk across the river outlet up a bank, which is grass. The river is only inches deep at the beach. The beach crowd is split. Half the people lie on the sand and half the people on the grass. There's a coffee and hot dog place and as the land turns out from the beach to the sea there are rocks. These rocks go out towards the sea then curl back towards the river inlet and beach."

"The curl doesn't quite make it," said one surfer we met at a party.

"You can dive off the rocks and surf to the beach, walk along the beach, over the river, up the bank, look at the girls, walk out on the rocks and dive into the swells and catch a wave . . . just so clean!" said another.

Scottburgh was named after John Scott, Governor of Natal, and was surveyed in 1860 as the first township south of Durban. Later, our history books told us, there was an attempt to make it a bay for sugar exports, but this failed because of the scant shelter for ships. The river's name Mpambanyoni (confuser of birds), was given because its course meanders so much, birds fail to find their own nesting sites. I thought that was confusing as well, when I read it, because birds fly half way around the world every year and on set times and still find their nests!

"Scottburgh is next," everyone agreed.

One month later we went to Scottburgh without reservations, little money, a wealth of expectations and an attitude of taking all the chances given.

◆

The soccer ball was thrown from surfer to surfer as about twenty surfers waited for a potential surf wave that would carry us to the beach. The surfing crowd was off the rocks at Scottburgh. Somebody said you wait for seven swells before the surfing wave comes. Trevor, Johnny, Doc, Zoni and I had been out there in Scottburgh bay for what seemed like ten minutes and the swells went by, lifting the body up and letting it come back down, till it was boring. At certain tide levels you sometimes could touch the ocean floor with your feet if you pushed yourself down. Right now we were playing 'Sea Polo'. The groups of surfers were throwing a soccer ball to each other. Suddenly the white caps appeared, and just as quick, at twenty-second intervals, the strong waves were breaking. We 'jumped in' by swimming hard towards the shore until the power surge of the water took our bodies at wave speed. Churning water was immediately in our faces and around our heads as we lay like torpedoes, with two hands out front, breaking the water roll. The power took us all the way to the beach. We walked and then ran out, with the water level below the knees, across the sand beach, across the river, up the grass beach and out onto the rocks, and dived back into the sea for the next wave. We completed a horseshoe in coming back to the water. This continued for some time. Finally the Andrew Street Mob dragged themselves out, after repeating the surfing and beach run about ten times. We walked to the grass and collapsed.

"I'm done," said Zoni.

"Me too," was echoed.

We had been swimming all afternoon after leaving Johannesburg at midnight on Friday and having checked into the Scottburgh Hotel, which was only 500 yards from the beach. This time we had collected, in many ways, enough money to stay for a week. Now we had to walk up the steep stairs from the beach, walk along the roadway, and then climb more stairs to the Annex of the hotel. On our budget the Annex was fine. There were about eight beds located against the wall in the dormitory-style room. Three other guys had checked in and so the Annex was full. Doc had said he was hoping for three girls to move in!

We informed him that in our conservative country that was an impossible dream!

"Dance tonight at the hotel with a live rock band," I said.

"You sure?" asked Trevor.

"Yes, I'm sure. I asked at the front desk!" I replied.

"Always talking to girls . . . Charl!" said Johnny.

"Why not?"

"Where do they dance?" asked Doc.

"It's like an open air atrium in the middle of the hotel. There's an open area to the sky, surrounded by a covered seating area. It's called 'The Merry Windmill'. Actually the roof is of straw and there's a bunch of timber poles, a thatched roof, I guess, and everyone sits around tables . . . you know!! There's a dance floor in the middle and a bar to one side."

I turned and opened my hands wide and in an Italian accent asked "So! Whatta else . . . you wanna know?"

"Nothing," said Zoni

"... An a place for da musicians," I added. "I wenta over myself jus to see!"

We showered, got dressed in smart pants and neat, short sleeved shirts and went to the hotel restaurant. This was the appropriate dress code in this sub-tropical paradise. Except for our 'Ducktail Haircuts'. We loved the style. The weather was perfect and the sumptuous eight-course dinner was devoured. We wandered into the bar and ordered 'Rainbows.' The bartender didn't like it. He looked at us for a long time in disgust.

"Are you sure?"

"Yes! Five Rainbows. We've come from Johannesburg and this is the only place that makes them! . . . So we've been told!"

He conceded. A Rainbow drink consisted of seven liqueurs, which were poured individually through a silk handkerchief, into a very small glass. It was done this way so that you could see seven layers of liqueur unmixed. We toasted the trip and 'all the girls in our life', and hoped that four or five new girls might add their names to our list . . . tonight!

"Let's try the 'Cane'." Johnny suggested. He had been talking about it for days!

"What's Cane?"

"Cane Spirit made in the South Coast from sugar cane. It's demonstrative to your tummy, boy!" said Trevor.

"Let's try it man!" said Doc.

"Seven Canes."

"We don't have to go anywhere!"

"We have a week to recover!"

People started to drift into the Merry Windmill and take up the tables. The band had arrived and put all the instruments together; each musician in their own particular way. They started to play dinner music and drinks were consumed everywhere. The clink of glasses became more frequent. We took a table and 'sighted' all the girls. Those with boyfriends were forever eliminated; those with parents almost eliminated and those by themselves became targets. Trevor and I got up simultaneously and went over to a table with five or six girls. We weren't sure!

"Can we buy you a drink?"

The girls looked at us . . . at each other . . . for what seemed a long, long time.

"Do you think we should let them?" asked one girl of all the others. The answers varied from "no" to "maybe" for a while. We stood there patiently, smiling and occasionally looking up into the sky above because it was there to see!

"Well! All right then!"

The girls were on vacation from Pietermaritzburg! I was immediately attracted to Linda, a very pretty, dark haired girl, slight, and a little shorter than Trevor in height. I noticed Trevor was making a move to this girl as well. He was the 'ladies' man' of the group. Johnny, Zoni and Doc came over and eventually the whole crowd spread out and was talking. The 'Rainbow Toast' had come true. The other three guys from the Annex dropped by and joined us for a drink. They were going for an all-day hike into the sub-tropical vegetation of the hills, starting early the next day. So they had one drink and left to go to bed. I was concentrating on Linda. I knew my dancing would help me, especially if she liked to rock, despite Trevor being pretty good at rocking as well. My major concern was that Trevor was so smooth with ladies, much like Errol Flynn. The night went on marvelously for everyone as the cares of the world disappeared. This was good fun and that's why we came here in the first place. The floor was hard and it was easier to dance in socks anyway, so the girls and then the boys took off their shoes.

Johnny danced. Zoni danced. Doc watched more than the rest of us. Despite some girls sitting out, Trevor and I danced whenever possible with Linda. I finally felt awkward and backed off. I didn't want to make this competitive. If Trevor liked her then he should have her. Besides we were just having fun anyway. We were laughing at everything, silence was measured in seconds and the social fun hit many, many peaks of joy. This was our outlet from a hard-driving life and the end of the night came too soon! Linda's brother came in and told her that her parents were waiting outside the hotel. She got up and said goodnight to the girls. This started a sequence of everyone finding and putting his or her shoes back on. Trevor couldn't find his shoes so he walked Linda to the car without them. I followed with her friend, being courteous and curious! As we got to the car Linda stepped on the grass, which was wet from watering, and Trevor stood in the grass helping her into the car. The parents greeted Trevor and talked to him as he slowly sunk in the muddy grass. He bowed as the car pulled off and walked back to the dance floor with mud on his socks. The rest of the crowd was laughing. Trevor just ignored us!

"Where are my shoes?" he asked out loud.

Nobody knew where they were. The dance had ended. The crowd dispersed with promises of some more activities together. Trevor crawled all around the tables looking for his shoes. Hardly anybody was left at the dance as we finally finished our drinks and got up to leave. A waitress came over.

"What are you looking for?"

"My shoes," said Trevor.

"There is a shoe on top of the thatch roof by your table!"

"Thank you," said Trevor. Sure enough, there were his shoes on top of the canopy roof.

"How the hell did they get up there?" asked Trevor.

Nobody replied . . . but a couple of us were smiling!

◆

The days were full of glorious sunshine and great weather. The bodies were turning brown and red depending on the skin texture. There were girls on the beach, we had many, many conversations and reveled in the pure enjoyment of meeting new friends. We were just having fun. The atmosphere had now totally removed activities related to work each day: studying, training for soccer and the economics of life. We were feeling free. The tropical weather of the South Coast was just perfect to be in and the background of blue skies, dark green trees and vegetation, bright sandy beaches and a deep blue sea provided a perfect place.

Each morning, Andries woke us up at 6:30 AM. He was one of the Annex boys. He had a coffee-pot in one hand and a bottle of brandy in the other.

"So, what do you want my friend? One black . . . one brown . . . or black and brown?"

The first morning everyone said no. The second was no plus a favorite curse word. On the third morning I tried the black and brown.

"Oh! My God, this hurts!"

"Well Charl, you have to become a Boilermaker to be able to drink this stuff."

The vacation was everything we had needed, surfing for days and days, dancing at night and drinking. Our money was gone. We could not afford to go to any dance or ask a girl on a date. So, the men in the Annex decided to have a 'stag night' and stay in the Annex. A couple of beach friends were asked and they brought liquor and beer to add to ours. The party was just to hang out, talk, laugh, tell jokes, and lie about the women we'd met! The Andrew Street boys had done this so many times before and we liked the whole thing. After a couple of hours of drinking we were sitting on the floor in a circle.

"Remember at Pat's, when his parents went away for the weekend? Charl, when you got so drunk and passed out?" said Doc.

"Yes! Or . . . No! Whichever you prefer!" I replied. The liquor was stirring in my head.

"And they found you the next morning in his parents' bed!"

"Yes!"

"Lucky they didn't come home!" said Doc.

"His brother came home unexpectedly though and Pat got shit anyway!" interrupted Zoni.

"Yes," I said, drinking my brandy and coke and quickly changing the subject. "I never understood why they kept that monkey in the yard as a pet. Wonder if he stayed on that chain all the time?"

"Don't know, Charl. What the hell has a monkey to do with you being in bed?"

"I don't know!" I replied. This was confusing!

The clock touched on 11 PM. The group was pretty drunk now. Trevor grabbed Doc, Zoni, John and me.

"Let's do our song."

"No! No! No!"

"Go for it man!" said the rest of the guys.

"Silence Please!" Announced Trevor in the appropriate announcer voice. *Damn, he is good at this,* went through my mind. Trevor looked at the audience, held his head high and said out loud. "The entertainment is about to begin . . .Please stay in your seats. Have the damn decency or courtesy not to talk, because! . . ." His hands were high. He turned his body and pointed to us. We were all over the place. Trevor pointed again and again. Then he faced the audience.

"The Scottburgh Annex Quartet." (There were five.)

We immediately got up, walked out the narrow side door, waited for a short while, laughed like hell, composed ourselves and went back into the Annex through the double doors, using them as a stage entrance. We were walking and singing 'All of Me'. We did a little shuffle to the left and then to the right, as we sang the verses. Trevor went down on his knees in front. Zoni fell over and got picked up. Doc was out of tune and I was bowing to the wall. John was acting like James Stewart. The antics continued for a long eight minutes! . . . A really long, long time for a short song! But the feelings of enjoyment from our audience just kept on coming through – so we continued. Then as if a secret baton dropped for the last phase, we all got together and ended with 'Take -- All -- of -- Meee!' But we were laughing and refused to end the song, as one after another kept singing 'All of Me' in different ways till we were all laughing at each other!

The audience was whistling and making comments like "Take it off! . . . Never take it off . . . you're ugly naked! . . . Oh! No!"

The audience stood up, clapped, cheered and shouted "More . . . More! . . . More!"

But 'The Scottburgh Annex Quartet' rejected the applause (we really only knew one song completely), got another drink and continued talking. Some of us were now lying on the floor.

Time went by.

"Where's Trevor?" asked Doc.

"He went out the door."

A bunch of us went outside. Trevor had thrown up on the concrete walkway.

"What are you doing?"

"Looking for my tooth."

"I'll get a stick," said Johnny.

He moved the stick through the stuff and sure enough there it was.
"You pick it out."

"Never!"

"Come on then Trev . . . you do it."

Trevor stumbled. So he got assisted out of the way. Doc went and got a towel and dug his tooth out and put it in the bathroom.

We went back into the dorm. The talking continued. Girls, philosophy, girls, soccer, rugby, girls, cricket, girls and movies with girls . . . all had a turn to be evaluated. Then it was short girls, tall girls and bad short and tall girls and even bad ugly girls.

"Where's Trevor?" was asked again.

"He changed into his shorts."

"Oh shit!"

Johnny, Doc, Zoni and I got up and looked.

"He's gone to the beach."

We sobered slightly and seemingly ran down the stairs of the hotel, down the road and down the stairs to the grass section and then onto the beach. I knew everyone's head was churning like a washing machine; mine was!

"Trevor!!" we yelled as loudly as possible.

"Trevor!" we yelled even louder than that!

The moon was bright and there were a couple of pole lights always left burning at night at the beach. The crests of the waves could be seen, because of the white-caps, but all the rest of the sea was black. We were scared of the treacherous currents, which occur at different times. They could so easily carry Trevor out to sea.

The liquor effects of the night were deep in the heads of Johnny and I, but we ran as hard as we could. Time seemed to stretch into a long duration before we finally reached the beach. Sure enough there was Trevor sitting in the waves.

"Trev! You alright?"

"Huh!"

Johnny, Doc, Zoni and I picked him up. We helped him to walk. All five of us were swaying. It was strenuous to support and walk him. We were determined to dump him in bed and maybe lock the door!

"Hey, did you find my tooth?" asked Trevor.

"Yes, but we sold it!"

"You bastards! Take a man's tooth and then sell it!"

Trevor paused and continued. "Did you bastards really sell it?"

"Yes!"

"Oh! Yes, someone without teeth went away happy."

It was tough going up the stairs, and then traversing the road, with Trevor seemingly getting heavier even though there were four of us. Finally we pulled him up the stairs, dragged him to the dorm, wiped him down with a towel and put him in bed. I threw a blanket over him.

"Trevor," I said in a loud voice.

"Yeah," he mumbled.

"Damn it Man! You shouldn't get so upset, just because I threw your shoes on the roof at the dance!"

"You bastard, Charl! . . .You wanted Linda so much . . .!" came back Trevor, "you probably sold my tooth!"

"I did that too!"

The trip back to Johannesburg during the following day continued our unfinished discussions in slow words and soft voices.

＊

CHAPTER 10

Inside Johannesburg

JOHANNESBURG WAS A VERY young city in the 1950s; it began as a mining camp in 1886 and had grown continuously since that time. This city was born from gold and thrived on the precious metal. The growth of the city was never easy and was subject to all the manifestations of rapid expansion in a new and young country with both newcomers and natives of the land. The excitement of discovery, opportunity for wealth, benefits of society, power struggles for position, politics, economic gain, the establishment of an industry, maintenance of family life, church and schooling, as well as the propagation of the arts, sports and musical entertainment added much interest for the adventuresome. It was a new lifestyle to all that lived there.

From the late 1880s, the area that became Johannesburg was first subject to the Boers of the Transvaal who wanted a farm community and a religious life, independent of the colonial and the imperial rules of England. These people were mostly Dutch descendants but there were many others, including British, and French Huguenots, that wanted the same separation. Paul Kruger, the leader of the Transvaal Republic, and his followers in the city of Pretoria, didn't want the Uitlanders (Outsiders): mostly resident in Johannesburg. The cities were located, 35 miles apart, in the vast Transvaal Republic. Despite Paul Kruger and his followers, almost every major country would endeavor to reap the profits of the gold discovery. England, America, Australia, New Zealand, Germany and many European countries were all interested. Besides the foreign interest and maneuvers, a further dimension was added: politics abounded because of the basic make-up of Dutch, British and black people of many different native tribes.

In schools and colleges we learnt about gold, diamonds and unique materials such as platinum and chrome because South Africa mined these minerals. As young engineers-to-be, we were required to learn to design and make the machinery, and design and construct facilities, to extract the pay dirt.

The gold ore body was different to the gold discoveries of California, Alaska and Australia. The surface panning of gold soon disappeared in the early years. Geologists, engineers and scientists of the mining game came to the conclusion that the ore body was large and deep. To mine the gold would require new mining methods, which involved complex structures above and below ground, to support and house the sophisticated, custom-designed and manufactured machinery. Mines could take six years to build before gold was separated from the rock. The problems were significant but as nature often deals both negative and positive hands, the positive element was that the gold discovery was the largest ever. Johannesburg is located midway between Springs and Randfontein, which encompasses the Witwatersrand ore body, however the gold area doesn't end there, it extends to Evander past Springs on the East Rand, and to the Carletonville and Klerksdorp areas on the Randfontein, West Rand side. The ore body then appears again in Welkom and Virginia in the Orange Free State. The total length of this crescent shaped gold bearing rock is in the order of 350 miles. Most of the gold is located in depths of 8000 feet plus below grade. The temperature of the rock increases about a degree centigrade for every hundred feet of depth.

The collars of the mines on the Rand were about 5-6,000 feet above sea level. The ore grade was very low, being quoted in pennyweights instead of ounces per ton (20 pennyweights per ounce); but it was consistent and this was the key element for the future. Hence the methods of mining could employ efficiency as a goal to lower costs. Later improvements were significant in the 1890s, the replacement of mercury in the process of Amalgamation which only extracted 60% of the gold, with the use of the cyanide process which increased the recovery factor to 90%. The use of the lightweight jackhammer improved the output of rock to be crushed. In the 1930s the mines had reached 8000 feet, 2000 feet below sea level, and much bigger stamping machines were being used to crush the ore. Cheap labor had been an advantage over Europe in terms of cost, but even that was in short supply. Chinese labor, and black labor from Mozambique, was imported. The mine labor eventually centered on black labor, as most of the Chinese were returned to China or sought work in other enterprises. The mines employed ten percent whites and ninety percent blacks. Blacks were paid ten percent of the white man's wages. Even with the use of these economic advantages, the gold production would not have been possible if the necessary energy source had not been reasonably low in cost. Johannesburg is located in the middle of the Witwatersrand (Ridge of the white waters) and there is no major water supply on the Rand, so water had to come from the Vaal River about 50 miles south and it had to be elevated. The large amount of energy needed to pump the water, sustain gold production and serve a large city was fortunately available using good quality coal from nearby coalfields, in the region of 60 miles from Johannesburg. Cheap coal was the most important ingredient to produce the gold ingot at competitive prices, and to produce more gold in fifty years than the rest of the world had known in four centuries.

Johannesburg was a unique city; in fact it was forever growing, despite setbacks, and therefore encompassing all the problems of a large expanding city. It was not that old, less than 70 years. It owed its existence to gold and to the many things the magic metal brought to the lifestyle of its followers. It was initially an area of farming, followed by the discovery of gold, mining exploration and the tremendous influx of people to mine and make money. Very quickly the early mining camps changed into a town. It became subject to all the forces of political and national goals as it expanded and became a city. People strove to make it a city of importance with a population of farmers, miners, tradesman and laborers as well as businessmen, architects, engineers, doctors, politicians, lawyers, accountants and all the others necessary to make a city work. These people, through all their complex backgrounds, had also strived to build museums, libraries, schools, opera houses, luxury hotels, and entertainment theaters as the culture advanced. They had succeeded. In fifty years of growth, the city had over a million people, skyscrapers, office buildings, hospitals, sports stadiums, opera houses, theaters and blocks of flats, and many suburbs with modern houses. There was a central transportation system, and a large water system pumping water up to the 6000-foot level. It had all the structural elements of a large city.

Inside Johannesburg was the major difference to most cities of the world. It was not historically bound by hundreds of years of religion and tradition; the people had come from almost everywhere. The whole of Europe and the Middle East was represented; Asia was represented heavily in Chinese and Indian cultures, (Russia, Japan and Korea had very little participation). Almost half the African countries, especially those below the equator, and people from Madagascar, had contributed with their tribal complexity as they sought a better life; even the promise of food and running water were sufficient reasons to come to Johannesburg. They entered South Africa from the north and many of them ended up in the Johannesburg mining game. Even some of the Malay descendants who lived primarily in the Cape had drifted into town. This was a lot more than a city of only Afrikaans and English speaking inhabitants with a black population; this was also more than a city with depressed blacks and rich whites and gold in the streets. In true contrast to the world's understanding there were also poor whites, there were blacks that were better off than blacks in the countries where they had been born. The people in Johannesburg were a cross-section of nearly all races. The gold was thousands of feet below the streets of Johannesburg. It would take hard work to get it out as well as a large potential risk in investment, to accomplish this feat. Finally, business and other activities had brought people from far away places of the world. Miners traveled everywhere. They were true adventurers and loved challenges. Gold recovery methods in Johannesburg were extremely complex technically and even more so in operations. The governmental political arguments added to the complex situation and the business risk and financial matters extended that complexity. It was an individual challenge to anyone. Different people brought different cultures and it all added to the melting pot of the city. It was possible inside Johannesburg to learn almost any language, learn to play any kind of music, eat any kind of meal and play many of the sports of the world, including ice hockey in a country without snow. The generations that followed these adventurous people of the late nineteenth and early twentieth centuries continued to build Johannesburg through to the 'fifties'. Our family and the Andrew Street Mob and their families were involved in all of this, we knew the subject well and we knew the price of gold was a primary factor in our lives. I was totally absorbed and learning every day.

◆

As I grew up with my friends, I found us continuing the tradition of hard work instilled by our parents. Our goal was to do well, but I didn't believe any of us knew where we wanted to go or what we wanted to be. It was obviously talked about relentlessly but not in great depth. We were glad the forties were over and although everything was hard to get, it was available, and simpler to obtain in this decade.

We remembered the forties, when South Africa had gone to war. Everyone we knew had worked to support our soldiers, sailors and airmen posted overseas. South Africa also provided facilities for rest and recuperation of British and South African men who fought in North Africa and Italy. We met the British soldiers. Despite the war having been far away, it had been followed daily. As kids we hadn't read that much but we'd checked the newspaper maps for the arrows showing the progress of the Allies across Europe and into Germany. The shortages of food and goods were very apparent due to the war but never assumed to be anywhere as bad as countries in Europe.

In the second half of the decade, after the war had ended, the town of Welkom was founded, as the gold mining spread to the Free State. Johannesburg celebrated its Diamond Jubilee in 1946 with a population of over 600,000. The new, very modern, Clarendon Theatre opened in Johannesburg and the Harrison Street Bridge was built. The Wanderers sports ground was sold and the club moved to Kent Park, Illovo, in the northern suburbs. There were thousands of cars in Johannesburg. The major change in the late forties was the Nationalist Party winning the elections. They had an immediate drive to remove the black-inhabited townships from the center of Johannesburg. The new expansions of the city had gone around and beyond these areas. Passes were made mandatory for blacks. The word 'Apartheid' was born (separate development was the translation—but never the meaning). We didn't understand it because most changes were negative to us. It truly was not understood why we should go backwards! . . . Still, positive elements of growth were apparent. A highlight in the late forties was the visit of the Royal Family, King George VI and Queen Elizabeth and their two daughters, Princesses Elizabeth and Margaret. Flying to London was down to less than four days. Technology was changing as the sound barrier had been broken, atomic bombs had been used, and now there was talk of nuclear-powered ships. Jet planes had been built and flown and the jet age had arrived. The Standard Theatre closed, built in 1891 based on Victorian Architecture. So there were hundreds of changes occurring and maybe we didn't appreciate deeply the values of change, because of our age, but learning and talking about them was exciting!

However, now my friends and I saw some of the results of the change of Government as the 1950s brought to life in Johannesburg everything that was feared in the days following the 1948 elections. The Government drove a wedge between white and black, and English and Afrikaans. 'Separate' was a daily word, 'Krugerism' was alive and growing. General Smuts had died after being made a Freeman of the city of Johannesburg. He had been world-renowned. The world became conscious of 'Apartheid' especially as the United States had outlawed segregation. However, the Government continued its goals and took on the University of the Witwatersrand, who had declared to uphold the principle of education to men and women without regard to race or color. The Government interfered with Johannesburg's planning as it enforced the removal of black slums in the Western Native Townships: Newclare, Sophiatown and Martindale and a township called Moroka. All freehold titles were withdrawn by the Prime Minister, Dr. Hendrik Verwoerd. The Pretoria vs. Johannesburg problems returned. Television was banned and the country relied on the government-controlled South African Broadcasting Corporation for its news on the radio. Newspaper content was continually in contrast, depending on whether the publication was pro-government or not.

Despite all the political overtones, Johannesburg grew and supplanted Cape Town as the entry-point to South Africa (previously by sea), as the world's first jet airliner, BOAC Comet, landed at the Johannesburg airport. The flight from London took 14 hours. Automobiles from all over the world were imported as the mineral wealth of the country increased. The Witwatersrand was now the largest producer of uranium in the world; in this case, uranium was a by-product of gold mining. Platinum was added to the gold and coal production. The gold mines were continually pushing technical mining barriers, as they were now well over 2000m deep, where rock bursts occurred and temperatures were unbearable. This demanded some of the largest air-cooling systems to be installed. Just south of Johannesburg the first commercial gasoline-from-coal plant commenced operation. Johannesburg expanded widely and houses in new townships were built on a one-third acre. A new railway station and a new airport were added as the city spread northwards and southwards. The Globe Theatre, first theater in Johannesburg, and the Palace Buildings both from Johannesburg's

'Camp Days' were demolished: the new replacing the old . . . sad in many ways!

What became truly interesting and exciting to our generation were things associated with dress and entertainment. The 'Sack Dress' was in fashion. 'Duck Tail' haircuts for young men dressed in stove-pipe pants were popular. The Rock-n-Roll era, tight fitting sweaters, full skirts, bobby socks, flat shoes or high heels and jeans, for the young girls, were 'In'. In contrast, formal dress was still appropriate for dances, theater and concerts. Drive-in cinemas were very popular. The atmosphere in Johannesburg was more happy than sad, despite the overwhelming seriousness of the Government. It was like, 'a stupid big brother that wouldn't let his younger sisters and brothers play fun games, in this area or in this or that way'! The arts and music of this time reflected that atmosphere. The black music of this era 'the Kwela' was happy, upbeat music. Black writing was satirically funny, and theater was creative. A large number of artists came out of this era from both black and white populations: Juliet Prowse, Glynis Johns, Lawrence Harvey, Eve Boswell, Maria Lester, Vincent Fortelli, Miriam Makeba, Hugh Masekela, Bloke Madisane and Lenny 'Special' Mabaso all became world famous.

Inside Johannesburg was intriguing. The most vibrant element to me, was its people, and their complex backgrounds of different families, religious beliefs and political views. The daily vibrancy stemmed from the interconnecting of people. The input waves of the various cultures came out of the mixing of various communities of African, Asian, Indian, Middle Eastern, European and American heritages, and added to the vigorous activities of the multi-generation South Africans, new South Africans and the traditional families of South Africa. All this meant some understanding would be necessary, as well as a sophisticated knowledge of people and their different worlds. The major stream of conversation centered on the differences between the British and Dutch backgrounds, British and Boer, Imperialism and Colonialism, a Republic, and ownership and independence. The papers covered these topics constantly. Churches propagated it. In the 'Fifties' adults discussed it to death. The young people in Johannesburg, as far as I knew, observed it, respected the arguments, but didn't care as much or as deeply about these topics. Equally discussed on many levels was black and white heritage, and their future needs and wants. The white people never wanted black rule. Even the most liberal didn't think it would work, judging by the results of other African countries that had become independent of Colonial or other types of rule.

It was not only daily contact through business and work that formed the personality of a 'Johannesburg man or woman', but also intermarriage among the different white people, with its complications. The blacks had similar problems due to inter-tribal marriages. Johannesburg was a lot more liberal than rural cities and the smaller communities of the country. The big city was therefore less understood, referred to as 'the bad place', 'despotic', and 'unreligious'. Johannesburg's basic personality then came from the people and families that survived the many transformations involved through the gold mining camps, power struggle of the British and Boers, the Boer War, a depression in the 1920s and the Second World War. The city buildings grew vertically despite the abundance of land in the surrounding countryside, and it was referred to as a 'Small Chicago': the similarity in the vast surrounding flat lands and tall buildings. Science and engineering benefited from the universities, colleges, and government research, and enterprises that manufactured commercial products constructed the mines, buildings, bridges, roads, railways and the usual infrastructure of a Western civilized country. The arts continued to be pursued relentlessly. Ballet, classical music, plays, opera, literature, painting, and sculpture flourished throughout the country. Sport was represented everywhere, and South Africans cherished any accomplishment in that endeavor. To win in Johannesburg was to win in South Africa. To win in sport was to be a 'star', equivalent to or better than any movie star. Sportsmanship and sports went very deep into the heart. As most sports activities were supposedly amateur the financial compensation was generally unknown!

◆

I preferred Johannesburg when I compared it to other cities; it always came out on top. To me this was mainly due to the excitement of the big city. I had played soccer in almost every city on the Rand as well as having competed in special tournaments in Pretoria. So, indirectly, I had visited, seen and talked about these cities and still ended up with the same result: Johannesburg to me was number one and I knew that was favoritism. There were travel trips, as a young kid, to the South Coast, Scottburgh and Durban. I went on one trip to Cape Town with Doc when I was thirteen. Cape Town was definitely beautiful sitting at the bottom of Africa and washed by two major oceans, the Indian and Atlantic, plus it had Table Mountain and a spectacular coastline; but it seemed small. Durban and it's subtropical weather and wonderful beaches was interesting and a good possibility for exciting living. Both these cities were more beautiful by a large extent than my hometown. However, Johannesburg was more exciting because it was the center for business, sports activities and entertainment. The 'Southern Suburbs' was my territory! It seemed as though I knew everyone. I knew that not all people knew me, but my curiosity had prompted me to seek out knowledge on anyone who had anything to do with my friends. My memory was also good. I knew all the sport places connected with cricket or soccer and I certainly knew all the places to dance. I was, despite minor complaints, a very happy person!

Also there was family. My father lived across town. Part of my extended family lived in the northern suburbs, some in the western part of Johannesburg, and some on the Witwatersrand, but mostly in the vicinity of Johannesburg. On my father's side there were some in the northern suburbs and some in the Cape. My dear Aunt Rachel, my father's sister, and her daughter Evelyn and husband, had recently moved to the Cape. They were fairly successful in business and always had lived in 'the nicer houses' such as those located in Northcliff. My father had other sons and daughters from different marriages but as they never associated with me very much while growing up, I didn't become deeply involved with them. There was one exception, and that was Charles, my father's newest arrival, born 13 years after me. They lived on the way out to the Johannesburg Zoo. I visited them more than anyone else in my father's family. Even then I didn't see them often because of my activities with college, soccer, work and when I had free time, my friends kept me very busy.

Johannesburg was definitely my hometown. I was at home in the big city and could go anywhere I wanted with confidence. I also knew where not to go. However, my freedom was severely curtailed by not having my own car. It was the biggest problem of my social life and a monster requirement for independence, which was my major goal in life, at that time!

The Andrew Street Mob had not seen white and black or white and Asian marriages. I had witnessed the problems in mixed English and Afrikaans marriages; there were even some minor problems in my family. I had avoided and remained distant in open conversations held on Boer and British, and black and white, because I felt my views were at least a little controversial, and mixed. This often made me feel as though I sat on the fence. I didn't like the British attitude, as my family had been subjected to British Imperialism, especially on my father's side, and therefore I supported the efforts of the Afrikaners to build the country without interference from foreign countries. I believed, as did many South Africans, that if you came to live in this country you become part of it i.e. 'Don't leave one foot in Europe'! But I certainly didn't like what the Government was doing in many areas. My aloofness from deep discussion was caused by the interactions of my mother's side of the family coming from England, and my father's side from the French Huguenots. The latter were historically combined with the Dutch in South Africa. My family was a combination of English and Afrikaans people, although we mostly spoke English, because it was the business language of Johannesburg. I definitely didn't like Apartheid and everything it represented. I also had many Afrikaans and English friends and this was a very normal situation in Johannesburg. What troubled me more than all of this was the question . . .'Where else could you, as a South African, go?' I asked myself many times. Some English speaking, mostly newer immigrants, could hardly integrate with local white people, never mind black people. Some of my casual friends couldn't marry each other because of their beliefs or their parent's beliefs. I knew the history of Johannesburg and South Africa and the history of England and Europe, as did all the teenagers, from schooling. The 'War' taught us many things, and we knew the history of America because we continually compared it to 'all other histories' almost every day. America seemed unique in its practice of freedom. It had many religions, but no overwhelming religious /governmental rules. There was a basic question to our lives . . . American style, or British or European style? Another question . . . what was the South African style? The working environment of foreign and domestic companies was continually compared as well. Most young people that worked for American companies believed they were better off. Parents didn't necessarily agree, for a number of unknown reasons. When my family talked about politics and history and life, I would not contradict my family, because it was not worth the arguments that followed. I applied that same premise to many groups that became emotional about these issues. This approach was in the Andrew Street Mob and it was very successful, and we practiced it all the time. It was also never planned, it came about naturally and adopted by everyone.

I was looking for a future. The American image re-entered my thinking for the hundredth time. Each occasion when the movie in my mind of America formed, I thought of how much better it would be than the Government in South Africa and its restrictive approach. Everything, to this body of men, was linked to the Voortrekkers' dream of owning and directing their own country. Now, that was okay, but why not open all the major social categories like the Americans had done? In business terms the Government had an American approach. In social terms that was not the case. To me there seemed to be more rules to social life than to business. 'Too close to the church,' I thought. All the changes to the black person's lifestyle were even more restrictive now than before. Even though all my friends were white, in South Africa's terms, they too were suffering indirectly at work and in business. Distrust, petty theft, loss of good attitude by the blacks and the overall atmosphere of a people being hounded back into a kraal and pushed from side to side because of all the restrictions imposed on them. What would be the result? Only a fool would say 'nothing!' The fences of the kraal would be broken and the people would eventually get out. History would then have repeated itself for the nth time.

I wondered how many other people thought this way? Was I wrong? Was there any way to find out? Did I want to find out?

The Andrew Street Mob was a haven from politics and the 'everyday bad'. We never got into these controversies and therefore we were very comfortable around each other. It was not the proverbial 'ostrich head in the sand attitude' but our discussions were probably a realistic view among friends. We knew what was happening, but declined to let it affect us. However, there was a definite departure from the many 'norms' of South African life. There were major differences between the parents of the crowd and the crowd itself. In general the kid's approach to the normal South African problems of heritage and religion were taken in a much lighter vein . . . it didn't seem so deeply important. 'Change is coming about and let's go with it.' There seemed to be a much less aggressive approach to historical grievances. Besides, we had all survived the Second World War, and 'wasn't that enough?' Wasn't it better to live in happiness than under a dictatorship? After all . . . 'freedom' . . . wasn't that what everyone in the world had fought for!

One factor that did not escape discussion in our Andrew Street Mob was the Nationalists coming into power in 1948. My thoughts were the same as many of my friends. We were afraid that South Africa would retrench into the old ways, the very, very, old ways of Pretoria vs. Johannesburg, and thereby become like a European Country, with all its traditions rolled over and over again. I knew inside and from what I had learnt that it had never worked historically. It just manifested wars. I loved this city, its people and everything that went about it; to me the good was so much better than the bad. And I believed, very much, that Gran was right, when she told me to 'judge a man on who he is . . . and a lot more on what he does.' I knew in my heart that this was the solution.

◆

The work at Main Reef Engineering was becoming interesting now that I had been there for three-plus years. I got to spend Fridays in the design/drafting office. This was an exciting departure for me. I had spent time learning the different facets of being a fitter and turner (machinist and millwright). I was excited because drafting and designing was more on the pathway towards becoming an engineer. I could also use the office, after work hours, to do some of my work from college. Somewhere, sometime, someone had suggested that an engineer with shop experience was a good thing, and had a better chance for a good job. The designer for the company was the owner, Mr. Funkey. His son, John, ran the shop. So I became the draftsman, and got to make drawings of a new 20-ton underground diesel locomotive. The main feature of Mr. Funkey's locomotive designs was the gearbox that allowed the locomotive to go from forward to reverse by pulling a large lever from one side to the other. This feature preserved the locomotive drive train because the drivers, mostly black men, in the mines, didn't clutch properly when changing gears. They had ruined many gearboxes of other types of locomotives, which were similar to clutch shifting (stick-shift) cars.

I had some very close friends at work: Sandy, Mr. Warren, Ginge and Laubscher. Sandy, about 32 years old, a good looking man, strong and very competent, was the journeyman who had taught me a lot about machining, especially how to machine fast, thus continuing the age-old journeyman/apprentice relationship. He was always challenging me to do better. Mr. Warren, a short, stocky man, bald, about fifty, was a hard worker and drove his black helpers to their limit of output. He didn't shirk in his effort. He matched anyone in output of work, so therein lay a manner of respect. When you worked with Mr. Warren there was little instruction, just watch and do as he did and do it fast. If you didn't, you got the frown look and it didn't go away till you got good and fast. Ginge, a redhead, good looking in an Irish way, with a friendly smile, was a senior apprentice. He was a quiet young man, about twenty. He and I shared many hours talking; we were work friends in lots of ways. Ginge had also entered the domain of the Andrew Street Mob but not to a large extent. Jazz was the close connective between him and me. It was discussed every day. Laubscher (affectionately called by his last name) was an operator. He was about 30 years old, did most of the drilling work required on the various parts of the locomotives, underground hoists and special equipment made for the gold mines.

The black men in our factory were good producers; they very much enjoyed the American style management, which included working hard and getting paid well. Our bosses were unusually attentive and helpful to all their workmen. The employees were willing and happy workers in all ways. The whole shop enjoyed a good relationship with each other. I was so thankful that some inner force had made me change my workplace to Main Reef Engineering.

◆

Ever since I had started work, Laubscher had promised to show me a night in Johannesburg that I'd never forget. I had reminded him many times that I was already eighteen and ready-to-go. Laubscher had declined my requests many times, but he knew that he would have to do it sometime, so he suggested the coming Friday night.

I was so excited as Laubcher and I caught the bus into town. We were headed towards Langlaagte, the very birthplace of this city. The maroon-colored bus left Industria, the factory area of Johannesburg, and proceeded down Central Road at 5 o'clock. Hundreds of people crossed the street leaving work to get to the railroad station. This bus was an express and literally flew through the area. The black people knew that these busses did not slow down as they went through the Mayfair and Fordsburg areas and into the west part of downtown Johannesburg. The drivers of these double-decker busses must have been specially trained, either to have instant reactions, or to have a definite goal in life to get people 'splattered all over the radiator'. Laubscher and I jumped off the bus at Harrison Street, totally relieved, and walked down the street to a bar. We sat down and had a beer. It was so delicious, a pint of Castle Lager after a long week's work. The week of work melted into oblivion.

Laubscher drank deeply as though it was his last drink. He smiled and then said, "Put some money in your front pocket and what you want to spend in your back pocket. For the rest of the night that's all you've got, no matter what anyone asks."

"Okay!" I said.

We had just been paid in cash. We threw the envelopes away and then sat talking about work, but that went away fast. I noticed the bar was old, and so was the furniture, but it was clean. A lot of mining people and tradesmen were having a beer. Conversations on rugby, women, soccer, were almost absorbed, or at least dulled by, the smoke, but not quite. The atmosphere was up-beat. I knew now why Grandpa Mick liked to go to the bar and get drunk. And these people, just finished a week's work, were talking and laughing, and were going to get drunk. I noticed it was 6:30 PM already.

"Let's get some curry and rice", Laubscher said as he stood up and went into the kitchen and right up to the stove.

The cook just stood there in the background. It was a help-yourself style dinner. Laubscher took two plates, opened up the pot, put some rice on his plate and continued to the next pot, which was filled with curried meat. I followed him and we ended up with two plates each, one with curry meat and rice, the other with condiments and bread. We went to the bar and each got our second Castle Lager beer, paid the bartender, then sat down and ate. It was super-delicious.

"Help-yourself style, Charl."

"Yes, and its good!"

The cold beer mixed with the hot curry-and-rice was magnificent . . . a very good mixture. We chewed and talked about Sandy and the boys at work. Laubscher agreed that Sandy, and the men of Main Reef Engineering, were some of the best things that had happened to him. I explained the freedom of Friday night to me. Having a pay-check in my hand, no school, no work and 'Saturday' coming up, which was my present religion. 'Free Saturday Religion' I called it. We both laughed at the many ways it was a good religion, and agreed that it could possibly become popular . . . worldwide.

"Playing soccer is so much a part of it! I can't explain," I added.

"That is nice Charl! . . . But it's good you are studying . . . keep it up my boy. You will not be sorry . . . some day!"

"My family agrees!"

We left the bar and Laubscher cautioned me that he had a friend whose daughter lived in an unusual way. He continued by saying that he helped her when he could, and not to be upset at what I would see. We walked towards the Johannesburg railroad station and then cut left down towards Chinatown and Indiatown, areas named according to their inhabitants. Walking a few more blocks, we reached the middle of this area and entered an old building: a boarding house from the early 1900s. It was run down and full of foul smells. There was a large courtyard and three floors of one bed roomed, old fashioned flats that encircled the courtyard. All floors had wrought iron railings and columns along the walkways. A fishpond was in the center of the ground floor but I refused to look inside the pond. We went up to the third floor. A woman greeted us, nice-looking, in her early twenties, dressed very cleanly in a tight dress. She was smiling with happiness as she greeted Laubscher.

"How are you?"

"This is Charl. We work together." She walked up, shook my hand and gave me a kiss on the cheek, very lightly. I went warm inside, and didn't understand the feeling. We went to a room. I sat on a chair. I looked at Laubscher across a table. He was a strong tall man, ruggedly handsome . . . a little scary, because he was generally quiet and stern. A good man to me though, and he always gave me a comfortable feeling like a friend . . . I respected him in many ways. I continued to notice things in this flat. It was dreary. I noticed a baby in a crib; he was standing up. Suddenly, a man came into the room and took money from the girl. He was swarthy and tough-looking, serious and 'taking care of things'. He nodded at Laubscher, went to the crib and then walked out, ignoring me completely.

"Her husband," said Laubscher.

The girl started to cry. The happy smile was gone. The man had taken all the money plus a coin Laubscher had given the kid in the crib. Laubscher talked to her for some time at the other end of the room. I felt uncomfortable but I knew of people like this in the 'Suburbs'. Some of my friends in the Andrew Street Mob and Bobby's Group knew all about the rougher side of Johannesburg. We had ventured there but

withdrawn. . . just knowing we should stay away. I sat in the chair looking at the kid, who was relatively cleanly dressed for the surroundings.
My God! What a mess! I thought . . . I almost said it out loud!

After an hour we had consumed a few glasses of 'Old Brown
Sherry' (a very cheap wine, known in South Africa to have changed the
color of white men to dark brown!). Then the woman came in to look
at the baby.

I had been standing at the crib and slipped three coins into the pil-
lowslip while everyone was talking.

"We'll walk with you," said Laubscher loudly, so I could hear.

"Yes, I need someone to go into the hotel with . . ."

"Let's go."

The woman knocked on a door as we went out. A scrubby-looking
woman opened the door.

"I'm leaving, go up to the baby."

"Yes!" was the insincere reply.

The three of us walked five blocks to the Sylvia Hotel and entered
through the front doors.

"You are all together?" asked the doorman, looking at the girl.

"Yes," said Laubscher.

"How old is the young man?" asked the doorman.

"Nineteen," replied Laubscher.

We sat down in the lounge and ordered a drink. There were quite
a few ladies in the lounge, each one supposedly with a man. Men came
in and out frequently. I noticed it and completed the story: because the
hotels could be charged for assisting prostitution, if solicitation took
place, they discouraged women being unescorted upon entering the
lounge.

Laubscher and I left the lady in the hotel lounge with some of her
friends and walked down the road to another place that had a very dark
entrance. There were no lights shining anywhere. Laubscher knocked
on the door and a man answered.

"Who's the kid?"

"He's okay. We work together, three years now."

"No trouble . . . Hey!"

"No trouble."

We entered a large three-storey house. It was a gambling house
and gambling went on in all rooms: illegal but alive. A lot of Chinese
men were playing poker and dice. The money changed hands quickly. I

knew my money would not last long in these games. I had played poker and loved it, but the stakes in this place were very high. What I had in my back pocket would be gone in minutes. I watched and had a brandy and coke, the most popular drink of the day with my buddies (we had replaced rum and coke), but unheard of in this place of older men.

Laubscher gambled and circulated for a long time. Sandy had told me that Laubscher had been in trouble for fighting and being drunk more than once. There was something mysterious about Laubscher, but he was very good to me, always, even on the worst of his hangover days. Gran's word about judging a man on what he does was deeply entrenched. So I didn't care about backgrounds: this extended to the black and white controversies. I already knew that there were just as many bad whites as bad blacks. Besides, I had naturally met more bad whites anyway! The whites had killed many, many people in the world for some very weird reasons. These thoughts went through my mind as I watched Chinese, whites, and one or two colored people playing poker together. Socially-indiscreet-in-South Africa-in-the-50s. The back streets of Johannesburg were loaded with indiscretions. There were black women who lived with white men; the reverse was never seen. Who was right? There were a number of young black girls serving in the club . . . every one definitely picked for their youth and figure! What was their true role? I had a lot of questions, but they were slowly answered in my mind and I decided tonight was not the night to find out.

"Want to play, son?" asked a big, burly man with a beard and a nice suit.

"No thanks," I said. "Not enough money."

He brought me a drink of straight brandy. "Story of life, son! The big story of life."

"Can I have a coke too?"

"Brandy and coke, are you mad?"

"No Sir! It's the popular drink now . . . also rum and coke."

"Really? Well, what can I say? The kids of today are crazy . . . I'll get it."

"Thank you."

The man was right. Brandy was a very respected drink and some people got upset if you even added water. About an hour later, Laubscher grabbed me by the shoulder.

"Let's get out of here, no luck . . . do you play snooker?"

"Yes", I said enthusiastically. Off we went.

"What's the time? Is it midnight yet?"

"Yes!"

"Okay."

We went back to the Sylvia Hotel. Laubscher got an offer—so did I! We both refused. My refusal was not based on lack of desire, but it seemed the thing to do. I did it in a nice way. Laubscher's friend wasn't there so we left immediately. Later, I thought it would have been very intriguing to accept the offer! But I felt obligated to follow Laubscher.

"Hope she made some money, otherwise the 'creepy bastard' will beat her up," said Laubscher. And added, "I am her 'brother-in–life!'"

We left the hotel and walked down to a snooker room.

Laubscher was a good shot and I was not bad. We played a couple of games and then got challenged for money.

"Gimme what you got Charl . . . from the back pocket now!"

I turned it over. Laubscher put money with it. "Enough for two games . . . losing."

We played for an hour before the money ran out . . . at least six games.

"Let's go," said Laubscher.

"We should have quit after we won those three games," I suggested.

"Doesn't work that way Charl! They'd make you stay until you lose it all. So you play till the money is gone . . . you leave . . . and they're happy. We'd be there till the sun came up and more, if you won! You still wouldn't get out of the place with their money!" We hit the street.

"Let's get some coffee."

The restaurants and coffee places were all closed, but we headed back towards the gambling place. Sure enough, around the corner was a small café, fly screen door almost worn out. We entered and sat down on hard wooden chairs, on dirty linoleum floors. I decided not to even look at the ceiling. I wiped the lip of the cup with a napkin and drank the coffee. I hoped no germs had fallen into the coffee.

We talked for a while. Laubscher said it was a quiet night and that we could do it again sometime. I agreed. He said he didn't like the situation of his friends' daughter, wished it could be better for her, and might help her more in the future.

"I'm going home, it's been a long day . . . and I've enjoyed your company . . . away from work as well. You're a good man!" said Laubscher, smiling slightly.

"I'll head home!" I stated. I believed it was a good time to depart.

"You all right?" asked Laubscher.

"Yes, it was fun and very interesting. I'd like to do it again!"

We left the coffee shop.

"See you Monday." I said walking away.

"Yes, my friend, I'll be there, at the machine . . . come over, okay?" suggested Laubscher, with a big smile.

I ran as soon as Laubscher was out of sight. Maybe the rock dance club was still open, and maybe I could get a ride to the Southern Suburbs. All the buses had stopped running hours ago. I ran for about 20 minutes. I felt the beer, the curry, the rums, the brandy, and the terrible coffee lurching inside, but I kept on going. Not many people were outside this time of night, only the familiar night-watch boys, sitting by their fires. They were usually Zulus armed only with a knobkerrie stick (a thin tree-branch, very strong, with a hard root bulb on the end). That was plenty protection for them. They could use it expertly, if needed. Stories were legendary how they had beat up to six or seven Tsotsis (young Black hoodlums). As the Zulus were honest, the storekeepers employed them.

The rock club was closed . . . no lights . . . sign on the door 'No more dances here'. It was the same problem. Johannesburg organizers would find a place to dance, the local rock bands would follow them and play, and the young Johannesburg dance crowd would be there. Eventually the crowd would get noisy or a fight would break out and they would be closed down. There were never any advertisements in the paper. It was all word of mouth as to where the new place would be and when the dances took place. The dances were held almost anywhere from Fordsburg to Hillbrow.

I set out to walk home. This wasn't too bad. I had ended up on the other side of town many times, especially when I went out with Rosemary, so I walked at a brisk pace, hands in pockets and jacket collar flipped up over my ears. The air was beautifully cool at 6,000 feet above sea level. I thought about Rosemary and what effect she had had on me. She was always on my mind. I hadn't met anybody who had moved me the way she did! It was hard to work it out and console myself that she was not available. I still thought that we could make it, if I gave in to being the good boyfriend. What drove me was the fact I did not want to be just a machinist. I already loved design and I loved gaining knowledge. I deep down wanted to know things, the more technical, the more pleasure I got out of it. I knew all my friends seemed happy in what they were doing. And they were all doing well. I drove hard because I did not want to be in the bottom of any barrel . . . especially if things changed in Johannesburg. I had seen Rosemary at these dances, and had actually danced with her a couple of times. It was always awkward for me, but not so much for her . . . or so it seemed. It was not healthy for my feelings. I knew I was not in her pathway. I couldn't afford the luxury of time needed to devote to her. I had to do my schooling and my soccer, they still were too important somehow . . . but I'd been over that too many times! *Interesting night,* the thought broke into my mind, as I wanted to change my thinking away from something I had loved so much and lost. I felt a smile come across my face, *always something going on in this city . . . always exciting.* I was extremely intrigued with adventure, different people, and different places. Movies were not enough. I couldn't understand friends settling down.

I wondered about my life at Main Reef Engineering as I walked. *Such a good bunch of people,* I thought, *and the boss is great.* Especially since John, the owner's son, ran the shop, after the previous foreman had left. Mr. Waffle had been a stern figure without much give, one way or the other. Probably got his training in the British Army. In fact, it was a great group at Main Reef Engineering! My thoughts solidified on that subject. Mr. Warren, who definitely drank about a bottle of brandy a day . . . I knew that because I had to jump out of the car every evening and get one from the Industria Bottle Store. Ginge, his hair red, almost an orange color, tight and curly, a young man of Irish descent, with freckles beyond belief, was the senior and only other apprentice at Main Reef Engineering. He had a really pleasant smile, was thin and strong.

Ginge was definitely my technical jazz fan buddy. He and I hit it off from the beginning. We even went into Johannesburg on Saturday mornings to hunt for jazz records. Besides the main record stores in the middle of Johannesburg, there were some record stores in on the West Side of the city near Ferreirasdorp (near Indiatown). Indians owned these shops and they had the greatest collection of 78s. Ginge and I would have to go through them one by one in boxes, or ask for them by name, if they were rare. Also, there were ten-inch and some twelve-inch long-playing records now. Very expensive, a third of a week's pay, but they did last 15 – 20 minutes as opposed to the 2 to 3 minutes of a 78-RPM record. And, you could lie on your bed and listen for a long time without listening to the automatic changer making noises every three minutes. Some of our favorites were Lionel Hampton, Duke Ellington, Buddy Rich, Gene Krupa, and Woody Herman. We both liked the harder driving bands in preference to the smoother styles of Glen Miller, Benny Goodman, or Tommy Dorsey. Ginge was even a little further out, liking Stan Kenton and June Christy, and some of the new Bop sounds from Dizzie Gillespie. Ginge tended towards the 'deep jazz'. My preference was leaning towards the new 'rock bands' only occasionally heard on the Johannesburg sound waves. There just weren't enough programs on jazz and rock and we didn't understand why . . . all our friends loved it.

◆

I had gone through Main Reef Engineering in a series of training jobs to be a machinist and millwright. My first job was learning to measure and cut steel, then weld and assemble simple parts, and work the drilling machines. Because of my training in school I went onto the shaper and small lathes fairly early, then after a while, I learnt to operate the gear-cutting machine. This was followed by working the vertical boring machine, and then onto one of the bigger lathes. It was a normal process. We worked hard in this comparatively small shop that produced custom mining machinery. The radio was on all the time; controlled by the fat old bookkeeper lady who sat in the office. She would never put on the Laurenço Marques Station, which played American music. Nobody in the shop cared for her selections and when she was off sick we were glad. We had a chance to change the station.

Joseph, a black man of about 30, very strong, good-looking and with a super smile, worked all the lathes. He kept them supplied with material and took away cuttings when the bottom trays filled up. He was a good worker and a good man. He talked to me quite a bit about his family. He had a wife and four children, primarily supported by him, as his wife could only get just a little housework. They lived in a very small two-room brick house. There was little furniture. Joseph came to work on the infamous commuter trains that were so overcrowded that the carriages actually had people hanging on the outside of the doors, as the train hit 20 to 30 miles per hour.

"The bodies dangle," said Joseph.

When the shift was over he would clean the machine and make it ready for the next day.

Picannin was an older black man. I thought he was about forty, but it was hard for me to tell the age of older black people. Some of them looked so good into there seventies, and I was often surprised when the black people said they were fifty or sixty. I could tell the age of white people only a little better. Picannin was always nicely dressed. He was a chauffeur for 'Old Man Funkey'. He was about 5'6" and had big eyes, receding hair, and always a great smile. Picannin was totally animated when he talked and usually put out a great story every time: Picannin's stories were famous. This was especially true when Sandy and Laubscher egged him into the telling of his experiences. Picannin was truly a gem!

The Funkeys were born in America. Mr. Funkey had chosen South Africa over Russia to try his business. He was born in Salt Lake City. 'The Old Man' as everyone called him, went home many times and always brought back a present for each of his employees. The way he looked after us was one of the reasons I was glad I worked at Main Reef Engineering. At the previous place everyone seemed down, never happy, always working hard and never looking up. The atmosphere here was bright, happy, and amplified by good, hard-working people. Blacks and whites got on very well. There was a lot of give and take and the white men in this company often tipped their helpers because of the low wages they received.

"They're good boys," one journeyman had said. "It's better to help them out . . . you know?"

I tipped Joseph despite my own meager earnings. It was a meager tip!

I had now rounded the Turffontein Race Course and I headed up Turf road, past La Rochelle to Rosettenville Corner. I saw only street-lights and a few lit shop fronts. A few rooms were lit in the Broadway Hotel. *They're still drinking!* I thought. *A bunch of them probably carried a shopping bag filled with liquor bottles to the room and continued drinking there after the bar closed. That's a drinking place!*

There were a few cars on the road; also a few people walking home. Then there were cyclists. All the people moving were white. You very seldom saw a black person at night in the neighborhood, except for the familiar 'night watchman', sitting behind his fire, Bantu blanket over his shoulder, a pipe in his mouth and the familiar knob kerrie in hand.

There was a reason: there was a curfew on black people in the suburbs at night. They had to have a pass and a reason to be out; if not, the police would pick them up and take them to jail. It always seemed so unfair to me. The black men and women that I had known were always nice. They were polite and yet could become exuberant when discussing different things. I mainly loved their upbeat approach despite their heavy tasks in life. I thought of Joseph and wondered how he coped. He earned less than me and had a wife and four children . . .

I pushed passed the Broadway Hotel and up Main Street. It was still a mile to my house on Andrew Street. I could walk up Main Street with my eyes closed; I had done it so many times. *Now for the game tomorrow*, as my mind drifted into the solid sequence of Saturday. I felt pretty happy because there was a party and I actually had a date. "That is the essence of my present Saturday religion!" I murmured with a smile. I had had a good time with Laubscher. As I got into bed the sky was brightening, and the very low light reflections came through the window. Today there would be a great soccer game.

❋

CHAPTER 11

The South Coast—Margate

ANY MENTION OF THE South Coast, and within milliseconds
I was there in spirit. Every time I had been there, I had had a
good time, an exciting time. The South Coast was also very
beautiful. I saved as much money as I could, because I wanted to go
to Margate. This town, located on the South Coast highway and the
Hibiscus Coast, lay south of Durban and Scottburgh. Margate had a
beautiful, long, fine sandy beach, many hotels, numerous nightclubs,
restaurants, and nearby golf courses. The whole town was geared for
young people and set up to accommodate youthful activities. I had
learned there were organized parties for young people at each of the
hotels, and between different hotels, and also friendly rivalry competitions between the hotel guests to win any kind of game. People I knew
talked about how each hotel would wear a specific color shell necklace
that hung almost to the belly button. This represented the hotel team.
There were unofficial initiation ceremonies to be endured after you
arrived. They took place during the introduction to other hotel guests
after your first dinner. There were competitions held between hotels
in running on the beach, volleyball, and dancing. I tried to get some
of the Andrew Street Mob to go, such as Johnny and Trevor, but they
were busy. It was around Xmas so family events tied up most of the
Andrew Street Mob. I convinced Bobby to go. Bobby in turn suggested
Tom and Mickey. I asked Viv and arrangements were made for Bobby
and I to go first and the rest to follow later.

Following the Potchefstroom era, I now hung out with both
Bobby's Group and the Andrew Street Mob. There was some intermin-
gling, but Bobby's Group was into the Johannesburg rock club lifestyle,

and the Andrew Street Mob group, especially Johnny, Billy, and Trevor, were more into the nightclub scene with swing and pop music style activities. The Andrew Street girls loved the dress-up entertainment with good manners and clean looks. I liked the formal side of life, but the rock and roll scene was becoming truly exciting. The two styles of life had other differences as well. The one was pleasant and straightforward and lots of fun, and the other offered a casual, flamboyant atmosphere with a large potential for unpredictable excitement. The Rock dances were the peak of fun times for me. I could get into the excitement very deeply. It suited me just fine.

Bobby and I drove all night and arrived in Margate early in the morning. The beautiful subtropical breeze of the South Coast swarmed over our faces as we got out of the car. Johannesburg air, because of its six thousand feet elevation, never gave that special 'air enclosure of the body' experienced in tropical climates. Bobby and I grabbed our bags and went into the hotel. We checked in, threw the bags on the bed, put on our swimsuits, grabbed our beach towels, ran to the beach, dropped the beach paraphernalia on the sand, speeded up our run and dived into the warm waves of the Indian Ocean. The smell of the sea, the freshness and the taste of salt on the lips, were just so different to anything in Johannesburg. The sensations in our bodies created by the complex forces of the water as the waves carried us in towards the beach, added to our enjoyment of being. We were surfing. Having learned many times before, to judge the waves for strength and break, we very seldom caught a bad wave. We also knew how to duck under the waves when swimming out to sea. These unrelenting swim out and surf back sequences would never have ended if we didn't get tired. However, after an hour, the energy loss took its toll. Our muscles grew weary to the point of hurt. Bobby and I decided to quit. We took our last wave, put our feet back on sand, and staggered up the very slight gradient of the beach. We reached for our towels, wiped our faces, threw the towels down and collapsed on them with fully outstretched bodies.

"I've been waiting to do this since September," I said.

"Not me," said Bobby. "I had a bath in November and don't really need to have another till January!"

"Well, it is good that you have one before Christmas," I suggested.

"Mickey, Tom and Viv should be here Thursday," said Bobby. Viv had grown up close to Andrew Street and was part of the Mob's party group. He had been part of the cycling group as well.

"Yeah, they'll miss the Wednesday dance at the Palm Grove," I said. "Wouldn't miss that for the world. Jeez! It's nice just to lie on the beach and look at all these cute girls."

"Where?"

"Over there by the coke stand."

"The big one with the elephant rear?"

"No!"

"The blonde with the silver satin suit standing next to the ugly, old bald guy."

"Looks like her boyfriend."

"Could be . . . it fits here in Margate!"

"What's this about Wednesdays?" asked Bobby.

"Every Wednesday night the Palm Grove has a singles night, with a bunch of rules," I continued. "It's famous for being different by reversing the roles of the boy and girl at dances. The Wednesday night thing is even known in Johannesburg."

"Go on," instructed Bobby, lying with his face pointing directly to the sky. I leaned on one elbow talking to Bobby's left ear.

"There are two lines when you enter, one for the girls and one for the boys, or women and men, you know. Inside is a big dance floor. The guys have to sit on the balcony outside, and the girls sit inside on the opposite side of the dance hall. If you have a girlfriend or you only want to watch, you sit near the entrance, opposite the dance band; there's a railing that separates you from the players; otherwise, you must take part in all the single events."

"What events?"

"The single dance events. Like, when the band starts, every girl must get up and go over to ask the boys. It's a reversal right? Otherwise, the band stops until all of the girls get up and go and ask someone to dance. They go! In return, the guys must dance if asked. They can't refuse a girl who asks. If they do, the girl reports them to the bandleader. They stop the music and the guy pays a forfeit, either by singing a song or they make him apologize to the girl in embarrassing ways . . . like on your knees! The girl can refuse the apology, if it's not sincere, then the guy must do it again."

"There won't be any dancing!" said Bobby, puzzled by the whole thing.

"No, it goes well. I hear everyone plays the game. I've also heard there's only a few times in the night that someone gets leveled in front of everyone."

"How do you know, you haven't been there."

"No, but Viv told me about it. So are we going tonight?"

"Sure," said Bobby. "Wait a minute, what music?"

"Rock and Roll . . . live band . . . all night. What more do you want?"

"All right, it's a deal!"

Bobby and I got dressed and walked down to the Palm Grove Dance Hall located on the beach and off the main street behind the Margate Hotel. The Margate Hotel was the most expensive in Margate. Lots of convertibles came and went. Lots of beautiful women with fancy dresses and a variety of men, young and old, were coming and going through the foyer of this most famous hotel. We passed the Margate Hotel, peering in the entrance, and went into the Palm Grove. We sat very close to the doorways going out to the balcony.

"The girls don't like to go onto the balcony very far. They just grab the guys near the door," I informed Bobby, who didn't seem to care anyway.

"You know all these rules."

"Engineers love to know rules, Bobby! Don't you know that!" I stopped a waitress and ordered two rum and cokes.

"When the music stops, the girls must go back to their seats, but first they have to bring the guys back to their tables. I like the switch . . . good hey?"

"Yes, Charl. When can you sit with the girls?"

"Only half-way through the dance. There is a long break for the band, like thirty minutes, and then everyone has to go back to their seats. These are the rules of the dance game! Man!"

Bobby and I got a fair share of dances. There were always more guys than girls and so a lot of beer went down smoothly and often. At the break two girls came over and sat with us and the five other guys at our table. The tables were long and seated about twelve people. Bobby and I got drawn into the conversation and found out these seven were all good friends and were planning a beach party after the dance. That is, everyone would go back to the hotel, change, and hit the beach. The girls invited Bobby and I and we agreed to go.

The two girls asked us to dance, as well as dancing with their friends. Bobby's partner Janette was definitely keen on him. My partner, Jean, just seemed to go along. The dance ended at 1:30 AM.

"We'll go with Bobby and Charl," said Janette. "They're staying at the same hotel as us and then we'll see you on the beach."

"Okay, cheers," said one of their friends.

We took a short cut that avoided the main street. The walk to the hotel was through a tropical growth along a pathway cut by people who liked short cuts. Bobby and Janette walked in front, arms around each other. They stopped quickly, kissed just as quickly, and walked on. I did the same, Jean responded slightly, but would only walk arm in arm. I felt excited by the events, especially meeting two girls so quickly. They had told us that their friends were just that and nothing else, which added to the intrigue.

Bobby broke from Janette, came over to me, and whispered in my ear.

"We're going to their room!"

So we went to the girls' hotel room. It was a large room, kitchenette at the entrance, a bathroom on the right, then a long bedroom. One bed at the window, at least thirty feet from the entrance, and a second bed located close to the bathroom. The beds were separated by almost 20 feet. Bobby and Janette went to the bed at the window.

"No lights, Jean," said Janette.

Jean and I sat down on her bed, talked for a while and then kissed, and lay back. A lot of time went by as whispering was going on in both areas of the room. Then there were active movements starting on Janette's bed. The room was dark but not that dark. I saw two figures wrestling nicely! I decided to do the same. Jean's response was mild, but she did not refuse any move . . . there was never a negative response. I wondered about the whole thing. Was she shy? Did she want to do something? We had partially undressed and I didn't know. But I was going to find out the answer! Suddenly there was a knock on the door.

"Janette, Jean, you coming to the beach or not?"

The girls said nothing as Janette came free from Bobby's grasp. The knocking was repeated but then subsided. So we all resumed our activities. The mood was much disturbed and my confidence shattered!

Bang! Bang! On the window scared the hell out of me. I got out of the bed and put my pants on. *Can't fight without my pants on*, went through my mind. Amazingly, Bobby was so cool. He just lay in the bed. I had known Bobby a long time. He was cool. I wished so much I could be like that, as I stood up and buckled my pants. Janette got out of bed as Sol yelled, "Let us in!"

"We're tired, Sol, we decided to go to bed," said Janette.

"Where's Bobby and Charl?"

"I don't know . . . they traveled all day today. I think they went to bed. Listen, see you guys in the morning, okay!"

"Okay," said Sol.

Smart lady, I thought.

There was a quiet time. Like waiting for something else to happen; nothing did. I decided to get back into bed before everything went away. We resumed the fun of 'pre-lovemaking'.

Knock-knock-knock, came from the window and the door, causing four hearts to leap.

"What the hell, you guys?" yelled Janette.

"Just checking," said Sol, "See you in the morning!"

"Okay! . . . Enough!"

"Cheers," said Sol, as the boys ran off laughing.

It took some time for that atmosphere to disappear. The disturbed dust did not settle down easily. *The mood must return,* I thought. It did, especially in Bobby's corner, where the bed started moving in an all too familiar rhythm. I decided to go for it, and I undressed Jean. She didn't stop me, so I took everything off her body. I was ecstatic! My body was almost painful with tinges of excitement. I then undressed with speed, my underpants and leg manipulations to remove my clothes all from my experience of getting to the shower first after a soccer game. I slid on top of Jean; all of Bobby's sounds were a galaxy away. Our skins touched with maximum envelope. Her legs opened and the ecstasy increased throughout the lovemaking to its final peak. The stars cleared when I opened my eyes. I rolled off Jean and lay next to her. I kissed her forehead and her shoulders. Then I put my arm under her head and lay on my back. Jean had hardly moved throughout the whole act, except near the end when her body accepted the fast rhythms. I was glad. There had at last been a response to the act of lovemaking.

The sounds of Bobby's corner returned. I turned over and put my head on the pillow.

I woke up as Jean said, "You'd better leave." I found Bobby up and dressed, Janette making coffee. I hugged Jean and rolled out of bed, got dressed and went to the bathroom. I came out and had some coffee.

"You guys went home last night, okay? Please!"

"Sure enough." The conversation was light.

"See Ya! On the beach." as we all hugged and kissed. Bobby and I left.

"What a start, Bobby."

"Let's take a shower and go and have some breakfast," said Bobby.

Outside the hotel was the warm air and atmosphere of a subtropical sunrise. The brightening sky and sight of just a few people up at 7 o'clock added to the birth of a day in the tropics. The sea was dark blue. The sky was light blue. The beach had not yet attained its bright shiny beige. The waves were presently empty of surfers, except for one or two diehards. Breakfast was really welcome as Bobby and I sat on the balcony of the Palm Grove looking out to sea . . . thinking.

"Amazing we got here six hours ago," said Bobby.

"This is the life," I said. Comparing, in a flash, the life in Johannesburg versus that of Margate. How could we live here permanently?

Tom, Mickey, and Viv arrived. Bobby and I were glad to see them. After settling into the hotel, they walked over to the Palm Grove for lunch with Bobby and me. The story of the night before was related, perhaps expanded with subtleties and innuendos, as the drinks went down. After lunch we walked around the town with a certain inability to focus. Finally, we went to the hotel room. Sleep assisted with resting and reviving our bodies. At 5:00 PM, with the afternoon sun still high in the sky, we went to surf, then scrambled out of the sea to go to the hotel, shower, and be in time for dinner and free cocktails.

The hotel had a large initiation cocktail party between 7:00 and 8:00 PM. Hotel guests assembled in the lounge room. The basic idea was to introduce newcomers by putting them in the middle of the group, sort-of center stage, and have them introduce themselves, plus perform through either singing or telling a story, or participating in a contrived trick. Newcomers were ushered to a separate room and were asked to come into the room one at a time.

A crew of five men and five women ran the Initiation Games. Bobby went first. He gave his name and said he would participate. Two guys blindfolded him and then they took his right hand and folded his fingers, moved his thumb so it stuck out from his hand. They lowered the thumb into an open can of Vaseline, pushed his thumb in and out quickly.

"What's that?" asked one of the guys.

"Grease," said Bobby.

"What do you do Bobby?"

"I'm a mechanic."

There were giggles from the audience!

Then they cleaned his thumb and pushed it into an orange which had the navel removed and pushed it in and out twice.

"What's that, Bobby?"

"An orange," he replied.

They took his blindfold off. "You're too good. Have you done this before?"

"No!" said Bobby looking totally bored.

The audience clapped.

Bobby was given a necklace of white shells.

"You have to wear this at all times now. Each hotel has a different color, so they know who we are if we compete on the beach."

After the initiation of two other people, I went to the center of the room.

They introduced me to a girl, named Elizabeth, who came up and lay down in front of me on her back. They told me to look at her very closely, and then blindfolded me. I was made to kneel on the other side of her, after which they took my left hand and guided it over her hair. The touch was gentle. They moved my hand over her face from left to right, very gently over her nose onto her lips. I could feel her lipstick; she kissed my hand, and touched it very softly. That sent a few pleasant feelings. Then they moved my hand onto the chin and lifted it.

"Is it the same girl that lay at your feet?" asked one of the men.

"Yes," I said.

People were clapping, yelling "Ja! Man! Yes man! Good!"

"Slowly now," instructed the man, guiding my hand as it was started at the top of the sweater and moved very slowly down the chest. I felt the sudden rise in the sweater.

"No," I thought. There is something different.

The crowd was in complete harmony and uttering in sequence, "Ooh! . . . Aah!"

My hand was guided slightly to the one side and then to the other. There was no mistake that it felt like a woman's breasts.

"Charl, what do you feel?"

I smiled. "A sweater!"

"Yes, we know . . . but Elizabeth is smiling."

"What else, Charl? Here, feel some more," as the guy guided my hand over the whole chest.

"Wow," I said, "feels nice!"

"Yes! . . . We know that! What is in the sweater?"

"Well! Ummm! I can't quite tell."

Then my hand was lifted and kissed!

Off came the blindfold and a guy, lying on the floor, was kissing my hand! A man with a wig had replaced the girl. He wore the same type of sweater she had had on, but he had falsies inside. Everyone burst out laughing. I just stood there and laughed. I also got a white shell necklace.

Mickey and Tom chose to tell jokes that were a little on the edge. Mickey was of Lebanese descent, dark complexion and black hair; he was short, had a great smile and was always laughing. Tom was quiet and unassuming. He and Mickey were quite a contrast, with Tom and his blue eyes and blond hair being just the opposite of Mickey. The jokes were mild to our standards, but not with this crowd. They were off-color! There was not much applause. This crowd preferred the skits.

The last to enter was Viv. Viv was a strong-looking man, tall and blond like Tom, with striking eyes; he looked almost scary sometimes. He disarmed people with his very attractive smile and great laugh.

Two girls introduced themselves and Viv smiled, they were pretty, he enjoyed that aspect. Then without hesitation, they put an oilcan funnel down the front of his short pants. The crowd chuckled. Viv was made to put his head back. The girls mounted a coin on his forehead, as they helped him stand upright, by putting their hands on his shoulders.

"Drop it in the can," he was instructed.

Viv brought his head forward; the coin fell, but missed the target. Viv tried again by bending his knees, looking awkward, and this time the coin dropped in. The crowd laughed at Viv's stance, but quickly applauded him as he had succeeded.

"Not finished," said one of the girls.

The girls then very gently blindfolded Viv and with lots of encouragement told him to try again. He took the crazy-looking position, brought his head forward and missed the can. The crowd hissed!

"Try again," said one girl, while the other put the coin back on Viv's forehead. This time as Viv tilted his head forward one of the girls emptied a glass of water down the funnel; the water ran into Viv's pants.

Bobby, Tom, Mickey and I were instantly very worried and scared at what Viv might do. We'd seen him drop somebody for a lot less! He could get aggressive, and could get mad quickly sometimes, and come out swinging or swearing.

Viv ripped the blindfold off, looked at the two girls, looked at his soggy pants. The crowd was still laughing but it had dropped when they saw the expression on Viv's face. Many seconds drifted past. . . . Viv laughed! The girls smiled and gave him a hug, the crowd applauded loudly, and for a long time. We were very relieved after having visions of a fight breaking out.

As the noise died down Viv asked, "Which of you girls is going to dry the pants?"

"Drop them off in the morning and we'll dry them out!" said one of the girls.

Viv just smiled. He got his shells.

Close call, I thought.

The party continued as different people went through the fun initiation. At the end, everyone was reminded that the string of shells were to be worn throughout Margate, if anyone were caught without them they would be called up on the carpet.

"Sort've high school stuff," said Tom, "Good thing they told everyone to wear old clothes to the Initiation!"

"Yup!"

◆

Bobby, Mickey, Tom, Viv and I had planned a week of vacation, plus getting into at least one big party. The game of wearing shells in Margate was not part of the plan. The daily routine was simple: a late breakfast, walk to the beach in thongs, wear a swimsuit, a shirt and a towel and carry money in the small pocket of the swimsuit. We put on dark glasses and had a comb stuck somewhere, or at least one comb between all of us. Smoothed-out hair was important for our looks. We also used Vitalis hair tonic but it came off instantly in the seawater. Sometimes suntan cream was taken, but we had such nice brown skin, it was not necessary. Anything extra was overloading. A suntan and swimming were the stated goals. The silent goals were girls and fun.

Each morning after breakfast we walked for about a half-mile along the lagoon in sub-tropical vegetation to the beach. We found a place for our stuff against the wall and went surfing. Body surfing was the method, as we did not use surfboards; expense was at least one of the reasons, plus you had to lug them everywhere and make sure nobody stole them. Margate currents are strong and the beaches are constantly patrolled by lifesavers: mostly white. There was always a black lifesaver in the beach shack. The black swimmers on this part of the coast were excellent, and very knowledgeable about the currents. They often swam a couple of miles in the sea, down or up the coast, for training, one of the few groups of black men known to do this. The safest areas were marked by flags, which were moved from day to day but were generally close to the south side of Margate beach, close to rocky cliffs. The shoreline consisted of beach and an outcrop of rocks that typically extended from the land into the sea. This separated the beaches and was a familiar sight all along the East Coast of South Africa. Surfboards were used, outside the flags, and away from the general public beach.

Our small Southern Suburbs group had the same routine for two days. On the third day, without any warning, a strong current changed and quickly swept about thirty swimmers out to sea, separating the thirty from the main bulk of swimmers by about 50 yards. A number of 'Surfo-Planes' were also swept out. Surfo-Planes were ribbed plastic, inflatable and 3 feet long by 2 feet wide, and fit under your chest for surfing. The siren went off and most people got out of the surf to allow the lifesavers space to operate. The waves were about 5 feet high and the current was moving fast. A couple of strong swimmers went with the current for a while and then headed for the shore. I didn't see any of my buddies, so I grabbed a loose Surfo-Plane and within minutes shared it with a woman who was swimming and getting tired. I asked her if she was all right.

"Yes," she said, and I helped her slide her body over the Surfo-Plane. We just held on and drifted. I didn't like this because it was moving parallel to the beach, away from the flags, and drifting slightly out to sea. A black lifesaver's head appeared without any inflatable. He asked me if I was okay and I said that I was fine. He turned the woman around and pulled her out. Two lifesavers were reeling in the rope on a winch. The rope was attached to a broad belt around the black man's stomach. He pulled out two people at a time. Two winches were working and six lifesavers were at work. Now I knew why the Australian lifeguards had a big rowboat in their arsenal.

I thought the lifesavers were rescuing all the women first, and decided that I would just try to swim to the shore. I swam for a long time; in fact, I noticed everyone had been pulled out of the sea by the time I reached 25 feet from shore. I wondered thirty times if I had done the right thing. Thoughts of my stupid statement of being okay resounded! I kept reminding myself not to panic, even though the urge was always there. The tide was strong, pushing against my chest and although I got very close to a person who was standing—it seemed I could almost reach out and touch him—it was too deep, where I was, to stand. I wanted to yell! But I felt it would be stupid.

Eventually, I decided to stop swimming and let the sea do what it wanted to do. I drifted sideways, parallel to the beach, for a while, and then the strength of the sea dissipated as a second current threw me out, almost like magic! I glided in with the next wave, walked onto the beach and collapsed. I was only 150 yards outside the flags and had probably gone unnoticed, until I let myself drift. I lay there absolutely exhausted, but relieved I was out of the sea. I didn't think I had 'done a smart thing' as my mother would say. I should have stayed with the Surfo-Plane. A lifesaver came up after a few minutes.

"You okay?"

"Yes, thanks," I replied. "It was stronger than I thought. I was mainly scared of being washed out to sea!" I stood up and felt okay.

"It does happen. By the way, we did get a boat out when we saw you drift out to sea."

"I could have touched the guy standing in the low water!"

"Yeah! The beach drops off steeply just about there. We never have the flags out that far."

We walked back together to the main beach. He confirmed that the woman had been rescued, and then I took off to go sunbathing for the rest of the day.

"Listen! Thanks a lot! I do appreciate you guys."

"Cheers!" he said, and headed back to the lifesavers stand on the beach. I was okay and finally frightened at what had happened.

After telling my story that night in the bar, even without exaggeration, nobody was impressed! I just wrote it off . . . damn scary though!

◆

Our group danced with many ladies and we talked to quite a few on the beach, none of whom stuck to us. Then we were finally invited to a party, in a house, on the lagoon. There were fifty people from everywhere. This was ideal; you could get drunk and walk to the hotel or anywhere in Margate. The cars were parked. Dancing, talking, pairing off, walking the premises, sitting by the lagoon, eating in the kitchen, were all the activities underway. Tom, Bobby, Viv and I were drinking in the house, having some luck but not much. After a couple of hours Mickey came out of the deepest part of the garden, disgusted. He called us together. He had worked pretty hard on a girl.

"I took her into the garden. We had drunk so much liquor! I didn't think we could do it. But she was eager and I got her to lie down on the grass behind the tree, like! We started to take clothes off," explained Mickey in a tone that would not excite anyone.

"And then what happened?" we all asked in unison.

"She threw up!" said Mickey with his arms stretched out and a serious look on his face. Mickey paused and pointed to the sky. "It went straight up in the air . . . Oh! God! . . . And fell right back down all over her face and clothes! . . . Yuck!"

"Oh shit," we were in chorus. "No!"

"Is she okay?" asked Viv.

"Yeah, I guess. She just lay there. Then she wiped it off with her hands. I went and got a towel and gave it to her but she didn't know what to do! I wiped her off. She couldn't get up! So I lifted her up onto a seat. Then I went to the bathroom . . . I was sure I got some of the shit on me!"

"So, where is she?" continued Viv with an Italian gesture.

"She's still sitting there," answered Mickey.

"You left her?"

"Oh God! Yes! Her clothes just reek!"

The party had broken into little groups: a bad sign! We didn't think there was any prospect of further fun and decided to leave. It was no longer our scene.

We went back to the hotel and sat in one of the rooms drinking rum and coke. It was already 4 AM and the light of the day was starting to creep into our space. We continued talking until about 6 AM, and then suddenly decided to go find a place to eat. A coffee shop had opened. We had oatmeal porridge, toast, papaya, and a few cups of coffee. I had sardines on toast; it was a favorite of mine. We sat there for an hour before walking back to the hotel. But we were not sleepy, so Mickey and I changed our clothes and walked to the beach. Bobby, Tom and Viv did the same but at a very slow walk. Mickey and I hit the beach. "First one in wins the Puke Girl for a week," said Mickey, about to run. I grabbed his arm.

"You have her number in Joh'burg?" I asked.

"Yes!" said Mickey.

"You're on!"

We ran as fast as we could but Mickey was no match for me. My head went into the first four-foot wave coming towards us. To my surprise, Mickey was right behind me. We swam out.

"Oh, it's a little cold," yelled Mickey. We surfed only twice, and staggered back towards the beach, arm in arm, laughing.

"You got the Puke Girl, Charl, she's all yours."

"Thanks! Mickey! I don't have one of those!"

We stood in the low waves looking at Tom, Bobby and Viv.

"You two want a beer?" asked Tom.

"Sure," was our answer.

"You two are stupid together," said Tom.

"Well, we were trained by the South African Army and by Potchefstroom's finest," I replied indignantly. "Oh, shit, you weren't with us Mickey!"

"Yes I was," replied Mickey in a slow tone.

"Okay, you were." I knew inside that with all the shit we went through he would have wanted to be with us. We went back into the water.

The boys yelled at us because a beach photographer came by and they wanted a photo. So despite the cost, Mickey and I had a photograph taken in the surf. Now I knew we were definitely drunk. We never posed for photos! Finally we staggered out knowing it was dangerous to swim on the South Coast of Natal without all your strength. We found a quiet spot near the wall, lay down on the finely ground beach sand, curled up and slept till the very warm sun woke us at noon.

◆

We met quite a few girls and guys on the beach and continued the vacation with one type of crowd on the beach and another type of crowd at night. We were all from South Africa, young, and came from all places and cities. Surprisingly many of us were from the Rand and

Johannesburg. The routine never changed. It was so good, we didn't want to change it. There were many sights to see, inland from Margate are tropical rivers and beautiful scenery, but we just stuck to the beach and the bars and the parties and dancing. Margate was so easy, we walked everywhere, no cars were needed as we picked up the girls at their hotels and walked to the dances and parties. Viv drank more than us and danced just a little. The rest of us were into the whole enjoyment.

Everyone had a friend and so we decided to go to the Palm Grove for the last night together. The girls were dressed nicely, looking just grand in high heels, slim-fitting dresses, with their hair nicely done and, of course, the 'tan' which made everyone look so good. There were two girls I thought were excruciatingly good-looking. I always felt I couldn't make it with girls like that because they had so many guys around. I didn't believe I would stand a chance. I would have to dance with them in order to have any confidence.

Our group reserved a large table on the verandah. A six-piece band played the latest popular songs, mostly from America. They also played rock music and then the traditional South African music with its complicated beat. This beat was not quite a true Afrikaans beat but a combination of part polka, part swing, and anything else that could be added. We loved these sessions where people sang and did crazy dances. We had fun because everyone was on vacation, young, and this was the first age of dancing apart, and to upbeat music. The boys danced with every girl at the table as a matter of friendliness. Then came the hopeful choice of someone you liked when the music was slow. We were very adept at the slow tunes! I was in ecstasy, being at the dance, talking and drinking with my buddies from the Southern Suburbs of Johannesburg.

I saw June, who I had befriended on the beach. I went over and asked her to dance a number of times. Most guys just had fun and danced and never took it seriously. The girls often had the same approach. June was different. I thought she was beautiful and had a wonderful smile. She was blonde and had these challenging eyes. She gave me her home phone number. The night seemed to last forever.

The dance shut down at 2 AM and was followed by a walk on the beach. June joined me for the walk. There were now maybe twenty to thirty of us. Margate was truly a tropical paradise. The wind on the beach was in the form of a warm, gentle breeze that caressed the face and body to soothe the sunburnt skin. The sand was cool and crisp and crunched as our feet broke the surface. We could tell because our shoes were in our hands. The sea continued its endless lapping at the beach and the sound was very pleasant, completely soothing and a perfect background for the arm-in-arm, hand-over-the-shoulder, arm-around-the-waist or just a holding-hands walk. I wondered how many millions of years it had been just like that . . . then I thought how little time we had spent here. The crowd talked in hushed tones for fear of disturbing the aura of this place. Laughter occasionally broke through the pure enjoyment of us young South Africans enjoying the magnificent beauty of our country.

◆

The trip home was always hard because the lifestyle in Margate was truly exceptional and exciting. The cars headed north with over 450 miles to go and 6000 feet to climb from sea level. The obvious questions were rampant: "Did you get a phone number, is she from Joh'burg?"

"Bobby I have Janette's and Jean's phone numbers, but . . . Jean said she didn't want me to call. I don't understand that!" I implored.

"Didn't you know she's getting married in three weeks?" answered Bobby.

"Bullshit No! I don't believe that!" I exclaimed in astonishment.

"Don't then," said Bobby.

"Well! Well! Well! There is a hysterical story . . . You were her last fling!" said Mickey with a smile. Then he drove home the punch line. "And, don't forget you won the Puke Girl as well!"

"What?" asked Viv.

"Nothing!" I interjected, "you don't have to know!"

"Come on!" teased Bobby.

"Nope!" I confirmed.

The vacation was a total success for all of us and in addition to all the fun we'd had, we were really happy because we were not entirely broke! Tom had met a nice girl. Mickey got to know a couple because he was always 'alive' with things to do. Viv had got drunk a couple more times than usual, and in his way had interested at least a few ladies. Bobby always seemed to succeed and treated it all as though it was nothing at all to scream about. I had danced a lot, surfed a lot, talked too much sometimes, met a couple of girls. The nicest one had been June, from Alberton. I really liked her, and she lived in a town close to Johannesburg. She had agreed that we should see each other again. I was amazed how good I felt about that! To me that was an exciting thing to look forward to. My best feelings on the trip came from being with this group of guys . . . we were essentially 'Southern Suburbs Brothers'.

CHAPTER 12

✳

Music Interweave

THE SOUNDS OF SCREAMING trumpets, punctuated by the smooth saxophone section, driven by multiple drums, all in harmony with the Mambo beat of the Perez Prado's very famous band, flowed loudly into the house from my bedroom.

"Close your door!" yelled my mom.

"Yes okay! . . . Mom!" I replied. I fell on my bed, almost exhausted from practicing the Mambo step in the three-foot gap between my bed and the wall.

Now in the early fifties, the Andrew Street Mob was experiencing a phenomenal interweave of music from many sources ranging from the traditional to the modern. It was having a major impact on our lifestyle. This effect included our outlook, which was so different to that of our parents. We adopted a freer and more open outlook between casual friends and our dress was continuing to move away from the very formal traditional ways. We were dancing in different styles. The ingredients came primarily from America. Europe had some influence as it modified American music in its way. South African black musicians were also contributing, adding their version of the American sounds and scenery. A young dynamic group of kids in Johannesburg was adding their influence to prewar music styles. The prime contribution to this complexity was the many different types of music from America and its effect on the changes in the style of dress: the two went hand in hand. This was especially true with formal clothes. The lack of suits and ties worn by the musicians in the presentation of entertainment; the use of wild styling and colors of dress on-stage. Added to this was the casualness of clothes with jeans, T-shirts with a myriad of designs, moccasins, loafers, white socks, and sweaters with large printed names, associated clubs and schools, plus wild bathing suits in two pieces! Modern sophisticated suits for American business activities contrasted this. The music and the clothes fueled the 'love of change' in young people and caused the roots of concern for our adults.

Teenagers of our time loved the various American beats. The exception was the conservatives, non-music types, and most kids from Afrikaans families who were tradition-bound. The Andrew Street Mob had always loved jazz, and in particular Johnny, Pat, Zoni, Trevor and Billy; Doc didn't seem to care. This love started with the blues, boogie-woogie and Dixieland jazz of the late thirties when it was played in the style of the 'Fifties'. Then the swing era, which changed and evolved into sophisticated Big Band music. In addition, there was the African-Jazz beat. This was a very exciting time from the point of music maturing in South Africa. African rhythms were being integrated with wonderful American melodies and played in an African lyrical style. Born in South Africa, this music style was growing fast in popularity.

Traditional music for many white South Africans had an old European style with background created with an accordion, music box, single trap drum, sometimes a guitar, and bass. It was Afrikaans music based on the foxtrot, polka and waltz rhythms. The 'vastrap' (foxtrot) was the popular beat, which was based on folk dancing, close to your partner, and whirling, skipping and walking at high speeds. The polka was similar to this dance step. The Country & Western music of America had identical rhythms. The American music influence had affected this traditional background a great deal, during the early part of the century, and had solidified its influence due to the entertainment impact of the war years. Country & Western music from America was liked by parents, because of its similarity in style to that of South African Folk music.

◆

Music was a wonderful thing in my life. I had become interested in it at an early age by listening intensely to the radio. I could remember being bored with all the talking on the radio that took up most of the broadcast. I had rapidly graduated from the age of twelve when I first learned to dance. I was now a sophisticated jive/rock dancer at the age of 19. At the age of twelve my cousin, Elaine, had taught me to dance the foxtrot; my mother taught me to waltz and tango, but I liked the jive, the modern jitterbug, rock and roll and all the new moves that were created by '*free dancing*' in which partners danced without formality: I loved that! It was so inventive! I had done it for years and could do it all and I had added steps from the Mambo, Samba and Cha-Cha into my dancing. Friends and teenagers of this time added new steps, and it seemed to change weekly, thereby becoming an instantly creative choreography. At parties in the Southern Suburbs, exceptional new steps were noted, and copied very quickly. Judging by what we saw in movies and on TV shorts that were filmed and shown in theatres, we even felt that we danced better than the Americans! Dancing was a great love of mine. It instilled a confidence in me for meeting and persuading girls to go out.

In this musical interweave, there was also the early traditional jazz played with a modern beat. Some of it, however, never needed changing. These included boogie-woogie, piano music by Fats Waller, Meade Lux Lewis, early Oscar Peterson, Nat King Cole, and the great Jelly Roll Morton and then later, Lionel Hampton. I was now heavily into the more sophisticated jazz pianists like Art Tatum, Duke Ellington, Stan Kenton, and Oscar Peterson. The music seemed boundless and it was new almost every week! The drummers I followed were Gene Krupa, Lionel Hampton, Buddy Rich, and the most famous solo 'Skin Deep' by Louis Bellson with Duke Ellington. In my mind I could recall the sequences of the many drum solo skits. There were many saxophone players that were added to my record collection and they included: Charles Barnett, Johnny Dankworth (Ted Heaths Band), Coleman Hawkins, Lester Young, Flip Phillips, and Illinois Jacket. My selections in trombone players were J. J. Johnson and Jack Teagarden, Buddy Morrow, and some Tommy Dorsey.

"I don't like the Big Band jazz! It drowns out the soloists and they only have a few bars of music to show what they feel," complained Ginge, and he was serious.

"True but there is a hellava feeling when the whole band backs the singer up!" I argued.

"You dancers are driven by heavy sound," came back Ginge.

"Yes! It goes all the way from the brain to the muscles and bones! . . . Agreed!" I replied.

Ginge and I would argue and agree on many aspects of jazz and the musicians. We were critical of everything. It had to be good, because jazz was not played on the radio very much, so we relied on records and they were very costly. This situation never affected our discussions on jazz and it just filled our conversations with no end in sight.

Ginge loved the clarinet solo the most, so I bought some of those records. Our record collections included the clarinet players, Benny Goodman, Artie Shaw, and mostly Woody Herman; the latter was also a great blues singer, who created unusual modern big band jazz with marvelous sounds! Finally, the bass players who kept our feet moving and tapping were Chubby Jackson, Eddie Safranski and Ray Brown.

These were names our parents were oblivious to. Many of them knew of Glenn Miller and that was it!

So as the big bands matured over time, the young people in South Africa, including me, followed them. Meeting people in record shops in Johannesburg city always conjured up lively discussion: Saturday mornings you could be guaranteed of talking to a bunch of people at the record shops in Johannesburg. We felt starved of information about these great artists, as radio and newspaper articles were scarce. The most prized dream thought amongst us was, "Wouldn't it be great to go to a live concert!"

Jazz fans I knew seemed to follow the music in the same sequence as the Americans. We saw the Glen Miller and Tommy Dorsey music change to a preference for Stan Kenton, Duke Ellington, Lionel Hampton, and Woody Herman. Then the Bebop era brought in Dizzy Gillespie and the smooth jazz bands. Bebop had actually started in the early 40s, but it was very popular in the late 40s and early 50s in Johannesburg.

Driven by my desires, and helped by the constant enthusiasm of Johnny and Ginge, I bought the records at great damage to my apprentice's paycheck. But the pleasure derived from the music drug, and the fact that my friends in the Andrew Street Mob were also intrigued, made this a very important part of my life. The Andrew Street Mob spent many, many Sunday nights lying on my bed, sitting on the floor in my room, and listening to the music of America. Johnny and Pat held similar sessions. The crowd discussed, listened, loved it, and combined all the music pleasure with teenage cuddling. Everyone knew the lights had to be out when listening to smooth jazz music for the true appreciation of the intricate melody and solo! We were not the 'Vastrap Generation'! We were interested only in modern American music.

The South African Broadcasting Corporation, which held all the rights to broadcasting in South Africa, did not provide satisfaction in this type of music. If there was a jazz program, it was obscured to the listeners. The broadcasting of such music was scheduled at some time when was improbable anyone would be available to listen to it. The Andrew Street Mob loved, and thanked God many times for, the Laurenço Marques Station broadcasting out of Mozambique, the only commercial station. It was the primary outlet for American music other than the record stores. David Davies, the listeners' favorite announcer, was also the most loved man of the time. Everyone looked forward to the return of his annual visits to America because he brought back the latest music of the time. We always knew the time and date of his reviews and we passed on the word. It was our 'Jazz and Rock and Roll Concert Attendance'.

South African parents were familiar with opera, classical music and the composers Bach, Beethoven, Wagner and others. Many people liked Strauss, Tchaikovsky; some of the composers of lighter classics. Added to this was the influence of European folk songs: Scottish, Welsh, English and Irish folk songs and ballads, and English light opera such as Gilbert and Sullivan. Then again the parents were heavily influenced by the South African traditional music, which was a mixture of folk songs, sung in both English and Afrikaans. I liked the music at dances with Afrikaans and English colloquiums that intermixed the languages at the root level: only South Africans could truly understand the words because it reflected the essence of people in South African life.

Although there was some popular music coming out of the British Isles and Europe, the most popular was continually and predominantly from the USA. It came in many forms and it seemed to be unending . . . every week there was a 'new hit'. The parents in South Africa were influenced by films and popular songs of crooners and so in the forties, Doris Day, Tony Martin, Bing Crosby, Frank Sinatra, and Perry Como were admired and in some strange way, set the standard for cleanliness and purity. Also, in the forties the movies poured out a magnificent library of songs from American songwriters and composers and the production seemed endless. Except for the occasional British or European tune and the tradition-based South African music from artists like Nico Carstens and Al Debbo, and traditional songs by the popular singers Marais and Miranda, the hit parade was essentially American. In fact, a few South Africa songs recorded by American artists had crept into the international arena; 'Skokiaan,' 'Wimoweh,' and 'Sugarbush' were amongst them.

The detailed knowledge of American music was not important to our parents . . . it was a 'teenage thing.' There was very little conversation with adults! They didn't understand that this music to us was 'freedom undefined'.

◆

The unending surges of wonderful music grew even greater in the late forties and early fifties when new popular singers seemed to appear every week. Surprisingly artists in the 'Forties' were getting stronger in the 'Fifties'. And it is in this time frame that possibly the largest interweave of music took place. All forms were still popular and the pressure for young people to choose was perplexing. In the late forties Nat King Cole, a foremost jazz artist, entered the hit parade singing 'Nature Boy', Les Paul sent ecstatic feelings through the body with his multiple guitar recordings of 'Brazil' and 'Lover', and Arthur Smith drove hard with 'Guitar Boogie'. Everyone loved Tennessee Ernie Ford with 'Smoky Mountain Boogie' and 'Shotgun Boogie'. Kay Starr's 'Wheel of Fortune', 'Bonaparte's Retreat', and the Ames Brothers with 'You, You are the One', 'Rag Mop' and 'Sentimental Me'. Doris Day sang 'It's Magic' in 1948, and in 1952 she just sank all South Africans with 'Sugar Bush', which was a traditional South African song 'Suiker Bossie'; 'Secret Love' increased her popularity intensely. Patti Page entered in 1950 with 'I don't Care if the Sun don't Shine', and had a shattering success with 'Tennessee Waltz' and later 'How much is that Doggie in the Window?' which made her a household name. Perry Como whose success in the late forties with 'Till the end of Time', 'Blue Moon', 'A You're Adorable' extended his popular run with 'Don't let the Stars get in your Eyes' and 'Papa Loves Mambo' in the early fifties. Tony Martin, along the same lines from his successes in the forties: 'To Each his Own' and 'There's no Tomorrow', extended his run into the fifties with 'I get Ideas', 'Kiss of Fire', and 'Stranger in Paradise'. Al Martino thrilled the teenagers in the early fifties with 'Here in my Heart', 'Take my Heart', and 'When you're Mine'. Guy Mitchell came out with Percy Faith's Orchestra in a rendition of 'My Heart Cries for You', and Percy Faith followed in 1953 with 'Delicado'. Billy Eckstine, sang 'My Foolish Heart', 'I Apologize and I Wanna be loved' and deepened his mark by transcending the forties to fifties. The Weavers formed by Peter Seeger gave the popular music lovers great feelings from 'Good night Irene' and 'Tzena, Tzena, Tzena' and then followed with folk song favorites like 'On Top of Ol' Smoky', 'So Long it's been good to know you' and 'Kisses Sweeter than Wine'.

These songs were in our lives every minute of the day that was not occupied with deep thinking. The Andrew Street Mob, all its friends, teenagers of the time, knew these songs, knew the words and loved to sing them in the back of trucks, at picnics, on the beach, when beer was being drunk, or any time people were having fun. The songs were upbeat, happy, inviting and expressed the feelings of the time. Music was so much a part of us.

"Just as soon as you think we've got the latest record in our crowd, they release another," complained Johnny.

"I can't buy them all! I have stuck to just the heavy jazz." I said.

"Maybe that's what we should do in the crowd. We each buy a different type of record," suggested Billy.

"That's what I do," said Pat.

Les Paul continued his modern sounds accompanied by his wife Mary, with 'Mockingbird Hill', 'The World is waiting for the Sunrise', 'Tiger Rag', and 'Vaya Con Dios', and the monster recording of, 'How High the Moon'. Rosemary Clooney singing with an amplified harpsichord had a sensational hit in 1951 with 'Come-on-a-my-House', followed with 'Too Old to Cut the Mustard'. Nat King Cole continued his popularity into the early fifties from his early forties jazz playing by singing songs 'Mona Lisa', 'Too Young', 'Unforgettable', 'Pretend', 'Answer Me My Love', and 'Ballerina'.

'Come-on-a-my-House' was an Andrew Street Mob phrase for a long, long time. Especially the line, 'I'm gonna give you a everything . . . everything!'

These were the popular artists and many of the songs were popular with adults and teenagers. Then the parents were driven crazy again! The teenagers became more enthralled by some of the offbeat, different and exciting new artists. Johnny Ray was one artist whose sensational voice (of crying) thrilled teenagers with his song style in 'Cry', 'The Little White Cloud that Cried', 'Please Mr. Sun', 'Here I am Broken Hearted' and 'Walking my Baby Back Home'. Parents could not understand it, so we liked him even more! Frankie Laine was equally sensational with 'That's my Desire', 'That Lucky Ol' Sun', 'Mule Train', 'The Cry of the Wild Goose', plus his super rendition of 'Jezebel', 'Hey Good Looking', and 'Sugar bush' (again) became a solid favorite. Billy Daniels wiped out the Andrew Street crowd with his rendition of

'Black Magic'; the words were engraved on everyone's tongue. These artists were top favorites of the Andrew Street Mob; records were literally worn out and some bought second recordings. We could sing any of the songs by Frankie Laine. You could say he was a truck favorite. The 'Wild Goose' song had more off-key singing than any other! But we didn't care.

◆

The loud and unusual music that teenagers were also intrigued by was associated with the Mambo beat. The Afro-Cuban rhythm with hot jazz riffs created by Machito, Tito Rodriguez, Tito Puente, and Benny More added hard, high-note trumpets and wind instrument chops with the Latin beat background to popular songs. Perez Prado was one of the most famous with recordings of 'Mambo #5', 'Mambo #8', 'Slow Mambo' and 'Cherry Pink and Apple Blossom White', which were played for many months. The cha -cha-cha swept Cuba in 1953 and not much later an old swing band, Tommy Dorsey, had 'Tea for Two Cha-Cha-Cha' on the hit parade. There was no let-up in this continuing surge of rhythm and song mixture.

From about 1948 onwards, the music, style and attitudes of the teenagers in Johannesburg surfaced and amazed many parents. The indifference of young kids to established lifestyles, and their lack of acceptance of the authority of government and administrative rules was apparent. Parents blamed it on the American influence, but it could have been the age-old recurring generation gap of 'teenagers against all others.'

In the fifties we saw a trend in the change of music, movies and dancing .The music influence came mostly from rock'n'roll which had its birth in 1948, under a guise of many other titles but eventually Bill Haley and the Comets had made sure everyone knew the beat in 1954, with 'Rock around the Clock', and 'Shake, Rattle and Roll'. From the movies came the sultry personality of Marlon Brando in 'On the Waterfront' and the deep, intriguing action-personality of James Dean in 'Rebel Without a Cause'. These two actors and their movies gave new images to replace the very stale personality of the generally acceptable nice guy with pressed pants, ironed shirts, shiny shoes, all well defined and in matching colors. Kids in Johannesburg were glad to see a change in the style of singing and dancing. The trend was going from the crooning and ballads by dark handsome men, singers like Doris Day, and impeccable but boring dancing by Fred Astaire, to something new. There were singers such as Fats Domino, large and happy and loose, with a rough voice, and dancers such as Gene Kelly, Donald O'Connor and Gene Nelson, who displayed an athletic type of dancing. We were influenced by this change. The stale English social expressions of 'delightful', 'how nice' were replaced with the jazz and rock words of 'dig', 'flip', 'jive', and 'cut-a-square'. In addition there were those made-up American words from the music of Chuck Berry songs like 'Maybelline' and Gene Vincent's, 'Be-Bop-a-Lula, She's my Baby'. This was happening a little later than it did in America but it was still a 'Jukebox and Jeans Generation'. At this stage I knew my brother Bazil had grown old because all he liked was Vaughn Monroe.

The swing era was definitely on its last legs, although helped occasionally by a movie or a good recording. 'Bop' the progressive jazz, had replaced the swing, but not the jazz. Dizzy Gillespie, Dave Brubeck, Gerry Mulligan, and Chet Baker would all play a few bars of a melody and then disappear into a string of notes with or without a hard beat rhythm. Stan Getz, Lee Konitz and Miles Davis were a little more understandable. This music only appealed to a small percentage of the teenage crowd. Being 'cool' with the impression of money and other assets that were beyond compare, together with an overbearing attitude, did not go with the 'Rock Teenager' who was not dressed very well and loved to be exuberant. Still, the big band popularity survived with a few of the Andrew Street Mob. Johnny would force us to listen to the singing of June Christy with Stan Kenton, with his progressive jazz style and superb musicians such as Art Pepper, Maynard Ferguson, Eddie Safranski, Bob Cooper and Kai Winding whose music left us breathless.

◆

If the voluminous recorded music background to our lives was not sufficient for choice, there was always the local jazz scene. There were many white bands interpreting the jazz of America. Local teenage groups, mostly with an amateur ability, played in our local municipal halls. Sophisticated trios and a number of really professional jazz bands played in Johannesburg clubs, such as Northcliff's Worldsview Night Club and The Coconut Grove. Our mob's sophisticated opinion rated the Dan Hill All Star Band as 'tops'.

In the background of all the music from overseas and the popular movie music was the local black music scene. The black musician of South Africa, whose love of jazz was a lot deeper than most people knew, was very active. Music by black people evolved in every part of South Africa over a long period of time. Sophiatown in Johannesburg was the source of a long series of major music creations.

Sophiatown, sometimes called 'A Harlem in Johannesburg' and 'Chicago of South Africa' was a most unique suburb in the area of entertainment and life associated with music, theater, art and night-life. Its history is fascinating. A speculator, Herman Tobiasky, bought 277 acres of land in 1897 and named it after his wife Sophia: hence Sophiatown. Years later the city built a sewage plant nearby and as none of the land sold, he offered it to Africans. The land was purchased by a large cross-section of people of many races, including whites. This resulted in a collection of musicians, writers, journalists, politicians and enterprising businesses because of no municipal ordinance restrictions, and no special permission being needed for Africans to live there.

Located five miles from the center of Johannesburg, formed in the 1910s, by 1946 Sophiatown had a population close to 400,000. Even by the 1940s the roads were not tarred; houses were of brick, wood, and galvanized iron sheets; sometimes constructed, but more often just assembled. There were also some well-built houses and shops belonging to the middle class Africans. All this was serviced by communal water taps and toilets. Music thrived in this location. The big difference in Sophiatown was the permitted ownership of real estate by black people, and that gave people in this part of Johannesburg a true sense of having something. (Black people were not allowed to own real estate elsewhere.) Sophiatown's Asian, white and colored residents were also part of the community.

Music and nightlife flourished here. The American influences were strong in drinking places such as 'Aunt Babes' and 'The Back of the Moon'. These hangouts became meeting places of the African businessmen, entertainers and underworld. They would bring to the table discussions of their world, and to the club floor, dancing to the latest American music with an African style. South African black bands first copied an interpretation of American influences of the swing, jitterbug, and Latin rhythm dances, but the African musicians, in their traditional way, soon developed their own style, called Tsaba-Tsaba. This dance involved two dancers dancing apart, shaking their legs and moving by means of body gyrations. It emphasized lots of footwork and moving towards each other, and just before touching, yelling "Tsaba", and then moving back and away. The most famous dance song was 'Skokiaan' which topped the American Hit Parade in 1954 as 'Happy Africa'. Louis Armstrong had also recorded 'Skokiaan'. This style was extended by street musicians into what was very popularly known as 'The Kwela', made famous by the penny whistle music. The music became very popular and a further style of dance called Patha-Patha (Touch-Touch) evolved, a very sexual form of jive dancing where dancers touched each other all over the body, again shouting, but this time using the word "Kwela" (jump up—jump in—join us). Penny whistle artists who played this music were popular with both black and white people. Artist Spokes Mashiyane was one of the first black musicians to record with some success.

Kwela-Kwela also means climb up - climb up, and comes from police raid instruction to get up on the truck. The Kwela, the most famous of all South African black music, began because musical instruments such as clarinets and saxophones were very expensive, and definitely out of reach of the black man. The penny whistle was the main instrument and the substitute; a metal tube, half-inch in diameter, about fourteen inches long, with one end flattened. The artist, from his interpretation of a combination of Scottish drum and fife music and American jazz, created its relatively simple melody. Some African tribes had traditionally used reed pipes and had contributed some of the background to rhythm and melody.

Black jazz bands started in the early forties and by the end of the decade, a major orchestra, the Jazz Maniacs with singer Emily Koene, was very popular, as were Sophiatown's Dolly Rathebe and Bulawayo's Dorothy Musuka. There were male quartets, tap dancers, minstrel choruses and Vaudeville reviews. The military hired the best African jazz bands to perform for black units. Some of them met Glenn Miller. The South African Broadcasting Corporation even had African music on the air. In the early forties African jazz bands played in white nightclubs, but were eventually banned due to white musician protest. The Jazz Maniacs, a Sophiatown band, were one of the first bands; ten years later they became very popular in the Jig Club. The declining popularity of dance bands in America influenced the South African scene. Still, these local Johannesburg bands that played into the early hours of the morning, created the Marabi, Kwela and Mbaqanga, the 'people's own jazz'. Mbaqanga had evolved from the late night jam sessions with solo after solo and support chorus and rhythm from the rest of the band. Saxophone, trumpet and trombone were the basic elements of music that were formed from the free flight of musical notes, unrehearsed and non-orchestrated African Jazz.

The black music scene in the late forties went through at least two major upheavals. The first problem was that the black-city youth formed gangs of Tsotsis who portrayed the American gangster lifestyle; a new type of black gangster evolved. Young city-bred men with a gift of the tongue. The term Tsotsi was based on a pronunciation of 'zoot suit' . . . the American flashy culture dress. A lot of the style came from American movies. Tsotsis were clever, not necessarily violent, and they were mostly young black teenagers. Purse- or handbag-snatching and shoplifting were the most popular activities. Older boys robbed and broke into houses and some stole from warehouses and trains. White South Africans could identify the Tsotsis because of their clothes. The cut and quality was not like the clothes of the hard-working black men. Also, their walk was musical, boastful and confident.

The Tsotsis and black gangs had an influence on the local bands because they admired jazz musicians and singers, and therefore the audience would be determined by their liking for the band. This following was not necessarily good for musicians as jealousy, ownership and power caused fights on behalf and against the performers. Miriam Makeba, Dolly Rathebe, Thoko Thomo and Susan Gabashne were all victims of assault in the early fifties. There were fights with other gangs from other black urban areas of Johannesburg and these included 'The Spoilers' from Pimville and the 'Msoni' gang from Alexandria. The gang called the 'Americans' controlled Sophiatown. The musicians were also 'located', the Manhattan Brothers were in Pimville, and the Jazz Maniacs were attached to Sophiatown.

The antics of the gangs forced people to stay away from clubs.

A major change to this music scene was caused by the Nationalist Party, which took control of South Africa in 1948. It started to impose the apartheid process. Restrictions, passes and the Urban Areas Act were designed to move black people out of segregated living areas. African music and lyrics of songs opposed this. There was success for 'Jazz at the Odin' jam sessions; the shows 'Jim comes to Johburg', 'The Magic Garden', and the film shows 'Zonk' and 'Song of Africa'. The talks and fashion shows and atmosphere of Sophiatown's nightclubs were coming to an end. Two devastating words made an entry: Soweto (SOuth WEstern TOwnships), where Sophiatown residents would eventually be forced to move to, and, Triomf, the name of a new suburb of Johannesburg, which would replace Sophiatown.

The early fifties for black South Africans were a golden age of creativity for artists, musicians and writers. Drum magazine was an example of this creativity, of white and black working together. Bloke Modisane and Can Themba were two journalists associated with Drum magazine. The African National Congress was becoming active. The legal offices of Nelson Mandela and Oliver Tambo were a center for information. However it was an upstream swim for preservation of the new creativity and integration; the Nationalist Government was intensifying segregation, and removing more and more of the black rights that already existed. Their goal for the city of Johannesburg was the removal of so called black areas from white urban areas. Sophiatown, a major source of black creativity, was greatly affected. The social mixture of drunks, prostitutes, and blacks of all kinds, the shebeens and speakeasies, and of the mixing of whites with blacks were not desirable elements in the view of the Nationalist Government. This situation was against all that they believed to be correct.

My interest in American music came through boogie-woogie and blues. It remained the music that entered my soul and caused emotion. The seedy dark spots and smoky nightclubs with dancing and a heavy music beat were beautiful to my eyes. I could not picture anything better than Duke Ellington's band playing 'Take the 'A' Train' with a beautiful singer in a nightclub and me sitting with some pretty lady, drinking rum and coke. In the dream was a dance competition with the band driving hard and the dance floor full of couples swinging, dancing free of each other and 'letting it go'.

The '*free dance*' to me was ultra-important because it let the music flow through the body. The music drove its energy inside for the mind to interpret the mood, the rhythm and the style, and signal the release of the body's energy in sequence and harmony with the song. It was very tiring to dance with someone whose body did not match the timing and flow of the music being played, no matter how beautiful they were or how outstanding their appearance. The dancing of black or white teenagers in America and the dancers in movies had a large influence our style in Johannesburg. Although the Andrew Street Mob could go to nightclubs neatly dressed and behave very nicely, if the music changed to the upbeat, we would break down any reserve very easily and form a space on the dance floor to 'rock it out'. The Worldsview Club, Coconut Grove, Hilton in Hillbrow and many social dances had witnessed this transformation. We were never stopped from doing 'rocking out', so we knew we were good! Music influenced many hours of the week and songs tended to remind us all of events, parties, sitting in a car with someone, going to the drive-in theaters and traveling, but mostly having fun with our friends.

Johnny, Trevor, Pat, Billy, Zoni, Doc and I sought out the clubs in Johannesburg and in the surrounding districts and we tried them all. Johnny and I went further and slipped into Sophiatown to see the famous black artists performing. Although these black clubs had a bad reputation, we didn't believe the talk and were not worried about the outcome. We found there were other white people in the crowd. The black people didn't necessarily like white people to be there because they weren't sure of their motives. Johnny and I mixed well with the crowd. People were friendlier when they saw that we were interested only in the music and willing to have fun. We were fine, we enjoyed it, and joined in with the way the crowd enjoyed themselves. It was difficult for us at first, because of the crowding and the roughness in the clubs. There was a big difference in the ways that people did things. Space was at a premium, so pushing past people was done continuously. The second time we went, we had a confidence in where to go, where to stand, and what to wear. In the end the music drove the problems away. It was a wonderful experience of people and music. It was different to anything Johnny and I had done before. Johnny was not as enthusiastic when we went to the rough white gang music scenes producing their equivalent rock music. In some ways the atmosphere in white clubs seemed more intent on ending with an altercation than the black clubs, where people seemed to just have a good time. Johnny and I never witnessed any fights in Sophiatown!

One evening, an astonishing event took place in La Rochelle in the Southern Suburbs: black musicians playing to a white audience, sponsored by white musicians; to us, this was unheard of. Johnny and I attended and came away very deeply impressed. As we left the hall, Johnny and I had some very personal discussions.

"Beautiful music with rhythm, the sax player was as good as any-body we've heard on records," said Johnny, as he walked with long strides. I always felt comfortable with him and somewhat looked to him for agreement on many things. We had done so much together and his demeanor was always positive. He was willing to do almost anything new. My mother said he was his mother's child. Never did our crowd ever think that our parents knew about each other!

"Their jazz music has that different sound. You can always hear what the black people are saying in the music, even though there are no singers," I added and then expressed an inner desire: "Wish I could do it!"

"Why don't you learn?" asked Johnny.

"It would be exciting but where do you go with it. Maybe hit the top by playing at Northcliff or Coconut Grove. . . . No! I'd rather be a dancer." I paused for a while. "Oh! I don't know, that probably wouldn't go anywhere either!" I said, knowing that it would take years of learning. "It's hard enough learning a trade and going to school."

"Where does the black man go?" asked Johnny.

"With his music, or his life?" I asked.

"Both."

"There is something I want to tell you, because I don't discuss this with anyone," I said to him softly, while feeling apprehensive about this topic. I didn't know why I spoke softly, there was no one else around!

"Shoot," said Johnny.

We continued to walk to the car. We had said nothing but we were automatically going to the Olympia Ice Rink Drive-in for a milk shake and a steak sandwich. It was automatic because the Southern Suburbs young people would go there whenever they could. It was 'the place' for young people in the Southern Suburbs.

"There are a lot of rules made by this government that upset me inside. I just don't care about their theories of what black people should or shouldn't do. Because, I believe, no matter who you are, if you have the ability or the talent, you should be able to use it and you should be able to be free to go anywhere with it." I looked at Johnny for a reaction. There was an interested look on his face.

"Imagine how well South Africa would do if black people could participate in the Olympic games . . . It's tough for us, as working class people, to get a university degree. Mostly our parents can't afford it. Granted, the kids in the northern suburbs can more easily do it." I paused, still not knowing how far to go, because Johnny could easily afford university, but didn't seem to be interested. He just liked what he was doing.

"So when you look at life to answer questions, we are placed in the Number 2 spot. But the black man's chances are impossible . . . well almost. I don't know but what do you think?" I stopped. It was time to find out Johnny's reaction.

"Go on . . . you've got a couple of good points," stated Johnny.

"So for you and I, given that we can excel as a musician, artist, singer, soccer player or whatever, all the chances are open here and if successful, there is even a chance to go to Europe or America."

There was silence as we reached the car, got in and drove off. I continued. "Now the black man can't go just anywhere in this country, and he definitely can't go out of the country because the government would most likely refuse to even give him a passport. There is something cruel in that Johnny! There cannot be anything worse than preventing a person from using all the talents that were given to him, or he has developed. Now! I don't mean bad talents!" I emphasized, smiling, trying not to make this super-serious.

"We all get a chance to practice those," said Johnny, pausing before replying. "I don't know what they do or where they go. And I agree it isn't fair!" he emphasized. "But a person feels so hopeless with the situation. There doesn't seem to be anything you and I can do anyway. Our family tries to help our girl and boy (expression for black house servants) as much as we can afford, but I don't think money is the only answer."

"My grandmother and mother do the same," I added. "You know Johnny, money seems so hard to get when you don't have it. Maybe you and I, given their situation, would steal for food . . . for our brothers or for us! Hard to tell! What makes me mad is that there are many whites who don't care about any of that, some of them think that blacks were born to do only the unwanted jobs," I stated emphatically. I paused and thought for a while. I knew this conversation was too deep, but I wanted to talk to someone. I had held a lot of this stuff inside for a long time. Who better than Johnny? So despite my wanting to continue, I changed my thought direction. I went back to the amazing feeling and revelation I had experienced while listening to 'the South African Blackman's jazz'.

"Maybe their love of freedom is so important that they get it out of music. It is the freedom to create the jazz in their style. You can see that in the way they sing so beautifully together. I love the chanting; especially when one singer sings a few words and all others follow. It's as good as the Welsh choirs. Also they do it without ever being out of rhythm or being off the right sound. So damn natural the way the chorus answers . . . very beautiful."

We reached the Olympia Ice Rink Drive-in, our eyes roving over the parking lot looking for friends or anyone we knew. A cute white girl appeared, like in the movies. She was dressed in a blouse, skirt and flat shoes. We ordered and the girl soon came back with the tray and hung it off the car's door, on the driver's side. Johnny passed the good stuff over. We dug into the sandwich and milkshake like hyenas because they were so good! I paused, thinking about the concert.

"I thought the tenor sax player was the best. He seemed to have a complete freedom when he played. And he was so ecstatic, after his solo, especially when the crowd clapped! So loud!" I said. I continued to open my mind to one of my best friends. "Johnny, black music has taught me something. I've been blind to for a long time."

"What's that?" asked Johnny, who had assumed the role of listener.

"I've been living in a world of family and friends and ignoring everything that's been going on around me. Every time I get to know of something that affects a black person in a bad way, I've felt it's none of my business or my problem. I've ignored it. I don't think that it is a good thing on my part . . . now it is like someone slapped my face. I've realized almost instantaneously that there are a lot of things wrong in the way we do things. The rigidity of classical, religious and old time music requires that you behave correctly, dress correctly, right? We don't like it."

"Yes! Right! What are you getting at my friend?" inquired Johnny, chewing away but listening attentively.

"It's not so with jazz, rock, swing, I mean it is not rigid and has a freedom connotation . . . and that's why black people love it enormously," I stated, as if I was a consultant.

"True! Yes! . . . Maybe No! . . . Yes! That sounds right!" answered Johnny.

I didn't know what he meant so I just continued. "So I feel really bad! Sophiatown is going to be flattened and rebuilt for whites and called 'Triomf' (Triumph). Alexandria has the same fate. All the clubs will disappear. I mean even if you don't believe the Government will do that . . . it will happen. Worst of all I don't know if we can do anything about it? The Government is so determined. They have the power to do it. So it will be done. You know what Johnny? I already hate the insidious rules. I mean if we were black, what could we do? Would we fight?"

"You've woken up a bit Charl, and that is good!" said Johnny with a look on his face that showed he didn't want to upset me.

"That's right and I'm mad at this lifestyle we create and I'm twice as mad at myself for being so dumb for so many years." I paused, finished off my milkshake, and continued with a lot of vigor, "I know now what it is! . . . I have never liked the interference of government in sports. Riding with the black riders on the road and not being allowed to compete against them! . . . So inane! It would only improve all of us. Politics and sports . . . politics and music . . . there should be a law against politics having anything to do with these two things at all!"

"We all have freedoms," said Johnny. "You're 'gone' when you dance. You disappear into another world!" Johnny laughed. "Some chaps do dagga (marijuana), some drink."

"Yes, that's true and we could name a few in the 'Suburbs'!" I agreed and laughed. "But . . . I want you to know something that has really made me happy. The connection that came about tonight between white and black through jazz music! Tonight here in La Rochelle it was so unbelievable how the white audience participated."

"Good jazz, and a great evening. Lots of people buy records and go to jazz places here in town," said Johnny. "Yeah . . . very distinctive . . . a little different to the Worldsview Club band."

"Very different. Many worlds apart in some sense and very close in others," I added.

We finished the milkshakes and Johnny drove me home to Andrew Street. I was so glad of my friend's philosophy and agreement. Johnny didn't say much, but I knew that he agreed with me, that was his nature! We didn't go to all these places to hear music for nothing. Johnny often proved that he was sympathetic to black people through the way he treated them at work and socially; every person was a good person to him. I felt great about the night out; the whole thing was very startling to me, because I suddenly admitted that I was aware of the social and work life of the blacks, and I had done nothing. Could I do something? I didn't think so!

◆

A crashing blow to jazz lovers in South Africa happened when Louis Armstrong, a beloved jazz artist to anyone who enjoyed his special music, was refused entry to South Africa by the Government.

A concert tour had been planned and the news was hot, everyone talked about it. Those that loved jazz hoped beyond hope that his tour would come true. Those that knew popular music thought it great. Deep down I knew that the Government wouldn't approve of Louis Armstrong's visit. I could see the cabinet assembly discussing how was it even possible that someone would make such a request for a black artist to come to South Africa and let us enjoy his talent. I also believed they would do everything to prevent it, even though I was not fully informed, I believed inside that I knew the atmosphere of the discussion.

I was mad when I finally heard the news of the refusal. I was totally upset. I told everyone I came in touch with and everyone that was home for dinner.

"This is exactly the reason that lots of people hate the Government and the people who run it. It's the church and its archaic ideas about who are God's people. If God created us all, why the hell are we dividing people up into groups that are allowed to go here and not allowed to go there? The earth is not ours, it belongs to everyone."

"So, who is Louis Armstrong?" asked my mom, totally ignoring my tirade.

"Oh! Mom! He is an unbelievable artist. He is a trumpet player from America who is revered by people all around the world. He was in the movie 'High Society' with your beloved Bing Crosby. Maybe some Americans don't like him because he is black, but they cannot dislike him for his music or his personality! I'll play you a record," I got up.

"Not now . . . maybe later," suggested my mom.

"Well okay, but this kind of thing makes me wonder how this country can change when we have a closed-minded government. We can't even vote them out. How can we get the United Party in? They have reapportioned all the voting areas. Thousands vote for the United Party in Johannesburg and we get one United Party person in parliament. Hundreds vote in the rural districts and the Nationalist Party gets a representative."

"That's probably true," said my Mom who didn't care for the Nationalist Party either.

"They reapportioned the constituencies and now six people in a rural area are equivalent to 6,000 city people!" I exclaimed in the heat of the moment.

"What is your problem with farmers, Charl?" my mother asked. "You came from farmers and a lot of your family are farmers!"

"That's very true Mom! . . . And I know that for sure . . . but I definitely don't mean farmers. They are like owners of a business; they have many things to consider with all kinds of headaches. We know that! . . . I mean the large number of people in small towns, which are far from big cities and don't know everything that goes on inside the cities. So they definitely do not face all the problems of a large city! I mean what do they know about science and technology and planning of big business? How can they vote for things they don't know anything about? How about jet planes, electronics, superstructures and nuclear power? All these new things are the future. If that's who you put in a government, how can you advance as a country?"

"Charl! Gran and I never taught you to be like that . . . you have to know a lot more things before being so opinionated!" stated my mom loudly . . . with an anger that matched my upset!

I calmed down. My mom and I very, very seldom got this confrontational.

"But Mom, you don't understand. We are living in a state ruled by people who don't want progress. To me they don't seem to know what black people can do. They don't seem to know that there are many, many whites that get on very well with blacks. Maybe some black people are gangsters, but most of them are nice. Isn't it the same with whites? Aren't they just as bad in what they do? Of course they do it with a lot more sophistication and with a lot more friends in high places that can help them out, and who may save them!"

"That's unfair Charl," protested my mom.

"Mom, I know black people who can read and write and are intelligent and get one-fifth of the money any body else gets!"

"Charl, calm down . . . you never talk like this!"

"Maybe I've something inside that's coming out," I replied. "I'm tired of rules and rules and rules and regulations and laws!"

"Well who isn't, Son? I'll never disagree with you that there are too many rules, nor do I believe the Government is right, but you should work at it in some other way than insulting everyone," stated my mom in a calm manner.

"Okay! Mom! I'm sorry! Music and sport are very important to me! . . . I think they are super important things in life. I do believe the Government should stay out of the game. Why don't we even have TV in this country? We're probably the last ones in the world to get it!" I knew my Mom was right. I didn't know what had got into me lately. Maybe the 'music scene' was driving home reality.

"Life is a hard road Son! By your going to college and learning, it has opened the world to your mind. You are learning about things Gran and I . . . or even the whole family, don't know anything about! When you tell us at dinner what you're doing, we often don't know what you're talking about!" said Mom in a soft voice. "And that's why I am so glad you're going to college!"

"Well! How do we get all these dumb situations to go away?" I asked in an equally soft tone. "All these things are driving a big nail in my body and it's beginning to rust. I want to get it out, but how can I do it? These rules are everywhere!"

"I don't know, Son! Maybe you should go overseas when you get older!" replied my mom. She was smiling. "It is good that you get it out . . . don't let these ideas fester within you. They will just damage you."

"I'm afraid you're right again, Mom! I guess I was drawn up in events in my life. I am so busy at work and college, and sport and music are a relief to me . . . and important to me. Now I have realized the Government interferes with that! I'm truly sorry Mom!" I gave her hug and it was warmly returned.

"See you in the morning . . .!"

"Good night Son!"

I went into the back yard for some fresh air. Pal was wagging his tail. I hugged him and untied him, so he could run around the yard. Pal did run, but he came back to me every twenty seconds. I now took another blow to the mind, as I realized there was a rule to keep him tied up at night, sort-of a neighbor's rule. Nearly all the houses had dogs. They were there as an alarm, to their owners, of any potential robbery. They were a guard of the best kind. Gran's dog, before they moved to 65 Andrew Street, would let anybody come onto the property, but wouldn't let them off! Gran or someone from the house would have to give him a command! The exception was the milkman. Then Gran and Uncle Mick's house was robbed. The police caught the man through investigation: it was the milkman!

I played with Pal and then went into the house . . . I didn't tie him up. I put a record on the player to listen to music. It would help soothe the mood. It was not by Louis Armstrong because that would further increase the torment.

"Jeez!" I said out loud.

＊

CHAPTER 13

Andrew Street IV

T HE BIG CITY OF Johannesburg had a complex society of people from all over the world. This society included many black people who were from many parts of Africa. Some of them were original natives, some of them first- and second-generation immigrants, and some of them new immigrants. Many were from fathers and mothers who had lived a very rural or tribal lifestyle. Johannesburg had been a raucous gold town at the turn of the century, full of bars and prostitution and miners from many parts of the world. Family lifestyles also existed in this young city that was using extremely sophisticated mining methods to dig out the gold from veins that were extending further and further underground. The gold in its quartzite rock was being removed each day now, by the drill and blast for production, and then the long drill and examination of the cores for the planning of further development of the mine. The city had gone through, directly and indirectly, three wars and a depression up to the present day's growth. The parents of our crowd were not politicians or financiers of the largest ore body of gold discovered. They were the pioneers and workers of the mines.

We in the Andrew Street Mob members were fortunate, due to our parents' great efforts in bringing us up well in an ever-changing Johannesburg. In addition, we were fortunate in that we were too young to participate in the Second World War. Some fathers, older brothers and relatives had served. However, luckily only a few of us knew the horrors of relatives not returning. We knew the history of the war very well. Some of us had seen the movies made of the atrocities. Although it had happened in far away places, it remained an unbelievable series of events and still left a huge impression on us. To most it was more gruesome than any movie ever made. Johannesburg had many ex-servicemen glad to be back from North Africa and Europe. Also, there were many immigrants from Europe who were glad to get away from Europe and the Middle East and start a new life. Some of them had sons and daughters. The Andrew Street Mob consisted now of direct descendants of these city pioneers. We were changing to the 'new things of the day'.

The picture of our lives was becoming clearer to us. We were not so spellbound by everything around us. We were in fact facing a lot more reality than we bargained for! A change was taking place. Late teens meant most of the kids were working hard to earn money and learn a trade. Aspirations of love adventures with the opposite sex were increasing at a phenomenal pace and to some it was the primary goal in their lives. The inherent need for excitement of teenagers approaching their early twenties was blossoming fast. Following a week's work, Fridays were still for the boys, Saturdays for dates, and Sundays were flexible for either situation. In a land of sunshine where summer lasted from September to April, water sports, tennis, golf, cricket, hiking, swimming, and picnics were all included in the activities. Soccer and rugby belonged to the so-called winter period.

Social success for young people, in Johannesburg, was primarily determined by the mode of transport. A car was success; a bus was not acceptable transport for a date. In the southern suburbs there were no proper dance clubs. Dancing happened at parties and there were parties almost every weekend. The lifestyle in the 'Suburbs' consisted of movies, bar drinking, sports, parties, dances on Saturday and outdoor activities on Sunday. There were dances held by various groups with live bands at meeting halls, but real 'club life' was found only in Johannesburg City, where there were hotels with professional live jazz bands. The girls were now becoming more demanding on dates, wanting to occasionally go to 'The Orange Grove Hotel' or the 'Hilton Hotel' in Johannesburg city; both were very popular. The 'Northcliff Club' located in the northern suburbs of Johannesburg (often referred to as the rich suburbs), was definitely a non-refusal date.

Restraining entertainment activities were, firstly, the strict liquor laws in South Africa, mostly predicated by the heavy religious backgrounds of the politicians. Drinking was legal at 18 years of age and no selling of alcohol was allowed on Sundays. The Sunday rule did not apply if you had a meal at an eating establishment, so if a person had lunch or dinner, beer and liquor could be served. Secondly, there was no television like in America and Europe, because our Government had banned it. Radio was the entertainment of parents. Records were the entertainment of their children. There were plays on the radio, some in English, some in Afrikaans. Obviously to our young crowd, anything away from home would be exciting, and we wanted to experience as much as we could get.

The Andrew Street Mob embraced everyone who came into it, and everybody who stayed in and contributed to the fun party atmosphere. The gang avoided trouble and created a twist to every event, even a formal dance was not straightforward. This seemed to be our inherent desire. Time causes change and the Mob was not exempt. We were now going through some major changes. The first was the Mob expanding when the original girls found older and other boys attractive. The second was the original Andrew Street crowd of kids moving in different directions as we pursued our current ambitions. Work had taken away 'street play', families had changed, and in general we were older. Third, new people from outside Andrew Street were joining us in our activities, and they came from other areas like cycling, social activity and life. We were now entering the wider scale of Johannesburg lifestyles.

The Kennedy Street girls had got different boyfriends. Beryl had in fact got married. I had helped her clean her wedding rings and asked why she was doing this so early . . . before she was twenty. I was losing a very close friend and I didn't like it. We had talked for many hours at her front gate over the years; I had a crush on her but I was a year too young, such a big difference as a teen, as I sadly discovered. Grace had met Otto; they started to go steady and he became a very enthusiastic member of the Mob. Ann also had a boyfriend.

The boys that made up the main core of our mob now consisted of Johnny, Trevor, Pat, Zoni, Doc, Billy, Norman, Mac, Viv, Tommy, Gerald and myself. Some of the Andrew Street Mob had changed direction. Juni had become a part-time member; he'd dropped off and pursued work and hobbies such as his MG. Helen, from next door to me, had a number of boyfriends and was busy with her activities. Her brother Bobby was also busy with other things and faded out of the crowd. Julius went back to Belgium for a year or so. Guy was no longer active but kept in touch. Many of the seventy street kids had drifted off into their respective worlds.

The Andrew Street boys' interest remained faithful to beer, sports activities and parties. The girls were interested in new teenage boyfriends. The original group of Andrew Street boys actually welcomed the new boyfriends and in the process became 'street brothers' of the girls they knew so well. We tended to be a little protective! The dancing and parties and picnics were in turn more fun because of the expanded number of people. There were budding romances for the original boys, but to enter long-term, tied-up linkages with ladies was not the most important thing to us.

Our young crowd was also growing in all directions as most of us were working. Johnny was working for his dad, Billy, Tommy, and I were working as machinists and millwrights, and Norman was a bricklayer—also working for his dad. Juni, Doc, and Pat were working as electricians and Zoni as a refrigerator mechanic. The girls were working in office-related jobs. The boys had a variety of cars and trucks that were being used; I was one of the few without transport. We were all following our parents to some degree, except most of the parents had never had cars at our age, and some still relied totally on public transport.

Very few of the crowd had the desire to go to college. We were from the blue-collar suburbs. Matriculation was a major achievement. Most of our parents had not attained even this wonder-crest of knowledge: they were tradesmen, some were in business, but mostly they were miners, plumbers, diamond cutters, carpenters, machinists, bookkeepers, and housewives. There were very few working mothers; my mother was an exception. The parents of the Andrew Street Mob were home people. Weekends at home, maybe picnics on Sunday, or a drive, if the family had a car.

The Andrew Street Mob continued to expand in all directions and it became difficult to remember all the names. At the same time the Mob went through a natural progression of forming small groups. The small groups would often go out to various functions such as the movies, but when parties, picnics or just 'get-togethers' occurred, this often attracted a big crowd. It was a marvelous time for all. Cars were available and the horizons expanded; almost everyone had been to parties and events outside the Southern Suburbs.

Johnny organized most of the social activities, and through him, Elizabeth joined, and added her friend Joanie. Viv had been turning up more often, Denise and Meridy also joined, and they became soul mates. Almost all of these people were single-single; that is, no attachments. Bobbie and Ron were still part of the social activities and still cycle racing. Joan P and Denise P, sisters who lived south of Meredale (we now had two Joans and two Denises!) in the crowd, continued to throw a wonderful set of parties. Nobody left these parties till 3 AM in the morning.

Joe, a good looking insurance salesman, joined, folded in quickly as he moved in with Zoni and Juni and Ron and added to the complications of Mimi's life.

The people that joined the Andrew Street Mob lifestyle were now from all over. Viv lived one block away, Mac six blocks away from Andrew Street and Norman lived up at the top of Lindhorst road, which cut across Andrew Street. Joanie came from Diering Street and Elizabeth, Johnny, Denise, Meridy and Billy came from the suburbs northeast of Andrew Street such as The Hill and Northern Rosettenville. The Andrew Street Mob continued to grow and the interaction was wonderful to everyone. It was impossible to find a conflict among us, and people just floated in and out at will.

The general trend continued as we were very often assembled in small groups during the week and in large numbers on weekends; always seeking fun.

◆

So the activities continued: I got to know Gloria very well and we became good dance partners. Our two body rhythms were a match and at parties we often had the crowd clear the floor to see us dance. The swing, jitterbug, bop, rock style was a copy of the American swing. Gloria and I added many unique moves to the basic rock and roll dance choreography. She was blonde, pretty, 5'6" and thin and light. I had grown into an active young man, 5'10" and strongly built at about 170 pounds. The key to our dancing excellence, so we were told, was our smoothness, combined rhythm and unique steps, plus our happy, joyous, smiling attitude.

Trevor, Pat, Zoni and Johnny were all good dancers. Billy liked the slow dances. So did Doc. Everybody danced in this crowd. Trevor, Zoni and Johnny could all 'go it'. Parties, dances, weddings and sports club events held in public halls were always enthusiastically enjoyed. Occasionally, when going to the Coconut Grove or the Northview

Club, which continued to be our best dream venue, Gloria and I would dance the same way.

Rock and Roll dancing competitions were often held in Johannesburg. Gloria and I won quite a few. Some of the most exciting competitions were often impromptu. One night a small Andrew Street Mob group went to a rock dance in Braamfontein.

Braamfontein, an infamous, small inner-suburb of Johannesburg, with one- to three-storey buildings, mostly from the early days, and close to downtown, was a tough neighborhood with a cross-section of all peoples and skin colors. Poor and tough, its population scratched out a living. It was a melting pot of the descendants of black, white, yellow and brown people, intermarried, single, or living together. In contrast, Hillbrow, close to Braamfontein and north of downtown Johannesburg, complete with tall modern buildings and located on a hill, was the richer side of town, with more cosmopolitan people. People from the nations of Europe, the Middle East, and Israel lived in this area of downtown Johannesburg. Hillbrow had all the clubs, out-door cafés, hotels, and parks, so well-suited for visitors to Johannesburg and residents who liked the high style of life and the European culture. Gay people adored the place. There were also many 'ladies of the night', discreetly available.

After entering, we became very nervous. There was a strong lo-cal atmosphere. There were gangs in Johannesburg made up of white men: semi gangsters, living by their wits. They were always around at these dances. The underground news wire informed them of the dance events. The Andrew Street Mob was out of its element there, so we usu-ally avoided these dances. I had been to a number of them with Bobby's Group and other friends introduced to me by Rosemary. Our group talked a little, and the consensus was that this dance seemed to have a rougher crowd than we were used to, and that the atmosphere was a little tight. The band was good. Everybody was dancing, drinking and having fun, and the tight atmosphere seemed to disappear. Towards the end of the evening, the band announced a jive competition and Gloria and I joined the competing dancers. The usual elimination took place. As the couples were touched on the shoulder by judges, they left the floor. The judges seemed to be self-appointed. Eventually, four couples were left, Gloria and I among them. The band stopped for a minute. The crowd formed a circle and the four remaining couples entered a new round. The band played and Gloria and I got into our dance. The band stopped; two couples were left: a local couple, and Gloria and I. I didn't really care about the consequences and said to our group that I was going to 'go for it'. The time was here to let loose; let everything go!

"So look out," I said, smiling.

But the Andrew Street group hinted in many ways: 'don't win! '

"Nah! It's okay!! I've known some of these guys from other dances and some from the soccer field."

"Different place, Charl."

"It's their place! Charl!!"

"Nah! It'll be okay!" I came back. I was just so excited to try and win, and Gloria was always supportive.

The final round started and Gloria and I rocked all the way through. I got into the dance with some good splits and low gyrations. Gloria matched my moves and twisted her body smoothly, complementary to the wild motions of a 'good rock'. We gave it everything we could and we were having a good time . . . talking and laughing while dancing. The crowd enjoyed it, clapping, yelling. Who could tell whom it was for? The music came to a stop on the drummer's last few loud beats in the smoky atmosphere and the competition ended. We left the floor, exhausted, to loud cheering, joined our group and waited.

An uneasy silence came over all of us. Although I wanted to win, Gloria and I knew we would gladly give it up in a second. We definitely did not want to show the locals up! Finally the judges got together and went to the mike. A loud roar from the crowd greeted the announcement by the main judge. I did not hear the names of the winners but I knew the other couple had won. Most of our crowd was relieved. Some said we were robbed, but then, they were friends!

Johnny added some wisdom and stated, "You can never tell as a dancer. You just dance and it's up to everyone else. Not bad though! Second-place in 'Braamie' is good man!"

As we drove home the talk was about our experience in Braamie. There was a definite agreement that it was better to come in second knowing that we could leave easily, than to be winners, and not know if we were going to sleep in a hospital bed or in the street!

◆

Sunday night, the last time of weekend freedom before work, school and controlled time, had to be entertaining for us. It was our philosophy. Those that could afford the purchase of records had to be enthusiastic, as they were very expensive. This was because 78 r.p.m. vinyl records were going out and 33 r.p.m. long-playing records were being bought, costing at least a day's pay. Johnny, Pat and I, one way or another, bought records. Sunday nights became a night of listening to music. At Pat's it was in his apartment, at Johnny's it was a large portion of his house 'Emoyeni', and at my house it was on top of my bed in my bedroom at 65 Andrew Street. It was amazing how many couples could squeeze on top of a bed, in the dark, listening to predominantly American music. At Johnny's and Pat's it was Nat King Cole, Billy Eckstine, Billy Daniels, Johnny Ray, Patti Page, Rosemary Clooney, Mitch Miller, Jo Stafford, and the latest hits—but only the romantic and slow. At my house the music was predominantly jazz. So we started with the latest recordings then, after some hard driving with Stan Kenton, Woody Herman, Tito Puento, and Jazz at the Philharmonic, the music would change to long sessions of smooth romantic jazz such as 'Stardust' by Lionel Hampton, Duke Ellington's 'Mood Indigo', and 'The Mooche', Artie Shaw's renditions of Cole Porter and anything by Ella Fitzgerald. I was not averse to also playing June Christy, Peggy Lee, Al Martino, Kay Starr and even Doris Day. There was no doubt I would never allow a Pat Boone record to be played, even if the request came from someone with a pretty face and soft pleading voice.

One of the ingredients for Sundays was beer and our famous, and most popular food, 'toasted cheese sandwiches'. They were made a special way. The cheese sandwich was made with two slices of bread, butter, cheese and sometimes tomato. But the secret was in spreading a little butter on the outside faces of the bread, wrapping the sandwich in greaseproof paper and ironing the whole thing with a hot iron. Very important in this procedure was the temperature of the iron. These sandwiches were mostly eaten between record playing. It was okay to interrupt a hard driving music set, but sacrilege to talk, munch, and groan during the romantic series. Although there were sometimes twenty or more people at these sessions, it also got down to four, six and eight: uneven numbers were okay but tended to be rare. 'Playing in the street' had all but come to an end.

The crowd was very active now, and our parties in the southern suburbs were known in advance, as hardly a weekend passed without at least one party to go to. This helped everyone, because taking out someone on a date was still very expensive. We were still apprentices and a major date took money from two paychecks. It was a daily thing to watch pennies disappear, and it was a source of anger in our life. We saw money flow, we saw American movies of affluence with cars and beautiful clothes and great places to dance. We couldn't believe the wages in the U.S.A. compared to ours on the same job basis. The related subjects were discussed so many, many times.

Activities at Mimi's house continued. Joe, one night, didn't quite like what Mimi had cooked and said so. Mimi didn't say anything; she just walked over, picked up the plate of food and dumped it all over him! Joe never complained again. A month later Mimi informed her house crowd that she was going to make pigeon pie. Two days later after the black servant had actually caught a number of them . . . the pie was served! It was on the menu for a week! Zoni and Juni now had a lot fewer pigeons flying around their cages in the backyard. Billy, who visited fairly often, came to visit one night and got thrown out for walking on the newly polished black and red walkway to the front door. He was not the first to walk up, get thrown out, and then try and figure out how one could get to the door any other way. The rest of the front yard was a complicated garden arrangement that defied walking through it from front to back. Mimi always went on Sunday nights to play cards with her friends. So the Mob ended up having crazy get-togethers in her absence—and in her house.

Aileen came to stay for a month; she was a good-looking red-head, taller than most of the boys and she had a most beautiful figure. Everyone pursued her. The best the crowd ever did was to convince her to play strip poker. Zoni, Juni, Ron B., Johnny, Joe, Billy, and I were included. Aileen beat us all. Some of us landed up on the cold chairs with only our underpants. Aileen did have to remove her bra but only because she chose to do it in place of her blouse, despite all the guys quoting the strip poker rules that clothes must be peeled off from outer to inner garment. Joe pursued Aileen relentlessly but never succeeded. Aileen only stayed for a short while and, against all our hopes and wishes, finally left for 'somewhere else' as she put it. We never saw her again.

◆

Rifle Range road, south of Kenilworth, was our route to Uncle Charlie's Restaurant and Roadhouse, located on the intersection of the Vereeniging and Potchefstroom roads. The crowd, now with cars, was drifting southward in pursuit of new places and this was one. Uncle Charlie's had a lion, leopard, a few buck and monkeys in the back yard locked in cages and behind tall fences. One Sunday, Mac and Norman loaded up the two half-ton trucks with the Andrew Street Mob, and we took off for a milkshake at Uncle Charlie's. Going down the Rifle Range road a challenge was made to jump from one truck to the other, so Mac pulled alongside Norman and the trucks drove down the road side by side. The guys jumped from one truck to the other until a loud shout informed everyone that a car was coming towards us in the opposite direction. Mac backed off and pulled in behind Norman.

Billy suggested loudly, "Maybe the Yanks should try this instead of playing 'Chicken'!"

The three-hour milkshake visit at Uncle Charlie's was filled with talk and banter; we were lost in our own amusement and great friendship.

Rifle Range road was to witness another event. Johnny had got a two-door, 1942 Studebaker with a 'Dickey Seat', and thirteen of our Andrew Street Mob squeezed into the car to go to Meredale. On the way back one of the girls wanted to drive and Johnny obliged. The crowd was yelling "Right!" "Left!" "Brake!" Four people that day learned to drive a car with a full load. I was lucky, excited as hell, as I shared the learning experience. I did scare the hell out of everyone by being a little rough on starting and stopping such a large car. It was my first drive on Johannesburg streets.

In the hot South African sun, nicely cooled by breezes at 6000 feet above sea level, swimming was loved, and combining swimming with picnics was even better. We worked hard to organize these events. Johannesburg's temperature ranged generally from 40 to 90 degrees F but for most of the year resided at 70 degrees. Our large, dispersed, Andrew Street Mob would come from everywhere to meet at Van Wyk's Rust, which had a natural spring of cold, cold water and a swimming bath a hundred feet in diameter. Trees surrounded the pool; with grass that surrounded the trees and allowed room to play minor soccer games, run, lie around, picnic, and generally have fun. There was a stream going past the picnic area that we could swim down, if we wanted to take a long walk up the bank first! It was so carefree and our young bodies were urged by our minds to try to exceed our abilities to run, swim and be athletic. As it was fifteen miles from the Southern Suburbs in a southwest direction, Norman's truck, Mac's truck or many cars were needed. As soon as the transport was arranged it was easy. Everyone usually met in Andrew Street, drove out along Rifle Range road to Uncle Charlie's, and then crossed straight over the Vereeniging road to get onto the Potchefstroom road that went to Van Wyk's Rust. The whole day was spent swimming, walking, playing with a ball in the water and lying around eating. The cold, cold water warmed up by midday, so as long as you broke the ice, after the first dip it became tolerable and very refreshing. The pool only averaged a depth of about three to four feet.

The crowd usually picked a section between the river and the pool. The reason for this was that mud fights were fun. The riverbanks provided a black, soft, and sticky mud just perfect to transform someone's neat look. Twenty guys would fling this gooey mess through the air and when it landed, it stuck. If the girls looked too comfortable, accidental missiles launched by the guys would just happen to land on the laid-back and complacent girls. This would force them to retaliate. The crowd would end up in a mess of black mud and white skin. As we had nearly been banned from Van Wyk's Rust for going into pool covered in mud, we had to go in the river to clean up. That was agony—the spring water was very cold. The days were full of fun as small soccer games, badminton, and cricket with a tennis ball took place almost continuously all day long, and swimming and sunbathing became a luxury. The activities only came to an end when the sun started to go down. The trucks would leave in the early evening and we would drive back to Andrew Street singing songs or just quietly talking. The South African sun burned our skin and the games tired our bodies and we loved it.

A second pleasure resort was Meredale. It was also past Uncle Charlie's roadhouse but then south on the road to Vereeniging. Meredale was a new resort and had become very popular because it had playgrounds, a high-diving board, a cable slide into the water, and a big rotating barrel about ten feet in diameter, located in the middle of the pool. We loved to go down the slide, into the water, over to the barrel, and fight like hell to stay on top of the rotating drum. Billy, Johnny, Trevor, Zoni, Juni, Doc, Joe, Norman, and I competed every time. The idea with the barrel was to run on top while it rotated and to see how long you could stay up. Something like the log-rolling competitions of the American and Canadian lumberjacks. All of us got very good at the barrel rolling. The competition got fierce and the barrel truly churned up the water: going one way, stopping it, and going the other way; people fell off, and it was dangerous for anyone to swim near the barrel until we had left.

The Andrew Street Mob also became so good at diving off the high-boards that the owners suggested we give a show one Sunday. There was a high-board at 30 feet, a second board at fifteen feet and two boards at 3 feet above poolside. Special costumes were made to depict the 1920s. The boys got dressed up and we individually attempted various comic dives off the boards. A lot of funny dives were done as we ran off the top board running in air until we hit the water. Clown dives of falling, springing off the board, and only hitting on one foot, thereby entering the water way to the side of the board, rather than straight ahead. Gerald dived off the top board without fooling, slipped, and hit the second board. Our mob rushed to the poolside with fear of injury but he came up out of the water with only red marks on the side of his body. He got a tremendous applause. The dives varied from the swallow to the pike. The grand finale was a dive of all divers off all the boards at the same time.

I went off the top board, with Joe, Zoni and Trevor off the second, and Gerald and Juni off the springboards, with the rest of the crew off the side of the pool. The group dive was successful. But my costume came halfway over my head as I hit the water. It was a woman's bathing suit from the 20s, suggested and made by my mother. It had pant legs that went below the knees, a full top and hat all made from brown flour sacks. My arms became half locked-in the top and I couldn't see out or use my arms. Pure instinct made me kick my legs furiously to head upwards to the surface, and then sideways toward the noise of people on the side of the pool. I was kicking and struggling at the side of the pool because I couldn't get free of the costume top, and I could not breathe. Apparently most of the crowd must've thought it was part of the act. I managed to draw some air in my mouth and so relaxed and sank down to the bottom of the pool, almost fifteen feet deep, before kicking up again. The sides of the pool sloped, so I pushed up against the side. I managed to get a little air, but the sack was wet, all over my head, and hard to breathe through. I went down again, and then kicked my way back up. I knew I was at the side of the pool. It seemed like ages but then suddenly it didn't. I kept going up again for the little bit of air I could get, hoping something would change. I didn't know which way to pull my arms out—it seemed as though the costume had twisted or something. I was thinking hard what to do, and preserving my breath. Suddenly, to my relief, I felt someone in the water near me, pulling me to the side. I relaxed. The man also pulled my costume top off. To my complete surprise, it was a black man. Those close-by pulled us both out of the water. The black man was a maintenance worker and had been cleaning the sides of the pool, picking up papers. He was not allowed (by South African law) to swim in the water at this resort. He was black and this was a white man's resort. He could have been fired for entering the water, even if he swam after the place was closed.

I thanked him. I shook his hand and remembered his face.

"We thought you were acting!" he said.

"No!" I said loudly. "It nearly got me. I could hardly breathe."

We went back to picnicking. I went to my street clothes and got five shillings out of my pocket, a day's pay at apprentice rates. It was definitely more than I could spare. I found the black man, shook his hand, and offered him the money.

"No Baas!"

"Yes! My man!" I demanded very emphatically. "You saved my life and this is just a little thanks."

"Tank! You Baas! . . .Very much!" His head tilted down, as he bent to his waist, his arms extended out in front of him with the money in his open flat hand.

◆

One night a small group of us young men and women decided on a midnight swim at Meredale. It was closed, so it was without permission. Norman drove the truck down the Vereeniging road and, about a mile away from Meredale, he switched off the lights and coasted quietly, hoping no one would see us actually stop at the front gate. The truck pulled in to the side of the fence; we jumped out and clambered over the fence and into the pool. It was a beautiful summer's night, full moon and warm air. The water was still warm from the sun's rays during the day. Our mixed group had a fun time in the water, cooling our bodies and whispering to each other. As though speaking would be louder than the splashing of water. Joe then challenged all of us to swim in the nude. Even though it was dark, the girls declined. The boys kept pleading but no success. The boys tried to lead the way by getting naked. I was also naked and got the shock of my life when I dove off the top board into the water. I had done this at least fifty times in my life. The descent time to the surface of the water, instead of taking seconds, seemed like minutes. Then I felt a sharp, excruciating sting between my legs as I hit the water! I grabbed what I had and swam to the side of the pool with one-armed strokes. I got out the water and just lay on the side of the pool for a long time. I heard a girlfriend of Joe's yelling, "Joe! Stay away!" as he pursued her in the water. The attempted enticement of swimming in the nude by the boys did not work. And we had planned it so well. Everyone went home . . .cold... at 2 AM.

The nudity antics did not end with that event. One Sunday afternoon, at Meredale, the crowd ripped the towel off Johnny's midriff as he attempted to put his swimming trunks on without going to the change house. There were a lot of people at Meredale that Sunday afternoon and they enjoyed seeing Johnny running after a fast-moving towel!

◆

A major 'Boys Only' Saturday-Sunday weekend was planned at the Vaal River. Johnny had got all the camping gear and twenty of the gang headed off for a summer weekend of drinking, swimming, talking, and fun. Billy, Tommy, Trevor, Zoni, Juni, Viv, Norman, Mac, Pat, Otto and I were among the twenty.

Two truck–loads: Mac and Norman, our faithful drivers, got us down to the river, after stopping at Uncle Charlie's for breakfast and driving a long way down the Vereeniging road. We found a picnic spot and set up camp. After everything was unloaded, we decided to walk to a store about a mile down the road. We had all the supplies and beer you could eat and drink for a week. So we were just exploring. It was summer, hot and dry, and very little wind. Short pants and t-shirts with sandals or running shoes without socks. This picnic style fashion of the afternoon probably wouldn't change or for the whole weekend. The Vaal River flowed past our picnic spot and took a wide turn before going under a bridge near the store. We were barefoot and the tarmac was too hot, so we walked in the brush on the side of the road. We continued down the tree-lined road over the bridge and went into the store. After drinking a number of cokes and cool drinks, and eating dried-up chocolate and country biltong (jerky), we left with very few goods. Trevor suggested that we swim back across the river, below the bridge, as it was so damn hot. Some declined, carried the goods and our wallets, and walked back over the bridge. Most of the crowd went off the bank and into the river. The water was flowing fairly fast but not excessively. We knew the swim would be diagonally across the river. We selected the landing on the other side. Zoni did not know whether to walk the bridge or swim. I stood next to him; we were last to go. Some had already reached the three-quarter mark across the river.

"Let's go Man!" I yelled. I dived in and Zoni followed. The current was a little strong but nothing big. The river was about two hundred yards at this point. We swam together, talking for a while and then almost at midpoint Zoni quietly said, "I'm going back."

"You're crazy, Zoni, we're half way there!" I suggested.

We treaded water and drifted with the current.

"No, I'm going back," said Zoni as he swam back to the store side of the river.

I put my head into the water and continued to the other side. As I got near the bank the boys were yelling, "Get out! . . . Get out!"

I was used to all the bullshit on these trips, so just kept swimming to the bank. As I reached the bank five or six of them were screaming, "Charl get out the damn water!" So I hurried and climbed out quickly.

"There's a likkewaan (iguana) in the water."

"What?"

"Yes, there he goes."

I could see his long tail in the water—he must have been eight feet long.

"Looks like a croc! Oh! Shit! I thought you guys were bullshit-ting!!"

"A whip of that tail can kill you," advised Billy in a very aggressive voice.

"Yeah! But Charl is ugly meat . . .so he didn't bother!"

"Thank you . . . thank you!" I replied.

We walked slowly back to the camp, and collapsed on the grass, under a tree, in the shade. Perfect—there was a small breeze. We were away from our Johannesburg routine. We could hear some people play-ing guitars and singing traditional Afrikaans songs. We sang with them even though they were a fair distance away. We started the fires for the braaivleis and drank beer and talked and told funny stories. Three hours later there was an old woman, apparently from nearby, drinking with us. She had no teeth and was about a tough 60. She was wiry, wrinkled, sunburned and with scraggly hair. Her hands showed years of hard work. She was telling stories of her youth and how pretty she once was and how the boys in the town were always at her verandah.

Tommy was trying to tell her how beautiful she still was, but he could hardly stand up. She went from English to Afrikaans very easily. She sang traditional Afrikaans songs and we all joined in yelling at the top of our voice ranges. Some songs went from Afrikaans to English and then back to Afrikaans; whatever we chose. The true Afrikaans song never really sounded good in English. There was definitely something missing, because these were traditional songs. The lady continued as the boys added to her drink. Her style of story telling was just like the Cape Coloreds of South Africa who could spellbind you with their words. Their expressions were always with a positive note and laughter. She had us laughing. She was so much fun. . . . We could not recall her leaving. Nobody could say they were the last to see her. We never saw her leave, we fell asleep drunk, but we all remembered her the next day. "Now we can say we met a great lady at the picnic," suggested Johnny. More swimming in the river, more eating, more talking all day Sunday, and then finally packing up and heading home. I was very, very happy with this great bunch of friends. Someone had suggested that South Africa had too much sand, another that we'd never get drunk again, and another that taking girls on the next camping trip would prevent Tommy from going after older women! And finally someone closed with a Churchill accent, "We wouldn't want that! . . . Now, would we!"

◆

Our all-boy Andrew Street group assembled again and headed off to the Rand Easter Show one Saturday afternoon. It was the biggest showcase for South African industries from cattle to cars, and, most important, the latest items from Europe and the USA. This sprawling show occupied the multi-acre fairgrounds in Johannesburg. It was very large and included agriculture, industrial displays, flowers, and food competitions. There were many restaurants, hamburger stands, game booths and many different rides including a large Ferris Wheel. It was the premier fair of the year.

We strolled through the exhibitions, really not interested in most of the displays and definitely not in agriculture. The latest radios, Hi Fidelity systems, tapes, records, music or clothes were keenly inspected. This was still a low priority in comparison to possible entertainment provided by girls. Girls just walking, just sitting, just being there. We talked to quite a few. As soon as we found out they were from some other province or small town we disappeared. We boys had our priorities. We loved watching the girls closely to determine their rating: dividing them into categories such as thick-ankles, too highbrow, wrong color hair, flat shoes, mother looks mean, probably doesn't own a car, walks like a horse, is too beautiful for the amount of money we make! We went on a couple of rides on the roller coasters, mainly because we had drunk a lot of beer by now. We finally ended up in a beer garden.

"Wonder why Chinese and Indian families are allowed on the rides but no blacks," asked Pat.

"I think nearly all the blacks are working the show!" said Viv.

"Yeah, maybe they're not even allowed to come in. I mean as general public," I added sarcastically.

"Weird," said someone.

The beer garden was not entertaining. There were mainly big fat old men in long khaki short pants and socks to the knees with shirts tucked in and a hat. This definitely was a sign of the older generation. The younger group had short shorts and low socks, rolled-up sleeves way above the bicep and the shirts hung out—sort've sloppy—and definitely no hat.

"We did not come here to talk to old men . . . let's go!" suggested Doc.

"I hear they have a new hi-fi tape system or something at the tower," suggested Trevor.

"Why don't we go there after the beers?" suggested Johnny.

"Yeah! After a lot of beers . . . it's boring walking around here," stated Viv.

"There's a drought in the female department," said Pat.

All efforts of the day to make contact with females had failed.

"What do you expect . . . you guys . . . there are twelve of us? The girls go around in twos and threes," suggested Norman.

"Not enough blondes anyway," complained Tommy.

"What do you think? Johnny," asked Doc.

"I like what we're doing . . . take it easy . . . it'll come if it comes!" replied Johnny.

"Great philosophy!" added Viv.

Quite a few rounds of beer went down. We got up slowly and walked towards the tower. Sure enough there was a hi-fi system being demonstrated. A very cute girl was demonstrating the amplifiers and speakers and describing the beautiful sounds.

"When the hell are we going to get television in the country?" asked Pat.

"When you change the government!"

"Yeah, they're scared of everyone knowing what goes on elsewhere in the world."

"We already know . . . some guys from the suburbs went to England for three months. Just got back," said Mac

"Too serious, you guys are too serious," said Viv.

"No! They didn't like England. They said it is hard to find a job . . . the girls speak funny and don't want to get to know you . . . the weather is the shits . . . but the television is great!!"

"Oh! Bullshit Mac!!"

"No they didn't like it . . . so they came home . . . glad to be here."

"This is a good place guys . . . we're just depressed . . . cause we can't find any girls."

We stood and watched the girl, a typical, beautiful South African girl with smooth skin, a well-tanned, athletic figure, nicely made-up (not to much), beautiful smile and whatever else goes through a young man's mind that makes a girl beautiful. I looked at the calmness in my buddies' faces. I agreed with them, without a word being spoken . . . she was gorgeous!

"Would one of you like to sing a song? We'll record it and play it back."

Trevor jumped in, "Anyone? . . . Anything?"

"Something all the audience can listen too," she replied with a smile.

"Good come back," said Johnny.

There were only a few people aside from our group at the stand.

"Did you know a song, Sir?" she asked Trevor, looking him in the eye with a challenge.

"Sir!" shouted a few of the guys . . . then questioned the title.

"You called him Sir!"

"Why not?" questioned Trevor, as though it should be obvious.

"Well, we'll call him 'Sir' for the time being!" replied the girl. "Doesn't it sound good, fellows?" she asked, knowing she now had a monster problem on her hand.

"Yes! Ma'am!" replied Trevor with courtesy.

"Then how about you singing?" she suggested, pointing to Trevor.

"No, that's alright, thanks," said Trevor very politely.

"C 'mon Trev!" yelled the boys.

"No, thanks fellows!" and Trevor stepped away.

"I'll sing a song," I volunteered, then realized I was enamored by this lady's beauty. I was determined not to stay in the background . . . whatever happened!

"Yah! You're crazy enough!" said the boys.

"Go for it!" was echoed.

I stepped up to the girl. Shivering inside, finding out that what I had said just removed all effects of the alcohol. Also not knowing what song to sing. But she was pretty and I didn't care. And the little bit of beer inside helped a lot!

"What's your name?" she asked, with such a sweet smile. I went as soft as a rose petal.

"Charl," I said sheepishly. Now this was not a good situation. But my buddies were laughing, and would support anyone who was stupid.

"Charl, that's nice. Here is the mike. Hold it about 3 inches away and sing your song."

My eyes tried to go blank to the audience. But it was about four deep now and growing; mainly due to the discussions going between the girl and the boys. I thought of the crowds at soccer and how I no longer was scared to play in front of them —despite knowing some of my friends were in there . . . this was just a smaller crowd! I wondered if I knew all the words of the song. I looked up, put the mike to my mouth, moved it away, started to tap my foot to a solid blues beat. I thought very quickly that I'd be all right if the first words came out good. The crowd did quiet down during the foot tapping. The girl looked at me and that was the last time I caught a glimpse of her as I disappeared into the song.

"Grab your coat and get your hat

"Leave your worries on the doorstep

"Just direct your feet

"To the sunny side of the street."

With my foot still tapping I heard my buddies start clapping to the blues beat. Just beautiful support to a damn nervous buddy. I walked a little from side to side . . . mike in hand . . . bent my knees a little and . . .

"Can't you hear that pit-a-pat?" I continued. The crowd loved it. I knew it wasn't professional, so I made it gutsy and it put feeling into the words, by growling 'Sunny', and 'Street'. We were having a good time, but I still had a non-confident emptiness in my body. *One more verse,* I thought, *then end it. Let's get out of here.*

I went through another verse and finished the song with the usual stalled finish.

"On the sunny . . . Oh! So sunny, sunny side of the stree-eet."

The crowd clapped and the boys cheered the hell out of me. I gave the mike back to the girl.

"Thanks," I said. Then I turned and bowed to the crowd. I just wanted to get into our mob and disappear.

"That was very good. Wait for the playback." she suggested.

"No, that's alright, got to go." I was embarrassed and I didn't know why.

"Wait," said the boys.

The girl played back the song. First time I had ever heard myself over the radio or the airwaves. I was embarrassed. I had such a keen ear for good music. I thought it was horrible!

"Let's go!"

"No!" said the boys.

The crowd listened and clapped at the end. The girl handed out brochures, called me over and gave me one. "Thanks! Very nice."

"Thank you . . . for being nice . . . Bye!"

"Bye!"

The boys walked off agreeing that had been fine.

"Did she put her telephone number in the brochure?" asked John.

I searched while they all looked. "No."

"Too bad!"

◆

Trevor acquired a beautiful old car. He arranged to show the crowd one Sunday night in Andrew Street. A small group of us waited on the corner, our favorite place. Pat, Zoni, Johnny, Doc, Billy, Viv, Norman and I were sitting on the ground just talking. A black car came around the corner. It was amazing. We had all heard the story but this was a little older than we had expected. The car was a 1929 Marquette, which had a straight eight Oldsmobile engine, with a manual spark and retard. W. H. Gross made the body in England. The car was assembled in Canada. It also had an external boot (trunk) and pumped-up red seats. It had a 12-volt system and 12-inch diameter lights. It was necessary to crank-start it (i.e. use a crank going through a hole under the radiator).

It looked like a black hearse. The discussion went on for hours. We insisted on going for a ride.

"Okay!" said Trevor.

Our little mob mounted all over the car on the back, on the running boards, hanging out the windows. We drove around the 'Suburbs' singing 'Mule Train' (made famous by Frankie Lane). This was done three times, up and down Andrew Street and Kennedy Street. The Broadway Hotel was considered but as we were already breaking the law, going to jail didn't seem worth it. We eventually drove through Turffontein and ended up at the Olympia Roadhouse. We left the car running because it might stall. The engine had a 'rock and roll' beat. The crowd got out of the car and started dancing to the definite beat of the engine. People in the crowd started to clap to the beat and joined the dancing. Trevor had the car for a long while and going out in the car was an experience for anyone.

The Andrew Street Mob had now reached about forty persons in count. But we were not sure! It had the same uncertainty as the number 70 for kids in the street many years before. About twenty of us were very active and the basic core of ten to twelve of us were together almost every weekend. The Mob had grown. We had very diverse activities, but still kept re-grouping to have fun. I had Bobby's Group as well. Others had their choices, but the Andrew Street Mob still remained intact. Although most mobs came and went, we expected ours to always be there! It was a Godsend for a lot of people, including myself. The friendship became an important integral part of the lives of most members. There never was an official leader. There were no rules and nothing was owed. Participation was very important to everyone and anyone was welcome. Fun was the goal and whenever time was available, we filled it with enjoyable activities. Politics, religious overtones and deep problems were solved in other places and at other times.

＊

CHAPTER 14

Discussions With Uncle Mick

I DIDN'T KNOW HOW OLD Gran and Uncle Mick were and I really didn't care. They were too important to me; they were ageless. I did know it was 1954; Uncle Dennis had been twenty when he was killed in 1942 in the war so I figured they had been married for at least 33 years. And as teenagers, it was easy to assume, that anyone over thirty was an old adult, and they all looked the same age until they hit the wheelchairs. Gran had been married before, so in rough numbers they were about 60 years of age. At first I had thought Uncle Mick looked younger than Gran, but his Irish descent had given him a love of drinking, and now they looked about even. There was always a big jug of wine, red stuff that could clean out drains, and one or two 200-pack cigarette boxes in his room. Cigarettes mainly came in twenties but didn't last long. There was also whiskey in the house but it was well hidden. So Uncle Mick drank wine and whiskey and Gran didn't drink any kind of liquor. My mom loved expensive brandy, straight, in the large bowl-shaped brandy snifters. I drank beer, brandy and coke, and rum and coke; I hardly smoked and didn't need any of it—I did it only with friends.

Uncle Mick and my dad had grown with Johannesburg. They were about the same age and they were there from at least the 1910s when my father arrived from Beaufort West in the Cape. Gran's family had come from the Orange Free State. Uncle Mick's family was large, as he had many brothers; they were in Johannesburg but we hardly saw any of them.

There was never much family history discussed in our family, because it was too damn complicated. The one story that remained basically the same was on my dad's side, where his father had achieved an amazing accomplishment. My true grandfather (Dad's father) was descended from the Huguenots. He had owned a very large ostrich farm in Oudtshoorn, in the Cape Province. My mom and dad continually argued about the number of kids he had sired. The highest number was over 20, with two English wives! My mom's number was lower than Dad's number but still in the double digits. I only saw my true grandfather once. He had come to Johannesburg with his youngest daughter, who was 24 and unmarried. She was not allowed out the house without a male escort. I thought that was funny because my grandfather was 93 and blind, so there were many ways to get around that instruction.

My family was so complicated compared to those of my friends. When growing up as a teenager, there was a tremendous lack of conversation between adults and children. The result of a question from a child to an adult was usually, "You don't need to know." My friends' families seemed a lot more stable. Well, Gran and Uncle Mick had been together a long time, and were my stability.

My mom was now a single mother, a bookkeeper and good with numbers. She loved the family; her favorite was Yvonne who had given her grandchildren, and she loved every minute of her time with the kids. This was not the only reason though; you could just see the excitement when they got together. My dad always wanted me to join when his family had get-togethers. I nearly always found an excuse. I was not a family participant. I preferred my Andrew Street friends. I generally showed my resentment at family gatherings, and though the family members tried hard to change my mind, it never worked very well.

◆

School continued to be interesting because I was learning to design structures and mechanical systems, and was moving forward with mathematics and industrial complex studies. Mining and manufacturing were the background of these studies. Gold was the major integrating spinal cord of the industry. I loved the historical aspects of gold. The stories of gold and its people were always fascinating. One night, after everyone had left the dining room table except Uncle Mick, and Gran was in the kitchen and Mom in the living room, I decided to corner him:

"How long have you been down in the mines Grandpa?"

He looked at me with astonishment.

"Since I was eighteen, but I was not down in the mines then—we had to go through a year or two on surface operations. We went through a lot of training before going underground."

"So was it around 1920 when you went underground?"

"That's close." His look didn't change. "I worked in the building where they process the ore. It's just keeping the gold and getting rid of the rock, which goes to the tailings dumps, the ones you see all around Johannesburg."

"Did you ever see gold?" I was relentless with my questions! It was hard to get Uncle Mick to talk.

"Yes, and Son! One time they even showed us the refining of the gold."

"You mean pouring of the gold? You mean you actually worked with actual gold?"

"Yes! But we were escorted into that room, because when they pour the gold, it splatters, and there is pure gold on the floor."

"Oh! So they didn't want you to pick it up? Pity you couldn't bring some home!"

"That's right! Actually Son, there was a person who took a lot of it home!"

"Really true? Without anyone knowing?"

"Yes! There was this one chap who put the gold splattering in his mouth, and when he got to his bike, he'd take the handlebar grip off put the splatterings in grease that was in the handlebars." Uncle Mick smiled.

"So when do they search you?" I asked, thinking that it seemed too easy to take the gold.

"Well, you have to go through showers and leave your working clothes on one side and street clothes on the other side."

"So he got away with a lot of gold?"

"Nobody knows how much, but they caught him!"

"How, Uncle Mick?"

"He did it for twelve years and said nothing to anybody. Then for some unknown reason, he told a friend!"

"No! And so they caught him!"

"Yes Son, and now he knows! If you're wanting to do something illegal—do it by yourself and say nothing," emphasized Uncle Mick. "I don't believe you should do it—but!"

"Hard not to trust a friend. Do you know them?" I asked.

"No!"

We paused for a while; Gran came in and gave Uncle Mick another cup of tea. She winked at me. I knew she was pleased. I was talking to the man of her life.

"I asked Gran what you'd done each day going down the mines. She said to ask you."

"Well it was a rigorous thing that I did. I'd go down the shaft at 7:00 AM, set up the drills, we'd drill for four or so hours, take a quick lunch break, set the dynamite charge, and wire up to the blast point. Then we'd clear the drift, clear the level, go up to the collar and head frame and then blast the rock. Then I'd come home and have a cup of tea! The night crew mucked out the rocks, preparing for the next day. That's what we did five days a week. The black men did the drilling and white men worked as trainers and supervisors. The underground workers that hauled the muck to chutes and those that operated conveyors were black men from South Africa and surrounding countries. The white men supervised all miners, and operated the underground and surface hoists; they were also the geologists and mining engineers who told us where the ore veins were going and how to get the maximum gold out without removing too much rock. They were the ones who looked after safety, ran all the operations and managed the mine. There were others who risked money. Now you know these white men were immigrants, sons and grandsons of immigrants, and some were South Africans with a heritage of over 200 years. Did you know that it was mostly black and white mining men that worked the Johannesburg mines, and that the Indians and Chinese people brought in to labor in the mines never made it?"

Uncle Mick seemed to enjoy telling me about his working life. Perhaps nobody else had asked him.

"Uncle Mick, I wanted to tell you that we're designing mining machinery at college and learning all about mining and mining methods. Some of the problems are hard to solve. We have to size the cage and skip hoisting systems. Our big problem now is trying to figure out the rope size for a 6500-foot hoisting system that carries the cage or skip down to those depths. Now, the teacher says that most ropes have a point of no return after about 5000 to 6000 feet."

"What do you mean, Son?"

"Well they always make it tricky. So you have to work at it. It means that the weight of the rope is becoming too heavy to support itself and any dynamic loads. Also it's a major factor in the choice and cost of machinery operating the rope system. So at about 5000 feet deep we have to have another hoist system to go down further—or put in an incline shaft."

"Didn't know that, Son! I'm just a miner."

We paused. I went to get a cup of tea and came back in the dining room. Uncle Mick continued: "I'm glad you're studying and won't have to go into the mines to work at the face. It's not a good career. The money isn't worth the risk. Talking about 5000 feet – I had to climb up from the stopes at 3000 feet, one day, all the way to the surface."

"Why?"

"The mine hoist system broke down and it was going to take a couple of days to fix it! I didn't want to sleep in the mine."

"But you could have walked to the steam hoist system! Supposedly that's why they put it in the middle of all the mines on the Witwatersrand. It's connected to all the mines with different drifts! Wasn't the steam hoist working?"

"Yes! The steam hoist was working. But everyone was saying it would be just as far to walk through the connecting drifts as to climb the ladders. We didn't have any maps Son, and we were concerned that we might get lost. So we climbed out."

"What, on the ladders, in the shaft?"

"Yes!"

"That is 3000 feet divided by about 20 feet per ladder which gives you 150 ladders. Wow!"

"Yes, Son! It took all morning and some of the afternoon. It would have been better to walk to the steam hoist. But, what can I tell you?"

I could tell Uncle Mick was enjoying this! So was I!

"We toured that steam hoist facility." I continued. "The college professor took us to see that operation. It's incredible. We went around the back of the building to see the black men throw the coal into the furnaces for the boilers. There were multiple boiler/steam engines side by side. Twenty or so black men throwing coal—I guess for eight hours. Then we went inside to see the hoist drums, with the ropes that carry the cage underground. They made us stand on the side of the piston and crank that drives the hoist drum. The crank, Uncle Mick, is as long as our house, and the piston must be three feet in diameter. We stood there for a while because they were going to show us how it operated." I paused. "We were talking. Suddenly it started, slowly, like a train pulls out of the station. Well, it's the same design, in principle. Then it started to move and we couldn't believe this big crank going around so fast. It was damn scary! The building rumbled. Well then, maybe we just imagined it!"

"The hoist is used as an emergency if all the electrical power goes out," said Uncle Mick as he paused and drank some tea.

I was so fired up, actually talking to someone in the family who knew what I was doing. My father and mother didn't know, and neither did my uncles!

"Doesn't all that machinery come from Europe or America?" asked Uncle Mick.

"Yes! But where I work, we make small hoists and locomotives for underground operations."

"I mean the big machines, Son!"

"Yes that's true. Because, on a second trip we went to see an electrical hoist system, made in Scotland, with two 3000 Horsepower motors (approximately), on each end of the hoist shaft. The hoist was for a 5000-foot descent into the mine. The hoist room and operation was so quiet and clean. Man! You could eat your lunch off the floor."

"The history of mining is very interesting in Johannesburg, Son, because the mines became so big. In the end, it truly put South Africa on the world map and especially as it followed the discovery and mining of diamonds."

"Yes I've read quite a lot about that as well." I added. "In fact there is a controversy as to who discovered the gold in the late 1880s!"

Uncle Mick interrupted me, "Man has always sought gold, and it often has a high price attached to separating it from bedrock . . . Gold miners know that only too well, Son!" He paused and looked at me with a clear seriousness. "You should not go down into the mines. It is not worth it. You must keep up your studies to make sure you don't have to! Now! I'm going to bed Son!"

"Okay Grandpa."

My uncle Mick, actually 'My Grandpa' in life terms, got up from the table and went to bed. I realized that we had lived together for over ten years and that I didn't see him enough. I wanted very much to talk some more. It was as though he had heard my thoughts, because he turned and said, "We'll talk more about the history of gold and your dad and I—next time. Goodnight Son!"

"Goodnight Grandpa!"

Gran came into the room after Uncle Mick went to bed.

"Son! We are so proud of how you are working and going to school. When you finish your apprenticeship, I have enough money for you to continue in university schools."

"Gran! Mom says we don't have that sort of money! Anyway you need it for you and Grandpa."

"I have some shares in First Electric." Gran paused and looked at me with joy. "We can use those!"

"Thank you Gran. But I think Mom is right, you've worked too hard for that money—I'll be all right."

"Keep going to school and we'll argue about this at some later date. Goodnight!"

"Goodnight Gran!" I gave her a hug and she went off to bed.

I went to my room. *It's not right for her to give me that kind of money,* I thought. *Couldn't even think about it!*

♦

My dad had worked for the Rand Daily Mail newspaper for thirty-plus years, including a seven-year apprenticeship. He was raised in Beaufort West in the Cape. He came to Johannesburg in the 1910s and his stories of the town were typical of those in the literature—rough and tough. My dad had chosen not to be in the mines. He had worked as an apprentice operator of newspaper machines and, as a journeyman, continued to operate the 15-meter-long machines, printing newspapers and magazines. I had seen them when I had been to visit my dad at his work. He was very good-looking: dark hair, green eyes and full of fight. He was short. His greatest claim to fame was riding a bucking bronco in a rodeo show from Australia. He got a bronze medal. He stayed on the horse for 12 seconds.

His tangled life ended up in three marriages and many hours at the racetrack and in the bar. South Africans referred to his favorite drink, brandy, as "rot gut". My father spoke Afrikaans and English but no French. My true grandfather was the last in the family to speak French. My father may not have liked the Government, but he definitely hated the pompous English. English-English he called them. He was a proud South African and definitely a Jan Smuts man. I didn't think my dad was as smart as my mother.

As life would have it he was 'fed up', as he put it, with the Rand Daily Mail. He told me he was going to work for the Vaderland, an

Afrikaans daily paper with opposing views in many ways to the Rand Daily Mail. He said that they had offered him more money. I didn't know what to believe! I thought it was because they let him rent a house cheaply and he had just got married to Bramie, an Afrikaans lady. I also thought it was good for him, because she was a very nice person, and my dad would no longer have to live alone in his dreary downtown Johannesburg apartment. I had met her a number of times. He had once taken me to a house party with Bramie. My dad had ended up on the piano singing funny Afrikaans/English colloquial songs—making everyone laugh. He was drunk. Then he got the crowd in stitches, when he suddenly turned from looking at the piano keys, and sang the song with the bottom set of his dentures upside-down in his mouth. I had never seen this side of him and, although I had felt embarrassed, I had also laughed like hell!

"Dad! You don't like what the newspaper prints. You told me many times." I confronted him on one of my visits to meet him at a bar in town.

"It will be okay Son! We'll get along. I have a good friend at work, Hendrik, he helped me get the job."

So my father went to work for the Vaderland. He ran the big printing presses that put out the daily papers. This particular machine could also do the weekly color supplements that went in the Sunday papers. I went to see him at work a couple of times, after his pleading many times for me to come and visit. I did it only because he loved it. I found out my father was very popular on the newsprint floor. He introduced the young girls to me, saying we should go out with each other. Then he told me later not to take them out.

"Why?" I asked.

"Because you should marry someone better." He made the statement emphatically. It confused me because both statements were opposite to my thinking. I would choose the girl and I wouldn't marry someone because of a recommendation. I didn't say anything because these 'thoughts and things' belonged to adults. Anyhow, I really got to like Hendrik, a great friend of my dad, and talked to him on every occasion I visited. He had done a good thing for my dad. I still didn't speak Afrikaans very well and I knew I had a weakness for languages. When I visited the Vaderland, they all spoke English to me. This was the one thing that continued to embarrass me. The problem was, my life was in English: at home, at work, at play, and especially at school.

I could never master Afrikaans and I couldn't express myself fluently, so I spoke English.

◆

One Saturday morning I walked into Uncle Mick's bedroom after knocking on the door.

"Hullo! Grandpa! Reading another Zane Grey?"

"Yes Son! Come in and sit yourself down—take a load off your feet. What can you tell me?"

"Not much—went to see my dad the other day. He told me about the Australian Rodeo that came to Johannesburg in the 1910s. So I wanted to know more about Johannesburg at that time."

"Oh! So I'll have to put me lovely cowboy book down and entertain you?" drawled Uncle Mick in his best Irish accent.

"Yes!"

"You want to know about a long time ago?"

I nodded and sat down at the foot of the bed.

"Well Johannesburg in the 1910s was not only a very young city—when you think of Dublin—'cause although it had new buildings, railway trams, horseless carriages, and also opera houses and sports grounds, it was truly just a sophisticated mining camp. There were many houses for the rich and the workers, but that was not enough to make it a city."

"Wasn't it growing fast?"

"Yes! But the gold had been panned out, Son! The surface gold was gone. And now all the mining was going to be underground, and it would take professional people to mine the gold. They had to drill many holes to find the ore body and sink mines that took six years to build before they went into producing gold. Our problem was these mines were all over the Rand. We miners had no idea which one would last a long time. We wanted to know! We all had families and needed something to last, so we didn't have to move from place to place!"

I went and fetched two cups of tea—very quickly. This was good and I loved it, because my uncle Mick had been there, and I was not sure some of our teachers had seen what they taught. I attributed that to Otiend's suggestion of teachers not having experienced what they taught.

"Thank you Son! Thirst is a terrible thing and I don't know if the one in the morning is more dangerous than the one in the evening!"

"It was the first time your dad and I had seen such tall buildings—American technology, someone said. We had come to this place with people from all over the world including, Americans and Chinese. They all came to make money. Then we worked for a couple of years and started to make money. But then the blacks wouldn't work. It truly was not a long time after the Boer War, and there was still a lot of political fighting between Pretoria and Johannesburg. The South Africans and especially the Afrikaners had not forgotten the four thousand Boers killed and over 20, 000 Boer women and children who died in the British concentration camps. That is the way the British were and the Afrikaners will never forget it. Well, for that matter, nor will anyone born in South Africa! The Boer Kommandos under Deneys Reitz, Louis Botha and Jan Smuts were very, very famous, Son."

"Do you like Jan Smuts, Grandpa?"

"Don't know! He did some good things and some bad things."

"What bad things?"

"He stopped the big strike by the miners—and it made the miners mad. You don't get paid if you don't work, and we were paid so little. And then again, when they replaced some white miners. Well! The blacks didn't want to work, so they brought in Chinese—the blacks came back and the Chinese went home. Then the big strike happened. It was bad Son!" Uncle Mick stalled, sipped his tea, and took a small break. "Martial law was declared when the strikers blew up a police station. That was too much! Smuts did that!"

I had listened intently. "So he declared martial law, and also, that's why we have a Chinatown in Johannesburg?" I asked.

"Yes; some didn't go home and stayed. Then we got Indians to come and work the sugar cane fields. Well Son, that didn't work either! They stayed, but they didn't work the fields very long, they became shop owners and worked in restaurants."

"That I know, and that's why we have an Indian section in Johannesburg—far away from sugar cane fields! Where did you and Gran live during these crazy times?"

"The mining business was in a turmoil. So we lived in houses without electricity; candles only, water boiled on a coal stove for eating or having a bath!"

"True, Grandpa?"

"Yes Son. But after a while we moved into mine houses with electricity, which was very good! Then we lived lower down in Kenilworth.

Later, your Uncle Bill bought this house, and we have rented it ever since!"

"Oh! You mean 65 Andrew Street? You rent it?"

"Yes! So he is not so bad! I know you don't like him, or Uncle Robbie!"

"I don't like them!"

"Well Son! We all have some bad spots on our skin, or we'll eventually get them."

Rented! I thought. My mother had extended the house, making it bigger. *I bet she will never see that money again,* I thought. This only added to my belief that adults didn't tell kids anything.

Uncle Mick sipped his tea. We were quiet for a while. He had said that my uncles were not so bad, and the look on his face told me we were entering dangerous territory. Then he smiled as he asked, "Do you have a girlfriend?"

"No, I can't afford one!"

Now his look changed and became very stern. "That's not very healthy! A good-looking young man like you!"

"Well! I do go out with the girls, but I'm studying and playing good soccer, Grandpa, and they don't want a boyfriend who's not around all the time."

I knew my heart was not in this discussion. I hated to admit my problem with girlfriends. Why would my grandpa want me to have a serious lady?

Suddenly, as if he had read my mind, he turned and said, "Don't worry Son! I wanted to make sure you weren't only buried in work and books. Young men should have girlfriends. But don't go marrying early like our generation—take your time. I want you to remember this! There is a famous Irish philosophy that 'a man shouldn't think about marriage till he's thirty-five—and then he should think about it for ten years!' And now I'm going back to my cowboy book!"

I laughed and got up to leave. "Bye Grandpa! Thank you!"

"Bye, Son! Have a good game today. Make yourself proud!"

I wondered why it was so hard to get things out of adults. It seemed like a club that teenagers weren't allowed to penetrate. Even Uncle Mick! I still didn't like my two uncles. Why? The answer came very quickly—I felt couldn't trust them.

◆

This was now a time in life when my parents had decided to show me off at work. My dad had loved it when I went to visit him at the Rand Daily Mail, and now my mom wanted me to go to her work. She had worked for Publix in the head office. It was a department store like the O.K. Bazaars, but not as big. Every person I had known had shopped at the O.K. Bazaars in Johannesburg city; it was a store with everything.

"You come in about 11:30 AM and we'll go to lunch afterwards," suggested my mother.

"Yes Mom!" I agreed reluctantly because I got confused when introduced to a group of people. I could never remember all the names. Now I would have to match a face with a name when my Mother talked about them at the dinner table. I'd have to know the good ones from the bad ones.

The Publix offices were located on Eloff Street Extension and so I could catch a bus at 11:00 AM, because it only took fifteen minutes to get there. Industrial shops and businesses abounded in the area. There was also a mine tailings dump in the background that probably had fifty different types of grasses on it. The mining industry had unsuccessfully tried to prevent the very fine tailings from blowing all over the Eloff Street Extension area and the Southern Suburbs of Johannesburg. Today was not windy so there was no problem.

The bus stopped almost at the door of the Publix building. I walked in and was directed to my mother's desk. She looked so pretty, dressed impeccably with a neatly ironed dress and her long hair brushed to the ends. I loved her very much but wasn't sure of everything that was going on! So the love was often confusing.

"Hullo Mom!"

"Hullo Son!" Her face beamed with pleasure. "You're on time!"

We sat and talked for a few minutes, then walked around. Everyone was so pleasant and complimentary. The men said that my mom had a fine-looking son and the women said I was handsome and strong! The compliments didn't vary very much. I refused to get embarrassed and ignored the compliments but couldn't help feeling pleasantly surprised.

"What do you do, Charl?" asked one man.

"I'm an apprentice machinist."

"And I hear you play for Marist Brothers."

"Yes Sir!"

"What level?"

"Under 21 League, Sir!"

"You must be good—what position do you play?"

"Mostly as a back, but sometimes up with the forwards."

"Very nice!"

"Thank you!"

"Sorry, but I support Germiston Callies!"

"That's okay, so does my brother-in-law James!"

"Oh! Well, you know how to take care of it!"

"Yes!"

We both smiled.

The introductions waned and my mom and I left the rows and rows of desks at Publix and went to a small sandwich shop. It was busy but we got a table.

"Thank you for coming Son. I wanted my friends to see whom I was talking about all the time."

"You told them about me?" I guess I was surprised.

"Yes! Son! You're doing so well!"

"I don't know Mom. There is a long way to go. I'm sure the mining industry requires a degree from Witwatersrand University!"

"You will do okay!"

"Well Mom. Your friends at work are very nice and I'm glad to see you have them around you!"

"We help each other. Most of the women are married and supported by a husband. There are others are like me—single Mothers with children!"

"But Dad gives you money. I know—I have to get it from the bars in Johannesburg!"

"I'm sorry, but he wants to see you—and that's one way! —"

"It's terrible Mom. All those men just drink to get drunk. My friends and I don't go to get drunk and fall out on the street! You once told me you would throw me out the house if you saw me lying outside the Broadway Hotel!"

"Did I say that?" asked my Mom with a gleam in her eyes. "Well not to worry. Although the maintenance money is not a lot, it helps us live with Gran and Uncle Mick, and I don't know what we'd do without them."

"I'm glad! I don't want to live anywhere else!"

"Good Son! I don't want to live anywhere else either!"

"This sandwich is good Mom. Maybe you should bring some home for dinner!"

"Your Gran would be insulted!"

"I know! She is such a good cook—we eat well!"

"I have to go now Son," said my mom, sounding sad.

I hugged and kissed my mom goodbye. She went back to work and I caught the bus home. I went to the upper deck front seat as always, sat down and started thinking. I always did a lot of thinking on a bus. My Mom was glad I had done this for her. She was happy and that made me happy.

◆

"Gran! What do you think is going to happen to the black people in the future?"

"Why do you ask?"

"Everything that some of my friends and I feared would happen, in the days following the 1948 elections, has happened. I have been worried about Lena and her husband's situation, plus the black people at work and in Vryburg. The Government have opened a gash between white and black, and English and Afrikaner. General Smuts is dead and the United Party is without a leader, and the Nationalists are doing whatever they want to!"

"I didn't know you were interested in politics," stated Gran.

"I'm generally not—except when it affects music and sports. You know, I believe we could win a lot more medals at the Olympics with black people than we do now."

"Do you think you could play soccer against a black team?"

"Oh! Yes! We may not win! But I would love playing against another style of soccer!"

"Well! I wouldn't know about all that!" said my gran.

"But there is unrest now, that we didn't have before 1948. The whole world knows about 'Apartheid' now, especially as the United States has outlawed segregation."

"The United States did that?"

"Yes!" I continued. "I mean the Government took on the University of the Witwatersrand, who wants to educate people without regard to race or color. They forced Johannesburg to remove the black slum areas in the Western Native Townships like Newclare and Sophiatown. Our Prime Minister, Dr. Hendrik Verwoerd, took away all the property that they owned. I hear next year they are moving Sophiatown residents to further South West areas of Johannesburg—a place called Soweto."

"They want to move the slums out of Johannesburg City. Those areas are full of crime, Son!"

"But they won't own the new houses and they are really small Gran, 15 feet by 15 feet for a family. I mean, I think of Lena and her husband—they can't live together like us!"

"There are many things wrong! But you must hope the future is better."

"I know. It bothers me though, why we can't just let everyone have a piece of land and live together without all this!"

I didn't know why I had brought this subject up. I wondered why it bothered me. My friends never talked this way about it.

"You must keep studying! You must become an engineer and run projects—like the one I read about in the paper. The big oil-from-coal plant they're building south of Johannesburg."

"Sasolburg is the name! Very interesting. They are building it because South Africa doesn't have oil."

"You see, you know all these thing!" said my gran.

"It's a long way away, to become a manager, Gran! You have to spend time in the design office, in construction and in many planning meetings to do that! It will also take a lot of time."

"Just get an education and it will follow that way! Time flows like a fast, fast river!"

"Uncle Mick also wants me to get out of the trade."

"Yes, but finish your apprenticeship first."

"Oh! I will do that Gran—it's less than a year and I will get all the money of a journeyman: double my salary!"

"You must keep studying even after that! I really mean it!" Gran said emphatically.

"I promise! I promise!" I replied.

"Would you give Pal some water?"

"Yes! Absolutely Gran!"

"I'm going to lie down, Son!" We hugged and kissed.

I went into the yard. Pal was tied up. I released him, hugged him and sat on the back step while Pal had his fun. I did this every time I could and Pal loved it. I loved to be with him as well.

I wondered why I had brought up the subject of the Government and 'Apartheid', the word for 'separate development'. I didn't do it very much with my friends—perhaps everyone just discussed it at home. I knew my mom got all heated about some of these things. It seemed so far removed from what Johannesburg young people were saying and doing. My thoughts became too serious! I hugged Pal, put him back in the kennel and left him un-tied. I knew I'd get into trouble. I grabbed my bike and went for a ride out on Rifle Range Road. It was so beautiful with a breeze at the 6000-foot altitude, sun shining down, green grasses on the side of the road, blue-blue sky, and only the sound of the bike's wheels, cranks and chain, joining the air rushing by. My thoughts continued.

I felt even better about my mom, Gran and Grandpa. They had opened up a little. They definitely wanted me to do better; even my dad did, in his way. I wondered where Gran would get the money for university. It was a large amount of money for those in the Southern Suburbs. Study, study, study; they all pushed it. Well I was!

The complications of a girlfriend always drove me crazy! Why couldn't the girls just be patient or something? Why couldn't I just get a car somehow! *Must think about that—it would be perfect!*

✳

CHAPTER 15

The Soccer Game

(Soccer World Johannesburg)

The Learning

IT STARTED IN THE street on a tarmac road: a tennis ball propelled by bare feet at the end of young legs of nine- to fourteen year-olds. They kicked the miniature soccer ball with scraped fuzz and a snake-like seam encircling the rubber compound sphere: it went in all directions.

We all knew it was not a soccer ball for over twenty reasons. The object was to beat the opposing players and then the goalie that stood between two jam tins placed in the middle of the street. If the ball was lost in play to the other team, they had the same incentive. The techniques were all natural; nobody coached us. We learned off each other and attempted in our individual ways to bring something new to the street game. It was so much fun to beat someone and score. This was such an ecstatic feeling and there was so much power in it! It was also just about as much fun to take the ball away and defend the goal. The surge in your body and the mental confidence just soared out of sight, and if your opponent was bigger or faster than you, it glorified the feeling. We relied on our natural abilities and likes and dislikes, and fell into the roles that suited us best. No parent was around to tell us where we played best: it came out from the necessity to play well. The tools were simple . . . bare feet, a tennis ball, preferably with a little fur on it, and talent. The ability to get the toes under the ball, move it left and right, pull it back, lift it off the street, volley the ball and hit it hard and straight was paramount. Then you learnt to lift the ball onto your knee, flip it onto your head and move it forward to someone on your team. The heading of the ball or the hooking of the ball into your body, your thighs and inside your legs and turning at the same time were some of the methods to keep control. 'Greedy' some called it but it felt good. The more you learnt, the better you played. Then there was protecting the ball, hitting the opposing player hard and fairly and not fouling: sportsmanship was our credo. The dress was simple . . . short pants and shirt. The payback was in the hours of enjoyment and, conversely, the hurt through scrapes and burns that were sore for days. The worst and most hated element was the voice of an adult yelling, "Dinner is ready!" and, "Come on home now!" . . . Didn't adults know that whoever left the street game broke up the rhythm and intrigue of play, and caused it to shatter into pieces? This however guaranteed the will to do it again the next day.

Soccer, born in the streets and alleys of the world, was no different in Andrew Street, Kenilworth, Johannesburg, than in any other blue-collar suburb. We saw this on film clips. The blacks did the same thing in the townships, mostly on sand roads or open patches between houses. The whites grew up to play in large stadiums . . . Rand Stadium was the top venue; the blacks were not that lucky. There was also no playing between black and white at any level.

The next stage in soccer was for my soccer friends and I to join the Boy Scouts, a church organization, or St. John's Ambulance Brigade. They taught kids all the principles of survival, first aid, and safety. They also had camps and lectures and tests. But the main reason that we joined was soccer. My choice was St. Johns—made by my mom. She had done a lot of volunteer work with them during the war. You could also see the volunteers, all neatly dressed in a dark uniform with shirt and tie, at any soccer games played in England and especially the very famous Cup Final.

So at the age of ten we had played on Wednesday afternoons for Rosettenville Central School and for St. John's Ambulance Brigade on Saturday morning. The kids in other parts of Johannesburg followed similar pathways. Pioneer Park was the venue for all our games in the Southern Suburbs and they were played on red sand pitches. The soccer shoes were high-topped or had enough leather to cover the ankle. The bottom of the shoes had three leather straps about 3/8 inches wide, one on the heel and two on the ball of the foot. About eight nails held each of the strips to the sole. The sand soccer fields ground the leather away and the nails came though the sole. Depending on our parent's money situation, we were treated to new leather strips, put on by the shoemaker, or otherwise we had to hammer the nails over flat. This was never enough for your foot comfort so we placed a newspaper cut out or cardboard strip inside the boot to avoid the pain: the latter, however, prevailed.

To play rugby was not popular with most Southern Suburbs kids. It was played at Forest High School but they were no competition for the Afrikaans schools that continuously beat them by large scores. Cricket was also played in the street and then in school. There was even an English professional cricket player who came to coach us at Rosettenville Central. I got two minutes of instruction, as did every young cricket player! There were no professional cricket players in South Africa, but some had very good jobs at certain companies heavily supportive of cricket! In the Southern Suburbs the kids preferred soccer.

I had loved soccer ever since I had started in the street at the age of eight. There was always the thrill of playing a game. There was no weather I knew of, no reason not to go, and no sickness I had experienced, including asthma, that would prevent me from playing. I was totally enthralled with the game. It was my first love of anything active. I was never the star, never the best, but I was damned determined to be good, and always willing to learn. This did not mean I had not shared any glory. I had started as a goalkeeper at Rosettenville Central School. After a season and a half, I got bored because my team won all the games, so I came out to play as a full-back (defender). Then, because of my speed, I moved up to half-back, and again to forward where I suddenly displayed a good sense of the goal and developed a good shot, and scored many goals. Later I found out that I had some shortcomings, in that: a forward had to have a third eye (in the back of his head), a sense of close surroundings, and be quick and clever, if you wanted to be very successful. So eventually I alternated between forward and back according to the coach's selection. I played for Marist Brothers almost every Saturday of every soccer season from the age of twelve.

The lowest league in Johannesburg was under 16 (based on January 1). Marist Brothers Organization was a full club having teams from under sixteen to First Division (The top division in the country). The group under 16 had four teams. So when a player was 13, he would play for the fourth team; at 14 the third team; and 15 the second team. If a player was exceptional he could play for the first team at any age, but very rarely was it before he was 15. Usually a kid was 16 for the

Under Sixteen League First teams. This was followed by 2 years in the Under 18 League and 3 years in the Under 21 League, then the Reserve League, which was open to all ages. The last was essentially the toughest league. It had players coming up from youth teams, and players going down from First Division. Players were very fast and very good, mainly because they were being scouted for the premier leagues: First and Second Divisions. These players were always perceived as the potential replacements for the top team. There were only a few moves from reserve to the major team. All games were played on Saturdays. The Reserve League was where soccer players either made it, or reluctantly chose to play in Sunday Leagues, or quit.

The Sunday League soccer in Southern Suburbs was played at Pioneer Park on its reddish-brown sand. This is where lesser-skilled players belonged—in social clubs. The Greeks, Lebanese, Italians, Dutch, Jewish, Scandinavians, and all the various ethnic groups of Europe and the Middle East, ran the clubs. There were also other clubs that South Africans had formed, those whose families had been in South Africa for a number of generations. Although Johannesburg was the center for soccer, there were leagues containing teams from all over the Witwatersrand, from the towns of Springs to Randfontein, a sixty-mile span. I grew up with the same team, Marist Brothers, all the way from age 12. Two of my friends, Desmond and Robbie, went all the way with me. We had a very successful team, as we grew older and benefited from the excellent soccer training, coaching, and playing together. Our team ended up winning the Under 16 League and Cup competitions and the Under 18 League; we lost the Under 18 Cup by a goal at the Rand Stadium. This was achieved as the first team in every category: that is, when Robbie, Desmond and I were 16 and 18. I had been a player on this team throughout, played consistently, and loved it all. It was a saving grace to me for many situations in life and it was fun with all the different players and all the 'bull' we got up to! Our team was now in the Under 21 League and Cup Competition and a lot more serious, because to be selected to play was a major accomplishment. Players from all over the Rand were competing to play in a team that was in the First Division. At this time the Transvaal League had ten teams in First Division: Germiston Callies (Caledonians), Benoni, Wanderers, Iscor, Delfos, Balfour Park, Marists, Berea Park, Ramblers and Boksburg. The Second Division also had ten teams: Benoni Callies, Brakpan,

United, Arcadia, Randfontein, Southern Suburbs, Germiston Rovers, Roodepoort and Pretoria Municipal.

When I was twelve, James (my sister's husband) and I went to see a team from Laurenço Marques play against Germiston Callies. I witnessed for the first time the Latin soccer style, which had beautiful ball control, a slower pace, and 'velvet' touches. Just before the game the captain bounced the ball off his foot and into the air. He did this maybe forty times without the ball touching the ground, and while talking to the captain of our local team. The soccer style obviously came from the Portuguese who at one time occupied Mozambique. They had taught the local players the game. The Laurenço Marques team did not survive against the aggressive style of South African soccer that day, but they left an indelible impression on me in the way that they handled the ball so gently and with such great finesse. I thought that a combination of their beautiful ball handling and our fast, aggressive play in soccer would result in the best soccer in the world.

Soccer competitions were held between the provinces, and also between Rhodesia, Laurenço Marques and South African teams.

The Bantu Social Club was the only place where I had seen black players in competition. Johnny and I, and sometimes Trevor and a few others in the Andrew Street Mob, would go to Johnny's father's business on Heidelberg Road in Johannesburg. We would take sandwiches and beer, go upstairs, and watch the games through the back windows. It was a beautiful seat for viewing the games. Anyway, we would not have been allowed in the small stadium. Even if they had let us in, we may never have got out! Below the windows were railway lines and then the stadium fence. The ground of hard red sand was surrounded by a minimum of terraced seats. The stadium was always full, people moving and jostling around, and very noisy. It was the weekend enjoyment for the black man. This Municipal stadium sold beer—legally—one of the very few outlets of beer for the black man. The beer was also very diluted and weak. So illegal beer was sold through the fence. The very famous 'Shebeen Queens' were the purveyors of the illegal brew. These black ladies made homemade beer. It was very strong and made in any sort of can, including old petrol (gasoline) cans. Many unknown chemicals were used to make the beer different. They were supposed to aid the fermentation process. However, the very famous Baragwanath Hospital (in Soweto) had to resolve the drinkers' problems. The hospital had recorded the largest variety of stomach ailments in the emergency wards of any hospital in the world! One analysis of the fermentation chemical resulted in torch (flashlight) batteries! Two process elements existed: the beer was made, and then buried to ferment. The cans were buried close to the railway line and there were so many holes dug that eventually the rail lines subsided. The Shebeen Queens were merciless. The authorities adopted the railway line problem and the beer problem and the whole situation was cleaned up. However, it was not long before the status quo eventually returned and the weekend soccer game enjoyment continued.

Johnny and I would discuss the merits of different players, the good play, and the teamwork, ad infinitum. We didn't know the players' names, but after watching many games we knew who they were! We also wondered how they would do against one of the top white teams.

"Their style is very different to our hard and fast handling of the ball. We tend to tackle very hard and move fast, Johnny," I noted one afternoon, looking at a game, out the back window.

"That's true. They maneuver the ball all over the ground and almost stand in place, tempting you to try and take it away," answered Johnny.

"Yes! Its like they've beaten you already! So why not move on? No! They want to beat you again!" I interjected.

"But then when they decide you're truly beaten, they move very fast, pass and go to get the ball again!" Johnny added.

We talked about how much stronger South Africa would be internationally with these very gifted black players. But we knew that many people would disagree with the idea.

One soccer game that Johnny and I watched had an unusual set of circumstances. We had seen monstrous fights, referees running for their lives, spectators coming onto the field, the crowd just going crazy at the scoring of a goal and the wild celebration after the team had won. This game was different. There was a very light-skinned, almost white, player on one of the teams. Johnny and I surmised he was from the Cape Province. Each time he got the ball he was booed, regardless of his good play. When he mishandled the ball or someone took it away, the stadium cheered. This became a game for Johnny and I to decipher. Knowing this man was of mixed blood but obviously partly African; the reactions raised the possibility of discrimination. Long conversations followed each action and reaction to any play he was involved in . . . was it his color? His ability? Or was he just a player on the opposition? Johnny and I finally agreed it was probably something that neither of us would ever find out. The problem, we thought, was that he was a very good player!

"After all, there is no commentator, we don't understand the language, and we are watching the game from an open window on the other side of the tracks!" I suggested.

"Is that a pun?" asked Johnny, laughing.

"No Sir!"

The final resolution, after at least four beers, was that hopefully the cheers and jeers were only determined by either his ability or his personality and nothing else. This would be the only reason that would satisfy our philosophy.

The game of soccer to Johnny and I was a separate thing to anything in our lives. It sometimes clashed with important events and was only relegated if circumstances were major: life itself, totally unavoidable situations such as not knowing or being misinformed, sickness causing inability to move, and some other events that are hard to imagine happening. Events such as weddings, baptisms, dates with girlfriends, government laws, and parental requests or demands, were always in jeopardy of being turned down or skipped. To me, in particular, the friendships with my soccer buddies that I grew up and played with, all over Johannesburg and the Witwatersrand, were ultra-important. These friends became very, very close in helping me to understand matters of life. I had so much respect and liking for these soccer-friends who played on dirt and grass, in new or broken shoes, with worn-out socks and pants, in good or bad weather; and who played their hearts out, sad in defeat, exultant and happy in victory, but who played with the same feeling of helping out each other, just to beat the opposition. I knew these friends formed a young man's bond through this sport process that was irreplaceable and would probably be remembered forever.

The Game

It was Saturday morning; our soccer team met at the Cenotaph in Johannesburg. The time was 10:00 AM and the game was in Krugersdorp. The coach came up to the team and said that our First Division Team needed a player as a backup to one of their players who was sick. They needed someone for the defense.

"Charl, you head off to Rand Stadium, report at 12:00 noon, game is at 2:00 PM."

"Me Sir?" I asked. Excitement flowed all over my body. I questioned my hearing for a split second but I knew it was my name.

"Yes! You can do it," replied the coach, "see you at practice next week."

"Good for you, Charl," said Desmond and Robbie, as both of them slapped me around playfully. A couple of my buddies joined in the good wishes. These player–friends and I had been together a long time. Anything good for one was good for all.

The rest of the team took off to Johannesburg's Park Station to catch the train to Krugersdorp. I didn't know what to do. I wanted to call a dozen friends, though I knew Johnny nearly always went to the Rand Stadium on Saturdays. Also, Sandy from work usually went; every Monday he would discuss the Saturday game, the plays, the players, the league and everything about the soccer day on the way to work. I decided to let it go; besides what if I didn't even get to play?

The Rand Stadium, opened in 1951, hosted the premier amateur soccer in South Africa as well as hosting visiting teams from Europe. I had played there before, in night games and curtain raisers for the big game of the day, and in most of our championship games. This was my first opportunity to play in the Saturday 'Match of the Week', as players had named it. Had my dreams on the bus finally come true?

I had a couple of hours before the game, which was in the afternoon. So, I walked through Johannesburg, thinking that I had many, many times wished I could play in an important game at the Rand Stadium. Now it might actually happen! The real dream of course was to be in a First Division team and play in the stadium throughout the season. I loved Saturdays because they were always different, especially compared to the routine of the week. The walk through Johannesburg was undertaken with a large amount of exuberance. I went into the Protea Milk Bar near the bus station at Escom House, so that I could catch any one of the many busses to the to Southern Suburbs. I ordered a milkshake. The waitress was really nice-looking but I paid little attention to her. I was so excited inside. Even if the player turned up, I might still have a chance to play. If I did not play, I would watch from the bench. There were no substitutions allowed in the game, except for the goalkeeper, and then only if he got injured. So the eleven players selected went on the field at the start and would be there for the whole 90 minutes. I knew I was fast and strong and had a powerful kick. I wasn't a tricky player with lots of moves, and that made me wonder why the coach hadn't chosen Robbie or Desmond or any other player. Maybe he didn't want to deplete his own team drastically. I agreed with that!

Suddenly I noticed a young guy talking to the really nice-looking waitress. The milk bar was shaped in a horseshoe with the round end at street level near the doorway. The folding doors were completely opened so that the people walking by the bar could almost touch people sitting on the high stools at the round end of the bar. The young man was definitely gay and standing at the round end. His arms were moving everywhere as he spoke. People at the bar were giggling!

"I know, Darling," he said to the waitress. "Some customers are absolutely hateful. They think you should be their slaves. Well . . . I . . . am . . . not . . . any . . . body's slave, unless I want to be. I resent that attitude!"

" That's really not what I said...and..." interjected the waitress, but she got cut-off.

"I'm telling you, it's almost disastrous you know. Nobody really cares. The tips are so small. I always tip big. You see Darling! I've been a waitress as well!" stated the gay man, lapping up all the attention, looking at all the people close to him and around him for recognition, and smirking. Then he looked straight at me!

"What do you think?"

"Ugh! Nothing . . . No! Whatever you say," I replied, and turned my head away looking for the men's toilet. I caught the waitress's eye. "Over there?" I pointed in the direction.

She nodded, perhaps recognizing my small embarrassment. "Yes," she said, and took the opportunity to walk away from the gay man, inside the counter, and alongside me as I moved toward a door at the back of the milk bar.

"Over there," she pointed.

"Thanks."

When I came out, the gay man was still talking to people in the street, and then to those at the milk bar, alternatively. He was loud, his hands continuously caressing the air around him.

Thoughts of Mel went through my head. He had turned gay. He had been in our Andrew Street Mob forever. All of the boys and girls in the crowd knew the stories of gay people. It was just something that you learned about when growing up. Eventually, Mel had slowly retracted from the crowd. One other friend and I continued to keep in touch. Mel went his way of life at 17. His parents eventually moved away. The kids in the Andrew Street Mob couldn't care less about Mel's leanings. He had grown up with us, he was one of us forever, and he had known that for years.

I decided to head for the stadium. But first I said good-bye to the waitress, and thanked her. I would try to come back and see her. I caught the bus to Rand Stadium.

I got off the bus and walked up to the players' gate. I gave my name.

"Oh, you're the reserve, go ahead. Good luck!"

"Thank you Sir!"

That put a hold in my feelings. Reserve? Well, maybe that's the way it was going to be! I made my way into the change room and reported to the coach. He was very busy scuffing around. He turned and looked at me.

"So you're the reserve?"

"Yes! Sir!"

"Well we're not sure of the situation. What position do you play?"

"Back or Wing."

"Which side?" asked the coach with a frown.

"Any side," I said nervously.

"Can you shoot?"

"Yes Sir!"

"How many goals have you scored this season?"

"About six!"

"Only six?"

"Yes Sir! But I played more than half the games as a back!"

"Six from the back position . . .Hmm! Not bad! Okay! Sit over there for a while and I'll let you know what's happening."

I went and sat down by the lockers. I didn't know what he was talking about. I had played both positions. Players came in, greeted me and went about their business of changing, sitting at their seats, and talking about almost everything but the game. Nobody talked to me so I just sat there! I hadn't experienced that feeling for some time.

To me it seemed the actions were like an everyday thing to all these players. I was so nervous inside and also so anxious to play. Because if I started as the reserve, the only chance I would get to play was if the goalkeeper got injured. I kept thinking, *Once the eleven-man team is named and given to the referee that's it! I'll have to sit on the bench and watch the game.* It also irritated me that this thought kept repeating itself. I leaned back and just sat and watched.

All the players were moving around; some naked, waiting for a massage; some finishing putting on their pants and their soccer shirts. Yellow and gold: *Great colors!* slid through my mind. I had worn them for years and years but now they really looked good, and seemed to mean more! I hoped so much that I could get dressed to play.

Activities went on for quite some time. It was now one o'clock; the game was at two. As always, there was a preliminary game between the Under-21 or Reserve League teams. I had played in many of these and I had also played a night game with a white ball. Now that was a beautiful experience! Since then I had really preferred it to the natural-leather brown ball. I wished they would use it during the day. It was easier to see unless the sun was in your eyes. It was a great feeling playing at night in cool air, with a white ball, moisture on the grass, and lights! At night, you could hear the crowd, but it was hard to see them.

My thoughts kept wandering all over the place. The crowd, for some reason, was never big at the pre-games, especially the ones I had played in. The stadium was seldom over half full. Most of the crowd turned up for the big game at 2:00 PM. I was now desperate to play. My inside energy wanted to be released. Run, pass the ball, intercept the play, move ahead, and think ahead too! Whatever—just make a good play. I felt I had sat on the bench in the change room for hours, but it was only 30 minutes.

The coach came into the room. "Shit, Johnson is too sick. You're on Charl. Get changed and see Joe for a uniform."

"Yes Sir!" The words were hardly out of his mouth and I was moving. My heart was pounding like never before. I was in turmoil! This was such an incredible feeling. My mind took me through the sequences of running on the field, the crowd cheering, and getting the ball from the kick-off. . . . It stopped there, that was enough thinking! This was the real thing. My body was quivering with ripples of excitement. I went to find Joe.

"Over here, son. Here's a shirt, but we're short of pants." Joe looked around but couldn't find a pair to fit. Amazing! I was 170 lbs. and 5'10", had slim hips and big legs and all the pants I tried hung like trash bags. It was not our team style anymore. Short tight pants felt so much better.

"I have a pair of blue shorts very close in color."

"Use them," said Joe.

"Over here, Charl, before you get dressed." It was the masseur. I got undressed, put on my soccer shorts and got up on the table.

So this is what it's all about, I thought. *Oh! I want to do this every week!* The masseur's hands went over my legs, working the muscles with his fingers. It almost hurt, but not really. Then his hands moved over my back and the pressure was lighter, but heavy again around the neck.

"No stiff necks from heading the ball," said the masseur. I just lay there . . . this was ecstasy.

"You're in good shape Son!"

"Thank you Sir!"

I couldn't wait to tell my friends. The masseur finished and I got dressed by adding my socks and shin pads, my shorts, and the soccer shirt. I packed my bag and left it on the bench. I had a pound and some change in my pocket. I decided to just leave it in the bag. I wasn't playing away in some other team's clubhouse, where money had mysteriously disappeared before. I put my boots on, tightening the laces from the toe to the ankle. I threw the laces around the foot only. I didn't tie the lace around the ankle, which was much the style. I liked my ankles to be totally free to move. My boots were also the new style of being low cut; high tops were commonly the order of the day. It had taken a major amount of my savings to buy these boots, and they were treasured. I would never have left *them* in the change room. I felt in style, and that was important to me in sport. It gave me confidence. I looked in the long vertical mirror . . . I looked professional! Well, why not!

I had never felt so good. I definitely was fit and that gave me confidence. The opposition would have to run, fight and protect everything they had! My mind was whirling. The coach called everybody to close in.

"Tough game! Important game today! Keep the ball on the ground. They're very physical and strong in the air. Don't fall asleep in the first few minutes. Charl is our new player today and he'll be playing left wing. Charl, this is Jock. Jock is inside left. Denny is center forward and Van is left back. Talk to each other, okay?"

"Yes coach," we replied.

I shook the hands of Denny, Jock, and Van. Some of the players introduced themselves, but at that moment my mind had no capacity for names.

Our team walked through the tunnel and at that very moment I felt the true excitement that something very good was going to happen, and there were just thousands and thousands of people going to watch it. We went to our benches. Germiston Callies, the other team, were already on their benches. The preliminary game was almost over. It had been dull and we knew that because the crowd was 'talking'. The game came to an end and the crowd clapped very lazily. I remembered this kind of enthusiasm very well. The two curtain-raiser teams cleared the field. The Germiston Callies team took off to the north goal and Marist Brothers went to the south goal. I trailed them. This was the end that Johnny sat in. Sandy usually sat in the middle of the field. We had about six soccer balls to kick around. I hoped very much that Johnny or some of the Southern Suburbs crowd would see me. Uh! They wouldn't see me till the game had gone on for a while. Right now I concentrated on passing the ball. I took a couple of hard shots at the goal; one went over the top. *Keep your head down,* I told myself. I felt so physically fit and so anxious that I wanted to say, *Don't rush the ball.* I knew all the training and running I did during the week would help now, and count as the game went on.

I was still anxious about not playing. I felt the coach might still change his mind or the regular player might turn up. My fears stopped when the referee blew his whistle and the game started. Now I knew I was in for the whole game! It was up to me entirely. The Germiston team kicked off and the ball moved from player to player in their team, and then they pressed forward down their right side. I ran back to help and the ball was intercepted by Van. He pushed up to Jock, Jock to Denny, and then onto the right wing. The ball went up and down the field. I touched it twice, but it seemed they never attempted to pass to me except in an emergency. I handled the ball well each time and passed it on, then ran into position to get it back, but it never came back me. Germiston scored a goal and by half-time the score was Germiston 1-Marist Brothers 0. I came off not even tired. I had run a lot, but had not been part of the team. The coach said a few words about tackling earlier and passing, but I felt disappointed. It was strange. The coach said nothing to me at half-time.

The second half started. I decided to come back more and one time took the ball off Van after he had tackled someone. I turned up-field and took the ball down the sideline. I beat one player by pure speed as he tried to tackle me. I then sent a long ball over the Germiston half-backs, onto what should have been a right wing running onto the ball. The Marist wing was not there and the ball went to waste.

"Easy Charl," said Derek, the right half-back.

"Okay!" I agreed. Then said to myself, *Shit! The winger should have been there! That's the way our team plays that sequence.*

The game continued with back and forward play. It was tough. These guys were hard to beat. Some of the players from this league had actually been to England; sometimes picked, sometimes on their own. Marist's pressure in the first part of the second half paid off, as a goal was scored by our inside right: 1–1 was the score.

I really got into the game now and didn't care if my team passed to me or not. I went to a position where I could possibly receive the ball . . . That's what I had been taught! "If you don't get the ball, do something about it." The game started to come to me more and more. I helped a lot towards the scoring of Marist's second goal. This woke up Germiston Callies who retaliated with tremendous pressure.

"Go back and help. We need to get the assurance goal!" Denny yelled.

I looked at him and thought a few things about his giving the instruction, but there was no time for that!

"I'm on my way!"

I went back and helped. Van and Jock showed their appreciation by giving me the ball. I lost it once, but got it back quickly. I worked hard. Fifteen minutes were left to go. Germiston continued to press hard. A good save by Franz, our goalkeeper, kept us in the game. Frustration mounted for Germiston and they pressed even harder. Franz picked up the ball one more time, but instead of throwing it short, he kicked it to the right wing. I saw this and took off down the left wing thinking, *If he...* Sure enough, the right wing put the ball just over the Germiston back and out of his reach. Denny took it and broke away with the back on his heels. He ran towards the goal. I cut as fast as I could towards the goal from the left wing position, and also towards Denny. Following my thinking again, but this time of a different, *If he...* All this so that, in case a loose ball from a tackle or something came out to my side, I would be there. Denny had the ball under control and slowed a little. The sweeper came out to tackle him, but Denny beat him and took his shot immediately. The goalkeeper dived and punched the ball out. I saw it coming towards me! . . . It was ten feet away! . . . I kept my eye on it! I slowed down: all this in a split second . . . I felt my left foot crack the ball, and instantly, I knew I had hit it well! The back of the net went blowing outwards as the ball's motion decelerated. It was a goal! Marists 3—Germiston Callies 1. The thirty thousand people screamed. It seemed to echo in my head forever . . . I had scored a killer goal! My new team players ran towards me and slapped me on the back.

"Yeah man!"

Someone hugged me: "Great shot!"

One pushed me on the grass, and then helped me up!

It was all over in seconds. We walked back to the kickoff. Germiston Callies' players were dejected. I was in absolute heaven. The game ended in a 3-1 win for us. The crowd started to file out. The players went back to the change room.

"It'll be in the paper, Charl," said the coach. "Great shot! Nice game, kid!"

We showered, changed and had a beer. The chatter was non-stop. This was just incredible to me! I could have stayed in the clubhouse all day and into the night.

"Great shorts, Charl!" said one player, who was younger.

"Little too short!" said another.

"New style my friend," said another. "They're coming off the knees. Just like his boots with low cut sides."

The players shook hands and I left, almost last. I thanked Joe and the masseur. I was savoring the day very deeply now and the inevitable was happening. The thrill was dying. I was happy-sad-happy. I had never experienced so much in a soccer game and I believed it was due to the large crowd. I had played differently with this team. Being in the under 16 and under 18 cup finals, winning the league cups, even all that, and having played at the Rand Stadium before, had not equaled the scoring of that goal. The bottom-line question was: would the top team pick me up, or would I have to go back to my buddies? I didn't want to leave them, but I believed, 'Fate will answer it'. However, I knew now definitely that I could play at this level of soccer and that was the great thing that had happened today! I was a fatalist, like my mother had been all her life. She had often said that fate takes care of many things.

I jumped on the familiar yellow-and-red bus to Rosettenville as I asked questions of myself. Should I stop at the Broadway Hotel? This is where the Saturday soccer crowd from the Southern Suburbs went after the game. I thought not. That was like putting yourself up on the stage.

I stayed on the bus and went home. As I walked from the bus stop on Main Street to my house, a couple of deep-rooted thoughts crossed my mind. I had learnt my soccer on this street. I loved it then and I loved it now. Adults, who talked about all the players at the Rand Stadium, had successfully driven my childhood dreams of wanting to play there. I wanted that! It was my dream of dreams. *It may not come true, but I have at least done it once.* I wondered where my dad was. I wondered where my mom was. It would've been great to have them at the game. But they never came to any of my sports activities: this second thought jumped quickly into my mind to stop me going to the deepest of my emotions. I really hoped Johnny had been at the game. I swung through the gate at 65.

"Hullo! Grandpa!"

"Hullo! Son. Did you win today?"

"Yes! Guess what? Grandpa, I played at the Rand Stadium!"

"Rand Stadium, on a Saturday! Top venue then! That's very good . . . so very good Son! I knew you would make it . . . you have worked so hard!" Uncle Mick paused. "Was your team promoted?"

"No, I just substituted for a sick player in Marist Brothers' top team."

"Son! That's wonderful! They may bring you up then . . . soon. Keep playing hard. Remember . . . toes-out in the middle of the field . . . toes-in when you get close to shooting at the goal."

I laughed. We hugged. "I will. Is Gran inside?"

"Yes! For sure!"

I went inside and sat with my gran at the kitchen table like we always did. Then Grandpa joined us. I told them the story in great, great detail. Gran was cooking and doing lots of things. She kept saying . . . "You did!" . . . "You are brave!" . . . "You liked that huh!" Finally at the end she looked me straight in the eye.

"That's marvelous!" Gran said and then turned around and gave me a kiss and a hug.

"Keep studying, though! Son! I know how you love sports and it makes you happy, and you've had a wonderful day . . . but nobody gets rich playing sports in South Africa!"

◆

The Forever Goal

Monday morning Sandy picked up me on the corner of Main and Andrew Streets like he always did. This ride was so much better than the three buses I had had to catch when I first started work. Then he picked up Laubscher in Johannesburg, and finally Mr. Warren. Mr. Warren, whose bottle of brandy a day partially came out of his body in the morning air, with the rest coming out as he worked and sweated during the day. We had done this for years.

I wanted to talk about the soccer because Sandy always went to the games. His wife went too. But every time I started, they changed the subject! The hour's drive became long. I thought how they always discussed everything about the game on the way to work. Now, why wouldn't they talk about the game?

"Anybody read the Sunday paper?" I asked loudly.

"No!" "No!" "No!" all three replied, followed by Sandy talking about his fishing trip. Laubscher had wanted to go but couldn't. So they discussed another potential trip while driving to work, and that took forever. Finally we all got out of the car and went into the Main Reef Engineering shops to start work. I was upset. I was proud of my Saturday and wanted to share it with my friends. I hadn't seen Johnny at all that weekend either, so my story was stuck inside of me.

At lunch everyone grabbed their sandwiches and went upstairs to the lunchroom. I opened my lunch, wishing I was on a team somewhere and we were practicing soccer drills. Most of the machinists and millwrights were talking. Sandy and Laubscher came in late. Sandy had a box. He threw it on the table and yelled loudly at me, "If you're going to play at the Rand Stadium, wear a pair of shorts that fit you! We could all see the hairs on your ass!"

Everyone in the lunchroom burst out laughing, making whooping sounds and pointing fingers in fun! The whole shop was in on it!

"Nice going, by the way," said Sandy. The rest laughed and cheered!

I felt so warm inside. These were people whom I worked with every day and they were just so nice. Sandy had taught me many things about machining. He was the fastest in the shop. Every journeyman and black helper had added something to my work abilities. It was a wonderful team and I would do anything for them.

Work that afternoon was a breeze. About 2 PM, Picannin, the boss's chauffeur, came up to me. He was always positive and full of smiles.

"Congratulations Baas! I hear you scored a magnificent goal on Saturday at the big Rand Stadium!"

"Yes!" I said, "thank you," not knowing how Picannin had found out. He had been gone all morning on some errand.

"Was it good?"

"Yes! Picannin, it was a very, very good feeling."

"You must be good to play at the famous Rand Stadium? Wow! Baas! What position do you play?"

"Left wing."

"Oh," said Picannin, pausing and moving his body into in a right wing position stance. "I am a right wing."

"You are?"

"Yes, and I played last Sunday." He smiled. "At the place of importance!"

"Your home?"

"Yes. In Alexandria we play every Sunday, and I was playing in the afternoon."

"Did you win?" I asked with a smile on my face, just knowing something was coming in this story.

"Yes! We did Baas! Can I tell you how I scored my goal?"

"Yes Picannin, the machine is running by itself, . . . go on."

"Well, I first collected the ball on about the half way line . . . between my feet," he pointed down. "When I looked up . . . Huh! There is one stupid man coming towards me, and he is small like this," Picannin pointed to a height of five feet. "He can't stop me. Stupid bugger! I just stepped to one side. He runs through like a rhinoceros. Stupid! Baas! So stupid! So I take the ball . . . I'm very fast . . . down the right side and who is coming to stop me? A big black man with a chest like a big baboon . . . I am thinking." Picannin pointed to his head. "So I stop the ball and I look at him. He still comes closer . . . maybe this is another stupid man. So I put my foot under the ball and flick it on his chest very accurately. The ball comes back to me because I very purposely flick it that way. This stupid man, Baas, still keeps coming towards me, so I flick it again and it comes back again. So I stop the ball." Picannin now stood as though he had a ball at his feet and his hands were upside down and pointed outwards . . . "Now! I must make a move. This man is not like a rhinoceros; he is coming like a Cape water buffalo." Picannin was looking straight at me. He paused, and he put his hands down on his hips. "So must I go right or must I go left? What must I do? . . . Man!" His arms came up and opened wider and then he pointed to his head again and looked straight at me. "I must make a decision. Every man must make a decision Baas! So . . . I push the ball in the air to the right, and I go left, and come around the Cape water buffalo. Why? Because I'm so fast, and before the ball touches the ground, . . . I catch it on my right foot." He bent and pointed to his right toe. "Yes Baas, before it touches the ground. The crowd loves me, Baas! They are shouting. I'm so fast and now here is the stupid goalkeeper. What! A stupid man! He is as slow as a giraffe. I run to the left, he moves a little. I run to the right, he moves a little. I run to the left, he moves a little. . . . I am tired of this Baas! I am so bored with him. So I just slip the ball between his legs and the net takes the ball and holds its speed to nothing! Baas! The crowd loves me! They dance, and we win again!"

Picannin looked at me straight in the eye and said, "Is your goal that good?"

"No! Picannin . . . not that good! . . . Congratulations!"

"Thank you, Baas. I must go now to drive the Big Baas to the center of the wonderful Johannesburg city."

"Bye Picannin," was all I could say! And a thought followed. *No wonder everyone loves him!*

✳

CHAPTER 16

Gran and Uncle Mick and Mom

JUST LIKE THAT, THE news was circulated that Uncle Bill wanted to sell 65 Andrew Street. The original family arrangement was that Gran and Uncle Mick could stay there for as long as they liked. Gran had paid for the house each month since the 40s. Vigorous family discussions ensued. There were complications. Where would Gran and Uncle Mick go? Where would my Mom and I go? What about me? Could anybody afford to go anywhere? The discussions seemed to go on forever. I wanted to put my suggestions forward, but I stayed clear. I had never liked Uncle Bill. He had continuously teased me in whatever I attempted and belittled everything I did. There was no recognition of what I had accomplished . . . no matter what! I remembered especially one time when I was nine years old and drying the dishes after dinner. I had dried a dish and put it on top of the sink with the cloth. I walked away, returned and grabbed the cloth, forgetting the dish was inside. The plate fell to the floor and broke!

Uncle Bill said, "That was stupid! . . . Well, what can you expect from one of the Marais' sons?"

I threw the cloth at the sink, and said in a broken voice, as loud as I could, without shouting: "You never did like my father, but you know what? He never liked you either! He also said you were a coward!"

I wanted everything to stay as it was!

The talks continued for a while and then before anyone knew it, all the arrangements were solidified. Gran and Uncle Mick would go to live with Uncle Rob in Benoni. I would live with my mom and her husband Mr. Boddington at 65 Andrew Street. Despite my efforts to question all the moves, no reason was given why everything had to change. Why were we staying at 65 and not Gran and Uncle Mick? I was to keep my room and continue to stay at 65! I said too many things that you couldn't print! My mom said to calm down! I added a few more unprintable statements. If anything was stupid this was it!!

It was a sad day when Gran and Uncle Mick moved. Many things were said about Gran's sons, Uncle Bill and Uncle Rob. The plus and minus game was too much for me. I was so damn sad that Gran and Uncle Mick were going to Benoni; I didn't know what to do. I was experiencing such a hollow feeling in my chest . . . I felt my body was like a paper bag . . .Then I got mad at everything! I couldn't care less about any of the uncles! I would have moved with Gran and Uncle Mick given the opportunity, but I already had a long way to go to work from Kenilworth to Industria; Benoni and Industria were on opposite sides of Johannesburg. My commute distance would double. Again decisions were made without explanation! Again my needs were neither considered, nor discussed and yet the results were to be accepted! These actions only cause erosion in many things!

I knew deep down I couldn't go. My routine was so rigid and all my friends were close to Andrew Street. What would I do in Benoni, anyway? The small towns on the East Rand always seemed so unsophisticated compared to Johannesburg. But my sadness just went so deep. Gran and Uncle Mick had been part of my everyday life for more than thirteen years. They were always there. They had raised me. Gran was the closest person to me . . . very, very deep feelings were there! My mom had been busy during the war years and the struggle after the war had not helped. Despite my mom being home all the time there was a gap between us, which didn't exist between Gran, Uncle Mick and myself; that bond was like the strongest glue. I always went to Gran for this or that, and she always had some help. It seemed like a million nights of routine had gone by, since I first played in the street, came home at 6 o'clock for dinner, saw my mom, had dinner, and then went to my room to study or go to bed. I actually didn't see my mom very much in the evenings. When I was young Gran greeted me after school, made me a sandwich, and then made me lie down for an hour before going out to play. Later on when I was working and going to night school the quick meal prepared by my gran was always ready. There was always talking between Gran, Uncle Mick and I, but not that much with my mom.

This was becoming a time of many family changes. My sister, Yvonne, was expecting her third child and was hoping for a boy. Her husband, James, wanted a boy. They got another girl. My brother, Bazil, got married for the second time. My dad had already married for the fourth time and was responsible for another son. But to me, none of these events had the deep emotions of Gran going to live in Benoni. This was a major cut into my life. I was totally unhappy with the new arrangement and increasingly disgusted with my uncles. Maybe they didn't even know, because I never told them!

The native girl, Lena, who had spent so many years with the family, wept for hours . . . then days . . . I had to comfort her! It seemed there was some reason she couldn't go to Benoni. She had been with the family for twelve years. To me she was part of the family. Her child had been born there. Lena loved Gran, and Gran loved her. They knew each other so well from talking in the kitchen during all those years. They had raised me through all the years as well. I wondered what Lena would do: what did black people do? Most white people didn't seem to care! I knew my family cared, especially Gran and Mom. My mom had gone to the black communities and taught small black kids for years . . . for nothing. Aunt Tillie and Aunt Eileen had the same caring. The black people who had worked for our family had our respect as well as our liking. I liked that very much, it seemed like the right thing to do.

I was developing a growing dislike for what the government was doing to the black people. Especially as all the black people I had ever met had always been nice to me. I recalled Otiend and Vryburg, the black men in the bicycle shop, all the black men at Main Reef Engineering, and all those black riders I had met when cycling. I had talked to so many and every time they were nice, helpful, and gentle. I couldn't understand either the English or the European immigrant attitude towards black people. They used words like 'uncivilized': *what the hell did that mean?* Neither did I understand the religious Calvinistic white person's belief that blacks were to be saved and brought into the church. In all the cases I had known, the black person ended up being a servant, helper, street sweeper, or a night watchman. The picture and monuments of a black man on his back, drill in his hand, thousands of feet below surface, in a four—foot high stope, drilling rock, were indelibly etched in my mind. I knew I was not as fortunate as to have come from a rich family, but I felt very lucky that I did not to have to do that kind of work. I had heard many bad conversations among white people about the black people: I never liked what I heard. So I stayed out of the talk and refused to get drawn in. So did most of the Andrew Street Mob! Was our crowd different or was this the norm? I asked myself this many, many times.

I thought more and more about Lena. What is there in a life of living in a small room in the backyard? Her husband was not there every night or even every weekend. Now the National Party was segregating the hell out of everything and moving people to new places. Changing the areas of Alexandria, Newclare, and Sophiatown, and making efforts to remove the so-called 'Black Spots' in Johannesburg. Where were they going to go? Lena was too important to the family to disappear to nowhere. This worried me. I was sure she would miss Gran, as much as me.

◆

My mom had been going out with a Mr. Boddington and they had decided to get married. So they did in a very small ceremony. Mr. Boddington had five sons, and one of them, Donald, moved into 65 Andrew Street. Donald was a happy man, 21 years of age; he had a pleasant face, he was plump, if compared against soccer players, and he was a gentle and very nice person. Donald was a buyer, which turned out to be very helpful at Xmas because he got all the unsolicited gifts of alcohol. He didn't have a girlfriend. I was worried that I would have to go out with him socially, and that it would interfere with my precious little fun time. It turned out to not be true and I was very happy. Donald also had a car, which did mean an occasional ride here and there. We got on well. Now, I was not sure, I knew everything about the moving of my Gran and uncle Mick.

I visited Gran and Uncle Mick every month after they had moved into the new place in Benoni. Each time I had the feeling that my Uncle Rob didn't want me there. I didn't care what the hell he wanted! One time, my gran told me to go and get a pair of long pants and charge it to her account. I was happy, because I needed a pair pretty badly. I went into the store where my uncle Rob worked, selected a pair of pants and told him how to charge it.

"Taking from your granny again!" My uncle Rob said.

"No I'm not. Gran suggested it and so she gave to me," I replied, thinking what a shithouse he was! I left.

Amazing, I thought. *When Gran was at 65 Andrew I'd never see my uncle Rob. In fact, he never visited his mother very much at all. Now she is in Benoni, suddenly he doesn't want anyone around her! Why is he so protective?* All this didn't sit well with me, and it played on my mind for a long time. I was never into the family maneuvers and somehow never completely trusted any of the outer family. I had been bumped around too much to sink all my emotions into anyone in the family except Gran, Uncle Mick, Mom and Yvonne. In fact, Yvonne's husband James, his father, Mr. Van, and his brothers, John and Peter, and their family, had been nicer to me than the so-called blood family uncles. On the money side, they knew my mom was battling against the economics of life, but I never saw a penny or a helping hand from any one of her kin.

◆

After about six months I was told my gran was in the hospital. So Mom, Mr. Boddington, Yvonne, Bazil, and I went to see her one night. I sat at Gran's bedside the whole time, talking. She said things like, "Keep up your studies; you must do well and become an engineer, like your Uncle Bill." I was going to say, "Gran, Uncle Bill is only a stationary engineer, he is not a real engineer, they have to . . ." but held it back. I knew that I, in my late teens, was already more qualified technically than anyone in our family; besides, all that didn't matter right now! I noticed there was a lonely sadness in Gran's voice. We both kept talking, while most of the family was discussing other things amongst themselves. Then, after the nurse had come in to end the visit, the family started to leave. My mom kept calling me to leave but I stayed; to me, every minute counted. Then it was every second that counted, as I stared into her marvelous face. It seemed so important to look and I didn't know why. The nurse almost picked me up physically. So I got up and walked out backwards, looking at Gran . . . *What a beautiful face,* I thought. "Good-bye, Gran . . . I'll see you soon."

But inside of me I suddenly felt so hollow! Something in my mind said, "Look again, it's the last time you'll see her." I didn't want to believe that and rejected the thought, but I followed the instruction and looked. I felt so very, very sad inside. There was a stream of teardrops just running down my cheeks, and tears blurred my eyes as I walked down the hospital corridors. I kept to the side and behind everybody else, so no one could see. I got into the back of the car, slid to the far window and didn't say anything to anyone. *Didn't anybody seem to see the seriousness of Gran's condition?* I questioned in thought. I got out of the car when we arrived home and went to bed. The tears and the thoughts would not leave me. I lay awake for hours, unable to go to sleep. I got up and made tea. I sat in the kitchen of my life! The room was empty!!! Thoughts kept streaming through my mind. Tears kept rolling down my face. Thinking kept bringing back the hard things that life kept dealing me. I never had any money, I couldn't keep a girlfriend because I was always studying or playing soccer. And now! My friends had cars and their families were always together. How come they always remained together? This had been such a sad breakup of the family. I would never forgive Uncle Bill or any of the adults in the family. Nobody asked me what I wanted!! The thoughts kept revolving in my mind. Finally, I convinced myself that studying would be worth it; it would get me where I wanted to go. I didn't know why, but that had been Gran's wish and it was good enough for me. I rolled over on my right side for the tenth time and fell asleep.

◆

A few days later, my mom came into my room. Her face was red and tired-looking and her eyes were full of tears. She told me that Gran had died! She began to cry and turned her face down. I hugged her. We sat for a long while together on the bed. We didn't say much . . . what was there to say? Mom got up and left. I just went out and got on my bike and rode it out of the yard. I didn't know if I had homework and I didn't care. I didn't really care about anything. I rode for hours but never physically felt anything. I must have ridden for fifty miles, out along Rifle Range Road. I knew I didn't want to talk to anyone that night. I just wanted to be alone. It was very, very late when I got home. The house was in darkness.

"Is that you Charl?"

"Yes."

"Where have you been?"

"Went for a ride, Mom."

"Are you alright?"

"Yes Mom! See you in the morning," I replied. Then I went to my room, closed the door and climbed into bed. I felt so empty in-side . . . tears were still coming down . . . I fell asleep, exhausted in many ways. My final thought, *She was so much to me, she loved me no matter what . . . Why? Why? Why?*

◆

I buried myself in my friends and activities. My mom and I talked a lot more than we had ever done before. We had now become very close, no doubt about it. The months went by quickly, or so it seemed. My mom, at dinner, announced that Lena was leaving.

"She told me that her baby and her husband are going to live together in Soweto, the new township!"

"Well, I think it is so nice that she is getting her family together. Also, Mom they are going to live in the same place." I said after some careful thought.

"I don't blame her, she wants to go" added Mom.

The dinner was quiet after the basic questions and answers.

I had deeply mixed emotions inside. I felt it was really good for her and she deserved it, but, to me, it was another piece going out of 65 Andrew Street. Thinking about Lena brought back the memories of her and Gran being there every day . . . I couldn't think anymore.

The farewells were sad. I hugged Lena despite her standing back, bowing her head, and clapping her hands towards me.

"I know that's respect," I said, "but I owe you so much! There is no way I can repay you!"

"No, Baas! You were very good to me . . . it is enough!"

"Happiness! . . . Oh! So much happiness . . . I hope for you. You must come and see us," I added.

Lena left.

I couldn't get rid of the thought that the government, because of its rules just continuously affected lives of black and white people

◆

A week later, Mom said she had interviewed a boy to do Lena's job.

"A boy! . . . A black man?" I asked.

"Yes, his name is Jonathan."

"Well, that's going to be different."

I went to find Donald. He was reading.

"Let's go somewhere tonight. This is too much. Lena's leaving, and now we have a man taking her place. Everything is becoming stupid . . . it's pretty sad."

"It's Sunday, Charl!"

"I know. Let's find a couple of girls and go somewhere."

"Okay!" agreed Donald. I was surprised.

I phoned Denise and Meridy. Denise said they weren't doing anything and would be delighted to go.

"Donald, you talk to Meridy," I said. "I'm really not her type."

"All right," said Donald.

Donald and I picked up Denise and Meridy and drove to the Zoo Lake in the northern suburbs of Johannesburg. Nothing was open in Johannesburg on Sundays. No movies, no bars, only some restaurants and hotels. Private clubs were open to members only. Nobody I knew (especially my teenager friends) belonged to clubs. They were out of reach. We talked about going to Hillbrow, but the Zoo Lake was chosen and we went there for tea. It was fun. Denise and I had been good friends for some time now and we enjoyed each other's company. The encounter proved to be very successful because Donald and Meridy hit it off. I was also glad that Donald would now occasionally have a date.

A few months went by as Donald dated Meridy. I loved it because if they stayed at home, I might get the occasional opportunity to use the car, which was seventh heaven. A date, a car on Saturday, meant the week went fast. I was anxious to get the car but careful not to ask too often.

Life did not change much for me on a day-to-day basis. I worked four days a week, went to college all day Friday and at night on Mondays, Tuesdays and Wednesdays. Soccer practice took up Thursdays and the games were on Saturday afternoons. I continued to sustain my position on the team and was still playing as a back, sometimes as a forward. Desmond and I were glad we were on the team together. Saturday nights were spent with Andrew Street Mob friends. Really there was little change in routine and I liked it, but I wanted to go out more with June. We only dated when I could get the car, because there was no way to get to Alberton without it. Therefore, I couldn't make a date until Donald had said yes! This complex circle drove me crazy!

While talking to Yvonne one day about my troubles with not having a car, knowing a very pretty girl, and my desires to see her, she told me about her husband's brother, John. He wanted his car fixed while he went on vacation for a month. I called, arrangements were made, and I went to get the car. It was hard to start and had to be pushed. But it was transport. It was a most beautiful sight to see! For two weeks, whenever I could, I missed classes, and ran the car down the road to get it going, so I could go and see June. Then, at June's home, I'd park it up the hill so that I could get it started when I left. Jonathan, our esteemed houseboy, a very meticulous black man, was always asked to help push to get me going.

Jonathan was a delight in my mind. He was so domesticated and loved cooking and cleaning, but didn't like anything too physical. He truly was a cook and a butler. Jonathan was not a boy, though! He was a man. In fact, he was about forty years old. He and I had gotten on very well except when he had to push the car or help carry large boxes. Then you heard his famous well-repeated statements just flow into the conversation.

"I am a Houseboy, I do not work in the garage. I am not qualified for that, Baas Charls!"

Despite gentle pleas and coercion he would put up a tremendous resistance to doing non-domestic work. Eventually he would succumb, but it was sometimes not worth it to me, because Jonathan had to rest a lot and his copious complaints would drive me crazy. The requests were avoided as much as possible. So Jonathan was happy peeling vegetables, going to the market, cooking, washing dishes, and gently cleaning the house.

"No Baas . . . my clothes are clean."

"Come on Jonathan! This is for my girlfriend."

"But, Baas, I must clean up the dishes."

"Jonathan! Come on, help me . . . the car gets going quickly when two push."

After forty excuses and two weeks of pleading, Jonathan knew he couldn't win. Finally, one day he said, "Baas! I pay for you to fix the car. Take my salary from the Missus. I'm not pushing the car. I am a Houseboy . . . I am not a Pusher!"

I finally realized that Jonathan was just that! He was always so clean, fastidious, never worked in the garden, and was very, very polite.

"I'm sorry Jonathan. You are right. I will fix the car and you won't have to push it again," I said. Now I felt very guilty for forcing him to help push the car. Actually, it was an easy thing to do, because when we pushed hard, I would jump in and the engine and clutch would kick in . . . Bang! Bang! Bang! And the stupid thing would go. Simple solution but....

One late night at June's, it was almost midnight and she went to bed. I left and walked up the road to the car. I was tired. I jumped in and the car rolled down the hill but wouldn't start. I lifted up the hood and took off the distributor cap and saw the rotor cam was loose. I had found the trouble. The bearings were worn in the distributor. So that was why it had to go fast in order to start... The distributor shaft would spin in the middle if the car went fast, and not flop all over the place. Why the hell hadn't I fixed it before? There was still some more down-hill left. I wasn't sure I could get it going fast enough to start. I needed to wait for someone to walk by or get June to help. I had left it too late; she would have been asleep already. But I was determined to try. I went back to the house and knocked on the door.

Her father answered, "Charl, this is very late, Son!"

"I can't get my car started."

"June is not going to push it, she's in bed."

"Yes, Sir! Goodnight."

"Goodnight! You kids must only go out on Saturdays now. The weekdays are for staying at home."

"Yes, Sir, goodnight." I agreed politely. *Another damn adult rule*, I thought.

I left. *Wow! This is just too much. My buddies seem to have cars that run. How do they do it? I don't even have a car. Nothing seems to work smoothly!*

"Oh, well, that old story is really old," I said out loud. "It is mid-night and I have to get up at 5:30 AM to go to work. Do I leave the car here and walk or what?" I reached the car, opened the door and sat on the seat, one leg outside. My hands went onto my head and I thought of just sleeping right there. *To hell with tomorrow, somebody will help me push in the morning.* I sat for a little while longer, my thoughts changing to all the negatives. *My dad never gives me any money, not for school, not for any damn thing. I have to give my mom half my wages, which is almost nothing! Actually I don't mind that... How the hell do I get out of this? I don't want to lose June! Girls always want to go out, but so do I! Just going to parties is not enough anymore. It would be nice to have a girlfriend that really understands. I think June would maybe be that! . . . Now look at this piece of shit of a car. I hate this!* My mind was swirling, my head was thick in thought. I decided just to sleep in the car.

"Charl!" It was June.

"What are you doing? Your dad will kill you!"

"I don't care. He's gone to bed; let's get the car going. I know it takes two."

I got out of the car and kissed her with passion!

"You're beautiful."

"Go," she said with a loving smile.

We pushed the car, sure enough it started, and I kept going. I opened the window and waved like mad, then opened the door, put my leg outside, shook it like crazy, and honked the horn. When I was confident the engine was warm, I turned the car around the drove back up the street to June's house. All was quiet. I blew a kiss to June who was somewhere inside. I slammed the accelerator and took off. I was now in mood #1.

◆

"Uncle Mick has been asking for you, Charl," said my mom.

"Let's go and see him," I suggested.

"Well, he doesn't respond to anyone after you greet him. He just sits and stares into the room."

"What's the matter?" I asked.

"Well, he hasn't been the same since Mom died."

"Let's go and see him this weekend."

"We can't go, we have to go down to Henley-on-Klip," My mom replied apologetically.

"You're always going there," I said.

"Well we bought the place for retirement and we have to continue to build each weekend. It's a very slow process."

"How long has Uncle Mick been like this, Mom?"

"About two months."

"Two months! Is this the first time he asked for me?"

"No, everyone in the family says he asks for you all the time."

"How come nobody told me? Come on! Mom, let's go!"

"No, I can't."

I figured I would try and go on the Sunday. I couldn't go Saturday. I called Uncle Mick and Uncle Rob answered. He told me they wouldn't be there Sunday. I didn't believe him and I knew he wouldn't let me come and see Uncle Mick by myself. I would have to go with my mom and she didn't want to talk to my Uncle Rob!

Early the next week, Uncle Mick died. It was only three months after Gran died. Life had leveled another punch at my body . . . taking my breath away!

My mom said she was going to the funeral. I had said I would do anything for Uncle Mick, but I had decided not to go, and I told her so. I didn't want to go to the funeral. I wanted to, in reality, but knew I couldn't take it. I stayed away from family gatherings for some time. I had just had it with everyone. I knew all my emotions would come out and I was not sure of the end result. I was not going near any of the family.

Two weeks later I was at June's house. Her parents had gone to a party and we had decided to stay in and cook something and drink a few beers. This was at my request. As we sat on the couch just enjoying each other with nobody else there, I told her the story of Gran, Uncle Mick and Mom. I told her of all the happy times. I brought her up to date about their departures. I got tearful when talking about Gran, so concentrated on Uncle Mick.

"My mom is upset on two accounts. The first was Uncle Mick dying. He was a father to her, for most of her years. I don't even know my mom's real father's name. She cried at the loss. We've had our share lately."

"What'd he die of?" asked June.

"Fretting."

"Fretting! . . . Charl that is not funny."

"No! No! It's not a joke; it's one of life's mysteries. We all thought he'd die of silicosis. He was a miner all his life. His life story is life against many odds. When a miner gets to the first stage of silicosis, which is caused from breathing dust in the mine, they give him a job on the surface. He doesn't go underground anymore. When he reaches the second stage of silicosis, they retire him and give him a pension. In the third stage of silicosis, they increase the miner's pension. Its simple! Because they know he won't live very long!" I smiled a little.

"Really? Isn't that being very considerate!" asked June with a questioning look on her face.

"Yes it is!" I replied while smirking. "And so, Uncle Mick lived for ten years in the third stage and got drunk every week. Well, only once a week, but every week! We found him in an alley one morning. He had been beaten up, but he still had his money on him. It was not in his pants pocket, where they probably looked, but in his shirt pocket. Whoever did him in, didn't look there!"

"Was he badly beaten? Did you find out who did it?" asked June.

"Yes! Badly beaten with bloody marks on his face. And, no! He was too drunk to remember!"

"Amazing!"

"My gran changed his allowance from weekly, on Fridays, to monthly. He then used to get drunk every month and disappear for two days. So my gran returned to giving him a weekly allowance, but this time she gave it to him every Monday morning!"

"Oh, so he wouldn't go get drunk with his friends on a Friday," suggested June.

"Yes, but that didn't work. Like a robot he'd go out on Monday morning, buy 400 cigarettes, a jug of wine, and about four Western novels. He'd bring all this home, put it in his room, and go out and get drunk," I paused to drink and continued, "Gran would wait for a day before going into the room because of the smell of wine. It's amazing to me but that particular wine smell didn't seem to be so bad."

"Honestly?"

"Yes! I loved him. He was a great grandpa . . . a kid's delight. When I was small I used to go into his room, after he came home drunk. Oh! The smell of liquor! And I'd ask him if I could clean his shoes. He'd always say, "Yes my son!" Then he'd give me ten pennies. In the morning when he sobered up, he'd find his shoes and I'd get another ten pennies."

"You didn't tell him?"

"No!"

"Charl, that's stealing."

"No, it's not, he just gave me the money on two different days!"

"Charl, all the black boys get on the street is ten pennies, come on!"

"It wasn't worth going into that smoky room for ten pennies."

"You're so bad!"

"My Grandpa, I mean Uncle Mick, was a character. I mean . . . his name . . . Mickey Flynn, is as Irish as it comes!" I drank some beer, smiled at June, leaned over and kissed her gently. She responded and I liked that very much. Then with a sparkle in my eye I added, "And in true tradition told me many stories . . ."

"So, tell me an Irish tale, would ya!" said June, pouring a beer, putting one knee to the side and slapping it with her hand.

"To be sure! I'll tell you a good one!" I replied, slapping my knee too. "There was this white miner, a shift boss, my Grandpa said, who only had one eye. He was sitting down on the 6,000-foot level watching the black drill crew drilling off the round. You know, the team goes down at 7 AM, sets up, and drills till twelve. Then the shift boss puts the dynamite in the holes, wires up the whole drill face and everybody evacuates that level. When all levels are clear and all men are on the surface of the mine they blast the rock. The night crew does the mucking up and you're ready to drill again the next day. Anyway, the drilling was the most boring time for this supervisor, and he wanted to go and have coffee with the other supervisors. The trouble was, if he left, the black miners would stop drilling, or be lazy about it. So he thought about this for many days and came up with a plan. One morning after setting up the drills, he called the black crew boss-man over. He put his false eye on the bench and he took his false teeth out and put them next to the eye.

"'Now, let me tell you . . . so you know,' he instructed the black crew boss. 'The eye will see if you are not working and the teeth will tell me if you don't work. So you better work hard or else you are in trouble. Understood?'

"'Yes Baas!' replied the crew boss.

"Well, this worked for some time."

"Is this true?" asked June.

"My grandpa told me. Of course it's true and as true as the Irish!" I replied and then continued. "It worked the first and second time, and he felt confident. He joked with his buddies and they laughed. So every day he set his eye and teeth on the bench and spent a couple of hours with his buddies. It was good for weeks."

"So they just kept drilling?" asked June.

"Yes! But one day after talking to his buddies the crew boss came back to the stope, where the black crew was drilling. As he approached the stope he had a funny feeling something was wrong. The sound was not right. *They couldn't have finished,* he thought. Sure enough, as he entered, the drills started up and the crew hustled back to the usual working position and started working.

"'Bastards!' he yelled. 'You lazy bastards!' The noise of drilling was very loud and his nice words disappeared. He went to the bench, to play the game he had described, and then pretend to name the culprit.

But much to his surprise, there was an inverted coffee cup over his eye and another one over his teeth!"

"Oh, hell, I don't believe it," said June, laughing out loud. She kept giggling as I got up, making funny gestures with the hands, pointing to my eye, my teeth and then my head.

"Minds are marvelous," I said, as I went into the kitchen.

I came back, gave June a beer, and sat down.

"So the doctor said it was fretting. The loss of a loved one, and it happens mostly with older people who have been together a long time."

"What was the second thing that upset your mother?" asked June.

"Well, when my gran died. Whatever she had would naturally go to Uncle Mick but a portion should have gone to her children: my uncle Bill, my aunt Amy, and my mom. I guess my uncle Rob would also have got some because he was Uncle Mick's son. Apparently, after my gran died, everyone didn't want to make a fuss in the family, or have arguments, so they let all the inheritance go to Uncle Mick."

"Oh! My God!" said June.

"You've got it! Perhaps with some understanding that they all split it later when Uncle Mick went. Well, surprise, surprise, now that Uncle Mick has died, legally it all goes to his son."

"Your uncle Rob?" Asked June.

"Yes."

"Oh, I bet you'll get a lot out of him. I've heard a lot of stories about inheritances," said June.

"Well my gran had said at one time that she had shares in First Electric and that there would be enough money for me to go to college, full time. You know how nice that would be. We had talked about that many times. I think it was part of her dream to have a grandson actually graduate."

"That would be marvelous," said June.

"Yes, but not a chance. My uncle Rob has kept it all. Even my mom, who lived with Gran and Uncle Mick, and who looked after them for thirteen years, didn't get anything! Now my mother refuses to speak to him. . . . My dad said I should contest the will. . . . I told him no! It is up to him to share!"

"Oh, those family things are horrible."

"Yes, I know . . . I guess you just have to look after yourself in the end. What you make, you get."

"Some are lucky though Charl," said June. "I think my brother and I are lucky, we have such nice parents."

"Except late on weekday nights!!" I suggested with a smile.

"Oh, yes!"

"I still think it was great of you to sneak out and help push . . . I truly owe you one."

"No you don't."

The talking subsided. We got closer together on the couch, touched each other and kissed and kissed and silently hoped nobody would come home!

CHAPTER 17

✳

Andrew Street V

O N THE HEELS OF Gran's and Uncle Mick's going away for-ever, and Lena leaving, the car belonging to John had to be returned. This would be really hard on me! It meant no trans-port to go and see June. This was a major problem and I felt helpless. The heavy loss of Gran and Uncle Mick had improved my relationship with my mom, until I asked her if I could borrow the car to go and see June. The answer was no. So, a total misunderstanding arose from the fact that her and Mr. Boddington's car sat in the garage every Friday night, plus she had asked me to help fix their car. Mr. Boddington wanted me to machine motor parts, which would save them money. I asked her where was the logic of 'give and get'. I refused to fix the car. My mom was now mad at me!

Family situations kept changing because my mom and Mr. Boddington were spending all their spare time building a house at Henley-on-Klip, close to the Klip River, about twenty miles outside of Johannesburg. I hardly saw them. My brother was totally involved with his family. My uncles and aunts, and cousins Elaine and Alicia, rarely visited. In addition, my dad was wrapped up in his new son, and any-way my dad's ability to take part in interesting conversations was null and void. His discussions were about horse racing, his wife, and his new son. Rarely did he talk about all the other children he had helped bring into the world, or if I had a girlfriend, was fit for soccer, had got an 'A' in my last exam, or whatever. My life schedule provided little time for my so-called new family. I preferred solitude. I was still coming off the loss of Gran and Uncle Mick. So I continued to be heavily involved with my friends despite the many changes going on in the Andrew

Street Mob. Donald knew my situation. I told him I thought things were unfair. He again offered me the use of his car when he didn't need it. Highlights were when Donald said I could use his car.

The Andrew Street Mob had leveled off and stabilized. The Mob was going through a stage of solid girlfriends and was becoming a little more serious about social activities. These events were now planned, and many of the crowd was less interested in the instantaneous, wilder, and more fun type of activities. Couples were emerging. Johnny had met Madge and was very strong in pursuing her socially. They were going together all the time. Madge was a pretty girl with long blond hair, always dressed very well, often the center of attraction and constantly smiling. Billy had suddenly dropped out of chasing all girls and ended up with one girl named Joy, who just happened to live close by in Rosettenville. Joy was also blond but different to Madge in that she was not the center of attention, was quiet, reserved and very nice to everyone. Doc was disappearing from many Andrew Street activities as he and Mary became entranced with each other. Mary was tall, dark haired, had a beautiful smile, and was pretty and friendly. Bobbie from cycling was going out with Joan. Gloria, my dance partner, had met Hobbs, and they were active together. Hobbs had come to one of the parties and showed his interest in Gloria. Hobbs was blond, medium height, nice looking and always willing to join in the fun with the crowd. Tommy, Billy's friend, had met Mavis, a really sharp-looking girl, with a great sense of humor, and they too were a couple. Tommy had also slowed down on the wild side of life. Zoni had met a girl named Maureen, very pleasant, good looking with long brown hair. She had a very warm attitude; they were 'sort of steady'. The crowd never knew if they were going together or not, and the question of the day was, "Did you fight again?" Otto and Grace were a couple. On the girls' side, Thelma, Liz, Denise, and Meridy, plus Joan, Denise, and Elaine from Mondeor, Elizabeth and Joanie were still single-single statuses, although a few of these girls had started to walk the dangerous path of love. On the boys' side, Norman, Trevor, Mac, Viv, Pat, Bobbie, Ron, and I, were still single-single. All others were in the single-couple status...and so the transformation of the Andrew Street Mob continued. Many of the single boys and girls would go out together. I went to the movies with Elizabeth a number of times.

The social activities were really enjoyable as different groups of the Andrew Street Gang turned up in random ways at the socially organized events. Saturdays continued to be scheduled with parties and dances. The parties were mostly house parties. The dances were at special venues and continued to include the Hilton Hotel in Hillbrow, the Worldsview Club in Northcliff, and the Orange Grove Hotel in Rosebank, but we had added the Roadside Rest on the way to Pretoria, and the new Wanderers club in Illovo. Sundays also continued being mostly outdoors and there was almost a non-stop set of picnics at Van Wyk's Rust and Meredale, and trips to the Vaal River. Johnny's family had purchased a place on the Vaal River and the crowd was learning to water ski. Sometimes this was on water skis! But we also skied on a board that was attached directly to the boat, and the skier held onto a short rope attached to the board. The skier's direction was primarily determined by his feet, which were placed on the two edges at the back of the board. Learning to water ski was especially a lot of fun for the non-athletic types, and the joy of athletic types to watch!

One Sunday a big crowd went to the Silverton Hotel on the road to Pretoria. Although the Pretoria area was never considered as a place for entertainment, the reason was simple: if you had lunch you could get alcoholic drinks. No bottle store (liquor outlet) was allowed to sell liquor on Sundays in South Africa, and that was due to Government laws. So everyone went to lunch, piled in at the large table, ordered lots of beer, then went swimming in the hotel pool. The staid Sunday crowd, mostly from Pretoria, was not appreciative of the 'young Joh'burg boys' and girls' antics'. We were asked to not come back again. There was always the feeling that Pretoria was conservative and that Johannesburg was wild and different; this was also a historical fact. No liquor for sale on Sunday anywhere in South Africa except illegally. Fat chance the Government could really win that one.

Sunday night parties varied in size and attendance but many late evenings continued to be enjoyed at Pat's, Johnny's, or my home. Jazz and records of popular songs were the theme. Music, toasted cheese sandwiches and something to drink, lights out, and a crowd of couples, were still the theme. Despite couples being couples we still loved our Sunday nights. If parents were away, the parties were big. Ginge, my friend from work, and a collector of jazz, was not a constant member of the Mob but knew a lot about them from me. He approached me with an idea of having a party at his house.

"At your house? With your parents?" I asked in total surprise.

"No! My parents are going on a 3-week vacation."

"Great—it's on!" I confirmed.

I loved the idea and was delighted to help Ginge put the party together. The Andrew Street Mob eventually ending up having three monster Saturday night parties. The neighbors told Ginge's parents and he was thrown out of the house the next week. We helped Ginge find a place to live.

Johnny's Austin A40, a four-seater, always had a minimum of three couples in between the four doors on Saturday nights, and even more on Sundays. On Saturdays it was tough on the girls when they got dressed up with beautifully ironed dresses and then had to contend with the tight squeeze. We shared the cost of petrol and whatever the night incurred. Whenever possible after a dance or party the group ended up at the Olympia Ice Rink Road House . . . the food was always so good. The routine just never got old.

A big party was planned for my house one Saturday. My mom and Mr. Boddington were gone for the weekend. A big crowd came and the back room was cleared as the Andrew Street Mob brought in food and drinks. The party went on into the morning and at 1 PM a knock on the door produced three guys from the Broadway Hotel.

"Hey! Charl, Howz-it going man! We heard you're having a party." It seemed the three guys, Du Toit, Eddie, and Erasmus, whom we knew from our activities at Rosettenville Corner, had the statement well rehearsed. My feelings sank. These guys spoiled things. They always looked for edges; they worked them into a confrontation and were experts at getting into fights. It was hard to turn them down. The boys and I had drunk with them so many, many times on the corner, as a matter of survival tactics. If you stayed out of their way, you never ended up in a fight. The boys from the 'Corner' had been in some terrible altercations but had never come on to the Andrew Street Mob. We were all from the 'Suburbs'. What could I do?

"Yeah, come in, but no tough stuff."

"No! We promise . . . not us. You know us Charl!" *Yeah,* I thought. Now I knew it had been a mistake to let them in!

The Andrew Street Mob had had many drinks at the Broadway Hotel with these boys from the 'Corner'. We were not a rival gang; we didn't get into their stuff. They would have won in a minute anyway. We had been at many parties where they were. We all had grown up in the Southern Suburbs. They were members of a tough gang. The party went on.

There was a lot of drinking and dancing and talking. Trevor, who was 5'6", about 165 lbs., and always a gentleman, was in the front hallway telling one of the guys from the 'Corner' to leave an Andrew Street girl alone. He kept explaining she didn't want anything to do with him.

"Who is going to make me?"

"Hey! Do us a favor, just leave her alone and everything will be alright." insisted Trevor.

I heard the scuffle and went to the front hallway, but before I could say anything, the guy took a shot at Trevor. Trevor got into the fight and then two others started fighting. Johnny got hit hard which landed him behind one of the doors and he decided to stay there. Trevor was doing all right, forcing the guy to the front door. All the Andrew Street guys got involved, but they were no match for the street fighters. Suddenly the three guys stopped fighting. I had been hit many times and I didn't even land a punch. But I was mad and didn't care. I pushed the one guy aside and yelled, "Get the hell out, you bastards!"

"Hey, sorry, Charl, but this guy started, so!"

"Okay! See you man! Cheers!"

They left. The party atmosphere never returned. People slowly got their stuff together and departed. Johnny, Doc, Billy, Zoni, Trevor, Pat, and I sat talking and having a beer. We consoled ourselves that it didn't really get nasty. We had seen a lot worse. We were pissed at one of our girls for getting herself into such a position. She had actually shown interest at first and that was her mistake. It wasn't a problem now.

"I apologize," said Trevor.

We replied in many ways not to even think about it, as we were proud that he stood up to them.

I finalized the discussion with a philosophical statement. "What can you do, they go to parties to fight."

◆

Maureen, who had been in and out of the crowd, went with me on a friendship date to join our crowd at a Wanderers Club dance. The whole crowd was going and we were the only ones without dates. Maureen was an only child, her parents had looked after her lovingly and obviously had helped in forming her very sweet personality, because they were that way too. I was glad of the chance to go to the dance and Maureen was one of the very few girls that anyone knew who had access to a car. So Maureen picked me up in her Morris Minor and we joined the Mob at the dance. They had reserved a big table as always. We joined in, talking and dancing. I was not in the mood for jovial extremes and sat quietly talking, and dancing occasionally with Maureen. As the night progressed, Trevor's date was dancing with everyone, so he came over and asked if he could dance with Maureen.

"Its up to her!" I replied with a congenial smile.

"Yes," said Maureen. They ended up dancing together all night. This particular event started a romance and eventually caused another pairing in the Andrew Street Mob. I did get a ride home! This was not breaking the unwritten rule in the Andrew St. Mob that when there were two together, no member of the mob would ever try to approach one of them romantically. Maureen and I were just friends. But I was happy because I got to tease Trevor incessantly! Cross dating was on a friendship and fun basis, when girls were single-single. We had done this for many years. It kept the crowd together and nobody was ever left out.

One Saturday, Johnny and Madge, Billy and Joy, and Denise and I went to the Worldsview Club in Johnny's Austin A40. In another car were Trevor and Maureen, Gloria and Hobbs, and Pat with a new date. It was more than an hour-long drive from the Southern Suburbs to Northcliff. Saving for this event and driving the long distance was worth it. We all just loved going to dance at the Worldsview Club. Dan Hill's Jazz Orchestra usually played at the Orange Grove. On this occasion they had formed an all-star band and were playing at the Worldsview Club. We considered them the best that anyone could dance to in Johannesburg, or even South Africa! It was expensive but everyone dug in, that way we usually got home without embarrassment! The Worldsview Club was unique in one way. The guests could take their own bottles of liquor and wine, and the club would provide service for tips, and very expensive mixes for drinks. So a Coca-Cola would cost about ten times that it would cost in the store. In this way it was a bargain, considering we got a very enjoyable atmosphere, an evening of dancing, talking with friends, and looking at all the lights of Johannesburg.

Our crowd looked very sharp. The girls were dressed in beautiful dance, ballroom-like, dresses and the guys in suits. The dancing was especially good as everyone danced with everyone and I got a chance to rock with Gloria. I always loved that very much. We were conservative though, and didn't 'rock out': this was not the place.

Johnny and Madge looked the part and definitely fitted into the club's atmosphere, her being tall, with long blond hair, always immaculately dressed and made up in the style of a model, and Johnny also being tall and slim, and looking in-control, with a friendly debonair look. Trevor and Maureen never stopped talking. The conversation seemed to overlap extensively! It was amazing how they understood what each other had said. Pat was strong and tall, always smiling or laughing, often telling fun stories. Billy looked debonair, and Joy was soft and very friendly. Hobbs and Gloria were a great match, both slim, good looking, alive, and always smiling. Denise, my date, was slim, very pretty, and full of many expressions, interesting topics, and challenging fun talk. She was younger than the main crowd.

I just loved the whole thing, and ventured a few sarcastic fun jokes to get the party going, but my main drive was to get our crowd dancing; it wasn't hard. Trevor very easily took over from me and he entertained with stories, gestures and antics. Pat got in the conversation with his laughter and anecdotes of the true stories that Trevor was telling! Billy would strongly suggest something different and then eventually agree with everyone else. The girls would always have statements that concurred with the guys, but said in such a way that the boys never knew if they agreed or not! Maureen would state something very definitely and be obstinate as to any change . . . but in a very nice way! Nobody continuously held center stage and therefore our getting together was never boring. The laughter never stopped. Serious subjects were strictly taboo; this was all fun stuff. In this group it wasn't necessary to be serious, and besides it wouldn't work. The crowd created an atmosphere that was continually synergistic to fun. This event to me was particularly nice. I had a good time this night, forgetting for a while about the departure of my Gran and Uncle Mick, and the many on-going changes in my life. This dance just confirmed my love for my friends and made me realize how lucky I was; they had in many ways been my saving grace while growing up in Andrew Street. We walked out of the dance at 1 AM . . . the last couples to leave. Johnny and I had gone up to the band and thanked them; we talked for quite a while about American jazz and the artists of the day, and then said our 'goodnights'.

Walking to the car, serious things returned to my mind. Denise had said many times that she had to be home early, by midnight, her father had warned her. Everyone had forgotten, so we took off in a rush, Johnny tearing his car up through Johannesburg, bypassing the

Olympic Ice Rink Roadhouse, up Main Street to Denise's house. I walked her up the driveway and her dad was waiting. He yelled at Denise and came after me with a belt. Billy saw this and yelled at Johnny who started the car. Billy opened the door and yelled, "In here mate!"

I just took off, and in two strides was out of range of the belt; ten more strides and I was in the car as it moved off.

"Damn," I said. "I hope he doesn't hit Denise!"

"You made it," said Billy. Everyone laughed!

"Wanna go to the rink?" I asked hopefully.

"No, we'll go home," said Johnny. He still had to drop off Billy and Joy in Rosettenville, and then he had to take Madge back into Johannesburg city, which was half way back to the Worldsview Club.

Johnny dropped me off.

"Thanks again, friend . . . lovely night . . . Cheers!"

"See you, maybe Tuesday," said Johnny.

"Goodnight," said Madge.

"Bye!"

I went into the house, and to my surprise my mom was in the kitchen.

"Hello Mom."

"Hi! Son!"

"What are you doing up so late?"

"Couldn't sleep."

"I know: you didn't go to Henley this weekend, and now you don't know what to do with yourself," I suggested.

"There is a lot to do here too!"

"I know."

"Want some coffee?"

"Yes," I answered.

"Want something to eat?"

"Fried eggs and toast!" I replied with a smile.

"Alright. Sit down at the table and I'll make it."

"Thanks Mom. We missed the Olympia tonight because of Denise's dad." I related the story and how bad I felt for Denise being treated like that!

"I know her father."

"You do, Mom? How?" this startled me.

"Well, that's not important, but I think he's a silly man!"

"Why is that?'

"Lots of men are silly, sometimes to the point of being stupid, Son!" Then my Mom stopped talking and fixed the 2 AM breakfast. As she put the plate on the table she said, "Don't these men know that if someone really wants to do something they can do it before midnight, or at lunch time!"

"Good point, Mom! Good point!" I agreed. "I just hope he didn't hit Denise, I would feel terrible if he did."

"Better call her tomorrow."

"No, you call, Mom, and ask to speak to her. If I call and he answers, he'll know it's me and he'll get mad again."

"No, just hang up," suggested my Mom

We changed the subject as we sat and talked about many things. Gran and Uncle Mick, her dislike of her stepbrother, Robbie, for doing what he did. She talked about the long struggle during the war, how she had had no choice but to send Yvonne and Bazil to boarding school, also her many years at Publix as a bookkeeper. She loved her brother Bill and all the family in Vryburg. She mentioned the good times she had always had with her sister Amy. I guessed my mom was now really off-loading her stories onto me. I welcomed it. She also talked about how much she loved being a grandmother, but not to tell anybody that she was a grandmother! Mom told me of all her struggles and the few rewards but she said she was now happy, especially with the facts that Yvonne and Bazil were married and comfortable. She got up and kissed me with two hands on my cheeks.

"You, Son! Have to continue to study. It will pay off! Believe me, it will pay off. I am very proud of what you have done, you must keep going!"

I ate the breakfast thinking this was so nice, talking to my mom; we didn't do that very often.

"I am transferring the title of a plot of land at Klip River to your name."

"Truly, Mom?"

"Yes, Son! There's also a plot for Yvonne and one for Bazil."

"Thanks, I'll have to go see it."

"Come down one weekend."

"I will," I promised. We sat quietly for a while then my mom turned her face toward me.

"When are you going to England?" she asked.

I was very surprised. "Wow, what a question," I replied. Mom had suggested this before, about going to see her friends over there.

"You'll be finished with your apprenticeship soon, and then after you're finished with school, you could go over and see something different," my mom suggested.

What was the motive? I wondered. The conversation continued on the pros and cons of the adventure, definitely intriguing to me. I would rather see a place than read about it.

"I want you to go and see my friends! . . . We have been writing since the war ended! . . . They will help guide you. You don't want to get married yet, Son! I see your crowd is changing . . . and very fast. You may change with them and end up with kids and dogs too soon. Then you won't see anything new."

"I won't. I don't have enough money!" I confirmed.

"Neither do all your friends, and they are going ahead! And they are going to do it soon! . . . Listen to what I say!! . . . I'm going to bed, Son!" She was smiling.

"Thanks for the food. I'll clean up."

I stood up and hugged her: unusual! She returned the hug for longer than I expected.

"Goodnight."

It was almost 4 AM. I went to bed wondering where that thunderbolt came from! Afterwards I had a thought that my mom had purposely stayed up to talk to me alone!

I liked talking to my mom without anybody else around. We never got a chance; there was always somebody around. Dinner had changed from having Gran and Uncle Mick, and Yvonne and Bazil at the table. Now there were the two Boddingtons, Mom and I. The conversation was dominated by information about the Boddingtons's five sons and the Henley-on-Klip house. Mom had bought about five lots around their house. I understood the motive. But the conversation with Mom this morning was warm, and with no confrontation on anything. I admitted to myself that even though most of the time it had been my gran bringing me up, my mom had always been there. Guiding me, spanking me, and boasting about me when I was introduced to her friends. She mostly loved Yvonne though; there was a true bond: mother and daughter. Even though Yvonne had been gone for a long time, they were always in touch. I also loved the way my mom broke the social rules. She drank brandy and talked politics, absolutely the wrong thing to do in South Africa, especially when amongst men! She had a lot of opinions about the government: its leaders and its programs. They were not complimentary. I can recall her giving her opinion one day and the men in the family all saying in different ways, "Maude, you're wrong."

My mom had replied, "And you men are stupid! You can't even see the other side! Never mind discuss it!"

One time she was asked why, if she was politically opinionated and liked to discuss politics with men, then why couldn't she also drink beer and smoke cigars. More specifically, why did she drink expensive brandy? A silly laugh had followed the challenging question.

"It's simple," was her reply, "anyone can follow the crowd, anyone can drink beer, and anyone can smell like burned tobacco, but learning to drink brandy takes time. A person has to learn to savor the taste, and so drinking brandy is an acquired taste, just like being able to be political." My mom got in trouble for that, but she didn't care. She was very smart. I admired that very, very much. But why she was suggesting England was not clear. *I'd have to find out.*

◆

Two events were coming up soon, around Christmas. I would be 'coming out of my time', an expression used for an apprentice's final day and being converted overnight to a journeyman. It was something to celebrate, because the salary was also doubled overnight. It was a major event in the Blue Collar World, when you became a professional. And, for our Mob, it was so important to have achieved your parents' desires. The first week in December 1954, I would receive my first paycheck as a journeyman. It was traditional that the apprentices spend it on the journeyman who taught him his trade. In my case it would be many journeymen.

Nearly all my friends in the Andrew Street Mob had already gone through this ceremony. They had in all respects honored their parents' wishes and made them very happy. Not one person had failed to complete their apprenticeship.

Main Reef Engineering organized a lunch, and everyone from work was there. The 'old man' Mr. Funkey, John, his son, the staff, and all the workmen from the shop jammed around as everyone roasted me. Individually they stood up and added their comments . . . my mistakes, my long times for machining even the simplest of shafts, my late arrivals at work . . . especially Mondays, my catching my finger in the gear shaper, my disregard for the South African Army, my terrible playing of soccer on any field, and my very bad game at Rand Stadium. Worst of all, was my short shorts, my bad jokes and my arriving late from the South Coast on a Monday morning and nearly falling asleep at the lathe. Also, they added, I was not good looking enough to meet girls and would probably be a bachelor for life . . . but that was mainly because I loved that dreadful American music. Ginge objected to that but was drowned out. They reminded me of nearly everything I did wrong as an apprentice. However, they added that I did survive, and now I was in the big money bracket. Because of that, Sandy, Laubscher, and Mr. Warren would take me for drinks after work, just to make sure I had no money left from my paycheck. The co-workers all cheered, clapped their hands and went back to work.

My three buddies, co-workers and commuters later in the afternoon took me to a bar on the way home from work. The more drinks I bought, the better machinist I had become, the better soccer player, the better draftsman, the nicer person! Till we all went home. Sandy dropped me off at the gate of 65.

Before falling asleep I thought how lucky I was. It had been a wonderful day and night. After lunch, I had thanked everyone individually for my training and for the help. I had also thanked the black men whom I had worked with; they had helped me as well. On that thought, my serious brain calculated that I had now doubled my wages, and would take home four times as much as any one of them, plus they had wives and children. My youth set that aside and I enjoyed my final moments of awareness before going to sleep, even knowing I had not a single penny in my pocket and would not have one till next pay day. I also believed I probably owed Sandy more than money for all the expertise and friendship and guidance given to me over four years. I had matured through my teenage years with his guidance. In fact Sandy, Laubscher, and Mr. Warren had taught me many, many things about work and life. I'd had four years of commuting from Kenilworth, Southern Suburbs, to Industria, some thirty miles across town. I'd survived four years of night school, and now I worked halftime as a machinist, and halftime as a draftsman and a designer on Mr. Funkey's new fourteen-ton locomotive. I felt proud. Then I remembered Picannin's comment about me being a big Baas and he would have to dress better! My head was swirling on the pillow. My last thoughts were: *Tomorrow is another day!*

◆

The Xmas holidays were coming up fast and I wanted to get out of Johannesburg and go to the coast. Norman had mentioned going but he wasn't sure. He had bought a 1952 MG-TD, a two-seater sports car: the ultimate dream of every young person that I had talked to about it. Norman's half-ton truck had taken the Andrew St. Mob everywhere. It was a legend and if only it was possible for a truck to have kept a diary, it would have been a best seller.

One night, Norman and I had got together to replace the clutch in the M.G. We had the car jacked up and had taken out the old clutch. The new clutch was in our hands.

"Which way does it go in?" asked Norman.

"Don't know," I answered. "It's not symmetrical: one side of the hub is longer than the other."

We looked at the old one, crawled under the car, and looked at the spline and the flywheel. We could not determine how it went in, long side first or short side.

"Let's wait until tomorrow," said Norman.

"No, I can't get time off work, and I have exams," I replied.

"Ah, let's just try it this way," I suggested. There was no description on British car part boxes. No manuals. We had no clue looking at the thing, even measuring the shafts and clearances.

"Go for it, Man!" said Norman.

We put the clutch in and the gearbox and tightened everything; it took over an hour. We tested the clutch. It didn't work!

"Shit! These damn British cars . . . they don't care once the car is sold!" It was 9 PM.

"We need to fix it, if we're going to go to Margate," said Norman.

"Are we going to go?" I asked in a high-pitched voice . . . due to my excitement.

"Yes, let's go!"

"Let's put the clutch in the other way then," I said, inspired. "It can only go in two ways . . . except!"

"Except what?" asked Norman.

"They gave us the wrong clutch!!"

"Never happens!" confirmed Norman.

"Now?"

"Yes!"

We decided to pull it apart and complete the installation. It was midnight when we finished and finally cleaned up the garage. The road test of the clutch was successful! We were so glad, as we disappeared into the night and went to bed.

The drive down to Durban was now so familiar, but in a car like the MG it was a different dream taking place. The MG had been the winner of many races, having a high-revving four-cylinder compact machine of the old style with disc wheels instead of spokes; very sturdy. It was capable of turning a corner at high speed and there were hundreds of those on the way to Margate.

Going through the hills, on a two-lane winding highway, from the Drakensburg through Pietermaritzburg and into Durban, was as thrilling as anyone could imagine. The roar out of the tail pipe as you downshifted brought purple pimples to your skin. Then the steady purr while cruising along the coast road and into Margate. This car definitely attracted girls, I mused. Within days Norman and I had met quite a few ladies. I knew it wasn't me! Viv had turned up from the suburbs and there was a confirmation that Doc and Mary, and Billy and Joy were coming down from Johannesburg.

Norman and I had a great time on the beach, and driving to Blue Lagoon, four-up in the car. I wore a blue beret to celebrate the venture. The French look hardly fitted my personality, even though half my family was Huguenot stock. Norm, Viv, the girls, and I went dancing at the Faerie Glen, a restaurant-nightclub on the river running into Margate. The restaurant was located about 3 miles from the beach. It was unique, with a low dance floor surrounded by a gently-rising ramp. The ramp had dinner tables all the way up. People eating dinner on the ramp could look down at the dance floor and the dinner tables around the dance floor. A further unusual aspect was that the band was on an island on the water twenty feet from the dance floor. A circular door system opened wide enough to see almost the whole water glen. On the far side of the glen was subtropical growth. If you swam over to the other side you couldn't get out of the water, the growth was so thick.

"We must come here for Xmas or New Year's," said one of the girls.

"I'm going back to Johannesburg," said Norman.

"No," cried out the girls, but despite their pleading to stay, Norman stood fast on his decision. I knew the reason. Norman's father had died recently and his mother would not enjoy Xmas and New Year alone. Also, a tradition in most Dutch and Afrikaans families was that the eldest son, upon the death of the father, not only became head-of-the-household in all matters, but was responsible for surviving members of the family, especially the mother. I would stay in Margate.

The next few days before Norman left were just as great as the other days. We bonded in our friendship with Viv and the group of girls. At one of the last dances together, I saw this beautiful girl amongst other girls at a table. I timed my move well and asked her to dance.

"I would like that!"

We danced and talked for a short time because she had to leave. I got the hotel number an'. . 'ed her for a beach date. She agreed. Her name was Jackie.

I told Norman the story. He said that he had seen her, and agreed with my compliments.

"She might go on the New Year's Eve date," suggested Norman.

"That is a nice idea! Norman! I thank you for that!"

"Do you want to go home for Xmas?" asked Norman

"No," I replied, "nobody is there!"

"Any reason?"

"I haven't been home for Xmas for years. I wouldn't know what to do, especially without my Gran and Uncle Mick. Also some of the crowd is down here. Some are going out. No, I think I'll stay . . .will you be all right, Norman, because I came down with you, and I'll go home with you if you want?"

"No! You stay and have fun. I have to be with the family," said Norman. "Will you be able to get home?"

"Yes! I'll be alright." I didn't have a clue as to how!

"Alles van die beste my vriend! (All the best, my friend)" said Norman.

Norman took off to Johannesburg. I was somewhat sad about that; we had been having a good time. I decided, however, to go and see if I could find Jackie. As I crossed the street I saw her with Tommy. I knew him. Tommy was 'Mr. Southern Suburbs'. A strong, tall, good-looking weight lifter: he was an acquaintance through some of my Southern Suburbs friends. Tommy, Horace and his brother Glen were part of the weight lifters' set in the Southern Suburbs. I decided not to get into a conversation with them and took off to find Doc and Billy.

Doc and Mary, and Billy and Joy were on the beach. I sat down and told them Norman's story.

"We've got tickets for New Year's at the Palm Grove. We got them from the hotel. Why don't you come with us?"

"I will. I don't have a date but I will come," I replied.

"Good! Don't worry, you still have seven days to get one," suggested Billy.

My good friends sat and talked about getting married and houses and kids all afternoon. I listened in astonishment. I took a break every now and then and went into the surf. We had never talked about these subjects before. What was happening? Was my mom right?

About two days later I got up the courage to go dig out Jackie. I was successful and we went to the beach. My 'natural luck' had Tommy walk by with his friends. He saw us and waved.

"Hullo! Jackie! . . . Hullo! Charl! So you're down here!"

"Yes!"

I decided not to touch the scene with a ten-foot-pole. I didn't know if he and Jackie were going out down here. We spent most of the time on the beach and then decided to leave. As we walked back to the hotel at dusk Jackie suggested some hamburgers and french fries. I agreed readily. I was glad.

About 9 o'clock we walked back to her hotel and I asked her if she'd be in Margate over New Year's.

"Oh, yes, I want to go to the New Year's dance. They really get dressed up."

"Do you have a date?" I plunged into the scene.

"No, but I'm with my friends."

"Would you go with me?"

"Are you sure?" asked Jackie.

"Yes, I'm absolutely sure."

"Yes, I'd love to Charl!"

Wow! Good-looking women had such a tremendous effect on my emotions. To me this was perfect; New Year's Eve with friends and a fun, very attractive girl.

We talked for an hour. We'd go with Billy and Joy and Doc and Mary. Everything was set. I took off to my room happy as could be. The next day I told everyone and the date was set.

◆

On New Year's Eve Jackie was waiting for me. I walked into her hotel. She looked terrific. I found out later that she was, in real life, a model.

We joined the crowd and went through the introductions. We had just the most wonderful time dancing all night. Billy and Doc were impressed, so were their girlfriends. I loved this group. I felt super-good; New Year's was brought in with a kiss. We walked the beach in our good shoes and I reluctantly took Jackie back to her hotel at about 4 AM. I walked home along the main street of Margate thinking about the offer she'd made. Her boss wanted someone to escort two models around South Africa. The job was to arrange transport, carry luggage, be present at the presentations of the models, keep the guys away and be a chaperone. Jackie was one of the models. I had just finished my apprenticeship contract and I needed desperately to earn some good money. So if I took the job it would have to pay good money, that was possible, but to find time to study would not be possible!

"What a job, though . . . I will definitely think about it," I said out loud. In the background I could hear the sound of waves hitting the beach. Margate was a dream place and paradise of fun to me.

After New Year's Day, Margate dies within a week. Major South African vacations drift to an end. Hundreds of people head back to Johannesburg and the Witwatersrand cities. Jackie, her girlfriends, and Doc and Billy and their girls took off early in the day. Viv had gone back with his friends. I had arranged to return with three guys that I met over the vacation in Margate, because all my friends' cars were full. I could definitely have got a ride with Billy and Doc but that would have meant five in a four-seat car, and ten hours was a long time.

I turned up at the meeting place in Margate at 6 AM. The three guys never showed. So after phoning without response, I got on the highway with my bag. The trouble was I had very little cash in my pocket. I stood with my thumb up for an hour. Finally, a commercial salesman, Jim, picked me up. He was only going to Durban, with three stops in between. So at Scottburgh he dropped me off and went to his first destination. I got out and hitched but no cars stopped. Then Jim came out the side road and picked me up again. He did this again in Amanzimtoti. We were now on our way to Durban. The conversations had covered both our lives to date. We laughed and expanded our philosophies about life!

"I'll take you to the north of Durban and put you on the Johannesburg road," offered Jim.

"Thank you Jim, but you don't have to do that."

"Oh! I know, but you still have to get back to Joh'burg."

"Thanks, thanks a lot, Jim! Our conversations have been really interesting for me."

We came to a stop. Jim got out the car and came around to my side. As I got out of the van, he stuck some money in my hand. I was amazed!

"I know you haven't eaten at all. Get a meal and get home safe, okay?"

"Okay! Wow! Thanks! You mean to do this?"

"Yes! You're a good chap! Enjoy it!"

"Please give me your card, Jim." He did that and then drove off.

I looked at the card. 'The Elephant Trading Company' was in nice blue letters on Jim's card. I vowed I would never forget.

Standing on the roadside for an hour again. A car stopped with a family going to Johannesburg. They were very nice and very religious.

"We're on our way to see Billy Graham," said the father. "Do you know him?"

"Yes! Sir! He's the American Evangelist," I replied. Then I sat back in the seat knowing that for eight hours I would be subjected to that subject. It was a long ride with over-pleasant conversation. I could not get over the world that I had been in, over the past two weeks. They dropped me off at the Johannesburg bus station and I caught a bus to the Southern Suburbs at 5:45 PM. Everyone was going home from work.

This was the end of the traditional South African holiday period. The first and second weeks of January had thousands upon thousands of South Africans going back to work to start another year. It was the middle of summer and after a couple of days, I finally met up with Johnny and Trevor and told them the story. I told my mother and I told Norman.

◆

Doc's stag party started in a house and then went to a bar and into downtown Johannesburg. The twenty or so friends and close mates wanted to make sure that one of the early Andrew Street Mob would dearly pay for breaking the ice and deciding to get married. So as the evening progressed Doc got drunker, and when he quieted down a little, the crowd knew he was on his way. Doc always laughed whenever a story was told; he was always upbeat. In one way he set the tone of the Andrew Street Mob by being positive. Always thinking of something to do. Restless was an insufficient word to describe his drive. Maybe it was his input that caused this group of friends never to walk in a straight line to do something, but to complete the event in a different way. The walk always had to be different with the Andrew Street Mob. It had to be a challenge; it had to involve more than a straightforward solution. You didn't just go to the movies, it had to involve something else . . . there had to be a party, there had to be a way that changed the normal routine . . . it just had to be different each time. So as Doc got drunk the plan evolved. The boys took Doc from the bar in Johannesburg at 10 PM. We had secured some rope from the bartender and walked Doc about two blocks to the Coliseum Theatre. We tied him to one of the lamps. We placed him cross-legged, facing the theater entrance, about twenty feet from the ticket booth. Then we placed a hat upside down in front of him and a sign in front of the hat, which read:

"I AM GETTING MARRIED TOMORROW . . . PLEASE HELP WITH YOUR CONTRIBUTION."

The set-up was complete, and not five minutes later the crowd came out the theater. The idea worked. Patrons started to mull around and the shillings started to fall into the hat; some gave pennies. The Andrew Street Mob stood up against the wall and occasionally one of them prodded the crowd by walking up to the hat, throwing a coin in, and passing a few remarks such as "Stupid", or "Ding-a-Ling". The people that saw Doc, laughed, stood back and looked around, then walked away talking. Nobody recognized him, which was a pity, because that would have completed the plan. We finally untied Doc, took him for another drink and then dragged him home to number 59 Andrew Street.

◆

Zoni moved out from Mimi's and into a flat for Maureen and himself. Zoni threw a stag party, which was a good reason to bring a lot of the crowd together. It always seemed that the tradition at these parties was to get absolutely drunk and talk about everything. Occasionally there was a stripper, but the parties became so bad that most of the strippers left early. Tommy got very drunk and we felt enclosed in Zoni's small flat; standing on the bed was not fun. So the crowd decided to go to the Olympia Ice Rink Roadhouse. Pat's Opel car had mudguards (fenders), and the crowd tied Tommy to the one mudguard with ropes. Two of us stood on the running boards, four got in the car and Pat drove off to the roadhouse. We were followed by three other cars. The drive was down Main Street, past the Broadway Hotel and Rosettenville Corner, to get the maximum exposure. The people watching this event stared and cheered. Occasionally some of them cringed at the horn blowing of all the cars. We passed the Rand Stadium and finally arrived at the Olympia Roadhouse. The crowd ordered their steak sandwiches and coffee while Tommy just lay on the mudguard. The roadhouse crowd was fascinated. The boys were amazed that no cops had seen us.

I had a strong feeling that we would be friends for life. Our friendship had come together from a street, and a love of having fun. We had survived our apprenticeships, which made our parents happy and relieved that they had given us a start in life. The ladies in our lives had become very important and the pathways of life were changing. Marriage was prominent. A large portion of the crowd was on their way and a second group was not far behind. I was definitely way behind, even though I had had thoughts about June. But I didn't know if we were ready for that challenge. There were never any discussions. So! Despite the changing shape of our lives, it seemed we could still get together and make something happen and that was cause for celebration. However, life was becoming very disconcerting for me.

CHAPTER 18

❋

Sandy

I
T WAS 7 AM Monday morning. I was standing on the corner of Main Street and Andrew Street. I had waited almost an hour for Sandy. This had never happened before. Sandy was incredibly reliable. The sun was already up and my ride was 45 minutes late. There was no phone nearby so I caught the bus into town. A walk across town took me to the bus that went to Industria. I was very late for work.

I changed and went into the shop. Laubscher was not there, but Mr. Warren, who was last to be picked up on our ride to work, was at the drilling machine working away. I walked over to him.

"Mr. Warren! Do you know what happened to Sandy this morning?"

"Yes! Son!" His voice broke up. He slowed down his machine, came over to me and put his hand on my shoulder. Instinctively, I felt that something was wrong . . . terribly wrong! I instantly looked around and noticed most people in the shop with their heads down just working away. There was an eerie quiet, suspended, in this loud machine and fabrication shop. Mr. Warren shut off his machine and walked me out of the shop. I didn't like this. We walked to where it was quiet.

"Sandy was killed over the weekend," he said in a sad, quiet voice. He looked into the ground. I knew there were tears on his face.

"My God!" came out of my mouth, as a monstrous hollow feeling went through my body in a wave. "No!" . . . I found my hands on my face. A hundred thoughts went screaming through my head, meaning nothing! I did not want to believe these words. But they came from Mr. Warren. It was true. Slowly, a profound thought crept into the mind mess. *How is it possible, we were laughing so hard on Friday at some silly joke . . . now Sandy is gone! . . . And forever!*

"It happened late Friday night," said Mr. Warren, hardly capable of holding back the water in his eyes. "He and Laubscher were going fishing, Son. On the way to the Vaal River." Mr. Warren paused for quite a while. I was frozen. "Sandy had his arm out the window, the way he always drove. A truck coming from the other direction sideswiped them. The truck severed his arm!"

"Oh! God!" came out again. "His wife? . . . How is she?" The image was not tolerable. I blanked it out.

"We don't know! Laubscher called John and told him the story. Laubscher is not coming to work," continued Mr. Warren.

"He's all right?"

"Yes, he got scratched up badly in the car crash, but he's okay."

I looked at Mr. Warren, there were tears on his cheeks. My eyes had started to water. The hollow feeling remained at full force.

"I'm sorry to bring you the news!" said Mr. Warren in broken tones.

We walked slowly back into the shop.

It was a long day. Very quiet up in the lunchroom. Most people ate their sandwiches and left. Sandy's machine stood quiet all day. A reminder that there was one noise missing. No chips were flying. No activity around the machine, such as parts that would normally come and go. It was amazing how the eyes of everyone looked over to the machine at different times. Everyone was relieved at 4:45 PM. This would allow recovery on an individual basis. I went to class and absorbed nothing. I left early and went home on the bus. There were just lights streaming by, no images, as the bus went to the Southern Suburbs. I couldn't think of anything!

◆

John the boss's son talked to me. He said I had been chosen to operate Sandy's machine.

I stood on the wooden platform of my mentor and sharpened the tools, loaded the chuck, set everything in place, started the machine, turned the hand wheels, and put out the parts. It took over a month before I felt near normal. Every morning it felt strange to walk to the machine and stand on the platform. The screaming machine putting out parts was, to some degree, a contribution to the man who had done it better than anyone ever had . . . I couldn't picture it any other way.

It was always a total relief to go up to the design office or to go off to college on Friday morning. The feelings inside lasted a long time.

One Thursday, John came over and told me that one of his clients had a copper mine near Warmbaths in the Northern Transvaal. Main Reef Engineering had sold him a hoist, and after installation it had jammed. They needed it repaired desperately, to pull out the ore, deliver it and meet a promised payday.

"They don't know the what the problem is. So we have to go up early Saturday," said John.

"I have a date and tickets to a big dance Saturday night," I explained, hoping to get out of this work. "Will we be back in time?"

"Yes, I'll make sure we will," said John. I had forgotten about the soccer game. It was not an important one, and I felt I couldn't add that too; this company had been so good to me.

Saturday morning at 6 AM I caught the bus into Johannesburg. John picked me up and we hit the road north towards Warmbaths. Just before getting there, John turned off the main highway and onto a sand road. Warmbaths was a town, north of Johannesburg. It was known for mineral spas and therapy for arthritis and a host of related ailments. Mostly old people vacationed there. It was a small town with lots of hotels and an old blockhouse. It was on the main road from Johannesburg that went through Pretoria, Nylstroom, Pietersburg and Louis Trichardt, directly north of Johannesburg and about 160 miles away.

The car hit bottom many times. It was now raining heavily as we approached the mine. The mining setup was truly small, a twenty-five foot high wooden headgear and a hole in the ground with rail tracks. It was essentially a starter hole, with a hoist, rails, coco-pans, dirt, timber, an electrical box, and a galvanized tin shack. It was called a mine, but more closely resembling a digging.

Mr. van Reenen, a farm owner, had done some drilling and found a strong copper vein 50 feet down. He didn't trust anybody, didn't want fly-by-night investors, and had decided to do the first stages by himself.

"Mr. van Reenen, this is Charl," said John.

"Goeie môre (Good morning)."

"Goeie môre, Meneer (Sir)."

The problem was explained. I was given two black helpers and a toolbox. I had brought my own toolbox, and the three of us disassembled the hoist. It started to rain harder and it reminded me of the fence repair with Southey on Aunt Eileen's farm. The hoist was out in the open. I found the problem. The clutch plate housing had the wrong size shoulder. It was too big and didn't clear the engagement plate properly. This caused the clutch to slip, especially while under load. I went to the shack where John and Mr. van Reenen were sitting. I explained the problem.

"It has to be machined," I said.

"The nearest place is in Warmbaths." He paused for a long time. "I will have to call Dirk at home to come and machine the plate," said Mr. van Reenen. "I certainly hope he is there."

I knew this delay would mess up Saturday night completely. It was already close to noon. I couldn't afford the time. My brain worked furiously, thinking of solutions. John and Mr. van Reenen discussed the trip, the phone call, and everything else. It was 15 minutes before they decided on the course of action. I couldn't see the dance in my mind. I had made a special date with Coralie. We had met just a few weeks ago. Also, I didn't want to miss the dance in Johannesburg with all my friends. This dance was one of the special ones, organized in a hall, with a band and everything, and where we would all get dressed up. How would I get to the dance if we left late? Johnny was going to give us a ride. He'd be gone by 7 PM. This was a serious situation!

"I'll chisel it off!" I exclaimed, totally surprised by my own statement. "Because if we machine the clutch plate rim size, the rivets holding the plate will end up too close to the edge of the plate. They may tear off and mess up everything. If we chisel the rim off, the clutch will work just fine! It'll take a little more than an hour. Then we'll send up a new part on Monday. I'll show the boys now how to put it back together, or I'll come up and install it myself."

"You'll get the clearance by chiseling?"

"Yes!"

"All right, that will be good," said Mr. van Reenen.

After half an hour, I had got half way round a 16″ diameter hub, chiseling away about a 1/4″ chamfer off the hub. It was still raining. The two black boys stood and watched, and helped whenever they could. They both had been given a chance to chisel, but were too slow. They also didn't understand the reason to hurry! There was only one chisel. It was after 1 PM when I finished chiseling and smoothing the edges with a file. The assembly of hoist with instruction took only a half an hour. I didn't know if the boys had learnt anything about the assembly, but I didn't care. I could come back and do it if necessary. I went back to the shack.

"It's ready to test."

"Regtig (Really)!!" exclaimed Mr. van Reenen, looking very surprised at the quick outcome.

We put the fuse back in the motor control, reactivated the power and switched on the hoist. The drum rotated, the clutch engaged, and the coco-pan full of rocks moved. It worked! All of us clapped and yelled! I was so happy it had worked.

"Kom hier, my vriend (Come here, my friend)."

Mr. van Reenen put his arm around me and led me into the shack.

"I have something good for you." He took a can off the fire, added a little water, and handed me a hot cup of coffee.

"Yes! Just the thing!" I said, realizing I hadn't had any lunch. I took a large mouthful. I was thirsty as well. "Oh my God!" I shouted. The coffee was heavily laced with brandy. It was good. "Thank you! Sir, it tastes damn good!"

"It better! It's a very good brandy, my friend," said Mr. van Reenen with a wonderful smile. He reminded me of the farmer in Potchefstroom who had helped us with the car when Rudy had fallen asleep and driven into the ditch. I liked Mr. van Reenen.

We tested everything again, and then went through the instructions to reassemble. Mr. van Reenen was very happy. "What a smart chap," he said with his best English accent. John and I smiled.

"I know, Mr. van Reenen, why he worked so hard," said John. "He has a date tonight!"

"Ag! Man! Those days were so much fun," reminisced Mr. van Reenen. "In any case, I appreciate you coming all this way and helping us. Now have a safe trip home."

"Dankie Meneer van Reenen, vir die lekker koffie! Totsiens! (Thanks Mr. van Reenen, for the very nice coffee! Goodbye!)"

"Totsiens, Charl!"

It was now 2.15 PM. John and I loaded up and took off. Next stop Pretoria. John had agreed to stop in Pretoria, so I could make some phone calls and grab a sandwich, and then we'd drive like hell to Johannesburg. We made good time to Pretoria and were there at 3:45 PM. I called Coralie, told her I would be late, and that I didn't know how we would get to the dance. I told her the story and added that I still had to change. She lived in the Southern Suburbs, only a few blocks away from Andrew Street. The dance was in the downtown area of Johannesburg City. John lived in the northern suburbs, closer to Pretoria than 65 Andrew Street by half an hour. She told me not to worry about being late, that we could catch a bus, but to please shower at least! I liked that very much, sarcasm or not: the fact that she would take the bus to the dance impressed me no end.

"Really nice of you, Coralie!" I said and hung up.

To my surprise, John took the short-cut road to the northern suburbs after leaving Pretoria.

"John . . . are you going home first?" I asked.

"You can take the car. Just bring it back in the morning," suggested John.

"Wow! Are you sure?"

"Yes, it's okay."

"Thank you! Thank you!" I didn't know how to be this glad.

The car was a two-door maroon 1947 Cadillac. Unbelievable looks and so classy. I just sat back in the seat and started dreaming of the night to come. Just to see the surprise on everyone's face. I just couldn't believe my luck. This was a dream movie being played in real life. I hadn't done anything like this ever! It was impossible to imagine I would ever have been so lucky to do something like this! I loved it.

The dream became reality as I picked up Coralie. I drove to Johannesburg. She was very excited at the car.

"I feel like an American movie star with a beautiful date!"

"You look the part, Charl!"

We laughed. I was extra careful and drove slowly just because of the 'dream aspects' of this night out in Johannesburg. The dance required men to dress in tuxedos, but Donald hadn't left his tux out for me. He had said he might use it himself. So I was dressed in my one and only dark suit. Coralie looked gorgeous in her evening gown. She was a redhead with some blonde and was wearing just enough make-up. Her smile was as nice as her personality, warm and affectionate. Coralie walked with a bounce. In my eyes, she was such a beautiful girl.

I found a parking spot right outside the entrance, somebody had left early: just my luck for the day. We went in to the dance and joined Johnny and the Andrew Street Mob. I introduced Coralie to the crowd. She was instantly approved. I could tell. We sat down at the table and then danced as much as possible. During the dances I realized how much I loved this lifestyle. I loved dancing, pretty ladies, talking while dancing, being nicely dressed, being among friends and having music that moved my heart and soul and stirred my feet to movement. *Yes it's basically American style, but Europeans do this as well and our South African group get an enormous amount of pleasure playing the part,* I thought. *The picture of what I wanted to do in the future was coming clear. If I could know a couple of girlfriends, have a car and some money, and could do this type of thing with friends, I would be very happy. I definitely was a 'city boy'. No way could I live the life of Mr. van Reenen . . . that was too isolated.*

Throughout the evening I primed my friends for the exit. When the dance ended, the Mob walked out together, and of course I headed for the Cadillac. They looked at the car in disbelief, thinking I was up to my usual clown antics as I got in the car. But when the key started the car, the Oohs! and Aahs! Gave great pleasure to Coralie and me. This was one of the big things missing in my life: a car!

Coralie and I very naturally went to the Olympia Roadhouse. I had had a special time and knew from our close dancing that we would probably kiss passionately. But I wasn't completely sure! We stopped at her home. We sat and kissed, but eventually, time was pushing 3 AM, and finally the long day took its toll. I said goodnight, drove to Andrew Street and went to bed. As I lay between the sheets, I thought how totally attractive Coralie was, and what an evening it had been! I was sure lucky sometimes!

Reality crept back into its ugly movie the next day. It was back to the hard way, as I drove the car to the northern suburbs, knowing I would have to use public transport to get home.

"Glad you had a good time, you deserved it," said John.

I thanked John over coffee, and then caught two empty busses back to Andrew Street.

◆

The Apprenticeship Act in South Africa had a rule that an apprentice, after finishing his contract, must leave the company within six months after becoming a journeyman. I left Main Reef Engineering with many, many sad good-byes, saying I would like to come back. I shook hands with everyone, thanking them sincerely for all I had learned. My job was guaranteed if I returned. I was confident, based on all I had learned, that I would do well. I silently thanked all the white journeymen and black men that had helped me throughout the years. There was also John, the boss, who had trained and guided my progress, and his dad, Mr. Funkey, who had given me a number of major breaks with my studies. But Sandy, most of all, was the mentor and guide of this young apprentice, in work, in life, and in inspiration. He had managed to make me add polish to the final products that I produced in my craft, and had then turned around and guided me in the same manner towards my attitude in life: a good finish, sincerity and laughter. He fostered my soccer craft almost every week. What a person! I knew I would see Ginge again, so leaving him was not emotional. Mr. Warren looked at me . . . I thought he had a tear in his eye. He wished me the best of luck. Joseph and I just stood apart and looked at each other—a thousand thoughts of all the hours of his help---we shook hands and bowed our heads to each other. I would truly miss Picannin and his humor. He had kept my head from going completely serious at work. His expressions and animation was just so unique. He never left your presence without you feeling on the upbeat. His stories left you laughing inside till it hurt. I said goodbye to all the boys in the shop, individually. Finally, Laubscher wanted to walk me out the gate, and so he did. We strolled in silence down the side of the shop . . . tears came to my eyes as I waved to those standing at the big double-doors. I had gone through them a hundred times or more. Laubscher put his hand on my shoulder.

"All I can say is thank you, Charl for being such a good friend to Sandy and me. We enjoyed your company very much. You made life fun and interesting for us both. You must come and see us . . . okay!"

"I will for sure!"

It seemed to be a sad day that was not necessary to have taken place.

◆

I got a job with Gardner-Denver on the south side of Johannesburg. I had again negotiated time off for school. I had made sure it was an American company. I had a major aversion to English and South African companies because of their rigid manner of business, plus the stories I had heard about low-paying jobs. This machine shop paid a basic salary plus a piecework bonus. I made a lot of money because I was fast. I continued my schoolwork. I started to retire the debts I had.

I met two people: a Dutchman, Gert, from Holland, who taught me about the fine points in sharpening cutting tools, and a German,

Heinz, who was always semi-depressed. Gert was always very busy and did not converse with many people. Heinz, although being gloomy, took a liking to me and talked freely. When I asked why he had come to South Africa, he replied that his story was sad and he hadn't told it to too many people. It seemed Heinz had been a prisoner-of-war in Russia for four years during World War II. He had given up meals in exchange for an extra letter to his wife in Germany. This meant he could write twice a month, rather than once, as had been negotiated by the Red Cross. When he returned to Germany at the end of the war, he found out his wife had been living with a German officer for three years. Devastated, he got a divorce and came to South Africa to start a new life. He liked it very much, the money was good, the food was good—but he didn't know if he would stay.

I thought deeply about the Europeans who came to my country and didn't like it, despite living well. *Why the hell don't they just go back, then?* was my thought. I also got mad inside, each time the immigrant story was told, about possibly not staying for life. I agreed with South Africa's wish: 'Not to put one foot in this country and leave the other one in Europe.'

I didn't like working at this place. I badly missed all my friends at Main Reef Engineering. This was just a production shop . . . no feelings . . . no laughter . . . no personality . . . just grinding work! I thought about Sandy, his beautiful wife—so nice. I thought about Sandy's work ethics of hard work, good quality, and high speed, and his coupling of all that with an attitude of fun. How much I had learned from Sandy and the boys! I truly missed them! It was a deep emotion, because I somehow knew I would not go back. I was becoming totally depressed with my situation. I wanted to get out of here, and soon! But what should I do? I was finally earning good money.

I quit Gardner-Denver after five months. Working under a piece-work scheme was a killer. Billy and Tommy, also machinists, had coerced me to come and work at their workplace.

＊

CHAPTER 19

Collision

A SHOT CAME OFF THE forward's foot with a resounding noise. The goalkeeper, spread-eagled, was in the air as the ball hit the goal post and came back into a group of players. The goalkeeper hit the ground. I ran towards the goal, intercepted the ball with the top of my right thigh and guided it down to my knees with my chest. As it fell to the ground, I protected the ball with my body. Instinct moved me to the right to find space and time needed to complete my defensive move. Moving away from the goal posts, protecting the ball, my eyes saw an opening, my body reflected the impulse, and I drove to the sideline. Suddenly, my knees buckled and I went crashing to the ground as my body twisted and I rolled on the moist grass. The images of people, earth and sky were out of focus as I slid ten feet with a body tangled in my legs. Instinctively, in slow motion, I rose from the slide to get free and ensure nothing was wrong with me. As I did so, I saw Jack, a forward on the opposing practice team, who had tackled me feet first.

"You bastard!" I shouted. "Jack, you bastard."

"I couldn't help it!" yelled Jack.

"Bullshit!"

I knew he'd taken me out too aggressively with his tenacious play. He had played this way, lately. I knew Jack was hoping to be noticed by the coaches, as a possible selection, for Saturday's game. He hadn't made the team for the past five games.

"Sure," I yelled. "Why don't you learn ball control instead?" Jack just walked away.

The coach blew the whistle for a foul. I placed the ball on the ground and, with my right foot, lofted it high into the air toward the right wing forward. Then continuing the kicking motion and running up the field towards Jack, I slammed my left elbow into his right chest as I ran past him.

"Sorry Jack didn't mean it."

Jack's "Ugh!" was followed by, "Screw you, Charl."

"Cut it out you two!" the coach yelled.

The practice game went on late into the moist-laden evening, until it was too dark to see the ball. Then our team of twenty players sprinted up and down the field until we couldn't see through the darkness and mist in front of us. Although this was an unofficial semi-pro league, most teams couldn't afford expensive overhead lights. The players broke for the showers, anticipating a beer at the local bar.

The soccer league in Johannesburg during 1955 was well organized. Based on the successful experience of 50 years of tradition, and on principles of encouraging players from schools to play for a club when kids were 13 to 14 years of age. The opportunities to play would continue for players through their twenties with the possibility of being a player in the club's top team. The major teams came out of Johannesburg, Germiston and other major cities close by. They competed on Saturday afternoons. The top event of the day was preceded by a highlighted youth game, usually under 18 or under 21 years of age. This took place at the Rand Stadium that accommodated about 20,000 people.

Desmond, Robbie, Jack and I were in the Reserve League fighting to make the team and then, of course, consideration for the Major League. We all played for the Marist Brothers Club, one of the many such clubs in Johannesburg and the surrounding areas. Desmond, Robbie and I had played for them since we were about 14 years of age. Jack had played since he was 18. Robbie was the best player amongst us and had the greatest chance of going to the top . . . whatever that meant.

I was twenty years old, and so were Desmond and Robbie. This was the time to make it in the soccer world and play at Rand Stadium. If you failed to make the team, your choices included playing for the reserves for a few years, or ending up in the Sunday leagues. These leagues were for any age and played at less important grounds such as Wemmer Pan, a recreational area east of Rand Stadium. The other choice was to quit!

After practice, I refused the short ride Desmond offered. This surprised him. "What's up?" he asked.

"Just wanna walk it. I'll be there for a beer," I answered.

Desmond slid off in his car murmuring something about everybody had already run about 15 miles and sprinted . . . I didn't hear the end.

My walk felt refreshing, especially the silence part. I hadn't had silence all day. Work and practice and travel to and from my work place had consumed all my time this Thursday. The dirty slide tackle hadn't hurt me, it was part of the game, but it had sparked other feelings inside. These feelings provoked my ongoing thoughts of what the hell was making me feel so aggravated all the time. I had been so happy for years, working, pursuing my college degree, and playing soccer. My friends were great. I had known most of them since I was ten years old, and some since I was six . . . great buddies. What was making me so dissatisfied inside, and so bitchy in all these different situations?

I walked towards the Broadway Hotel bar. By eight o'clock in the evening, most of the blue-collar workers would have left, and the bar would only have its steady customers drifting in after dinner, or those who had broken away from drinking earlier to have a plate of food at the Crystal Café next door. It was possible to eat at the hotel where the bar was located, but everyone knew that would be a health hazard. You could get an idea what was cooking from the smell on the way to the men's room. You could also see what was being cooked from the passageway between the barroom and the men's room, but that was not advisable!

I did not look at the shops or the people passing by as I stretched one leg after the other in a slow deliberate manner. My body clicked into autopilot as I went through the crosswalks, easily deciphering the safe, progressive path to the bar. I reflected on my frustration of doing pretty well in many things and yet feeling so deeply dissatisfied. One major reason, I knew, was that many of my close friends were in the process of getting married. Some had moved into there twenties. I was one of the youngest in the so-called Andrew Street Mob. I really missed the Saturday night parties with my buddies, when they had been single. Now I got invitations to dinner on Saturdays; however, each one of my friends outlined the evening's entertainment the same way. "My wife will cook and then we can all sit around and shoot the breeze." But that was so much boredom after one or two of these dinners. *Why does everyone get so old when they get married?* This was 'instant old!'

Then I said it out loud.

"Instant old . . . Dammit!"

I remembered my thoughts on the subject of getting old. *Why would anyone want to live after twenty-nine? I mean thirty is a monstrous number!* I was glad to be going through this experience though, because it set my mind at rest about how I felt about getting married. Man! All my friends were tying the knot. And even though I knew definitely that marriage was out of my range, mentally and financially, there was a pressure to just join my friends in their new adventure. My mom was getting so worried about the 'marriage drug-cloud effect'. She had said that it was perpetuated by the actions of friends who were getting married. Was I becoming one of the last singles? My mom had been married at seventeen, had two kids by nineteen, and that's all she had at twenty. Her husband drank incessantly and she had eventually thrown him out permanently. So, I agreed to let her warn me so many times.

"Why don't you go to England?" she had said again and again. "I have some friends there. Finish your studies. Save some money and go see the world for a little while." The same conversation increased many-fold when I went out with same girl more than two or three times. Why all this damn pressure?

Peer pressure came from school. My main teacher at college was a Frenchman, Dr. Beaucamp. He had helped inspire me this year to continue my final design project in mechanical engineering. This was a most important part of the Mechanical Engineering curriculum. I had gone to him in June saying that I did not see how I could attend army reserves, work, play soccer, do all the other subjects, and complete my chosen design of a drilling machine. The design had to be from first principles and be complete with neatly done calculations, three draw-ings, including a cross-sectional view, and a sketch of the final product completed in ink on linen. It had crossed my mind many times that there was barely enough time to do all my other subjects and live life, never mind doing this mechanical project paper as well.

I thought about the conversation we had had in June, as I walked towards the hotel. This teacher, Dr. Jon Beaucamp, had graduated from the Sorbonne University in France and had taught for many years in his home country. He had decided to come to South Africa because he was tired of French university politics. Besides, the offer of a house, plus a three-year contract, renewable for two years at his option, was just too good to turn down.

I recalled the conversation: "Sir, I asked for this interview to see what would happen if I dropped the mechanical design project. I just don't have enough time to do the whole thing. And I admit . . . I have wasted a lot of time just trying to work out the power required to drive the drill through steel, never mind at different speeds and different feed rates."

"Charl, the first thing is that you won't graduate." Dr. Beaucamp had this beautiful French accent that made English sound great and I was very intrigued. "Then you will have to wait . . . for another year . . . to take the exam. Because of the normal curriculum of the college, the design next year will be different. That means . . . all the work you have done so far this year . . . will just be for nothing! I can assure you of that! Also, if you knew that time was not available, why did you pick the most difficult design?"

"I found that out too late, Sir! The drill has nine speeds and four feeds, and that means you have to have two gearboxes. You can't drive off the drill gear box . . . very easily!" The sarcasm fell on the floor.

"Why didn't you choose the internal combustion engine design project? It is the same as the Volkswagen engine, an air-cooled horizontally-opposed cylinder design."

"I didn't think I knew enough about it. But I did look into it. I found so many references on internal combustion (IC) engines, and next to nothing on drilling machines. It was a bad decision! Now I know there is no time to switch."

"Well, it seems to me that you have at least done some research work on the design. It is just a little late to do an IC engine," said Dr Beaucamp with a little smile. "I could allow you to change your choice of design, even though your selection was supposed to be submitted in March."

"Uh! I'm thinking of dropping everything," I said, turning away, getting up from the chair and walking across the room. "It just doesn't seem worth it. I have very little money after I pay for my textbooks, college fees, room and board and bus fare!"

In my mind, I was thinking that it was also so hard to have a girlfriend, with no time to go to movies during the week, or to go out every weekend. Girls went out with you if you consistently confirmed dates, way ahead in time. Besides, who could afford to pay for themselves through school, and also pay for a steady lady every weekend? I couldn't manage all this, despite the fact I was now earning good money.

"Charl, you came with a question, but it seems you want me to confirm that you do not wish to continue," said Dr. Beaucamp. "I have a question for you."

"What's that?" I asked.

"You see this letter addressed to me? What can you recognize on the envelope that's just a little different to what you get at home?"

"Dr. Beaucamp," I replied.

"How are letters addressed to you?" he asked.

"Mr. Marais," I replied.

"What's the difference?" asked Dr. Beaucamp.

"Dr. before your name," I said, "and there are a million with 'Mr.'"

"Right! Very good! You are a smart man! . . . That qualification means I can be accepted fairly quickly and work in many countries, many cities. I can possibly choose where I would like to work and ensure that it would be pleasant." He paused. "What does it mean in South Africa to you? The South African society will eventually change. And, the black people are studying hard and, in twenty years, any one of them could be your boss," he suggested.

"It doesn't matter to me that they could become a boss or supervise me. I know a lot of people would rather die than be under a black person, but I don't have all those traditional problems. If he is good enough it is all right by me. I don't have the upbringing for power and politics. In fact I sometimes just dislike it!" I paused. Where was I going with this? I noticed his blank look. I came back to the topic of discussion. "Sir, your suggestion of working in other places sounds interesting. I would truly like to have that experience and come back to South Africa with an overseas résumé; I believe that would be an advantage for me . . . and even a better one, if I had completed my studies." I paused and saw Dr. Beaucamp had a small smile. "I guess what you're saying is finish and then decide what to do." Then I thought that a qualification sounded very good to me!

"Yes, Charl. You are, again, an intelligent young man, and you think things out. Think about the future a little further. You have already done that by fighting hard to get through school. When you are finished, go to France or anywhere in Europe and work in a factory where 20,000 people clock out at 4:30 PM."

"Wow! 20,000 people in one factory," I said out loud, then thought for a few seconds. "There's nothing like that in South Africa, is there? What about the girls in France? Maybe learn French?" My mind had drifted, but came back quickly, as I remembered this was a serious conversation.

"Furthermore, I am willing to help you as much as I can as your teacher. I may have a reference on the forces a drill encounters when shearing through steel, which will help you determine the power requirements for your design project. Also, you could work through the winter break, which means the whole of July. Let's meet after July and see what is 'left to be done' before November 20th. You know that's the last date for submission," offered Dr. Beaucamp.

"Yes," I said. I got up from the chair. "I have made up my mind on what I should do. I would like to do exactly what you suggested. It seems the best! My answer is . . .Yes, I agree!"

"Very good Charl!" stated Dr. Beaucamp, with a smile.

"Thank you very much, Sir! Europe sounds like a great idea . . . Thanks! Bye Sir!"

"Goodbye young man! You know your name is deeply French!"

"Yes Sir! Many people think it is Afrikaans! . . . Goodbye and thank you again!"

◆

I recognized the familiar hotel bar from a block away. I had been working hard on my design project and had progressed very well, after the interview with Dr. Beaucamp in July. Everything had been settled to finish by November 20th, but it was going to be tight. There were about six weeks to go.

I wish I could get rid of this frustration. It's getting to me. It's driving me crazy, were the thoughts drifting in my mind, as my muscles drove my legs. The walk had been worth it!

I entered the bar, "Hi, Desmond. Who's the spare Lion beer for?"

"You! Sit down, grouch!"

Most of the team members were in the bar. They sat at tables, varying from two to six. Desmond and I sat together because we always did. We had known each other since forever, played together since we could remember, and had gone through the important friendship years, when you're growing, from ten to twenty. We knew each other well. He never became a part of the Andrew Street Mob. He was an entrenched friend.

"So, are you going to tell me why you walked from practice?" asked Desmond, with a double frown look and split-lip smile. Desmond was nice looking, with strong features; he was normally quiet, serious in many ways, but had a cutting humor, and it had got worse as he got older.

"Just needed some time to think," I replied. "I have many things coming to a head right now! The Andrew Street Mob is changing fast, the family is changing due to the loss of my gran and grandpa and it is still very hard to go on a date due to having no car. Also, the Army still irritates me, and I am still not going to stop studying. This led me to thinking of my big interview with Dr. Beaucamp and what he said . . . you know, the interview in June, about my mechanical engineering project."

"Yeah, I remember," said Desmond, who took a comfortable position over his beer glass, knowing that this was leading into a long conversation.

"Well, he made a statement about the blacks becoming supervisors in twenty years. He thought that it might be worth studying a little harder, to make sure a person didn't land up down the road, in a position under a black man." I took a big sip of beer. "It doesn't bother me, but I'm thinking of all these guys we know, a lot of them don't ever want to live side-by-side or mix with the blacks. Hey! They're not studying. What is going to happen to them? What are they going to do? It's got to come. Just look at their numbers!" I emphasized the point by raising my voice slightly.

"They'll probably rely on the government to make it the same as it is today," replied Desmond, seemingly not very concerned, but interested. "Some of them don't even care what happens or what they do. But, in fact, I know one or two who've slept with black women."

"You're kidding! Some of our players?" I asked.

"Yes, some of them have been down to Braamfontein. You can get a white woman too, if you want," replied Desmond.

"Well, if I went for that, I'd go to Hillbrow," I said. "Pay more and come out safely."

"What do you mean by that?" asked Desmond. Now he showed some interest and finally perked up from his bored position.

"Oh! Nothing! Well, let's say I'm not sure I'd like to be pursued by a bunch of blacks after I was caught doing something they didn't like!"

"No different than a bunch of whites from Braamie," said Desmond.

"You're right, Desmond. You're right," I admitted.

We were hungry but did not want to eat in the Broadway Hotel.

"What's happening with the Andrew Street crowd?" asked Desmond, changing the subject.

"Complicated as hell. I don't know where everybody is going . . . there is some peculiar love wave going through everyone. Looks like we've been hit by moonbeams! Most of my friends are starry-eyed. Could be that we're changing, or times are changing. It's some kind of disease. There's restlessness too!" I said.

"Like what?"

"Uh! Maybe something that doesn't want us to exist the way we are right now. I don't really know!" I replied almost apologetically.

"Well! That answer explains everything!" Desmond sipped on his beer. "So! What are you thinking of doing? Are you going to become a super soccer star? A lover of all women? A dancer? An architect of nations and cities? Or a 'Southern Suburbs Joller (hangabout)'," asked Desmond, without a smile, but peering over his mug of beer as he swallowed another mouthful.

"I am a lover!"

"Of whom?"

"You'd love to know . . . I said that I was a lover . . . not a news service!"

"Oh! Yeah! I get it. Won't tell them cause you don't know either!"

"Most correct Sir!" I paused for a while. But as I knew Desmond was earnest in his questions, I continued, "I don't know what to do now, Desmond! It is driving me crazy. I know I'm not finished at college but I'm trying to work through the changes in my friends and family. Now my friends are doing weird things! I believe that will only unfold slowly. There's truly nothing I can do! The family is so complicated. It may be time for me to go live somewhere else. But, I've no idea where or how!"

"Oh! Like getting married . . . that's not weird Charl!"

"Yeah I know! But my choices are wide in selecting something to pursue! Soccer is interesting! I love it deeply, but I hardly think it is a career here in South Africa. Engineering or design of new things is beautiful and maybe that's my ambition. Basically, I want to do something and be good at it!" I sipped on my beer thinking I was talking too much. "I am definitely scared of being just a 'Joller'. To me it is just a dead-end lousy life, as you get older. Just look at them. There are some in this bar! They are hard work to be around. Now, when you suggest my being a dancer, you know my weakness and that is not fair! But let me remind you, I could be famous within months if I really pursued it!!"

"Oh shit here we go again!" came back Desmond.

"Des . . . I really don't know right now. All I know is I'm feeling weak and I don't like it. Come on I'll buy the last round!"

"I'm agreeing with all my heart!" Desmond answered, and shoved his beer mug across the table.

"Desmond, what do you think about the black people you work with? What are your feelings?" I asked, challenging him. Then I went and got two beers and returned.

Desmond, who was an apprentice mechanic, looked surprised at the question, but answered, "They're okay people. They really have a lot to learn to catch up. Most of them can't read or write so they do all the hard work. But it fits in . . . somebody has to do it. Actually, I like them. We get on well at work. Living with some of them could be okay, but most of them aren't too clean."

"Squeaky clean?" I inserted.

"The Zulus are extremely clean, they're also the most trustworthy; strong people. Sort of the Romans of Africa, I guess. I mean, you look at the ones that are at my workplace. Some of them are over 65 or something . . . they look great.

"Maybe twenty years will make a difference, but right now there are so many tribes . . . many of them have never worked in the city. Remember Johan, the white guy from the Free State? We sat talking to him for hours, about a month ago. He worked in the mines or something! Man! He hated blacks. I know he'd never be supervised. Probably not by anyone!" said Desmond.

"True!" I agreed.

"But I sometimes think the immigrants to our country are worse than us. Actually, they have some weird idea or notion that *we're* uncivilized and blacks have just come out of the bush. So they treat them even worse than we do!!" said Desmond.

"I can't agree more . . . we actually get mad at the way they treat the blacks." I said.

We stopped for a while, enjoyed our beer, and looked around. This was a crummy bar, the décor was nondescript, the floor slightly wet with beer spills mixed with dirt from the boots of the workers, but everyone came here, and the population was diverse and interesting. The noise was loud. Sometimes, when you heard shouting by more than one person, you flinched and looked for the door. Mostly though it was a man's bar to bullshit in!

"Back to their experience." I broke our silence. "A good proportion of the blacks that come to work in the gold mines have to go through at least three months of training. I know, my granddad told me. He said that they have to be taught to read simple signs, not to walk in front of buses, to wash! Hey! There was this accident in the mine where an underground locomotive ran right into the mineshaft gate, deep down in the mine. I mean, the locos have to stop ten yards from the gate. The driver was still at the controls; his head was almost completely severed off. The miners think he stood up while driving in a low-clearance drift."

"Oh! God!" Desmond squirmed. "Was he dead?"

"Yes!" I said and continued, adding some emotion. "They also teach them hygiene . . . all kind of things . . . before they even do a day's work." I continued drinking more beer and chewing on some biltong (jerky). "Ah! This is all too much to think about . . . I'm too busy studying and stuff."

I got up and went to the bathroom. I couldn't get all this out of my mind because I couldn't understand why there was so much hatred and belligerence towards the black people. They had been nice to me, almost every one. There was never any trouble; I always approached them sincerely and in a friendly way, and had never been treated badly, in fact, just the opposite. They had always treated me the same way; so we got on fine . . . the attitude of the Government, to me, was beyond comprehension. I returned to find that Desmond had bought two more beers and placed them on the table.

"Nice guy! How did you know? Thanks."

"What's Jack's problem?" asked Desmond.

"He wants to make the team for Saturday's game," I replied. "He'd probably be okay. I like him playing with us. That way the other team can suffer the injuries!"

"Come on Charl," said Desmond. "He hardly hurt you."

"I know! Actually it's me. I like Jack. He sure tries hard. He may go all the way someday."

"What's all the way? In soccer? Here in Johannesburg?" responded Desmond with an exclamation of aggression and a sarcastic look. He continued, "There is nothing here, my friend. This is a bush country league compared to Europe."

"A couple of players have gone to Scotland. One to England to play," I said in a weak defense of our sport in Johannesburg.

"They'll be back," said Desmond. "Put them in a big game in England and you won't see them . . . except for their mistakes. They can't keep up with ball control at a fast speed. Jack has the speed, but ball control, never! He needs a basket on each foot!"

"You're right. Maybe you should try to go. You and Robbie!" I suggested earnestly.

"Nah! I don't like the English. Maybe Scotland, but that place is too damn cold. South Africa's my place. I love the warm weather, and the girls are pretty nice too."

"You have the talent to go. Not for girls, though!" I liked my entry into Desmond's statement: it was like intercepting a ball in soccer . . . disbelief by the ball carrier.

"You wanna bet?" growled Desmond, getting a little uppity.

"Yeah!" I agreed.

"Buy beers on Saturday after the game, and I'll tell you a few stories. Then my friend, I'll show you a few good tricks," said Desmond.

"Deal!"

The big hand was on six and the small hand past eleven. We left the bar with arms around each other's shoulders.

"Cheers Hey! See you!" We both agreed, and went our separate ways. Desmond had an errand to run.

I headed home, catching the bus outside the hotel on Main Street, and then jumping off at Andrew Street. I walked past the houses without seeing them. I turned into 65 Andrew Street, swung my soccer bag to one side, so it would clear everything, took three steps to the door, opened it, and quietly slipped inside to the passageway, to the bathroom, and finally into bed. I was tired, but couldn't sleep. My mind reviewed quickly all the major things I had done in life. I felt experienced. But that wasn't true! South Africa wasn't like Europe, or the U.S.A., or England. The English immigrants reminded us South Africans of that every day, even to the point that it made South Africans dislike them. Why was it I felt old? Why did my friends change from being so exciting, adventurous and instantaneous, to being so laid-back and relaxed after they got married? Why hadn't they done something different than just meeting a girl and getting married and living in Johannesburg? They ignored all the chances of becoming 'world-wise' by not traveling and getting tied down before they were twenty-five. They had become lovers of a fulltime mate: couch sitting, bed lying, and taking a 'hellava' long time to have lunch and dinner. It was now very clear to me that there were only two types of people in the world: those that bought couches, and those that traveled!

CHAPTER 20

The Time Has Come

Somewhere beyond the sea
Someone is waiting for me.
My lover stands on golden sands…

SITTING ON THE BENCH at work, I was eating my sandwich and thinking of the song La Mer. I wondered, "was my fate over the sea?" I reminisced deeply about my talk with Desmond in the Broadway Hotel. There was so much more I had wanted to talk about but had held it back. I wasn't sure if I should talk about it ---, shouldn't I solve figure out my own future? After all, I had decided between soccer and cycling, and sticking to the miserable schedule of college, work and commuting. Nobody told me to go to school. There was no real outside pressure, forcing me, certainly not from my mom or dad. In fact they had both remarried, and were busy with their lives. My Dad didn't care. My Mom was busy with her new life.

I had been so enamored by America all through my teens. What a place, judging from the movies, Coca Cola, music, dancing, beautiful houses, new cars, New York with its tall buildings, the Grand Canyon, and Las Vegas! The list seemed to go on and on. Since I had talked with Desmond, I had accumulated so many things I wanted to go and see!

I had just changed jobs for the second time since leaving Main Reef Engineering. I was doing very well, especially in earning money. The social scene was opening up to a wide expanse, making me feel like I had been in a cocoon for five years. Was there a desire in my body to do something major? I did know the changes up to now were not enough to satisfy me. I was sure that it should be something more significant! The major setbacks of losing Gran, Uncle Mick, Lena and Sandy made me understand I was on my own. There was no doubt it was up to me!

The twenty-first birthday was a major milestone for young men in South Africa. It was a celebration and tradition passed down from generation to generation. When you turned twenty-one you were a 'man of your own'. It really meant you were about to become independent of your parents' instruction. The event is celebrated with friends and family, with parents being the center for congratulations. The parents hand over 'the key to the door', a symbol of freedom. I was getting close, but this independence had been mine since I was sixteen, maybe even late fifteen when I started work. I had contributed to my support since I was sixteen without a thought. I had done what I wanted. It had been a long and hard road chasing a college degree. The single thought, 'they can't take away knowledge,' had been my driving force to eventually get out of the no-money lifestyle. "Money and power comes and goes," someone had said, and, "Very quickly sometimes," another person had added. I knew how hard my mom and dad, and Uncle Mick and Gran had worked. I saw how all the parents of the Andrew Street Mob left early and came home late, every weekday of the year, and still they had little of the frills of life. Absolutely nothing like the American movies where tradesmen had houses and cars. The thought that our parents, despite having worked most of their life, didn't end up having expensive furniture and beautiful homes, plus the fact that many of them had never had a car, always circulated in my thoughts. I knew knowledge could get me out. Even though I had tried hard to study and complete my degree, it was not yet finished. My head was on a track to burst. My thoughts were endless about what to do now. I would be twenty-one next February 14th, a magic day in love affairs, Valentine's Day! My problems were more about myself. I wanted a change. I wanted something exciting and new. Maybe it was over the sea? But there were many things still unfinished right here that I needed to do.

◆

I had worked for two American companies and had liked the way the bosses treated the workers. I never forgot how my first boss, Mr. Funkey, went home to Salt Lake City, in the U.S.A., every year. When he returned, he had a present for everyone in the company. It was like he bought one for each employee individually. Main Reef Engineering had been my apprenticeship firm for some four years. I may never have left except for the South African Apprenticeship Contract law, requiring apprentices to leave for at least a year. I had done that, and now, Joy Manufacturing was my new place of work. I had got the job through Billy and had started as a machinist. There were a lot of nice things about this place; it was modern, a bigger factory than the privately owned Main Reef Engineering, and it had a great cafeteria. It was also an American company.

The interview had been held on a Monday with the shop foreman, Leonard, who was firm and very pleasant. My interview ended with Leonard saying that if I was not worth high pay we would not have an agreement. I had a two-week trial. I was very happy and smiled and thanked him. I met Tommy and Billy for lunch. Told them about the interview.

"You'll make it, from what you told us. Unless of course . . .!"

"Come on you two! This is serious."

"We know! Don't worry!" said Billy.

I had to get the job. It would be so embarrassing to not get it, because of Billy and Tommy having helped me to get the interview, plus they were friends, and they were definitely teasers.

I anxiously started in the new machine shop on the Tuesday. I was not confident despite the feeling that I had good experience. I was directed to an old lathe machine where two hundred bearing covers needing to be machined to fairly accurate tolerances. The machine was really old, and probably in worse condition than anything I had worked on since I was a second-year apprentice. As I started to machine, the chuck that held the first cover shook. The cutting tool chattered: either the slides on the lathe bed weren't adjusted properly, or the bearings on the chuck shaft were too loose. I took the tool out and sharpened it, tried once more; same result. I quickly decided on an alternate way to get the job done. I opened up the gearbox and made a few shims for the loose bearings. I placed the shims into the bearing housing and rotated the chuck; it was free. I attacked the tool housing- and tool carriage slides on the lathe bed. First, I cleaned them, added small screws, and completed some hand filing on the slides. I then adjusted them so they slid freely, but had no 'play' (looseness). The repair took the whole morning. After lunch I continued fixing other things and finally started machining at 3 o'clock. The lathe ran beautifully! On Wednesday morning at 11 o'clock, I was finished. The checker came over and checked a number of the machined parts; they passed; the batch of covers was approved. I was relieved! I went and got another job and completed it. On Friday, Leonard called me into the office. He looked at me with a smile.

"You have a job if you want it."

"Yes, I do!" I said with the excitement of having been approved. "See you Monday!"

I anxiously arrived the next Monday. Leonard led me to the back of the shop to a row of machines.

"You are assigned to this new Dean, Smith and Grace lathe. Arrangements have also been made for you to continue college."

"Thanks Leonard . . . very much!" I was ecstatic. I was on my way!

I worked there for months without looking up. I greeted Bjorn, a Danish machinist who worked in front of me on the next machine, each morning and evening. I went to lunch with Billy and Tommy in the cafeteria every day. We caught up with our stories of going to parties with and without the Andrew Street Mob. Billy and Tommy were talking about going into business together. I definitely didn't have money to contribute, so I just listened. I went to school on Fridays and continued my studies. The lifestyle was easier than when I went to Main Reef Engineering because Joy Sullivan was on the way to Alberton, and considerably closer. I was very happy now with my new set of things to do.

It was not until one day, when I stayed at the lathe for lunch, that I actually sat with Bjorn and talked for a long time. He opened up a serious conversation.

"You're a good machinist . . . and fast," said Bjorn.

"Yes, like the time I machined that big flange and it was a quarter of an inch under the size. I remember the boys rolling it down to the welding shop to be built up for re-machining . . . Yeah?"

"I liked the writing on the flange, 'From Charl's Machine'," laughed Bjorn. I joined the laughter.

"I had many good teachers and one really excellent one," I said, thinking of Sandy.

"Well we all have good teachers, but you're fast. Better enjoy it now because after a while you will slow down a little and hang on to accuracy . . . no mistakes".

The conversation moved on to soccer, then Bjorn got up and went to his machine.

◆

Some days later, I was sitting on the bench with the song 'La Mer' in my head. My thoughts turned to what Bjorn had said many days ago. I had realized I was at the back of a row of machines. There were six machines in a row and our particular row in the machine shop did specialty machining. There was an 'automatics' section that machined big productions of standard parts; Billy was in charge of this section.

I had looked down the row and realized each machinist was older than the one behind him. Bjorn was older than me and the closest in age to my 20 years. Fred was older than Bjorn, and so it progressed. A chilling thought when looking at a possible future life style. This was the machinist's life! I didn't want that at all! This would turn out to be like the 'Andrew Street Parents' syndrome', where people just worked in the same boring job their whole lives. It seemed crazy that I had the most interesting job and I was the youngest!

I went to the phone and called Desmond.

"Can you get the two dates like you promised in the Broadway Hotel?"

"Certainly! How about I'll get my brother's car. I'll also get two dates for Saturday, because you can't get them, and you can't get a car . . . and we'll go to the Roadside Rest in Wynberg. Okay?"

"Yes! My friend, it's a smart idea. You are really wise and capable. I'll see you at the game first and get all the details".

Desmond and I played on the Saturday afternoon in Krugersdorp. We hustled back home to shower, dress up and look good. Desmond picked me up at 7 PM and introduced me to Pattie and Laura. They were sitting in the back seat: a well-planned maneuver by Desmond. No pairing-off of couples from the start.

"Where is the Roadside Rest?" asked Pattie.

"On the way to Pretoria," replied Desmond

"Is it a dance place?"

"Yes! It is an easy-going dinner place with a bar, and has a jukebox with all the American songs."

"Oh! Very good! Do you dance . . . well, I mean rock and roll?"

"Yes! I love to rock and roll."

"Desmond says you're good."

"He's my friend Pattie, and you know what that means!"

"He's my friend too. He'd never lie to me!"

"Well I won't pass him the ball if he doesn't say nice things!"

Laura slipped into the conversation. "Well that means that we all can dance. I know we all can eat. I guess only Desmond can't drink. So this should be fun!"

"We can all drink! Laura!" corrected Desmond.

"All of us can drink! I know!"

"Oh! Like the last time we all went out!"

Desmond turned to me and explained that they had spent a long day of drinking and having fun. He had passed out early. Laura just laughed. I had a feeling that this would be a good night just as Desmond had promised.

Pattie and Laura were both blondes. Pattie looked a little taller and bigger. Laura was almost petite but not quite. They were well-dressed, as though they wanted to impress. We got out of the car and went into the Roadside Rest. It was an American style diner. I noticed both the girls walked with a spring in their step and I liked that very much. I didn't like girls that walked with a heavy breadbasket on their backs. Tables were available and we sat down and ordered drinks, Desmond and I sitting across one corner, and Pattie and Laura sitting across the other. After looking over the menu we ordered food. This was a place for young people and it was always crowded, mostly with a noisy and active crowd.

Laura was first to speak after we had all joined glasses. "I wish us all a good evening of fun." She continued, "Desmond told us you were a machinist but that you were also going to college. Isn't that hard to do?"

"Well maybe, but quite a few guys in the class are doing the same thing. So we don't think its unusual or anything more than what sports-crazy people do!" I replied.

"At least it's trying to do better," complimented Laura.

"Doesn't help my dancing though!" I replied.

They laughed.

"He wants to be a dancer," explained Desmond with a quirky look.

"Desmond, you're in trouble mate. Stay out of the secrets!" I said with a finger pointing down the table.

"Oh! So what's the finger for?" quipped Desmond.

"I won't pass you the ball next week now, or help you out again!" I suggested with a look of honesty as displayed by politicians. "By the way, Laura, I'm the only one on the team that actually passes him the ball."

"Why is that?" Laura fell in the trap as the straight man.

"Because nobody else likes him!"

"You're mean!" added Pattie.

"No! I'm joking! Our team truly loves him!"

The drinks went down and the dinner was eaten and I got brave enough to ask Pattie for a dance. I judged and hoped that it was the right choice! It turned out to be a good decision because I watched Desmond and Laura dance and their bodies were very close. I now felt glad the night would go well. Pattie was a good dancer and lively. She was also fun. Her blue eyes were striking, especially in the dance floor lights. We had a lot of small inquisitive talk, finding out about each other. The talk split at the table as well. The girls finally went to the powder room.

"Charl, remember Henry from Rosettenville Central School?" asked Desmond.

"Yes! We helped him down the stairs, almost every day," I answered.

"Remember he had iron braces on his legs from polio?"

"Yes!"

"Well I spoke to him the other day and he told me he had just completed the Johannesburg to Paarl Cycle Race. You know, South Africa's 'Tour de France'."

"Unbelievable! Its 800 miles or so!" I exclaimed. "So he's walking and riding. I would not have believed that possible." I paused. "Funny, just when you think you're struggling but still doing really well, you find it is nothing compared to great stories like that! Just shows, we worry about small things."

"Ah! Yes my friend!" agreed Desmond.

We both agreed, with happy thoughts, that Henry had accomplished something that neither of us had thought was possible, in any way!

"Not to change the subject, but very nice Des! Glad you pulled this night together. It's medicine needed to get me out of my stinking mood. You know what I mean."

"Charl, I don't want you to get upset, go away, make big changes and break up the team. I mean, you're my very good friend, that's what I care about . . . more than the team. Uh! Shit! You know what I'm saying!"

"Yes! And I'm glad we have been friends for such a long time," I said, trying to avoid the compliment. "Now stop with all this nice stuff." I looked away to the dance floor to see what was happening, then turned back to look at Desmond. "I'll buy you a beer anyway!"

I got up, went to the bar, and bought a round of drinks for everyone. My feelings and thoughts combined. I could sit here with Desmond,

Laura and Pattie through all the necessary hours required and see the sun come up. This was a nice evening. Walking back to the table with the drinks. I felt this gentle ankle tap as one foot collided with another. I turned around and it was Pattie smiling.

"Heard that you get upset with people who kick you on the ankles!"

"Boy! That Desmond! I'll get him!"

Pattie took her and Laura's drink from me. I sat down and put both the other drinks in front of me.

"Go and get your own, Desmond!"

"What's the damn problem now?"

"Absolutely nothing about tackling!"

"Pattie! . . . I told you about that in confidence," scolded Desmond.

"I know, but it was fun!"

We had a great evening, acting like two young couples. We regretfully had to leave before the owners threw us out. We rearranged the seating on the way home. Laura sat in the front. Pattie was definitely inquisitive about me. I had told her many things but avoided any of the complexity of my present thinking. I was determined to have fun. Desmond dropped me off first. Pattie gave me a very nice kiss. I went 'warm and melty' inside. She smiled. I said goodnight and they drove off. The sun was not up yet.

"Oh! Well! Next time!" I said out loud as I went through the gate at 65.

◆

On Monday morning at work I could not wait for the lunch break. When it came, I ran to the phone and talked to Desmond for a long while. I concluded by saying, "Thanks a million for Saturday, it was definitely a night to remember."

"Pattie says to give her a call."

"Will do that for sure," I replied. "See you on Thursday?"

"See you Thursday!" agreed Desmond.

I went back to the bench with coffee and a sandwich. I was not going to the cafeteria today, I had decided to sit outside the building on the wall near my machine. I needed some thinking time. I went into deep thought.

I had finished my mechanical project and submitted it to Dr. Beaucamp. I had also written the technical exam and ended up with a distinction in the mechanical project. I was so very happy about that, because I now had only two more courses of study and final exams at this college, to graduate. I was so tired of the constant effort. I felt it held up doing other things in life. I had gone to see Dr. Beaucamp to thank him. He had congratulated me on my 'come from behind' effort and then turned around to me, as I was leaving the formal interview, and asked a peculiar question: "Charl, can I ask you something?"

"Yes Sir! Anything!"

"Do you think you can do a better report . . . next time?"

After a succession of thoughts I replied, "Yes! . . . Definitely! . . . Much better! And I would plan it better."

"Good," said Dr. Beaucamp. "Very good! Remember that deeply, Charl. Design work will always involve many iterations before it is a final product."

"I will remember that!"

"Charl, you have shown me you can do something, and do it well!" He shook my hand. "I must go now. Goodbye and good luck . . . or just *au revoir* my friend!"

"Goodbye Sir! Thank you Sir! Very much!"

"You are welcome, Charl!"

I walked away thinking that I would love to have his great accent, his French-come-English. His intelligence. What a nice man!

◆

I enjoyed working at Joy Manufacturing and especially the camaraderie of my two Andrew Street Mob friends, Billy and Tommy. I had worked into December. I reached my decision to make a move to break out of machine shop work: Billy and Tommy, who were also going to break away, helped drive me towards making the decision. However, they were going to start their own business, and that idea would have to wait for me. I was now earning some good money. I could not go back and battle life with small funds for another long period of time.

In the lunchroom Billy whispered, "I have a friend looking for a partner to help start his business."

The conversation went into detail.

"I'm interested and I'd like to help him but without any investment," I replied.

"This could be a good chance to become a working partner with a chance for a piece of the business eventually," suggested Billy.

"That's an idea! I'll let you know soon. Thanks Bill!"

Once before, I had been offered a business opportunity through a close friend of my mom. It was with Kaplan and Company. The owner, Mr. Kaplan, was born in the late 1800s. A Jewish immigrant, he came to South Africa in the early 1900s, and eventually manufactured and sold canvas. When he died he left a legacy of money to his seven children. My mom had known one of the brothers for a long time. He had agreed to set his son and me up in business. I had refused and my mom had been furious.

"Why not?" she asked.

"Because if you don't put money in—and I don't have any—you will continue to work for the owner. Besides Mom, his son knows nothing about machining parts or how a workshop is run. He's a good guy, but I don't want to work for him, build up a business and end up having between ten per cent and nothing."

"It's a good chance, Charl. You don't understand, it's a break and Frank will make sure you get a share!"

"No Mom, there are too many hidden pathways."

I was definitely not popular for a long time. My mom couldn't understand the turning down of such an opportunity.

◆

What I didn't say, in truth, is that I wasn't sure now, if I wanted to stay in Johannesburg, continue to be in the army, study and work, or save money and start a business. This would inevitably lead to getting married and having kids like everyone else. It seemed this pathway would prevent me from seeing England or Europe or even the very distant possibility of going to the United States. I knew I could work in the United Kingdom, because South Africa was part of the Commonwealth. France, I had heard that you needed a work permit for, and this was a good possibility, but the U.S.A. required that you be part of the quota for immigrants, and South Africa's quota was small, and already filled for at least the next 3 years. I was now definitely confused and a little troubled, at the fast pace of all these possibilities taking place.

◆

Many of my friends had got married during the last year or so. Doc and Mary got married and went to the Free State. Billy and Joy got married and lived in the Southern Suburbs. Tommy and Mavis got married. Beryl was married and Guy had moved away. The Andrew Street Mob was breaking up and going into different avenues of life. Trevor and Maureen were going very steady and so were Johnny and Madge. Zoni had got married to Maureen in a wild reception with 60 people in a two-bedroom apartment. We were actually standing and sitting on the beds talking. All the Andrew Street girls were going steady or tied down! Beryl was the first of my long-time friends to get married, and she was gone. Grace was going steady with Otto; he and his brother were good friends of mine. Nearly all the couples were from the Southern Suburbs. Thelma had a boyfriend too. Gloria was still going steady with Hobbs. The Andrew Street Mob boys were all dating new faces, girls from Krugersdorp to Benoni. Anything further out on the Rand was still considered absolutely too far away. Parties were held everywhere for engagements followed by weddings and invitations were never turned down. It had been a very expensive year mainly because of gifts. I would not give my friends a cheap wedding gift. My mom consoled me by saying I would get it all back on my wedding day!

I knew that girls needed attention! I had learned that well. Now this was the first time I had money to spend, and all of my close friends were tied up. So my social life alternated between sets of friends. When I didn't go out with close friends in the Andrew Street Mob, I was out with Viv, Norman or Mac occasionally, and alternatively with Bobby, Tom, Mike and Abie, or Desmond. I also had other acquaintances in the Southern Suburbs who were single, so I got invited to parties and movies.

Coralie and June weren't going steady, and I loved to go out with them, but it remained difficult logistically.

I had to think of other things!!

Cling! Cling! Cling! The bell for work rang and I went inside, threw the sandwich bag in a bin, and went back to my lathe. Within seconds the steel chips were flying and the hours went by as I machined part after part.

My mind came alive again, as the work progressed: I remembered Jonathan and the 'Houseboy' expression that had really stuck in my mind. Did it come from the British or the Dutch? Definitely British Colonialism had left its mark in the world, and in too many places in my opinion. I did not like the 'British Way' or the 'Dutch Way' of doing things. All through my life I had been subjected to rules manifested by one or the other. That was the reason I had had so many conflicts in the family and in school. I spent less and less time within 'the circle of rules' so that eventually they spun out of my social life. I absolutely preferred avoiding the precarious nature of political mind games and physical altercations. Some people would fight over any little deviation to such subjects as black and white, English and Dutch, boss and worker, mixed relationships, etc. My thoughts were, why would someone argue about German, English, Afrikaans, and how correct and how right certain languages were? All these languages had horrible sounds when it came to expressing love, poetry or beauty. The French, Spanish, and Italian languages sounded beautiful even if you didn't understand them. In fact, they could be swearing at you in a gentle voice and you wouldn't know it. But why fight about something that was not important. If the language enables you to tell other people things that have to be told, and they understand . . . who cares? Also, why did all these people ridicule American slang? Take the expression "Hey Guy." It was clear to me what it meant. It was a lot simpler than words out of a mouth with marbles, or from a face with a frown, or words that sounded like the end of the world was coming.

How many times had I heard that whites shouldn't mix with blacks? I mean, they did mix, every day, in many places. I knew some that did more than most people could envision. I knew I had learned something from the black people, especially Otiend, whom I had secretly wished could've transferred all his intelligence to my father. They had good rules of life and a feeling of love and compassion. So I questioned, if that was the black man's way of treating children, then why did white people think they were superior? Otiend's attitude towards me had been very kind. Otiend had discussed many subjects and was clear in his philosophy . . . teaching, telling, and talking without rules. Of course there are rules of behavior, learning and tribal laws. But, the gentleness of black people, their love of their children and the natural earth had impressed me. Also, their simple laughter at simple things was something we could learn from. I knew inside I had never had cause to treat any one badly. Nor did I want to. Certainly I had been frustrated with some of the ways of the black people, and I didn't understand them all, but perhaps I just needed to know more. I knew they could be violent, but hell, look at the other races of the world . . . violence abounded. The profound question of "Why?" stuck in my mind.

I recalled my decision to not believe in religion, after I had been caught not going to church. Every Sunday Yvonne and I would go to whichever service our mom didn't go to. Sometimes Bazil would go with us. But we actually never went into the church. Instead, we went into the park and spent time on the swings and sitting under the trees. Finally, the minister called our mom asking why Yvonne, Bazil and I, did not come to his church. Mom was so mad! She scolded us and talked at length about deceit and dishonesty. A long while after that occasion, my mom turned to me and asked why I didn't go into the church.

"I don't believe I have to fear God, if he created me! They teach you that." I replied.

"You have to study what fear means," she answered.

"Fear is fear Mom. It goes right to your stomach and back into your brain and then you either panic or you don't! I also don't agree with a lot of their rules," I added. "Why do black people have to sit at the back of the church? Why must there not be more than one row of them? Why do they have to leave before everyone else and never shake the minister's hand? That is more social bull than religious belief," I said. "They were made by God as well!"

"Anyway, I want you to go to church at least twice a month and that's it," Mom instructed me. I did that until I started work, and then never went again.

I also recalled the funniest thing about going to church when I was about eleven. Helen and Bobby from next door had also had to go. And we always sat together. The problem was, Helen always giggled when she heard the bell ring for communion. The more it rang, the more she giggled! Grown-ups would put their finger on their lips to indicate silence, and many times Helen would have to leave the church. One Sunday, in church, I suggested that she stuff her handkerchief in her mouth just before communion. It would be easy to do because we knew every part of the ceremony, it was always the same, and she could time it perfectly. So Helen did just that at the correct time. Helen, Bobby and I knelt while the communion bells rang. I turned towards Helen to see why she was so quiet. Her cheeks were blown up, she was red, and a small corner of the handkerchief was sticking out of her lips. I burst out laughing, Helen spat the handkerchief out in frustration and she laughed. Bobby laughed! We got up and ran out of the church quietly and quickly. Then, when we entered the street, we broke into a total release of laughter until our stomachs hurt with pain.

Of course, this was reported to the parents and so another series of lectures took place on the sanctity of the church, and so on and so forth!

My confrontations with my family continued every time I explicitly stated, whenever asked, about my feelings on religion. "God created man and that's good. Man created religion and that's not so good." I found that it irritated people but I didn't care. In my mind a lot of wars had been started because of religion . . . Well! . . . That was what the books said!

Another driving factor to break away from living life in Johannesburg, or even South Africa, was the army training. If ever there was a reason not to put your life on the line for your country, it was the incredible lack of understanding I had experienced during my training, teaching, and use of arms. The continuous boring practice, practice, and practice made the learning soldier feel like he was the dumbest of all animals on earth. Almost everything we had done in the period of two years could have been learned in the first three months of induction. And I still had two more years to go with maneuvers each year and parades each month. The boring parades, polishing boots, cleaning uniforms, and making the beds was all so like 'playing a game with a thousand rules, of which only twenty percent count'. This I thought definitely came from the British. It must have come from the same place as the pure stupidity to fight in the South African bush with red coats on their backs. Why do hunters sometimes wear orange vests? So the other hunters won't shoot them! Why would you wear red in a brown terrain when you didn't want your enemy to see you? And so the South African kommandos fought the British for two years after the Boer War was supposedly over. Still, the British never changed the redcoat uniform. Instead, they used the worst tactics of all, vengeance and spite, powered by their numbers and money. It was only the power of money that provided many more soldiers for the British than the Kommandos could pay, and so in the end the Boers lost the war.

What was so controversial and contradictory in my thoughts on the army was the fact that the South African soldiers and airmen had received so many compliments for their participation in World War II. Did they really go through all that bullshit before being thrown into a war? I didn't think so, . . . but I didn't know.

I recalled the story that I had told Johannes at camp in Potchefstroom. The story my dad had told me about his side of the family, during the period after the Boer War had been declared over by the British. A horse can only run for about 40 miles at a very fast pace. So the South African kommandos would hit the British camps with surprise raids, ride right through, not even stop for a fallen comrade, and ride like hell for the 30 to 40 miles. The British couldn't catch them because, firstly, they took a long time to react, and then after the 30 to 40 miles, the kommandos would change horses at a predetermined farm, and ride off on fresh horses. This continued for nearly two years. The British were being laughed at in Europe.

So the British did the fateful thing: declared it illegal for anyone to help the kommandos in any way. If a farmer helped a kommando, the British shot all the men on the farm and took the women and children to concentration camps. My grandfather, who was a Huguenot and spoke French, never liked the British. He helped the kommandos. And his farm in the Cape, near Oudtshoorn, which reputedly took three days to ride round, was burnt to the ground and the women put into concentration camps. I wondered how this had happened . . . nothing had been confirmed . . . I didn't know how my father had got away, or how my grandfather and his family had survived. . . . My dad never saw many in his family again and he didn't know if they had ended up in the concentration camps or what. There were reputedly more than twenty brothers and sisters from two mothers. My grandfather must have got away and eventually ended up visiting Johannesburg. My dad grew up in Beaufort West and eventually also went to Johannesburg. The story was so confusing!

My only memories of my grandfather were that he had been blind and ninety-three years old. He would not let his youngest daughter, who was twenty-three, go out unescorted, even to the shops. She obviously disobeyed him, especially when he fell asleep. I had met my grandfather only once. He spoke French and Afrikaans and I couldn't understand him very well. When he died he took the last words of French spoken in the family with him. His family had come to South Africa over 200 years earlier.

If I ever fought for my country, it would be as a kommando. This parade stuff was just too much for me. I was a good shot. I had proven this in Potchefstroom and knew the basis of survival in the bush. I would not allow some stupid leader have me march into the enemy as a sacrifice, or as just another number. I hated the army routine; it was a waste of time and interfered with my need to learn.

I also didn't want to continue this college, army and work program, with very little time for soccer and still not enough money to have a car. I wanted to take girls out without worrying about where we went, in case it cost too much, or how they'd get there because of no car, and how I had to get home after taking my date to her house and staying late. I'd love to have the freedom of not borrowing a car or asking for a ride. I had done that so many times and each time it was an embarrassment. I thought to myself that a car would solve all my problems. I would now put any thought of going overseas on hold. It would just be perfect. As I hadn't saved very much money, I'd talk to my mom, or whatever.

Suddenly the bell rang again. I shut off the machine and headed home. I really didn't know if I had machined all the pieces correctly, and I didn't care for once. I would check them in the morning. Right now I was going to play soccer on Thursday and Saturday and that was all that counted!

◆

Soccer was a major mainstay in my life. The constant activity was physically rewarding and playing in the top leagues was a monstrous uplift. But even soccer was changing rapidly. Many of my friends in soccer were reaching their limitations. The Reserve League was tough, hard hitting and fast. It drew players from all over the country. If you played in Johannesburg there was a chance, however small, of being seen by a soccer representative from Europe. The Scottish Leagues had picked up at least ten of our players over the past few years. The English Leagues, with four divisions, had picked up even more. There was no doubt that if you were to be a movie star equivalent in South Africa, it would be through sport. South Africans always had a wonderfully deep respect for anyone who excelled in sport; in any sport.

I knew I had little chance of excelling, even at the young age of twenty: I could be a good journeyman player, and that was fine. My love of the sport was my reward. Although you can never judge your play against that of other players, you can measure your contribution over a period of time. I wanted to be honest with the thing in my life that had provided me with something that I had been able to look forward to for over ten years. So I considered that there were many players deemed much better and there were many I considered I could handle. The downside of the soccer was, you could go to England or Scotland and play soccer professionally, but you wouldn't earn more money than a qualified journeyman would in South Africa; all the soccer players knew it. Then there was the weather; we all thought it would be atrocious to live in such constant rain. The parents of the Southern Suburbs had made sure that their sons and daughters had a trade, especially the sons. The stories of returning players had confirmed that there was a special pleasure in being a player from South Africa, playing in the United Kingdom. The pressures were great, and the British players had had better coaches in their learning curve, but still, a few South African players, like Johnny Hubbard, Ken Zeising, Horace Smethurst, Gordon Falconer and Wally Warren had held up the honor of South African soccer.

◆

Saturday came quickly and Desmond, Robbie and I played again. Robbie, who played right wing in our team, was extremely talented. He was just so natural in his body co-ordination. He was fast, tricky, and had a good shot. He was walking with me after the game. Robbie smoked, which was common among many players. To me it was most unbelievable when done straight after a game.

"That's it, I quit!" Robbie said to me.

"No! Don't say that . . . you're crazy!" I said in a startled voice.

"No! I've had enough! I'm really not interested any more, the training, the practices. I'm going to Sunday League, it's more fun."

"But Robbie, you've carried us into finals, won finals, and been our best player for years. You're the one player who could go to England. There isn't a better player in our team and there are not many in other teams who would have a chance to go!" I pleaded.

"I don't want to go to England. The English chaps want to come here!"

"But just for a few years," I came back. "What's to lose?"

"No, I'm happy here in Johannesburg. My family is great and I've got a girlfriend. It's too much trouble. We wouldn't save any money . . . Charl, there are no guarantees!"

We walked for a while. I was dumbfounded and speechless.

"Well, we could talk for hours," I continued. "I've had this funny feeling our team is breaking up. We've been together for almost nine years . . . you . . .Desmond . . . and I. I was talking about this heavy stuff just this week, with Desmond!"

"Charl we've been soccer friends forever it seems, but it's time for change. Come and play in the Sunday Leagues. This stuff is too serious and I feel it's more hard work than fun! Sometimes it's really good but only half the teams are competitive."

"Agreed! What does your brother think?" I asked. Robbie's brother played for the Marist Brothers' top team and many of Robbie's teammates, including me, thought Robbie was better than his brother.

"I don't know. He's in his own world, and besides, he may go to Scotland." Robbie paused. "Charl what are you going to do?"

"Shit. All my friends are getting married. They're slightly older than me, but it seems everything is breaking up now. Soccer has always been steady. A lot of things are happening in my life. But I'm not as good a player as you are, nor will I ever be, and I envy your talent. I would like to see you 'use it' as we say. Maybe I envy your choices."

"Forget that!" said Robbie. "What about you, you're a good player, very strong, very fast. You're extremely hard to beat in defense . . . that's definite! Yes! Man! What about you?"

"Robbie, I could spend hours telling you. I have some school to finish. Friends are disappearing into marriage, plus some family changes. I am confused! But I'm excited. I'm happy. Couple of girls in my life, what else you want to know?"

"How's the school? You must be finished by now. Shit, it's been years and years."

"Oh, it's fine. I'm taking French next year! Just kidding!" I continued in a serious vein. "I'm very much thinking of just buying a car and having a good time."

"That's alright."

"Yes, it's okay, but I think I'd like to go to America. Please! I haven't told anyone except you and Desmond."

"I'll say nothing! But you can't get into America. The waiting list is two to three years."

"Yes, I know, Rob. Maybe I'll go to England first or something."

"Well, Pal! You think about the Sunday League at Pioneer Park. Seriously, there's room for you on my friend's team. I wouldn't ask you if I didn't think you were good enough! Forget about your crazy dreams! Stay in South Africa and marry a beautiful woman!"

Robbie laughed! I laughed!

"It's not a bad suggestion!!" I replied.

We shook hands and hugged.

"Cheers!"

"Cheers!"

I walked away thinking that my friends were in a marriage frenzy!!

◆

I really loved Johannesburg and when I compared it to other cities, it always came out on top, and mainly because of the excitement of the big city. I had played soccer in almost every city on the Rand as well as having competed in special tournaments in Germiston and Pretoria. So, indirectly I had visited, seen and talked about these cities. But in comparison the result still ended up the same: Johannesburg was number one. There were many trips to Durban and one trip with Doc to Cape Town when I was thirteen. Cape town was nice but seemed small. Durban had the ocean and beaches and a good possibility for exciting living. I didn't know anyone there though, so it too was discounted. Johannesburg was the big center for business, sports activities and entertainment. The Southern Suburbs was my territory and Johannesburg downtown just twenty minutes away. How could you beat that? I felt at home anywhere in the city and sometimes it seemed as though I knew everyone in the Suburbs. My curiosity had sought out knowledge on anyone who had anything to do with my friends. My memory was also good. I knew all the sport places connected with cricket or soccer and I certainly knew all the places to dance. Johannesburg was such a positive factor and it always made me happy to go downtown. I was at home in the big city and could go anywhere I liked with confidence. I also knew where not to go, and kept up with where to go and when to go.

◆

All these thoughts kept bringing me back to the feeling that my true family included my friends. Problem: they were slowly going their own ways. First, as a steady girl- and boyfriend, then as married couples, all of which had the most dubious effect on their availability.

Zee marriage is zee guillotine of zee friends, especially zee single ones! I thought. So I also thought about changing cities, but that was not easy because I was not finished with college, and I was not finished with the South African Army. A job change to be an engineering designer instead of a machinist meant I might have to take a drop in wages. This did not suit my liking because I had just started to enjoy the higher journeyman's wages. Other restrictions were the cost of renting a flat and buying a car, and then buying and cooking food, buying clothes to look sharp, and the costs of going out. So the end result was that I still lived with my mom, her husband, and Donald. Privacy was nil.

The slow disintegration of the Andrew Street Mob activities meant that a more individualistic approach was needed, but I ignored that aspect. I was looking for a future and the American image re-entered my thinking for the hundredth time. Each occasion when the movie formed in my mind of America and its freedom, I thought how much better it would be than the Government in South Africa and its restrictive approach to life. Everything to this body of men in the Government was linked to the Voortrekker's dream of owning and directing their own country. Now that was okay, but why not open all the major social categories like the Americans had done. In business terms they had an American approach, but not in social terms. To me there seemed to be more rules to social life than to business. *Too close to the church,* I thought. All the recent changes to the black lifestyle were now even more restrictive than before and it was as though the black man had to go back to something in history that they didn't like. All their social gains, no matter how small, were wiped out in one stroke. Even though all my friends were white, in South Africa's terms, they were, because of the Government, suffering indirectly at work or in business. There was distrust, petty theft, and loss of good attitude by the blacks. Also the overall atmosphere of restriction due to the segregation rules and the dividing line in social graces had its effect on normal relaxed lifestyle. Anything not in a line with the politicians' traditional ways was harnessed. The black people were changing their acceptance of all Government rules and were showing it through defiance. The atmosphere had changed, already there were fewer places to be safe in Johannesburg: my beloved city.

All these deep thoughts questioned my future in Johannesburg. I knew my friends would remain in South Africa, because none of them had ever expressed a view to live overseas, nor did they seem to worry about the changes. If they did it was not discussed. Actually none of them, including me, had even wanted to go to the copper mines in Rhodesia less than a thousand miles away. There you could earn a lot of money in a two-year assignment, at least enough to put down on the purchase of a house. Any European attraction or idea of going to England fell away as my friends approached their marriage dreams. Perhaps they were now on different pathways. I was also starting on a different path. It was exciting. It was also very, very sad.

◆

Invitations to dinner with my best friends on a Saturday night became boring. All they talked about was the house, the presents they got, and the furniture they bought. I loved them very much, and so I went to some dinners, but it was not what I wanted to do. The latest events in my life confirmed my feelings of staying single, especially every time I went to dinner with friends. I didn't want marriage yet.

So I went back to the social scene. The jazz music continually drove me towards the 'Rock Scene' and American-style dancing. My first love was in clear view to me on Fridays and Saturdays. Musicians in rock bands were the hit. Jazz was also very prominent, but drew the older crowds. There had finally come an entertainment split in the Andrew Street Mob. As my close friends had found steady girlfriends and entered the marriage scenario, I alternated between what was left of the Andrew Street Mob and Bobby's Group and the 'Rock Crowd'. I was drifting from my long-standing basic social crowd, but still driving hard in playing soccer, working, and studying.

Then I went out with Joan. She lived in the northern suburbs. This tall beautiful girl with dark hair and a smiling face fitted into a dream girl category. We went out a number of times, but the cost was killing me. I also had to beg my stepbrother, Donald, for a loan of his suit, so that she didn't think that I had only one suit. And, because she lived on the other side of town, I also had to beg for Donald's car: not an easy task as we both wanted to go out on Saturday nights. I had only partially solved the problem by introducing Donald to Meridy, who loved to stay home on Saturdays! The major frustration was that good etiquette and common sense required that young men ask the young lady to go out—a week before the date. But too often, it was Saturday morning before I found out if I could have the car. So I had to scramble for a date. My frustration continued to mount over not having a car. Joan was really beautiful and was a driving force. I was earning good money and could spend a lot more if I quit college. Then I could go and see Joan during the week as well and not suffer the same problem, which had caused me to lose June. My thoughts continued on this theme because there was no alternative. Girls would not just see you on a Saturday night. If they liked you, they wanted to see you during the week too. Calling up late, wondering about transport, hoping everything would work out was becoming old, really old. I had done that for too long. Studying on Sundays 'SoS' crossed my mind: *Same as in the war, I'm in trouble here! I'm tired of studying, going to school, one night of practice. This is the same old routine!! I am not going to do it!! Anymore!! I'll talk to Mom!*

So I decided to look in the papers for a car and found it exciting. I went to see some of the cars and finally to my delight I found one, a Citroen. A French car, a two door (both doors opened to on-coming traffic) and a stick shift on the dash. The seller wanted 200 pounds, a fair price, but not in my pocket. I went to see Mom.

"Mom, what do you think? I really need this car to live!"

"How are you going to pay for it?" she asked.

"Well, if you buy it, I'll pay you back 4 pounds a week. It'll be done in a year!"

"How about license, insurance, etc.?"

"Same thing Mom, I'll pay you back," I confirmed.

"If it breaks down . . . "

"I'll fix it. I've fixed your car, Mr. Boddington's car, James' brother's car, and John's car! That's not a problem and it's simple!"

"The money is hard to come by though Charl, and I think it will upset your routine with college and you'll stop going."

"No I won't! No! It won't upset my life!" I almost pleaded. "I'm in such a predicament always borrowing a car, Mom!"

"I don't know! I'll have to think about it and talk to Donnie."

"What's Mr. Boddington got to do with it?"

"We are married you know . . . !"

"Yes, everyone is married. It's becoming dumb! If this is what happens to everyone, I'm not going to get married!!!" I said, totally frustrated.

"Good," my mom said. She got up and walked out of the room very quietly.

I knew it was a problem. It was a major problem.

◆

After about two days, after dinner one night, my mom called me in to my room.

"We can't do it," she said. "We're trying to build a place out at the Klip river and we owe too much money. Sorry Son!"

"I should have fought for Gran's money," I said, not knowing where that thought came from. "No matter what I do, it boils down to money-money-money. You can't ignore it. I had lousy old used bicycles for racing. I still have to spend everything on books, bus fare, and college dues. All my friends seem okay, all they have to do is go to work and play! I don't even have enough clothes to go to Northcliff dancing twice a month with the same girl. I have to take a different date because they'll think that's the only suit I have! Mom, this is serious. I'm earning good money now. I need a car to be independent. I hate depending on Donald's car, or your car, or whatever. I've bummed off everybody for years, getting rides, having to ask girls on dates hoping Johnny was going to the same place. . . . I've never asked anyone for money!!"

"Son! You admit you don't have enough money for clothes, but you want a car," my mom interrupted.

"They don't look at your clothes, Mom, when you have a car!" I said smiling. "Besides, I'll have more time than now when I have to catch buses and wait for trains to get somewhere. I have to have a car!"

"You have worked very hard for an education. Stick to it Son! Don't let the girls drive you into spending all this money. You've nearly finished with all your college. You're a qualified machinist. Your world will change radically in your twenties. We can't afford to go another 200 pounds in debt. Sorry Son!" My mom left the room.

◆

This whole life subject was really burning inside. My thoughts went into the unfair category of life. I knew I had worked damn hard to get ahead . . . studied . . . worked hard . . . got raises, but still no satisfaction. I had put up with a lot of pain knowing most of my friends seemed to afford the lifestyle a lot easier. Who helped them? Uh! Maybe they had the same problem. Well they never said they couldn't. I had battled now for five years. Maybe I was impatient and should work and save for a year for a good down payment on a better car. But another year seemed like an eternity. Joan was really beautiful and classy. She walked so elegantly and was so nice to talk to, and the enjoyment of being with her into the early hours of the morning was very special. It made my hard work seem worthwhile. The soccer was dragging, school was dragging, and I really, really hated the Army routines.

Something has to give, was my last thought as I took off out of the house to catch the bus once more to go to soccer. The bus was my place to calm down, think things out and work up a plan. I had always liked riding on buses; you were alone-in-yourself, but not alone in life. So I tackled life there, almost like an observer. I just wondered why I was questioning all these subjects of life, and in so much detail. It was becoming a major confusion.

The bus took off and I went into the thought process: *Is there a concern with Johannesburg, maybe South Africa?* I thought. *No it's not with South Africa.* I hadn't seen the whole country. How could I tell? The prisoner-like feeling induced by the Government seem to disappear at work or playing sports, but there always seemed to be reminders. The way Government agencies—the Post Office, the police force—acted or spoke to you as a person always perpetrated methods of dominance and control. I cared for none of that and yet there were so many nice places to go, friendships were never in short supply. There were rough gangs in the 'Suburbs', a violence aspect, but they were known and that was not a great deterrent. The rough gang activities were easily counterbalanced by being with the large numbers of nice people around you. As a white, I never really witnessed the physical black/white problems; there were enough problems among the whites: the normal forces of young and old, new and traditional, deeply and moderately religious, European background (new immigrants) and native South African, lazy and industrious, rich and poor, and hard and soft. Of course, there was always the complication of the unfair laws against black people. I had never had more than casual interactions with Asian or Indian people. There seemed to be no problems with them at all. Despite all these complex situations my belief that South Africa could survive as a multi-race country was always positive. There was enough land and food to share. The more I read about America, the more I didn't want to go to Europe, England or Asia. I didn't want to prejudge these countries, but all the history, the behavior of immigrants, and current news didn't lean in their favor. So I never really sat down and talked about this aspect with anybody. I tested the thought with a lot of people and with my friends, but I had no intention of influencing anybody. No one person had received the full blast of all my thoughts, especially my close friends. Maybe I was scared of their reaction! Overall, I was definitely feeling like I was being squeezed in a corner with too many rules. So! When my brain became overloaded, I played soccer, went dancing or met with my friends. *Why not!* I concluded.

CHAPTER 21

❄

Making A Move

BILLY AND TOMMY HAD talked so much about starting their own business that I got caught up in the fever. They were waiting for Christmas to pass before starting their planned move to quit Joy Sullivan. Billy, understanding my anxiousness, made arrangements for discussions to take place between his friend Dan and me. The interview took place and it all seemed reasonable but very different to what I had been doing. Dan's company made swings and playground equipment for kids. He had about eight black people in the fabrication shop. Dan needed somebody in between sales and shop fabrication to work the factory system. Also, he needed a designer to create new ideas. I liked that very much. I was to get the same salary as my present job as well as the promise of a share in the company. I signed on to start after the Christmas holidays. Billy and Tommy formed their engineering company and so the three of us were now definitely leaving Joy Manufacturing. Len was displeased as hell, losing three good men. In the end he somehow understood our craziness and offered us a job if things didn't work out. I thanked Bjorn for his good friendship at work and his help.

On my first day, early in January, at the job, after discussions with Dan, I started on a welding job. I hadn't welded anything for four years. The shop routine was straightforward: cut, shape, drill, weld, assemble, weld, clean, paint. There were no lathes, grinding machines, or boring mills. After ten days I was very frustrated. First there was nothing to do, and then there was a mad rush during which I didn't know what to do. So I decided to design a jig whereby the parts of the swing were laid in, cut and welded—no measurements. Then I found out the swings always changed in size. Dan felt the jig would become too complicated if it were adjustable. I believed I could make it work. I got the feeling that Dan didn't really need someone new; he needed two Dan's. I couldn't seem to contribute anything substantial, no matter what I tried. This very quickly became a difficult situation and I saw Dan's frustration. Despite all the questions on my new job, I just kept a positive side up. I did not say anything to my friends. To my family, "everything is fine!" was my answer to their questions. Inside I knew I had made a mistake. It was a terrible error in judgment. I definitely had got caught up in the scheme of things.

On a Thursday in the middle of January, just ten days after starting, I took my lunch into Dan's office.

"Dan, it's not going to work!"

Dan looked at me and then smiled. He sat back to give the upcoming subject his fullest attention.

"Yeah, I think it's a mistake, Charl," Dan replied almost sympathetically. "In fact I've a feeling that I was in too much of a hurry to hire someone. It's mainly because I'm so frustrated with doing it all myself."

"No, I was in a hurry for an opportunity. This move seemed so good, I just leapt at the chance of getting into a business with some sort of partnership." I came back. "Now I'm feeling I don't have a way to make a contribution." I paused. "It's costing you money as well."

"No, Charl, I see your potential. I think you would make it. I just need someone now who could do it without me training them. I don't have the time to train someone. Time is what I am willing to buy. It's my mistake."

"Well . . . " I started.

"Listen Man! I pulled you from a good job. It's my fault. If you could find another job it would make me feel better. In the mean time, I'll pay you full wages until you do. I don't mind, Charl—I don't mind at all."

"That's fine. I'll go look." I paused. "It's okay! In fact, I want to take this afternoon off. Is that alright?" I asked, not knowing what my options were while saying it. I felt my current situation was like a slot machine, where the reels kept running and no three items lined up. I was now going to do something about it.

"Please Charl, go ahead, take your time, we'll work it out."

"Thanks" I answered, feeling a little relieved that this whole thing had come to a head. I did not want to be anywhere I wasn't wanted.

I got changed and walked towards the center of downtown into the abyss of tall buildings. It was not a long distance from Dan's shop in the southern part of Johannesburg City. The walk was doing me a lot of good. The pinwheels in my mind were turning . . . stopping . . . restarting . . . moving on and repeating the process every time I had a new thought. I was going through all my thoughts of the past year and I just knew that a solution would come out: it had to!

The traffic was very busy. The streets were crowded with shoppers. There was a continuous mixed flow of moving people and cars, and people that didn't move but just looked. The traffic lights changed, and the people and cars swapped space. The same rhythm, on and on, non-stop from morning till night. I didn't know where I was going but when I reached Eloff and Commissioner streets, I cut left, and after a couple of turns, I was standing outside the Castle Shipping Line offices. I decided to go inside.

"When does the next boat leave for England?" I asked a pretty young lady behind the counter.

"We're all booked up until April, Sir."

Sir! I thought. *Wow! That's nice.*

"Towards the end of April," she continued.

"Too late!" I said emphatically. "I need a boat leaving soon."

"Let me see in the shipping guide. I'll see if another line has a ship."

"Thank you," I said, thinking she was pretty and had such a nice voice. *That's probably why she got the job . . . Ah! No! Not really!*

"Shaw Savill Line has a boat leaving February 12th from Cape Town."

"Truly? Where is their office, please?" I asked, trying to be polite.

"Two blocks down the street on the left."

"Oh! Thank you . . . very much!"

I ran down the street into the Shaw Savill offices. After twenty questions, many answers, and the signing of some papers, I ran out of their office, down to the government offices, and filled out the forms for my passport. I came out of the government office onto the street; it was 3 o'clock. The South African Government office doors closed. I had just made it. A chill, a very deep chill of excitement, went through my body. These three hours had been so exciting. Things were moving! I was sailing on February 12, 1956. In four weeks, I would sail out of Cape Town to England. I had not the slightest idea where I was going to get all the money for the trip. It cost 65 pounds for the ship alone, about four weeks' wages. I'd find it! I'd get it! My body was shaking with excitement and it wouldn't stop! So I ran to Escom House to catch the bus to the Southern Suburbs. I was dying to tell someone what I had done.

Mr. Boddington sat down at the table, Donald came in late, and Mom sat down just as we started supper. The same table that all the aunts and uncles, and cousins, had sat at. It was the same table where Lena had so often brought me a plate of food. I loved her for that, and the many other things she did. The table had served Bazil and Yvonne. It had witnessed a million conversations encompassing so many of my friends in the Andrew Street Mob. They had been allowed to come in late at night, sit down, and have a fried egg sandwich after partying all night. Bobby and Helen from next door and many kids on the block had eaten there. My mom had always welcomed them. It was the same table at which Gran and Uncle Mick and Wolf had watched me growing in my seat, until I had no longer needed a cushion. I'd thrown everything that I hated to eat under this table. Wolf had eaten it all. It was here that I'd talked to Gran for more hours than I could ever imagine. *Tonight is significant,* I thought as I sat there. I didn't know whether I should wait for Johnny to drop by for dessert, or let the family know my news right away. The silence at the table was eventually broken.

"You look happy," my mom said, smiling. "Did you have a nice day?"

"Yes," I said, jumping in, following such a perfect opening by my mom. I had a smirk on my face, and I knew it. "I got fired and I'm going to England in February."

Everyone looked up while they chewed on their food.

"Charl, stop that nonsense."

"No Mom! It's true! February 12th . . . 1956."

My mom wasn't sure whether I was joking or not. She was being careful. So she said she thought it was a good idea and put forward many questions. I answered them. Finally she asked the hard one.

"What about money?"

"Don't know, but I'll do it," I said. I knew the news was a shock, and that maybe they didn't believe me, and that I didn't have all the arrangements in place yet, but I was going to go, and I knew it.

Mr. Boddington said nothing. He had for many years not interfered in matters between my mom and I. Donald was equally quiet.

I don't think they believed me . . . surprisingly!

◆

I went into work the next day and told my story to Dan.

"I don't believe you did that!" He had an astonished look on his face. "You must have been thinking about going overseas before."

"No! It had crossed my mind in the last few months, but I had no real plans! I just went downtown and did it!"

"You're damn lucky to be able to do that! I've always wanted to go to Europe. This business and my family keeps me from doing that . . .!" He smiled. "Didn't mean to drive you out of the country!" said Dan, laughing and twisting his head, "just 'cause we didn't work out!"

"My urge to do something really different has been some time coming, Dan," I said, laughing. "But now you understand that you're part of the catalyst." I continued with a big smile, "Thanks!"

Dan continued talking for some time about the many choices in life that were there but never taken. He then discussed the details of my commitments and his promised contribution. Despite my arguments of no-fault between us, I was very happy with the much-needed money that Dan said he would give me.

"I can't thank you enough," I said. I was truly earnest in my gratitude to this nice person.

"That's the way I want to do it . . . just let me know when you get back. We'll get together and I'll listen to your stories. I'm only saying goodbye *for now*, Charls, and good luck!"

"Bye," I said as I left, thinking what a good man he was. He was the second person who had assumed that I would be back soon . . . the first had been my mom.

Johnny hadn't come for dessert for the second night in a row. So that night I took the bus to Rosettenville Corner and went into the Broadway Hotel bar. I was desperately hoping I would see someone. The everyday crowd was there. It was noisy, smoky and, as always, upbeat: probably its key to success. The day's activities were being discussed.

After sitting with a beer for a while, something I seldom did alone, I heard familiar voices. Much to my surprise, and of all people I had expected, Bobby and Abie came in and sat down with me. "I'm glad to see you guys!"

"Hullo Charl!"

We drank and slopped our beer all over. It was a fun old dirty bar.

"Got too much money?" I asked.

"What money?" asked Abie.

"The money you're throwing on the table. It's sacrilege to spill beer!" I said.

"Alright, how's the new job?" asked Bobby.

Perfect entry, I thought. I started my story, with all the excitement of a child. I told them about the change in job, Dan and the shop and the problems, and finished with the booking on the S.S. Southern Cross and why I had done it. Then I got up to get another three beers—it was hard to get waitresses to work this bar, they never lasted very long. In fact I wasn't sure how many years ago I had last seen one come to the tables. I dropped the beers off and went to the men's room. The smell was worse than any construction site temporary shack, used for the same purpose. Also, I remembered that you could see into the kitchen down the hall, so I didn't look. My design sense could never figure that one out. I came back to the table.

"We're going to go," said Bobby.

"Go where?" I asked.

"To England!"

"Bullshit! . . . Oh! . . . Just like that!"

"Yes!"

"Come on! You've just got nothing to do . . . your bank account is full . . . so you're ready to go!" I challenged.

"No! We wouldn't want you to travel alone! You could get lost!"

"Don't mess me around, you two! This is something that is super-important!"

"We're going to go, Charl!"

"Marvelous . . . bloody marvelous." I yelled. "The three of us. Oh my God!" I felt a thrilling surge, like I hadn't felt for some time, go through my body. This had all been inconceivable just a few days ago.

"We've nothing to lose."

"That's right!"

"Abie wants to fight in England and I want to stop being a car mechanic," said Bobby.

"I want to beat up the Pommies!" added Abie, laughing. I knew he was serious!

"This could be a great adventure. What about Tommy?"

"Don't know," answered Bobby.

We were totally exhilarated. The hours flew by like seconds, as we discussed the plans and dreams of us three 'Suburbs Boys' going to a foreign country. It became apparent that the trip was going to be a truly unknown adventure. We didn't know where to go, where to stay, or what to do about a job, after we got off the ship. Money was hardly discussed. Girls were discussed in every possible detail. All three of us came to the conclusion we were bored in one-way or another. We knew the 'Suburbs' and Johannesburg backwards. We could almost go anywhere in our city, blindfolded, and find any place. Girls were looking to get married or were evolving into something other than just a good time. The new set of girls was younger, maybe too young? Or was it the embarrassment of being seen with someone not our age. The situation was boring and without excitement! There was no doubt that the three of us had worked through our respective apprenticeships, qualified, and would now be glad to go see another world. The guys from the 'Suburbs' who had gone to Europe, and come back with scintillating stories, may also have prompted all this 'travel nonsense'. Regardless of how they expanded their stories, it was intriguing, listening to the different ways other people did things, the change of scenery, the stories about the girls. In our discussions tonight we refused to believe them and agreed that we would go and see for ourselves.

The three of us rolled out of the Broadway Hotel as it closed. The first bus was going up Main Street. I jumped on and just stood in the well of the double-decker bus, as I only had about four stops to go. I walked the forty paces after the bus stop, and as I turned into Andrew Street, I passed by Zoni and Juni's house, Gloria's house, Thelma's flat and the Joostes' house, then the Loxtons' house. I thought of all my friends. I went down the list of neighbors I'd known since I was a six-year-old. Very, very few had moved away. I had known these people for fifteen years. Amazing! There had been a change, and most of the 70 kids had drifted into different pathways of life, but they were still in Andrew Street. The bigger question was the Andrew Street Mob . . . was this crowd of very close friends truly breaking up forever? I went through the gate at 65 and into the house. No matter, anyway! I had committed myself, and I knew I was going to go. I kept saying it, to make sure. There was no way I could back down now!

On Friday, Johnny dropped in for dessert, as he had done for many years. The family and John sat around the table for hours, talking about my trip. It was amazing that from Monday to Friday that week, so much had been learned about traveling and the country of England. I hoped with all my heart that Johnny would go too. I asked. Johnny replied that business and school would not allow, but that maybe he could come over for a visit.

"Yes! Please, John!" I pleaded.

Following that discussion my mom realized her son was really going away. How I could manage it, was yet to be answered. I was so happy inside. My physical element was so alive.

"We're going to have a 'helluva' going away party," John said.

"Right here," said mom. "We'll celebrate your twenty-first birthday before you reach it!"

"Okay, Mom! I would just love that . . . thanks!" I got up and kissed her.

"I'm only letting you have the house! You do the rest!"

"Okay!" I agreed, knowing that she would do all kinds of things to help.

At the end of the weekend, almost everyone knew about my news. The party would be on the Saturday the week before the train left for Cape Town.

◆

I played my last game with the Marist Brothers' team. It wasn't such a big deal to most of them. A number of guys asked if I was going to play in England. The answer was that I didn't know. I had told Desmond and Robbie before the game. I had actually called Desmond a few days before, and, in our conversation, he had revealed his disappointment. The three of us sat on the bench after the game and talked about many things. The emotion almost made me cancel my trip! I told them there was no reason that I would not come back, and then maybe play on Sundays. I felt so close to these two guys. I also felt some guilt for the change to the team, but Robbie had already said he was leaving the team. Besides, we knew that most players would go elsewhere; our training was complete. What Desmond would do, was my concern! We shook hands and they agreed to come to the party. I left, not feeling very good.

The complex logistics of leaving the country became apparent. There were so many things to do. I was counting on my holiday pay, and to get this I had to guarantee the Machinist and Millwrights Union that I would not work for three weeks after receiving the money. The

Union collected a portion of my pay every week, and dispensed the money when the holiday pay had been earned, usually at forty-nine weeks. There was a rule to ensure employees did take a holiday, and didn't work during that time. I signed a paper to ensure that I would not work in England until the three weeks was up. I wouldn't get my money until two days before catching the train. No reason was given. *Typical of this society*, I grumbled to myself. The other major piece of paper to get was permission to get out of my army service. Incredibly, it was not that complicated. I told them I was going to leave South Africa, work in England, and try out for professional soccer. The army gave me a letter of discharge. I was absolutely ecstatic inside. I just couldn't believe it. I was told, of course, that if I came back during my four year term, I was obliged to notify them. I agreed. The passport application also went without a hitch, and now I just had to pay for my ticket. Big question: sixty-five pounds—four weeks' full salary. I had about fifty pounds in my savings account. So what could I do, what could I sell? I knew I couldn't borrow . . . that would be funny! "Hey! Lend me fifty quid (pounds). I'll give it to you when I return!"

Besides the money, the big issues had been solved. The thought pattern of other things continued. I thought of how I was going to say goodbye to everybody, such as family and friends, and then a couple of close girlfriends. At one time I thought it might be better to stay and not go. What suitcase could I use? What should I take? Did I take my tools? What about my records? I mean, I had made a record cabinet in James' shop to hold my three hundred or so jazz records. Then the inevitable problem of money: how much would be enough? If I didn't get a job in England right away, I'd be in big trouble, with no one to turn to. Bobby and I had discussed that, and agreed we would take any job at first, and then look around while working. Even collecting trash. However, many things were starting to work out. My mom said that I could forget about the rent, which was a plus, but still, I did not have enough money. So I took a piecework machinist's job—and quit after ten days! That made the foreman mad! Perhaps because I produced more than his other workers. I was confronted at first with the foreman's pleading, but when he saw I was not going to stay, he lashed out with all his venom! I didn't care! It added almost thirty-six pounds to my kitty. I had really worked hard. So I bought my ticket for the sea passage, and my train ticket to Cape Town, and that made me feel good, because everything else would be money for living.

I was quickly realizing how complicated the trip to England was becoming. Besides the many things to do to make it happen, there were other events every day to complicate my coming change of lifestyle. I realized the planning wasn't simple; it was not just moving to Durban where I could pack up my clothes, toolbox, and record collection, and go. There was a difference between saying "goodbye" and saying "see you later." Every aspect of going to England was more complex. It was easy to hitchhike back from Durban with no money . . . I had done that . . . but how did I get back from England, if it didn't work out? My best, and most positive, estimate, was to arrive in London with two weeks' of money. I would have to get a job within ten days to still have at least a few pounds in the bank. I also wasn't sure what Bobbie and Abie would do. They might take off in some other direction, and then I wouldn't know anybody! Should I change my mind? . . . No! No! No! Not with my commitment, and the excitement of going. I just couldn't see myself going back to work in Johannesburg, finishing school, and being in the army until I was twenty-two. This would take at least another year. Besides, my soccer performance was peaking . . . I wasn't going anywhere. I needed to live alone or with a buddy—but who? They were all getting married, or getting complicated. I wanted a car and that seemed impossible; I wouldn't stay without having one. These things kept repeating in my mind. It just reinforced my own argument that a change in lifestyle, and the trip to England, it was the right thing for me!

Going to the dance with Coralie, when I had the car, confirmed my idea of a good time. A nice girl, a neat car, a good dance . . . and looking good. What else would a person want? I would get there, but not yet. The excitement of change was just too much. Could I get to America? Well, that was just an impossible thought and a crazy fantasy, right now. Maybe I'd learn to travel, perhaps it was easier from England. Then again, I might want to just come back to South Africa. Now that would be fine, but I had to go! Once again I convinced myself I was doing the right thing.

The complication of how to say goodbye to everyone I knew was reduced greatly by having a party. Also, we were catching a train, and some people would come to that event. Family pressure would require aunts, uncles and cousins to say their farewells. I still had a lot of arrangements to make.

I called the South African Railways and booked on a train to Cape Town leaving Wednesday night at 8 PM. The trip to Cape Town would take about 30 hours. I would arrive four days before the S.S. Southern Cross left Cape Town for Southampton.

I bumped into Dai at Rosettenville Corner and we talked about college. Dai and I had attended many classes together, and, more recently, the number of joint classes had increased. Dai was working on civil-structural subjects. I had broadened my perspective by taking on a combination of mechanical and structural courses. There was encouragement to engineering students in South Africa to take on two disciplines. For mechanical engineering the choice was electro-mechanical or structural-mechanical. This was a small country, and two disciplines were definitely better than one. Dai lived on Kennedy Street, about three blocks from me, and, being the same age, we had been at many parties together throughout the years. We hadn't seen each other socially much though, since the Army sign-up. Dai had met some of the Andrew Street Mob but did not participate regularly.

"I would like to go too," said Dai.

"Really?" I asked.

"Yes!" said Dai. "Well, my parents are from Wales, and I have a lot of relatives there. I could go and see them. My mom and dad have always wanted me to go."

I wondered about the mixture of guys. Bobby and Abie were definitely not Dai's type. It didn't matter, the more the merrier, I concluded.

"Bobby and Abie are going to come to the bar tomorrow night and we'll talk it out."

"Okay," said Dai, and he took off.

◆

Bobby, Abie, Dai and I met at the Broadway Hotel bar. The conversation was exciting as well as perplexing. How many suitcases? How much money? Who would do what? What to do when we arrived! How to get a job? What tools to take? The beer went down and the questions died out as positive themes took over from the hard stuff.

"Look," I said, "book on the train for Wednesday, get your ticket for the boat, get a date for the party at my house and we'll worry about the details later!"

"Now you're talking," said Abie. "Let's just go—no more talk about money and stuff. I'm going to talk to my boxing manager tomorrow. I'll get some fights organized in England."

"I'm with you," said Bobby. "I talked to Ian."

"Who's that?"

"My cousin, he is in England and looking to get us a place to stay."

"I'm going, for sure," said Dai.

"Good, four is easy, we can get a compartment on the train and a cabin on the boat," I suggested. "I don't care if I get on the boat with only one pound left—we eat free until England."

"When's the party?" asked Abie.

"Next Saturday, and we leave the next Wednesday night on the train," I answered. "Everyone got it? . . . Let me know if you get tickets."

We all got up and left.

How did I say goodbye to everyone? I thought an awful lot about that. How would I say goodbye to June, Joan and Coralie? I wasn't going steady with any of them but I wanted it to be more than an average effort to say goodbye. It was one of those complications of going a long way . . . like overseas. This was definitely a big jump. Then there were people who had been big in my life; I went down the list. Norman, Mac and all the boys; the party would take care of them. I would definitely like to go out with June, Coralie and Joan, but how, and when? Something reminded me of Rosemary and Jackie. Rosemary had called me before Xmas to say she was going to Cape Town to get married or something . . . I decided I would call her mother. The family list became more and more important: Mr. Van, for sure, Yvonne and James, my dad. Then there was Main Reef Engineering, the professors at college and the guys on the soccer team. No! This was becoming too much. Why shouldn't I treat it as though I was going for only a month? I knew that going to Europe was a big thing in our circle. Nobody just went there for a holiday or short business trip.

◆

I went to Main Reef Engineering and arrived just as lunch had begun. I walked down the side of the factory where most of the black men sat eating their lunch. As I approached, I noticed some new faces, and some very familiar faces. Those that knew me stood up and told the others to stand up. They touched their hands together like clapping hands with slow movement but no sound. I had never seen this before, but had heard about it. It was a sign of respect . . . I did the same. They gathered around and I told them I was going to England.

"Do you have a nice suit?" asked Picannin.

"No! But if it is necessary I will steal one from my brother!" I replied, knowing I was being set up by Picannin.

"Ah," said Picannin. "Then you can go to see the Queen and tell her about us. Tell her we have been working very hard and we want to become rich like her . . . and stop working . . . and then we just play soccer!"

"Yes Picannin! I will tell her for sure," I said, with a big smile.

They all laughed. "To the Queen," said Picannin, as he held up his can of Coca-Cola.

"To the Queen," came the chorus.

I went in to see John, the boss's son, and we talked for a long time. All I could think of was that I would never return to this machine shop again . . . this was all over! I said goodbye. John wished me well.

The timing was good, it was lunchtime, and so I went into the shop lunchroom, sat down and talked for a while to the men I had worked with.

"Funny that you're going there to work, and they all want to come *here* to machine," said Mr. Warren.

"I just want to do something different," I said. "Maybe not machining, but just anything . . . you know, be a waiter or something."

"You'll have to join a union over there. Everybody belongs to a union," said Mr. Warren.

"Yes, I guess so."

The men and I all shook hands and said our goodbyes. Ginge and I agreed we'd see each other later.

Laubscher and I went for a walk. We talked for a while, and in the conversation we talked about Sandy. Laubscher was a tough man and had seen more than I could ever expect to. We were from different eras and had different lifestyles, yet we shared such a wonderful bond that had really no definition in any advanced social dissemination. Sometimes it was 'stop and talk' . . . sometimes it was 'don't'. It didn't take words to acknowledge the need. It didn't take much to laugh. This time it was sad. Laubscher hadn't said anything in the lunchroom. I sensed his quiet. But I felt the deep emotion that was evolving now. Two buddies from the past, probably never to socialize again. Laubscher was going to leave Main Reef Engineering for a change in life. I had the feeling that since Sandy was killed, and I had left, Laubscher had found a void too big to fill in the same place. Sandy's absence was a big part of his despair. We walked a long distance . . . silent, for most of the time.

"All the best, my friend" said Laubscher, in broken tones.

"Shit!" I said, with moisture gathering in my eyes. "Everything is changing so fast."

"Don't panic Charl. You will do well, you are so talented, so intelligent," my friend of five years responded. He put a lot of emphasis in the statement.

"I hate to leave friends, lose friends, like Sandy," I added. Then there was silence again. "Laubscher! . . . . I truly thank you so much . . . you do not know. I will call when I come back. Leave details of your future place with John."

"All the best, my very good friend. I thank you too!"

We parted.

I caught the bus back into downtown Johannesburg. I went to the Carlton Hotel, climbed the stairs and sat in the lounge. I ordered a Castle Lager and my mind revolved. I saw no one as I sat and thought of all this lifestyle coming to an end. I would be away from my family, friends, and this city I loved so much. I sat in almost the same set of chairs that my dad, Aunt Bramie, their new son and I had sat in, one Saturday, a long time ago. My dad loved to go to the lounge at the Carlton Hotel. It was a symbol of success to him. It was probably where he could be at ease. I could not see that as a goal. The lounges seemed to foster pretentiousness . . . I didn't like that. To Dad it was different. As I sat there thinking, I began to understand the draw of the room's atmosphere, after comparing this beautifully decorated room to my dad's awkward ways and life history. The thoughts got too emotional. I drank my beer and got up and left.

On the bus going home I split the list three ways: one, to go and see, two, to phone, and three, to come to the party or the train. Relatives would be invited to the train. I couldn't see all my friends, so they were invited to the party . . . Oh! That included Bobbie and Abie's friends and Dai. *Oh well, if they can't get in 65 that is just too bad.*

As I walked up the street I thought of Rosemary again. I went into the house and called. Her mom answered and said that she was out and would be back soon. I put down the phone and wondered why she was at home and not in Cape Town. I was completely surprised!

Bobby, Abie, and Dai called and confirmed the train compartment: we would all be together. However, we would be split into two cabins in the boat. The whole thing was coming together. The positives blew out the negatives. I worked out my money. If I got everything and paid for everything, I would land in England with fifty pounds. I probably could live for four weeks on that amount. I was happy. I couldn't spend a lot of money on going out or the party; otherwise it would cut into the fifty. *Well, here goes,* I thought.

Rosemary called and wanted to see me. I wanted to find out what was happening in her life, so I went out to Rosebank. But this time I knew I would catch the bus home. She explained that she had got cold feet and cancelled her marriage plans. We had a great time together, and suddenly she suggested, "How about tomorrow and Saturday?"

I told her about the party and she said she would come. Now suddenly, the light pressure of 'no free time' had just become a surge monster!

I went to see Mr. and Mrs. Van. Then I went to see my dad and his wife and son and tell them of the trip. We had dinner together. Bramie was a good cook. My dad, however, was more interested in when I was coming back. He had no excitement for my trip. Why I was going for more than a month didn't make sense to him! Where had I got the money? What about a job? Then, what was my reason to leave? I rode the tidal wave of questions in an easy manner. But I did jump positively on my dad's suggestion to see my stepbrother Ivan and my Aunt Rachel, my father's sister, in Cape Town. All that would be arranged, and my dad was coming to the station. Again, I had taken two buses to see my dad and two buses home. I confirmed one more time that my dad knew very little about me!

I had tried very hard to get any one of my very close friends, Johnny, Billy, Trevor, Zoni, Juni, Norman, or Doc, to go to England. They were all tied up. No one even got excited. I remembered that Pat had slipped quietly out of the country and gone to Chicago, and there hadn't been a major explosion of sentiment. In fact, Pat was supposed to be in London when I arrived. I didn't know where he lived. Maybe my friends just weren't interested in going to work, live, or even read about, overseas. I would get Pat's phone number.

I called Coralie on the Friday, but she was busy that night. We talked for a long time with me avoiding an invitation for her to come to the Saturday night party: Rosemary would be there. All the questions about going were answered for the umpteenth time. But it was nice to hear Coralie's reaction to my adventure. Coralie said she might come to Park Station. Although I had shown interest, many times, in going out a lot with Coralie, she had been very careful to not get too serious. We liked each other though, so when we did go out, it was always very enjoyable. I got off the phone and went into the backyard looking for Pal.

"Pal . . . come here boy!" He just stared at me as though I had done something wrong. Pal never moved . . . very, very unusual. Then I realized this running around had been going on for over two weeks and I had ignored him. But, ever since the day I came home after booking the passage to England, Pal had been this way! *No! That could not be so!* I thought. I went over to Pal and stroked him from head to tail. Pal did not respond. Pal's eyes were also very sad. I went inside.

"Mom, have you noticed Pal lately, is he sick?"

"No! He is alright."

"Does he wag his tail with you?"

"Well, come to think of it, he has not been very lively."

"I think that's been true for almost two weeks," I added.

"No, Son!"

"Dogs know a lot of things, Mom, that we don't. Yes! It's uncanny. Ever read Jock of the Bushveld?"

"Yes! I cried as well! I'll go look at Pal,"

I continued on my run of things to do. Then I started out the door to go and get a bus to Rosemary. "This is becoming a weird turn of events," I murmured, as I walked through the kitchen.

"What events?" asked my mom.

"Oh! Nothing! Lots of things are strange! First, everything is routine for a long time and now, Hell is breaking out all over!" I suggested.

"Oh! By the way, Pal wagged his tail for me."

"That is just one example, Mom!"

"Are you coming home?"

"Yes! But I'll be late. Bye!"

These dates with Rosemary were becoming very intense. The next big thing was the party.

◆

I picked up Rosemary on the afternoon of the party, and we arrived at 65 Andrew Street at 5:30 PM. At 6 o'clock there were already thirty people there. Many neighbors had dropped by early to wish me a safe trip, including the Adamses, Mutches, Gilberts, Joostes, and the Loxtons of course. This had been at my mom's suggestion. Although the party was scheduled for 8 PM, eighty people had arrived before then. This wasn't a big house! As it was summer, some people went into the backyard, some stayed out on the sidewalk, and some in the street. Andrew Street was filled with cars. It was very seldom that the kids of this block saw so many cars. A changing sign of the times! However, these kids were now in their twenties and many still lived on the street of their youth. I could not count the well-wishes, handshakes, and kisses on the cheek. At 9 PM the full Andrew Street Mob was there, including Trevor and Maureen, Johnny and Madge, Zoni and Maureen, Juni, Gloria and Hobbs, and Doc and Mary. Then there was Denise, Meridy, Ann, Grace and Otto, Thelma, Tommy and Mavis, Bobbie, Ron Joan and Denise, and Ginge and his girlfriend. Donald Boddington and his new girl Margaret arrived. She had actually grown up on Andrew Street in the next block. Norman brought a new friend Sheila, and Mac and Viv turned up late at 10 o'clock. In addition there was Dai, Bobby, Abie, Tom, Mickey and friends, until it became a blur to me. Rosemary and I tried to spend some time together but it seemed impossible. My mom reminded me to circulate many, many times. I wondered how. I circulated with everyone, leaving Rosemary in the kitchen with a drink. Desmond and Robbie dropped by with their girls, and we talked for a while, and then they seemed to disappear. The party was too big, but what else could be done? The people were inside and trying to dance in the back room, the marvelous extension to the house built by my mom. People were also standing outside among the fruit trees, talking and laughing, as the music floated into the neighborhood. There would be no complaints from the neighbors. They all knew the reason for the event, and besides, it was like a little village here in the Southern Suburbs. They were also celebrating the coming of age and wishing of a Bon Voyage to one of the kids that grew up in this Andrew Street Village. This was summer, and parties should be taking place. I wished someone would make a movie!!

Everyone was dressed up and looking good, laughing, talking. The dancing was strictly rock and roll, wherever it could be done. It was tight despite all the furniture of the room extension having been moved to one of the bedrooms. The rock and roll recordings from our era were played, and some of the favorites played more than once: this was a unification of the crowd and our music. Then a session of Afrikaans music got the dancers sweaty. The backroom and the kitchen were packed. My room, that had housed those wonderful Sunday night parties, had coats packed on the bed six feet high. It was a wonderful gathering of friends, acquaintances, neighbors and people who knew each other so well they could all be called 'family'. The majority of people here had known each other through the most important years of their youth.

At 11 PM my mom turned off the record player and asked for the crowd to make a small space in the back room. As many people as possible squeezed in. A hole in the crowd managed to take form. My mom stood on one side, and I stood on the other. She took out a gold key, about 8 inches long and 4 inches wide at the broadest point. Someone pushed a cake into the middle of the opening with candles burning.

"Happy birthday Son! May God travel with you everywhere, and keep you safe." Her voice stammered. "Also . . . here is the key to the door on your twenty-first birthday."

"Thank you Mom!" We hugged for quite a while, kissed, and I blew out the candles. The crowd sang the traditional Happy Birthday song, and then the sarcastic version:

"Why was he born so beautiful?
Why was he born at all!
He's no bloody good to anyone!
He's no bloody good at all!"

The well wishing continued. The party did not let up. Finally, after a lot of circulating, I spent some time with Rosemary, dancing and talking, and then we disappeared into the backyard.

"It seems like history passes by my eyes in a flash when I stand in this yard. I remember every tree, branch and corner from the house to the wall at the back lane," I said to Rosemary. "Most vivid is the fact that it was my dog Wolf's home, and now it's Pal's. Wolf could clear that back wall, six feet high, by just touching his paws on the top. This is where I played at soldiers when I was little. This is where my uncle tried to get me to chop off a chicken's head with an ax . . . I couldn't! So he did, and the chicken's body jumped around for quite a while. I ran in the house yelling 'Gran!'"

Rosemary laughed.

"After that I always asked if the chicken had come from the butcher!" I continued. "My brother had pigeons in those cages, wonder where they went. And this is Lena's room where she watched me grow up. I never knew why her room was in one corner of the yard, and the outside lavatory in the other.

"This is where we dug a trench three feet deep, filled it with coal and let it burn until it was red, then we put meat and chicken wrapped in silver paper and wet towels and covered up with sand. Some time later we dug it all out and ate it. What a braai (barbecue). I hear they do that in Hawaii or someplace.

"Let's go and find Pal."

We went to the kennel and there was Pal . . . but he still would not respond. I told Rosemary the story. Pal had become really excited, two days before I arrived back from army camp, when I had been away for three months. And now, before I had even bought the ticket to England, Pal had refused to respond to anything I do. "It's like he is mad at me!"

"Incredible," said Rosemary, "and you such a nice guy! You are a nice person, you know!"

"Yes I know!!" I smiled at the sarcasm.

There were still a number of guests in the backyard so any passion of the moment had to be delayed. *Dumb*, I thought, *who cares?*

"Charl!" my mom yelled, "some of your guests are leaving!"

I only saw Desmond and Robbie once. As the party continued, some friends and neighbors drifted home, but the music kept playing and the 'kids of Andrew Street' were still dancing. The core group hung on to the end; the room walls became a 'lean-back', and the floor became a seat, as we pretty much collapsed and relaxed. The crosstalk from wall to wall covered all subjects of the day. South African life was being discussed, from the perspective of my young friends. Mom, as always mixing with youth, was also sitting on the floor. Some of the girls were picking up the empty bottles and glasses.

It was 4:30 PM before the last few left. Johnny had taken Madge home and come back. Trevor and Maureen were still there. Rosemary and my mom were among those cleaning up. Mom's rule was simple: 'We don't care how long the party lasts, or how late it is, we are not going to get up in the morning and have to smell or clean up the liquor stuff.'

Johnny drove Rosemary and I back to Rosebank, and dropped her off at home. I was especially going to miss Johnny. How many times had we done this? The talks were terrific, our philosophy the same: 'See good, do good, have fun!'

"Rosemary is not coming to the station," I said.

"Whoa!" said Johnny, "why not?"

"Doesn't want to go through it, or I don't know why. So we're going to spend a day or so together," I said with a laugh. "I don't know, John, the Andrew Street Mob has gone out together so many times . . . we know each other's freckles. This party tonight makes you re-think your thoughts. For a while I thought we were all breaking up because of the marriages. New solid-type girlfriends are causing the guys to spend almost every night with them. My soccer team is also breaking up because of girls . . . players like Robbie are quitting because they are no longer interested or are interested in something else." I felt a little drunk. "Have we all got to the stage where picnics and sloppy Sunday evening parties are boring? We don't go to Margate in a crowd of more than four. We used to be ten or twelve of us going everywhere without all these monstrous arrangements. Maybe it's money? Back then we didn't have any pennies. Now we all are earning good money and can afford reasonable things . . . perhaps we've become independent." I paused for a while, but I didn't want Johnny to comment. I slipped back in the unilateral discussion. "It is almost impossible to get eight of us to go to a dance. So now we all pick a girl, go to a show, go to a place and sleep late on Sunday. Are we getting old? Actually the party tonight diffused all those thoughts, kind've mixed up my mind."

We rode for a while in silence.

"You're just a little sad you're leaving, and you should be glad you're going. Most of us would like to go," said Johnny.

"Really? I think most of us *could* go! I think we are getting old! Pretty soon there will be kids running around the houses. God, John, we're not thirty years of age. It's like society is separating us because we've been working for a long while."

"Charl! You're too emotional on this subject." He laughed.

I laughed and said very sincerely, "You're right, good buddy!"

"We'll all be friends forever, and maybe have picnics with our kids", added Johnny.

There was silence for a while, then I spoke. "You haven't been going out with Madge for a while. What's going on?"

"I think it has ended. We're not going out on any basis. We're just friends."

"I love the story of your first or second date."

"What story?"

"When you wanted to impress her on your first date! You were driving in the car, and she was all nicely dressed, and she lowered the visor to check on her make-up, and a pack of condoms fell on her lap! Shoot! . . . I'd have died on the spot!" We laughed and laughed.

"We've done some crazy things," added Johnny.

"Did your brother Allen put them there? That's the kinda thing he would do."

"No! He didn't. They came with the car when I bought it!" replied Johnny.

"Sure!"

"Talking about my brother, he and Denise are going out on a steady basis."

"Oh! Wow! I like Denise . . . hope it works out."

"Meridy has a new friend as well."

"Yes! I know her and Donald are not going out anymore . . . changing world."

"Norman, I believe, is going out with Sheila."

"True. And she is very pretty."

"Yes!"

We sat in silence as the Austin A40 went through Hillbrow. The car drifted down Eloff Street Extension towards Rand Stadium

"I wish we could go for a steak sandwich breakfast at the drive-in," I said. I did not want this time to end. And I definitely did not want to go home to sleep; I was wide-awake. "But it's closed for sure!"

"Sure was a good party!" complimented Johnny. "So good to see everybody. Your mom has been terrific Charl. One of the few parents who always had an open house for us kids."

"I never thought about that!"

"It's true hey! Think about that, not many of us were welcome in each other's homes. But everyone could come to your house."

"I know most of the parents made us go around the back of the house, and not go past the kitchen door into the living room or anything. Yes! You're right. Good old 65! Good for my mom . . . She's a little sad I'm leaving."

The car stopped outside 65 Andrew Street. It wasn't a mansion by any means. It was packed with memories though, and they were all flowing through my head as I thanked Johnny for driving through Johannesburg twice.

"This is heavy duty, John, lots of things on a man's mind. Suddenly it's not Andrew Street, it not the Southern Suburbs, it's not even Johannesburg, it's a country, South Africa, it's South Africans. It's who the hell we are and what the hell we do. It is complicated, it's house and food and money and jobs and lifestyle. It's girls, John," I shouted. "It's a million or more English girls, John, just waiting for us. They're tired of the tame old English boys with manners and conservative ways, John. They're looking forward to meeting crazy hot blooded South Africans, well tanned, good looking and good dancers!"

"You set it up," said John laughing, "and I'll come over."

"Do it, John! . . . Please! . . . Plan it and do it! It would be the best thing that could happen to me."

"I will try," said John.

Johnny drove off and I knew his route to the inch: up main Street, down Verona, right on Prairie and into the garage at 'Emoyeni'. A very appropriate name, meaning 'In the Wind'.

My last thoughts as my head hit the pillow, were that all my friends had shown their friendship, good wishes and eagerness for a fun journey. Rosemary had shown much interest in me during the last week or so. I was amazed at her change in feelings towards me; they were on the crest of seriousness. I was not sure. Johnny seemed as though he would miss me, and the reverse was very true. My lingering question was, what would I come back to? It was now becoming a sad thing to be leaving, instead of a delight. Consoled by the thought that I could come back to South Africa anytime, happiness, tiredness and sleep took me away from consciousness.

◆

There was a good reason that I had not invited Joan, June or Coralie to the party. It would've been a disaster. These were very nice friends in many ways, and I had just avoided talking to them before the party. I felt bad about it. So I called June and Joan, as I had called Coralie. I explained that I had an opportunity to go overseas, would be leaving pretty quickly, and would write. I desperately wanted to see them all but to do that would be almost impossible without transport. I felt as though I had let a couple of good friends down. Should I say that I would be back? Yes! I was beginning to think that way . . . Ah! I didn't know!

I went into Johannesburg to get my holiday money from the Union, then went home and packed. There wasn't much to pack. Thoughts crossed my mind as to this significance. *I've worked a long time but everything I have fits into a couple of cases. I am leaving my bike, tools, records, a lot of my books, some clothes, and a fabulous set of jazz records. Most of what I own is in my hands and my head! Well... that's all right!*

Everybody was at work so I walked down Main Street to Rosettenville Corner, went into the Broadway Hotel and ordered a beer. I drank it very slowly and spent the time people-watching and realizing what an icon this place was in the Southern Suburbs. I then walked out and caught the bus to town on my way to Rosemary's.

I spent a very nice evening and night with Rosemary. It was very emotional and we talked continuously. Rosemary wanted me to promise to come back within three months. "You must come back!"

I didn't know what she meant. If she was looking towards us getting together that would be serious stuff . . . right now!

I had to leave soon, to catch the last set of busses home. I did not want to leave. We embraced, knowing it would be a while before we saw each other again.

"I'll call you from the station."

"Promise?"

"Promise."

The next day flew by so fast; I was packing, getting toothpaste, checking tickets and wrapping up my room contents for a later time. Tommy said he'd hold onto my tools, and Ginge took my records. I was very happy with both of those arrangements. Helen and Bobby came to say the very last goodbye.

"Don't you marry one of those English girls now! You come back and marry a South African, right?" suggested Helen. We hugged.

"I won't . . . they speak funny!"

"Bye!"

"Bye Bobby. Bye Helen!"

I wasn't sure I had said goodbye to everyone. Rosemary and I had complicated the schedule; however, that had been my decision. I decided to make do with phone calls to June and Joan. The conversations were long, and they both said to write; I agreed. The list of people I had to write to was now becoming enormous. The three ladies had all asked if I would be back in a couple of months. I had replied that I didn't know how long exactly. I was getting the feeling that nearly everyone

I knew was considering this venture as a holiday. Perhaps that was because all the people that we knew who had gone overseas, had all come back. To a person, they had said that going overseas was very nice, but that South Africa was the place to be. Europe was too crowded, too busy, too many people and 'Old'.

◆

The money, the tickets, the bags were ready. I went out to the backyard to say goodbye to Pal. He slinked away, I pursued, but when he was cornered he shot past me. It was at least ten minutes before I managed to grab him. I ran my hand over his head and then his legs. I hugged him three or four times, but there was no response and no tail wag. I was in tears as I walked up the back stairs and into the house. I turned to look at Pal. It was uncanny that Pal and Wolf had sensed my problems. Wolf when I was a kid at 9 Main Street, and then Pal, with me going away to camp. Now he hadn't wagged his tail since I had booked my passage on the ship. I waved. Pal just stood there looking at me, very silent, not moving, eyes directly focused on me. It was a deep, long-lost look that could only bring sadness into a person's heart. Tears came into my eyes for a second time; I turned and went into the house. God, I had loved Wolf, and I loved Pal.

The next thing I knew, I was in the car with Mr. Boddington and Mom. She wanted me to go and see her friends from World War II, or at least show my face. She was talking, and then suddenly started to cry.

"What's the matter Mom?" I asked.

"I didn't really need you to go overseas, Son. I am just now enjoying you very much . . . watching you become a beautiful man!"

I was about to say, "*but Mom, you're the one who suggested it,*" and then realized that was out of place. Instead, I said in consolation, "I'm just tired of doing the same thing Mom!" I paused, thinking hard. "It's just like everything is changing and I need a break in what I'm doing. I need a change, especially while all my friends go in their directions. I don't want to get married!"

"Yes, I know, Son, that is good . . . that is so good!"

The car went over the bridge and down Eloff Street. I had requested that route. The tall buildings that created the city canyon were equipped with lights that lit up the streets. When would I see them again? This significant thought sat in my mind while Mr. Boddington talked. I heard nothing. Park station loomed up ahead.

"Son, if you need to come home, or need anything, go to Barclays Bank, Piccadilly Branch, and I'll wire you a draft."

"I'll be okay, Mom! I've got two trades and I'm better than the English at one of them."

"Good! Very good! Don't forget to go and see my friends."

"I will, Mom, I will. I promise."

The car was parked. I took my two cases. One was a square box, about 18" x 24" x 15". I had converted it from a portable record player by putting hinges and a lock on it. The second was an old leather suitcase with a belt around the middle, not very big. The contents included a suit, a sports jacket, casual pants, two pairs of shoes, soccer boots, shirts, a swimsuit, 'tackies' (running shoes), and a towel. The rest was engineering books.

It was two hours before the train was to leave. I had promised to meet my dad in the bar. I checked everything and left my mom to go to the bar. My dad was there.

"I'm always on time," my dad said.

"Hullo Dad!"

We hugged, sat down to a couple of beers, and talked.

"You're the first one in the family to go to college, and the first to go overseas."

"Well, Bazil, James and Uncle Dennis went over to Europe."

"Yes, but that was in the army, they had to go."

"True, but it's not such a big thing, Dad!"

The conversation continued but I was not there. My dad kept asking me to do two things: to come back to South Africa soon, and not to marry any English woman. I had no idea where this came from. Why was my dad interested in me now? He'd never seen me play a soccer game, or ride in a bicycle race. Only once had he and my mom come to a game. I had been thirteen. They had sat on the bench and argued. I had looked at them from the field about twenty times, and they had been arguing every time.

"Here's a present, Son, for your 21st birthday, and the trip."

"Thanks Dad!" I hugged him, and wondered a thousand thoughts on who he was...

I broke away to a telephone and talked to Rosemary for the second time that day. This call was short and sad. In a parting shot, I very seriously suggested she come over to England. She said she'd really think about it.

Ginge walked in and the conversation changed as the bar got packed with friends and relatives. They were all talking at an elevated volume, laughing, bullshitting, shaking hands and hugging. Bobby, Abie and Dai had arrived with their buddies and their families. All my immediate family was there, including Yvonne and James, Bazil, Aunt Amy and my cousins Elaine and Alicia. Donald Boddington and Margaret were there, with some of his brothers. It seemed to me as that there were over a hundred people spilling out the bar. More than had been at the party! Amazing! I was circulating. Almost the entire Andrew Street Mob was there, laughing, talking, and telling me to have a good time and not to get married to any English girl, because the South African girls were good stock, had beautiful figures, didn't turn that awful red in the sun, and didn't talk with grapes in their mouth.

The crowd drifted towards the train.

Desmond and I hugged, maybe for the first time! We said our goodbyes.

"You crazy bastard, play soccer! . . . Try a Second Division Club," ordered Desmond.

"I will! All the best, Desmond!"

I grabbed Mickey and said, "Best friend I ever got drunk with on a beach, and in the morning!" We embraced strongly.

"Go well!" said Mickey.

"You too Mike! Come and join us when you can!" I added.

Bobby, Abie, Dai and I saw each other in glimpses only. I had made sure we were all here and then let it go. I saw them with their relatives and friends. There were some girls there as well, and I was going to ask them questions for sure!

Johnny and Trevor had found the coach and the compartment. There was a slow wave of laughter as each group got to the coach. There was toilet paper streaming down the sides of the carriages, coming out of the windows and onto the steps . . . probably ten rolls of decoration. There was writing all around the compartment:

'Look out England here they come.'

'Keep you legs together English ladies.'

'Don't give them a job! . . . Send them back! . . . NO! . . . MAYBE KEEP THEM!'

'Another Springbok Wave coming ashore!'

'Bobby, I love you!!'

'The Andrew Street Mob'

I said goodbye to Yvonne, and hugged her. She promised to write, as long as I sent a card from all the places I visited. Donald and Margaret said goodbye, as did my Aunt Amy, Alicia and Elaine. It all was becoming a blur!

The engine let out its steam blast a number of times. The last round of hugs and kisses went on as the conductor yelled, "All Aboard!"

I said goodbye to Johnny and Trevor with large hugs.

I hugged my mom intensely. I knew I would miss her badly!

The train started moving. My mom was at the steps; she started to walk with the train as I hugged her. I jumped on the step and kissed my mom, but she held my hand and wouldn't let go.

"I'll write, Mom, I love you!"

She still wouldn't let go. Johnny ran with her as she almost stumbled. He grabbed her.

"I love you Son!" she blew a kiss.

The crowd was screaming, cheering and clapping . . . darkness came fast.

The four of us made our way to the compartment. It was in the middle of the coach. We came from both sides, as we had split between the two entrances to the coach. There were so many people there for the four of us. This was a typical coach with little verandahs on each end. We sat down, Dai and I on one side, Abie and Bobbie on the other. We were very lucky; we were only four, in a six-bunk compartment.

"Shit, what a send-off," said Abie.

"Yes! What a crowd."

"Maybe they wanted us to go?"

"We are so popular!"

There was silence

"Mike was very sad," said Bobby.

"Yeah! And a few others," added Abie with a smile. "All my girl-friends!"

"What about your married friends, Charl?" asked Dai. "Why didn't some of them come to the station?"

"Don't know. Oh! Billy and Joy are on holiday in the Cape."

"Your mom is a great person," added Dai. "She always tried to talk us into going overseas."

"Yes! She truly is," I said sadly, and then I brightened up. "And she pushed me to go, and I know now that's not what she truly wanted . . . Well!"

Then silence fell around us adventurers; only the noise of the train wheels was significant. We were transfixed in silence. We sat for quite a while looking through the two windows of darkness with the lights of the city in the background. Johannesburg was going away! We were going away!

"Well, we've done it," said Dai.

"Yes," said Bobby.

"Here we go," I added.

"Super, super, super man!" yelled the other three, as though they were all shouting at the scary silence.

"I've got a bottle of brandy," said Abie, as he got up and opened it.

"Good man Abie!!"

We drank and talked about who was there, and who didn't make it, and what they'd brought, and how they'd got there. The drinks went down hard. Even Dai had a few. We got drunker and drunker and slowly made our beds, climbed into the bunks, had another drink, and then went to the bathroom, down the corridor of the train, in our underpants. Our twisting minds slowly stopped thinking as the train continued across the West Rand and through Potchefstroom. We all toasted that town, despite the fact that Dai had – luckily—never seen it.

"Lucky bastard!" we all chimed.

"Why didn't Tom come?" I asked Bobby.

"He had too much work to do."

"What's with Rosemary now?" asked Abie.

"What's going on? You haven't been out with her for years!" said Bobby.

"A good question. Maybe a deep question!"

I related the basic events of the last month. "I've always liked her . . ."

"Loved her! . . . We know!" said Bobby.

"True!" I wanted to move away from that issue. "I was amazed at her response to my call. Thought it might have been because she had broken up a relationship, but it was very nice to see her again. We are older you know!! I'm going to see what happens. I was in a different position during our first months of going out."

"Okay, we are going to let you off the hook!" said Abie.

"Thank you guys . . . Appreciate it!" I felt very tired.

"Let's go back tomorrow! I didn't know we were so popular!" suggested Abie.

"No!" said Bobby, "they're glad to see us go!"

We agreed, and fell asleep within seconds. The train was due to arrive in Kimberley in the morning.

＊

CHAPTER 22

Cape Town

Thursday

WE WOKE UP WITH hangovers in Kimberley. My thoughts were all exciting. No work today and who knows what we do tomorrow.

Kimberley—and its world famous 'Big Hole'. The largest crater made by man seeking diamonds, it was 4000 feet deep and a mile in circumference. The fabulous volcanic pits that contained blue-colored soil, rich in diamonds, had drawn thousands of prospectors and fortune-seeking men from all over the world. The diamond field was discovered on a farm called Vooruitzicht that was owned by Johannes and Diederik de Beer. They sold it to an agent John Reitz for 6000 pounds. The De Beers name became historical even though they never gained a single royalty and never participated in the mining. Kimberley was the start of change to industrial life in South Africa. The discoveries of diamonds in 1871 not only turned Kimberley into 'The Diamond City' but also helped finance and provide a mining community for the gold rush in 1886, which formed the Johannesburg Mining Camp. Almost 15 million carats of diamonds were removed before the mine closed in 1914. The land around Kimberley is flat and semi-desert, seemingly without water.

We had breakfast and got off the train in Kimberley. We stretched, ran a few yards and got back on before it rolled out and headed for Beaufort West. My father had lived there as a kid, but he had never told me any of his stories. A long hot day on the train going through the Great Karoo, a huge area believed to have been a great swamp over 300 million years ago, a third of the size of South Africa. There are many sites with dinosaurs' footprints and fossils. It is desolate and barren but the Karoo bush is abundant, and subterranean water provides the essentials for sheep farming. The countryside is famous for the multitude of flowers that grow following the spring rains.

We were severely hung-over and the dust came in the train windows when we opened them to get some non-existent cool air. There was no air conditioning. Standing on the verandahs only added soot, from the funnels of the steam engine, to the sand blown by the wind, which landed in our hair. Lunch was the big event of the day, complete with silver cutlery and white tablecloths, in the dining carriage. The four of us sat there till we were thrown out. The train, traveling at 30 miles per hour, seemed to drag on forever. We reached Beaufort West in the evening. We were told that if we got up, really early around 2 AM, we would be able to witness the addition of another engine at Touwsriver before the descent through the famous Hex River Valley Pass. Touwsriver had been a famous locomotive depot in the 1800,s.

Friday

I woke up at 4 AM and went and sat on the verandah railing. The train was swaying slowly from side to side. It was still dark but changing to the lighter edge of darkness. The air was cool but not cold. Inside I felt a distinct feeling of freedom . . . marvelous! But there was also a feeling of seriousness, a responsibility creeping in, for everything from daily food to places to live. All decisions were mine now. I had made some big ones already, and independently of people in my life. I had been forced to do that many times in the past too, because of the lack of a distinct father role in my life: I now had to do it all.

My thoughts changed. I had been amazed at my tears for Pal; nothing else had affected me that deeply in the process of leaving home. Interesting and deep, as it seemed he had known that he might not see me again! Too sad! I shook off the thoughts to enjoy the quietness, the beauty of this magnificent land that my forefathers had traveled by horse, ox-wagon, and foot. They must have blessed their fortunes, despite their hardships, looking at the same beauty. They must have been scared of the chances they were taking, trekking through the Karoo with no surface water. My love of traveling and adventure was perhaps just being born! The excitement was feverish, and I knew I was going to 'give it a go' as the Southern Suburbs boys used to say.

The train went down the pass very slowly. The beautiful, deep, blue-gray background of the sky accentuated the dark, sharp peaks and large mountains of the Hex River Valley. The train crawled very slowly down the steep grade and I could see the steam engines almost continuously by moving from one side of the verandah to the other. The train resembled a snake on wheels. The grinding of the flat-faced wheels against the curved track gave out a continuous screeching, not obtrusive to the ear but enough to realize the seriousness of this tricky operation. If the train went over the side, its fall would be through thousands of feet directly down. This would certainly crush the iron and steel cars into a compressed hulk. It took hours before we finally reached a level grade. We were close to the bottom of the mountains and the outline of vineyards and Dutch architecture buildings could be seen in sunlight, as the train went through Worcester, Paarl and Stellenbosch: all famous towns in South African history.

The train was now traveling through the area of the country where my ancestors had arrived and lived almost three centuries ago. The first Huguenots, arriving in 1688 from France, via Belgium, quickly migrated to the Paarl, Stellenbosch and Drakenstein areas. They built small communities of grape and fruit farms, churches and schools. The differences in their religion to that of the earlier settlers, such as the Dutch, caused a conflict for half a century, until they eventually became part of the Afrikaans heritage in South Africa. I wondered how they had got to Oudtshoorn where my Grandfather had farmed. My thoughts were interrupted when Dai came out onto the verandah.

"I've been looking through the window. This is so beautiful," he exclaimed.

Now the towns and houses were more numerous. The roads were filled with cars. The clickety-clack of the train wheels hitting the rail joints was still the loudest thing. The sky was brightening. Next stop . . . Cape Town.

◆

The train pulled into Cape Town at 8 AM—a most beautiful city, located near the southern tip of the African continent. Not quite the most southern point, but undoubtedly the center of a magnificent part of the world. The Khoikhoi (Hottentots-no longer used) pastoral and the San (Bushmen) hunters and gatherers, were the original inhabitants of much of Southern Africa before the blacks or whites arrived. In 1487,

Bartolomeu Dias rounded the Cape of Good Hope, followed a decade later by Vasco da Gama. These Portuguese sailors were seeking a route to India even before the first American colonists had moved inland in their country. Jan van Riebeeck of the Dutch East India Company arrived at the Cape of Good Hope in 1652. In 1688 a group of French Huguenots arrived and the story of Cape Town evolved. The Khoikhoi integrated or moved northwards and the San moved out and towards the Northwest. Since the early times the city has seen many changes in occupancy from the Dutch to the English, back to the Dutch and eventually to the 'South Africans'.

The train entered Cape Town Station with Table Mountain on the left, the sea on the right, and the city straight ahead. I had a sense of belonging here, a spiritual link, perhaps, to my ancestors who had fled religious persecution. It was the same feeling I'd had when I came down with Doc so many years before. It was as though I was at home, and Johannesburg had just 'happened'. This inexplicable feeling puzzled me. . . . *Nah!* I rejected the fanciful image. It was just the outrageous freedom I was experiencing!

Cape Town is the 'Mother City' of South Africa. It is blessed with Table Mountain, a Mediterranean climate, thousands of different flowers and plants, and some of the finest bathing beaches in the world. It is graced by two oceans: the Atlantic, and the Indian. Table Mountain often has a cloud over its top, which is appropriately called 'The Table Cloth'. Just as the weather can be beautiful, it can also change in a very short time to unpleasant conditions. The Portuguese named it 'The Cape of Storms'. The wind and dark clouds are referred to as 'The Vacuum Cleaner', which cleans the city and leaves it as fresh as you can imagine.

We got off the train, carrying all our belongings ourselves. The weather was beautiful, the sun already bright, and everything around us was new.

I had the phone number of my half-brother Ivan. We shared the same father, but Ivan had a different last name. Our father's sister had raised Ivan; she was known as Aunt Rachel, and he used her married name. Ivan was a devout bachelor, 40 years of age, and a wonderful classical pianist. He lived with his friend Johnny.

I called Ivan, who arranged to meet me at lunchtime at his workplace. "Bring your bags, Charl and stay with us until you leave," he suggested.

"All right," I agreed, being glad to be able to spend a night. Some of the sadness of leaving Johannesburg had lifted. *This is what traveling is all about,* I thought. I replaced the phone and ran down the station to catch up with my buddies.

"I won't see Ivan till lunch. I'll walk with you to find a place to stay."

"Have you got any ideas?" asked Abie.

"No," I replied.

We four vagabonds walked from the station towards the tall buildings of the city. The station was reasonably close to downtown. As we walked, the realization ng in this beautiful place hit us. A jumbled discussion took place.

"Look at the mountain!"

"With its table cloth."

"Table Mountain and its cloth."

"What a view, man!"

"Nothing like the pictures..."

"Anybody bring a camera?" I asked.

Three replies of "No!"

"Must get one," I said. "Maybe they're cheaper in England."

We walked, looking at all the new scenery

"Wow! Look at that lady . . . just cherry!" said Abie.

"Cape Colored," said Bobby.

"Really?" asked Abie, surprised. "Wow, she's beautiful."

"The saying is that they age very quickly," said Bobby.

"That's crap," said Dai. "We all age quickly."

"No," I injected. "I think whites age more rapidly than the Zulus. Look how hard it is to tell their age when they get older. They have great bodies . . . good looking, and age with dignity. We all just shrivel up and look like twisted white wheat pancakes with bumps and freckles!"

"This town has had so many different people come through it for some three hundred years. There's no telling who you're going out with," said Bobby.

"Who cares," said Abie. "Take her out and have a good time and leave!"

"Why not?"

"I don't know if you could do that in Johannesburg..."

"Well maybe you can go out with them in Cape Town!"

"Let's find a shitty hotel and then go dancing tonight," suggested Bobby.

"I'm going to stay with my brother tonight, so maybe I'll meet you later or something."

"Hey! We're on holiday. Let's have fun . . . when does the boat leave, again?" asked Bobby.

"Sunday," replied Dai.

"Good, just a few days of looking around," suggested Bobby as though he hadn't known.

We walked into the city. It was 9 AM and everyone was going to work. We found a coffeehouse with chairs outside, sat down, and put our bags down where we could see them: basic training in South Africa, otherwise they'd be gone when you next looked around. We ordered breakfast. All our meals were paid, for the two weeks on the ship. Truly our only urgency was that we would all have to get jobs as soon as we got off the boat in England. Our one security was that Bobby's cousin, Ian, had arranged a flat in London where we could stay. We just sat there watching our South African buddies go to work, some running, some depressed and walking slowly, not wanting to go but forcing each leg to move forward in turn . . . dragging themselves to the inevitable. Some were very nicely dressed, 'looking sharp'. We commented on a girl passing by. We noticed the girls over the boys by a ratio of twenty to one, and perhaps even a magnitude more.

"Some of these people dress like they're going to a wedding. I've never worn a tie to work."

"Who wants to?"

"Am I dreaming, or does everyone look a little lighter?" asked Dai.

The conversation changed. "Look at those two ladies."

"Let's ask them to go out tonight."

"Hey! Man! Hey! They're coming to the café."

The two ladies came to the cafe and went inside.

"Damn," said Abie.

Within three minutes they came out again, and sat at the next table. They were talking about work, and some problem with their last couple of dates. We were silent . . . hanging on every word. I was listening, and waiting for a break in the conversation. The two girls sat back and, taking their coffee cups in hand, sipped on the coffee carefully, taking a few minutes to relax. I jumped at the opportunity.

"Excuse me, we've just got off the train from Johannesburg . . . and not knowing anybody, wondered where we could stay for a few nights . . . cheaply!"

"Oh!" exclaimed one of the girls. "Never had to stay in town."

"Neither have I," said the other. Continuing, she asked, "What are you doing in Cape Town?"

"We're on our way to London," I answered, my thoughts flowing rapidly, *Wow! It sounds exciting and important and true and whatever!*

"How wonderful," said the first girl. "You know," she continued, "there is the YMCA and some cheaper hotels down this road here, about five blocks." She pointed to a street.

"We could try that," I said, trying to show thankfulness in my smile. Then without a moment's delay, I surged forth with the second question.

"We'd also like to go to a good dance place . . . rock and roll! . . . American music! Well . . . also with hundreds of girls and no guys!" I added, smiling.

"Paradise for you, of course," said one of the girls, sarcastically.

"Well, yes!" I agreed. "We all like to dance . . . meet some people." My thoughts were moving fast, backed by the entire street talk learnt in Johannesburg. "We are also thinking of coming back to live in Cape Town for a while . . . after the London trip."

Bobby, Abie and Dai looked at me simultaneously with curious looks.

"Well, there is a club called 'The Ring'," said the first girl.

"It's pretty rough sometimes, but the music is good," said the second girl.

"Do you go there?" Bobby wandered into the conversation.

"Yes, occasionally."

"Listen, this is Charl. He is not our spokesman! This is Abie and this is Dai. I'm Bobby. We really did just get off the train and would like your help."

"That's okay, I'm Kathy and this is Bettie," she pointed. "We've been to the club, but we usually go with dates."

Kathy was medium height for a girl, and had a shapely figure. She was blonde, had short-cut hair and beautiful blue-green eyes, soft looks and a pretty face. Bettie was opposite in looks with dark brown hair, brown eyes, a pretty face but harder looks, and the outstanding figure that had caught all eight of the Johannesburg tourists' eyes. I thought Kathy looked just . . . so . . . nice!

"Well," continued Bobby, "I already know where we're going tonight, and if you want, we'll meet you outside at 8:30 PM. Is that a good time to get there?"

"Well, I don't know . . . the club only starts at 9 PM."

"Listen," I interjected. "We'll leave it up to you. But we'll be there exactly at 9 PM and we'll wait fifteen minutes. We promise! Otherwise, we'll be inside. It'll be fun."

"Thank you," said Kathy.

Bettie said, "We have to go or we'll be late for work."

The girls got up and said goodbye.

"See you tonight," said Abie.

"Man, I knew this trip to England would be great!" Dai commented, and he was actually smiling.

"You're pretty smooth!" said Bobby, looking at me. "We've never discussed coming back to Cape Town!"

"Well! We didn't plan to go to 'The Ring' either and now we're going!" I came back, smiling.

This agreement to go places without a moment's notice was typical of how we had operated forever. Go, and find out what happens next!

We left the cafe and wandered down the street. The commuter traffic had died. We continued down the suggested street and, sure enough, there were the cheaper hotels. We found a hotel room. The guys checked in, threw their stuff in the room, and we headed back to downtown Cape Town.

"God, what a beautiful city," said Abie.

"Maybe we should just fake the London trip and stay here," I suggested.

"No," said Dai. "I'm going to England. I didn't . . . "

"Don't be so serious, Man!" said Abie.

"Seriously! Lets get a refund on our tickets, find a job after two weeks . . . stay here for a couple of months. We could read about England and then go back to Johannesburg!" I persisted with a smile.

"Charl . . . forget it!"

We walked the city for a couple of hours. The air was so crisp and fresh, the sunshine warmed the day, and everything looked new and clean. We just liked it all, especially the air—it was so different to Johannesburg. After arranging to meet my buddies at The Ring at 8:45

PM, I went off to meet Ivan. He worked at a piano store very close to Greenmarket Square, a very popular place for tourists.

Greenmarket Square is the second oldest square in Cape Town. In the 19th Century it was a fruit and vegetable marketplace, and in 1834 the declaration of the freeing of all slaves was made there. Historical buildings surround the square.

There were hundreds of people hanging around, selling and buying, and partaking of life, in this active marketplace.

I walked into Ivan's store, looking in the spaces for this tall man with light skin, penetrating eyes, and arms that moved expressively. Ivan came over. There was that instant pause in which both people realize that the picture in the mind from before is slightly different than the picture seen now. We approached each other, fairly sure of the outcome.

"Hey, Boet (brother)," said Ivan.

"Hello Ivan," I replied. We shook hands and embraced.

"God, you look good," said Ivan.

We talked for a while about how long ago it was since we were together, and about our unusual father and his new family: this was his fourth. We touched on his many antics. The upbeat mannerisms of my half brother were familiar; I had seen them many times before. Ivan stowed my bags in the back of the store, and we went to lunch in a restaurant right on Greenmarket Square. We sat on the verandah of the restaurant near a railing where you could almost touch the people walking past. Cape Colored musicians entertained the restaurant crowd from the square: a given right and freedom. Police would seldom interfere with them, unless they were really drunk and disorderly. Following each musician's show he or she would pass a hat around.

"How's Dad?" asked Ivan.

"He's all right. I saw him two nights ago. He came to see me off."

"That was nice."

"Yes, I guess. He also gave me my twenty-first birthday present."

"Was it a box of 'French Letters' (condoms)?"

"No! . . . Shit, Ivan! I don't think he cares about my love escapades."

"He should," said Ivan. "He has helped produce a large number of children," pointing to himself and to me, "and with many wives."

"Oh, I know," I said. "This family tree has overburdened branches with all his fruit."

"That's a good way to put it," said Ivan. "I love that. So what was the present? The big present of your coming-of-age party?"

"A plastic Gillette razor with two blades!" I replied, laughing.

"No!" exclaimed Ivan throwing his arms up. "My God, that's terrible. He probably bought it on the way to the train station."

"Glad you said it!"

My voice had a neutral tone when discussing my dad.

"Charl," said Ivan, "we know what Dad did and does. He's very much involved in his own life. Aunt Rachel told me many stories!"

"Oh! Are we going to see Aunt Rachel, Evelyn and Ron?" I asked.

"Yes, and they're coming to see you off on the boat. Saturday, isn't it?"

"Sunday," I corrected.

Ivan paid the lunch bill and we walked back to the store. He gave me all the directions and time to meet in a very precise manner.

"See you tonight," said Ivan. "I'll take your bags home and you can roam free!"

"Thank you!"

I walked off down the streets of Cape Town. Wow! I was so glad! So free! And I would be in England in two weeks! Just wonderful! I took a walk towards the Government House gardens. It was so comfortable in the sunshine. The gardens were beautiful and the flowers so very bright due to the sky, a magnificent, clear, light blue. This was mid-summer and the weather was perfect. I was looking in the shop windows. *This is good,* I thought, *even though I'm not interested in buying anything at all.* Deep in thought, I crossed the street and looked into the car coming towards me. I could not believe my eyes!

"Billy," I yelled. "Joy," I yelled louder.

It was Billy and Joy from the Andrew Street Mob in Johannesburg. They pulled over and I ran up to the car.

"This is unbelievable!"

Billy and Joy got out of the car. We hugged, looked around and decided to sit on the brickwork ledge of a building.

"We've been in Cape Town. That's why we couldn't come and see you off at the station. Was it crowded?" asked Billy.

"Oh! Everybody was there. Couldn't believe it . . . just about the whole Andrew Street Mob. Well, that's not possible, but just a helluva lot of them!"

"So you're going to England, Mate!" said Billy.

"Yes, going to conquer the Rooineks (Rednecks – English)."

"More like the women!"

"Well, they also get their necks burned bright red in the South African sunshine."

"True!"

"Don't marry one of those girls," said Joy.

"No, I won't . . . they have that funny sweet accent that makes their tongue come out their mouth," I answered smiling. "But Joy, you're the third or fourth person that has told me not to . . ."

"It's because we want you back!"

"Nice thoughts . . . thank you both!"

We then talked for an hour. Like always, it was about everyone and all the recent events. Billy and Joy, knowing that my time in Cape Town was going to be spent visiting my family, agreed to come down to the boat and help cheer me off the shores of South Africa. They said goodbye and drove off.

I spent the rest of the day walking Cape Town, feeling the return of the sadness of leaving some very special friends behind. I finally headed to Ivan's flat. I went up the stairs and knocked on the door. It opened.

"Hello, Charl."

"You must be Johnny."

"Yes."

I was shown my room. Ivan came out of the bathroom and we sat out on the verandah and had drinks.

"What a super view," I exclaimed.

The breeze from the sea was warm, and moved slowly in the tropical calm. The whole scene, of the expansive sea and sky, and uniquely built Cape Town with its white houses and light colored buildings, some of them with lights already on, made it magic.

"We like it very much. It's a ritual," said Johnny, "Every night we have this drink which transforms us from day to night people."

"Yeah!" I said. "Nothing like this in Johannesburg."

"No, there's nothing like it. The view is breathless."

We finally sat down to dinner. Johnny had cooked the meal. We ate and talked about the trip to England. Ivan was a classical pianist, and had gone over there to try out as a soloist for a concert in London. He'd first had to go to Birmingham, and play in a concert there. This was the proving ground, or test venue, for London concerts. Ivan never made the London concert.

"England is fabulous," stated Ivan. "You'll love it. Watch out for the Cockneys. They're sneaky little devils! Lots of Gypsy blood in them!"

"I will! I've met a few in Johannesburg," I said as we got up from the dinner table. "I'm going to meet my travel friends now, for our first night out in Cape Town."

"Okay, take a key Charl," said Ivan, "but don't make any dates for tomorrow night."

"I won't," I promised as I disappeared out the door. I was so excited about going out at night in a new city. The feeling was intense. I ran down the stairs.

I walked through the streets of Cape Town. The buildings ranged from very old to very new. Some of them had curled railings and banisters, like the courtyard where Laubscher and I had been on our night out. Some buildings seemed even older. They made a wild contrast to the towering new buildings, straight up, glass and metal, impressive but not exciting. I had found out the location of The Ring. I walked down a couple of side streets, my thoughts centered primarily on the two girls. I preferred Kathy, although I figured there was little chance of ever seeing the two girls again—I didn't think they would come through *this* area, unescorted. As I walked, the streets seemed to become better lit, and finally, I saw The Ring. It didn't look too bad. Bobby, Abie and Dai were already there.

"Hullo! Good you're here," said Bobby.

"What about Kathy and Bettie?" I asked.

"They won't come . . . we've been here ten minutes. Let's go in before the main crowd gets here. Also, if the girls come, we'll have to pay for them."

"No, you guys go in. I'll wait."

"Deal."

I waited till 9:15 PM. I was somewhat dejected, despite my positive assumption that they would come. I decided to go in. I had to stand in a long line. It felt strange—I didn't know anybody at all. Everything was new. There wasn't that comfortable feeling of knowing people around you. I wasn't sure who was who. Who were the bad guys? Just before the cashier, about four people away, I saw Kathy. My heart leaped.

"Kathy" I yelled, trying to hold back the joy.

"Charl, get two more tickets."

"Done!"

I got the tickets and walked over to Kathy and Bettie.

"Very glad you came . . . this is fabulous."

"Well! It is Friday, you know, and we had nothing planned for the weekend. Maybe this will start a roll," said Kathy, smiling warmly at me. I got another ripple of excitement through my body. I showed what little shyness I had, and coupled it with a smile.

"Bobby, Abie and Dai are already inside?"

"Yes."

"And you waited in the hopes we'd come! What a nice chap!" said Kathy, with a quirky smile.

Putting my arms behind my back, I said, "They forced me!"

"Sure they did!"

We went into The Ring and shifted around until we found Bobby, Abie and Dai. Then the girls suggested we move to the other side of the hall.

The Ring was a converted old warehouse, but nicely done. It had a red and black color motif on the walls, a stage for the band, and a dance area. There were many tables on each side of the dance floor, and a standing space at the end opposite to the bandstand. The layout divided the crowd naturally into singles standing, and couples sitting. The band consisted of eight musicians. The music was rock, sometimes played straight, as per the American way, sometimes with the distinctive African beat, and even more often with the Cape Colored flair. The latter was a little faster, not so solid, accentuated with a swaying rhythm, making the music move from side to side and accentuating the music notes, so that they were not just plain rock or jazz. This style introduction by the Cape Colored people to American and South African music was exactly why they were famous. There weren't any ukuleles in this band, but you'd swear you could hear them!

Dai found a table and we sat down and ordered drinks. The band was playing, but nobody was dancing.

"It'll start going at about ten or so," said Bettie. "Hope you can dance!"

"Yes, we learned to do the fox trot and waltz while we were in the army," said Abie.

"You were in the army?"

"Yes, the Royal Stupid-Something Irish Twenty First Regiment. Bobby, Charl and I were there," said Abie. "Dai took up knitting while we did our training!"

"You didn't serve?" said Bettie looking at Dai.

"No, I was exempted."

"Exempted?" exclaimed Bobby. "Dai, your name wasn't on the ballot --- so you didn't have to go through four years of training!"

"I know! Lucky in some ways."

"All the ways you can think of!" said Bobby

"Okay, it's a stupid system, some people get to go in for four years, and others don't have to do a thing. It's our wonderful government." I paused. "Sorry if you are a keen supporter!"

"No," said Kathy, "definitely not. I can't . . ." she paused for a long while . . . "understand what they are doing. Going back to the 'old ages' or just being pig-headed."

I jumped in because this was great. "They are holding onto something that will slip out of their hands, and they fear the problem of not being able to handle it. The adults can't see it, but young people can!" The sound of that line went through my head again. As it echoed, I realized I had never said that aloud to anyone before.

"Charl, let's talk about real life," said Bobby.

"Yes Sir!" I answered immediately, with a nice smile.

"Agreed! We're leaving all this stuff behind us."

"Have you known each other for a long time?" asked Kathy.

"Yes! Since we were teenagers. We all grew up in the Southern Suburbs of Johannesburg," said Dai.

"What do you do?"

"Bobby's a mechanic, Charl's a machinist-come engineer, I'm an engineer and Abie is a professional boxer," replied Dai.

"Abie, you're a pro boxer?"

"Yes, I was South African Champion." Abie stopped, then continued because the girls looked as though they were interested. "I'm thinking of fighting in England."

"Are you really going to fight in England?"

"Yes," interjected Bobby, "we need the money."

"You're his manager?" asked Bettie.

"No," I answered, "we're all on our own, but we need Abie to make money, so we can have a flat in Soho, London, and be visited by . . . famous people. Or girls we've met in Cape Town!"

"Interesting!"

The time went past 10 PM. Abie got up and walked around. Dai got up and danced with a girl from one of the nearby tables. Bobby talked to Bettie, and I to Kathy. It just worked out that way, from our seating arrangement. I asked Kathy to dance, she liked it, and so Kathy and I danced a lot. Dai danced with a girl three times from the standing crowd. It was weird how he managed to do that, because she was surrounded by a group of guys. Bobby suggested he quit that 'cause the guys didn't seem to like it.

"No, they're not worried," said Dai.

"Dai, we buddies have a feeling, *we're* worried," said Bobby. "What do you girls think?"

"Yeah, I would stay away," replied Bettie.

"Do it," I said firmly. "We don't want any trouble mate!"

"She's nice," replied Dai.

"Let's not be stupid, Man!"

At midnight, I sensed that the crowd opposite us was becoming hostile. I decided the fun was over and asked Kathy and Bettie if they wanted to go for a drink, elsewhere. They agreed. Dai was pushed out of shape. Bobby and Abie did not care and did not waste any time in getting up to go.

As we left, one of the guys in the standing group suggested loudly, "Take him with you!"

"We will!" I gladly agreed.

We walked out.

"It's okay," said Bobby, to console everyone.

"It's no matter."

"It's like that sometimes," said Kathy.

"We've been to so many clubs in Johannesburg like this, it's the same. We can sense trouble early and we prefer to avoid it. Besides, we're strangers here. We know who the strangers are in Johannesburg—they know we're the strangers here," continued Bobby.

"They'd like to have some fun and rumble," said Abie. "It's like the club in Vrededorp."

"Yeah, but there's a difference. Lots of Cape Colored people in this club tonight, don't see that many in Johannesburg," said Dai.

"That's true . . . so what's the difference anyway?" asked Bobby.

The talking subsided; the subject was exhausted. We wandered into the late night, agreed on a coffee place, and sat in a booth. We talked until 2 AM. I had been up since 4 AM and started to feel that drawn-out affect, despite the exciting time I was having with Kathy. The girls took a taxi. I agreed to meet the boys on Saturday, during the day, at the Seapoint Baths, the only place I could remember from my visit with Doc. I had made a tentative lunch date with Kathy. Bobby, Abie and Dai made no plans; they didn't want to spend precious money. We parted. I walked home very slowly, without a care through this magnificent old city.

I crept into the apartment and quietly went to bed. I fell asleep with a beautiful feeling of freedom that was starting to be commonplace in my life.

Saturday

The Saturday morning sunshine was strong by the time I came back to the world. Ivan had gone to work. Johnny was around. "Welcome to the day," he said. "Want some breakfast?"

"Maybe coffee."

"Okay."

I showered quickly and got dressed to go.

"What's happening today?" I asked Johnny.

"Ivan said to make sure you're here by seven tonight, for dinner. Your cousins Evelyn and Ron will pick you up tomorrow to go out to Camps Bay, and we're all gonna see you off tomorrow."

"Wow, that's great. This is a big family, Johnny even my grandfather sowed many seeds."

"Yes, and it's complicated, too!" Johnny agreed.

I finished breakfast, thanked Johnny, and left the apartment after calling Kathy. I was headed to meet her for lunch. I would catch up with the boys at Sea Point Swimming Baths later.

I saw her waiting outside her work. *Gee! . . . Kathy is really pretty!* Went through my mind.

"Hello there!" I greeted her with a big smile.

"Good day, Charl," replied Kathy, showing her gladness to see me. "Shorts hey!"

"Oh, yes!" I said with exuberance. "I'm becoming the total tourist."

"Nice legs," she continued.

"Oh, you can't miss if you play soccer. The legs come with the soccer ball!"

"Sure!" Kathy agreed with a snicker. "In truth, I think you have to work at it. I've seen scary . . . skinny . . . hairy legs, kicking the ball!" stated Kathy emphatically, laughing at the same time.

I put my arm around her shoulder. Kathy folded warmly under my arm. I felt very comfortable, and very happy to be her date. This was exciting stuff!

"Glad I asked the question yesterday at the coffee table," I said, looking up into the sky. "Thank you, Cape Town!"

"Oh, I'm glad the train was on time. You may have missed us going to work."

We walked down the road. Then I explained the schedule of Saturday.

"Do you want to have lunch in Sea Point and then come swimming?" I asked.

"Yes! We can forget the lunch, unless you're hungry?"

"Okay! I don't need lunch. Do you want to get a swimming costume (bathing suit)?"

"No," Kathy said, showing me her bag.

"Oh, you came prepared?" I asked.

"Yes! If you hadn't turned up I was going to go swimming."

"Well done," I said sheepishly. *Women are uncanny,* I thought. *They are just as sneaky as men are, even sneakier, perhaps. How come they know? Oh, forget it!*

We caught the bus from Cape Town out to Seapoint. We sat upstairs on the double-decker and looked at the beautiful scenery. On our left were the mountains and on our right was the sea, which went all the way to the Antarctic.

Cape Town is in the unique position of helping to divide two oceans. There are two currents flowing into the area off Cape Town. The Benguela current, bringing the cold water up from the South Atlantic, circulating in an anti-clockwise direction, and the Agulhas current, one of the world's strongest and fastest currents, coming down from the equator through the warm Indian Ocean, fed by the West Madagascar and Mozambique Currents. There is an upwelling in the Benguela Current, which nurtures sea life by providing vast quantities of plankton. There are large shoals of fish, giving this region a large fishing industry. The two ocean streams touch each other at the tip of Africa. Taking a twenty-minute bus ride from the city, you can swim in both oceans, in cold and warm surf.

Kathy and I were going to Seapoint, a delightful suburb of Cape Town, east of the city and perched on the side of the hills running into the sea. Some precarious-looking houses were built on stilts off the main road, with 10 -12 foot backyards, and front decks open to the ocean breeze. No land to walk on! The short bridges that connected the houses to the road were very important structurally: first to hold onto the house, and second to support a car's accelerating or braking. Seapoint was still extremely busy. February was slightly cooler than December, but still very warm at 80°F.

The bus ride was delightful. People, feeling the summer sun, passed on the warmth in the bus with loud conversation. I detected the Cape accent, very different to that of Johannesburg, probably because of the Cape Colored influence.

The descendants from Malaysia and other places had evolved into a people who loved music, laughter and conversation. They were part of the complex population and mixed cultures of this city, formed from the multitude of sailors and immigrants who had come through this point of Africa over a period of about five hundred years. Those that stayed joined the pastoral Khoikhoi, the original South Africans, to form a new culture. The Coon Carnival on New Year's Day could match most large city celebrations of the world. The bands and dancers and singers marched through Cape Town. Dressed in very colorful shiny clothes, they walked and danced and sang and laughed for hours. It was a Cape Town event I had heard about many times but never seen except on the screen.

"Let's go," said Kathy. "It's the next stop."

We walked down to Seapoint Baths, entered, went to the separate change rooms and met at the deep pool. The pool was the usual T-shape with the stem of the T being the 16-foot-deep pool with a 33-foot high (10-meter) board. The rest of the pool went from 3 to 6 feet deep. Twenty feet of tiles separated the long side of the pool from the sea and rocks. The Seapoint Baths was built on the rocky edge of the sea.

Kathy and I saw the boys, and put our towels down next to the group. "Hi, everybody."

"Yes! . . . Hello!" said Abie. "Good place Charl. Lots of ladies."

"Is Bettie coming?"

"No," said Kathy. "She's gone shopping with her mom."

We collapsed to the prone position or just sat upright soaking up the sun, being lazy, and of course watching people. After an hour, I was tempted by the thought of cool water. I looked at the diving tower, wondering if I could do the dive. I had dived off this 10-meter board when I was thirteen. Doc had taken pictures so I could prove it! I liked a challenge. So I got up off my towel, climbed straight up to the top of the high board, and stood at the board's edge. It was a solid platform, four feet wide. I took about 10 seconds. It was a long way down, but I was up there, and there was no way I'd back off. I took a deep breath and went off the board in a pike dive. The amazing rush of water around my head and the cool sensation of water was delightful after being in the hot sun. I came out of the water and heard my buddies clapping and yelling, "Yeah!" It was all sarcastic action!

"He always does that in front of girls," said Bobby.

"Yeah, but that's the first time he went in head first," said Abie.

"True," said Dai.

Kathy looked at the boys for a second with a questioning face, and then said, "I'd say it was a pretty good dive anyway."

"Nah!" said Abie.

Kathy dived into the water. I caught up with her and we swam to the other side of the pool, away from the boys. We hung on the side of the pool. I put my arm around her shoulder. We kissed very lightly, lips wet with water. A surge went through my body. It was the same as when we had danced the night before. *Strange! Very nice!* I thought. *Why is this happening so quickly after leaving home?* How could I get these feelings? Rosemary and I had just, somewhat, come back together! Maybe it was part of the freedom phase.

"Wow!" I said loudly.

"Nice," said Kathy.

We swam around the pool together, got out and went to the edge of the wall to watch the waves come in to the rocks, a relentless cycle of crash and spray that varied and mesmerized the mind, a satisfying, normalizing, emotional stream of consciousness, passing continuously through the webs within the body. We sat for some time; feelings of anxiety flowed through us, even as we enjoyed each other.

"Can you come over tonight? Later?" asked Kathy.

"I can't." I explained the story of Ivan and Johnny, and the relationships with my family. "I owe them this evening. It would be tasteless if I missed it."

"You leave tomorrow?"

"Yes . . . 4 PM."

"Tell you what," said Kathy.

"What?"

"You have to be there by seven tonight?"

"Yes!"

"Then let's go to my place for a drink, before you go to your brother's," suggested Kathy.

"Definitely, you're on."

We got up from the wall and walked over to the boys. I said, "I'm going over to Kathy's. Catch up with you later."

"You're at your brother's tonight?" asked Dai.

"Yes! See you at the boat . . . Tomorrow!!!" I emphasized.

"See you later," said Bobby.

Kathy and I left, rode the Seapoint bus going towards Cape Town for a short distance, then got off. We ran, for the fun of it, up the hill to a small house, very white, very quaint, with a little verandah, windows and a doorway, all painted green. It was well over 100 years old. As we went in I could smell the mustiness of sea and moisture. The furniture was quaint and pretty and pictures hung on the walls. The inside contained one bedroom, a living room, a bathroom and even a kitchen. And it had a pantry!

"Make yourself at home."

"This is beautiful," I said. "I would have given anything to have a small house like this in Johannesburg. A bachelor's pad."

"It is a bachelor's pad. Only I'm a female."

"Yes, I already know you're a fine woman!"

"Thank you! That's a compliment."

"Do you rent it?"

"Yes, and my father helps a bit."

"You're very lucky, Kathy. This is super," I said, with a lot of envy.

It was already two o'clock in the afternoon. We sat on the couch drinking beer and talking. The windows were all open and the curtains flapped in the sea breeze. The house was on the side of the hill.

"Why are you going to England, besides to have fun?" asked Kathy.

"Serious question?" I asked.

"Yes! Very serious."

"It's lot of reasons. Maybe lots and lots of reasons."

"Why is that?"

"Well, because when I first wanted to go, it was for fun and excitement. First in line were American music and dancing, then adventure, and then it was because my mother wanted me to go. After talking to all my friends in Johannesburg, I realized that I had told different people different reasons. Not lying or bullshitting, but because maybe I didn't know. There are some feelings, though, that are very deep, and I've never told anyone those reasons, because again, I'm not sure. How is that for a confusing non-answer?"

"You can tell me," said Kathy.

"I don't know if I could, I hardly know you. Some of my friends that you've met, I've known a long time, some over 10 years. I haven't told them." I picked up my beer and took a long drink. "Although if I feel comfortable with someone . . . I could spill the feelings!" I said with a tease.

"I already like you," said Kathy. "I've not brought anybody to this house for some time. I don't know why I did it." She paused. "Perhaps I am very interested in what you're doing, and I didn't think I could find out with your friends around you..."

"Well, it's exciting, this whole thing, being away from everybody at home and having just a little money to get to England. And maybe that's the reason," I said, with confusion about what I was really saying. "I mean, everybody seems interested, and it's nice." *That didn't help,* I thought, so I pushed on.

"You're very nice, Kathy, it seems such a pity I'm leaving tomorrow. I'd like to go out some more with you." *Now those words drifted and they sounded like avoidance.* My thoughts continued to intermingle with my statements. I was definitely overpowered by Kathy's presence.

"Thank you," said Kathy, with the nicest smile. "I think you're a nice person too! So tell me some of your thoughts then." She got up, wiggled her way across the room, turned and smiled, and made animation signs of going to fetch two more beers. They were Castle Lager beers, fairly strong, and there were already six of them on the table. I slipped off the couch and sat on the carpet leaning up against the couch. Kathy slid down as well, moving closer to me.

"Most of my very close friends got married. So the crowd that went out together for many years, and I mean many years . . .we called it the Andrew Street Mob . . . a good mob, not a bad mob . . . is breaking up. We're not really going out anymore. It has splintered. I was the youngest, and I didn't want to get married. Life in Johannesburg changed, it didn't seem the same going to places with different people, so I decided to do something." I spoke sincerely. I didn't believe this was the only reason, but right now it would do.

"You have a girlfriend?"

"No," I said. I felt a little guilty about Rosemary, but it was essentially true . . . things had been said about coming back soon, but I had not, and would not, agree to anything that held me down.

"Good!" said Kathy with enthusiasm.

"The second reason," I said quickly, "was because the army was driving me crazy with all their bullshit."

"You're running away from the army?"

"No! You can get discharged if you leave the country. Bobby and Abie got a discharge as well."

"How about Dai?"

"He never had to go. We tend to be a bit mad at him, because he didn't have to serve like us."

"Oh! Yes! I remember. Does his father know somebody?"

"No, it's like a ballot system. If they pull your name out of the hat when you are eighteen, you belong to them for four years. . ." I took a slug of beer, " . . . and you go! His name wasn't called." I paused. "So, what's your story, Kathy? You're kinda cute and nice-looking. You have a boyfriend?" I asked, desperate for a change in subject.

"No, I told you. It's been some time. Bettie and I just go out to parties and stuff." She paused. "What do you mean kinda cute?"

"Oh just kidding, really cute then!" I replied sheepishly, and then laughed.

Kathy told me how she had lived in Cape Town all her life. Her parents were born there, so was she, and she had gone to school in Seapoint. As she continued, I drank some more beer and began to realize how attractive Kathy was, especially in the way she smiled while talking. Why should I catch the boat? Nah! I couldn't desert my buddies. Oh! Yes, I could! I immediately decided that I would return through Cape Town. *That's it!* Then I thought, *No strings! Oh! It doesn't matter!* Kathy had continued talking, I hadn't heard the last few explanations . . . and then she stopped, drank some beer, and looked me right in the eyes.

I took the opportunity. I slid over closer to her, touched her chin with my left hand, and kissed her. Her response was immediate and we sat up awkwardly to embrace until it hurt the stretched muscles. So we slid down to a horizontal position on the carpet. We never let up, as our bodies got closer. I could feel her legs with mine as my left leg went over her body. Her legs opened and I could feel nearly all of her body next to mine. I did not want to stop the rhythm and progression.

I didn't know what to do. We were closely embraced and here was that moment in which a girl might back off. But there was no sign. I shifted over more and she opened more until I lay on top of her. She broke her lips from mine.

"I think it would be nice, but I'm scared I've moved too fast," said Kathy, with some doubt in her face but no sign of it in her body as she held on tightly.

"No! I've moved too fast," I said. "But it's so damn good. I mean, the feelings."

We kissed gently. I felt her relax. I knew it would end at this point but decided just to lie there.

The few moments lasted for a few minutes but felt like an eternity. Thoughts ran through my mind that were usually inconceivable. They were deeply related to what life was all about: love and fun. I wondered why this didn't happen more often. That's what repeatedly went through my mind: Why didn't it happen more often?

"Come on," Kathy suddenly said. She pushed me off, grabbed my hand and pulled me into the bedroom. She closed the door and drew the curtains while opening the window slightly. In less than two minutes we were naked together, under the sheets, ferociously feeling, touching and rolling around. Our lovemaking was ecstatic and after the 'eternity of love time', finally that magnificent drain on all the senses. We lay there exhausted, arms in arms, legs around legs, and totally satisfied. I couldn't believe what we had done. It was so good!

"I don't know about you, Charl!"

"Well I like all about you, Kathy . . . and that cancels any bad in me."

"No, don't do that. I like the bad."

We lay in bed just touching; enjoying every moment, whispering stupid things and laughing . . . we were there for an hour. I did still not believe what had happened to me. There were so many questions of Why . . .?

"Oh shit! What's the time?"

"You really have to go?"

"Oh! Yes! I couldn't miss this dinner. Like I said, I'd be dead as far as the family is concerned."

We got up and talked some more over coffee at the kitchen table. I ran out the door at 6:15 PM, the last possible moment. I arrived at

Ivan's and Johnny's at 6:55 PM. They were already dressed and ready. The dinner table was set.

"I won't be long," I said.

"Don't worry. Take a shower and get dressed in your best casual fine pants!" said Ivan, laughing. "You don't have to look your best, you know!" The thought crossed my mind: *Casual fine pants, for a dinner at home, I'm really moving up!*

I came out clean, dressed in a white shirt, one of the two I had brought with me, long pants and my only dress-shoes.

Ivan poured me a drink and made a short toast. "Here's to our darling dad and his most recent family," I tipped my glass with Johnny and Ivan.

"Charl," said Ivan "We're going for a short drive, then coming back to dinner."

We descended the stairs and got into the car. It was still light outside. The sun was setting. We drove through this most picturesque city and started up Signal Hill. The street was now tree-lined, in contrast to the house-next-to-house suburbs of downtown Cape Town. The road wound left and right and we could see Table Mountain clearly, and where the houses and roads stopped and the mountain's vertical slope took over. Only caves would possibly house people at that stage of the hill. Table Mountain went up straight almost a thousand feet from that point to its flat top.

"This city is so beautiful," I said. "They should build a restaurant on top of Table Mountain."

"There is a tea room," said Johnny.

"General Smuts loved this mountain," said Ivan. "He used to walk up and down that mountain when he was sixty. Think! Oh! Yes, definitely sixty."

"Is there's a trail to the top?" I asked.

"Yes, I believe it's on the other side of that flat vertical face," said Johnny.

Ivan drove up further to a car park on top of Signal Hill. We got out of the car and sat on the railing, facing the city of Cape Town some 1,800 feet below. To the left was the sea, stretching to the Antarctic, behind us the Indian Ocean to Australia. If our eyes could see over the Cape Strand and hills beyond, and could see far enough, we could have seen Argentina, Brazil and South America. We sat there for some time. I got up and walked around. Despite all the beauty of the surroundings, I was thinking of Kathy. *I'd like to have her up here,* I thought. I could've brought her but I didn't like explanations. Family one side, work one side, love, life and enjoyment one side and one side for everything else: 'The Box of Life.' Then I felt a little guilty and agreed with myself that Ivan and Johnny were being so very nice. And they were in a different place, that's all. The sun slowly went down and the lights of Cape Town were brighter to the eye.

"Just beautiful . . . I keep saying that," I said.

"You can come up here after some bastard didn't buy a piano, after you worked his mind into a corner, and after your boss got mad at you for no sale. You'll forget it all," exploded Ivan, with lots of gestures. "It seems so insignificant, all that work stuff." After a while he admitted, "It's my favorite place. It's so peaceful. I wish that it had an 'Ivan's Park Only' sign."

We laughed.

"Neon sign, maybe!" I paused. "Cape Town seems a long way from Johannesburg today," I said. Wondering, *Why did I say that?* After the words had rolled from my tongue without a thought in my head.

"Maybe you will come and live here after your overseas trip," suggested Ivan.

"Yes, who knows? That could be nice," I answered, thinking, *Uncanny, that suggestion . . . maybe I won't even go to England.*

We walked back to the car. The winds off the sea were increasing in velocity, bending the trees; the lights from the city seemed to flicker in agreement with all this beauty. The ride down to the city was as though we were descending from the white clouds of a dark universe into a lighted fairyland.

As the three of us sat down to dinner, Ivan opened a bottle of champagne and made a toast. "To your trip, Charl. Glad to have you visit us."

"Thank you for having me. Sorry it is so short," I replied.

The food was delicious. Johnny had been a chef on the Blue Train, the luxurious, world famous, air-conditioned train that ran between Cape Town and Johannesburg.

"John has a story from the Blue Train," said Ivan. "He was on there when the King and Queen of England, and Princess Margaret and Princess Elizabeth toured in 1947."

"No!" I exclaimed.

"Funny stories on that train," said Ivan.

"What stories?" I asked.

"About the Princesses," said Ivan. "Tell," he suggested to Johnny.

"Well," Johnny began, "all the newspapers stated that the Princesses had colds and would not be able to appear with the Royal Family when the train stopped in Bloemfontein. Many, many people were mad because they were more interested in the Princesses than the stuffy King and Queen. The truth of the matter was that they had been carrying on, talking, flirting, or whatever kids do, with some of the waiters. They were caught sneaking into parts of the train they weren't allowed to go to. So the King and Queen forbade them to get off the train in Bloemfontein."

"Well, they probably thought they wouldn't miss much, so it was worth the flirtation," I said, jokingly. "What a great story though."

"All the staff on the train were called together and told not to talk to reporters, and not to fraternize with the Princesses," said Johnny.

"I think Princess Margaret is the nicest," I said.

"She is very 'spirited,'" said Ivan, in his best interpretation of a British accent.

After dinner we sat in the sitting room. The champagne was gone and Ivan brought out a bottle of Van Der Hum, South Africa's premium liqueur brandy. He poured three glasses for us and put the bottle on top of the piano. It was a beautiful, chromium black, grand piano. Ivan sat down and looked at Johnny. "Shall I start?"

"Yes, of course," said John.

Ivan's fingers took off on the piano keys. His eyes closed as he played a series of short classical phrases, jumping from one piece to the other, a potpourri of classical melodies. He sat there playing for about ten minutes, then abruptly got up. He bowed to our loud clapping.

"Johnny," he beckoned.

Johnny took a slug of brandy, sat down and played in much the same manner. He went through various classical melodies for 10 minutes. I was amazed. Nothing in my lifestyle came close to this. I loved music but had drifted more towards jazz than the classics. Classical music was played in our house through radio programs. Nobody in my immediate family could even beat a drum. Ivan sat down at the piano, took his glass of Van Der Hum, and downed it. He then went into a beautiful classical piece by Beethoven, swaying slightly as he played. I also took a slug of brandy, sat back and relaxed.

I listened to the intricate sequences of the keys, the changes in tempo, and tried to identify the melody. My mind drifted to my mom, who had taken me to see a touring Italian opera company production of 'Il Travatore'. I remembered being so glad when the intermission came and we went out for refreshments. Then I was even gladder after the second part of the opera was completed. The lights had come on and everybody had got up and gone to the foyer, but they hadn't left. To my dismay I found out it was a second intermission, and that I had to go back again. I had enjoyed the 'Anvil Chorus' though.

Then I remembered Gran sending me to piano lessons, to the big fat lady off Main Street. I had agreed to go, on the understanding that I would get a soccer ball. After the soccer ball wore out, I gave up the piano. Now I realized how stupid I had been to give up. Looking at Ivan, he was in heaven, and he played almost anything. It seemed such a nice thing to do . . . play the piano.

Ivan and Johnny played in alternating sequences for almost 3 hours. Each time the classical piece got longer and more complicated, and the bottle of Van Der Ham got emptier. There were some mistakes. At those points Johnny and Ivan would laugh. Eventually I got up.

"Goodnight," I said.

Johnny was at the piano. He stopped his classical piece and broke into 'Goodnight Irene', a popular tune on our 50s hit parade. Only they sang, "Goodnight Charl, Goodnight Charl, we'll see you in our dreams."

I slipped into bed. I went over the day's events in my mind, feeling ecstatic with all of them, my thoughts continually returning to Kathy. What a nice thing to have happened to me. Nothing that good had ever happened that fast! Kathy had a lot of class and I was amazed at what the two of us had experienced. I was so very anxious to see her again, and had to work out a plan before 4 PM tomorrow. I couldn't let go the image of this beautiful girl. I could see her face as clear as if she was in front of me. I fell asleep easily, lulled by both the Van Der Hum and the classical music.

Sunday

I woke up with a monster hangover. I had drunk champagne, a lot of Van Der Hum, plus all the beers with Kathy. Nobody was up as I went to the bathroom, then out onto the balcony. I looked out over Cape Town. *Nothing in Johannesburg can compare*, I thought. *Wonder if Kathy is up.* I remembered that Ivan had said we would meet my Aunt Rachel and Evelyn *later* in the morning. So I took a chance. I called Kathy.

A sleepy voice answered the phone. "Morning Charl. What is the time?"

"Eight o'clock."

"Oh my God! And it's Sunday."

"Yes! Listen, I don't have to meet my relatives until close to 12. Want to have breakfast?"

"Yes!" said Kathy with joy. "Can you come over here? I'll make breakfast."

"Absolutely!"

"Bring some bread. I have eggs."

"Done, I'll be there quick. Bye!"

I showered, wrote a note and caught the bus after running like hell down the hill. I got to Seapoint, bought bread, ran up to Kathy's house and knocked on the door. I was breathing fast from the running. I waited. I knocked louder. It opened.

"Oh! You were so fast. It's only 8:45 AM."

"Yes."

I grabbed her, wrapped my arms around her, and gave her a kiss. The response was slow but then came the melt. Her arms went around me and we stood there for a complete minute.

"Come on! You start the breakfast and I'll shower."

"I'll help you shower," I suggested, laughing.

"No! Charl . . . you make the breakfast."

We sat in the little kitchen sipping coffee, the breakfast dishes all in the sink. We were feeling both happy and sad. Neither of us touched the subject of leaving . . . or love. I was scared of both subjects. My anticipation of going overseas had been deeply challenged by this girl. I would like to have made love to her again but that was not important. We touched, kissed, hugged, laughed, sang songs, and sometimes just stared at each other. It was so nice . . . just to be with her. Table talk took care of time as it flew by like a swift arrow.

"I have to meet the rest of my Cape Town family, and then meet Bobby and my friends and catch a boat. Can you come and see us off? I would like that very much."

"Yes, Charl. I wouldn't miss it. Bettie is coming as well."

I got up and went to the door. "I don't know . . . but I just wanted to see you this morning." I said looking into her eyes.

"So did I," said Kathy with a beautiful, warm smile.

Kathy came to the door. 'This is so sad,' I thought. We hugged and kissed until the last second.

I got back to the apartment. Aunt Rachel, my cousins Ron and Evelyn, and their children Ron and Bluebell, were already there. They were seated, and all got up as hugs and kisses were exchanged.

"You look wonderful," said Evelyn. "Just a little like your father."

"Don't ever say that Evelyn!" interjected Ivan. "We don't want to look like him."

I grabbed my travel bags and we went down to the cars. Ivan and Johnny were going in their own car. I climbed into Evelyn's car. We drove out on Camps Bay Drive.

This popular road starts in Cape Town and leads to various scenic routes: through Hout Bay and out towards Cape Point, or over the hills to Muizenberg. The road passes through wealthy Cape Town suburbs, past beautiful beaches, and ends up 200–300 feet above sea level in some parts on the mountain slope, the gradient nearly 70° at times, leading down to the sea. When the road roams at sea level, the beaches are a stone's throw away. At St. James and Muizenberg, the beaches have very gentle shelving. You can walk out a half a mile into the sea and the water is still at waist-level.

The conversation was relaxed but full of questions, such as, what was I going to do in England? Had I finished college? How was my dad? These were typical family questions. I answered each with an appropriate answer but felt like I was in an interrupted dream. People were preparing to say goodbye. I started to feel that I was going overseas, but felt guilty because I hadn't seen enough of my own country. So my answers finally fell in the category that I'd be back in 3–6 months, at most it would be a year!

"You'll have to come and live in Cape Town," said Evelyn's daughter, Bluebell. She was about eighteen, and a ballet dancer in Cape Town's Ballet Company, which regularly supplied dancers to the Sadler's Wells Ballet in London. Bluebell was enamored with my trip and fired off lots of questions. Ron and his father did not say very much.

As we neared Cape Point, we suddenly stopped. All the cars had come to a halt. Evelyn moved off to the side of the road. There was a group of baboons on the road, with one sitting right in the middle of the road, refusing to move. This was a main highway, very busy on Sundays. We all got out the car and walked along the edge of the road.

The pathway between the road and the drop to the sea was only two to three feet wide. We leaned up against a railing, and Ivan took pictures of the monkeys (baboons), and then of the family. Evelyn wanted them as keepsakes.

Aunt Rachel was my dad's sister. Evelyn, Aunt Rachel's daughter, had married Ronald, and they had obviously done well. Earlier, they had lived in the Northern Suburbs of Johannesburg in a very nice house. I had always associated this part of my family with money. They dressed well, drove late model cars and lived in nice houses. I was a little embarrassed in their company, despite the fact that they always treated me like family. Every time I had been to see them in Johannesburg they had been kind to me. I loved Aunt Rachel she was a beautiful person. Her hair had been white hair since her thirties. Evelyn's black hair had also started to grey. Everyone in the family was good-looking.

We got back in the cars and returned to Camps Bay. We had a quick brunch in Camps Bay and then headed to the Cape Town docks around 2.30 PM. The ship was to leave at 4 PM, but you could go aboard with visitors at 2 PM. We parked the car and walked to the ship's berth. It was a big ship, the S.S. Southern Cross, from the Shaw-Savill line. The smoke stack was at the stern, one of the first luxury liners to be designed that way.

I went ahead up the stairs, got my cabin number, dropped off my bags in the cabin, and came back to the dock. There were too many people there, so I went up to a railing above the gangplank for a better view. Bobby, Abie and Dai appeared and completed their trips to the cabins. Then I saw Kathy and Bettie, so I went down the gangplank again. Billy and Joy turned up at the same time I got to the dock. We all dragged ourselves up the long gangplank again.

Introductions were made all around. I introduced Kathy by first putting my arm around her waist and then pointing to the circle of friends and family.

"My mother said that it is bad to point, so step forward upon the sound of your name," I proclaimed, in an English sailor's accent.

"You sound like the Captain," said Aunt Evelyn.

"You're right!" I repeated in the appropriate accent.

"Very good," said Bettie.

"Have to practice my new language."

"Oh! You're going to have so much fun," said Bluebell.

"Well, we'll be okay if we can get jobs quickly. Otherwise—see you in a month," said Abie. "Maybe we'll come and stay in Cape Town for a while."

"I'd like that!" said Kathy.

"How long have you known Charl?" asked Bluebell, looking at Kathy.

"It seems like years!" I interjected.

"Where did you meet?"

"Oh! In a bar! No, I'm kidding, at a restaurant." I replied.

Kathy's face had a puzzled expression, but she went along with it.

Ivan and Johnny caught up with us, and soon everyone was talking. Billy and Joy were talking to Bobby and Abie. I slipped away with Kathy and as soon as we were out of sight I kissed her. Her response was so good, sending high-energy volts through my body. We didn't say much, just held each other's hands and looked at each other.

"I don't quite believe this," I said. "I'd have given anything to have met you in Johannesburg."

"Ditto," said Kathy.

"Have to come back."

"Right," said Kathy.

We reluctantly rejoined the crowd: some had noticed our absence, some had not.

Finally, the announcement came for visitors to disembark.

I said goodbye to Aunt Rachel with a big hug and kiss.

"God bless you, Son! Please come back safe."

"I will," I promised.

"Thanks a span, Boetie," I said to Ivan. I winked at Johnny and shook his hand.

"Okay brother, anytime. Don't forget, Cape Town is the place to return to!"

Evelyn gave me an envelope. "A little present, for your birthday," she said, "from all of us."

I hugged and kissed her, and then Bluebell. "So nice to have met you."

"Keep in touch," said Bluebell.

"I will."

Billy, Joy and I hugged and we said our goodbyes with a lot of feeling.

They all went down the gangplank to the dock. Kathy and I kissed and hugged, then she said, "You write, or I'll spank you!"

"I will! I promise, faithfully!"

Everyone was on the dock as the ship slowly backed away, the engines grinding and moaning at the start of two weeks of constant revolutions. A large Cape Colored band on the dock was playing all the South African traditional songs, their ukuleles strumming. Streamers were being thrown from all over the boat, and the crowd on the dock were singing to the band and waving, as they grew smaller and smaller. The last song the band played was 'Sarie Marais.' The crowd followed the band and sang in Afrikaans:

"My Sarie Marais is so far from my heart
And I'm longing to see her again,
She lived on a farm on the Mooi River bank,
Before I left on this campaign.
Oh, bring me back to the old Transvaal,
That's where I long to be,
There yonder 'mongst the mealies by the green thorn tree,
Sarie is waiting for me!
I wonder if I'll ever see that green thorn tree,
There where she's waiting for me!"

The song's sound waves rippled across the amphitheater of the Cape of Good Hope. My three strong young buddies and I, all born in South Africa, had tears in our eyes, on our cheeks and on our shirts.

◆

Land was fast disappearing on the horizon. My friends said they were going to the Tavern on the ship. I said I would join them soon. I had no idea why they had really joined me on this trip. I watched Table Mountain disappear in the dusk of the day. I was sad because the song Sarie Marais is about a soldier wanting to see his girl again . . . and he is at war in a foreign land. The song is very dear to South Africans. The slow movement of the ship provided time to watch the shore of South Africa slowly disappear on the horizon. I continued to lean on the railings, and looked at the water churning on the side of the boat. I looked at my country, South Africa, disappearing quickly. It already seemed so far away. I was entering a new world almost immediately. I was excited about the unknowns and didn't feel scared at all . . . my body and soul were very calm and that was good!

There was still a great number of feelings swirling in my body from the last four days of leaving Andrew Street, saying goodbye at Johannesburg station, the train trip, and the joyful and exciting time in Cape Town. Kathy was especially responsible for bouncing my emotions all over the place. I finally decided there would be time to think about that later, and that I would instead think about what I should do in the near future. But it was not that easy.

I felt I had recently been through a cyclone, in my life. I had no single reason for doing what I was doing. There was the excitement of travelling to see new things, meet new people, and experience something different. It bothered me that South Africa was slowly disappearing into the distance. Had I made a mistake? Now that I'd gone up the gangplank, was I subject to fate? My mother believed in fate. I liked the idea. They said it took courage to step off the dock. I knew I couldn't go back after only a month . . . that would be just like a vacation. It wouldn't warrant the send off I'd got at Johannesburg Station and at the docks in Cape Town. Did my friends and family believe I was going for a long time? Or forever?

I knew I would not live in Andrew Street again; that time was past. But it had been marvelous, what some seventy kids had got up to. As kids, we had listened to all the adult discussions on blacks, religions, farmers, fighting gangs, complaining immigrants, tough times, sports and on many other subjects; also, we experienced the edicts of our parents, who were essentially conservative, and old fashioned in many ways. We knew how to sit and eat at the dinner table, how to stand up when someone came into the room, that ladies should go first, and we certainly knew how to remain quiet and not interrupt. However, the pioneer spirit in the adults challenged us to do things: take them apart and put them back together, and to always finish something we started, plus finish it well; the development of our determination of not giving up! The early Andrew Street Mob played in the street and talked and yelled. We very often sat on the curb and discussed all the events in our life, and, in turn, got to know each other well. Our subjects included the games we played, servants, parents, relatives and what they'd all said. We held back nothing, solved our problems in no time, and moved on, wondering, but never knowing, why the adults kept trying and trying to work it out. We knew the answers! Us kids of Andrew Street transferred our knowledge to anyone who joined, and newcomers were welcomed. We were very careful of strangers, they were analyzed instantly, and little did they know what we knew, so quickly. None of us kids were ever harmed by outsiders!

I had graduated from Andrew Street. There was no future for me in that wonderful place. It was much like Main Reef Engineering. I knew I was never going to be a machinist again. In an emergency, yes! The design field had taken over. It was so exhilarating. The challenge was superb. New designs, new challenges and new thinking were all the things I wanted to have happen.

I stopped thinking and just stared at the sea, but came back to reality a little later. My brain would not allow me to think of nothing. I went and sat in a chair on the deck. I arranged my body comfortably; I rested my head back on the back of the seat and smiled. My thoughts returned: this was becoming serious. I was caught between being sad for leaving, and excited because everything was going to be new. I had very recently realized that it was Gran and my mom who truly raised me. My sister was always there, and so was Grandpa Mick. Lena was my constant friend. My mother, being a single mom, had battled in many ways. Despite that, she'd allowed me an 'open house and dinner table', and had welcomed any of my friends, at any time. I had no idea of where Gran had got her money. But they were the solid core that saw me through. Tears welled my eyes again. I regretted not having got to know more about my mom. *Gran and Uncle Mick should have lived longer . . . that would have been nice.* A tear always came into my eye when I thought of Gran. Gran and Uncle Mick were both gone. I believed I would see them again. My beautiful mother who worked to make my life easier, and who had taught me respect, and love, and freedom, and adventure, and who now had finally found her own happiness in her grandchildren. Uncle Mick and his non-interfering ways, and contributions unknown to me . . . I loved him too. My dad, whom I never really understood, but who had some nice qualities, and then some crazy ones too, always, wanted to be positive. I thought of my sister Yvonne, who had saved me so many times from everyone, and had taken the edge off my nastiness! Then there was my brother Bazil who was a quiet person, and didn't talk to me very much. What about my dog Pal, who had instinctively known I was going away . . . did it mean the dog, knew it would be for a long time? And Wolf, who was had been my first real friend, at the start of my play-life. Wolf, my beautiful friend, who nurtured me until I was seven. Pal, who was probably sent by Wolf, who looked after me till I was twenty, and that was perhaps why he was so mad at me when I left to go overseas.

My wonderful relatives in Vryburg, who had accelerated my learning at warp speed, changed my whole way of thinking, and maturing me in so many ways. Southey had mostly been responsible, but the Harveys had been close behind in making sure I took 'Vryburg Ways' home with me. Otiend was a diamond in the rough . . . I had wished so many times for his company in my life. I believed he could have been the chief of a nation. His working of problems was so smooth.

Adding to my fortune had been my work friends who'd taught me how to work well: Sandy, Mr. Warren, Laubscher and John Funkey, plus Picannin and the boys, and Ginge, my Jazz and Work Soul mate.

I kept wondering why I was going over all these things now? Perhaps I'd had no chance to do it after I'd bought the boat ticket to England. I had always broken things down into detail. I had always thought of how I could do it better! So here I was, doing it again, but a little late and large in comparison to anything I'd done before. I moved over in the chair and noticed there was nothing but ocean on the horizon. There sure was a lot of water on this earth.

And what of South Africa itself? Would it become more like America over time, and less like Britain and Europe? It could perhaps turn out like Australia and New Zealand, even though the racial complexity was different. What of the English/Afrikaans dilemma, and the black and white separation, and the many people caught in between the two dominant colors? I had confronted these thoughts before and they were still too deep. Now I needed to think of survival—like I had always had to. I had already found out that survival sorts out many issues and brings the important ones to the top. Why was I leaving this paradise of friends and beautiful countryside with family spread everywhere? Why had I chosen to leave? Was it just American music and American lifestyle? Did I, deep down, want to go there? Maybe! I just couldn't answer anyone who asked the question.

I thought of the black people who had been in my life: Otiend had made a great impact on me . . . yet he had never really told me what I should do. How could he? He had never seen the commercial world of western ways, yet he understood the essence of its lifestyle. I had wished so deeply for a father like Otiend: not instructive, yet persuasive. He was wise, calm, and gentle. Most of my friends had had a father at home.

Picannin was another person who had made a deep impression on me. His positive personality and wonderful expressions had kept his audiences in a mesmerized state. I had become wiser by listening to Picannin's illustration, through his soccer story, that my one major soccer accomplishment was not such a magnificent feat. So I scored a goal in front of 20,000 people! Was it that glorious? What could Robbie have done if he hadn't given up top soccer? He'd had all the talent our team had wished for.

The black bike riders I had ridden with and talked to; Joseph and the other black men at Main Reef Engineering, and at Huth's bicycle shop; all had been very nice to be around. All the people in the Sophiatown nightclubs had been friendly and fun to be with.

Lena had looked after me for a very long time; she was so forgiving, and felt like family. She and her husband were finally living together . . . but they'd had to wait such a very long time. Why? I wondered why my black friends had been so very nice to me. I was going to miss the black South Africans.

I drifted back to thoughts of my country. South Africa seemed so very complicated; it was not like the American movies, which painted life as easy, comfortable, and exciting. But I loved South Africa deeply and was very proud of many things it had achieved: its multiracial society was diverse and interesting, and had contributed to our complex personalities. The seriousness was sometimes too disturbing, and I'd had trouble following all the ultra-conservative rules. People were tough in South Africa, but it took tough people to make the earth give up its bounty, and to build such a diverse society. Many of those pioneers had been trying to escape Europe and its rules. I laughed out aloud . . . *I'm going to the country that initiated most of the rules I hate, England!* But my main complaint against the South African Government was their not allowing more freedom in music and sports, and in life itself. It was my belief that all the black people in my life needed to have a better education. If they gained more knowledge, it would make it easier for everybody. They had very little chance to attain the better knowledge and I believed the whites were at fault in not advancing everybody, or at least giving them a chance. I had found it hard to advance, even with the opportunity to complete my studies.

I rolled over and wondered why all these thoughts were streaming through my mind. Was the rhythm of the ship forcing these thoughts to materialize, or what?

My friends were enormously special: so many feelings of love, and friendship, and caring and, more importantly, the drive to have fun. I had been so lucky. What a great and wonderful time I'd had in Andrew Street. It had started with Helen and Bobby next door, and Zoni, Juni and Doc, whom I'd met when I first moved into Andrew Street. I went through the list of all the 70 kids on the block, remembering the hundreds and hundreds of games we'd played in the street, and sometimes almost laughing out loud at some of our antics. Then came the meeting of the Kennedy Street Girls: Beryl, Ann and Grace; the joining to the Mob of what were now some of my closest friends: Johnny, Trevor, Billy, Norman, Pat, Viv and Guy, and the continuing friendship of Zoni, Juni and Doc. Then Gloria, Thelma and Hobbs and Julius had joined. The circle of friends expanded with Bobbie, Joan, Elaine and Denise joining from cycling, and Meridy and Denise.

Besides the Andrew Street Mob, I had met and gone out with Bobby's Group, Abie, Mickey and Tom. We had been in the Army together, and had hung out at the Rock and Roll scenes. I'd had my soccer buddies, together with my special friends Desmond and Robbie, through eight years with Marist Brothers.

Most of all, it was the unending spirit of the Andrew Street Mob I would miss: our continuing antics, parties and discussions. We had grown up together. We had accomplished many, many things in a very complicated society. We had come through a very complex living situation, certainly not with ease. There were thousands of incidents that had been handled without major provocation. We had also arrived at a point in life qualified at something, at least, to help us go forward, and to stay in front during the upcoming changes that we had all surmised would come about. All the rules imposed from many directions had been worked out and the answers seemed insignificant. We'd had a simple philosophy, we'd done little harm to anyone, and we had ignored the rhetoric of grown-ups and stuck to the simple and enjoyable things of life. We had so many times wondered why the edicts and rules of the government had to be enforced. Was there not an easier solution?

Now, it all seemed like a beautiful cloud that was breaking up and drifting away in many directions, floating all over the sky. There was no way to hold it, no way to influence the pathways of all these wonderful people and events that had unfolded into a matrix that was, for the longest time, inconceivable. Yet it had worked for us. We were not a 'Vastrap Generation'; we were a young, modern thinking group, so it was bound to change! It was amazing how quickly and suddenly almost everyone was going in different directions.

We were many, many people together . . . It would never happen again . . . but the beauty was, that it did happen!

I thought of the girls whom I'd enjoyed spending time with, and who had raised passion in me: Beryl, Rosemary, June, Coralie, Joan, Rosemary again, and now Kathy. How things changed and rotated! Beryl's wonderful friendship until she got married; Rosemary, my first love, who had truly wiped me out at one time and had remained in my thoughts all through her two-year absence, and then her confusing return and change of attitude towards me. The most delightful times spent with June, followed by really good friendships with Coralie and Joan. The meeting, and instant, profound, liking of Kathy, her presence that was so exciting the memories went through me like a shockwave. I missed them all already.

My Andrew Street Mob friends and Bobby's Group had formed my lifestyle. I can say they saved my life by providing excitement, and laughter, and serious discussion, and love and friendship . . . I had no doubt our bonds would last for a very, very long time. We had done almost everything there was to be done, growing up and we'd done it well . . . what else could anyone want?

England would not have an Otiend or a Picannin, with all their wisdom and story telling. All their animals were locked up; ours lived the same way they had for centuries. England would not have the beautiful vastness of South Africa, with the landscape changing from sea and sand, to bushes and grass, to mountains and trees, rivers and lakes, and then tropical, dense vegetation that shut out the light; and all this embraced by a cold and a warm ocean, with endless waves and surf, all dangerous and beautiful beyond any photograph or movie. How could I leave all this?

I already believed England was not for me, just because of the weather. I was not born in rain. But there was nothing wrong in trying to find out! I wanted to see London because it was so famous and historical, and the buildings were incredible. We knew from engineering that they couldn't build them as high as in America, because London sits on a marsh and it would be very expensive. But there were so many different types of buildings, and the museums, and the palaces, and the bridges...

Even more exciting were the music and nightclubs, and soccer, all beyond anything I knew. I so loved to dance. It expressed many things in a person's personality. It also was the easiest way to meet someone. Also, my passion for playing soccer was extreme. I would even play at night without light. I had many dreams now in my freedom. There was a catch! I had enough money for two weeks after arriving in London, and then nothing . . . so I would have to find a job very quickly!

However, these issues were background to an exciting life. I did have underlying problems. Rosemary was a big question. She had surprised me in many complicated ways. I had been totally taken with her, and she'd caused so many deep feelings that they'd made me scared of what I might do. I'd almost given up everything to be with her. These were feelings, which still persisted: they wouldn't go away easily. I had never felt like that about any girl, till I met her. The devastating break up had, however, taken a heavy toll and had made me very reluctant to go steady again, till I'd met June. As fortune would have it, the same problem of no time and no car took that beauty away. Then Kathy had entered the scene, disrupting my mind and starting the movie again. *I could easily go back to Cape Town and continue with her . . . definitely an unfinished scene.*

I didn't really know why I'd done what I had about four weeks ago, just buying a ticket to England, and all I knew now was that everything around me was changing fast, and perhaps becoming complicated. I had always believed the future was indeterminate. The timing of the future was infinite, in a sense. To make it simple, I postulated that maybe I would spend the next eight years having fun—because there was no reason to live past 29! Everybody acted so old. I would complete my studies, earn a degree, and that would fulfill my promise to Gran. Then I'd have a year of dancing, a year of soccer, a year with a car and a year with crazy English women. Then four years of all that together, and that would be that! The future was really just that simple.

Right now I was a tanned, physically fit South African with happy spirits, intending to love London. I had been so free from the time I'd boarded the train at Johannesburg Park Station. I'd never before felt that total 'ownership' of myself. I at last had the possibility to do exactly what I chose, and it had thus far resulted in every day having been a gem.

The ship was sailing smoothly. I felt I could sit in the chair and reminisce for a long time. But my friends were in the Tavern, and, as

Abie had said so many times, "Let's just have a drink and have some fun."

I got up to go and join them for the fun of the evening . . . I was so very contented inside, and so peaceful. The future could roll in, and I would welcome it.

Beauty of the Southern Lady

You cannot ignore the beauty of the Southern Lady
Man has not destroyed it -- yet
Walk from the subtropical forest to the desert land
    into the veld where sparse trees yawn at the sun
      through grasses and wheat fields
        sitting up like a porcupines prickly shell
Sit beneath the willow trees alongside the gentle river
    watching the animals feed and water
Lie upon the beaches in the moonlight
    in the warmth of Africa's air
Watch the bounding waves sparkle in the moonlight
    rough seas smashing against the rocky shores
    or waves lapping against the beach
      then disappearing in the tropical forest lagoon
The beach is yours -- there is no one around
Miles and miles of coastline without man
Sunrays fall upon this Southern Lady
Her beauty leaves you breathless
As you recognize the charm about her person
    a gentle beauty -- so rare
    it is like the eiderdown on your bed
Your soul is captured in the passion for loveliness
You cannot resist
There is no reason for your soul to do so
Fine sands ground from nature's machine
    disappear through your toes
Desert breezes disarrange your hair
    if you are not African
    their bodies long time ago agreed with Africa's clime
Intrigue does not come from force

but from the awe-inspiring silence
from the floor of the land into the heaven
that silence of the deserts and rich green hills
walks through your soul
telling of the magnificence of Mother Nature
of animals
of flora
of trees
and birds
Stretched forth across the eye – the horizon
where there are always expectations of change
an alteration in this magnificent beauty
a difference in this land
when you arrive
there is no change
your expectation is refuted
Because it is the same -- the same -- the same
Never ending trek across the land

The stars do not move
they too spellbound by the beauty
and gazing down upon this useless human ant

Where do you go insignificant one

To the promised land of the future
a green pasture at the foot of a beautiful mountain
like a picture painted by the artist of life
who transferred all his desires
inside a three-sided frame
A life of abundance with an escape to heaven --
Is it here in the Southern Lady's bosom
What price for your framed picture -- with one side open
your religion -- your philosophy -- your culture -- your soul
Do you wish to buy
You do not know
You do not know
Oh! God! You do not know

Brian Marais

Further Reading

The background of this book has a fascinating compilation of stories intimating the diverse lifestyles of a very complex society, residing in a most beautiful country, surrounded by two magnificent oceans and the rest of Africa.

The following are suggested readings, which will expand the reader's enjoyment of pertinent information in this book:

1. *Sof'town Blues*
   Jurgen Schadeburg (Anthony Sampson)
   ISBN 0 9583980 1 1   1994
   Creda Press/Cape Town

2. *Like it was   1887—1987 100 Years in Johannesburg*
   The Star Newspaper
   ISBN 0 620 09389 7
   Argus Printing and Publishing Company/Johannesburg

3. *In Township Tonight!*
   David B. Coplan
   ISBN 0 869725 228 6 1985
   Ravan Press Johannesburg

4. *Vryburg 1882-1982*
   Town Council of Vryburg,
   P. O. Box 35 Vryburg, 8500
   Republic of South Africa

5. *The Coast of Southern Africa*
   John Kench   Ken Gerhardt
   C. Struik Publishers, Cape Town
   Republic of South Africa
   ISBN 0 86977 205 8

6. *Our First Half – Century 1910-1960*
   Published by Da Gama Publications Ltd.
   Johannesburg.   MCMLX

7. *Johannesburg One Hundred Years*
   Published by Chris van Rensburg
   Publications (PTY) Limited
   Johannesburg
   ISBN 0 86846 036 2

8. *The Gold Miners*
   A P Cartwright/ Illustrations-B. Gruzin
   Purnell and Sons (SA) Pty Ltd
   Cape Town   Johannesburg

Breinigsville, PA USA
28 May 2010
238872BV00003B/1/P